CIMA

STUDY TEXT

Foundation Paper 3a

Economics for Business

IN THIS JULY 2002 EDITION

- Targeted to the **syllabus** and **learning outcomes**
- **Quizzes** and **questions** to check your understanding
- Clear layout and style designed to save you time
- Plenty of **exam-style questions**
- **Chapter Roundups** and summaries to help revision
- **Mind Maps** to integrate the key points

NEW IN THIS JULY 2002 EDITION

- Revised coverage to reflect recent examinations

BPP's **MCQ cards** and **i-Learn and i-Pass** products also support this paper.

BPP Publishing
July 2002

First edition July 2000
Third edition July 2002

ISBN 0 7517 3750 X (previous edition 0 7517 3157 9)

British Library Cataloguing-in-Publication Data
A catalogue record for this book
is available from the British Library

Published by

BPP Publishing Ltd
Aldine House, Aldine Place
London W12 8AW

www.bpp.com

Printed in Great Britain by

WM Print
45-47 Frederick Street
Walsall
West Midlands, WS2 9NE

We are grateful to the Chartered Institute of Management Accountants for permission to reproduce past examination questions and questions from the pilot paper. The suggested solutions to the illustrative questions have been prepared by BPP Publishing Limited.

Contents

Page

THE BPP STUDY TEXT (v)

HELP YOURSELF STUDY FOR YOUR CIMA EXAMS (vii)
The right approach - developing your - suggested study sequence
personal study plan

SYLLABUS AND LEARNING OUTCOMES (xii)

THE EXAM PAPER (xvi)

WHAT THE EXAMINER MEANS (xviii)

TACKLING MULTIPLE CHOICE QUESTIONS (xix)

TACKLING OBJECTIVE TEST QUESTIONS IN COMPUTER BASED ASSESSMENT (xx)

TACKLING OBJECTIVE TEST QUESTIONS IN THE PAPER BASED EXAM (xxi)

PART A: THE ECONOMY AND THE GROWTH OF ECONOMIC WELFARE

1 The allocation of scarce resources 3

PART B: THE MARKET SYSTEM AND THE COMPETITIVE PROCESS

2 The price mechanism: demand and supply 19
3 Elasticities of demand and supply 39
4 Market failure, externalities and intervention 56
5 Theory of the firm: production and costs 70
6 Factor markets 90
7 Organisations in a mixed economy 116
8 Perfect competition and monopoly 131
9 Monopolistic competition and oligopoly 149
10 Public policy and competition 161

PART C: THE MACROECONOMIC FRAMEWORK

11 The nature of money and credit 175
12 Financial institutions and sources of finance 193
13 National income and its measurement 211
14 The determination of national income 226
15 Money and inflation 257
16 Monetary policy, unemployment and inflation 277
17 Fiscal policy and taxation 294

PART D: THE OPEN ECONOMY

18 International trade 313
19 The balance of payments and exchange rates 325

QUESTION BANK 351

ANSWER BANK 367

INDEX 387

REVIEW FORM & FREE PRIZE DRAW

ORDER FORM

MULTIPLE CHOICE QUESTION CARDS

Multiple choice questions form a large part of the exam. To give you further practice in this style of question, we have produced a bank of **150 multiple choice question cards**, covering the syllabus. This bank contains exam style questions in a format to help you **revise on the move**.

COMPUTER-BASED LEARNING PRODUCTS FROM BPP

If you want to reinforce your studies by **interactive** learning, try BPP's **i-Learn** product, covering major syllabus areas in an interactive format. For **self-testing**, try **i-Pass,** which offers a large number of **objective test questions**, particularly useful where objective test questions form part of the exam.

See the order form at the back of this text for details of these innovative learning tools.

VIRTUAL CAMPUS

The Virtual Campus uses BPP's wealth of teaching experience to produce a fully **interactive** e-learning resource **delivered via the Internet**. The site offers comprehensive **tutor support** and features areas such as **study**, **practice**, **email service**, **revision** and **useful resources**.

Visit our website www.bpp.com/virtualcampus/cima to sample aspects of the campus free of charge.

LEARNING TO LEARN ACCOUNTANCY

BPP's ground-breaking **Learning to learn accountancy** book is designed to be used both at the outset of your CIMA studies and throughout the process of learning accountancy. It challenges you to consider how you study and gives you helpful hints about how to approach the various types of paper which you will encounter. It can help you **get your studies both subject and exam focused**, enabling you to **acquire knowledge, practice and revise efficiently and effectively**.

THE BPP STUDY TEXT

Aims of this Study Text

To provide you with the knowledge and understanding, skills and application techniques that you need if you are to be successful in your exams

This Study Text has been written around the **Economic for Business** syllabus.

- It is **comprehensive.** It covers the syllabus content. No more, no less.
- It is written at the **right level**. Each chapter is written with CIMA's precise learning outcomes in mind.
- It is targeted to the **exam**. We have taken account of the pilot paper and the papers set to date, questions put to the examiner and the assessment methodology.

To allow you to study in the way that best suits your learning style and the time you have available, by following your personal Study Plan (see page (viii))

You may be studying at home on your own until the date of the exam, or you may be attending a full-time course. You may like to (and have time to) read every word, or you may prefer to (or only have time to) skim-read and devote the remainder of your time to question practice. Wherever you fall in the spectrum, you will find the BPP Study Text meets your needs in designing and following your personal Study Plan.

To tie in with the other components of the BPP Effective Study Package to ensure you have the best possible chance of passing the exam (see page (vi))

BPP STUDY TEXTS AND THE CIMA CERTIFICATE IN BUSINESS ACCOUNTING

In supporting your Foundation level studies, this text is your passport to success in the **CIMA Certificate in Business Accounting**, awarded from May 2002 to students who complete their Foundation level exams.

Recommended period of use	Elements of the BPP Effective Study Package
From the outset and throughout	**Learning to learn accountancy** Read this invaluable book as you begin your studies and refer to it as you work through the various elements of the BPP Effective Study Package. It will help you to acquire knowledge, practice and revise, both efficiently and effectively.
Three to twelve months before the exam	**Study Text and i-Learn** Use the Study Text to acquire knowledge, understanding, skills and the ability to use application techniques. Use BPP's **i-Learn** product to reinforce your learning.
Throughout	**Virtual Campus** Study, practice, revise and take advantage of other useful resources with BPP's fully interactive e-learning site with comprehensive tutor support.
Throughout	**MCQ cards and i-Pass** Revise your knowledge and ability to use application techniques, as well as practising this key exam question format, with 150 multiple choice questions. **i-Pass**, our computer-based testing package, provides objective test questions in a variety of formats and is ideal for self-assessment.
One to six months before the exam	**Practice & Revision Kit** Try the numerous examination-format questions, for which there are realistic suggested solutions prepared by BPP's own authors. Then attempt the two mock exams.
From three months before the exam until the last minute	**Passcards** Work through these short, memorable notes which are focused on what is most likely to come up in the exam you will be sitting.
One to six months before the exam	**Success Tapes** These audio tapes cover the vital elements of your syllabus in less than 90 minutes per subject. Each tape also contains exam hints to help you fine tune your strategy.
Three to twelve months before the exam	**Breakthrough Videos** Use a Breakthrough Video to supplement your Study Text. They give you clear tuition on key exam subjects and allow you the luxury of being able to pause or repeat sections until you have fully grasped the topic.

HELP YOURSELF STUDY FOR YOUR CIMA EXAMS

Exams for professional bodies such as CIMA are very different from those you have taken at college or university. You will be under **greater time pressure before** the exam - as you may be combining your study with work. There are many different ways of learning and so the BPP Study Text offers you a number of different tools to help you through. Here are some hints and tips: they are not plucked out of the air, but **based on research and experience**. (You don't need to know that long-term memory is in the same part of the brain as emotions and feelings - but it's a fact anyway.)

The right approach

1 **The right attitude**

Believe in yourself	Yes, there is a lot to learn. Yes, it is a challenge. But thousands have succeeded before and you can too.
Remember why you're doing it	Studying might seem a grind at times, but you are doing it for a reason: to advance your career.

2 **The right focus**

Read through the Syllabus and learning outcomes	These tell you what you are expected to know and are supplemented by Exam Focus Points in the text.
Study the Exam Paper section	Past papers are a reasonable guide of what you should expect in the exam.

3 **The right method**

The big picture	You need to grasp the detail - but keeping in mind how everything fits into the big picture will help you understand better. • The **Introduction** of each chapter puts the material in context. • The **Syllabus content, learning outcomes** and **Exam focus points** show you what you need to **grasp.** • **Mind Maps** show the links and key issues in key topics.
In your own words	To absorb the information (and to practise your written communication skills), it helps to **put it into your own words.** • **Take notes.** • Answer the **questions** in each chapter. As well as helping you absorb the information, you will practise the assessment formats used in the exam and your written communication skills, which become increasingly important as you progress through your CIMA exams. • Draw **mind maps.** We have some examples. • Try 'teaching' a subject to a colleague or friend.

Give yourself cues to jog your memory	The BPP Study Text uses **bold** to **highlight key points** and **icons** to identify key features, such as **Exam focus points** and **Key terms.** • Try **colour coding** with a highlighter pen. • Write **key points** on cards.

4 **The right review**

Review, review, review	It is a **fact** that regularly reviewing a topic in summary form can **fix it in your memory**. Because **review** is so important, the BPP Study Text helps you to do so in many ways. • **Chapter roundups** summarise the key points in each chapter. Use them to recap each study session. • The **Quick quiz** is another review technique to ensure that you have grasped the essentials. • Go through the **Examples** in each chapter a second or third time.

Developing your personal Study Plan

One thing that the BPP Learning to learn accountancy book emphasises (see page (iv)) is the need to prepare (and use) a study plan. Planning and sticking to the plan are key elements of learning success.

There are four steps you should work through.

Step 1. How do you learn?

First you need to be aware of your style of learning. The BPP Learning to learn accountancy book commits a chapter to this **self-discovery**. What types of intelligence do you display when learning? You might be advised to brush up on certain study skills before launching into this Study Text.

BPP's **Learning to learn accountancy** book helps you to identify what intelligences you show more strongly and then details how you can tailor your study process through your preferences. It also includes handy hints on how to develop intelligences you exhibit less strongly, but which might be needed as you study accountancy.

Are you a **theorist** or are you more **practical**? If you would rather get to grips with a theory before trying to apply it in practice, you should follow the study sequence on page (ix). If the reverse is true (you like to know why you are learning theory before you do so), you might be advised to flick through Study Text chapters and look at questions, case studies and examples (Steps 7, 8 and 9 in the **suggested study sequence**) before reading through the detailed theory.

Step 2. How much time do you have?

Work out the time you have available per week, given the following.

- The standard you have set yourself
- The time you need to set aside later for work on the Practice & Revision Kit and Passcards
- The other exam(s) you are sitting
- Very importantly, practical matters such as work, travel, exercise, sleep and social life

Hours

Note your time available in box A. A [ ]

Step 3. Allocate your time

- Take the time you have available per week for this Study Text shown in box A, multiply it by the number of weeks available and insert the result in box B. B [ ]
- Divide the figure in Box B by the number of chapters in this text and insert the result in box C. C [ ]

Remember that this is only a rough guide. Some of the chapters in this book are longer and more complicated than others, and you will find some subjects easier to understand than others.

Step 4. Implement

Set about studying each chapter in the time shown in box C, following the key study steps in the order suggested by your particular learning style.

This is your personal **Study Plan**. You should try and combine it with the study sequence outlined below. You may want to modify the sequence a little (as has been suggested above) to adapt it to your **personal style**.

Suggested study sequence

It is likely that the best way to approach this Study Text is to tackle the chapters in the order in which you find them. Taking into account your individual learning style, you could follow this sequence.

Key study steps	Activity
Step 1 **Topic list**	Each numbered topic is a numbered section in the chapter.
Step 2 **Introduction**	This gives you the **big picture** in terms of the **context** of the chapter, the **content** you will cover, and the **learning outcomes** the chapter assesses - in other words, it sets your **objectives for study.**
Step 3 **Knowledge brought forward boxes**	In these we highlight information and techniques that it is assumed you have 'brought forward' with you from your earlier studies. If there are topics which have changed recently due to legislation for example, these topics are explained in more detail.
Step 4 **Explanations**	Proceed methodically through the chapter, reading each section thoroughly and making sure you understand.

Key study steps	Activity
Step 5 **Key terms and Exam focus points**	• **Key terms** can often earn you *easy marks* if you state them clearly and correctly in an appropriate exam answer (and they are highlighted in the index at the back of the text). • **Exam focus points** give you a good idea of how we think the examiner intends to examine certain topics.
Step 6 **Note taking**	Take brief notes, if you wish. Avoid the temptation to copy out too much. Remember that being able to put something into your own words is a sign of being able to understand it. If you find you cannot explain something you have read, read it again before you make the notes.
Step 7 **Examples**	Follow each through to its solution very carefully.
Step 8 **Case examples**	Study each one, and try to add flesh to them from your own experience – they are designed to show how the topics you are studying come alive (and often come unstuck) in the real world.
Step 9 **Questions**	Make a very good attempt at each one.
Step 10 **Answers**	Check yours against ours, and make sure you understand any discrepancies.
Step 11 **Chapter roundup**	Work through it very carefully, to make sure you have grasped the major points it is highlighting.
Step 12 **Quick quiz**	When you are happy that you have covered the chapter, use the **Quick quiz** to check how much you have remembered of the topics covered and to practise questions in a variety of formats.
Step 13 **Question(s) in the Exam Question bank**	Either at this point, or later when you are thinking about revising, make a full attempt at the **Question(s)** suggested at the very end of the chapter. You can find these at the end of the Study Text, along with the **Answers** so you can see how you did. If you have purchased the **MCQ cards** or **i-Pass**, use these too.

Short of time: Skim study technique?

You may find you simply do not have the time available to follow all the key study steps for each chapter, however you adapt them for your particular learning style. If this is the case, follow the **skim study** technique below (the icons in the Study Text will help you to do this).

- Study the chapters in the order you find them in the Study Text.
- For each chapter, follow the key study steps 1-3, and then skim-read through step 4. Jump to step 11, and then go back to step 5. Follow through steps 7 and 8, and prepare outline answers to questions (steps 9/10). Try the Quick quiz (step 12), following up any items you can't answer, then do a plan for the Question (step 13), comparing it against our answers. You should probably still follow step 6 (note-taking), although you may decide simply to rely on the BPP Passcards for this.

Moving on...

However you study, when you are ready to embark on the practice and revision phase of the BPP Effective Study Package, you should still refer back to this Study Text, both as a source of **reference** (you should find the index particularly helpful for this) and as a way to **review** (the Chapter roundups and Quick quizzes help you here).

And remember to keep careful hold of this Study Text – you will find it invaluable in your work.

SYLLABUS AND LEARNING OUTCOMES

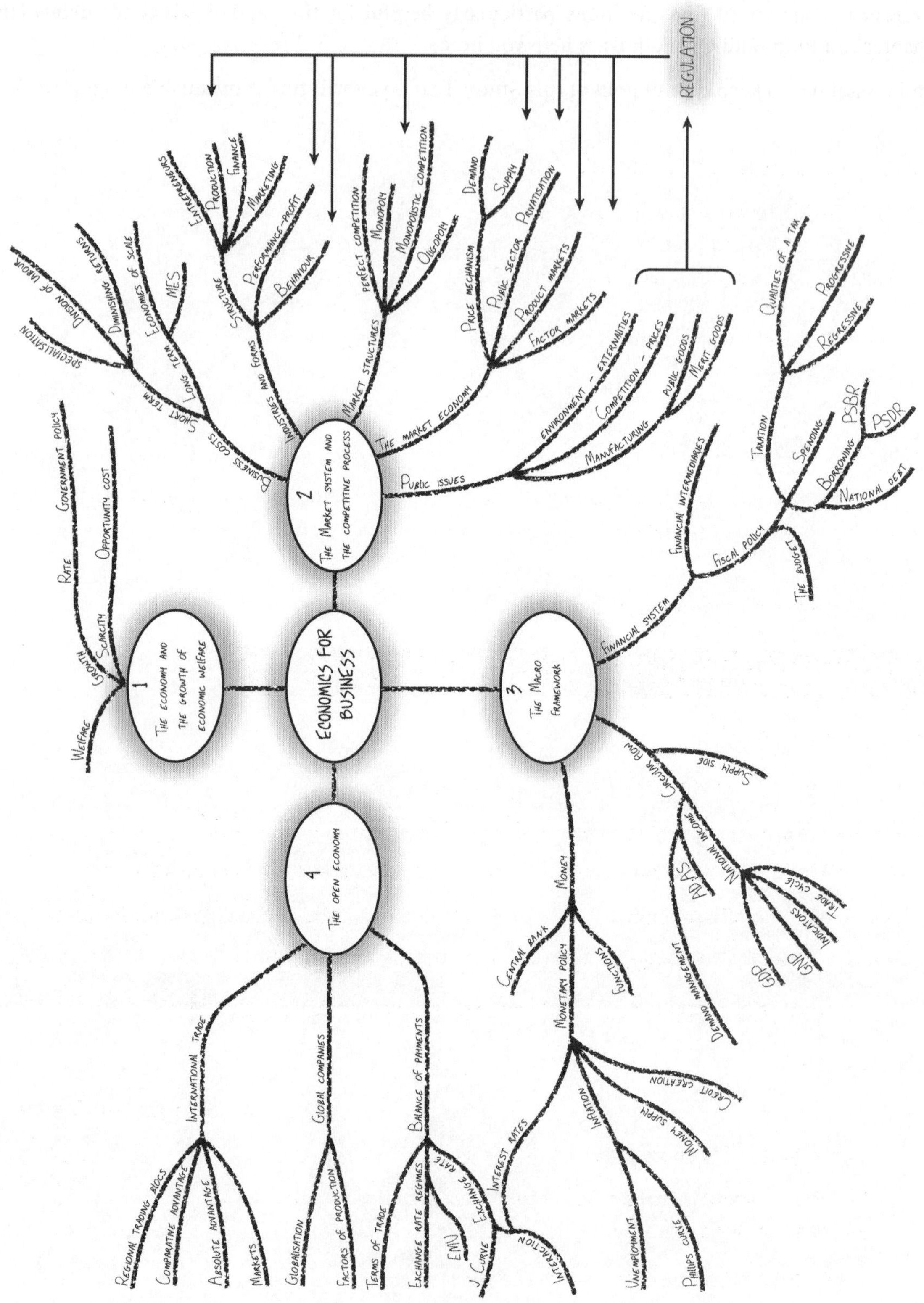

SYLLABUS AND LEARNING OUTCOMES

Syllabus overview

This syllabus is designed to enable students to acquire a knowledge and understanding of the fundamental economic concepts necessary for the work of the Management Accountant.

Aims

This syllabus aims to test the candidate's ability to:

- Identify how a market economy functions and the role of government within it
- explain the economic environment within which businesses operate
- Identify the economic factors which influence the behaviour and performance of firms and industries
- Prepare the economic analysis that informs and guides the advice given to business decision-makers

Assessment

There will be a written paper of 2 hours. Initially objective testing will form a minimum of 50% of the marks awarded on this paper.

Learning outcomes and syllabus content

3a (i) The economy and the growth of Economic Welfare - 10%

Learning outcomes

On completion of their studies students should be able to:

- Explain the principal issues related to economic welfare and its growth
- Explain the main trends in the rate and structure of economic growth in recent years
- Explain the central economic problem and the concepts of scarcity and opportunity cost
- Explain the main factors determining the rate of economic growth
- Explain the main elements of government policy towards economic growth

Syllabus content

	Covered in chapter
• The concept of economic welfare	1
• Economic growth: trends in economic growth; factors in economic growth	1
• Economic welfare and sustainable growth	1
• Issues in economic growth and growth policy	1

3a (ii) The Market System and the Competitive Process - 40%

Learning outcomes

On completion of their studies students should be able to:

- Explain the functioning of a market economy
- Explain how the price system works by applying appropriate economic concepts and principles
- Explain and illustrate how product and factor markets operate
- Apply basic economic analysis to explain economic and business issues
- Explain the behaviour of business costs in both the short and long run
- Explain the economic factors which affect the structure, behaviour and performance of individual businesses and industries
- Analyse the process of competition in different market structures
- Identify the public issues that are raised by business activity
- Explain how governments might respond to the effects of business and the environment

Syllabus content

	Covered in chapter
• The business environment and the structure of economic activity	7
• Business firms: legal, economic and organisational features; entrepreneurship and profit	5, 7
• Business functions: production and costs, finance and marketing	5
• The market process: supply and demand and their determinants	2
• The price mechanism: the demand and supply model and its applications	2, 3, 6
• Forms of market structure: competition and economic welfare; competition policy; regulation and deregulation; the public sector and privatisation	8, 9
• Business and the environment; externalities and public policy	4, 10

3a (iii) The Macroeconomic Framework - 30%

Learning outcomes

On completion of their studies students should be able to:

- Identify the appropriate macroeconomic concepts to explain the measurement and determination of national income
- Explain macroeconomic phenomena by demonstrating a simple circular flow of income model
- Identify the main indicators of macroeconomic performance and demonstrate their significance
- Identify the main elements of the monetary and financial system
- Explain the importance of the monetary environment to the business sector

- Explain the economic role of government through fiscal and monetary policy and demonstrate the impact of such policies on the business sector
- Explain the nature of the trade cycle, its causes and consequences
- Explain the debates concerning the nature of the macroeconomy and appropriate government policy

Syllabus content

	Covered in chapter
• National income: its measurement and determination; the circular flow of income and a simple aggregate demand and supply model; unemployment and the price level	13, 16
• The monetary environment: inflation and the money supply; the banking and financial system; interest rates and monetary policy	11, 12, 15
• The fiscal environment: taxation and public spending; the budget and government borrowing; demand management and supply side policy	17
• Macroeconomic stability; economic fluctuations and their causes; macroeconomic forecasting and stabilisation policy	14

3a (iv) The Open Economy- 20%

Learning outcomes

On completion of their studies students should be able to:

- Explain patterns of international trade and the source of international specialisation
- Identify the international movement of factors of production and the role of transnational companies in this process
- Identify and explain the concepts and consequences of globalisation for business and national economies
- Explain the concept of the balance of payments and its determinants
- Distinguish between different exchange rate regimes and explain their implications for the business sector
- Identify the main elements of national policy with respect to external economic relations, especially in the context of regional trading blocs

Syllabus content

	Covered in chapter
• Patterns of international trade and trade policy; regional trading blocs; the globalisation of production	18
• International factor movements; international capital markets; international investment flows; the movement of labour and technology; the nature and role of transnational companies	18
• The Balance of Payments; structure and determinants of the balance of payments; foreign exchange markets and exchange rate regimes; European Monetary Union	19

THE EXAM PAPER

Format of the paper

		Number of marks
Section A:	26 compulsory multiple choice questions (MCQs)	52
Section B:	3 compulsory data response/stimulus questions (16 marks each)	48
		100

Time allowed: 2 hours

Analysis of papers

May 2002

Section A

1 26 MCQs covering the complete syllabus

Section B

2 Trade cycle; monetary and fiscal policy
3 Monopoly
4 Taxation and government spending

Before May 2002 there was a choice of 3 from 5 questions in Section B of the exam

November 2001

Section A

1 26 MCQs covering the complete syllabus

Section B

2 Economic growth and inflation
3 Price elasticity of demand and supply; factors influencing demand
4 Economics of scale and industrial structure
5 Economic growth, inflation and monetary policy
6 Foreign trade; tariffs

May 2001

Section A

1 26 MCQs covering the complete syllabus

Section B

2 Production possibility frontier
3 Analysis of price and cost schedules
4 Positive aspects of monopoly
5 National income and influences upon it
6 Balance of payments accounts and exchange rates

Pilot Paper

Section A

1 26 MCQs covering the complete syllabus

Section B

2 Economies of scale
3 Costs and revenues for a monopoly; barriers to entry
4 Circular flow, injections and withdrawals
5 Absolute and comparative advantage in international trade
6 Taxation; the Laffer curve

The examiner

The examiner for the Economics for Business paper used to be the examiner for the equivalent paper in the old syllabus, Economic Environment. We expect that the emphasis in the new examination will be similar to that in the old and have prepared this Study Text accordingly.

WHAT THE EXAMINER MEANS

The table below has been prepared by CIMA to help you interpret exam questions.

Learning objective	Verbs used	Definition
1 Knowledge What you are expected to know	• List • State • Define	• Make a list of • Express, fully or clearly, the details of/facts of • Give the exact meaning of
2 Comprehension What you are expected to understand	• Describe • Distinguish • Explain • Identify • Illustrate	• Communicate the key features of • Highlight the differences between • Make clear or intelligible/state the meaning of • Recognise, establish or select after consideration • Use an example to describe or explain something
3 Application Can you apply your knowledge?	• Apply • Calculate/ compute • Demonstrate • Prepare • Reconcile • Solve • Tabulate	• To put to practical use • To ascertain or reckon mathematically • To prove with certainty or to exhibit by practical means • To make or get ready for use • To make or prove consistent/compatible • Find an answer to • Arrange in a table
4 Analysis Can you analyse the detail of what you have learned?	• Analyse • Categorise • Compare and contrast • Construct • Discuss • Interpret • Produce	• Examine in detail the structure of • Place into a defined class or division • Show the similarities and/or differences between • To build up or compile • To examine in detail by argument • To translate into intelligible or familiar terms • To create or bring into existence
5 Evaluation Can you use your learning to evaluate, make decisions or recommendations?	• Advise • Evaluate • Recommend	• To counsel, inform or notify • To appraise or assess the value of • To advise on a course of action

TACKLING MULTIPLE CHOICE QUESTIONS

The MCQs in your exam contain four possible answers. You have to **choose the option that best answers the question**. The three incorrect options are called distracters. There is a skill in answering MCQs quickly and correctly. By practising MCQs you can develop this skill, giving you a better chance of passing the exam.

You may wish to follow the approach outlined below, or you may prefer to adapt it.

Step 1. Skim read all the MCQs and identify what appear to be the easier questions.

Step 2. Attempt each question – **starting with the easier questions** identified in Step 1. Read the question thoroughly. You may prefer to work out the answer before looking at the options, or you may prefer to look at the options at the beginning. Adopt the method that works best for you.

Step 3. Read the four options and see if one matches your own answer. Be careful with numerical questions, as the distracters are designed to match answers that incorporate common errors. Check that your calculation is correct. Have you followed the requirement exactly? Have you included every stage of the calculation?

Step 4. You may find that none of the options matches your answer.

- Re-read the question to ensure that you understand it and are answering the requirement
- Eliminate any obviously wrong answers
- Consider which of the remaining answers is the most likely to be correct and select the option

Step 5. If you are still unsure make a note and continue to the next question.

Step 6. Revisit unanswered questions. When you come back to a question after a break you often find you are able to answer it correctly straight away. If you are still unsure have a guess. You are not penalised for incorrect answers, so **never leave a question unanswered!**

After extensive practice and revision of MCQs, you may find that you recognise a question when you sit the exam. Be aware that the detail and/or requirement may be different. If the question seems familiar read the requirement and options carefully – do not assume that it is identical.

TACKLING OBJECTIVE TEST QUESTIONS IN COMPUTER-BASED ASSESSMENT

What is an objective test question?

An objective test (**OT**) question is made up of some form of **stimulus**, usually a question, and a **requirement** to do something.

(a) **Filling in a blank or blanks in a sentence**

(b) **Listing items in rank order**

(c) **Stating a definition**

(d) **Identifying a key issue, term or figure**

(e) **Calculating a specific figure**

(f) **Completing gaps in a set of data where the relevant numbers can be calculated from the information given**

(g) **Identifying points/zones/ranges/areas on graphs or diagrams**

(h) **Matching items or statements**

(i) **Stating whether statements are true or false**

(j) **Writing brief (in a specified number of words) explanations to the data given**

Multiple choice questions (MCQs) – selecting the most appropriate option from a number of options provided – are the most common form of OT question. We looked at them in detail on page (xix).

OT questions in computer-based assessment

The CBA will not be divided into sections. There will be a total forty questions and you will need to answer **ALL** of them in the time allowed, 1½ hours. The computer will automatically work out your result and state your mark as a percentage. It will also indicate whether you have passed or failed.

TACKLING OBJECTIVE TEST QUESTIONS IN THE PAPER-BASED EXAM

What is an objective test question?

An objective test (**OT**) question is made up of some form of **stimulus**, usually a question, and a **requirement** to do something.

(a) **Filling in a blank or blanks in a sentence**

(b) **Listing items in rank order**

(c) **Stating a definition**

(d) **Identifying a key issue, term or figure**

(e) **Calculating a specific figure**

(f) **Completing gaps in a set of data where the relevant numbers can be calculated from the information given**

(g) **Identifying points/zones/ranges/areas on graphs or diagrams**

(h) **Matching items or statements**

(i) **Stating whether statements are true or false**

(j) **Writing brief (in a specified number of words) explanations to the data given**

Multiple choice questions (MCQs) – selecting the most appropriate option from a number of options provided – are the most common form of OT questions. We looked at them in detail on page (x).

OT questions in the paper-based exam

Section A of the paper will consist of 25 MCQs worth 50 marks.

In Section B of the paper, which will be worth **50 marks**, you will be provided with two or more **scenarios** and will be asked **several OT questions** about each scenario.

There will be **no optional questions**, you will have to attempt all the questions in both sections.

CIMA has offered the following **guidance** about OT questions in the exam.

- **Only your answers will be marked**, not workings or any justifications.
- If you **exceed a specified limit on the number of words** you can use in an answer, you will **not be awarded any marks**.
- If you make **more than one attempt** at a question, clearly **cross through** any answers that you do not want to submit. If you don't do this, only your first answer will be marked.

We strongly suggest therefore, that you **take note of the guidance given above when answering OT questions in the paper-based exam.**

Part A

The economy and the growth of economic welfare

Chapter 1

THE ALLOCATION OF SCARCE RESOURCES

	Topic list	Syllabus reference	Ability required
1	Economics as a social science	(i)	Comprehension
2	Scarcity of resources	(i)	Comprehension
3	Exchange, specialisation and economic wealth	(i)	Comprehension
4	Economic growth	(i)	Comprehension

Introduction

We begin our study of economics by introducing some fundamental concepts and considering the problems which economics attempts to address.

An important theme in this introductory chapter is economic growth and its relationship with economic welfare.

Learning outcomes covered in this chapter

- Explain the principal issues related to economic welfare and its growth
- Explain the main trends in the rate and structure of economic growth in recent years
- Explain the central economic problem and the concepts of scarcity and opportunity cost
- Explain the main factors determining the rate of economic growth
- Explain the main elements of government policy towards economic growth

Syllabus content covered in this chapter

- The concept of economic welfare
- Economic growth: trends in economic growth; factors in economic growth
- Economic welfare and sustainable growth
- Issues in economic growth and growth policy

1 ECONOMICS AS A SOCIAL SCIENCE

1.1 Economics is a social science which is concerned with the production and consumption of goods and services. It studies the ways in which society decides **what** to produce, **how** to produce it and **who** to produce it for. Economic activity is undertaken by people as a natural part of their pursuit of survival, prosperity and wealth. In a primitive economy it consists of hunting and gathering, and later of subsistence farming. More advanced economies display great specialisation of economic activity and measure it in money terms, but the end result is the same. We are all economic agents and economic activity is what we do to make a living.

KEY TERM

Ceteris paribus: 'other things being equal'

1.2 Because economics is a **social** science, concerned with human behaviour, it is extremely difficult to reach firm conclusions, and there are wide areas of disagreement among economists. The theories are based on observation of society as it exists rather than on laboratory experiment and the phrase *ceteris paribus* is often used. In fact, other things rarely do remain the same, and there is frequent debate about the meaning and implications of a particular set of observations. Nevertheless, economics is a science rather than an art since the scientific method of critical examination of theory in the light of observed data is employed.

1.3 Economists assume that people behave rationally at all times and always seek to improve their circumstances. This assumption leads to more specific assumptions.

- Producers will seek to maximise their profits.
- Consumers will seek to maximise the benefits (their 'utility') from their income.
- Governments will seek to maximise the welfare of their populations.

1.4 Both the basic assumption of rationality and the more detailed assumptions may be challenged. A further complication is that concepts such as utility and welfare are not only open to interpretation, but that the interpretation will change over time.

1.5 **Positive economics** is concerned with objective statements and explanations of what has happened and logical forecasts of what is going to happen. It is the truly scientific aspect of economics, and it is the approach we will take.

1.6 **Normative economics** is about economic and social value judgements and what people think **ought** to happen in an ideal world.

1.7 **Microeconomics** is the study of individual economic units; these are called **households** and **firms.**

1.8 **Macroeconomics** is the study of the aggregated effects of the decisions of economic units. It looks at a complete national economy or the international economic system as a whole.

1.9 In this text we shall examine microeconomics first and macroeconomics in later chapters.

2 SCARCITY OF RESOURCES 5/01, 5/02

2.1 It is a fact of life that there are limits to available **resources.**

(a) For the individual **consumer** the scarcity of goods and services might seem obvious enough. Most people would like to have more: perhaps a car, or more clothes, or a house of their own. Examples of services include live theatre performances, public passenger transport and child-minding.

(b) In the case of producers, we can identify four types of resource, which are also called **factors of production.**

- Land
- Labour
- Capital
- Entrepreneurship

Land refers to the natural resources which a firm uses, and so this will include oil and minerals. The definition of **capital** in economics is different from that used in accounting: as well as money, it means plant and buildings. **Entrepreneurship** or **enterprise** is the 'organising' factor of production. A firm must face the fact that the factors of production available to it, which it combines to produce goods and services, are limited.

(c) Consider now the national economy. Each country is endowed with natural resources of limited quantity and of different types. Some countries have plentiful mineral resources while others have hardly any, or none. Some countries have more skilled labour than others. Some countries have a relatively undeveloped manufacturing infrastructure (factories, machinery and so on). We shall see later how such differences provide a basis for international trade.

(d) For the world as a whole, resources available to serve human consumption are limited. For example, as we all know, the supply of non-renewable energy resources is, by definition, limited. The amount of many minerals which it is feasible to extract from the earth (for example, metals of various kinds) is also limited.

(e) Some resources are not scarce. Air to breathe is not normally scarce unless, perhaps, you are trapped underwater or underground. Ice is not scarce in Antarctica, and sand is plentiful in the Sahara desert.

KEY TERMS

Scarcity: the excess of human wants over what can actually be produced. A **scarce resource** is a resource for which the quantity demanded at a nil price would exceed the available supply.

2.2 Since resources for production are scarce and there are not enough goods and services to satisfy the total potential demand, choices must be made. Choice is only necessary because resources are scarce.

(a) Consumers must choose what goods and services they will have.

(b) Producers must choose how to use their available resources, and what to produce with them.

Economics studies the nature of these choices. What will be produced? What will be consumed? And who will benefit from the consumption?

The production possibility curve: illustrating the limits of production 5/01, 11/01, 5/02

2.3 We can approach the central questions of economics by looking first at the possibilities of production. Suppose, to take a simple example, that an imaginary society can use its available resources to produce two products, A and B. The society's resources are limited. Therefore there are restrictions on the amounts of A and B that can be made, which can be shown by a **production possibility curve** (or **frontier**).

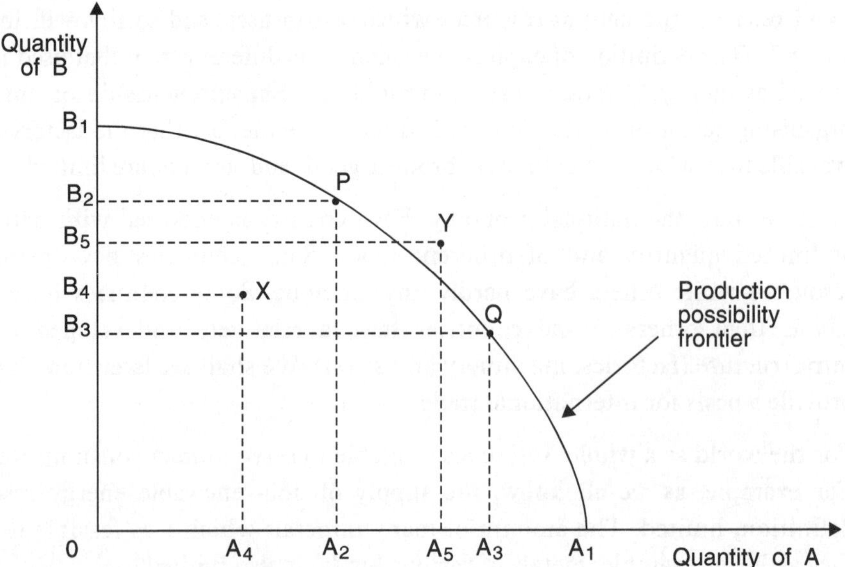

Figure 1 Production possibility curve

2.4 The curve from A_1 round to B_1 in Figure 1 shows the various combinations of A and B that a society can make, if it uses its limited resources efficiently.

(a) The society can choose to make up to:

- A_1 units of A and no B
- B_1 units of B and no A
- A_2 units of A and B_2 of B (point P on the curve)
- A_3 units of A and B_3 of B (point Q on the curve).

(b) The combination of A_4 units of A and B_4 units of B plotted at point X is within the production possibility curve. More than these quantities can be made of either or both of A and B. Point X is therefore an inefficient production point for the economy, and if the society were to make only A_4 of A and B_4 of B, it would be using its limited resources inefficiently.

(c) Note that the production possibility curve is just what it says: it defines what is achievable if **all** productive resources are fully employed. It follows that changes in the level of unemployment have no effect upon it. Similarly, changes in price levels will affect the **monetary value** of what can be produced, but not the **volume**.

Question 1

What can you say about the combination of A and B indicated by point Y in Figure 1?

Answer

Point Y lies outside the production possibility curve. Even with efficient use of resources it is impossible to produce this combination of A and B. To reach point Y either current resources must be increased or production methods must be improved - perhaps by developments in technology.

2.5 The production possibility curve is an important idea in economics which illustrates the **need to make a choice about what to produce when it is not possible to have everything** - that is, when there is scarcity. Although we have characterised the products of our hypothetical economy as A and B, we can generalise the production possibility curve to show the production possibilities for different types of good, and also for some 'good X' on one axis and 'all other goods' on the other axis.

Opportunity cost: the cost of one use for resources rather than another 11/01

2.6 Choice involves sacrifice. If there is a choice between having A and having B, and a country chooses to have A, it will be giving up B to have A. The cost of having a certain amount of A can therefore be regarded as the sacrifice of not being able to have a certain amount of B. There is a sacrifice involved in the choices of consumers and firms (producers), as well as the choices of governments at the level of national economy.

2.7 Suppose a consumer has a limited amount of money, and chooses to buy some eggs. One measurement of the cost of the eggs is their money price. Another way of looking at the cost is to consider the sacrifice involved in choosing eggs rather than, say, milk. If the consumer has some eggs, he or she is giving up the opportunity to have some milk, and the benefits that the milk would have provided.

KEY TERM

The cost of an item measured in terms of the alternatives forgone is called its **opportunity cost.**

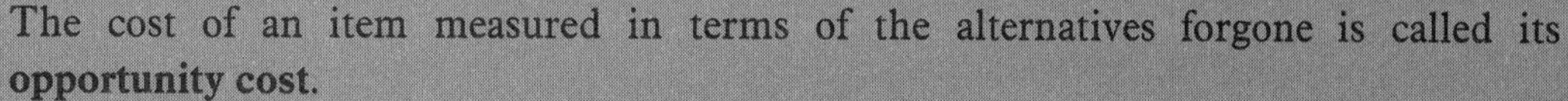

2.8 For example, the opportunity cost of buying six eggs can be measured as the two pints of milk or the one bus ride that could have been bought instead. Similarly, at a national level the opportunity cost of a country having a hospital could be measured in terms of the number of schools that could have been built and staffed with the same amount of resources.

2.9 A production possibility curve illustrates opportunity costs. For example, if in Figure 1 it is decided to switch from making A_3 units of A and B_3 units of B (point Q) to making A_2 units of A and B_2 units of B (point P), then **the opportunity cost of making ($B_2 - B_3$) more units of B would be the lost production of ($A_3 - A_2$) units of A.**

2.10 The production possibility line is a **curve** and not a straight line because opportunity costs change as we move away from a situation in which production is wholly devoted to either A or B. Thus, as we move away from point A_1, and introduce an increasing level of production of B, the amount of B that we gain from losing each unit of A progressively diminishes.

2.11 At the level of the firm, the production possibility curve can be seen as showing the maximum output of different alternative goods which the firm can produce when all of its resources are fully used - for example, a firm might operate production lines capable of producing washing machines or refrigerators. Producing more washing machines bears the opportunity cost of a lower level of production of refrigerators.

Shifts in the production possibility curve

2.12 When the availability of resources changes, or there is a development in technology, the production possibility curve may shift. Changes are made possible by developments such as a bigger labour force, more efficient methods of working, more efficient machinery, or a new discovery of natural resources, such as oil, natural gas or minerals.

(a) If the production possibility curve moves outwards, to the right, it means that the economy is capable of producing more goods and services in total than it could before, and there is **economic growth.**

(b) If it moves to the left (inwards) it means that the economy cannot produce as much as before (for example because of a significant decline in population or the exhaustion of a natural resource).

Note that the production possibility curve is concerned with **fundamental productive capacity**. Thus, an increase in the size of the labour force shifts the position of the curve but a fall in unemployment does not: it merely moves *actual* output closer to *potential* output. Similarly, an increase in available capital will increase potential output, but changes in prices do not.

2.13 In Figure 2, curve M represents greater production possibilities than curve N. If a society's production possibility curve shifts out from N to M, there is economic growth. The society could now switch from making A_1 of A and B_1 of B (point X) to making A_2 of A and B_2 of B (point Y).

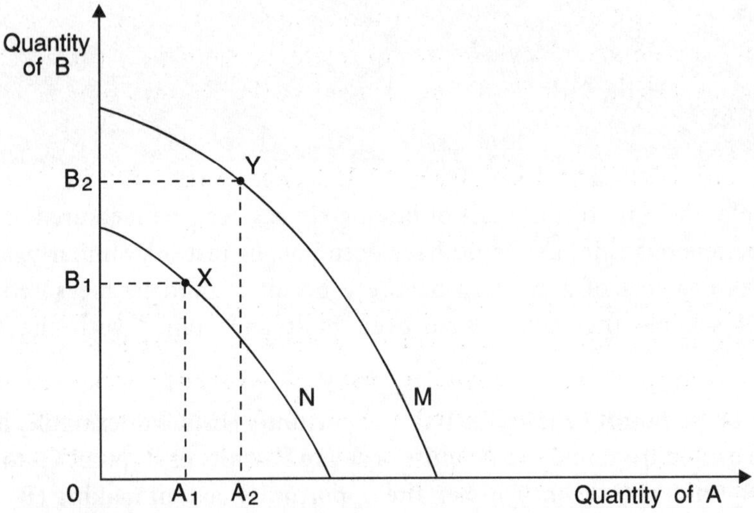

Figure 2 Shift in the production possibility curve

Economic systems **11/01**

2.14 The way in which the resource allocation choices are made, the way value is measured and the forms of ownership of economic wealth will vary according to the type of **economic system** that exists in a society.

(a) In a **centrally planned** or **command economy,** the decisions and choices about resource allocation are made by the government. Money values are attached to resources and to goods and services, but it is the government that decides what resources should be used, how much should be paid for them, what goods should be made and what their price should be. Although the individual might be allowed to own some personal possessions, most kinds of wealth would not be available for ownership by individuals.

(b) In a **market economy,** the decisions and choices about resource allocation are left to **market forces of supply and demand,** and the workings of the price mechanism. In the market economy, most wealth is owned by individuals, with a minimum being collectively owned.

(c) In a **mixed economy** the decisions and choices are made partly by free market forces of supply and demand, and partly by government decisions. Economic wealth is divided between the private sector and the public sector. In practice, all modern national

economies are mixed economies, although with differing proportions of free market and centrally planned decision-making from one country to the next.

2.15 The market economy brings social problems. Individual prosperity and even survival depend upon talent, enterprise and luck. Many people do not have the ability to prosper, especially in times of economic slow down.

2.16 The widespread deprivation typical of the newly industrialised western economies of the nineteenth century provoked the erection of economic theories based on public ownership of productive resources, central direction by government of economic activity and egalitarian distribution of national income.

2.17 Unfortunately, the experience of every country that has attempted to implement a planned economy is that the theory does not work: such economies are for less productive than those that allow market forces to take effect. The result is that apart from a few poverty-stricken dictatorships such as Cuba, North Korea and Zimbabwe, the mixed economy model is now used world-wide. This combines the wealth creating potential of the market economy with a varying degree of welfare provision and seems to be the least bad approach.

3 EXCHANGE, SPECIALISATION AND ECONOMIC WEALTH

Exchange value

3.1 As we mentioned earlier, there is an abundance of some things, such as air and seawater. Because these are not scarce, people will not generally pay money to acquire them. When a resource is scarce, it has an economic value or **exchange value**. Producers will give something in exchange for the natural resources, labour and equipment that they need to help them to produce goods and services. Consumers will give something in exchange for the goods and services that they can obtain.

3.2 For resources to have an exchange value, there is a presupposition that exchange can take place. If everyone were self-sufficient, producing goods only for their own individual needs, exchange would not be necessary. However, the vast range and complexity of goods and services in a modern society means that individuals cannot produce everything for themselves. They must **specialise** in one role and use their income from that role to purchase what they need. Exchange is thus fundamental to any economy and goes hand-in-hand with specialisation.

Specialisation and the division of labour

3.3 Specialisation allows the **division of labour** within an industry. Production is divided up so that specialists can develop and use their particular skills to the full. This increases the efficiency of operations and thus shifts the production possibility frontier to the right.

KEY TERMS

Specialisation means that individual workers do not undertake the whole possible range of economic activity themselves.

The **division of labour** refers to specialisation within a single industry. The manufacture of one product sometimes calls for the work to be divided up into sub-specialities in which workers can become expert; for example, in the making of motor cars, there are car body builders, paint sprayers and engine tuners.

3.4 In practice, most workers sell their labour to a firm (or to the government) in exchange for money wages. **Money is the medium of exchange which permits them to buy other goods and services.** By getting a worker to specialise in just one part of the production process, he or she will develop expert skills, and will be able to work more quickly, produce more output, and produce work of a better quality and with less wastage.

3.5 Specialisation applies to land, capital and entrepreneurship, as well as to labour. Specialised machinery is a common feature of production; some entrepreneurs specialise in a certain type of industry or market, and land can have a specialised use.

Question 2

Why do you think that specialisation of labour has become so much a part of modern economics? What benefits does it bring?

Answer

The main reason is that specialisation of labour leads to greater production efficiency. Workers engaged in just one part of the production process will be able to develop expert skills, and will work more quickly to produce output of higher quality. You might also be aware of the criticisms levelled at specialisation - that it leads to boredom and frustration for the workers involved, and that workers' ignorance of how their own contribution fits into the overall scheme can lead to inefficiencies - but that takes us beyond the point under consideration.

Economic wealth

3.6 Economics must take account of the processes by which **wealth** is created in an economy. Some economists are also concerned with the distribution of wealth in a society.

3.7 Economic wealth can be viewed as the **stock of net assets** owned by households, firms and the State. Another way to consider economic wealth is in terms of the total stock of goods of a society at a given time. Four qualities can be specified in order to define the nature of such goods.

In order for goods to be considered as wealth, they must conform to the conditions below.

(a) **They must possess utility**. In other words, they must be capable of yielding satisfaction.

(b) **They must have a monetary value**.

(c) **They must be limited in supply**. Goods are scarce in the sense that the resources available to society are insufficient to meet all wants to the level of complete satiety. Given their relative scarcity in relation to demand, scarce goods will have a price or money value.

(d) **Ownership must be possible**. The ownership of such goods must be capable of being transferred from one person to another.

3.8 The definition of wealth implied in the above would exclude intangible things such as acquired skills. A craftsman, such as a carpenter, would count his tools as part of his personal stock of wealth, but would exclude his skill in using them, as skills are not transferable in the sense mentioned above. In speaking of a nation's wealth, however, it would be appropriate to include the quality of the labour as represented by the stock of human capital where maintenance is determined in part by the level of education and training. And so we can define economic wealth as the total stock of tangible and intangible possessions.

3.9 It is possible to distinguish three classes of ownership of wealth.

(a) **Personal wealth** comprises personal belongings such as clothes, cars, books and consumer durables. It would also include houses, land, paintings, jewellery and other property owned by individuals. All these things presumably give satisfaction to their owner, or we may suggest that they would not have been acquired; all have a money value, all are limited in supply, and in general, ownership is transferable from one person to another.

(b) **Business wealth** comprises such things as factory buildings, machinery, raw materials and stocks of finished goods. These things also possess all the attributes of wealth, although they do not yield satisfaction for their own sake. They are derived merely to assist the production of other things and are usually termed capital.

(c) **Social wealth** consists of wealth owned collectively and includes all property owned by the national government and local authorities, for example roads, schools, public libraries and museums. It is possible to transfer wealth from the private sector to the social sector and *vice versa*.

Economic welfare 5/01

3.10 **Welfare** in its broadest sense is health, happiness and prosperity. The idea can be applied both to individuals and to society as a whole. It is more a matter for philosophy than social science to establish just what the best balance of health, happiness and prosperity would be, or, indeed, whether other matters such as freedom and faith should be included in the equation.

3.11 In simple economic terms, we may say that **prosperity is fundamental to welfare**. This is because economic wealth can certainly be used to provide the material aspects of welfare and may make possible the pursuit of any desired non-material components. For our purposes then, an increase in economic wealth implies an increase in welfare. Such an increase would be called **economic growth**.

3.12 Economic growth is usually thought of as an increase in the level of output of goods and services. Such increases normally arise in two ways.

- An increase in the **size** of the working population
- An increase in the **productivity** of individual work people

The first is influenced by a variety of demographic factors such as net immigration and the birth rate; the second by capital investment and technological advance.
This is measured in money terms and this immediately raises the problem of **output that is not traded**. Such output is not measurable in conventional economic terms and is not included in conventional measures of output such as national income. There is no easy solution to this problem, but it is always worth remembering that performing unpaid domestic tasks or do-it-yourself activities do contribute to economic welfare.

3.13 Another important consideration is that economic welfare can actually be reduced by the side effects of economic activities. Noise, dirt, chemical pollution and mental illness are all examples of such social costs. Social **benefits** can also arise and should also be considered when assessing economic welfare. Social costs and benefits are known as **externalities**: that is, they arise from transactions, but affect people who are not parties to those transactions.

3.14 We will deal with measuring economic wealth and with externalities in later chapters. For now, be aware that economic welfare is as much about quality of life as it is about production and output.

4 ECONOMIC GROWTH

4.1 It is widely accepted that economic growth is desirable because it increases welfare in the economic sense. It makes more and better **consumer goods and services** available to more people through the normal market process and enables governments to provide improved **public services.** It may be remarked that economic growth may also have undesirable side effects, such as increased pollution. However, as we will see in a later chapter, it is possible for such **externalities** to be regulated. Wealth is usually measured in terms of Gross National Product (GNP). We consider GNP in more detail later. For now, we may think of it as a nation's total output of goods and services in one year.

(a) Measuring **real** GNP removes increases in GNP caused solely by **price inflation**.

(b) Increases in the average standard of living of a population are measured by GNP per head of population. If a country's GNP is rising annually by, say, 3% but the population is also increasing by 3% annually, it would be concluded that the increase in living standards in the country is really zero.

4.2 The achievement of economic growth is thus central to government economic policy in all developed countries.

4.3 Economic growth may be balanced or unbalanced. With **balanced growth** all sectors of the economy expand together. When growth is **unbalanced** there may be a specialisation in areas of the economy so that some sectors of the economy grow faster than others. This imbalance often has a geographical effect with some regions becoming more prosperous than others.

4.4 Less developed countries in particular find it difficult to achieve economic growth, because many of the factors necessary for growth are absent in these countries.

4.5 **Actual economic growth** is the annual percentage increase in national output, which typically fluctuates in accordance with the trade cycle. **Potential economic growth** is the rate at which the economy would grow if all resources (eg people and machinery) were utilised.

Potential growth

4.6 Growth in potential output is determined by the **capacity of the economy** to produce. There are two aspects to this.

(a) There may be increases in the **amount of resources** available.

(i) **Land and raw materials**. Land is virtually in fixed supply, but new natural resources are continually being discovered.

(ii) **Labour.** In developed countries, about half of the average total growth comes from the increasing size of the working population. The **participation rate** is the proportion of the population which actually contributes to economic output.

(iii) **Capital** such as plant and machinery is increased by **investment**.

(iv) **Entrepreneurship.** The UK government has encouraged enterprise.

(b) Increases in the **productivity of resources** may result from technological progress or changed labour practices, for example.

Factors needed for sustained economic growth

4.7 **Sustained economic growth** depends heavily on an adequate level of **new investment,** which will be undertaken if there are **expectations of future growth in demand**. But there is no reason why the actual level of income should end up increasing as much as the investing business people thought it would. It follows that **investment,** a factor in growth, **is dependent on business confidence** in the future, which is reflected in expectations of growth in consumption.

Natural resources

4.8 The rate of extraction of natural resources will impose a limit on the rate of growth. Production which uses up a country's natural resources, such as oil, coal and other minerals, depletes the stock of available resources; it is therefore in a sense **disinvestment**.

Technological progress

4.9 Technological progress is a very important source of faster economic growth.

- The same amounts of the factors of production can produce a higher output.
- New products will be developed, thus adding to output growth.

4.10 There can be technical progress in the labour force. If workers are better educated and better trained they will be able to produce more. For example, if there is a fault in the production process, a skilled worker will be able to deal with it quickly, whereas an unskilled one might have to call for a superior instead.

4.11 Technological progress can be divided into three types.

(a) **Capital-saving**: technical advances that use less capital and the same amount of labour per unit of output

(b) **Neutral**: technical advances that require labour and capital in the same proportions as before, using less of each per unit of output

(c) **Labour-saving**: technical advance that uses less labour and the same amount of capital per unit of output.

4.12 If technological progress is labour saving, then **unemployment will rise** unless there is either a simultaneous expansion of demand or a reduction in hours worked by each person, in which case there is no productivity increase associated with the technological progress.

4.13 Technological progress may therefore stimulate growth but at the same time conflict with the goal of full employment. A further consequence of this could be that those people in work would benefit from economic growth in the form of higher wages, but those people put out of work by the new technology would be left with a lower income. There is thus a danger that the rich will get richer and the poor will get poorer in spite of economic growth, and this would be regarded by many people as an undesirable development.

External trade influences on economic growth

4.14 An improvement in the **terms of trade** (the quantity of imports that can be bought in exchange for a given quantity of exports) means that more imports can be bought or alternatively a given volume of exports will earn higher profits. This will boost investment and hence growth.

Exam focus point

The **terms of trade** is a concept you need to grasp for the exam: we return to it later in this Study Text.

4.15 The rate of growth of the rest of the world is important for an economy that has a large foreign trade sector. If trading partners have slow growth, the amount of exports a country can sell to them will grow only slowly, and this limits the country's own opportunities for investment and growth.

Advantages and disadvantages of economic growth

4.16 Economic growth should mean that the population as a whole will be able to raise its standard of living in material terms, and that there should also be an improvement in economic welfare. A country with economic growth is more easily able to provide a welfare state service without creating intolerable tax burdens on the community.

4.17 There are potential disadvantages to growth, however.

(a) Growth implies faster use of natural resources. Without growth, these resources would last longer.

(b) Much economic activity tends to create pollution, such as acid rain and nuclear waste. It leads to emissions which threaten to produce disruptive climatic changes through an increase in the 'greenhouse effect'. It results in more roads, cultivated farmland, new and larger towns, and less unspoilt countryside.

(c) There is a danger that some sections of the population, unable to adapt to the demands for new skills and more training, will not find jobs in the developing economy. This structural unemployment might create a large section of the community which gains no benefit from the increase in national income.

There potential disadvantages are recognised by governments. Pollution is controlled by regulation of various types. Training and re-training may be subsidised by grants, loans and direct provision. Structural unemployment is often concentrated in depressed regions and this is tackled by special regional measures to attract new businesses.

Economic reorganisation

4.18 Economic reorganisation is a term which refers to the economic changes which must be made within a country when its old industries are facing decline and new industries need to be developed to take their place, in order to prevent economic decline. Much of the UK's older industrial base is in decline or has already disappeared. Examples are shipbuilding, steel production and textiles.

4.19 **Task of economic reorganisation**

(a) To encourage firms to move into new, growth industries

(b) To encourage new investment by firms, in order to increase output capacity

(c) To encourage training, so that a skilled labour force is available to do the work in the new industries

4.20 In recent years, growth in most developed countries has averaged about 2.5%. However, it has varied quite significantly from country to country and from year to year. We discuss the **economic cycle** later in this study text. For now, be aware that achieving **continuous and stable growth is a goal which has eluded most countries**.

4.21 Differences between countries are quite marked. Most of the countries of the EU are growing rather sluggishly compared with the USA which has enjoyed an unusually long period of high growth. It has been suggested that this has two causes.

(a) The economies of the European countries are more subject to **government regulation** and costs are higher as a result.

(b) The US economy has undergone a transformation as a result of **technological developments** in general and the rise of electronic business methods based on the Internet in particular.

It should be noted, however, that some less wealthy European countries such as Spain and Ireland have enjoyed continuing high rates of growth, largely because of injections of EU funds and other special circumstances.

4.22 During the last 50 years, many economies in Asia grew extremely rapidly. Much of this growth came from increases in the participation rate. Even after the recent severe financial crisis that affected much of Asia, many Asian countries have recovered and are once again growing at high rates.

Exam focus point

The material in this section is not often examined in detail, but it is fundamental to much of what follows. Think about it and try to understand it in terms of what you see happening in daily life.

Chapter roundup

- Economics is concerned with how resources are allocated and how choices are made about resources. We have seen that economic decisions are about what gets produced, what gets consumed and who gets what.
- The need to make economic decisions, about what to produce or what to buy, arises because economic resources are scarce. Making decisions involves the sacrifice of benefits that could have been obtained from using resources in an alternative course of action: these benefits forgone are called opportunity costs.
- Scarce resources, and the output produced by scarce resources, have an exchange value. In modern economic societies, exchange values are measured by money, and the value of products is their selling price. Efficiency is enhanced by specialisation in the use of resources, and by the division of labour.

Quick quiz

1 Name the four resources or 'factors of production' available to producers.

2 Give examples of how the concept of opportunity cost is relevant to:

(a) an individual
(b) a government
(c) a firm

3 What is meant by specialisation and the division of labour?

4 What are the basic economic choices regarding the allocation of resources?

5 What is meant by unbalanced economic growth?

6 What are the causes of growth in potential output?

7 What types of technological progress can be distinguished?

8 What is meant by 'economic reorganisation'?

Answers to quick quiz

1 Land, labour, entrepreneurship, capital

2 A consumer who chooses to buy a particular good must give up another. A government which chooses to spend tax revenue on education cannot spend that money on railways. A firm which chooses to produce radios must give up some production of video recorders.

3 Specialisation means that people do not undertake the whole range of economic activity in person. The division of labour is specialisation by people within a single industry.

4 What will be produced? What resources will be used? Who will consume the goods and services produced?

5 Growth in which some sectors grow faster than others.

6 Growth in potential output depends on either increases in the quantity of resources available or increases in the productivity of resources.

7 Capital-saving, labour-saving and neutral

8 The replacement of declining industries by expanding ones.

Now try the questions below from the Question Bank

Number	Level	Marks	Time
Q1	Introductory	8	10 mins
Q2	Exam - MCQ	–	–
Q3	Introductory - MCQ	–	–

Part B

The market system and the competitive process

Chapter 2

THE PRICE MECHANISM: DEMAND AND SUPPLY

	Topic list	Syllabus reference	Ability required
1	The concept of a market	(ii)	Application
2	The demand schedule	(ii)	Application
3	The supply schedule	(ii)	Application
4	The equilibrium price	(ii)	Application
5	Maximum and minimum prices	(ii)	Application

Introduction

The distinction between the microeconomic level and the macroeconomic level was mentioned in Chapter 1.

In this chapter, we start looking in more depth at the microeconomic level of the individual firm, individual markets and consumers (or households). This means analysing how price and output are determined through the interaction of demand and supply.

Learning outcomes covered in this chapter

- Explain the functioning of a market economy
- Explain how the price system works by applying appropriate economic concepts and principles
- Apply basic economic analysis to explain economic and business issues
- Explain how governments might respond to the effects of business and the environment

Syllabus content covered in this chapter

- The market process: supply and demand and their determinants
- The price mechanism: the demand and supply model and its applications

1 THE CONCEPT OF A MARKET

What is a market?

1.1 The concept of a market in economics goes beyond the idea of a single geographical place where people meet to buy and sell goods. It means **the buyers and sellers of a good who influence its price**. Markets can be worldwide, as in the case of oil, wheat, cotton and copper for example. Others are more localised, such as the housing market or the market for second-hand cars.

KEY TERM

A **market** can be defined as a situation in which potential buyers and potential sellers (*suppliers*) of a good or service come together for the purpose of exchange.

1.2 Suppliers and potential suppliers are referred to in economics as **firms**. The potential purchasers of consumer goods are known as **households**.

1.3 Some markets have buyers who are other firms or government authorities. For example, a manufacturing firm buys raw materials and components to go into the products that it makes. Service industries and government departments must similarly buy in supplies in order to do their own work. The demand for goods by firms and government authorities is a **derived demand** in that it depends on the demand from households for the goods and services that they produce and provide.

1.4 Markets for different goods or commodities are often inter-related. All commodities compete for households' income so that if more is spent in one market, there will be less to spend in other markets. Further, if markets for similar goods are separated geographically, there will be some price differential at which it will be worthwhile for the consumer to buy in the lower price market and pay shipping costs, rather than buy in a geographically nearer market.

Price theory and the market

1.5 Price theory is concerned with how market prices for goods are arrived at, through the interaction of demand and supply.

1.6 A good or service has a **price** if it is **useful** as well as **scarce**. Its usefulness is shown by the fact that consumers demand it. In a world populated entirely by vegetarians, meat would not command a price, no matter how few cows or sheep there were.

Utility

1.7 **Utility** is the word used to describe the pleasure or satisfaction or benefit derived by a person from the consumption of goods. **Total utility** is then the total satisfaction that people derive from spending their income and consuming goods.

1.8 **Marginal utility** is the **satisfaction gained** from consuming one **additional** unit of a good or the **satisfaction forgone** by consuming one unit **less**. If someone eats six apples and then eats a seventh, total utility refers to the satisfaction he derives from all seven apples together, while marginal utility refers to the additional satisfaction from eating the seventh apple, having already eaten six.

Assumptions about consumer rationality

1.9 The following assumptions are made.

(a) Generally the consumer prefers more goods to less.

(b) Generally the consumer is willing to substitute one good for another provided its price is right.

(c) **Choices are transitive**. This means that if at a given time a commodity A is preferred to B and B is preferred to C then we can conclude that commodity A is preferred to commodity C.

1.10 Acting rationally means that the consumer attempts to **maximise the total utility** attainable with a limited income. When the consumer decides to buy another unit of a good he is deciding that its marginal utility exceeds the marginal utility that would be yielded by any **alternative** use of the price he pays.

1.11 If a person has maximised his total utility, it follows that he has allocated his expenditure in such a way that the utility gained from spending the last penny spent on each good will be equal.

1.12 We shall now look at demand and supply in turn, and then consider how demand and supply interact through the price mechanism.

2 THE DEMAND SCHEDULE

The concept of demand

KEY TERM

Demand for a good is the quantity of that good that potential purchasers would buy, or attempt to buy, if the price of the good were at a certain level.

2.1 Demand might be satisfied, and so actual quantities bought would equal demand. On the other hand, some demand might be unsatisfied, with more would-be purchasers trying to buy a good that is in insufficient supply, and so there are then not enough units of the good to go around.

2.2 Demand does not mean the quantity that potential purchasers **wish** they could buy. For example, a million households might wish that they owned a luxury yacht, but there might only be actual attempts to buy one hundred luxury yachts at a given price.

The demand schedule and the demand curve

2.3 The relationship between demand and price can be shown graphically as a **demand curve**. The demand curve of a single consumer or household is derived by estimating how much of the good the consumer or household would demand at various hypothetical market prices. Suppose that the following **demand schedule** shows demand for biscuits by one household over a period of one month.

Price per kg	*Quantity demanded*
£	kg
1	9.75
2	8
3	6.25
4	4.5
5	2.75
6	1

2.4 Notice that we show demand falling off as price increases. This is what normally happens with most goods. This is because purchasers have a limited amount of money to spend and must choose between goods that compete for their attention. When the price of one good rises, it is likely that other goods will seem relatively more attractive and so demand will switch away from the more expensive good.

2.5 We can show this schedule graphically, with **price on the y axis** and **quantity demanded on the x axis.** If we assume that there is complete divisibility, so that price and quantity can both change in infinitely small steps, we can draw a demand curve by joining the points represented in the schedule by a continuous line (Figure 1). This is the household's demand curve for biscuits in the particular market we are looking at.

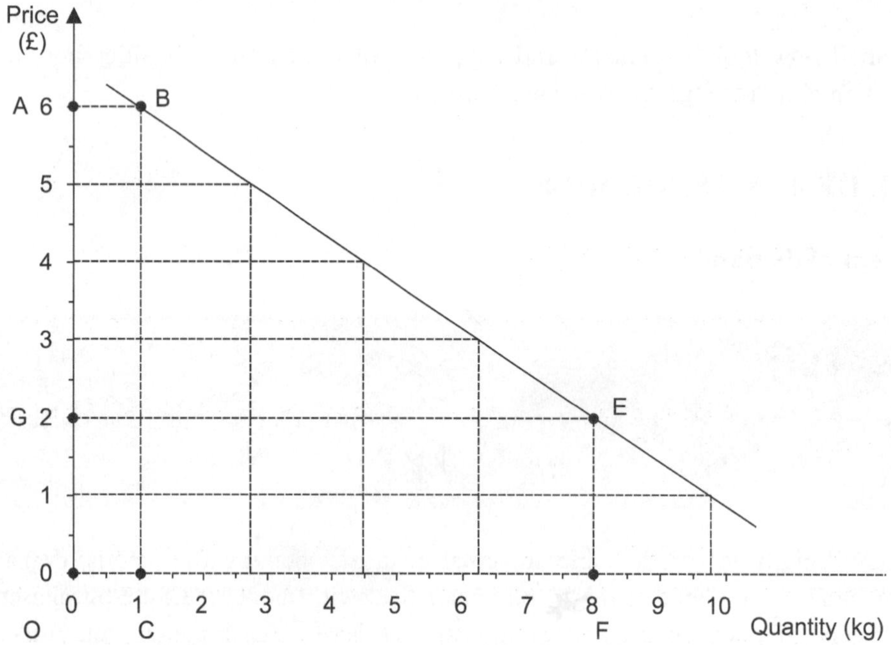

Figure 1 Graph of a demand schedule

2.6 The area of each rectangle in Figure 1 represents consumers' total money outlay at the price in question. For example, at a price of £6, demand would be 1 kilogram and total spending would be £6, represented by rectangle ABCO. Similarly, at a price of £2, demand would be 8 kilograms and the total spending of £16 is represented by rectangle GEFO.

Exam focus point

Sketching demand and supply curves is often a useful way of analysing an exam question.

2.7 In Figure 1, the demand curve happens to be a straight line. Straight line demand curves are often used as an illustration in economics because it is convenient to draw them this way. In reality, a demand curve is more likely to be a curved line convex to the origin. As you will be able to appreciate, such a demand curve means that there are progressively larger increases in quantity demanded as price falls (Figure 2).This happens because of the fall in marginal utility experienced as consumption of a good increases.

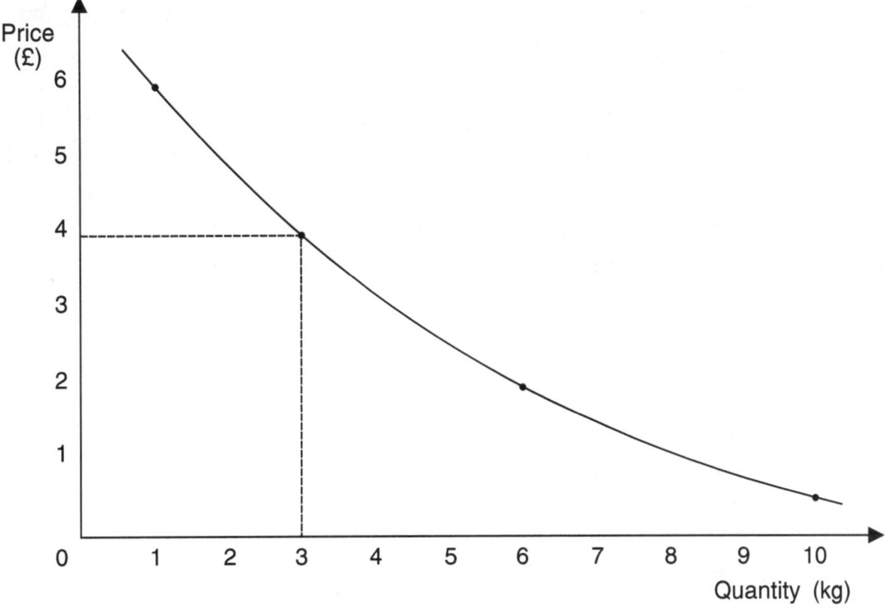

Figure 2 Demand curve convex to the origin

Question 1

Refer to Figure 2. Suppose the price of the commodity is £3. What would be the (approximate) demand for the commodity? And if the price fell to £2?

Answer

Demand is about 4.5 kilos at a price of £3 per kilo, rising to 6 kilos at the reduced price of £2 per kilo.

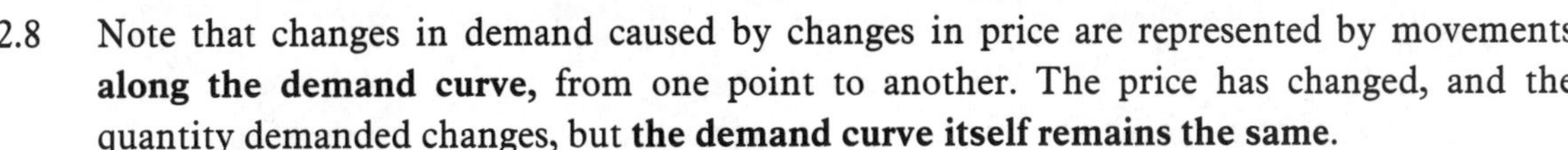

2.8 Note that changes in demand caused by changes in price are represented by movements **along the demand curve,** from one point to another. The price has changed, and the quantity demanded changes, but **the demand curve itself remains the same**.

The market demand curve 11/01

2.9 In the example above, we have been looking at the demand schedule of a single household. A **market demand curve** is a similar curve, drawn from a demand schedule, expressing the expected total quantity of the good that would be demanded by **all consumers together**, at any given price.

2.10 **Market demand** is the total quantity of a product that **all** purchasers would want to buy at each price level. A market demand schedule and a market demand curve are therefore simply the sum of all the individual demand schedules and demand curves put together. Market demand curves would be similar to those in Figures 1 and 2, but with quantities demanded (total market demand) being higher at each price level.

2.11 A **demand curve generally slopes down from left to right.**

(a) As discussed earlier, if the **relative price** of the good that is important. A fall in the relative price of a good increases demand for it.

(b) A fall in the good's price means that households with lower incomes will also be able to afford it. The overall size of the market for the good increases. The converse argument applies to an increase in prices; as a price goes up, consumers with lower incomes will

no longer be able to afford the good, or will buy something else whose price is relatively cheaper, and the size of the market will shrink.

2.12 Several factors influence the total market demand for a good. One of these factors is obviously its price, but there are other factors too, and to help you to appreciate some of these other factors, you need to recognise that households buy not just one good with their money but a whole range of goods and services. There are a number of factors which determine the level of demand.

- The **price** of the good
- The price of other goods (products and services)
- The size of households' income
- Tastes and fashion
- Expectations of future price changes
- The distribution of income among households.

2.13 A demand curve shows how the quantity demanded will change in response to a change in price **provided that all other conditions affecting demand are unchanged** - that is, provided that there is no change in the prices of other goods, tastes, expectations or the distribution of household income. (*Ceteris paribus*, remember, is the assumption that all other things remain equal.)

Substitutes and complements 5/02

KEY TERMS

Substitute goods are goods that are alternatives to each other, so that an **increase** in the demand for one is likely to cause a **decrease** in the demand for another. Switching demand from one good to another 'rival' good is **substitution**

Complements are goods that tend to be bought and used together, so that an **increase** in the demand for one is likely to cause an **increase** in the demand for the other.

2.14 A change in the price of one good will not necessarily change the demand for another good. For example, we would not expect an increase in the price of cocoa to affect the demand for motor cars. However, there are goods for which the market demand is inter-connected. These inter-related goods are referred to as either **substitutes** or **complements**.

Examples of substitute goods and services

- Rival brands of the same commodity, like Coca-Cola and Pepsi-Cola
- Tea and coffee
- Some different forms of entertainment

Substitution takes place when the price of one good rises relative to a substitute good.

Examples of complements

- Cups and saucers
- Bread and butter
- Motor cars and the components and raw materials that go into their manufacture

Question 2

What might be the effect of an increase in the ownership of domestic deep freezers on the demand for perishable food products?

Answer

(a) Domestic deep freezers and perishable products are complements because people buy deep freezers to store perishable products.

(b) Perishable products are supplied either as fresh produce (for example, fresh meat and fresh vegetables) or as frozen produce, which can be kept for a short time in a refrigerator but for longer in a freezer. The demand for frozen produce will rise, while the demand for fresh produce will fall.

(c) Wider ownership of deep freezers is likely to increase bulk buying of perishable products. Suppliers can save some packaging costs, and can therefore offer lower prices for bulk purchases.

Household income and demand: normal goods and inferior goods 11/01

2.15 As you might imagine, more income will give households more to spend, and they will want to buy more goods at existing prices. However, a rise in household income will not increase market demand for all goods and services. The effect of a rise in income on demand for an individual good will depend on the nature of the good.

2.16 Demand and the level of income may be related in different ways.

(a) A rise in household income may increase demand for a good. This is what we might normally expect to happen, and goods for which demand rises as household income increases are called **normal goods**.

(b) Demand may rise with income up to a certain point but then fall as income rises beyond that point. Goods whose demand eventually falls as income rises are called **inferior goods**: examples might include tripe and cheap wine. The reason for falling demand is that as incomes rise, demand switches to superior products, for example beef instead of tripe; better quality wines instead of a cheaper variety.

Demand, fashion and expectations

2.17 A change in fashion will alter the demand for a product. For example, if it becomes fashionable for middle class households in the UK to drink wine with their meals, expenditure on wine will increase. There may be passing 'crazes', such as roller blades or skateboards.

2.18 If consumers believe that prices will rise, or that shortages will occur, they may attempt to stock up on the product, thereby creating excess demand in the short term which will increase prices. This can then lead to panic buying. Examples of things producing this effect include fear of war, the budget, the effect of strikes or a rumour.

Market demand and the distribution of income

2.19 Market demand for a good is influenced by the way in which the national income is shared among households.

2.20 In a country with many rich and many poor households and few middle income ones, we might expect a relatively large demand for luxury cars and yachts and also for bread and

potatoes. In a country with many middle-income households, we might expect high demand for medium-sized cars and TV sets, and other middle income goods.

Question 3

What do you think might be the demand for swimming pools amongst a population of five households enjoying total annual income of £1m, if the distribution of income is either as under assumption 1 or as under assumption 2.

	Annual income	
	Assumption 1	*Assumption 2*
	£	£
Household 1	950,000	200,000
Household 2	12,500	200,000
Household 3	12,500	200,000
Household 4	12,500	200,000
Household 5	12,500	200,000

Answer

Under assumption 1, the demand for swimming pools will be confined to household 1. Even if this household owns three or four properties, the demand for swimming pools is likely to be less than under assumption 2, where potentially all five households might want one.

Changes in demand

2.21 If the price of a good goes up or down, given no changes in the other factors that affect price, then there will be a change in the quantity demanded, depicted as a movement **along** the demand curve.

Shifts of the demand curve

2.22 When there is a **change in other factors that affect demand,** the relationship between demand quantity and price will also change, and there will be a different price/quantity demand schedule and so **a different demand curve**. We refer to such a change as a **shift of the demand curve.**

2.23 Figure 3 depicts a rise in demand at each price level, with the demand curve shifting to the right, from D_0 to D_1. For example, at price P_1, demand for the good would rise from X to Y. This shift could be caused by any of the following factors.

- A rise in household income
- A rise in the price of substitutes
- A fall in the price of complements
- A change in tastes towards this product
- An expected rise in the price of the product.

2.24 It should be easy for you to appreciate that a fall in demand at each price level would be represented by a shift in the opposite direction: to the **left** of the demand curve. Such a shift may be caused by the opposite of the changes described in the previous paragraph.

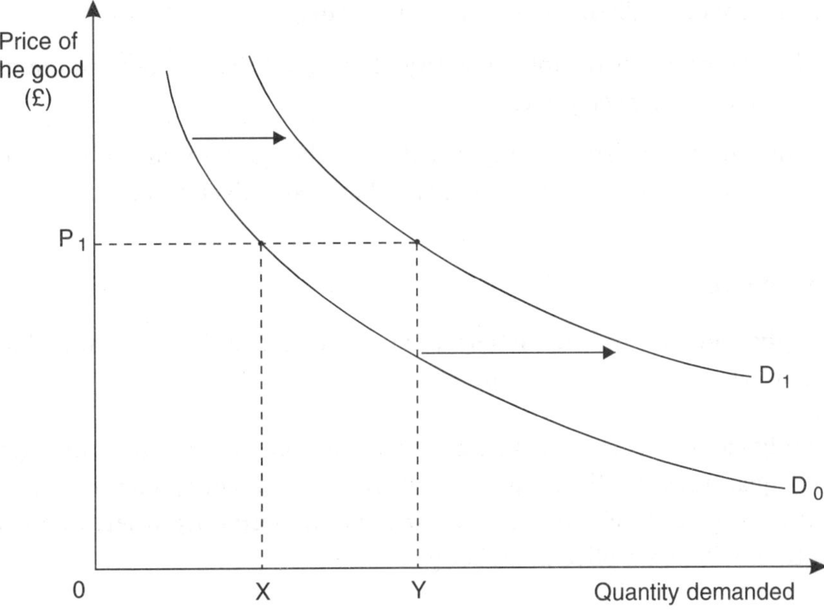

Figure 3 Outward shift of the demand curve

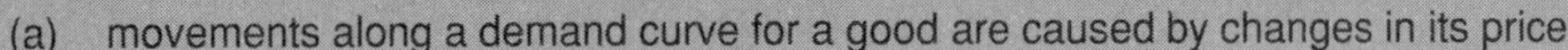

Exam focus point

The difference between a change in demand and a shift of the demand curve is of fundamental importance. You must not mix them up in the exam. Remember:

(a) movements along a demand curve for a good are caused by changes in its price

(b) shifts in the demand curve for a good are caused by any of the other factors which affect demand for a good, other than its price.

3 THE SUPPLY SCHEDULE

KEY TERM

Supply refers to the quantity of a good that existing suppliers or would-be suppliers would want to produce for the market at a given price.

The concept of supply

3.1 As with demand, supply relates to a period of time - for example, we might refer to an annual rate of supply or to a monthly rate.

3.2 The quantity of a good supplied to a market varies up or down for two reasons.

(a) Existing suppliers may increase or reduce their output quantities.

(b) Firms may stop production altogether and leave the market, or new firms may enter the market and start to produce the good.

3.3 If the quantity that firms want to produce at a given price exceeds the quantity that purchasers would demand, there will be an **excess of supply**, with firms competing to win what sales demand there is. Over-supply and competition would then be expected to result in price-competitiveness and **a fall in prices**.

3.4 As with demand, a distinction needs to be made.

(a) Market supply is the total quantity of the good that all firms in the market would want to supply at a given price.

(b) An individual firm's supply schedule is the quantity of the good that the individual firm would want to supply to the market at any given price.

The supply curve

3.5 A **supply schedule** and **supply curve** can be created both for an individual supplier and for all firms which produce the good.

3.6 A supply curve is constructed in a similar manner to a demand curve (from a schedule of supply quantities at different prices) but shows the quantity suppliers are willing to produce at different price levels. It is an **upward sloping curve from left to right,** because greater quantities will be supplied at higher prices.

3.7 Suppose, for example, that the supply schedule for product Y is as follows.

Price per unit	*Quantity that suppliers would supply at this price*
£	Units
100	10,000
150	20,000
300	30,000
500	40,000

3.8 The relationship between output and price is shown as a supply curve in Figure 4.

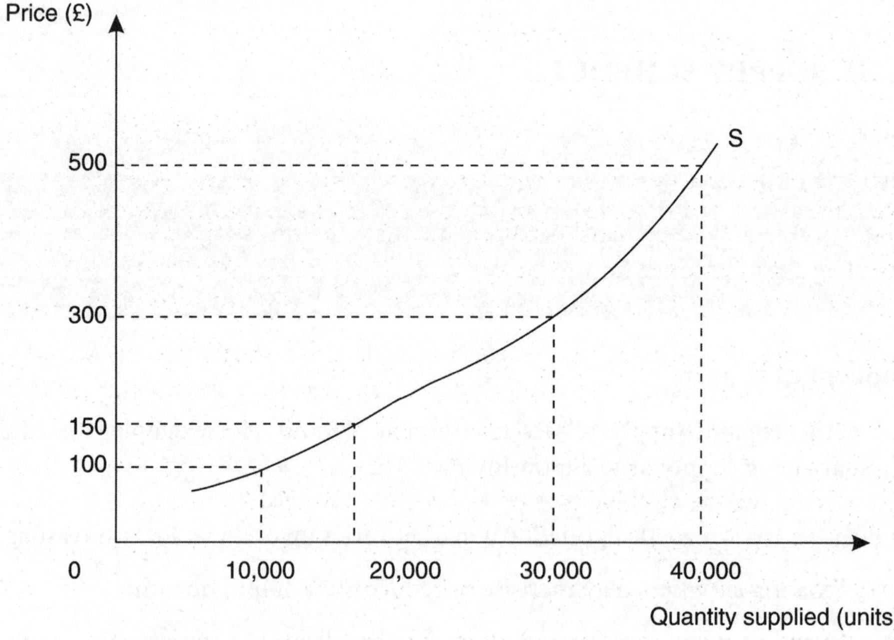

Figure 4 Supply curve

Factors which influence the supply quantity

3.9 The quantity supplied of a good depends, as you might expect, on prices and costs. More specifically, it depends on the following factors.

(a) **Expectations of price changes.**

(b) The **prices of other goods**. When a supplier can switch readily from supplying one good to another, the goods concerned are called **substitutes in supply**. An increase in the price of one such good would make the supply of a good whose price does not rise **less attractive** to suppliers. **Goods in joint supply** include leather and beef. If the price of beef rises, more will be supplied and there will be an accompanying increase in the supply of leather

(c) The **costs of making the good.** These include raw materials costs, which ultimately depend on the prices of factors of production (wages, interest rates, land rents and profit expectations)

(d) **Changes in technology**. Technological developments which reduce costs of production (and increase productivity) will raise the quantity of supply of a good at a given price

(e) **Other factors**, such as changes in the weather (for example, in the case of agricultural goods), natural disasters or industrial disruption

3.10 The supply curve shows how the quantity supplied will change in response to a change in price. If **supply conditions** alter, a different supply curve must be drawn. In other words, **a change in price will cause a shift in supply along the supply curve. A change in other supply conditions will cause a shift in the supply curve itself.**

Exam focus point

This distinction is just as important as the similar distinction relating to demand.

Shifts of the market supply curve

3.11 The **market supply curve** is the aggregate of the supply curves of individual firms in the market. A shift of the market supply curve occurs when supply conditions (other than the price of the good itself) change. Figure 5 shows a shift in the supply curve from S_0 to S_1. A rightward shift of the curve shows an expansion of supply and may be caused by the factors below.

(a) A fall in the cost of factors of production

(b) A fall in the price of other goods. The production of other goods becomes relatively less attractive as their price falls. Firms are therefore likely to shift resources away from a good whose price is falling and into the production of higher priced goods that offer increased profits. We therefore expect that (ceteris paribus) the supply of one good will rise as the prices of other goods fall (and vice versa)

(c) Technological progress, which reduces unit costs and also increases production capabilities

3.12 A shift of the supply curve is the result of changes in costs, either in absolute terms or relative to the costs of other goods (Figure 5). If the price of the good is P_1, suppliers would be willing to increase supply from Q_0 to Q_1 under the new supply conditions.

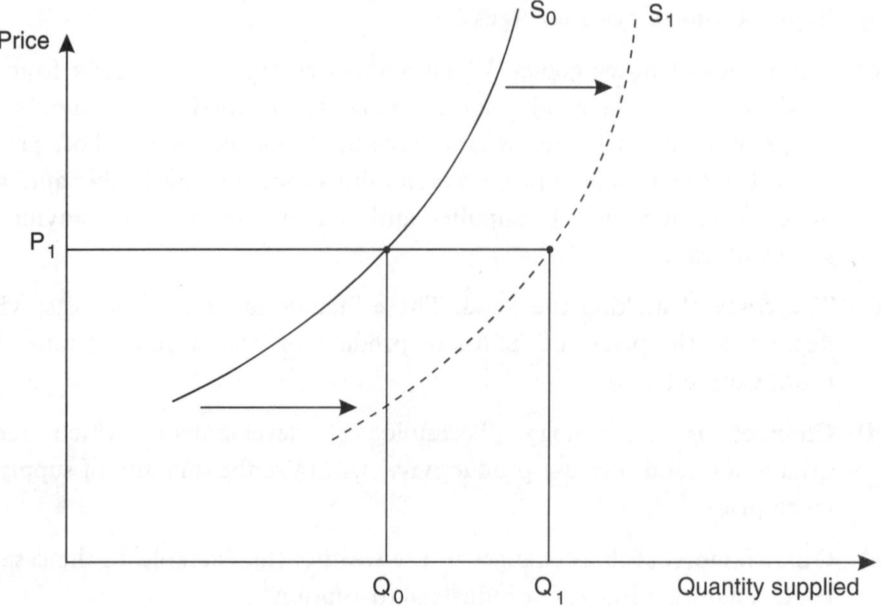

Figure 5 Outward shift of the supply curve

3.13 Note that we need to distinguish between short run and long run responses of both supply and demand. **In the short run** both supply and demand are **relatively unresponsive** to changes in price, as compared to the **long run**.

(a) **In the case of supply**, changes in the quantity of a good supplied often require the laying off or hiring of new workers, or the installation of new machinery. All of these changes, brought about by management decisions, must take some time to implement.

(b) **In the case of demand**, it takes time for consumers to adjust their buying patterns, although demand will often respond more rapidly than supply to changes in price or other demand conditions.

3.14 In some markets, responses to changes in price are relatively rapid. In others, response times are much longer. In stock markets for example, the supply and demand for company shares respond very rapidly to price changes, whereas in the markets for fuel oils or agrichemicals response times are much longer.

Question 4

In a stock market the 'products' bought and sold include shares in companies. What can you say about the supply of and demand for these 'products', and how quickly does their price change in response to changes in supply and demand factors?

Answer

The supply of shares in a particular company is relatively static, although new shares will be issued from time to time. Demand for a company's shares will depend largely on how well the company is performing, although broader economic considerations are also influential. The price mechanism responds very rapidly - a share price may fluctuate up and down at very short intervals, sometimes undergoing several changes in the course of a single day.

4 THE EQUILIBRIUM PRICE

Functions of the price mechanism 11/01, 5/02

4.1 People only have a limited income and they must decide what to buy with the money they have. The prices of the goods they want will affect their buying decisions.

4.2 Firms' output decisions will be influenced by both demand and supply considerations.

(a) Market demand conditions influence the price that a firm will get for its output. Prices act as **signals** to producers, and changes in prices should stimulate a response from a firm to change its production quantities.

(b) Supply is influenced by production costs and profits. The objective of maximising profits provides the **incentive** for firms to respond to changes in price or cost by changing their production quantities.

(c) When a firm operates efficiently, responding to changes in market prices and controlling its costs it is **rewarded** with profit.

4.3 Decisions by firms about what industry to operate in and what markets to produce goods for will be influenced by prices obtainable. Although some firms have been established in one industry for many years, others are continually opening up, closing down or switching to new industries and new markets. Over time, firms in an industry might also increase or reduce the volume of goods they sell.

The equilibrium price

KEY TERM

The price mechanism brings demand and supply into equilibrium and the **equilibrium price** for a good is the price at which the volume demanded by consumers and the volume that firms would be willing to supply are the same. This is also known as the **market clearing price** since at this price there will be neither surplus nor shortage in the market.

4.4 This can be illustrated by drawing the market demand curve and the market supply curve on the same graph (Figure 6).

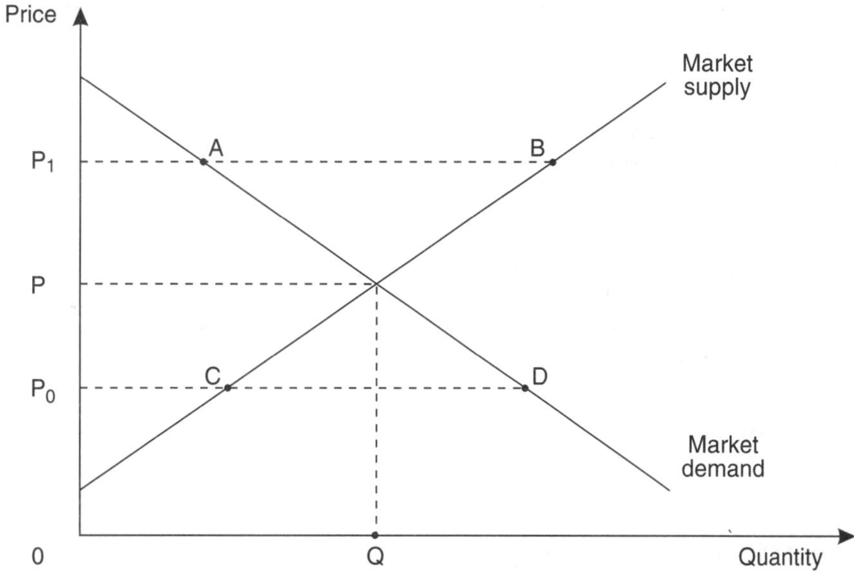

Figure 6 Market equilibrium

4.5 At price P_1 in Figure 6, there is an excess quantity that suppliers want to produce over the quantity demanded at that price, equal to the distance AB. Suppliers would react as unsold stocks accumulate.

(a) They would cut down the current level of production in order to sell unwanted stocks (de-stock).

(b) They would also reduce prices in order to encourage sales.

4.6 The opposite will happen at price P_0 where there is an excess of demand over supply shown by the distance CD. Output and price would increase. Faced with an excess of demand, manufacturers would be able to raise their prices. This would make supplying the good more profitable and supply would increase.

4.7 At price P the amount that sellers are willing to supply is equal to the amount that customers are willing to buy. Consumers will be willing to spend a total of $(P \times Q)$ on buying Q units of the product, and suppliers will be willing to supply Q units to earn revenue of $(P \times Q)$. P is the **equilibrium price**.

4.8 The forces of supply and demand push a market to its equilibrium price and quantity. Note carefully the following key points.

(a) If there is no change in conditions of supply or demand, the **equilibrium price will prevail** in the market and will remain stable.

(b) If price is not at the equilibrium, the market is in **disequilibrium** and supply and demand will push prices towards the equilibrium price.

(c) Shifts in the supply curve or demand curve will change the equilibrium price (and the quantity traded).

4.9 The **marginal utility** derived by different consumers from consumption of a unit quantity of a good will vary and so, therefore, will the price they would offer. Because of this, consumers may be able to buy the good at a prevailing market price **lower than the price they were prepared to pay**: you will be familiar with this idea from your own experience. This is called a **consumer surplus**, which can be represented as shown in Figure 7.

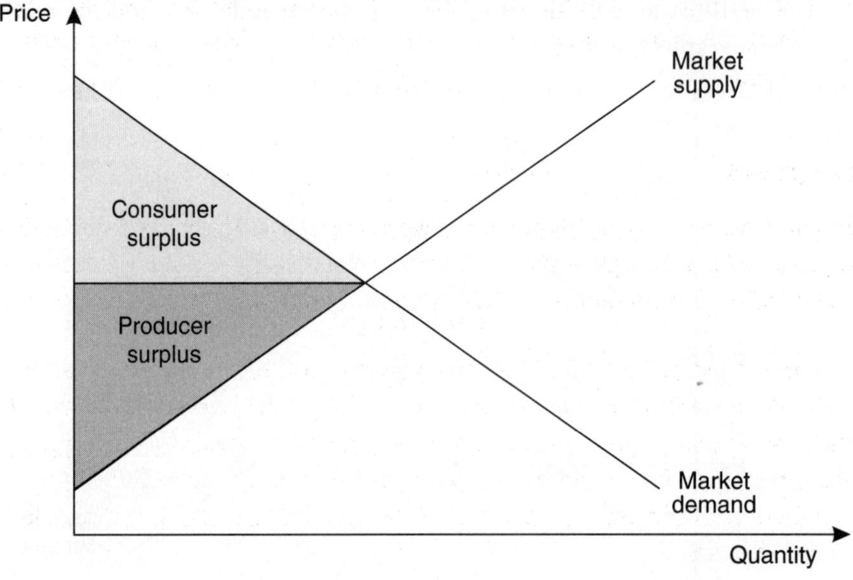

Figure 7 Consumer surplus and producer surplus

The **producer surplus** shown in Figure 7 arises because there will be suppliers in the market who will be prepared to sell quantities of the good at **less than the market price**.

Question 5

The diagram shows an individual's demand for fresh pasta. A special offer coupon makes it possible for this person to buy fresh pasta at a reduced price P_R rather than at the normal price P.

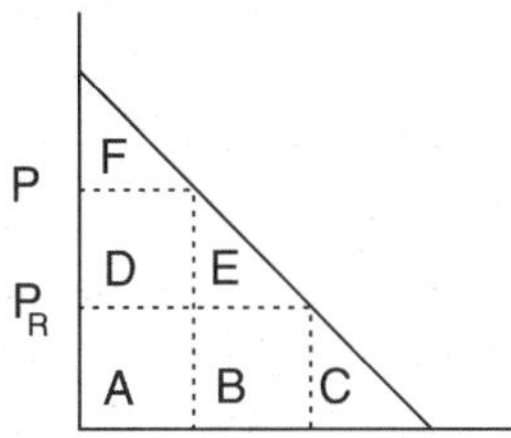

Which area shows the addition to the person's consumer surplus?

A D + E

B F + E + D

C F

D E + B

Answer

A F + E + D is the *total* consumer surplus with the coupon. F is the consumer surplus *without* the coupon. E + B has no significance.

5 MAXIMUM AND MINIMUM PRICES

Price regulation

5.1 The regulation of prices provides an illustration of how demand and supply analysis can be applied. Governments might try to control prices in two ways.

(a) They might set a **maximum** price for a good, perhaps as part of an anti-inflationary economic policy (such as a prices and incomes policy).

(b) They might set a **minimum** price for a good. The EU Common Agricultural Policy (CAP) aims to ensure that farmers receive at least the minimum prices for their produce.

Maximum prices

5.2 The government may try to prevent prices of goods rising by establishing a price ceiling. If the price ceiling is higher than the equilibrium price, setting a price ceiling will have no effect at all on the operation of market forces. Make sure that you can see why this is so.

5.3 If the maximum price M is lower than what the equilibrium price would be, there will be an excess of demand over supply (Figure 8). The low price attracts customers, but deters suppliers. Because the price ceiling M is below the equilibrium price P, producers will reduce the quantity of goods supplied to the market place from Q to A. The quantity demanded will increase from Q to B because of the fall in price. The excess quantity demanded is AB.

5.4 To prevent an unfair allocation of the A units of the good that are available, the government might have to introduce **rationing** (as with petrol coupons) or a **waiting list** (as for local

authority housing). Rationing and **black marketeers** tend to go together. In Figure 8 consumers demand quantity B but can only get A. However, for quantity A they are prepared to pay price Z, which is well above the official price M. The black marketeers step in to exploit the gap. The commodity may be sold on ration at the official price M, but black marketeers may sell illicit production at price Z.

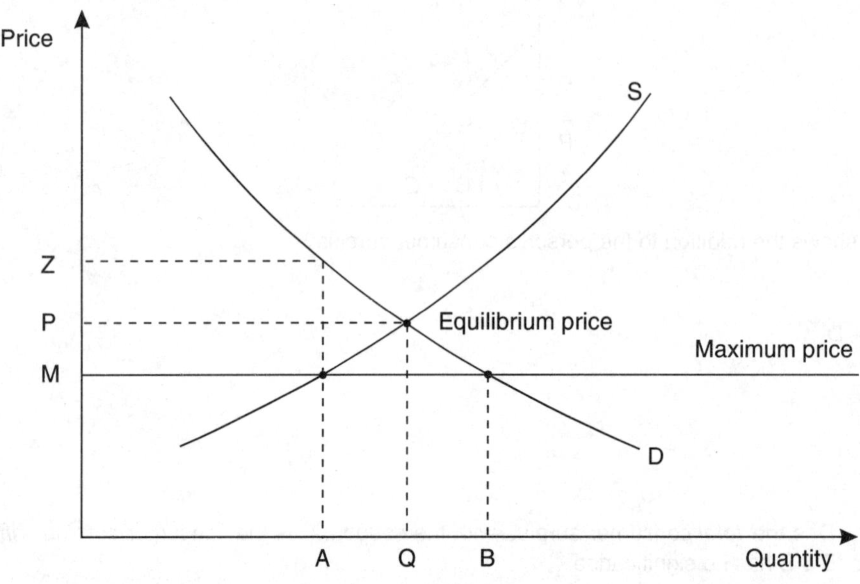

Figure 8 Maximum price below equilibrium price

Question 6

Supply of and demand for good Q are initially in equilibrium as shown in the diagram below.

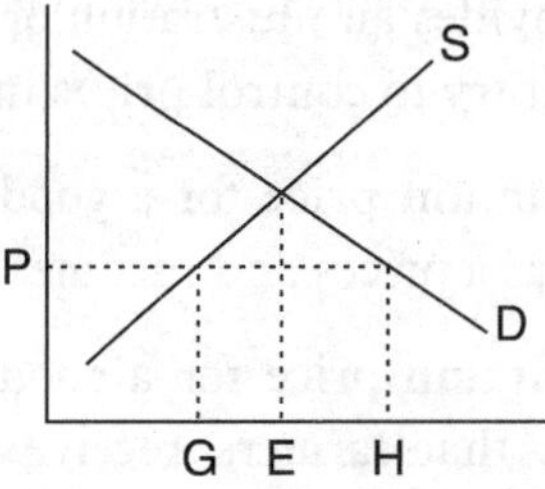

The government introduces a maximum price P. What effect will this have on the quantity of good Q purchased?

A It will rise from G to E

B It will rise from E to H

C It will fall from H to G

D It will fall from E to G

Answer

D Quantity demanded at the controlled price P will be H. However, only quantity G will be supplied and purchases will therefore be limited to this moment.

Minimum prices

5.5 Minimum price legislation aims to ensure that suppliers earn at least the minimum price for each unit of output they sell.

5.6 If the minimum price is set below the market equilibrium there is no effect. But if it is set above the market price, it will cause an excess supply of AB (as in Figure 9). This has been a recurring problem in Europe, resulting in the 'butter mountains' and 'wine lakes' of past years.

5.7 In Figure 9, the minimum price M is set above the equilibrium price P. The quantity demanded falls from Q to A but the quantity supplied increases to B. There is excess supply equal to the quantity AB.

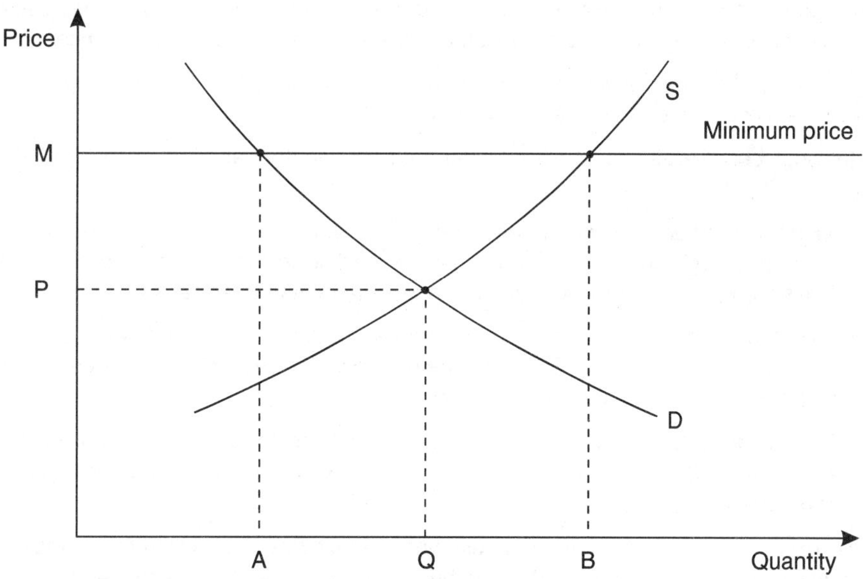

Figure 9 Minimum price above equilibrium price

5.8 When there is an excess of supply over demand, there is a danger that more of the good will be produced than can be sold at the minimum price, and so surplus quantities will build up, which suppliers might sell off at low prices just to get rid of them.

5.9 To try to prevent over-supply and 'dumping' of excess supply at low prices, a system of **production quotas** might be introduced whereby each supplier is allowed to produce up to a maximum quantity and no more. For some types of produce, the EU tried to overcome the problem of excess supply by imposing quotas on farmers. Since 1992, the EU Common Agricultural Policy has begun to oblige farmers to take land out of production: this is called 'set-aside'.

Question 7

Many governments impose controls on the rents of private property with the object of assisting lower-paid workers. What are the likely consequences of such policies?

Answer

You should see this question as a variation of maximum price legislation, which can be answered accordingly by supply and demand analysis. In addition, you could add points about:

(a) the deteriorating quality of rented accommodation if rents are held down, with landlords reluctant to pay for repairs and maintenance

(b) the creation of a black market in rented property

(c) discouraging new investment in building rented property.

Case example

The extract below gives an account of conditions in the markets for hazelnuts, almonds and pistachio nuts in the run-up to Christmas. As you read it, note down the different influences on the prices of each type of nut which are described in the extract.

'*Revellers may have to shell out more for nuts*'

'Consumers had better get cracking if they want to make sure of a crunchy Christmas. A looming shortage has pushed up prices of almonds and pistachios, while the cost of hazelnuts has jumped by 35 per cent since August after the Turkish government intervened to bolster prices.

Good-quality almonds are almost sold out and prices are up 20 per cent in the past six weeks following a poor Californian crop for the second year running.

Pistachio prices are also 20 per cent higher after bad weather affected almost half of this year's Iranian crop ...

Californian almond prices have more than doubled over the past two years as cold and windy weather during the important growing periods caused a decline in the harvest and poor-quality nuts. After a disastrous crop in 1995 there were no stocks to carry over to this season.

Pistachio prices have risen from $3,200 a tonne in July to $4,000 (£2,400), and [it is believed that] there will be a further rise of $50-$100 before next summer when supplies will run out. The new season's crop comes to market in November.

The Turkish government's farm co-operative has so far bought 25 per cent of this year's hazelnut harvest at almost $1,000 a tonne higher than the free market price in an effort to push up prices from their low base of recent years.

"It will encourage a lot more farmers to plant nuts and in five years when those trees produce, there will be a whole spate of deliveries," said a nut buyer for a leading UK confectioner.

Free market prices have risen to $3,800 a tonne, but remain below the $4,100 a tonne which the Turkish co-operative is believed to be paying farmers.'

(Financial Times, 5 December 1996)

Chapter roundup

- In a free market, the price mechanism signals demand and supply conditions to producers and consumers. It therefore determines the activities of both producers and consumers, influencing the levels of demand for and the supply of goods.
- We have seen in this chapter how the competitive market process results in an **equilibrium price**, which is the price at which market supply and market demand quantities are in balance. In any market, the equilibrium price will change if market demand or supply conditions change.
- Note in particular how the position of the **demand curve** is determined by the demand conditions, which include consumers' tastes and preferences, and consumers' incomes.
- The **supply curve** shows the quantity of a good which would be supplied by producers at a given price.
- Where **maximum prices** are imposed, there will be **excess demand**: rationing may be necessary, and black marketeers may seek to operate.
- Where **minimum prices** are imposed, producers will make **excess supply**.

Quick quiz

1 What factors influence demand for a good?

2 What are (a) substitutes and (b) complements?

3 What factors affect the supply quantity?

4 What is meant by equilibrium price?

5 A demand curve is drawn on all *except* which of the following assumptions?

A Incomes do not change.
B Prices of substitutes are fixed.
C Price of the good is constant.
D There are no changes in tastes and preferences.

6 The diagram shown relates to the demand for and supply of Scotch. The market is initially in equilibrium at point X. The government imposes a specific tax on Scotch whilst at the same time, the price of Irish Whiskey (a substitute for Scotch) rises. Which point, A, B, C or D represents the new market equilibrium?

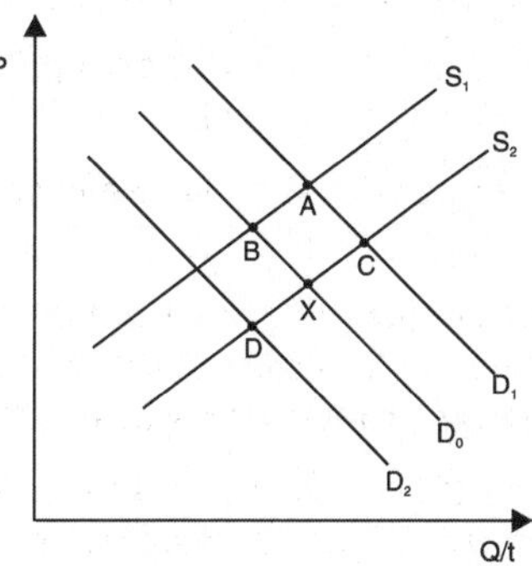

7 A price ceiling set above the equilibrium market price will result in:

A Market failure
B A perpetual surplus
C Market equilibrium
D An alternative (to price) rationing system

8 Which one of the following would normally cause a rightward shift in the demand curve for a product?

A A fall in the price of a substitute product.
B A reduction in direct taxation on incomes.
C A reduction in price of the product.
D An increase in the price of a complementary product.

9 What is an inferior good?

A A good of such poor quality that demand for it is very weak.
B A good of lesser quality than a substitute good, so that the price of the substitute is higher.
C A good for which the cross elasticity of demand with a substitute product is greater than 1.
D A good for which demand will fall as household income rises.

10 In the diagram below, point 5 represents equilibrium. There is now a fall in the price of another product which is a close substitute for the commodity. What will the new equilibrium be?

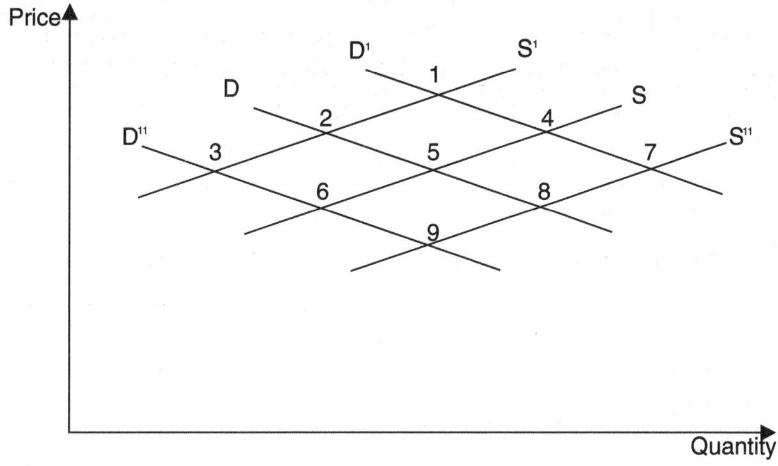

A Point 2
B Point 4
C Point 6
D Point 8

Answers to quick quiz

1 The price of the good
The price of other goods
Household income
Taste and fashion

2 Substitutes are goods that are alternatives to each other
Complements are goods which are bought and used together

3 The price obtainable for the good
The prices obtainable for other goods, particularly goods in joint supply
The costs of making the good
Disruptions such as bad weather and strikes

4 The price at which the volume of demand and the volume of supply are equal; there is neither surplus nor shortage.

5 C Demand curves express the quantity demanded at each given market price. Non-price determinants such as income must be held constant when looking at the effect of price movements in isolation.

6 A Supply shifts from S_0 to S_1, reflecting the per-unit tax. Demand shifts from D_0 to D_1 as the price of a substitute (Irish whiskey) rises.

7 C If the price ceiling is above the equilibrium market price, it will not interfere with the working of the price mechanism. The market will not be forced from its current equilibrium.

8 B A reduction in income tax will increase 'real' household income, and so demand for normal products will shift to the right, ie. quantity demanded will be greater at any given price.

A fall in the price of a substitute good would entice consumers away from the original good. This would cause a leftward shift in the demand curve.

A change in the price of the good itself does not cause a shift in the curve but a movement along it.

Complementary products tend to be bought and used together, so an increase in the price of one will lead to a reduction in demand for the other, reflected in a leftward shift in the demand curve.

9 D Inferior goods are defined in terms of the relationship between quantity demanded and income. The issue of substitutes is not relevant.

10 C The effect of a fall in the price of a substitute product will be to increase demand for this substitute, and so reduce demand for the commodity in the question. The demand curve will shift to the left, to the line going through points 3, 6 and 9. The new equilibrium will be at point 6.

Now try the questions below from the Question Bank

Number	Level	Marks	Time
Q4	Introductory	16	20 mins
Q5	Introductory - MCQ	–	–
Q6	Introductory - Interactive	–	–

Chapter 3

ELASTICITIES OF DEMAND AND SUPPLY

Topic list	Syllabus reference	Ability required
1 Elasticity of demand	(ii)	Application
2 Elasticity of supply	(ii)	Application

Introduction

We have discussed earlier the direction of changes in demand and supply when prices change. When price goes up, the quantity demanded will fall, and the quantity suppliers will be willing to produce will go up.

In this chapter, we consider the extent of such changes, which is measured by means of the concept of elasticity. You need to have a good understanding of this concept, which could be relevant in a number of different contexts in exam questions.

Learning outcomes covered in this chapter

- Explain how the price system works by applying appropriate economic concepts and principles
- Apply basic economic analysis to explain economic and business issues
- Explain the economic factors which affect the structure, behaviour and performance of individual businesses and industries

Syllabus content covered in this chapter

- The price mechanism: the demand and supply model and its applications

1 ELASTICITY OF DEMAND 5/01, 11/01, 5/02

Exam focus point

Elasticity is a favourite exam topic. it is also of great practical importance in the real world of business

The price elasticity of demand

1.1 If prices went **up** by 10% would the quantity demanded **fall** by the same percentage?

KEY TERM

Price elasticity of demand (PED) is a measure of the extent of change in market demand for a good in response to a change in its price.

PED is measured as:

$$\frac{\text{The change in quantity demanded, as a \% of demand}}{\text{The change in price, as a \% of the price}}$$

Since demand usually increases when the price falls, and decreases when the price rises, elasticity has a negative value. **However, it is usual to ignore the minus sign.**

1.2 This can be expressed as:

$$\frac{\frac{\Delta Q}{Q}\times 100}{\frac{\Delta P}{P}\times 100}\text{, which is equivalent to } \frac{\Delta Q}{Q}\times\frac{P}{\Delta P} \text{ and to } \frac{\Delta Q}{\Delta P}\times\frac{P}{Q}$$

where Δ is the symbol for 'change in'
Q is the quantity demanded of the good
P is the price of the good

1.3 If we are measuring the responsiveness of demand to a large change in price, we can measure elasticity between two points on the demand curve, and the resulting measure is called the **arc elasticity of demand**. We calculate the arc elasticity of demand from the percentage change in quantity relative to **average** quantity for the relevant range of output and from the percentage price change relative to the **average** of the corresponding price range.

1.4 If we wish to measure the responsiveness of demand at a particular point in the demand curve, we can calculate a **point elasticity of demand,** without averaging price and quantity over a range. In doing so, it is convenient to assume that the demand curve is a straight line unless told otherwise.

1.5 EXAMPLE: ARC ELASTICITY OF DEMAND 11/01

The price of a good is £1.20 per unit and annual demand is 800,000 units. Market research indicates that an increase in price of 10 pence per unit will result in a fall in annual demand of 70,000 units.

What is the price elasticity of demand measuring the responsiveness of demand over this range of price increase?

1.6 SOLUTION

Annual demand at £1.20 per unit is 800,000 units.
Annual demand at £1.30 per unit is 730,000 units.

Average quantity over the range is 765,000 units.
Average price is £1.25.

% change in demand $\frac{70{,}000}{765{,}000}\times 100\% = 9.15\%$

% change in price $\frac{10p}{125p}\times 100\% = 8\%$

Price elasticity of demand $= \frac{-9.15}{8} = -1.14$

Ignoring the minus sign, the arc elasticity is 1.14.

The demand for this good, over the range of annual demand 730,000 to 800,000 units, is elastic because the price elasticity of demand is greater than 1. Now try the following exercise yourself.

Question 1

If the price per unit of X rises from £1.40 to £1.60, it is expected that monthly demand will fall from 220,000 units to 200,000 units.

What is the arc price elasticity of demand over these ranges of price and output?

Answer

Monthly demand at £1.40 per unit = 220,000 units

Monthly demand at £1.60 per unit = 200,000 units

Average quantity = 210,000 units

Average price = £1.50

% change in demand $\frac{20{,}000}{210{,}000} \times 100\% = 9.52\%$

% change in price $\frac{20}{150} \times 100\% = 13.33\%$

Arc price elasticity of demand = $\frac{-9.52}{13.33} = -0.71\%$

Demand is inelastic over the demand range considered, because the price elasticity of demand (ignoring the minus sign) is less than 1.

1.7 EXAMPLE: POINT ELASTICITY OF DEMAND

Refer to the details in the example in Paragraph 1.5.

Required

Calculate the elasticity of demand when the price is £1.20.

1.8 SOLUTION

We are asked to calculate the elasticity at a particular price. We assume that the demand curve is a straight line.

At a price of £1.20, annual demand is 800,000 units. For a price rise:

% change in demand $\frac{70{,}000}{800{,}000} \times 100\% = 8.75\%$ (fall)

% change in price $\frac{10p}{120p} \times 100\% = 8.33\%$ (rise)

Price elasticity of demand at price £1.20 $= \frac{-8.75}{8.33} = -1.05$

Ignoring the minus sign, the price elasticity at this point is 1.05. Demand is **elastic** at this point, because the elasticity is greater than unity.

Question 2

Using the same details as in Paragraph 1.5 above, calculate the elasticity of demand when the price is £1.30.

Answer

We can use the same price/quantity change data, assuming that the demand curve is a straight line, although we are now looking at a different point on the curve.

At a price of £1.30, annual demand is 730,000 units.

For a price fall from £1.30 of 10 pence:

% change in demand $\frac{70{,}000}{730{,}000} \times 100\% = 9.59\%$ (rise)

% change in price $\frac{10\text{p}}{130\text{p}} \times 100\% = 7.69\%$ (fall)

Price elasticity of demand = $\frac{9.59}{-7.69} = -1.25$,

or 1.25 ignoring the minus sign.

Demand is **elastic** at this point.

1.9 If it is not clear from the details of an exam question whether you are required to calculate arc or point elasticity, then calculate the **point** elasticity.

Question 3

A shop sells 100 shirts each month at a price of £20. When the price is increased to £24, the total sales revenue rises by 14%. Within which range does the price elasticity of demand lie?

A Under 0.15

B Greater than 0.15 and less than 0.8

C Greater than 0.8 and less than 1.5

D Greater than 1.5

Answer

B Total revenue of £20 = 100 × £20 = £2,000

Total revenue at £24 = £2,000 × 1.14 = £2,280

Number sold at £24 = £2,280 ÷ 24 = £95

Price elasticity of demand

Point method

$$\frac{\frac{5}{100} \times 100}{\frac{4}{20} \times 100} = \frac{5\%}{20\%} = 0.25$$

Arc method

$$\frac{\frac{5}{97\frac{1}{2}} \times 100}{\frac{4}{22} \times 100} = \frac{5.13\%}{18.2\%} = 0.28$$

Elastic and inelastic demand

1.10 The value of demand elasticity may be anything from zero to infinity.

- Demand is **inelastic** if the absolute value is less than 1
- Demand is **elastic** if the absolute value is greater than 1

Think about what this means if there is a price reduction. Where demand is **inelastic,** the quantity demanded falls by a smaller percentage than the fall in price. Where demand is elastic, demand falls by a larger percentage than the rise in price.

Price elasticity and the slope of the demand curve

1.11 Generally, demand curves slope downwards. Consumers are willing to buy more at lower prices than at higher prices. Except in certain special cases (which we look at below), **elasticity will vary in value along the length of a demand curve.** This is illustrated by Exercise 2 above together with the example which preceded it.

1.12 It is therefore not possible merely by looking at the slopes of any two curves to state their comparative elasticities over different price ranges. However, it is possible to say that if a downward sloping demand curve shifts to become **steeper** over a particular range of quantity, then demand is becoming more **inelastic.** Conversely, a demand curve becoming **shallower** over a particular range indicates more **elastic** demand.

1.13 The ranges of price elasticity (η) at different points on a downward sloping straight line demand curve are illustrated in Figure 1. Check the arithmetic yourself and make sure you understand this.

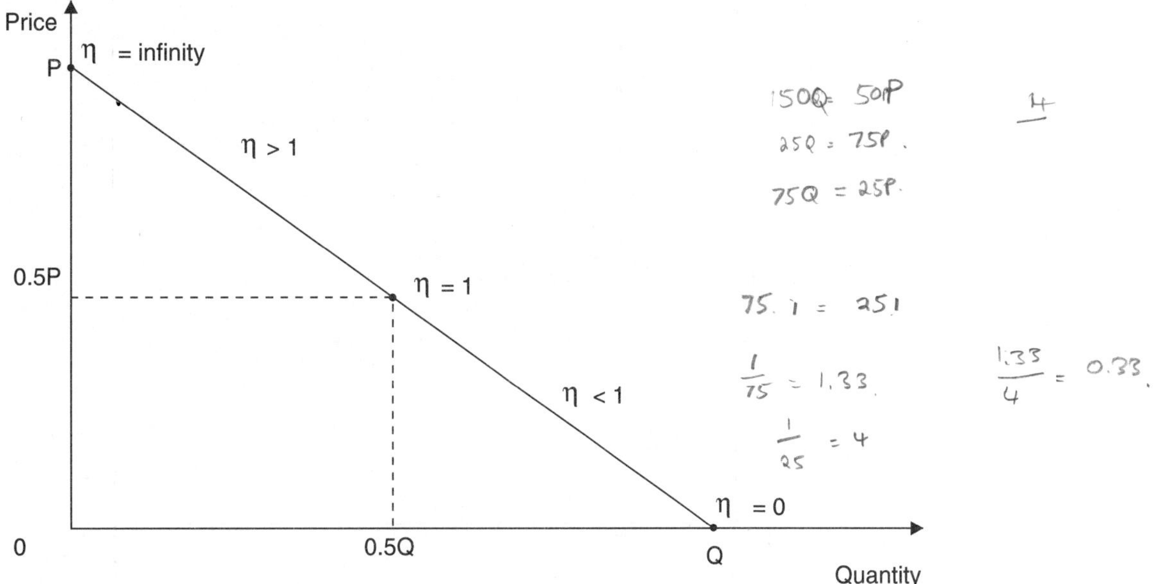

Figure 1 Ranges of price elasticity

1.14 At higher prices on a straight line demand curve (the top of the demand curve), **small** percentage price reductions can bring **large** percentage increases in quantity demanded. This means that demand is **elastic** over these ranges.

1.15 At lower prices on a straight line demand curve (the bottom of the demand curve), large percentage price reductions can bring small percentage increases in quantity. This means that demand is **inelastic** over these price ranges.

Special values of price elasticity of demand

1.16 There are three special values of price elasticity of demand: 0, 1 and infinity.

(a) **Demand is perfectly inelastic:** η = 0. There is no change in quantity demanded, regardless of the change in price. This is the case where the demand curve is a **vertical straight line.**

(b) **Perfectly elastic demand**: $\eta = \infty$ (infinitely elastic). Consumers will want to buy an infinite amount, but only up to a particular price level. Any price increase above this level will reduce demand to zero. This is the case where the demand curve is a **horizontal straight line.**

(c) **Unit elasticity of demand**: $\eta = 1$. Total revenue for suppliers (which is the same as total spending on the product by households) does not change when the price changes. The demand curve of a good whose price elasticity of demand is 1 over its entire range is a **rectangular hyperbola** (Figure 2).

(d) This means that in Figure 2, rectangles OABC, ODEF and OGHJ all have the same area, since the areas of these rectangles represent total spending by customers at each price.

(i) If the selling price were D, total demand would be F and total spending on the product would be D × F (rectangle ODEF).

(ii) If the selling price were A, total demand would be C, and total spending on the product would be A × C (rectangle OABC).

(iii) If the selling price were G, total demand would be J and total spending on the product would be G × J (rectangle OGHJ).

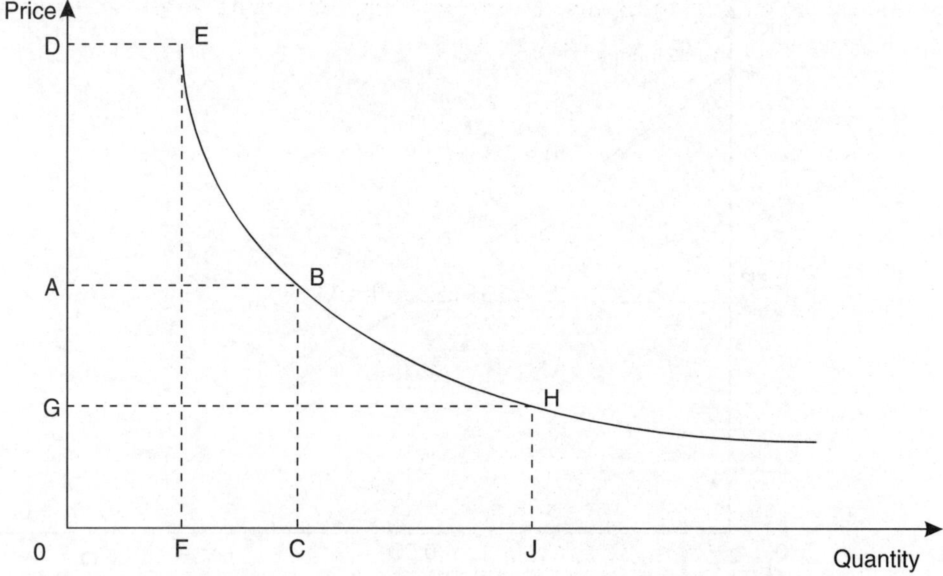

Figure 2 Unit elasticity of demand

The significance of price elasticity of demand

1.17 **The price elasticity of demand is relevant to total spending** on a good or service. Total expenditure is a matter of interest to both suppliers, to whom sales revenue accrues, and to government, who may receive a proportion of total expenditure in the form of taxation.

1.18 When demand is **elastic,** an increase in price will result in a fall in the quantity demanded, and **total expenditure will fall.** In Figure 3, total expenditure at price A is represented by the area OP_AAQ_A and total expenditure at price B is represented by the area OP_BBQ_B. Area OP_AAQ_A is greater than area OP_BBQ_B: this can be seen by observing that area Y (expenditure lost on a rise in price from A to B) is greater than area X (expenditure gained).

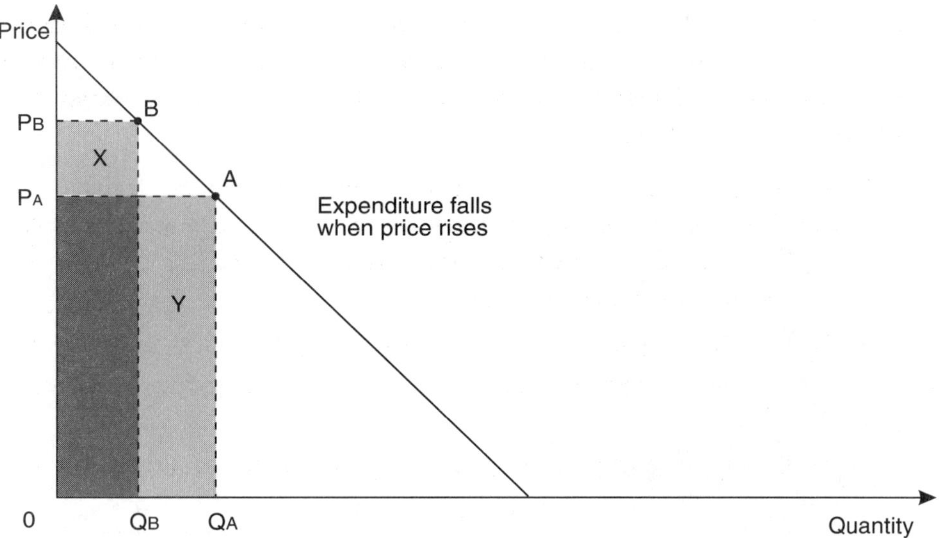

Figure 3 Elastic demand

1.19 When demand is **inelastic,** an increase in price will still result in a fall in quantity demanded, but **total expenditure will rise**. In Figure 4, area X (expenditure gained) is greater than area Y (expenditure lost).

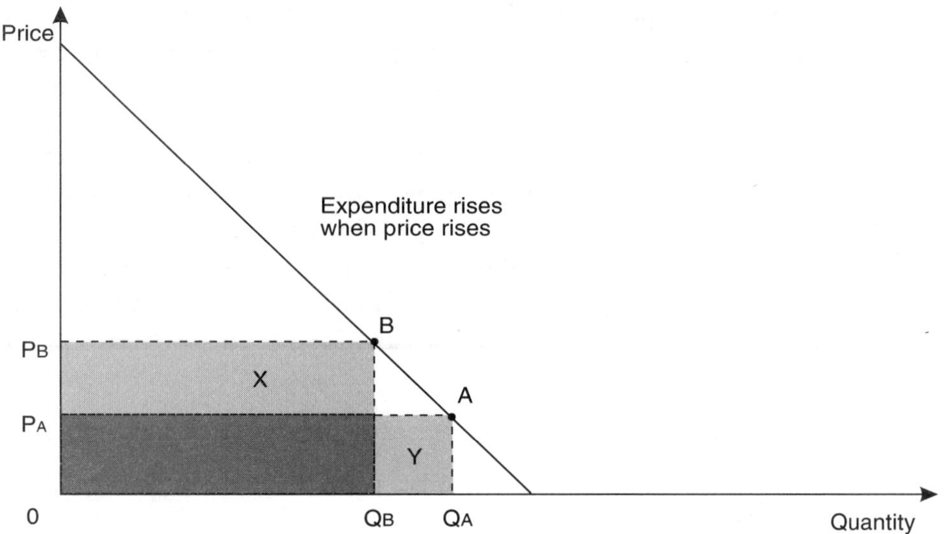

Figure 4 Inelastic demand

1.20 With **unit elasticity, expenditure will stay constant** on a change in price. In Figure 5, area X and area Y are the same.

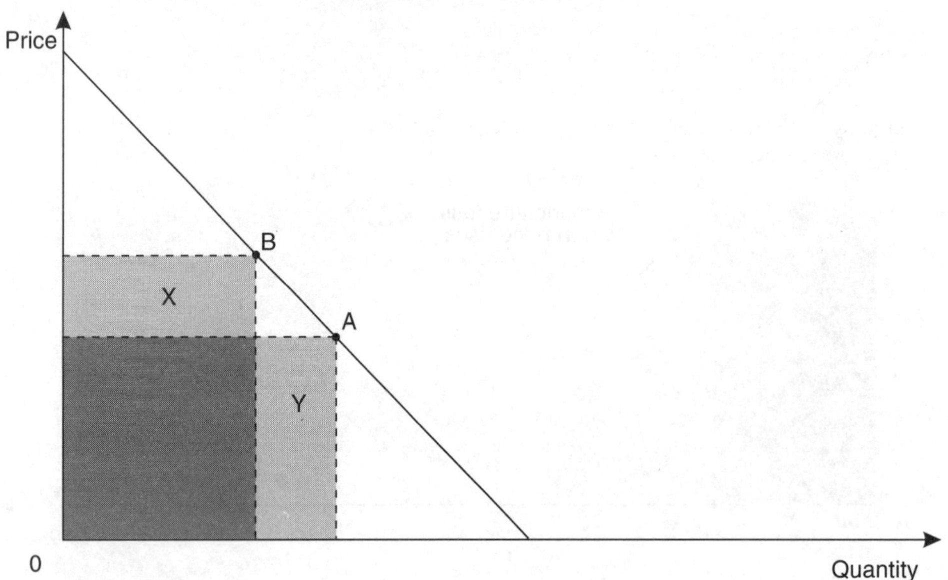

Figure 5 Unit elasticity

1.21 Information on price elasticity of demand indicates how **consumers can be expected to respond to different prices**. Business people can make use of information on how consumers will react to pricing decisions as it is possible to trace the effect of different prices on total revenue and profits. Information on price elasticities of demand will be useful to a business which needs to know the price decrease necessary to clear a surplus (excess supply) or the price increase necessary to eliminate a shortage (excess demand).

1.22 Government policy makers can also use information about elasticity, for example when making decisions about indirect taxation. Items with a low price elasticity of demand such as cigarettes and alcohol tend to be useful targets for taxation since by increasing taxes on these, total revenue can be increased. If demand for cigarettes was price elastic, increases in taxation would be counter-productive as they would result in lower government revenue.

Question 4

Suppose that there are two products, A and B.

Product A currently sells for £5, and demand at this price is 1,700 units. If the price fell to £4.60, demand would increase to 2,000 units.

Product B currently sells for £8 and demand at this price is 9,500 units. if the price fell to £7.50, demand would increase to 10,000 units.

In each of these cases, calculate:

(a) the price elasticity of demand (PED) for the price changes given

(b) the effect on total revenue, if demand is met in full at both the old and the new prices, of the change in price.

Answer

(a) Product A

At price £5:

Change in quantity $\frac{300}{1{,}700} = 17.7\%$

Change in price $\frac{40p}{£5} = 8\%$

$$PED = -\frac{17.7\%}{8\%} = -2.2$$

Demand is elastic and a fall in price should result in such a large increase in quantity demanded that total revenue will rise.

	£
Revenue at old price of £5 (× 1,700)	8,500
Revenue at new price of £4.60 (× 2,000)	9,200
Increase in total revenue	700

(b) Product B

At price £8:

Change in quantity $\frac{500}{9,500} = 5.3\%$

Change in price $\frac{50p}{£8} = 6.25\%$

$$PED = -\frac{5.3\%}{6.25\%} = -0.85$$

Demand is inelastic and a fall in price should result in only a relatively small increase in quantity demanded. Total revenue falls.

	£
Revenue at old price of £8 (× 9,500)	76,000
Revenue at new price of £7.50 (× 10,000)	75,000
Fall in total revenue	1,000

Positive price elasticities of demand. Giffen goods

1.23 When the price of a good rises, there will be a **substitution effect**: consumers will buy other goods instead because they are now relatively cheaper. But there will also be an **income effect** in that the rise in price will reduce consumers' real incomes, and will therefore affect their ability to buy goods and services. The 19th century economist Sir Robert Giffen observed that this **income effect could be so great** for certain goods (called **Giffen goods**) that the demand curve would be **upward sloping**. The price elasticity of demand in such a case would be positive. Giffen observed that among the labouring classes of his day, consumption of bread rose when its price rose. This could happen because the increase in price of a commodity which made up a high proportion of individuals' consumption could have a significant effect on real incomes. People would have to increase their consumption of bread because they were no longer able to afford more expensive foods.

1.24 The demand curve for a good might also slope upwards if it is bought **for purposes of ostentation**, so that having a higher price tag makes the good more desirable to consumers and thus increases demand.

Factors influencing price elasticity of demand for a good

1.25 Factors that determine price elasticity of demand are similar to the factors other than price that affect the volume of demand. The PED is really a measure of the strength of these other influences on demand.

1.26 **Main factors affecting PED**

- Availability of substitutes

- The time horizon
- Pricing policies of competitors

Availability of substitutes

1.27 The more substitutes there are for a good, especially close substitutes, the more elastic will be the price elasticity of demand for the good. For example, in a greengrocer's shop, a rise in the price of one vegetable such as carrots or cucumbers is likely to result in a switch of customer demand to other vegetables, many vegetables being fairly close substitutes for each other. To give a second example, the elasticity of demand for a particular brand of breakfast cereals will be much greater than the elasticity of demand for breakfast cereals as a whole, because the former have much closer substitutes. **Availability of substitutes is probably the most important influence on price elasticity of demand.**

The time horizon

1.28 **Over time, consumers' demand patterns are likely to change** and so, if the price of a good is increased, initially, there might be very little change in demand. Then, as consumers adjust their buying habits in response to the price increase, demand might fall substantially. The time horizon influences elasticity largely because the longer the period of time which we consider, the greater the **knowledge** of substitution possibilities by consumers and the **provision** of substitutes by producers.

Competitors' pricing

1.29 If the response of competitors to a price increase by one firm is to keep their prices unchanged, the firm raising its prices is likely to face elastic demand for its goods at higher prices. If the response of competitors to a reduction in price by one firm is to match the price reduction themselves, the firm is likely to face inelastic demand at lower prices. This is a situation which probably faces many large firms with one or two major competitors (ie oligopolies).

Income elasticity of demand 11/01

1.30 It is possible to construct other elasticity measures, and an important one which you need to know about is the **income elasticity of demand**. The income elasticity of demand for a good indicates the responsiveness of demand to changes in **household incomes.**

$$\text{Income elasticity of demand} = \frac{\text{\% change in quantity demanded}}{\text{\% change in household income}}$$

(a) Demand for a good is **income elastic** if income elasticity is greater than 1 so that quantity demanded rises by a larger percentage than the rise in income. For example, if the demand for compact discs will rise by 10% if household income rises by 7%, we would say that the demand for compact discs is income elastic.

(b) Demand for a good is **income inelastic** if income elasticity is between 0 and 1 and the quantity demanded rises less than the proportionate increase in income. For example, if the demand for books will rise by 6% if household income rises by 10%, we would say that the demand for books is income inelastic.

The change in quantity demanded takes the form of a **shift in the position of the demand curve,** not a movement along it, since it is **not** stimulated by a change in price.

1.31 Goods whose income elasticity of demand is positive are said to be **normal goods,** meaning that demand for them will rise when household income rises. If income elasticity is negative, the commodity is called an **inferior good** since demand for it falls as income rises.

1.32 For most commodities, an increase in income will increase demand. The exact effect on demand will depend on the type of product. For example the demand for some products like bread will not increase much as income rises. Therefore, bread has a low income elasticity of demand. In contrast, the demand for luxuries increases rapidly as income rises and luxury goods therefore have a high income elasticity of demand.

Question 5

What will be the effect on price and quantity demanded and supplied of sailing boats, given a significant reduction in income tax?

Answer

The demand curve for sailing boats will shift to the right. Both price and quantity demanded/supplied will go up. The effect of a cut in income tax is to leave households with more to spend. Sailing boats are a luxury good, and the income elasticity of demand is likely to be quite high. The percentage increase in demand for boats is therefore likely to be greater than the percentage increase in after-tax household income.

Cross elasticity of demand

KEY TERM

Cross elasticity of demand is the responsiveness of demand for one good to changes in the price of another good

1.33 Cross elasticity of demand = $\dfrac{\text{\% change in quantity of good A demanded}^{\star}}{\text{\% change in the price of good B}}$

*(given no change in the price of A)

1.34 The cross elasticity depends upon the degree to which goods are **substitutes or complements.**

(a) If the two goods are **substitutes, cross elasticity will be positive** and a fall in the price of one will reduce the amount demanded of the other.

(b) If the goods are **complements, cross elasticity will be negative** and a fall in the price of one will raise demand for the other.

1.35 Cross elasticity involves a comparison between two products. The concept is a useful one in the context of considering substitutes and complementary products.

2 ELASTICITY OF SUPPLY 11/01

KEY TERM

The **price elasticity of supply** indicates the responsiveness of supply to a change in price.

2.1 Elasticity of supply = $\frac{\%\text{ change in quantity supplied}}{\%\text{ change in price}}$

2.2 Where the supply of goods is **fixed** whatever price is offered, for example in the case of antiques, vintage wines and land, supply is **perfectly inelastic** and the elasticity of supply is **zero. The supply curve is a vertical straight line.**

2.3 Where the supply of goods varies proportionately with the price, elasticity of supply equals one and the supply curve is a straight line passing through the origin. (Note that a demand curve with unit elasticity along all of its length is **not** a straight line, but a supply curve with unit elasticity **is** a straight line.)

2.4 Where the producers will **supply any amount at a given price** but none at all at a slightly lower price, elasticity of supply is infinite, or **perfectly elastic. The supply curve is a horizontal straight line.**

2.5 Perfectly inelastic supply, unit elastic supply and perfectly elastic supply are illustrated in Figure 6.

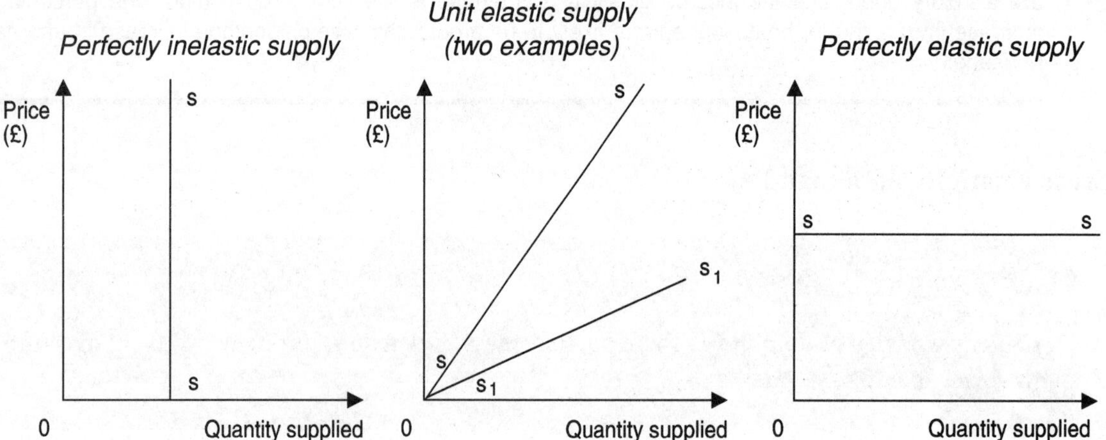

Figure 6 Elasticity of supply

2.6 Supply is **elastic** (greater than 1) when the percentage change in the amount producers want to supply exceeds the percentage change in price. Supply is **inelastic** (less than 1) when the amount producers want to supply changes by a smaller percentage than the percentage change in price.

Factors affecting elasticity of supply

2.7 Elasticity of supply is a measure of firms' ability to adjust the quantity of goods they supply. This depends on a number of constraints.

(a) **Existence of stocks of finished goods**: perishability or shelf life are important considerations.

(b) **Availability of labour**: when unemployment is low it may be difficult to find workpeople with the appropriate skills.

(c) **Availability of raw materials and components**. The existence and location of stocks is important, as is perishability, just as for finished goods.

(d) **Barriers to entry** are covered in more detail later in this study text. Here it is sufficient to point out that if firms can move into the market easily and start supplying elasticity of supply will be increased.

(e) The **time scale** is dealt with in the next paragraph.

Elasticity of supply and time

2.8 As with elasticity of demand, **the elasticity of supply of a product varies according to the time period over which it is measured.** For analytical purposes, four lengths of time period may be considered.

(a) **The market period** is so short that supplies of the commodity in question are limited to existing stocks. In effect, supply is fixed.

(b) **The short run** is a period long enough for supplies of the commodity to be altered by increases or decreases in current output, but not long enough for the fixed equipment (plant, machinery and so on) used in production to be altered. This means that suppliers can produce larger quantities only if they are not already operating at full capacity; they can reduce output fairly quickly by means of lay-offs and redundancies.

(c) **The long run** is a period sufficiently long to allow firms' fixed equipment to be altered. There is time to build new factories and machines, and time for old ones to be closed down. New firms can enter the industry in the long run.

(d) **The secular period** is so long that underlying economic factors such as population growth, supplies of raw materials (such as oil) and the general conditions of capital supply may alter. ('Secular' is derived from the Latin word 'saecula' meaning 'centuries'.) The secular period is ignored by economists except in the theory of economic growth.

Response to changes in demand

2.9 The price elasticity of supply can be seen as a measure of the readiness with which an industry responds following a shift in the demand curve.

2.10 Suppose that there is an increase in the demand for restaurant meals in a city, shown by the rightward shift in the demand curve in Figure 7 from D_1 to D_2. The capacity of the industry is limited in the short run by the number of restaurants in operation. The restaurants can be used more **intensively** to a certain extent, and so supply (S_1) is not perfectly inelastic, but there is a limit to this process. As a result, in the short run there is a large increase in the price from P_1 to P_2.

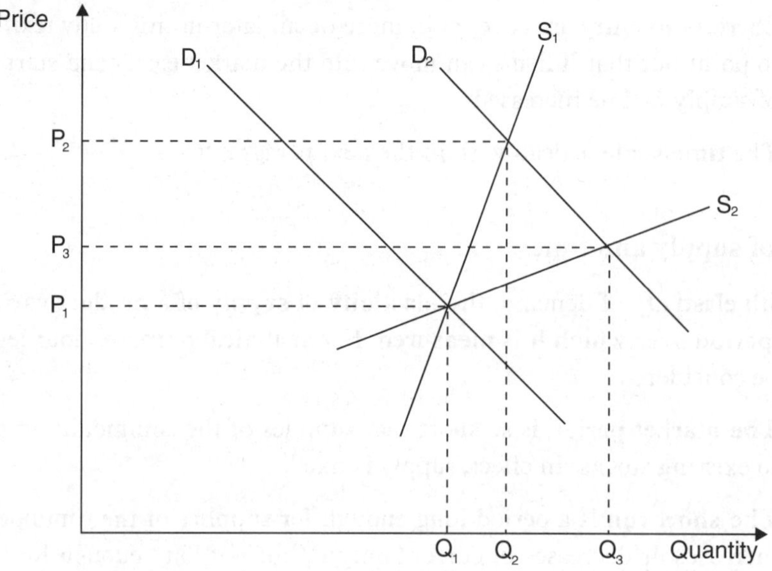

Figure 7 Response to a shift in the demand curve

2.11 The rise in price in the **short run** will encourage entrepreneurs to open new restaurants to take advantage of the profits to be earned. In the **long run**, supply is consequently **more elastic** and is shown by supply curve S_2. The expanded output in the industry leads to a new equilibrium at a lower price P_3 with the new level of output being Q_3.

Question 6

Which diagram shows perfectly elastic demand?

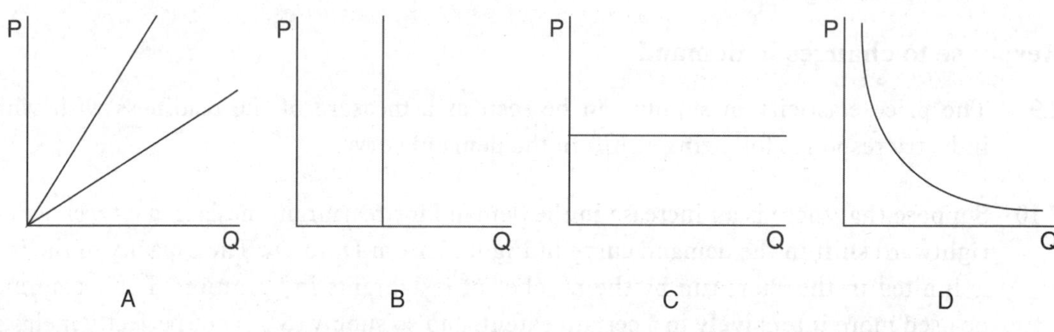

Answer

C A is unit elastic supply (two examples). B is perfectly inelastic demand (or supply), D is unit elastic demand. C also shows perfectly elastic supply.

Chapter roundup

- Demand for a good depends largely on price, household income and the relative price of substitutes or complementary goods. Changes in any of these will cause either a movement along the demand curve or a shift in the demand curve.
- We have seen that elasticity of demand measures how much of a movement or a shift there will be. Price elasticity of demand indicates the responsiveness of total expenditure in a market for a good to price changes.
- Note that the elasticity of demand mainly reflects the availability of substitute goods and the relative importance of the good in the consumer's budget.
- For the *Economics for Business* exam, you need to be able:
    - to distinguish between the factors influencing elasticity
    - to measure price elasticity from given price and demand data, and to draw appropriate conclusions from such information
    - in particular, to draw the correct implications for the total revenue of the producer of changes in the price of the product
- Income elasticity of demand measures the responsiveness of demand to changes in household income. Cross elasticity of demand is determined by the availability of substitute (competitors') products.
- As a measure of the responsiveness of supply to changes in price, the elasticity of supply is an indicator of the readiness of an industry to respond following a shift in the demand curve.

Quick quiz

1 What is meant by the price elasticity of demand (PED) for a commodity?

2 What is the significance of PED to:

(a) a manufacturer?
(b) the Chancellor of the Exchequer?

3 What determines the cross elasticity of demand between two goods?

4 If the absolute value of the price elasticity of demand for dry white wine is greater than one, a decrease in the price of all wine would result in:

A a more than proportional decrease in the quantity of dry white wine purchased
B a less than proportional decrease in the quantity of dry white wine purchased
C a less than proportional increase in the quantity of dry white wine purchased
D a more than proportional increase in the quantity of dry white wine purchased

5 Which combination of demand and supply curves would be appropriate for a firm attempting to increase its profits by increasing its market share?

A Inelastic demand, inelastic supply
B Elastic demand, elastic supply
C Inelastic demand, elastic supply
D Elastic demand, inelastic supply

6 Which of the following statements about the goods A, B and C is correct?

A 5% increase in the price of	Leads to the following % changes in purchases due to price change A	B	C
A	-3	-3	-2
B	-2	-10	+3
C	-1	+5	-1

A A and B are substitutes, A and C have inelastic demand
B A and C are substitutes, A and B have elastic demand
C A and C are complements, A and C have inelastic demand
D An increase in the price of C leads to a fall in C's revenue

7 Using the point method, what is the price elasticity of demand of product X as price falls from £20 to £15?

	X	X
Price	20	15
Quantity	10	15

A 0.5
B 1
C 1.5
D 2

8 Which of the following statements is true? 1. If the price elasticity of demand is more than 1, a fall in price will result in a fall in total expenditure on the good; 2. The income elasticity of demand will only be zero in the case of inferior goods; 3. The cross-elasticity of demand for complementary goods will always be positive.

A None of them are true
B Statement 1 only is true
C Statement 2 only is true
D Statement 3 only is true

9 Elasticity is not constant along a straight line demand curve.

Put the correct values for elasticity in the boxes on this diagram.

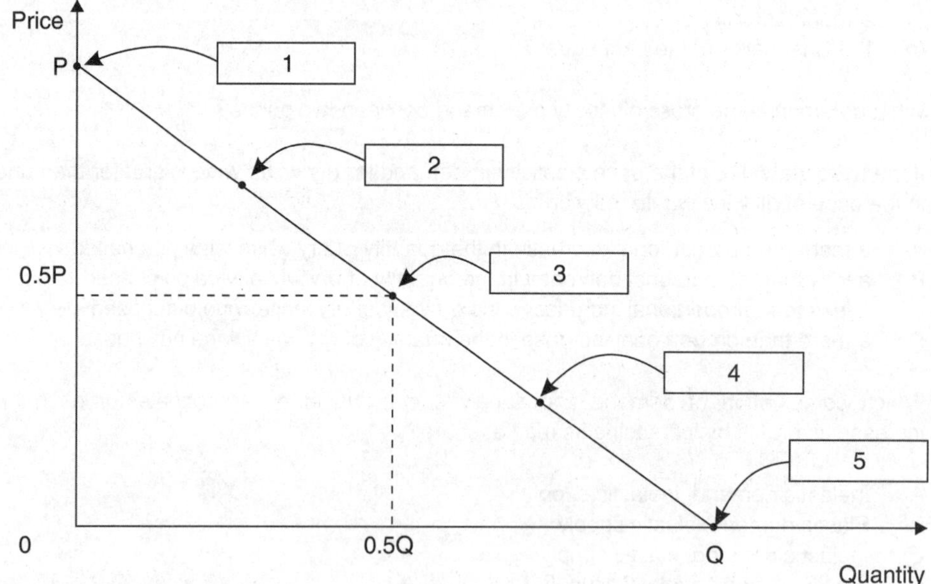

A 1
B Less than 1
C Greater than1
D Zero
E Infinity

10 Which diagram shows perfectly inelastic supply?

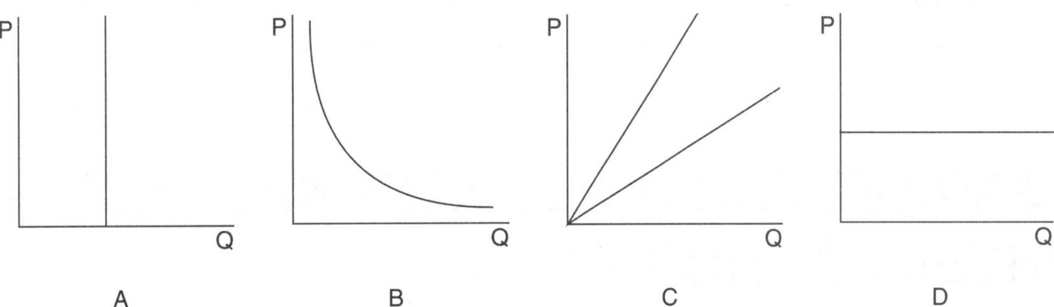

Answers to quick quiz

1 A measure of the extent to which market demand changes proportionately in response to a change in price.

2 If a good has low elasticity of demand, the manufacturer can increase the price without losing much sales revenue, and the Chancellor can impose a tax on it and expect to collect revenue. People will buy almost the same amount of the good even if its price goes up.

3 Cross elasticity of demand is the responsiveness of demand for one good to changes in the price of another. It is determined by the extent that the goods are substitutes or complements. Substitutes display positive cross elasticity and complements, negative cross elasticity.

4 D Assuming a normal good, a decrease in price results in a greater quantity being demanded. Given that demand is price elastic, the increase in quantity will be proportionally greater than the price fall.

5 B To increase market share requires greater quantities both demanded and supplied. To sell more, a firm needs to lower price. For this to be profitable, demand must be elastic. To produce more, supply must also be elastic.

6 C Demand moves in the same direction for A and B in response to changes in their price. Therefore they are not substitutes.

A and C are complements. Also A has inelastic demand.

C is price inelastic, therefore revenue would rise if price rises.

7 D Percentage change in quantity = 50%. Percentage change in price = 25%.

8 A Statement 1 is incorrect. When demand is price elastic, a fall in price will increase total spending on the good. Statement 2 is incorrect, because when household income rises, demand for an inferior good will fall: income elasticity of demand will be negative, not zero. Statement 3 is incorrect. If goods A and B are complements, a rise in the price of B will cause a fall in the demand for A, and so cross elasticity of demand is negative.

9
1 E Change in quantity from or to zero is infinitely large.
2 C % change in quantity is larger than % change in price.
3 A % change in quantity and price are identical.
4 B % change in price is larger than % change in quantity.
5 D Change in price from or to zero is infinitely large.

10 A B is unit elastic demand, C is unit elastic supply (two examples), D is perfectly elastic supply or demand. A also shows perfectly inelastic *demand.*

Now try the questions below from the Question Bank

Number	Level	Marks	Time
Q7	Exam	16	20 mins
Q8	Exam - MCQ	–	–
Q9	Introductory - Interactive	–	–

Chapter 4

MARKET FAILURE, EXTERNALITIES AND INTERVENTION

Topic list		Syllabus reference	Ability required
1	**Market failure**	(ii)	Comprehension
2	**Externalities and government intervention**	(ii)	Comprehension
3	**Indirect taxes and subsidies**	(ii)	Comprehension

Introduction

In this chapter, we are concerned with why a free market would result in an allocation of resources that is not optimal – that is, not the best possible.

Learning outcomes covered in this chapter

- Explain the functioning of a market economy
- Apply basic economic analysis to explain economic and business issues
- Identify the public issues that are raised by business activity
- Explain how governments might respond to the effects of business on the environment

Syllabus content covered in this chapter

- Business and the environment: externalities and public policy

1 MARKET FAILURE 5/01

The case for a free market

1.1 What is the general case for allowing market forces to set prices? The following arguments are put forward by advocates of the free market.

(a) Free markets are **efficient**. Suppliers and consumers react fairly quickly to changes in market conditions in making their output and purchasing decisions; **resource allocation** within the economy is quick to adapt to the new conditions.

(b) The market is **impersonal**. Prices and levels of output are arrived at as a result of numerous decisions of consumers and suppliers, and not as the result of bureaucratic or political regulation.

1.2 Advocates of a free market economy argue that the market forces of supply and demand will result in an **efficient allocation of economic resources**.

(a) Consumers will want lower prices and producers will want higher prices; a balance of supply and demand is struck in the market through the price mechanism.

(b) Producers will decide what goods to produce, and in what quantities, by relating their prices to the costs of production (and the costs of the scarce resources needed to produce them).

(c) If the price of a product is too high, consumers will want to buy less of it. If the price is too low, producers will make less of it and switch their production resources into making something different.

1.3 However, the arguments in favour of a free market are based on the assumption that there is **perfect competition**. Perfect competition has a number of prerequisites.

(a) Markets each have a large number of competing firms, each producing a homogeneous product and each having only a small share of the market.

(b) Consumers and producers have perfect information about markets and prices.

(c) There is perfect mobility of factors of production, which can be switched easily from making one type of good into making another, and free entry and exit of firms into and out of the market.

1.4 In reality, these assumptions are not often completely valid. However, the markets for many goods approximate to conditions of perfect competition.

Market failure

KEY TERM

Market failure occurs when a free market mechanism fails to produce the most efficient allocation of resources.

1.5 Market failure is caused by a number of factors.

- Imperfections in a market
- Divergence between private costs and social costs (externalities)
- The need to provide public goods
- The need to consider non-market goals, such as the consumption of merit goods

1.6 Market imperfection describes any situation where actual behaviour in the market differs from what it would be if there were perfect competition in the market (which we discuss in more detail in a later chapter). The following are examples of market imperfection.

(a) If a monopoly firm controls a market, it might prevent other firms from entering the market (for example by claiming patent rights, or launching a strong marketing campaign with the intention of keeping customers away from the new firms). By restricting supply in this way, the monopolist may keep prices higher than they would be in a competitive market. (Monopoly is a subject of a later chapter.)

(b) Just as monopolies are firms which dominate supply to a market, monopsony buyers are large individual buyers who dominate demand in a market. Monopsonists may exert control over the market, exacting low prices or other favourable conditions from suppliers.

(c) Consumers may make bad purchasing decisions because they do not have complete and accurate information about all goods and services that are available.

(d) It takes time for the price mechanism to work. Firms cannot suddenly enter a new market or shut down operations. The slow response of the price mechanism to changes in demand creates some short term inefficiency in resource allocation.

Exam focus point

A question on the price mechanism (which we covered in Chapter 2) may also ask you to describe why this mechanism can sometimes 'fail'.

2 EXTERNALITIES AND GOVERNMENT INTERVENTION

Social costs and private costs

2.1 In a free market, suppliers and households make their output and buying decisions for their own private benefit, and these decisions determine how the economy's scarce resources will be allocated to production and consumption. Private costs and private benefits therefore determine what goods are made and bought in a free market.

- **Private cost** measures the cost **to the firm** of the resources it uses to produce a good.
- **Social cost** measures the cost **to society as a whole** of the resources that a firm uses.
- **Private benefit** measures the benefit obtained directly by a supplier or by a consumer.
- **Social benefit** measures the total benefit to society from a transaction.

2.2 It can be argued that a free market system would result in a satisfactory allocation of resources, **provided that** private costs are the same as social costs and private benefits are the same as social benefits. In this situation, suppliers will maximise profits by supplying goods and services that benefit customers, and that customers want to buy. By producing their goods and services, suppliers are giving benefit to both themselves and the community.

2.3 However, there are other possibilities.

(a) Members of the economy (suppliers or households) may do things which give benefit to others, but no reward to themselves.

(b) Members of the economy may do things which are harmful to others, but at no cost to themselves.

2.4 When private benefit is **not** the same as social benefit, or when private cost is **not** the same as social cost, an allocation of resources which reflects private costs and benefits only **may not be socially acceptable**.

2.5 Here are some examples of situations where **private cost and social cost differ**.

(a) A firm produces a good and, during the production process, pollution is discharged into the air. The private cost to the firm is the cost of the resources needed to make the good. The social cost consists of the private cost plus the additional 'costs' incurred by other members of society, who suffer from the pollution.

(b) The private cost of transporting goods by road is the cost to the haulage firm of the resources to provide the transport. The social cost of road haulage would consist of the private cost plus the cost of repairs and maintenance of the road system (which sustains serious damage from heavy goods vehicles) plus any environmental costs, such as harm to wildlife habitats from road building.

Private benefit and social benefit

2.6 Here are some examples of situations where **private benefit and social benefit differ**.

(a) Customers at a café in a piazza benefit from the entertainment provided by professional musicians, who are hired by the café. The customers of the café are paying for the service in the prices they pay, and they obtain a private benefit from it. At the same time, other people in the piazza, who are not customers of the café, might stop and listen to the music. They will obtain a benefit, but at no cost to themselves. They are **free riders**, taking advantage of the service without contributing to its cost. The social benefit from the musicians' service is greater than the private benefit to the café's customers.

(b) Suppose that a large firm pays for the training of employees as accountants, expecting a certain proportion of these employees to leave the firm in search of a better job once they have qualified. The private benefits to the firm are the benefits of the training of those employees who continue to work for it. The total social benefit includes the enhanced economic output resulting from the training of those employees who go to work for other firms.

Question 1

Think of some situations other than those mentioned above in which private costs differ from social costs and private benefits differ from social benefits. How might these differences be prevented or compensated for in each situation?

Externalities 11/01

KEY TERM

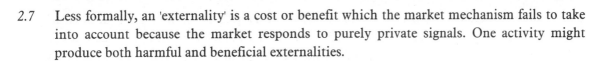

Externalities are effects of a transaction which extend beyond the parties to the transaction. The differences between the private and the social costs, or benefits, arising from an activity are externalities.

2.7 Less formally, an 'externality' is a cost or benefit which the market mechanism fails to take into account because the market responds to purely private signals. One activity might produce both harmful and beneficial externalities.

2.8 We can use demand and supply analysis to illustrate the consequences of externalities. If an adverse externality exists, so that the social cost of supplying a good is greater than the private cost to the supplier firm, then a supply curve which reflects total social costs will be above the (private cost) market supply curve.

2.9 Figure 1 shows two possibilities.

(a) If a free market exists, the amount of the good produced will be determined by the interaction of demand (curve D) and supply curve S. Here, output would be Y, at price P_y

(b) If social costs are taken into account, and the market operated successfully, the amount of the good produced should be X, at price P_x.

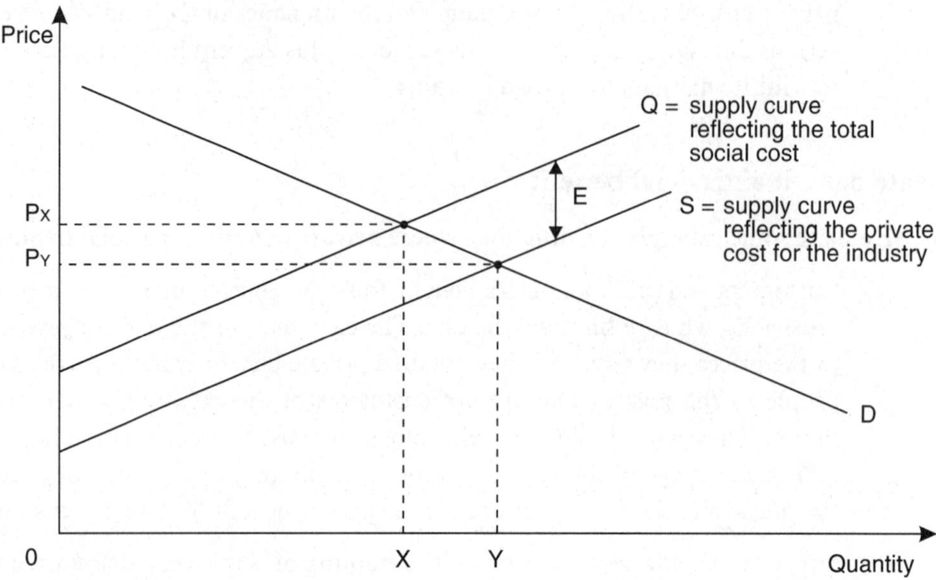

Figure 1 Externalities

2.10 Given a free market, output of the good will exceed what it ideally should be, and so resources will have been over-allocated to production of this particular good.

Public goods 11/01, 5/02

KEY TERM

Some goods, by their very nature, involve so much 'spill-over' of externalities that they are difficult to provide except as **public goods** whose production is organised by the government.

2.11 In the case of public goods, the consumption of the good by one individual or group **does not significantly reduce the amount available for others**. Furthermore, it is often difficult or impossible to **exclude** anyone from its benefits, once the good has been provided. As a result, in a free market, individuals benefiting from the good would have no economic incentive to pay for them, since they might as well be **free riders** if they can, enjoying the good while others pay for it.

2.12 National defence is perhaps the most obvious examples of a public good. It is clearly not practicable for individuals to buy their own defence systems. Policing is sometimes cited as another example of a public good, although the growth of private security firms in the private sector illustrates how some areas of policing are now becoming privatised.

Merit goods

2.13 The existence of market failure and of externalities suggests the need for intervention in markets by the government, in order to improve the allocation of resources. Another possible reason for intervention is to **increase** the consumption of **merit goods**.

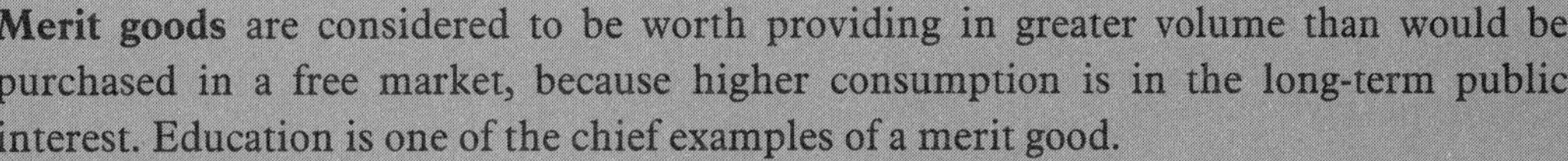

KEY TERM

Merit goods are considered to be worth providing in greater volume than would be purchased in a free market, because higher consumption is in the long-term public interest. Education is one of the chief examples of a merit good.

2.14 On the other hand, many governments want to see **less** consumption of certain **demerit goods,** such as tobacco.

2.15 Apart from providing public goods and merit goods, a government might choose to intervene in the workings of markets by other methods.

(a) Controlling the means of production (for example, through state ownership of industries)

(b) Influencing markets through legislation and regulation (regulation of monopolies, bans on dangerous drugs, enforcement of the use of some goods such as car seat belts, laws on pollution control and so on) or by persuasion (for example, using anti-tobacco advertising)

(c) Redistributing wealth, perhaps by taxing relatively wealthy members of society and redistributing this tax income so as to benefit the poorer members

(d) Influencing market supply and demand in various ways

- Price legislation
- Indirect taxation
- Subsidies

(e) Creating a demand for output that creates employment is labour-creating. A free price mechanism will result in a total demand for goods and services that would be met by a matching total supply, but this total supply quantity might be insufficient to create full employment within the economy. Government might therefore wish to intervene to create a demand for output in order to create more jobs.

2.16 Some externalities, particularly the problems of pollution and the environment, appear to call for international co-operation between governments. The UN Conference on the Environment and Development held in Rio de Janeiro in 1992 led to a convention on climate change which included commitments about emission reduction and was signed by 166 states.

Question 2

An industrial company alters its production methods to reduce the amount of waste discharged from its factory into the local river. What will be the effect (increase or decrease) on:

(a) private costs
(b) external benefits
(c) social costs

Answer

(a) Private costs of the company will presumably increase: the anti-pollution measures will have involved a financial outlay.

(b) External benefits will presumably increase: the public will benefit from a cleaner river.

(c) Social costs may stay the same: the increase in private costs may be balanced by the reduction the external costs to society.

Pollution policy

2.17 One area often discussed in relation to externalities is that of pollution. If polluters take little or no account of their actions on others, this generally results in the output of polluting industries being greater than is optimal. If polluters were forced to pay for any externalities they impose on society, producers would almost certainly change their production techniques so as to minimise pollution and consumers would choose to consume less of those goods which cause pollution.

2.18 One solution is to levy a tax on polluters equal to the cost of removing the effect of the externality they generate: this is called the 'polluter pays' principle. This approach is generally held to be preferable to regulation, as this can be difficult to enforce and provides less incentive to reduce pollution levels permanently.

2.19 Apart from the imposition of a tax, there are a number of other measures open to the government in attempting to reduce pollution. One of the main measures available is the application of subsidies which may be used either to persuade polluters to reduce output and hence pollution, or to assist with expenditure on production processes, such as new machinery and air cleaning equipment, which reduce levels of pollution.

2.20 A problem with using subsidies is that, unlike taxes, they do not provide an incentive to reduce pollution any further: indeed, profits are increased under subsidies which may have the perverse effect of encouraging more pollution to be generated in order to qualify for a subsidy. In addition, this is likely to be an expensive option for the government whereas imposing a tax actually provides the government with additional revenue.

2.21 An example of a subsidy to encourage a specific environmental alternative is that provided to a garbage burning power station opened in Lewisham, South London in 1994. The station receives a guaranteed high price for its power, which is effectively subsidised by electricity consumers. The subsidy thus actually encourages the plant to burn garbage wastefully.

3 INDIRECT TAXES AND SUBSIDIES 11/01

Indirect taxes

KEY TERM

Indirect taxes are levied on expenditure on goods or services as opposed to direct taxation which is applied to incomes. A **selective** indirect tax is imposed on some goods but not on others (or which is imposed at a higher rate)

3.1 We looked at the effects of one form of government intervention in markets - price regulation - earlier. An alternative form of price and output regulation is **indirect taxation.**

3.2 If an indirect tax is imposed on one good, the tax will shift the supply curve **upwards** by the amount the tax adds to the price of each item. This is because the price to **consumers** includes the tax, but the suppliers still only receive the **net-of-tax price**. For example, in Figure 2:

- The supply curve net of tax is S_0

- The supply curve including the cost of the tax is S_1
- The tax is equal to P_1 - P_2 or the distance A - B.

So if demand is for X_1 units the price to suppliers will be P_2 (or B) but the price with tax to the consumer would be P_1 (or A) - and the tax would be $(P_1 - P_2)$ or distance AB.

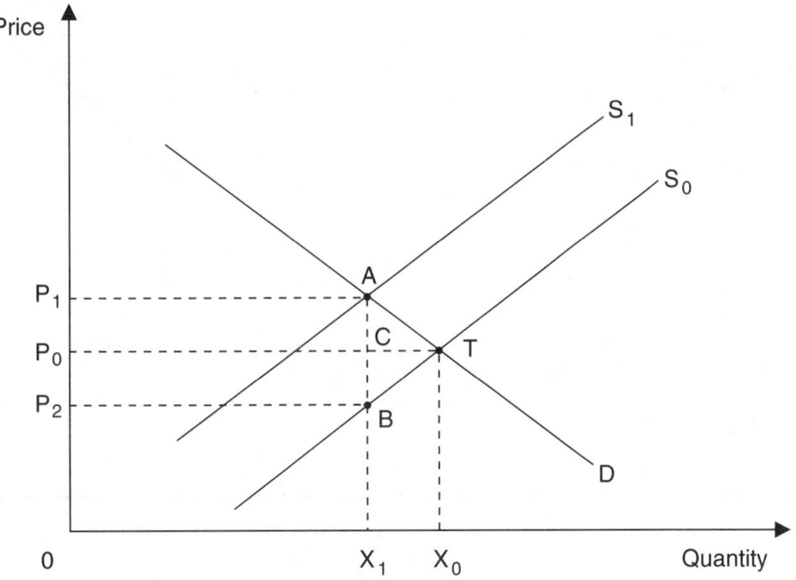

Figure 2 Selective indirect tax

3.3 Without the tax, output would be X_0 and price P_0. Total expenditure is shown by the rectangle OP_0TX_0.

(a) After the tax has been imposed, output falls to X_1 and price with tax rises to P_1. Total expenditure is OP_1AX_1, of which P_2P_1AB is tax revenue and OP_2BX_1 is producers' total revenue.

(b) A new equilibrium arises at point A.

(i) Price to the customer has risen from P_0 to P_1.

(ii) Average revenue received by producers has fallen from P_0 to P_2.

(iii) The tax burden is therefore shared between the producers and consumers, with CB borne by the supplier and AC borne by consumers.

3.4 Consumers pay P_0P_1AC of total tax revenue and producers pay P_2P_0CB.

3.5 The proportion of the tax which is passed on to the consumer rather than being borne by the supplier depends upon the elasticities of demand and supply in the market.

3.6 Figures 3(a) and 3(b) illustrate the extreme cases of perfectly elastic demand and perfectly inelastic demand respectively.

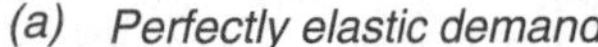

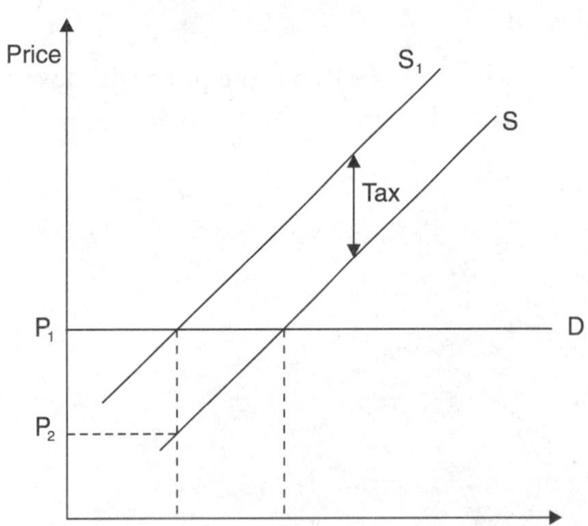

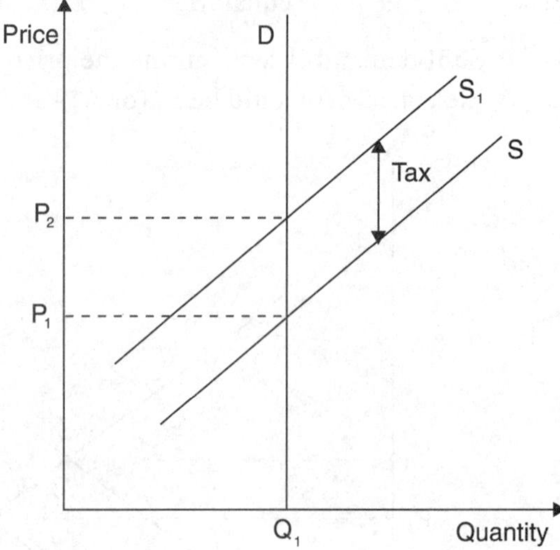

Figure 3 Elasticity of demand

Question 3

Try to work out yourself (from general principles, or from study of Figure 3) who bears the burden of taxation in each of these extreme cases.

Answer

In Figure 3(a), with perfectly elastic demand, demand falls to zero if the price is raised. Consequently, the supplier must bear the full burden of the tax. In spite of the imposition of the tax, the market price remains the same but there is a fall in the quantity supplied from Q_1 to Q_2. The supplier only receives P_2.

In the case of perfectly inelastic demand (Figure 3(b)), the supplier can pass on the full amount of the tax to the consumer by increasing the price from P_1 to P_2 by the full amount of the tax. The quantity supplied remains unchanged.

3.7 The elasticity of supply is also relevant. Figure 4 shows that for a given demand curve, the more inelastic is the supply curve, the greater is the proportion of the tax that is borne by the supplier.

(a) Figure 4(a) shows a relatively inelastic supply curve S. Imposition of the tax shifts the supply curve vertically upwards to S1 and the equilibrium price rises from P1 to P2. The price to the consumer rises by AB per unit, while the supply price to the producer falls by BC per unit. Thus, the greater burden is borne by the supplier.

(b) Figure 4(b) in contrast shows a relatively elastic supply curve S. With the imposition of the tax, the supply curve shifts to S1 and the equilibrium price rises to P2. The price to the consumer rises by AB per unit, and the supply price to the producer falls by BC per unit.

It can be appreciated from Figure 4 that the consumer bears a greater proportion of the tax burden the more elastic is the supply curve. Figure 4 also shows that, for a given demand curve, the price rise and the fall in the equilibrium quantity will both be greater when the supply curve is more elastic.

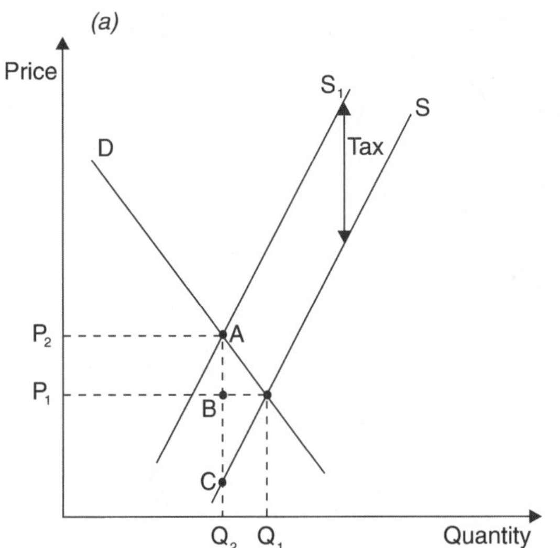

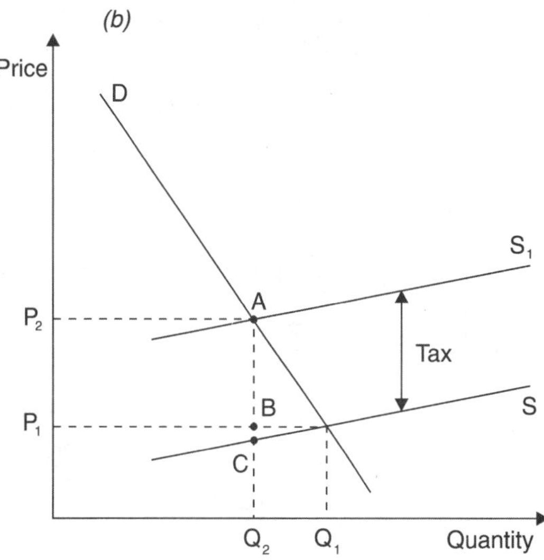

Figure 4 The effect of elasticity illustrated

3.8 In general, the greater the elasticities of demand and supply, the greater will be the effect of a tax in reducing the quantity sold in and therefore produced for the market.

3.9 It can be shown that:

$$\frac{\text{Consumers' share of tax}}{\text{Producers' share of tax}} = \frac{\text{Elasticity of supply}}{\text{Elasticity of demand}}$$

(though proof is omitted here).

3.10 Thus if a selective indirect tax of 10p is placed on a product where supply elasticity is 1.2 and demand elasticity is 0.8, the consumer would pay 6p and the supplier would pay 4p of the tax of 10p per unit and the price of the good would rise by 6p.

3.11 **Further points to note**

(a) **Since such a tax reduces output, it may be harmful to an industry**. For some companies, the reduction in quantities produced may lead to significant rises in the unit costs of production. This could have adverse consequences on the competitive position of the firm if it competes in domestic or overseas markets with foreign firms which are not subject to the same tax.

(b) Indirect taxation may be used to create an improvement in the **allocation of resources** when there are damaging externalities.

Subsidies

3.12 A subsidy is a payment to the supplier of a good by the government. The payment may be made for a variety of reasons.

(a) **To encourage more production of the good**, by offering a further incentive to suppliers

(b) **To keep prices lower for socially desirable goods** whose production the government wishes to encourage

(c) **To protect a vital industry** such as agriculture, when demand in the short term is low and threatening to cause an excessive contraction of the industry.

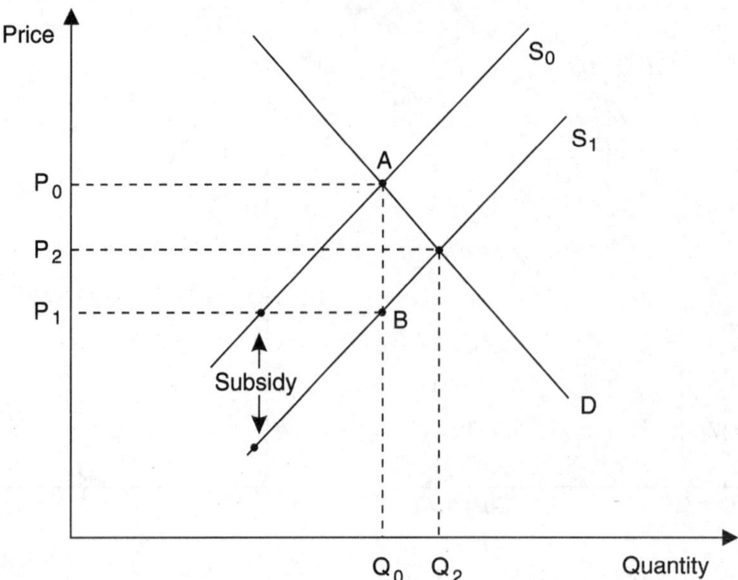

Figure 5 Subsidy

3.13 **A subsidy is rather like indirect taxation in reverse.**

- In Figure 5, supply curve S_0 is what the supply curve would be if no subsidy existed
- Payment of the subsidy moves the supply curve downwards to S_1.

3.14 If there was no subsidy, the free market equilibrium price would be P_0, and output Q_0. A subsidy per unit equivalent to AB is introduced so that suppliers would now be willing to produce Q_0 at a lower price (P_1 rather than at P_0). In other words, the supply curve shifts from S_0 to S_1. But there will be a shift in the equilibrium quantity produced to Q_2, which can be sold on the market for P_2. Thus, the subsidy will have two effects.

- The amount supplied in equilibrium will increase.
- The price will fall, but the decrease in price will be less than the value of the subsidy itself.

Question 4

By reference to Figure 5, analyse the extent to which the benefit of the subsidy falls to:

(a) the consumer
(b) the supplier

Who bears the cost of the subsidy?

Answer

The benefit of the subsidy will be shared between the consumer and the supplier.

(a) Consumers benefit by the lowering of prices from P_0 to P_2.

(b) Suppliers benefit because although they receive a lower price, P_2, they receive the subsidy AB per unit.

(c) The cost of the subsidy is borne by the government (in effect, the taxpayer).

Chapter roundup

- In this chapter, we have discussed why free markets may not lead to an ideal allocation of resources, and have discussed methods of regulating markets.
- Note in particular the following concepts.

  Market failure - the failure of a market to produce a satisfactory allocation of resources.

  Social costs - the total costs to society of using economic resources.

  Social benefits - the total gains to society as a whole flowing from an economic decision.

  Externalities - the differences between private and social costs.

  Public goods - goods which cannot be provided privately because if they are provided at all, all will benefit from them: as a result, individuals would have no incentive to pay for them.

  Merit goods - goods which need to be provided in the long-term public interest.
- Demand and supply analysis can be used to examine the effects on a market of imposing an indirect tax or a subsidy.

Quick quiz

1 What is the general case in favour of allowing a free market to operate?

2 What is market failure, and what are its main causes?

3 What is an externality?

4 List the various forms of government intervention in markets.

5 Which of the following are imperfections in a market? 1. Consumer brand loyalty to a firm's branded goods, regardless of price; 2. The lack of completely accurate information for consumers about all goods and services available; 3. The slow response of firms to price changes and the relatively inelastic supply of a good in the short run.

A Items 1 and 2 only
B Items 2 and 3 only
C Items 1 and 3 only
D Items 1, 2 and 3

6 Which of the following are weaknesses of a completely free-enterprise economic system? 1. It only reflects private costs and private benefits; 2. It may lead to serious inequalities in the distribution of income and wealth; 3. It may lead to production inefficiencies and a wastage of resources.

A 1 and 2 only
B 2 and 3 only
C 1 and 3 only
D 1, 2 and 3

7 Muddy Waters Ltd is an industrial company which has altered its production methods so that it has reduced the amount of waste discharged from its factory into the local river. Which of the following is most likely to be reduced?

A Total private costs
B Social costs
C External benefit
D Variable costs

8 Much Wapping is a small town in Hampshire where a municipal swimming pool and sports centre have just been built by a private firm Hands Nielsen Bumpsydaisy Ltd. Which of the following is an external benefit of the project?

A The increased trade of local shops
B The increased traffic in the neighbourhood
C The increased profits for the sports firm
D The increased building on previous open land

9 The chancellor increases the tax on tobacco. Assuming that the demand for cigarettes is completely inelastic, who pays the tax?

A It is shared between supplier and consumer in proportions equal to the relative prices before and after the increase.

B The supplier

C The consumer

D It is shared between supplier and consumer in proportions equal to the relative quantities sold before and after the increase.

10 In Ruritania, the government has recently introduced minimum price legislation for agricultural products, whereby the government buys up surplus produce which is not purchased by consumers at the minimum price. The minimum price for most agricultural products is well in excess of the free market price that has been obtained in the markets in recent years.

Which of the following statements is untrue?

A The supply of agricultural produce will increase, because more resources will be put into production

B Demand for agricultural produce will be unaffected, because the government will buy up all surplus food supplies

C The minimum price legislation will encourage some farmers to be less efficient, and to produce at high unit costs of output

D There will not be any black market in the sale of agricultural produce at free market prices

Quick quiz answers

1 Free markets are efficient in that they adjust quickly to changing demand and supply and they operate automatically, without need for direction or control.

2 Market failure occurs when a free market mechanism produces an allocation of resources which can be criticised on efficiency, social or political grounds.

3 An externality is an effect caused by an economic transaction which extends beyond the parties to the transaction.

4 Controlling the means of production

Legal regulation of products and prices

Indirect taxation

Subsidies

Redistributing income via taxation and welfare payments

5 D Brand loyalty can make consumers pay more for a good, without getting any greater total satisfaction from consuming it. Lack of information to consumers will result in 'bad' purchasing decisions. The slowness to price changes is a further market imperfection.

6 D The need to limit or avoid these weaknesses is the chief argument in favour of some government involvement in the allocation of economic resources - ie in favour of a mixed economy or even a command economy.

7 B Social cost is the sum of the private cost to a firm *plus* the external cost to society as a whole. Here, social cost is the sum of production costs (private costs) plus the cost of pollution (external cost). The firm's private costs might have been increased by the measures to reduce pollution, but the external costs will have fallen, so that total social costs should have fallen too.

8 A This is correct because the benefits to local shops are additional to the private benefits of the sports firm and as such are external benefits.

B is an external *cost* of the project, since increased volumes of traffic are harmful to the environment.

C is a private benefit for the firm.

D would only be an external benefit if a building is better for society than the use of open land, which is unlikely.

9 C As the consumer's consumption is not altered by the price rise, the supplier can pass it on in full.

10 B

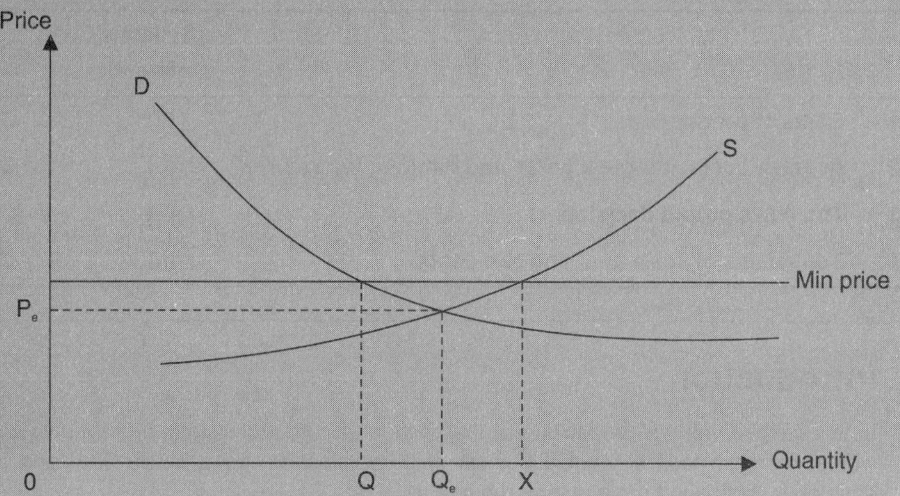

Statement B is incorrect because demand will fall for Q_e to Q, although the government *will* have to buy up the surplus production, which is (X – Q) in the diagram above. *Statement A* is correct, since supply will increase from Qe to X. *Statement C* is correct, because farmers can still make profits even when they incur higher costs - this is likely to create some production inefficiencies. *Statement D* is correct - although the negative statement might have confused you. Black markets are associated with maximum price legislation, not minimum prices.

Now try the questions below from the Question Bank

Number	Level	Marks	Time
Q10	Introductory	8	10 mins
Q11	Introductory - Interactive	–	–
Q12	Introductory - MCQ	–	–

Chapter 5

THEORY OF THE FIRM: PRODUCTION AND COSTS

	Topic list	Syllabus reference	Ability required
1	Costs of production	(ii)	Comprehension
2	Average costs, marginal costs and diminishing returns	(ii)	Comprehension
3	The firm's output decision	(ii)	Comprehension
4	Economies of scale and long run costs	(ii)	Comprehension

Introduction

In this chapter we shall be looking at the costs and output decisions of an *individual* firm. In other words, we shall look at what the costs of production are for a single firm, and how these are affected by both short run and long run factors.

We contrast the concept of *opportunity cost*, which was introduced in Chapter 1, with financial cost as seen from the accountant's point of view.

We also consider how much output a firm will produce at a given market price. The aggregate amount of goods supplied by every individual firm adds up to the market supply; by studying an individual firm we are looking at the 'building blocks' of market supply.

Learning outcome covered in this chapter

- Explain the behaviour of business costs in the both the short and long run

Syllabus content covered in this chapter

- Business functions: production and costs, finance and marketing

1 COSTS OF PRODUCTION

Exam focus point

The theory of costs and revenue is of great importance in later stages of the CIMA examinations, as well as in the *Economics for Business* paper.

Short run and long run costs

1.1 Production is carried out by firms using the factors of production which must be paid or rewarded for their use. The cost of production is the cost of the factors used.

Factor of production	Its cost
Land	rent
Labour	wages
Capital	interest
Enterprise	normal profit

1.2 **Notice that normal profit is viewed as a cost.** This may seem odd to an accountant, who thinks of profit as the difference between revenue and cost - a point we shall return to later. Any profit earned in excess of the profit needed to reward the entrepreneur (in other words, the **opportunity cost** of keeping the entrepreneur from **going elsewhere**) is called **supernormal, abnormal or excess profit.**

1.3 The behaviour of costs is usually analysed under two sets of conditions: the short run and the long run.

KEY TERMS

The **short run** is a time period in which the amount of at least one input is fixed

The **long run** is sufficiently long to allow full flexibility in all the inputs used

Fixed costs and variable costs

1.4 In the short run, certain costs are fixed because the availability of resources is restricted. Decisions must therefore be taken for the short run within the restriction of having some resources in fixed supply. In the longer run, however, most costs are variable, because the supply of skilled labour, machinery, buildings and so on can be increased or decreased. Decisions in the long run are therefore subject to fewer restrictions about resource availability.

1.5 Inputs are variable at the decision of management. For example, management might decide to buy more raw materials, hire more labour, start overtime working and so on.

(a) **Labour is usually considered to be variable** in the short run. Inputs which are treated as **fixed** in the short run will include **capital items**, such as buildings and machinery, for which a significant lead time might be needed before their quantities are changed.

(b) All inputs are variable in the long run. A decision to change the quantity of an input variable which is fixed in the short run will involve a change in the **scale of production**.

Short run costs: total costs, average costs and marginal costs

1.6 Let us now turn our attention to short run costs: the costs of output during a time period in which only some resources of production are variable in availability and the remaining resources of production are fixed in quantity. Figure 1 shows how the various elements of cost vary as output changes.

Exam focus point

This diagram is very important and you should learn to draw it from memory.

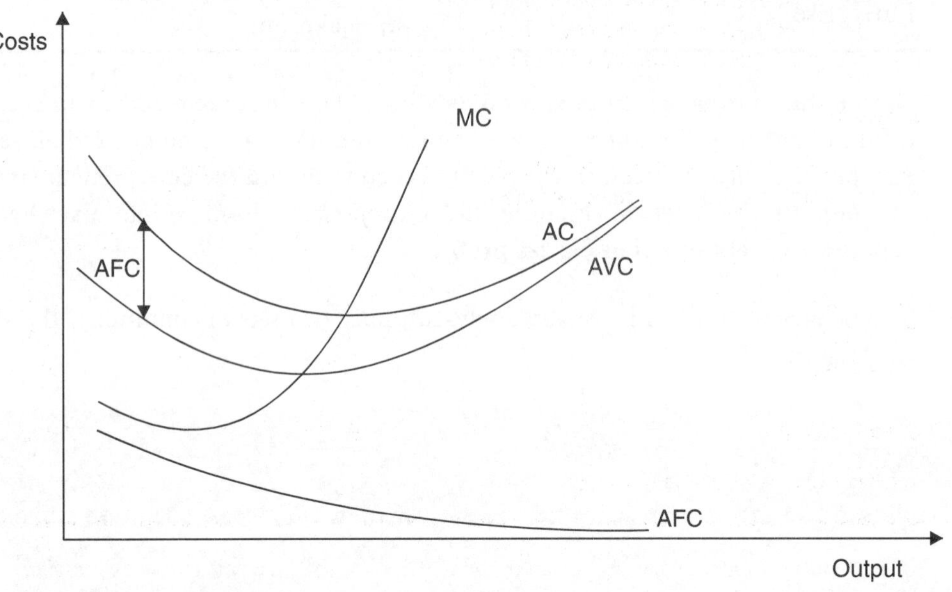

Figure 1 Components of a firm's short run costs

1.7 There are several components of cost to be considered.

KEY TERMS

- **Total cost** (TC). Total cost for a given level of output comprises total fixed cost (TFC) and total variable cost (TVC)
- **Average cost** (AC). Average cost for a given level of output is simply the total cost divided by the total quantity produced.

  Average cost is made up of an average fixed cost per unit plus an average variable cost per unit.

  $$AC = \frac{TC}{N} = \frac{TFC}{N} + \frac{TVC}{N}$$

  $$AC = AFC + AVC$$

  Average fixed cost per unit (AFC) will get smaller as more units (N) are produced. This is because TFC is the same amount regardless of the volume of output, so as N gets bigger, AFC must get smaller.

  Average variable costs per unit (AVC) will change as output volume increases.

- **Marginal cost** (MC). This is the addition to total cost of producing one more unit of output. For example, the marginal cost for a firm of producing the 50th unit of output is the total cost of making the first 50 units minus the total cost of making the first 49 units.

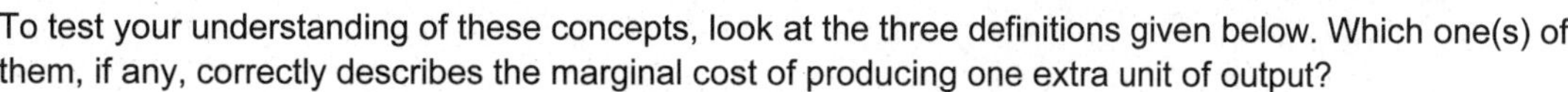

Question 1

To test your understanding of these concepts, look at the three definitions given below. Which one(s) of them, if any, correctly describes the marginal cost of producing one extra unit of output?

(a) MC = increase in total cost of production
(b) MC = increase in variable cost of production
(c) MC = increase in average cost of production

Answer

(a) and (b) are correct; (c) is incorrect. An example might help. Suppose a firm has made 100 units of output, and now goes on to produce one more. The costs might be as follows.

	Cost of 100 units	*Cost of 101 units*
	£	£
Total variable cost	200	202
Total fixed cost	100	100
Total cost	300	302
Average cost	£3.00	£2.99

Marginal cost = 302p – 300p = 2p.

Numerical illustration

1.8 Let us suppose that a firm employs a given amount of capital which is a fixed (invariable) input in the short run: in other words, it is not possible to obtain extra amounts of capital quickly. The firm may combine with this capital different amounts of labour, which we assume to be an input which is variable in the short term. Thus fixed capital and variable labour can be combined to produce different levels of output.

1.9 Here is an illustration of the relationship between the different definitions of the firm's costs. (The figures used are hypothetical.)

Units of output	*Total cost*	*Average cost*	*Marginal cost*	
n	*TC*	*AC*	*MC*	
	£	£	£	
1	1.10	1.10	1.10	
2	1.60	0.80	0.50	(1.60 – 1.10)
3	1.75	0.58	0.15	(1.75 – 1.60)
4	2.00	0.50	0.25	(2.00 – 1.75)
5	2.50	0.50	0.50	(2.50 – 2.00)
6	3.12	0.52	0.62	(3.12 – 2.50)
7	3.99	0.57	0.87	(3.99 – 3.12)
8	5.12	0.64	1.13	(5.12 – 3.99)
9	6.30	0.70	1.18	(6.30 – 5.12)
10	8.00	0.80	1.70	(8.00 – 6.30)

(a) **Total cost** is the sum of labour costs plus capital costs, since these are by assumption the only two inputs.

(b) **Average cost** is the cost per unit of output, ie $AC = \frac{TC}{output} = \frac{TC}{n}$

(c) **Marginal cost** is the total cost of producing n units minus the total cost of producing one less unit, ie (n – 1) units.

1.10 Note the following points on this set of figures.

(a) **Total cost**. Total costs of production carry on rising as more and more units are produced.

(b) **Average cost**. AC changes as output increases. It starts by falling, reaches a lowest level, and then starts rising again.

(c) **Marginal cost**. The MC of each extra unit of output also changes with each unit produced. It too starts by falling, fairly quickly reaches a lowest level, and then starts rising.

(d) **AC and MC compared**. At lowest levels of output, MC is less than AC. At highest levels of output, though, MC is higher than AC. There is a 'cross-over' point, where MC is exactly equal to AC. In this example, it is at 5 units of output.

Economists' and accountants' concepts of cost

1.11 As we have already mentioned, to an economist, cost includes an amount for normal profit which is the reward for entrepreneurship. **Normal profit is the opportunity cost of entrepreneurship**, because it is the amount of profit that an entrepreneur could earn elsewhere, and so it is the profit that he must earn to persuade him to keep on with his investment in his current enterprise.

1.12 A further feature of **cost accounting** is that costs can be divided into fixed costs and variable costs. Total fixed costs per period are a given amount, regardless of the volume of production and sales. Cost accountants usually assume that the variable cost per unit is a **constant amount,** so that the total **variable cost** of sales is directly proportional to the **volume** of sales.

1.13 Economists do not take this approach. In the short run, there are fixed costs and variable costs, but the variable cost of making an extra unit of output need not be the same for each extra unit that is made. As a result, the marginal cost of each extra unit is not constant, either.

1.14 **Accounting profits** consist of sales revenue minus the **explicit costs** of the business. Explicit costs are those which are clearly stated and recorded; some examples are given below.

- Materials costs - prices paid to suppliers
- Labour costs - wages paid
- Depreciation costs on fixed assets
- Other expenses, such as rates and building rental

1.15 **Economic profit** consists of sales revenue minus both the explicit costs and the **implicit costs** of the business. Implicit costs are benefits forgone by not using the factors of production in their next most profitable way.

1.16 It is a well established principle in accounting and economics that relevant costs for decision-making purposes are **future costs incurred as a consequence of the decision**. Past or 'sunk' costs are not relevant to our decisions now, because we cannot change them: they have already been incurred. Relevant future costs are the **opportunity costs** of the input resources to be used.

1.17 EXAMPLE: ECONOMIC PROFITS AND OPPORTUNITY COSTS

Suppose that a sole trader in 19X7 sells goods worth £200,000. He incurs materials costs of £70,000, hired labour costs of £85,000, and other expenses of £20,000. He has no fixed assets other than the building, on which depreciation is not charged. In accounting terms, his profit would be as follows.

	£	£
Sales		200,000
Materials	70,000	
Labour	85,000	
Other expenses	20,000	
		(175,000)
Profit		25,000

1.18 But suppose the buildings he uses in his business could have been put to another use to earn £15,000, and his own labour as business manager could get him a job with a salary of £20,000. The position of the business in economic terms would be as follows.

	£
Sales less explicit costs	25,000
Implicit costs	(35,000)
Loss	(10,000)

1.19 In economic terms, the business has made a loss. It would pay the trader to put his buildings and capital to their alternative uses, and employ his own labour another way, working for someone else at a salary of £20,000.

Question 2

Wilbur Proffit set up his business one year ago. In that time, his firm has earned total revenue of £160,000, and incurred costs of £125,000, including his own salary of £12,000. Before, he had been a salaried employee of Dead End Ventures Ltd, earning an annual salary of £20,000.

To finance the business, Wilbur had to sell his investment of £200,000 in government securities which earned interest of 10% pa. He used £80,000 of this to buy a warehouse, whose annual commercial rental value would be £11,000 pa. The remaining £120,000 has been used to finance business operations.

Required

Calculate:

- The accounting profit earned by Wilbur in the last year
- The economic profit or loss earned

Answer

Accounting profit

	£
Revenue	160,000
Costs	125,000
Profit	35,000

Economic profit

	£	£
Revenue		160,000
Accounting costs	125,000	
Opportunity cost of owner's time - extra salary forgone		
From alternative employment (20,000 – 12,000)	8,000	
Rental of factory (opportunity cost of £80,000)	11,000	
Opportunity cost of other capital tied up in the business		
(10% of £120,000)	12,000	
		156,000
Economic profit		4,000

2 AVERAGE COSTS, MARGINAL COSTS AND DIMINISHING RETURNS 5/01

The relationship between AC and MC

2.1 The relationships between average and marginal costs are important.

(a) **When the average cost schedule is rising, the marginal cost will always be higher than the average cost.** If the cost of making one extra unit of output exceeds the average cost of making all the previous units, then making the extra unit will clearly cause an increase in the average unit cost.

(b) In our example in Paragraph 1.9, the average cost schedule rises from six units of output onwards and MC is bigger than AC at all these levels of output (6 – 10 units).

(c) **When the average cost curve is falling, marginal cost lies below it.** This follows similar logic. If the cost of making an extra unit is less than the average cost of making all the previous units, the effect of making the extra unit must be a reduction in average unit cost. In our example, this happens between production of one and four units.

(d) **When the average cost curve is horizontal, marginal cost is equal to it.** In our example in Paragraph 1.9, when there are five units of output, the average cost stays at £0.50 and the marginal cost of the fifth unit is also £0.50.

Question 3

(a) It is possible for the average total cost curve to be falling while the average variable cost curve is rising. True or false?

(b) Marginal fixed costs per unit will fall as output increases. True or false?

Answer

(a) True. Average total cost (AC) comprises average fixed cost (AFC) and average variable cost (AVC). AFC falls as output rises, and the fall may be sufficient to outweigh a possible increase in AVC. In such a case, AC will fall while AVC rises.

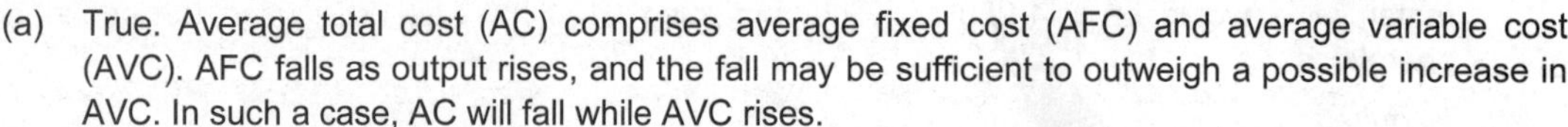

(b) False. It is *average* fixed costs per unit that fall as output increases. *Marginal* fixed costs = 0.

2.2 The marginal cost curve always cuts through the average cost curve at the lowest point of the average cost curve (see Figure 1 earlier).

2.3 The short run average cost curve (AC in Figure 1) is U shaped. We now consider why.

2.4 Fixed costs per unit of output, ie average fixed costs, will fall as the level of output rises. Thus if fixed costs are £10,000 and we make 10,000 units, the average fixed cost (AFC) will be £1 per unit. If output increases to 12,500 units the AFC will fall to 80p (10,000 ÷ 12,500) and if output increases to 15,000 units, the AFC will fall again to 67p (10,000 ÷ 15,000), and so on. Spreading fixed costs over a larger amount of output is a major reason why (short run) average costs per unit fall as output increases.

2.5 Variable costs are made up from the cost of the factors of production whose use can be varied in the short run – for example wages, fuel bills and raw material purchases. **Total variable costs therefore vary with output in the short run as well as in the long run.**

(a) The accountant's assumption about short run variable costs is that **up to a certain level of output, the variable cost per unit is more or less constant** (eg wages costs and materials costs per unit of output are unchanged). If the average fixed cost per unit is falling as output rises and the average variable cost per unit is constant, it follows that the average total cost per unit will be falling too as output increases.

(b) However, there are other reasons for the initial fall in average total cost. The first are the effects of the **division of labour** and **specialisation**. Imagine a small but fully equipped factory, with a variety of machinery and equipment and a workforce of, say, ten. If each person attempts to perform all the operations on a single item, production is likely to be low.

   (i) They will be unable to develop a high level of skill at every one of the jobs

   (ii) Time will be lost as they move from machine to machine

   (iii) Individual variability will produce a high rate of defects, perhaps with each person tending to produce different faults

   (iv) Individuals will work at different rates on different operations: as a result, queues will form at some machines and others will be under-utilised

   If there is a degree of specialisation, expertise and speed will rise, machines will be run at optimum rates and output will rise. Average costs will therefore fall.

(c) **The second reason is the utilisation of indivisibilities.** If a machine has an output capacity of 100 units per day but is only used to produce 50 units per day, the machinery cost of each of those 50 units will be twice the level it would be if the machine was used to capacity. Operation of a plant below normal output is uneconomical, so there are cost savings as production is increased up to capacity level.

The law of diminishing returns

KEY TERM

Eventually, as output increases, average costs will tend to rise. **The law of diminishing returns** says that if one or more factors of production are fixed, but the input of another is increased, **the extra output generated by each extra unit of input will eventually begin to fall.** In our factory, as we add staff, we start to see queues forming at machines; it becomes more difficult to co-ordinate work; machinery starts to break down through over-use and there simply is not enough space to work efficiently.

2.6 The law of diminishing returns states that, given the present state of technology, as more units of a variable input factor are added to input factors that are fixed in supply in the short run, the resulting increments to total production will eventually and progressively decline. In other words, as more units of a variable factor (eg labour) are added to a quantity of a fixed factor (eg a hectare of land), there may be some **increasing returns** or **constant returns** as more units of the variable factor (eg labour) are added, but eventually, **diminishing returns** will set in. Putting more people to work on a hectare of land will increase the yield up to a point, but eventually it will be costing more to employ additional labour than is being earned in additional yield. Observation of agriculture is the origin of the law of diminishing returns.

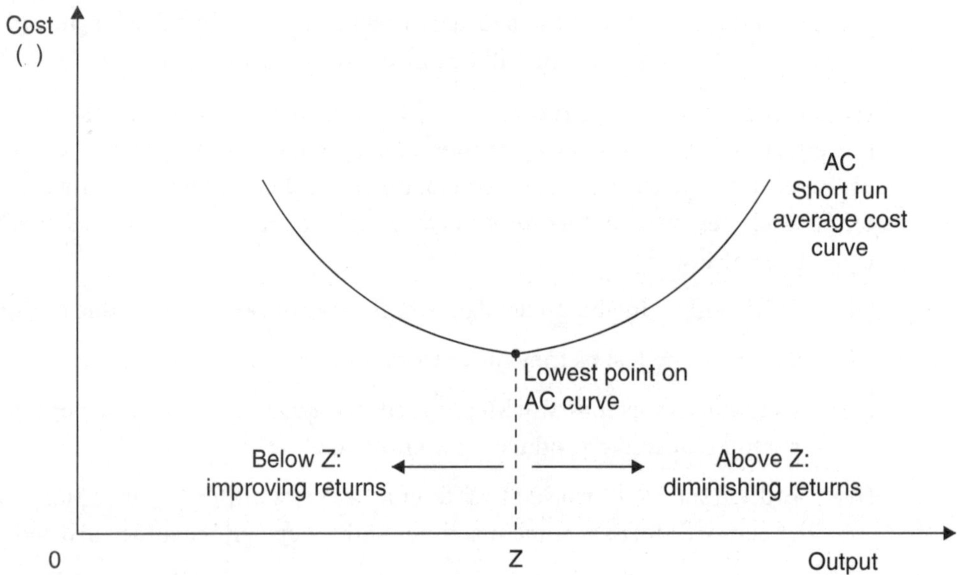

Figure 2 U shaped short run cost curve and diminishing returns

Exam focus point

Remember that this is a **short run** phenomenon; at least one factor of production is fixed.

2.7 The law of diminishing returns is expressed in production quantities, but it obviously has direct implications for short run average and marginal **costs**. Resources cost money, and the average and marginal costs of output will depend on the quantities of resources needed to produce the given output.

Question 4

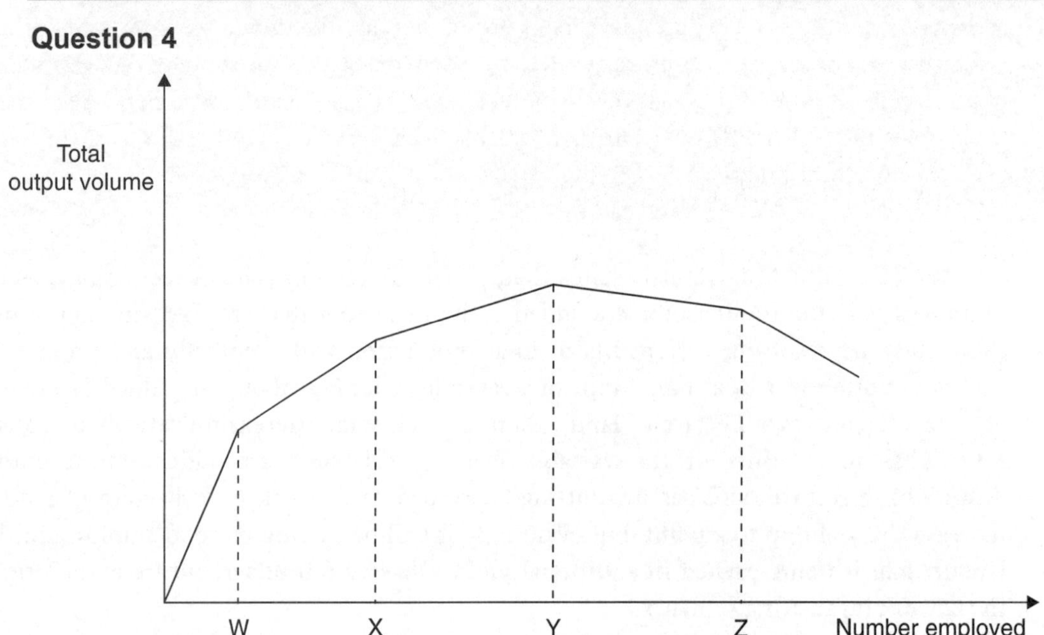

In the diagram above, from what level of employment do diminishing returns start to occur?

Answer

Diminishing returns occur when the marginal physical product of extra units of labour starts to decline. This begins to happen at output W, when the rate of increase in total output starts to decline as numbers employed continue to increase.

3 THE FIRM'S OUTPUT DECISION 5/01

3.1 The assumption of **profit maximisation** provides a basis for beginning to look at the output decisions of individual firms.

KEY TERM

Profit is equal to total revenue minus total cost of any level of output.

Total revenue, average revenue and marginal revenue

3.2 There are three aspects of revenue to consider.

(a) **Total revenue** (TR) is the total income obtained from selling a given quantity of output. We can think of this as quantity sold multiplied by the price per unit.

(b) **Average revenue** (AR) we can think of as the price per unit sold.

(c) **Marginal revenue** (MR) is the addition to total revenue earned from the sale of one extra unit of output.

3.3 When a firm can sell all its extra output at the same price, the AR 'curve' will be a straight horizontal line on a graph. The **marginal revenue** per unit from selling extra units at a fixed price must be the same as the **average revenue** (see Figure 4).

3.4 If the price per unit must be cut in order to sell more units, then the marginal revenue per unit obtained from selling extra units will be less than the previous price per unit (see Figure 5). In other words, when the AR is falling as more units are sold, the MR must be less than the AR.

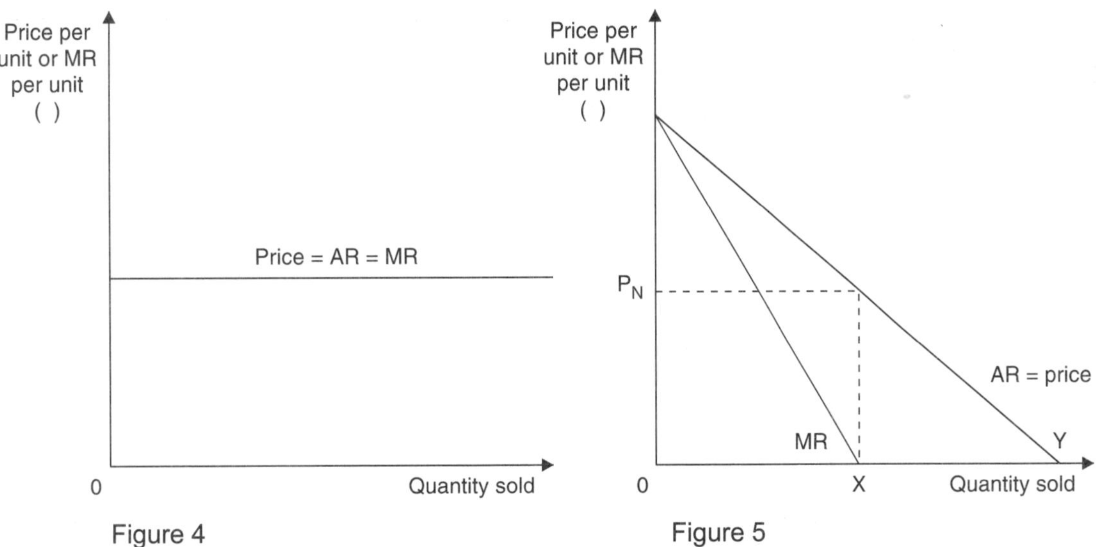

Figure 4

Figure 5

In Figure 5, with straight line MR and AR curves, the length OX is exactly half of the length OY.

Exam focus point

Figure 5 is another important diagram and forms the basis of other more detailed illustrations.

3.5 Note that in Figure 5, at any given level of sales, **all units are sold at the same price**. The firm has to reduce its price to sell more, but the price must be reduced for *all* units sold, not just for the extra units. This is because we are assuming that all output is produced for a single market, where a single price will prevail.

3.6 When the price per unit has to be reduced in order to increase the firm's sales the marginal revenue can become negative. This happens in Figure 5 at price P_N when a reduction in price does not increase output sufficiently to earn the same total revenue as before. In this situation, demand would be price inelastic.

3.7 We have defined profit as TR minus TC.

(a) Figure 6 shows, in simplified form, how TR and TC vary with output. As you might expect, TC increases as output rises. The effect of increasing marginal cost (caused by diminishing returns) is that the rise in TC accelerates as output increases and so the TC curve becomes steeper.

(b) Conversely, the gradient of the TR curve reduces as output and sales increase. This is because most firms operate under the conditions illustrated in Figure 5. That is to say, they must reduce their prices in order to sell more. The rate of growth of TR therefore declines.

(c) Notice carefully that the vertical axis of Figure 6 shows total values whereas in Figures 4 and 5, it shows value per unit.

(d) Profits are at a maximum where the vertical distance AB between the TC and TR curves is greatest.

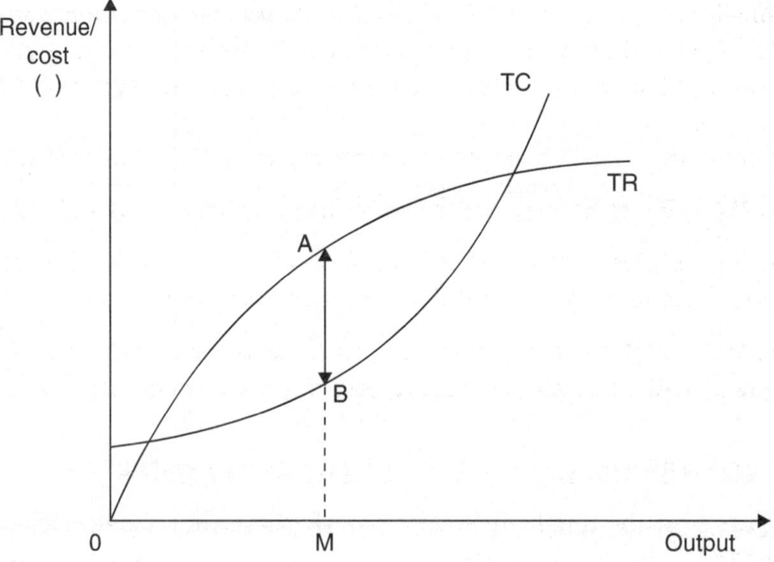

Figure 6 Profit maximisation

Profit maximisation: MC = MR **5/01, 11/01, 5/02**

3.8 As a firm produces and sells more units, its total costs will increase and its total revenues will also increase (unless demand is price inelastic and MR has become negative).

(a) Provided that the extra cost of making an extra unit is **less than** the extra revenue obtained from selling it, the firm will increase its profits by making and selling the extra unit.

(b) If the extra cost of making an extra unit of output **exceeds** the extra revenue obtainable from selling it, the firm's profits would be reduced by making and selling the extra unit.

(c) If the extra cost of making an extra unit of output is **exactly equal** to the extra revenue obtainable from selling it, bearing in mind that economic cost includes an amount for normal profit, it will be worth the firm's while to make and sell the extra unit. And since the extra cost of yet another unit would be higher (the law of diminishing returns applies) whereas extra revenue per unit from selling extra units is never higher, the profit-maximising output is reached at this point where MC = MR.

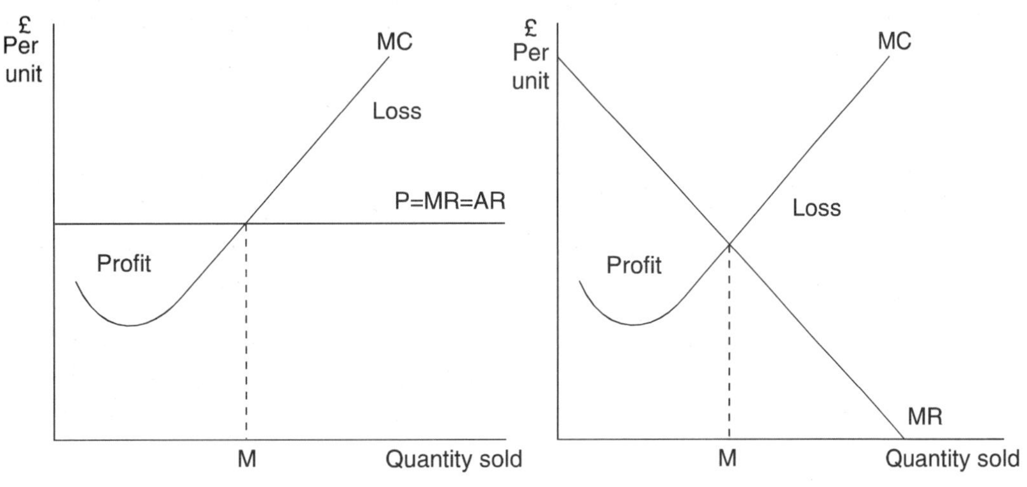

Figure 7 *Figure 8*

(d) Figures 7 and 8 show the profit maximising output quantity M for the 2 types of firm shown in Figures 4 and 5. In both cases, the marginal cost function is as discussed earlier in this chapter. The firm makes a profit on each extra item it produces, albeit a smaller one, until output M is reached. At this level of output the MC and MR curves cross. The addition to total revenue from the next unit is less than the increase in total cost which it causes. This level of output corresponds to the level M shown in Figure 6.

3.9 In other words, given the objective of profit maximisation there are **three possibilities**.

(a) If MC is less than MR, profits will be increased by making and selling more.

(b) If MC is greater than MR, profits will fall if more units are made and sold, and a profit-maximising firm would not make the extra output.

(c) If MC = MR, the profit-maximising output has been reached, and so this is the output quantity that a profit-maximising firm will decide to supply.

4 ECONOMIES OF SCALE AND LONG RUN COSTS 11/01

4.1 We have not yet considered a firm's long run costs of output. In the long run, all inputs are variable, so the problems associated with the diminishing returns to variable factors do not arise; in other words, the law of diminishing returns applies only to short run costs and not to long run costs. Whereas short run output decisions are concerned with diminishing returns given fixed factors of production, **long run output decisions** are concerned with **economies of scale** when all factor inputs are variable.

4.2 Output will vary with variations in inputs, such as labour and capital.

(a) If output increases in the **same proportion** as inputs (for example doubling all inputs doubles output) there are **constant returns to scale**.

(b) If output increases **more than in proportion** to inputs (for example doubling all inputs trebles output) there are **economies of scale** and in the long run average costs of production will continue to fall as output volume rises.

(c) If output increases **less than in proportion** to inputs (for example trebling all inputs only doubles output) there are **diseconomies of scale** and in the long run average costs of production will rise as output volume rises.

4.3 Returns to scale are, for example, concerned with improvements or declines in productivity **by increasing the scale of production**, for example by mass-producing instead of producing in small batch quantities.

Constant returns to scale 5/02

4.4 A feature of constant returns to scale is that **long run** average costs and marginal costs per unit remain constant. For example:

Output	*Total cost (with constant returns)*	*Average cost per unit*	*Marginal cost per unit*
	£	£	£
1	6	6	6
2	12 (2 × 6)	6	6
3	18 (3 × 6)	6	6
4	24 (4 × 6)	6	6

4.5 In the real world, the duplication of all inputs might be impossible if one incorporates qualitative as well as quantitative characteristics in inputs. One such input is entrepreneurship. Doubling the size of the firm does not necessarily double the inputs of organisational and managerial skills, even if the firm does hire extra managers and directors. The input of entrepreneurship might be intangible and indivisible.

Economies of scale 11/01

KEY TERM

Economies of scale: factors which cause average cost to decline in the long run as output increases.

4.6 The effect of economies of scale is to shift the whole cost structure downwards and to the right on the graph. A long run average cost curve (LRAC) can be drawn as the 'envelope' of all the short run average cost curves (SRAC) of firms producing on different scales of output. The LRAC is tangential to each of the SRAC curves. Figure 9 shows the shape of such a long run average cost curve if there are increasing returns to scale - economies of scale - up to a certain output volume and then constant returns to scale thereafter.

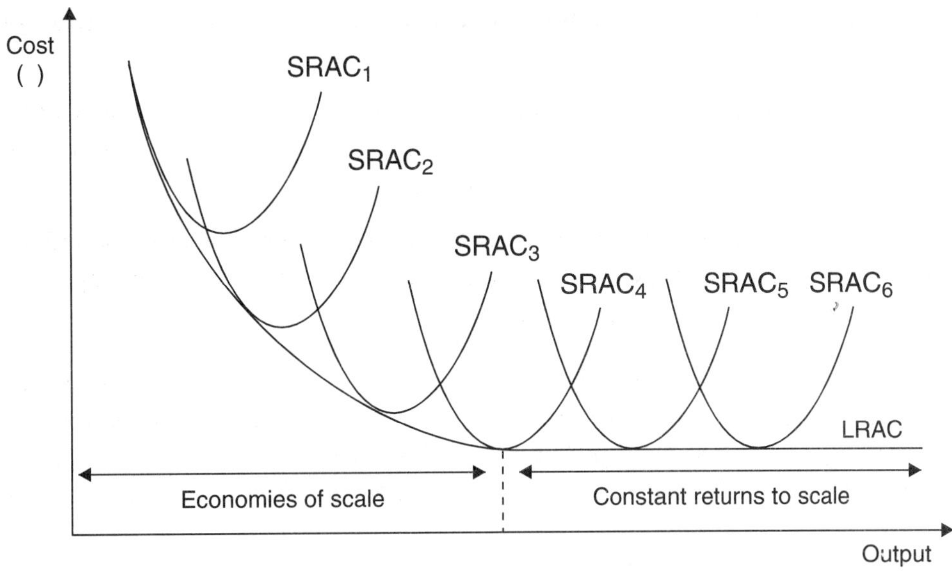

Figure 9 Economies of scale

Diseconomies of scale

4.7 It may be that the flat part of the LRAC curve is never reached, or it may be that diseconomies of scale are encountered. Diseconomies of scale might arise when a firm gets so large that it cannot operate efficiently or it is too large to manage efficiently, so that average costs begin to rise.

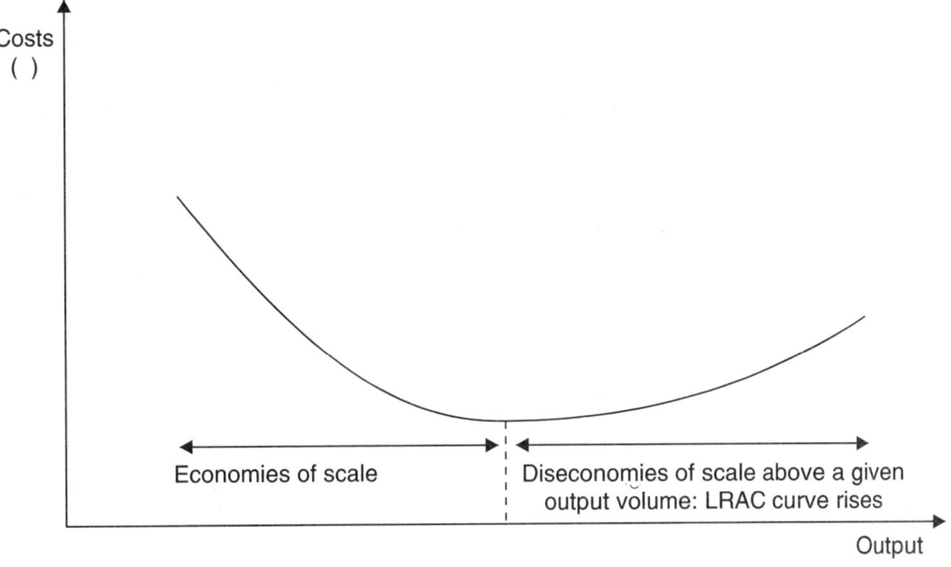

Figure 10 Diseconomies of scale

4.8 A firm should try to minimise its average costs in the long run, and to do this it ought to try to produce output on a scale where the LRAC curve is at its lowest point. While there are economies of scale, a firm should always be trying to grow.

Reasons for economies of scale

4.9 The economies of scale attainable from large scale production fall into two categories.

(a) **Internal economies**: economies **arising within** the firm from the organisation of production.

(b) **External economies**: economies attainable by the firm because of the growth of the industry as a whole.

Internal economies of scale

Technical economies

4.10 Technical economies arise in the production process. They are also called **plant economies of scale** because they depend on the size of the factory or piece of equipment.

4.11 Large undertakings can make use of **larger and more specialised machinery**. If smaller undertakings tried to use similar machinery, the costs would be excessive because the machines would become obsolete before their physical life ends (ie their economic life would be shorter than their physical life). Obsolescence is caused by falling demand for the product made on the machine, or by the development of newer and better machines.

4.12 **Indivisibility of operations**

(a) There are operations which must be carried out at the same cost, regardless of whether the business is small or large; these are fixed costs and **average fixed costs always decline as production increases.**

(b) Similarly, other operations' costs vary a little, but not proportionately, with size (ie having 'semi-fixed' costs).

(c) Some operations are not worth considering below a certain level of output (eg advertising campaigns).

4.13 **Dimensional economies of scale** arise from the relationship between the volume of output and the size of equipment (eg storage tanks) needed to hold or process the output. The cost of a container for 10,000 gallons of product will be much less than ten times the cost of a container for just 1,000 gallons.

Commercial or marketing economies

4.14 **Buying economies** may be available, reducing the cost of material purchases through bulk purchase discounts. Similarly, **stockholding** becomes more efficient. The most economic quantities of inventory to hold increase with the scale of operations, but at a lower proportionate rate of increase.

Organisational economies

4.15 When the firm is large, centralisation of functions such as administration, R&D and marketing may reduce the burden of overheads on individual operating locations.

Financial economies

4.16 Large firms may find it easier to obtain loan finance at attractive rates of interest. It is also feasible for them to sell shares to the public via a stock exchange.

Question 5

The above list is not exhaustive. Can you add to it?

Answer

(a) Large firms attract *better quality employees* if the employees see better career prospects than in a small firm.

(b) Specialisation of labour applies to management, and there are thus *managerial economies*; the cost per unit of management will fall as output rises.

(c) *Marketing economies* are available, because a firm can make more effective use of advertising, specialist salesmen, and specialised channels of distribution.

(d) Large companies are able to devote more resources to *research and development* (R & D). In an industry where R & D is essential for survival, large companies are more likely to prosper.

(e) Large companies find raising finance easier and can often do so more cheaply. Quoted public limited companies have access to the Stock Exchange for new share issues. They are also able to borrow money more readily.

External economies of scale

4.17 External economies of scale occur as an **industry** grows in size. Here are two examples.

- **A large skilled labour force is created** and educational services can be geared towards training new entrants.
- **Specialised ancillary industries will develop** to provide components, transport finished goods, trade in by-products, provide special services and so on. For instance, law firms may be set up to specialise in the affairs of the industry.

The effect of size

4.18 The extent to which both internal and external economies of scale can be achieved will vary from industry to industry, depending on the conditions in that industry. In other words, big-sized firms are better suited to some industries than others.

(a) **Internal economies of scale** are potentially more significant than external economies to a supplier of a product or service for which there is a large consumer market. It may be necessary for a firm in such an industry to grow to a certain size in order to benefit fully from potential economies of scale, and thereby be cost-competitive and capable of making profits and surviving (see para 4.21).

(b) **External economies of scale** are potentially significant to smaller firms who specialise in the ancillary services to a larger industry. For example, the development of a large world-wide industry in drilling for oil and natural gas off-shore has led to the creation of many new specialist supplier firms, making drilling rigs, and various types of equipment. Thus, a specialist firm may benefit more from the market demand created by a large customer industry than from its own internal economies of scale.

Diseconomies of scale

4.19 Economic theory predicts that there will be **diseconomies of scale** in the long run costs of a firm, once the firm gets beyond an ideal size. The main reasons for possible diseconomies of scale are human and behavioural problems of managing a large firm. In a large firm employing many people, with many levels in the hierarchy of management, there may be a number of undesirable effects.

- Communicating information and instructions may become difficult.
- Chains of command may become excessively long.
- Morale and motivation amongst staff may deteriorate.
- Senior management may have difficulty in assimilating all the information they need in sufficient detail to make good quality decisions.

4.20 There will not usually be **technical** factors producing diseconomies of scale. The technology of higher volume equipment, on the contrary, is more likely to create further economies of scale.

4.21 The implication of diseconomies of scale is that companies should achieve a certain size to benefit fully from scale economies, but should not become too big, when cost controls might slacken and organisational inefficiency is likely to develop.

Minimum efficient scale 11/01

KEY TERM

Given the idea of economies of scale, it is generally accepted that in any industry, there is a **minimum efficient scale** of production which is necessary for a firm to achieve the full potential economies of scale.

4.22 Just what this **minimum efficient scale** (MES) is will vary from industry to industry. In the paint manufacturing industry, for example, it might be necessary to have a 15% share of the market in order to achieve maximum scale economies, whereas in frozen food production, a 25% share of the market might be necessary, and so on. If a firm has a production capacity below the minimum economic scale, its unit costs of production will be higher than the unit costs of its bigger competitors, and so it will not compete successfully and it will make lower profits, or even losses. A profit maximising firm should be attempting to minimise its unit costs, and this means striving to achieve maximum scale economies, which in turn may mean having to grow bigger.

Question 6

Explain in detail the difference between economies of scale and diminishing returns to a factor.

Answer

Diminishing returns. In the short run, some factors of production are fixed, and some are variable. This means that a firm can increase the volume of its output in the short run, but only within the constraint of having some fixed factors. As a result, the short run average cost curve is U shaped, because of increasing and then diminishing marginal returns.

Diminishing marginal returns occur within a given production capacity limit. For example, if a company has a given capacity limit of 100,000 units, with fixed costs of £300,000 per period and variable costs of £2 per unit, there is a decreasing average cost per unit as output is increased.

Output	*Variable costs*	*Fixed costs*	*Total costs*	*Average costs*
Units	£	£	£	£
50,000	100,000	300,000	400,000	8.00
75,000	150,000	300,000	450,000	6.40
100,000	200,000	300,000	500,000	5.00

However, when marginal costs per unit begin to increase above £2 per unit (for example because of overtime premiums on labour costs) there will be diminishing returns to scale.

Economies of scale. In the long run, all factors of production are variable and so a firm can increase the scale of its output in the long run without any constraints of fixed factors. By increasing output capacity in this way, a firm might be able to reduce its unit costs, for example by mass-producing with bigger and more efficient machines or more specialised machines. These cost reductions are economies of scale.

Economies of scale occur when a firm re-organises its production capacity and is able to produce more output. For example, suppose that a firm which had an output capacity of 100,000 units, with fixed costs per unit of £300,000 and unit variable costs of £2, now doubles its output capacity to 200,000 units, when fixed costs are £400,000 and unit variable costs are £1.50. There will be economies of scale, because both average unit costs (above a certain level of output) and marginal costs have fallen.

Output	*Fixed costs*	*Variable costs at capacity*	*Total costs at capacity*	*Average costs at capacity*
Units	£	£	£	£
100,000 (old capacity)	300,000	200,000	500,000	5.00
200,000 (new capacity)	400,000	300,000	700,000	3.50

If economies of scale are sufficiently great, average costs and more particularly marginal unit costs will fall to the point where suppliers are able to reduce their selling prices and still maximise profits at the lower selling price. MC has fallen, and so MR will fall too, at the profit-maximising output level.

Economies of scale explain the L shape of a firm's long run average cost curve.

Chapter roundup

- It has been emphasised that economic costs are different from accounting costs, and represent the opportunity costs of the factors of production that are used.
- A firm's output decisions should be seen in both the short run, when some factors of production are fixed and the long run, when all factors of production can be varied.
- In the short run, a firm's average cost (SRAC) curve is U shaped, due to diminishing returns beyond a certain output level. In the short run, a firm will maximise its profits where MR = MC.
- In the long run, a firm's SRAC curve can be shifted, and a firm's minimum achievable average costs at any level of output can be depicted by a long run average cost (LRAC) curve.
- The shape of the LRAC depends on whether there are increasing, constant or decreasing returns to scale. There are some economies of scale, and even if increasing returns to scale are not achievable indefinitely as output rises, up to a certain minimum efficient scale of production (MES) there will be increasing returns to scale. Firms will reduce their average costs by producing on a larger scale up to the MES.
- Whether there are constant or decreasing returns to scale beyond the MES will vary between industries and firms. Similarly, whether economies of scale are significant will vary between industries.
- Technological progress results in shifts in the LRAC, and since technology changes are continual, a firm's LRAC can probably never be 'stabilised' and unchanging for long.
- If economies of scale are significant, there is a strong argument in favour of growth by firms, which might occur either through organic growth (building up the firm's own resources) or through mergers and takeovers.
- Before going on, make sure that you understand two things.

  The concepts of fixed and variable costs and their relationship to average and marginal costs

  The relationships between price, average revenue and marginal revenue
- Questions in the examination may require you to make calculations from limited cost and revenue data.

Quick quiz

1 Explain the distinction between long run and short run costs.

2 What is the law of diminishing returns?

3 At what point is the firm's profit maximised?

4 Why might there be diseconomies of scale?

5 Which of the following is an example of an external economy of scale?

A Increased wage costs due to falling unemployment in the region.

B The employment of specialist managers by a firm to cope with higher output levels.

C The extension of low-cost telecommunication links to an area of the country not previously served by such links.

D Cheaper finance in recognition of the firm's increased share of the market and therefore its stability.

6 Which of the following cannot be true? In the short run as output falls:

A Average variable costs falls
B Average total cost falls
C Average fixed cost falls
D Marginal costs falls

7 The tendency for unit costs to fall as output increases in the short run is due to the operation of:

A Economies of scale
B The experience of diminishing marginal returns
C Falling marginal revenue
D Increasing marginal returns

8 Which of the following cannot be true in the short run as output rises:

A Average variable cost rises
B Average total cost rises
C Average fixed cost rises
D Marginal cost rises

9 Harold Ippoli employs 30 people in his factory which manufactures sweets and puddings. He pays them £5 per hour and they all work maximum hours. To employ one more person he would have to raise the wage rate to £5.50 per hour. If all other costs remain constant, the marginal cost of labour is:

A £20.50
B £15.00
C £5.50
D £0.50

10 Which of the statements below best defines the difference between the short run and the long run?

A Labour costs are fixed in the short run and variable in the long run.

B Economies of scale are present in the long run but not in the short run.

C At least one factor of production is fixed in the short run but in the long run it is possible to vary them all.

D None of the factors of production is fixed in the short run

Answers to quick quiz

1 The distinction between the short run and the long run is that in the long run, all resource inputs are variable. In the short run, probably only the amount of labour input is variable.

2 If one or more factors of production are fixed, but the input of another is increased, the extra output generated by each extra unit of input will eventually begin to fall.

3 At the level of output at which marginal cost equals marginal revenue

4 Diseconomies of scale are problems of size and tend to arise when the firm grows so large that it cannot be managed efficiently. Communications may become difficult, motivation may deteriorate because of alienation and senior management may find it difficult to identify the information they need in the vast volumes available.

5 C This is an external economy of scale.
A is a diseconomy of scale.
B is an internal economy of scale.
D is an internal economy of scale.

6 C Factual knowledge. The key to this question is to draw a diagram of the cost curves.

7 D The benefits of specialisation and the division of labour
Economies of scale only operate in the long run.
B results in *rising* unit costs in the short run.
C is nothing to do with costs.

8 C Average fixed cost must continue to fall as output rises in the short term. This is a mathematical fact.

9 A

	£
Cost of 31 people (at £5.50 per hour)	170.50
Cost of 30 people (at £5.00 per hour)	150.00
Marginal cost	20.50

10 C

Now try the questions below from the Question Bank

Number	Level	Marks	Time
Q13	Exam	16	20 mins
Q14	Introductory - MCQ	–	–
Q15	Introductory - Interactive	–	–

Chapter 6

FACTOR MARKETS

Topic list		Syllabus reference	Ability required
1	Basic features of factor markets	(ii)	Comprehension
2	Capital and interest	(ii)	Comprehension
3	Labour and wages	(ii)	Comprehension
4	Effects of taxation on the labour market	(ii) (iii)	Comprehension
5	Land and rent	(ii)	Comprehension
6	Entrepreneurship and profit	(ii)	Comprehension
7	Transfer earnings and economic rent	(ii)	Comprehension

Introduction

The four factors of production have been mentioned already in this Study Text.

Now we look at them in more detail, analysing the markets for them in terms of demand and supply.

Learning outcome covered in this chapter

- Explain and illustrate how product and factor markets operate

Syllabus content covered in this chapter

- Business firms: legal, economic and organisational features; entrepreneurship and profit
- The price mechanism: the demand and supply model and its applications

1 BASIC FEATURES OF FACTOR MARKETS

1.1 Each scarce economic resource has a value, and the owner of the resource or factor of production is rewarded for giving it up to someone else. Firms are rewarded for the goods and services they produce by the price customers will pay for them. The resources used in production are also rewarded, by the price that firms pay for them.

(a) **Land** is rewarded with **rent**. Although it is easy to think of land as property, the economic definition of land is not quite what you might suppose. Land consists not only of property (the land element only: buildings are capital) but also the natural resources that grow on the land or that are extracted from it, such as timber and coal.

(b) **Labour** is rewarded with **wages** (including salaries). Labour consists of both the mental and the physical resources of human beings.

(c) **Capital** is rewarded with **interest**. It is easy to think of capital as financial resources, and the rate of interest is the price mechanism in balancing the supply and demand for money. However, capital in an economic sense is not 'money in the bank'. Rather, it refers to man-made items such as plant, machinery and tools which are made and used not for their own sake, but to aid the production of other goods and services. The cost of using machinery and plant and so on is **interest**.

(d) **Entrepreneurship** or enterprise is a fourth type of factor of production. An entrepreneur is someone who undertakes the task of organising the other three factors of production in a business enterprise, and in doing so, bears the risk of the venture. He creates new business ventures and the reward for the risk he takes is **profit**.

Factor prices

1.2 The prices paid to each factor of production are referred to as **factor prices**. The prices for land, labour and capital are determined by supply and demand. Entrepreneurship and profit are rather different and will be discussed later.

Factor demand as a derived demand

1.3 The demand for factors of production is a **derived demand**. By this we mean that the factors of production are not demanded for their own sake. They are demanded because a firm needs them to make goods, which are then sold to households. It is the demand by households for goods from which the demand by firms for the factors of production is derived.

1.4 Firms want to make goods because of the revenue they get from selling them, and the profit that they can make. Firms will not want to pay for factors of production if their marginal cost (and so the marginal cost of producing the good) exceeds the marginal revenue that can be earned from selling the good.

KEY TERM

Derived demand: firms demand for factors of production is derived from households' demand for the goods and services the firms produce.

Question 1

Think carefully about what is, and what is not, a factor reward. Which of the following earnings are factor rewards?

(a) Commission charges earned by an insurance salesman
(b) Dividends received on shares
(c) Cash paid to a window cleaner
(d) The pension earned by an ex-army officer now working for a security firm

Answer

All of these are factor rewards, with the exception of (d). The pension relates to a former employment.

1.5 Having set out some basic points about the markets for factors of production, we now look at each in turn.

2 CAPITAL AND INTEREST

2.1 Interest is the reward for capital. Capital as a factor of production has two aspects.

- Stocks of finished goods
- **Producer goods** (machines, tools, buildings, office equipment and so on)

2.2 The rate of interest, according to traditional economic theory, is determined by supply and demand.

(a) The demand for capital comes from firms, which expect to invest in stocks and equipment so as to create more output, make more sales and earn more profit.

(b) The supply of capital (finance to acquire stocks, equipment and so on) comes from investors.

2.3 Firms will only demand capital if they can make an adequate return: the return must exceed the cost of obtaining the capital. Investors will only supply capital if the interest they are paid makes it worth their while to invest.

The marginal efficiency of capital

2.4 The demand by firms to borrow capital is explained in traditional economic theory by the **marginal efficiency of capital (MEC)**.

2.5 Firms should always seek to invest in the opportunities that offer the highest returns, and once these have been invested in, remaining opportunities will not offer such high returns. As more and more investments are made, the returns from additional capital investments will gradually decline. A firm's marginal return is the return on its latest investment. You should be aware that the return we are speaking of is the **internal rate of return** of the project. This is dealt with in detail in your Business Maths Study Text.

2.6 The declining size of return as the volume of investment increases is called the **marginal efficiency of capital**. This can be illustrated by a **marginal efficiency of capital curve** as shown in Figure 1. A small number of investment opportunities offer a very high rate of return. As the volume of capital invested increases, less profitable opportunities must be taken up. The MEC curve is a demand curve for capital, with the demand being provided by firms.

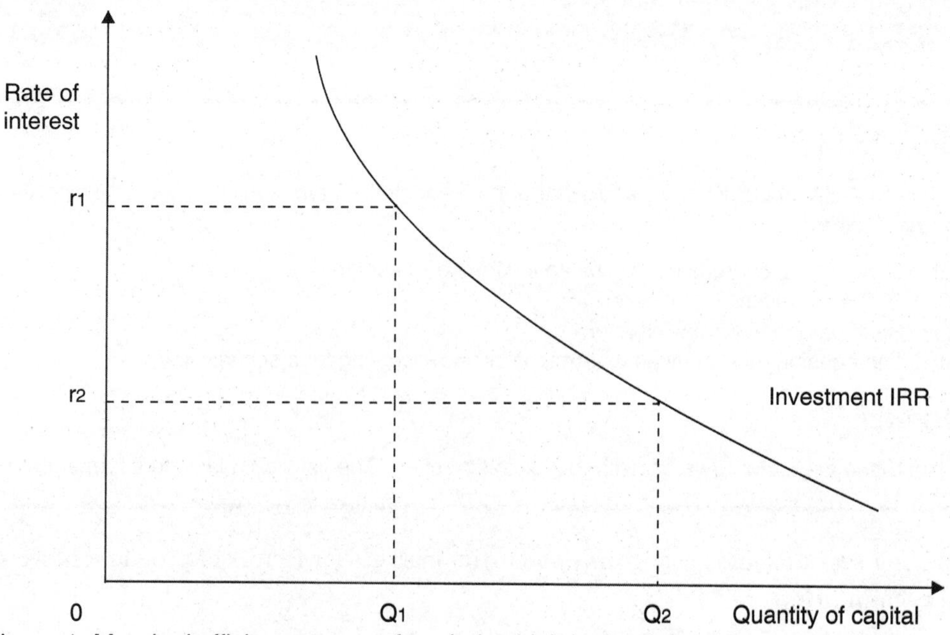

Figure 1 Marginal efficiency curve of capital, which is the demand curve for capital

2.7 Firms should be willing to borrow capital up to the point where MEC is equal to the interest rate the firm has to pay, because on investments up to that amount, they would earn a return in excess of the rate of interest. In Figure 1, if the interest rate is r_1, firms should be willing to borrow up to £Q_1 of capital to invest.

Question 2

Remembering the basic principles of supply and demand, how would an increased demand by firms (interest rates remaining unchanged) be represented on the above diagram?

Answer

The increase in demand would be represented by a rightward shift in the MEC curve.

2.8 The MEC curve for all the firms in an industry is the industry's demand curve for capital, and it is the sum of the demand curves (MEC curves) of all the individual firms in the industry. An industry's MEC curve and an individual firm's MEC curve have the same basic shape, as shown in Figure 1.

2.9 The assumption that firms are profit maximisers ensures that the **rate of interest** becomes an important determinant in an investment decision, because **it represents the cost to the firm of the investment capital**. When interest rates are high, say at r_1 in Figure 1, few investments will earn adequate return to cover such high costs and yield a profit and the demand for funds will therefore be low at Q_1. Conversely, many investments are profitable when interest rates are low, say at r_2, and therefore demand for funds will be much greater atQ_2 (subject to the intervention of national monetary authorities when they set a minimum level for interest rates).

The supply of capital

2.10 The rate of interest also depends on the **supply of capital** from investors, and **the interaction of supply and demand establishes interest rates**. The supply of capital comes from savers. Savings are the resources that are needed to produce capital (to pay for the materials and labour that produce the capital) and which could have been used for current consumption instead. Savings lead to investment and the creation of capital, but savings are only made by sacrificing some current consumption.

2.11 Savers choose to save in order to make possible the production of even more outputs in the future, and so the amount of savings is determined by comparing two things.

(a) What the available wealth could be used to obtain now from the current consumption
(b) How much extra wealth will be obtained in the future from saving

2.12 This extra wealth in the future, which makes savers prefer to save rather than consume their wealth now, is represented by interest. Higher interest will make saving more attractive, and the supply of savings will therefore increase.

Exam focus point

Do not confuse savings with investment, as many students do. Thus, it would be incorrect to suppose that investment will also increase if interest rates rise.

2.13 **The price of capital (the interest rate) should therefore be determined by the interaction of supply (savings) and demand (marginal efficiency of capital).** In Figure 2, the equilibrium interest rate would be r, with quantity Q of capital supplied by savers and demanded by firms.

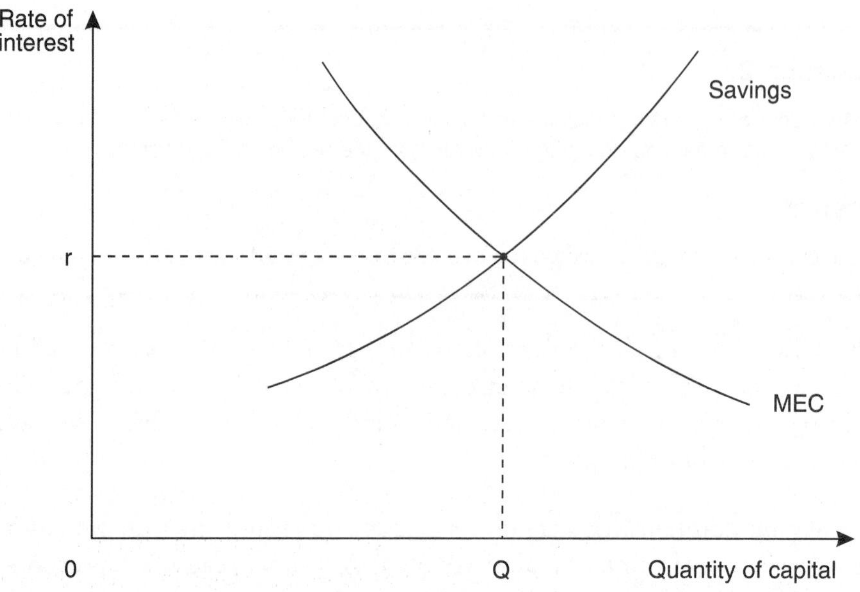

Figure 2 Demand for and supply of capital

Differences in interest rates

2.14 **In practice, different rates of interest apply to different firms. This is mainly because there are different levels of risk involved for the lender.** A lender will usually expect a higher rate of interest from a newer small company borrower than from a large long established company in the same industry because there is an increased risk that the company will be liquidated and the debt not repaid in full. Another factor affecting the price of capital (the rate of interest) is the economies of scale which a lender can gain from larger scale lending, which makes such lending cheaper.

Imperfections in the market for capital

2.15 In reality, the interest rate for capital is not determined just by the free market forces of supply and demand operating in this way. Several imperfections in the capital market affect savings, investment decisions and interest rates as follows.

2.16 **Monetary factors.** Interest rates are probably influenced not just by investment factors and savings versus consumption factors, but by monetary factors too. Keynes' theory about the influence on interest rates of the demand for money is described in a later chapter.

2.17 **Investment factors.** The theory of the marginal efficiency of capital does not properly explain the pattern of investments made by firms.

(a) Investments cover a period of several years into the future. The returns from an investment cannot be predicted with much certainty over a long period of time. A firm may even decide to invest in a project in anticipation of future profitability, even though at present short-term and long-term interest rates would counsel against such an investment. **Expectations** therefore play an important role in the decision to invest. These expectations may prove well founded, but they might be wrong too.

(b) Some firms have a more ready access to finance than others: for example, large firms can usually borrow more easily than small firms. Small firms might have difficulty in raising capital for efficient investments, because lenders of finance consider lending to a small undiversified enterprise to be more risky.

(c) The level of investment undertaken by a firm will depend on the age of its capital stock. A company with a high proportion of old capital equipment which needs renewing will tend to spend more on investment than a firm with modern machinery.

(d) A firm which is operating close to full capacity will need to invest in order to continue to expand, whereas investment may be largely unnecessary for the firm working at half capacity.

2.18 **Savings factors**. Savings decisions are not just determined by a simple choice between saving and consumption of wealth.

(a) Many savings decisions are made by the management of firms on behalf of shareholders, by retaining profits for investment.

(b) The split of national income between poorer and richer households could be significant, because poorer households need most of their income for consumption whereas richer ones have more available to save.

(c) Consumption and savings patterns are not determined by interest rates alone, but also by social attitudes towards thrift. A government might also make saving unattractive by taxing interest earnings at a high rate. It does not necessarily follow that a rise in interest rates will lower consumption and increase savings.

3 LABOUR AND WAGES 5/01

The demand for labour and marginal productivity theory

3.1 A similar demand and supply analysis can be made for labour and the price of labour (wages). Like the demand for capital, the demand for labour by firms is a derived demand, arising from consumer demand for the firms' output.

3.2 In our basic analysis below, we shall assume that the amount of other factors of production is in fixed supply, so that any additions to a firm's output and revenue can only come from additions to the labour force. In other words, labour is a variable factor of production.

3.3 The **marginal revenue product (MRP)** of labour is the marginal revenue value of the **marginal physical product of labour (MPP)**. This is the extra revenue that firms in the industry would obtain from the extra output provided by each extra recruit to the workforce.

3.4 The MRP of labour is similar in concept to the marginal efficiency curve of capital. The MRP curve for labour slopes downwards because of diminishing returns. The first person employed will generate a given MRP; subsequent employees will generate progressively smaller MRP as the law of diminishing returns takes effect. They will all, however, be paid the same wage. Firms should be willing to pay for labour provided that the marginal revenue product of labour exceeds the cost of employing the labour. Quite simply, if a firm can make an extra £150 per week from hiring an extra employee, it should be willing to hire the employee provided that the weekly wage does not exceed £150. In Figure 3, if the MRP of labour for a certain type of job, job type A, is as shown, and the wage level for job type A is W, then the industry would want to employ X employees in job type A, because the MRP of labour exceeds the wage rate up to X. The MRP curve thus represents the demand curve for labour.

3.5 In contrast, job type B has a higher marginal productivity value than job type A, and so the industry would be willing to do one of two things.

- Pay a higher wage for the same quantity of employees as job type A
- Employ more employees into job type B than job type A if the wage rate for both were W

In either case, the **total revenue** is equal to the area under the MRP curve.

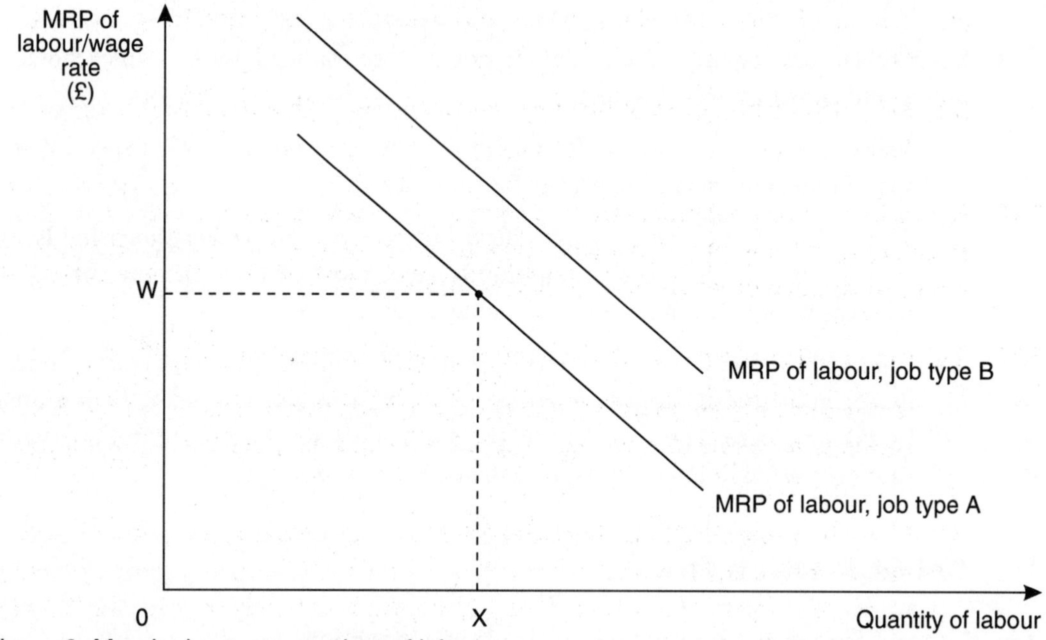

Figure 3 Marginal revenue product of labour

The supply of labour

3.6 This analysis of the MRP of labour only considers the **demand** by firms for labour of different types and skills. It does not consider the **supply** of labour.

3.7 According to marginal productivity theory, wage levels are determined by the interaction of the demand for and the supply of labour. According to traditional theory, the supply of labour is, not surprisingly perhaps, influenced by wage rates. Higher wages will attract more people willing to do the work. The **supply curve for labour** can therefore be shown as the marginal cost of the labour, in other words the extra total wage payments needed to increase total labour supply by each marginal extra amount.

3.8 For example, suppose that at a wage level of £160 per week, the supply of labour into a job would be 8 men. At a wage level of £170 per week, the willing supply would be 9 men, and at £180 per week, 10 men would be willing to do the job. The marginal cost of the 9th and 10th men would be as in the table below.

Wage = average cost of labour (AC_L)	*Supply (number of men)*	*Total wages*	*Marginal cost of labour (MC_L)*
£		£	£
160	8	1,280	-
170	9	1,530	250 (1,530 – 1,280)
180	10	1,800	270 (1,800 – 1,530)

Don't forget that all 10 men receive the higher rate of £180.

3.9 These figures illustrate that when higher wages must be paid to attract more labour two things will be happening.

(a) The supply curve for labour, which is the marginal cost curve for labour (MC_L), will be rising.

(b) **MC_L will be higher than the wage level**; that is, higher than the average cost of labour AC_L.

3.10 Returning to marginal productivity theory, we therefore have wage levels determined by the interaction of supply and demand, which is where the MC_L curve intersects with the marginal revenue product curve for labour (MRP_L).

3.11 The wage level also depends on the nature of the labour market.

(a) If it is **perfectly competitive**, and firms can obtain extra quantities of labour freely at a constant wage rate, the average cost of labour and marginal cost of labour are the same ($AC_L = MC_L$)

(b) If it is **imperfectly competitive**, for example dominated by a single firm (a **monopsonist** buyer of the labour) who can only obtain more labour by paying higher wages to attract more labour into the industry, the supply curve for labour will be upward-sloping.

The effect of wage rate changes on labour supply

3.12 The supply of labour is measured by the number of hours an individual offers to work at a given wage rate. The decision will be based on the individual seeking to maximise his utility, which he gains both from working, and hence earning income, and from leisure.

3.13 A rise in the wage rate will affect the labour supply decision in two ways.

(a) Firstly, there is a **substitution effect**: a rise in the wage rate increases the opportunity cost of leisure as each hour spent not working involves a greater sacrifice in terms of the amount of income forgone. The substitution effect hence leads the individual to **substitute work for leisure.**

(b) In addition, there is an **income effect**: the higher wage rate increases the individual's real income, leading them to consume more. Leisure can be thought of as a good, and **increased income** means that people can afford to 'consume' more of it by **working less**.

3.14 As the income and substitution effects work in opposite directions, the ultimate effect of the higher wage rate will depend on which dominates. Empirical evidence suggests that the substitution effect tends to dominate in the earlier stages of economic progress such that higher wage rates increase the supply of labour, but as an economy becomes increasingly developed the income effect becomes more pronounced. This can produce a situation in which, as wage rates rise, the supply of labour falls.

Limitations of marginal productivity theory

3.15 The marginal productivity theory of wages cannot account wholly for the determination of wage rates and wage differentials because the assumptions on which it is based do not apply in reality.

(a) It is often difficult to calculate the marginal productivity of labour, especially in administrative work or service industries.

(b) Marginal productivity theory for labour assumes that all other factors of production are held in constant supply. This is unlikely to be so, especially in the case of capital. As the amount of labour employed changes, so too would the amount of capital. (There is substitutability between labour and capital; alternatively more capital might be combined with more labour to increase total output.) If other factors of production are not held constant, it becomes difficult, if not impossible, to measure MRP, and so an MRP curve could not be drawn with accuracy.

(c) A further assumption of the marginal productivity theory of wages is that labour is free to enter the market or leave it for alternative employment elsewhere. In practice, this might not be the case, and there might be imperfections in the labour market.

Imperfections in the labour market

3.16 In a perfect labour market, the supply of labour would shift rapidly to whatever use provides the highest reward. Factor mobility is the term used to describe the readiness and speed with which a factor of production can switch from one use to another. The ease with which labour moves between industries is one factor determining the elasticity of supply of labour, measured as:

$$\frac{\text{Percentage change in labour supply}}{\text{Percentage change in wage rate}}$$

Labour immobility is an imperfection in the labour market which helps to explain pay differentials between different industries, jobs and regions. The more mobile labour is, the greater will be the elasticity of labour supply.

3.17 In a perfect market, labour would be perfectly mobile in response to different wage rates in different regions. Labour would move from regions with low wage rates to regions with high wage rates. This movement of labour would continue until, with wages rising in low pay regions and falling in high pay regions, equilibrium would be achieved when wage levels in all regions were the same. Similarly, the supply of labour should move from lower paid occupations to higher paid occupations.

3.18 In practice, there are restrictions which create a certain amount of labour immobility with two important effects.

(a) The level of unemployment may vary regionally.

(b) In the same region, there may be job vacancies for some types of worker but excess supply and unemployment amongst others.

Question 3

Consider two or three types of employment (including, perhaps, your own plus others with which you are familiar) and list the factors which you think might discourage mobility of labour in each case.

Compare your answer with the list below.

3.19 There are many causes of labour immobility.

(a) **Professional barriers**, where professional associations restrict entry by means of examinations

(b) Ignorance of employment **opportunities**

(c) A **housing system** which makes moving between regions difficult, for example where there are high costs of housing in regions with better job opportunities

(d) **Non-monetary considerations** (for example friends, social life outside work) which make individuals reluctant to move to a different region

(e) High natural **ability** required in certain labour markets, barring people without the necessary ability

(f) **Linguistic** and **cultural differences**, making some jobs more socially acceptable than others for some people

(g) **Discrimination** in the allocation of jobs, such as illegal discrimination on the basis of sex or race

3.20 The problem of the **geographical immobility** of labour could be alleviated by encouraging jobs to go to the regions with unemployment rather than expecting labour to go to the jobs. A government's regional policies might be directed at paying firms (or giving concessions to them) to invest in depressed areas, and in the UK, the government has had some success in shifting jobs between regions. Lower pay in depressed regions might be an added incentive to invest, but trade unions often organise labour so that national wage agreements are enforced.

3.21 Government retraining schemes and a job-oriented education policy might be necessary to overcome the problems of **occupational immobility** of labour.

Barriers to entry into labour markets

3.22 In some labour markets there are **barriers to entry**, such as regulations restricting entry into certain jobs to those belonging to a professional association. Barriers to entry prevent the supply curve from shifting far to the right.

Trade unions and the bargaining theory of wages

3.23 Although we have looked at marginal productivity theory and the view that wage levels are set by demand and supply factors, it should also be recognised that trade unions try to negotiate higher wages for labour. There is a 'bargaining theory' of wages which states that wage levels are set by negotiation between unions and management.

3.24 **Collective bargaining** is a term which refers to the process by which unions negotiate and reach agreements with employers. It is common for collective bargaining to involve a single monopolist seller of labour (the trade union) and one buyer or monopsonist (a single firm or an employers' federation). As such, annual wage claims may be one of a trial of strength between two 'giants'.

Exam focus point

You are not expected to have knowledge of institutional aspects of trade unions and the process of wage bargaining. You do however need to be able to analyse labour markets and to show the effects on such markets of imperfections, such as trade unions and minimum wage legislation (discussed later).

3.25 The role of trade unions, in economic terms, has two aspects.

(a) To erect and maintain **barriers to entry** into jobs in the industry, thus ensuring high earnings for the existing members

(b) To **monopolise** the supply of labour in the industry. If the demand for labour is in the hands of a single employer or employers' federation, this can influence the price at which labour is bought. If the supply of labour is in the hands of a collective body as opposed to individuals, this can influence the price at which it can be sold.

3.26 By restricting entry to the labour force, trade unions might force wages to move from W_0 to W_1 by effectively changing the supply curve from S_0 to S_1 in Figure 4. This will however result in fewer jobs. The number employed will fall from L_0 to L_1.

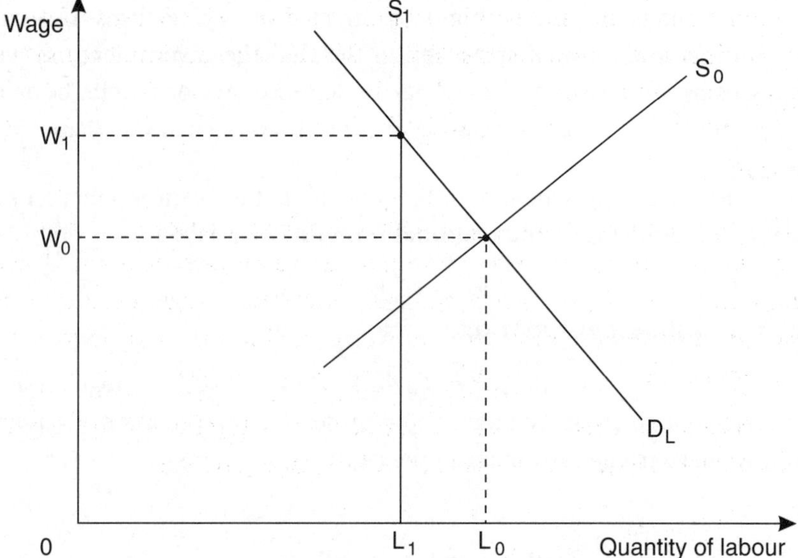

Figure 4 The effect of unionisation

3.27 However, once wage rates have been given an **initial** increase by the unionisation of the work force, any **further** pay rises, given no change in the marginal revenue product (MRP) of labour, will probably reduce the total demand for labour by employers.

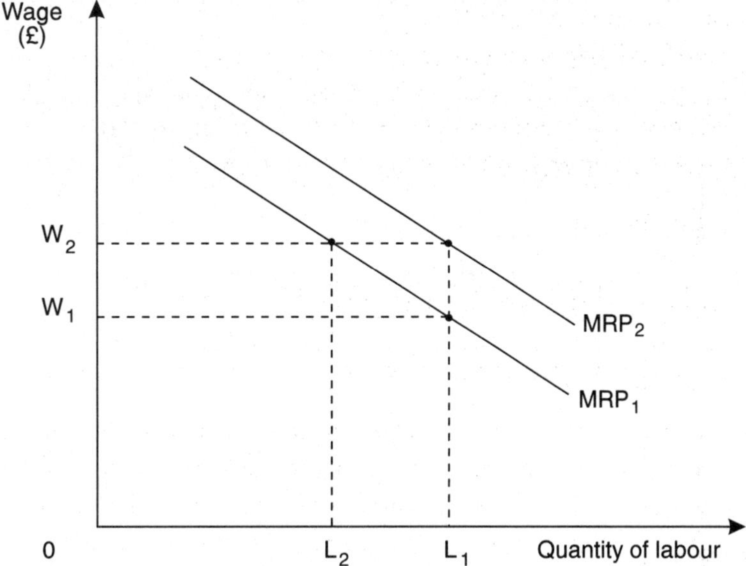

Figure 5 Wage increase

3.28 When wages rise from W_1 to W_2, the demand for labour will fall from L_1 to L_2 (Figure 5), given no change in the MRP of labour (initially MRP_1). However, if the labour force agrees to an improvement in productivity so that the marginal revenue product of labour shifts to MRP_2, an increase in wages from W_1 to W_2 could be achieved without changing the total workforce employed from L_1.

Minimum wages 5/02

3.29 The UK now has minimum wage legislation. The purpose of a minimum wage is to ensure that low-paid workers earn enough to have an acceptable standard of living. If a minimum wage is enforced by legislation (a **statutory minimum wage**) or negotiated nationally for an industry by a trade union the minimum wage will probably be above the current wage level for the jobs concerned. This would have two consequences.

- To raise wage levels for workers employed to a level above the 'equilibrium' wage rate
- To reduce the demand for labour and so cause job losses

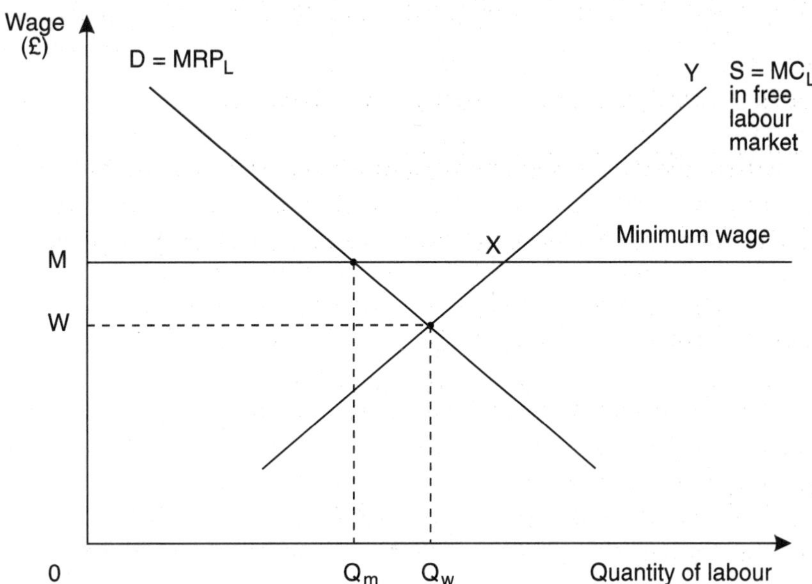

Figure 6 Minimum wage

Without a minimum wage, OQ_w workers would be employed at wage rate W (Figure 6).

Question 5

By reference to Figure 6, work out what happens when a minimum wage M, higher than the existing rate W, is imposed.

Answer

The supply curve for labour is now the line MXY.

Demand for labour from employers will fall to OQ_m, but OQ_m workers will at least earn a higher wage.

3.30 Despite this common sense result, there is some evidence that the imposition of a minimum wage can actually **increase** the numbers employed. This can occur with **monopoly** purchasers of labour and is particularly apparent in markets for lower grade labour. Where such employers hold wages to a low level, they will generally have vacancies since employment with them is unattractive. Where a higher wage is imposed by law, they will find it easier to recruit and their numbers on payroll may actually rise. Their need for labour outweighs the market forces that would otherwise lead to reductions in numbers employed.

Imperfections in labour supply: conclusion

3.31 In spite of imperfections in the labour markets, there is a lot of common sense in the general principle that the willingness of firms to hire workers and the willingness of workers to accept jobs will depend largely on wage levels. In other words, there is a strong element of truth in the theory that an industry's wages are influenced by supply and demand, and that an individual firm's demand for labour will be influenced by wage levels and marginal productivity.

The substitutability of capital for labour

3.32 Substitution between factors of production (for example between labour and capital) may take place provided that substitution is practical or technologically feasible (for example, machines can be made to do the work previously carried out by labour, or that labour can physically do the work of machines). Substitution is likely when the price or productivity of one factor of production **rises relative to another**. If wages go up, the marginal cost of labour will rise, and firms will want less labour at this higher cost. Labour will also become more expensive in relation to capital, and there will be some **substitution of capital for labour**. The net result of an increase in wages will be a reduction in the quantity of labour employed - unless the productivity of labour can be increased at the same time, to strengthen the demand for labour.

The elasticity of demand for labour

3.33 The change in demand for labour in response to a change in wage rates can be measured by the elasticity of demand for labour. This is:

$$\frac{\text{\% change in numbers employed}}{\text{\% change in wages}}$$

3.34 **Principal factors influencing the degree of elasticity of demand for labour**

(a) **The technical ease** with which employers could **substitute** other factors of production (mainly capital) for labour.

(b) **The elasticity of demand for the final product.** If the product made by the work force has an inelastic demand, producers can pass on higher wage costs more easily to consumers by raising prices. However, if demand for the end-product has a high price elasticity, an increase in wages will result, through higher prices, in a sharp fall in demand for labour.

(c) **The elasticity of supply of alternative factors of production.** Even if it is technically possible to substitute labour with, say, capital, it might be too costly for producers to do so if the elasticity of supply of capital is low. An increase in supply would then only be achieved by paying significantly more for the substitute factor (capital), and so in spite of higher wages costs, it might still be less costly to use labour than to switch to capital as a substitute factor.

(d) **The proportion of labour costs to total costs.**

Question 6

How does this last factor affect the elasticity of demand for labour?

Answer

When labour costs are small in proportion to total costs an increase in wages will be relatively insignificant and demand for labour will be little affected. In this case, the demand for labour is inelastic. But if wage costs form a major part of total costs, demand for labour will be elastic.

Labour productivity

3.35 Labour productivity can be defined as the output per worker over a given period of time and is influenced by a number of factors.

(a) The **quality of the labour**, which will depend on the amount of education and training which it has received. Education and training is a form of investment in human capital which can raise productivity, not only by equipping workers with direct vocational skills but also by encouraging people to become more innovative, more flexible and more capable of taking on work responsibilities.

(b) The **degree of combination of other factors of production** with labour also influences labour productivity. Physical capital in the form of modern technology can dramatically increase the amount and quality of output which a worker can produce. Such new technology may require additional training in some cases; in other cases a worker with a lower level of skill may take on the same task.

(c) The **pattern of remuneration of employees** and the associated perceived effect of the **tax burden** operating on them are further possible determinants of labour productivity. Profit-related pay and employee share option schemes represent two types of remuneration which are designed to make employees feel more motivated to ensure the success of the firm in which they work. Increased motivation will accordingly increase output per worker. It is also sometimes argued that the structure of taxation has an effect on the motivation of workers.

(d) **Other macroeconomic factors** can influence labour productivity. A steadily growing economy is likely to produce conditions more conducive to high labour productivity than an economy with a more erratic economic cycle, in which periodic recessionary conditions may inhibit a firm from maximising output effectively.

(e) The **economies of scale** which larger firms can often achieve will enhance the productivity of labour. **Specialisation** will be most readily achieved in larger productive units; where it occurs, workers are likely to be more productive when engaged in specialised work. High levels of labour productivity will only be achieved in firms or organisations in which the factors of production are organised to maximise efficiency, so avoiding wasted effort.

4 EFFECTS OF TAXATION ON THE LABOUR MARKET

The effect of a direct tax

4.1 A government is likely to impose direct taxes on earnings (as distinct from indirect taxation on expenditure). In the UK, for example, direct taxes consist mainly of income tax and National Insurance contributions.

We need to consider what the effect of a direct tax might be on supply and demand for labour, and on wage levels.

4.2 Some fairly basic points might seem clear, if you think about a situation in which a government which has never imposed direct taxes before now imposes an income tax on wages.

(a) In Figure 7, the original equilibrium is at point A, that is with average wage W_0 with L_0 labour employed. When the tax is imposed, employees will receive less take-home pay because the tax will be deducted from their wages. As a result, the labour supply curve will shift upwards by the amount of the tax, that is, the distance A-B in Figure 7. Workpeople demand higher wages to protect their take-home pay. Without any change in wages, workers will substitute leisure for employment and the supply of labour will fall.

(b) A new equilibrium now arises at point C, with average gross wage W_1 and L_1 labour employed. However, the net (after tax) wage is only W_2. Gross wages have risen, net wages have fallen and the quantity of labour employed has fallen.

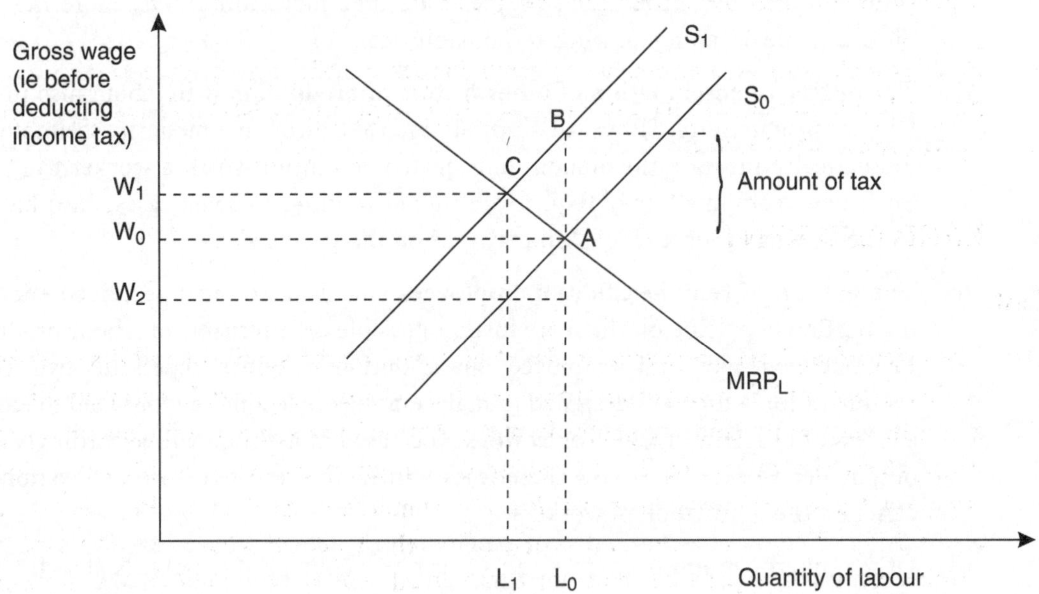

Figure 7 Effects of a direct tax

The incidence of a direct tax: example

4.3 A numerical example helps to explain who bears the burden of a direct tax, employer or employee. Suppose that labour in an industry is paid £180 per week, and pays no income tax. The government now imposes income tax at the rate of 25% of gross wages. This has three consequences.

- Gross wages go up from £180 to £200 (from W_0 to W_1 in Figure 7).
- Income tax is (25% of £200) = £50.
- Take-home pay for labour is now £150.

4.4 The incidence of the income tax of £50 is shared partly by each of the employers and employees.

- Employers pay £20 more than before in gross wages (£200 – £180).
- Employees receive £30 less than before in take-home pay (£180 – £150).

Taxation and labour productivity

4.5 It is sometimes claimed that high levels of taxation of personal incomes erode work incentives. A rise in levels of personal taxation will lead, *ceteris paribus*, to a fall in personal disposable income. In theory, the resultant **income effect** will lead the individual to work harder so as to regain the income lost through additional taxation. By the **substitution effect,** the person will tend to work less hard because the opportunity cost (in disposable income) of choosing more leisure is now reduced. If the substitution effect outweighs the income effect, a government could increase labour productivity by cutting taxes on personal incomes. The evidence on whether this effect can be achieved in practice is, however, inconclusive.

4.6 Other aspects of taxation policy may also influence labour productivity. Corporation tax changes, for example changes in capital allowances, may enhance incentives for firms to invest in new capital equipment. Tax concessions may also be applied to encourage firms to implement training schemes or to provide personal tax relief for individuals in respect of expenditure on their own education and training.

4.7 Policies such as those mentioned above which seek to influence the pace of development of physical and human capital (ie labour) need to be seen as long-term policies which are likely to take some time to work.

5 LAND AND RENT

Rent

5.1 The price of land, which is rent, is also determined by the supply of and demand for land. In discussing land, it is important to get our basic definitions clear. In everyday language, if a person buys some land, we probably mean that he buys some buildings with a supply of water, electricity and so on. To the economist, buildings and water supply are capital; land is the earth and its natural resources. It is also common to speak of renting a house, a car or a television. This is **commercial rent** paid to the landlord who is an owner of capital. Neither **rent** as the price of land nor commercial rent are the same as the more specific concept of **economic rent,** which refers to a payment made in excess of the payment needed to keep a factor of production, such as land, labour or capital, in current use.

The price of land

5.2 The special definitions of land and rent which are used by economists derive from those first used by *David Ricardo* in the 19th century. Ricardo was concerned, not with how much rent is paid for land used for a particular purpose, but how much rent is paid for land as a whole. His theory about land and rent has two points.

(a) The total amount of land available is fixed, therefore the supply of land is inelastic, regardless of how much rent is paid for it.

(b) Since the supply of land is inelastic, rent will be determined by the market price of the goods produced from the land.

Land and rent

5.3 As a simplified example, let us suppose that a piece of land (fixed in size) has only one use, which is to grow carrots; has a perfectly elastic labour force to work on it; and has no capital employed on it.

5.4 Figure 8 shows two things.

(a) The wage rate of labour, W, which is constant regardless of the number of workers employed, because labour supply is perfectly elastic.

(b) The marginal revenue product of labour curves for two different price levels, P_0 and P_1 of carrots.

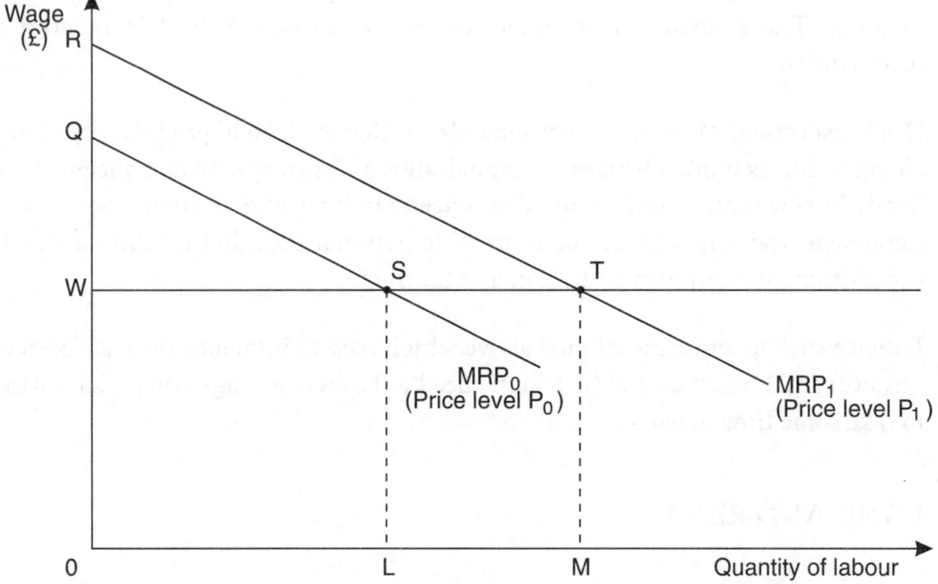

Figure 8 Rent, with land in fixed supply

5.5 If the price of carrots is P_0, OL workers will be employed at the given wage rate.

- The total cost of labour will be represented by the area OWSL.
- The total revenue from the sale of carrots will be area OQSL.
- The difference, area WQS, is rent.

5.6 If the price of carrots rises to P_1, **the MRP of labour will improve.** OM workers will be employed.

- The total cost of labour is now OWTM

- The total revenue is ORTM
- Therefore rent has risen to WRT

We conclude that when land is in fixed supply, the size of the rent depends on the price of the goods produced on the land.

The price of land for specific uses

5.7 We can extend this principle to cover the situation where the supply of land is not perfectly inelastic (Figure 9). This situation arises where we are considering the supply of land for a particular purpose, for example, office development or agricultural use. Since it is usually possible to change the use of a piece of land, the supply of land for a particular purpose should not normally be considered fixed. If the price of agricultural land in the UK went up we would expect a transfer of land from (say) the domestic housing sector to the agricultural sector. In fact, the supply curve of agricultural land slopes upward from left to right. The equilibrium price and quantity of agricultural land are determined by the intersection of the demand curve (derived from the price of goods produced on the land) and the supply curve (derived from the price which prevents a quantity of land being transferred to any other use).

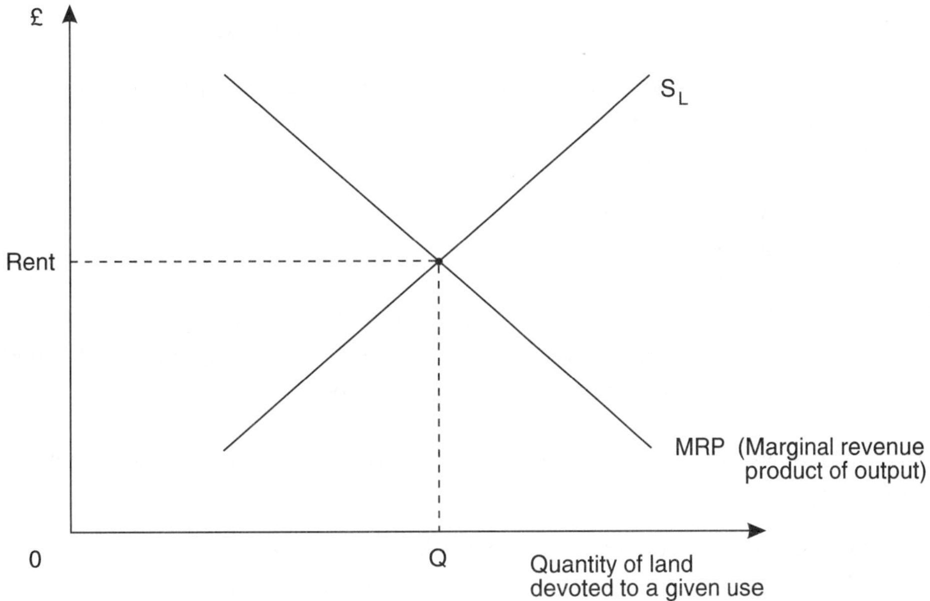

Figure 9 Price of land in a specific use

6 ENTREPRENEURSHIP AND PROFIT

6.1 As indicated earlier, entrepreneurship or enterprise can be viewed as a factor of production. The function of the entrepreneur is to combine the other three factors, natural resources, labour and capital, so as to maximise the efficiency of resource utilisation and to maximise the firm's profits. Business enterprise involves risk and uncertainty, and actual profits might be higher or lower than expected; it is the entrepreneur's role to bear the burden of this uncertainty. His reward, profit, is what is left over after the other three factors of production have been rewarded; if there is nothing left over the entrepreneur will make no profits or even a loss.

The function of the entrepreneur

6.2 It is the role of entrepreneurs to make decisions about new business ventures and to organise production. Their reward for doing this is profit.

6.3 Entrepreneurship is possibly most apparent in partnerships and small private limited companies, where the owners of the business (partners or shareholders) are often also the senior managers. They organise production, make the decisions, and earn the profits for themselves.

6.4 A **sole trader** might hire labour to help him, and might borrow money to set up his business.

- He might own the land which the business uses (eg a farmer).
- He will supply labour himself to the business.
- He will provide capital himself.
- He will organise production and make the business decisions.

In other words, a sole trader provides his own entrepreneurship, but also his own land, labour and capital, and his total reward in an economic sense will be a mixture of rent, wages, interest and profit.

6.5 In a public limited company (plc), there is a **separation of functions.**

(a) The people who organise production and perform the function of stewardship are the management team, led by the board of directors. These people provide a skilled kind of labour and receive wages.

(b) The owners (ie the shareholders) of the business take the risks, earn the profits and get the dividends.

6.6 The shareholder is making an entrepreneurial decision in investing in some particular shares. However, entrepreneurial decisions in the running of the business itself are effectively delegated by shareholders to the company's management.

6.7 In a similar way to public limited companies, there is a separation of function in state-run industries.

- Management are the organisers of production resources.
- The government, on behalf of the public, are the owners.

The nature of profit

6.8 Unlike land, labour and capital, which are rewarded by rents, wages and interest respectively, the entrepreneur cannot be sure of gaining a reward (making a profit) because his business might make unanticipated losses.

6.9 **Profit is the reward of the entrepreneur for the risks he takes. The entrepreneur bears the burden of business risk and uncertainty.** Production decisions are made on the basis of the best knowledge that is available at the time, but the passage of time and changing circumstances means that the actual outcome cannot be predicted with certainty. Sometimes circumstances might change for the better, but they might also change for the worse.

Risk and uncertainty

6.10 Business decisions about what to produce, and what investments to make, are taken (on the whole) with regard to the expected costs and benefits that will arise as a consequence. Any decision taken now will relate to the future. It takes time to implement a decision, and earn the benefits that arise from it. Some decisions relate to the short-term future, others to a longer term future.

6.11 What will happen in the future can be guessed at, or predicted, but the future cannot be foreseen with 100% certainty. It follows that any business decision involves risk or uncertainty. The terms are often used interchangeably, but may be used with more specific meanings.

(a) **Risk** involves situations or events which may or may not occur but whose probability of occurrence can be calculated statistically and the frequency of their occurrence predicted. It then follows that risks are insurable.

(b) **Uncertain events** are those which cannot usually be insured against. Their outcome cannot be predicted with sufficient statistical confidence.

Uncertainty

6.12 Uncertainty arises from three main sources.

(a) **External sources**. The decision maker will only have a limited view of political and economic factors affecting the situation under review. For example, a tobacco company launching a new brand may be caught out if the government suddenly prohibits all tobacco advertising. External sources of uncertainty include the state of national economies, world trade, potential legislation and political change. Changes in consumer tastes, perhaps because of competitors' actions or perhaps for social reasons (such as attitudes to alcohol and tobacco) might also create uncertainty for a firm.

(b) **Internal sources**. The organisation may not be able to react to challenges or crises, because it does not have the resources or the experience to do so.

(c) **Finance**. If the company is partly debt financed there is the problem of ensuring that debt interest can be paid out of profits before interest and tax.

(Somewhat confusingly, in the world of strategic financial management, internal and external sources of uncertainty are regarded as producing '**business risk**', while the specific uncertainty associated with **debt finance** is called '**financial risk**'.)

6.13 Uncertainty is not normally insurable. The chances of a new brand of soap or of a new model of car selling well can only be guessed at and cannot be calculated.

6.14 Commercial ventures are never identical and do not take place under identical circumstances, and so it is impossible to use past experience to predict the future with sufficient confidence in the accuracy of the prediction.

KEY TERMS

Normal profit is earned when total revenues equal the total opportunity costs of all input resources. If revenues are just enough to equal opportunity costs, this means that the input resources are being used as well as they could be used anywhere else.

If actual economic profit is below normal profit the firm would do better to leave the business it is in and put the resources at its disposal to better, more profitable use.

When total revenues exceed the total opportunity costs of input resources, the firm will be earning profit in excess of normal profits, and so resources are earning more than they could in an alternative occupation. These excess profits are called **supernormal profits**.

6.15 Firms will obviously benefit from any supernormal profits that exist, and will wish to enjoy them if they are available. Supernormal profits indicate to entrepreneurs the best markets for new investments or for a switch of their existing investments. When a firm makes supernormal profits, other firms will want to enter the industry if they can, to grab a share of the high profits that are available. In competitive industries, supernormal profits therefore tend to be temporary, because they are eventually eroded by competition.

6.16 We will see later in this Study Text how a firm which enjoys a monopoly position in a market can earn supernormal profits, while in fully competitive conditions this may not be possible.

(a) Entrepreneurs of better ability should be able to earn supernormal profits when others are making only normal profits.

(b) Monopolists can make supernormal profits by constructing entry barriers which prevent or deter rival firms from entering the market as competitors.

Risk premium

6.17 Firms in high risk industries should expect to earn a higher return than firms in low risk industries. The higher the risk, the higher the risk premium required. (Risk premium can be defined as the additional return in excess of a risk-free return needed to compensate an investor for making the risky investment.)

6.18 Since **normal profit** means a sufficient return to prevent the firm's owner from liquidating his investment and investing it elsewhere, normal profit must make allowance for the risk characteristics of the business, and what could be earned from an alternative investment of comparable risk. Thus, normal profit will be higher in a more risky market than in a safer market.

7 TRANSFER EARNINGS AND ECONOMIC RENT

7.1 We have discussed the supply and price of each factor. We will now consider some principles of factor pricing which may be applied to **every factor of production**.

7.2 The owners of factors of production will transfer their factors to another use unless the present usage provides the greatest rewards. This reward may be divided into two parts: transfer earnings and economic rent.

KEY TERMS

Transfer earnings are the reward the factor would receive in its next best employment, ie its **opportunity cost**. Transfer earnings are therefore the amount needed to keep the factor in its present employment

Economic rent is the difference between its transfer earnings and its actual reward for its present use, ie it is the surplus above transfer earnings.

For example, if a football player can earn a salary of £75,000, while his next best alternative employment would be as a salesman earning £15,000, the 'rent' paid to him as a football player is £60,000. If working as a salesman is the only alternative, any payment above £15,000 should be sufficient to keep the person as a football player.

7.3 To measure the contribution of transfer earnings and economic rent to the reward for factors it is necessary to study the elasticity of supply because the size of the economic rent is determined by the elasticity of supply of the factor of production.

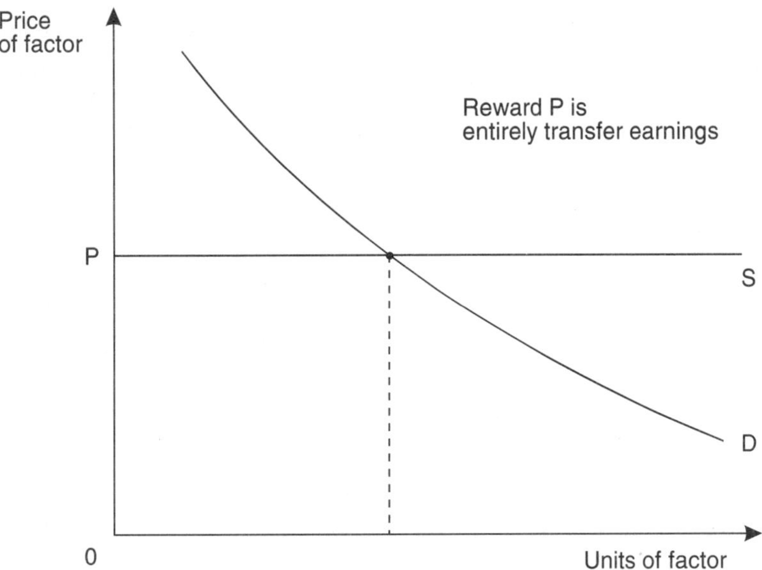

Figure 10 Perfectly elastic supply

7.4 **Where the supply is perfectly elastic (Figure 10), all income is transfer earnings.** If the price is not paid for the factor the whole supply will move to a new use. On the other hand, **where the supply of a factor is fixed and has only one use (Figure 11), the whole reward may be entirely economic rent**. The factor cannot transfer to another use; therefore there are no transfer earnings.

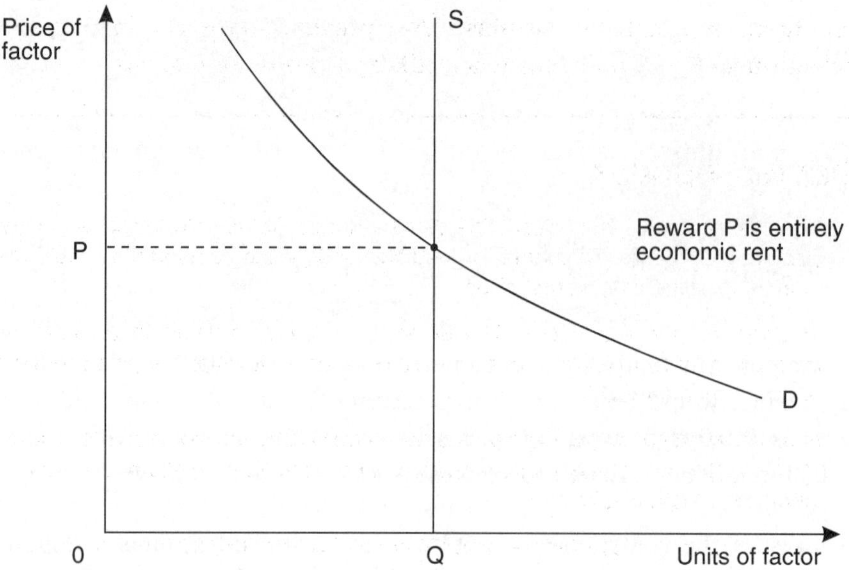

Figure 11 Perfectly inelastic supply

7.5 Where the elasticity of supply is nearer to unit elasticity it is possible to measure the transfer earnings by considering the payment of each unit on the supply curve.

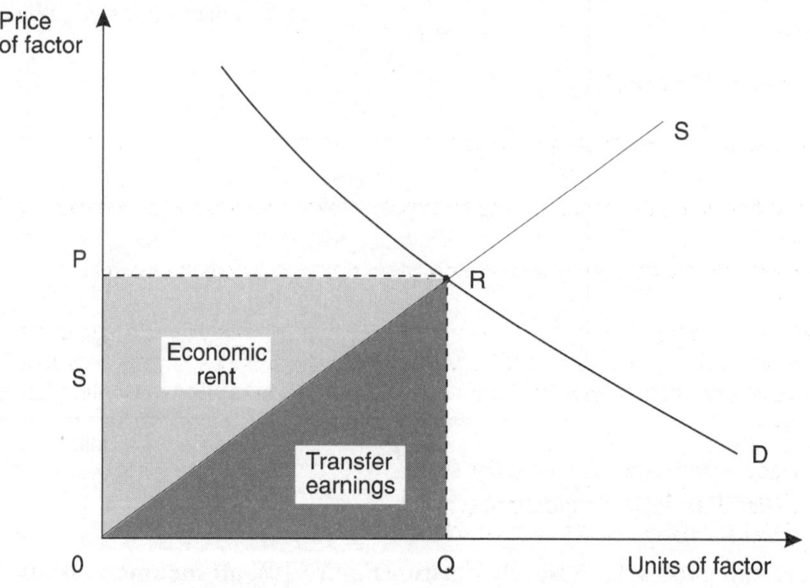

Figure 12 Economic rent and transfer earnings

7.6 In Figure 12, the area OPRQ represents the total income earned by the factor. The area within OPRQ but below the supply curve (SRQ) represents the transfer earnings and the area above the supply curve (OPRS) represents the economic rent. The more elastic the supply curve becomes, the less economic rent is paid. The more inelastic the supply curve becomes, the less transfer earnings are paid.

A note on terminology

7.7 Do not confuse **transfer earnings and transfer payments**. Transfer earnings were defined above. Transfer payments are grants or other payments **not** made in return for a productive service (for example state pensions, unemployment benefit and charitable donations by companies). Also, if you refer back to Chapter 2, you will see that economic rent is much the same thing as **producer surplus.** Use 'producer surplus' when discussing the price mechanism and 'economic rent' when talking about factor markets.

Chapter roundup

- The cost of capital is interest. The demand for capital is determined largely by the marginal efficiency of capital. It might be argued that supply and demand for capital interact (in a free market) to determine interest rates.
- The cost of labour is wages. The demand for labour is determined largely by the marginal productivity of labour, which declines as more labour is employed, in accordance with the law of diminishing returns.
- In a market economy, wage levels are determined by the interaction of supply and demand. However, there are various imperfections in the labour market which influence the supply of labour and wage levels.
- Land, which has a special meaning in economics, is a third factor of production whose market is governed by demand and supply. The price of land is rent.
- The reward of entrepreneurship is profit. Normal profit is, to the economist, part of the total costs of input resources.

Quick quiz

1 What is derived demand?

2 What are the MPP and MRP of labour?

3 What is likely to be the consequence for employment of minimum wage levels in an industry?

4 Outline the function of the entrepreneur and the nature of his or her reward.

5 Which of the following responses are correct? Trade unions are in a strong bargaining position with employers when: 1. The demand for labour is greater than the supply of labour; 2. Marginal revenue product is more than wages; 3. There is inelastic demand for the good that the trade union members produce.

A Responses 1 and 2 only are correct
B Responses 1 and 3 only are correct
C Responses 2 and 3 only are correct
D Responses 1, 2 and 3 are all correct

6 The table shows details of labour productivity in a firm, Second and Cloves Ltd. What is the marginal revenue product of the 12th unit of labour?

Number of people employed	Total output (units)	Sales value or price of output (per unit) £
10	300	10.0
11	400	9.5
12	450	9.0

A £250
B £450
C £475
D £525

7 Plowden Scatter Ltd produces packets of flower seeds. Data about labour productivity and selling prices are shown in the table. What is the marginal revenue product (MRP) of the ninth employee, and what is the average revenue product (ARP) of nine employees?

Number employed	Number of packets output per week	Sales price per packet
8	4,000	£1.60
9	4,320	£1.50

A MRP £80, ARP £720
B MRP £80, ARP £768
C MRP £480, ARP £720
D MRP £480, ARP £768

8 Which of the following statements is correct?

A For a monopsony buyer of labour, the marginal cost of labour is less than the wage rate.

B When a monopoly trade union negotiates with a monopsony employer, the resulting negotiated wage rate will be settled at the competitive level.

C A downward-sloping demand curve for labour can be a constraint on a trade union's ability and willingness to demand higher wages.

D In a free and competitive labour market, all labour of the same kind would earn the same wage.

9 Consultant surgeons are paid a higher wage than traffic wardens. According to traditional theory, which of the following factors might explain this differential in wage levels? 1. Surgeons have a higher marginal revenue product than traffic wardens. 2. The opportunity cost of working as a surgeon is higher than the opportunity cost of being a traffic warden. 3.The supply of surgeons is much more inelastic than the supply of traffic wardens.

A Factors 1, 2 and 3
B Factors 1 and 2 only
C Factors 2 and 3 only
D Factors 1 and 3 only

10 The mobility of labour can be increased by which of the following items?

1 Improving the frequency of the inter-city passenger train services
2 Increasing the specialisation of labour
3 Providing more labour retraining schemes

A Items 1 and 2 only
B Items 2 and 3 only
C Items 1 and 3 only
D Items 1, 2 and 3

Answers to quick quiz

1 The demand for the factors of production arises not because they are required in themselves, but rather because firms need them to produce goods which can be sold to households.

2 The marginal physical product (MPP) of labour is the extra output arising from the recruitment of one more worker. The marginal revenue product of labour is the value of the MPP.

3 A minimum wage set above the market determined rate is likely to have the same effect as any other minimum price set above the equilibrium price: a reduction in the demand for labour, but higher wages for those lucky enough to be in work.

4 The function of entrepreneurs is to make decisions about new business ventures and to organise production. Their reward for doing this is profit.

5 All are correct. When demand exceeds supply, the price of labour can be negotiated upwards by a trade union with relative ease. With inelastic demand for the end-product, the firm will be able to pass on much of the cost of higher wages to the consumer, by raising prices, without suffering a large fall in demand.

6 MRP of 12th employer = £4,040 - £3,800 = £250

Number employed	Output unit	Price	Total revenue
		£	£
11	400	9.5	3,800
12	450	9.0	4,050

7 MRP = £6,480 - £6,400 = £80, ARP = 480 * £1.50 = £720

Total employees	Price per output	Total packet	Average revenue	output
		£	£	
8	4,000	1.60	6,400	500 packets
9	4,320	1.50	6,480	480 packets

8 C

A is incorrect, since MC > AC.

B is not necessarily correct, although collective bargaining *might* result in competitive wage level.

D is incorrect, because even in a free and competitive market, non-monetary factors in a job would influence the amount that individuals would be willing to receive. For example, an accountant in a university might be willing to earn less than an accountant in industry because of the better quality of life in a university job. Job security, perks (e.g. cheap canteen meals) and unsociable working hours, in one job compared with another, will create wage differentials.

9 All are correct. 'Traditional' theory refers to the marginal productivity theory of wages. Surgeons have a higher MRP than traffic wardens (although physical product and revenue product must be difficult to measure in practice) and so demand for surgeons is stronger. The opportunity cost of being a surgeon is higher, and so surgeons expect bigger salaries. A more inelastic supply of surgeons means that if the MRP of surgeons and traffic wardens increased by the same amount, surgeons' wages would rises by more than the wages of traffic wardens.

10 C

Labour immobility is caused by the reluctance or inability of labour to switch from areas and industries where there is unemployment to areas and industries where there is a demand for workers. There can be reluctance of workers to move to another geographical area to find work, but an improved railway system (item 1) might provide a solution to some of the problem (eg getting managers living in the north of England to take up jobs in London). *Occupational* immobility of labour can be overcome by retraining schemes (item 3) to train workers with 'out-of-date' skills to learn skills for which there is a demand from employers.

Greater specialisation of labour (item 2) might result in greater labour productivity, but this has no bearing on the mobility of labour.

Now try the questions below from the Question Bank

Number	Level	Marks	Time
Q16	Introductory	8	10 mins
Q17	Introductory - MCQ	–	–
Q18	Introductory - Interactive	–	–

Chapter 7

ORGANISATIONS IN A MIXED ECONOMY

Topic list	Syllabus reference	Ability required
1 Sectors of the economy	(ii)	Application
2 Objectives of firms	(ii)	Application
3 Growth of firms	(ii)	Application
4 Industry location decisions	(ii)	Application

Introduction

Most major industrialised economies are mixed economies with a large private sector but a substantial public (government) sector too. As well as looking at the different forms of organisation in the mixed economy, we will be looking in this chapter at how the development of different sectors of the economy can be traced.

We also look at the objectives of firms, at reasons why firms grow and forms of business growth, and at the factors which influence where industry is located.

Learning outcomes covered in this chapter

- Explain the functioning of a market economy
- Apply basic economic analysis to explain economic and business issues
- Explain the economic factors which affect the structure, behaviour and performance of individual businesses and industries

Syllabus contents covered in this chapter

- The business environment and the structure of economic activity
- Business firms: legal, economic and organisational features; entrepreneurship and profit

1 SECTORS OF THE ECONOMY 5/02

The public and private sectors

1.1 The economy of a developed country can usually be divided into two sectors: public and private. Private sector organisations, also called businesses, are owned and operated by private individuals or institutions, while organisations in the public sector are owned by the state. Private sector organisations are of two main types: those which **seek profit** for their owners and those which have other objectives. Non-profit seeking organisations include co-operatives and mutual organisations; charities; and clubs, societies and associations.

1.2 **The economy is driven by the profit-seeking part of the private sector.** It is businesses which undertake the most enterprising aspects of economic activity; provide the bulk of employment opportunities and tax revenue; and create the growth needed to enhance economic welfare. Businesses are of two main types, distinguished by the extent to which the owners are liable for the debts of the undertaking.

(a) An individual may set up business on his own account as a **sole trader** or in **partnership** with others. In either case, the law will not distinguish between the private assets and liabilities of the owners and those of the enterprise. The owners have **unlimited liability** for the debts of their businesses.

(b) This degree of risk is unattractive to many potential investors, so to enable them to invest and thus release more funds for wealth-producing enterprise, the legal systems of developed countries provide for some form of **limited liability** enterprise. Such businesses are referred to as corporations or **companies**.

In the UK, there are two forms of limited liability company. They both limit the liability of investors to the nominal value of their share holdings; they differ in the extent to which they are permitted to solicit investment from the general public. **Private limited companies** may not offer their securities to the public; **public limited companies** may. Note carefully the rather confusing terminology: **public limited companies** are owned by **private** investors; they are **not** part of the **public sector**.

1.3 Public sector organisations are of two types.

(a) Central government owned and local government owned service organisations, such as hospitals, schools, the armed forces, the fire service and police service, public libraries, leisure centres and public museums and art galleries

(b) State-owned ('nationalised') industries which charge for their services and aim to make profits. In the UK, this includes the Royal Mail postal service and London Transport but most other major nationalised industries have now been sold or are soon to be sold to the private sector.

Some services in the UK National Health Service (NHS) are provided by self-governing trusts. These trusts sell their services to the NHS.

Exam focus point

You are not expected to have detailed knowledge of the economics of particular industries, but an answer may be improved by citing relevant examples.

Primary, secondary and tertiary sectors of the economy

1.4 The distinction between the primary, secondary and tertiary sectors of the economy and trends in these sectors can be illustrated using data on the UK economy, as set out in the table below.

Distribution of UK national output

	% share of GDP in each sector			
	1969	*1979*	*1989*	*1995*
Primary sector	4.3	6.7	4.4	4.4
of which:				
Agriculture, forestry, fishing	1.8	2.2	1.9	2.0
Mining	2.5	1.3	0.7	} 2.4
Oil and gas	-	3.2	1.8	
Secondary sector	42.0	36.7	34.1	29.7
of which:				
Manufacturing	30.7	27.3	24.3	21.8
Construction	8.4	6.2	7.4	5.3
Energy and water	2.9	3.2	2.4	2.6
Tertiary sector	53.0	56.5	61.5	65.9
of which:				
Distribution, hotels, catering	13.3	12.7	14.1	14.0
Transport and communications	6.3	7.3	8.4	8.4
Banking, finance, insurance	8.6	11.0	18.5	21.1
Public services	14.1	14.2	16.9	18.6
Others	10.7	11.3	3.6	3.8

The primary sector

1.5 The primary sector of the economy consists of industries which produce **raw materials** such as crops and minerals. Over the long term, the trend for the UK is one of decline in this sector when measured in terms of its share of gross domestic product (GDP). Viewed against the process of economic growth, this declining share reflects **the rising absolute level** of output of other industries.

1.6 The data show how, within the primary sector, the beginning of North Sea oil and gas production in the 1970s increased the overall importance of the sector within the UK economy. By 1989, however, the share of oil and gas within GDP had fallen to 56% of its 1979 share. Agriculture, forestry and fishing increased its share of GDP slightly from 1969 to 1979, but the fall in share from 2.2 per cent in 1979 and to 2 per cent in 1995 is more consistent with the long-term trend of declining importance for these industries. Mining shows a progressive decline over the period from 1969 (2.5 per cent) to 1989 (0.7 per cent), reflecting the progressive rundown of the coal industry in favour of other fuels. The relatively high share of 6.7 per cent for the primary sector as a whole in 1979 mainly reflects the advent of North Sea oil.

The secondary sector

1.7 The secondary sector consists of industries which **process raw materials**, and is sometimes referred to as 'industry'. This sector normally grows rapidly during the early stages of economic development; the data show how the UK has reached a later stage of decline in this sector. The major part of the decline in GDP share for the sector from 42.0 per cent in 1969 to 29.7 per cent in 1995 is attributable to a **decline in manufacturing**, which is the part of the sector most heavily involved in international trade, as opposed to construction and energy and water. The decline in the secondary sector has led to a **reduction in employment** in the sector bringing some problems of severe unemployment in regions which have been heavily dependent on particular industries.

The tertiary sector

1.8 The tertiary sector is made up mainly of **goods distribution and service industries. This sector has become the predominant provider of employment and output in the UK economy in recent decades**, growing steadily from a 53.0 per cent share in 1969 to a 65.9 per cent share in 1995.

1.9 The data shows that the main reason for the continuing growth in this sector during the 1970s and 1980s has been the rapid expansion in the banking, finance and insurance sectors, which more than doubled their GDP share (from 8.6 per cent to 21.4 per cent) between 1969 and 1995.

Shifts in output between sectors

1.10 Within the primary sector, the most significant factor affecting the change in GDP shares over the period from 1969 has been the discovery and exploitation of North Sea oil, and later gas. In the earlier years, as well as benefiting from the peak in absolute output from the North Sea, this sector benefited from relatively high energy prices compared with more recent years.

1.11 The term **de-industrialisation** is often used to describe the long-term decline in the importance of manufacturing industry and the secondary sector in general. Although we have so far considered GDP shares of the different sectors of the economy, as remarkable as the decline in the share of manufacturing is the fact that the level of manufacturing output has shown no upward trend in the UK since the early 1970s.

1.12 **Some argue that the decline of the secondary sector and the rise of the tertiary sector is an inevitable consequence of economic development**. As in earlier stages of economic development, the agricultural sector declines with the growth of the secondary sector, and so the latter sector declines as demand shifts, relatively, from goods to services. International comparisons offer some support for this explanation, since recent years have seen a decline in the share of employment accounted for by manufacturing in almost all advanced capitalist economies. However, a special feature to note regarding the UK is that manufacturing employment reached its peak rather earlier (1955) than in many other countries, including West Germany (1970), which faced major economic reconstruction following World War II. Some point out that **Britain was the first country to industrialise,** and during much of this century relative economic decline has been apparent in the UK, with many other industrialised countries overtaking the UK in GDP per head.

1.13 It is important to note that domestic output supplies both domestic demand and exports. A relative decline in manufacturing output may be the result of a shift of demand away from UK-manufactured goods towards foreign manufactured goods coupled with a failure of UK manufacturing industries to meet demand. This explanation is borne out by the shift from a UK trade surplus in manufactured goods during the 1970s to significant deficits in manufactured goods during the 1980s and 1990s.

1.14 Within the tertiary sector, the rising share of banking, finance and insurance reflects a number of factors.

(a) London has built on its reputation as one of the leading financial centres of the world, and in some areas (eg the foreign exchange markets) it is pre-eminent. The strong position of 'the City' (the London financial community) makes it a large exporter of financial services.

(b) Increasing affluence and changing social factors (eg increasing levels of owner-occupation of housing during the 1970s and 1980s) have increased domestic demand for financial products of various kinds (eg current accounts, mortgages and insurance products).

(c) The abolition of exchange controls in 1979 and the deregulation of financial markets during the 1980s (for example the Stock Exchange 'Big Bang' and the Building Societies Act of 1986) served to free supply as well as intensify competition in this subsector.

International trade and the sectors of the UK economy

1.15 The UK has historically been a net exporter of manufactured goods, with the result that the surplus foreign exchange earned allowed the economy to have a trade deficit (with more imports than exports) in the foods and raw materials sector.

1.16 More recently, the trade deficits in manufactures have been offset by surpluses in oil exports, the service sector and in earnings from assets owned overseas (for example, profits of overseas subsidiaries of UK companies).

1.17 A major problem is that by their very nature, **many services cannot be traded internationally**. This problem accounts for why the international market for manufactured goods is so much larger than the international market for services.

1.18 An exception here which we have already mentioned is that of financial services, which the UK, with its major world financial centre in the City of London, has been very successful in trading internationally. However, the UK's share of the world market in services ('invisibles') still declined from 12% in 1978 to 8.5% in 1989.

General problems with changes in economic structure

1.19 **Major structural changes may make the economy ill-equipped to respond to future economic changes**. For example, a country might have substantial oil and gas resources. Increasing employment in this industry and a buoyant exchange rate might lead to decline in manufacturing. When the oil and gas resources run down, the diminished manufacturing industry may be unable to make up for the lost oil and gas output rapidly enough. Domestic manufactured goods will be replaced by imports and the balance of payments will suffer.

1.20 **A change in world market conditions,** for example, a change in commodity prices, may adversely affect an economy. An economy may gain from having a widely based economic structure rather than one which is heavily reliant on particular sectors.

1.21 Some changes in economic structure reflect **economic and technological progress** and the trend towards **globalisation**. 'Sunrise' industries include information technology and genetics; their importance is increasing worldwide. 'Sunset' industries in the western economies include steel and shipbuilding whose prices have been undercut by more efficient producers in the Pacific Basin.

1.22 Industrial decline brings **unemployment**, particularly where there is heavy geographical concentration, as in the case of shipbuilding and coal mining. The effects can be severe: as well as the immediate problem of unemployment, there may be knock-on effects as consumers' spending power is reduced and people begin to leave the area. Such problems may be mitigated by government policies on training, support for new employment

opportunities in the affected areas and the encouragement of geographical and occupational mobility of labour.

1.23 **Rapid expansion of certain sectors may also present problems.** In Britain during the 1980s, expansion of the banking, finance and insurance industries put strains on the economic infrastructure and brought high house price inflation in the South. With improved technology, it is becoming easier for firms to move administrative departments to low cost areas in other regions or other countries.

2 OBJECTIVES OF FIRMS

The firm

KEY TERM

Firm is a wide term for any organisation which carries on a business.

2.1 In spite of their structural differences, firms will be treated as single, consistent decision-taking units and, for the purposes of economic analysis, we ignore any differences in decision-making procedures and economic structures between them.

Profit maximisation and other objectives

2.2 **Profit maximisation is assumed to be the goal of the firm in most economic textbooks and in a great deal of economic theory**. Where the entrepreneur is in full managerial control of the firm, as in the case of a small owner-managed company or partnership, this assumption would seem to be very reasonable. Even in companies owned by shareholders but run by non-shareholding managers, if the manager is serving the company's (that is, the shareholders') interests, we might expect that the profit maximisation assumption should be close to the truth. However, some writers have suggested that objectives other than profit maximisation might be pursued by firms. We discuss some of these alternative models below.

Stakeholders and constituents

2.3 We have discussed the position of proprietors of businesses and the role of entre-preneurs. Taking now a wider perspective, there is a variety of different groups or individuals whose interests are affected by the activities of a firm. These groups or individuals may be referred to as **stakeholders** in the firm. *Sharplin* (*Strategic Management*) has listed the various stakeholder groups in a firm as follows.

Common shareholders
Preferred shareholders
Trade creditors
Holders of unsecured debt securities
Holders of secured debt securities
Intermediate (business) customers
Final (consumer) customers
Suppliers
Employees
Past employees
Retirees
Competitors
Neighbours
The immediate community
The national society
The world society
Corporate management
Organisational strategists
The chief executive
The board of directors
Government
Special interest groups

2.4 Many managers acknowledge that the interests of some stakeholder groups - for example themselves and employees - should be recognised and provided for, even if this means that the interests of shareholders might be adversely affected. Not all stakeholder group interests can be given specific attention in the decisions of management, but those stakeholders for whom management recognises and accepts a responsibility are referred to as **constituents** of the firm.

Profit maximisation

2.5 If the interests of the ordinary shareholders were the only stakeholder interests that are recognised, the goal of the firm should be **profit maximisation**. There is reasonable logic to support the idea that firms seek to maximise profits, because competition from profit maximising firms could force non profit maximising firms out of business.

2.6 Entrepreneurs are interested in maximising profits over time. In order to do this, costs will have to be incurred today in order to generate returns in the future, and so a profit-maximising firm will seek to make investments - in physical capital, human capital, advertising and so on - and it would be wrong to think of profit maximisation as a 'short-term' motive.

Alternative managerial goals

2.7 In many large companies, the management is divorced from the ownership. Managers and shareholders are different individuals, and managers have the responsibility of running their company in the interests of their shareholders. Managers act as the agents for their shareholders (the principals).

2.8 The goal of profit maximisation might not explain management behaviour, because managers have interests of their own. If directors' remuneration schemes reward directors on the basis of a criterion other than maximising profit, then directors have an incentive to pursue that criterion.

2.9 **Managers will not necessarily make pricing decisions that will maximise profits.**

(a) They have no **personal interests** at stake in the size of profits earned, except in so far as they are accountable to shareholders for the profits they make.

(b) There may be a **lack of competitive pressure** in the market to be efficient, minimise costs and maximise profits, for example where there are few firms in the market.

2.10 It has been suggested that price and output decisions will be taken by managers with **managerial objectives** in mind. Rather than seeking to **maximise** profits, managers may choose to achieve a **satisfactory** profit for a firm: this is called **satisficing**.

2.11 One managerial model of the firm - *Baumol's* **sales maximisation model** - assumes that the firm acts to **maximise sales revenue** rather than profits. The management of a firm might opt for sales revenue maximisation in order to maintain or increase its market share, ensure survival, and discourage competition. Managers benefit personally because of the prestige of running a large and successful company, and also because salaries and other perks are likely to be higher in bigger companies than in smaller ones.

2.12 Another managerial model - *Williamson's* **management discretion model** - assumes that managers act to further their own interests and so maximise their own utility or satisfaction, subject to a minimum profit requirement. Utility may be thought of in terms of prestige, influence and other personal satisfactions. The profit aimed for will not be maximum profit, because of management's wish for expenditure on themselves, their staff and the perquisites of management.

2.13 *Cyert and March* suggested that a firm is an **organisational coalition** of shareholders, managers, employees and customers, with each group having different goals, and so there is a need for **political compromise** in establishing the goals of the firm. Each group must settle for less than it would ideally want to have. Shareholders must settle for less than maximum profits, and managers for less than maximum utility, and so on.

3 GROWTH OF FIRMS 5/02

3.1 The possibility of achieving economies of scale through expansion should encourage firms to try to grow in size. There are two broad methods of obtaining growth in sales and output volumes, and growth in profits.

(a) **Organic growth,** which is growth through a gradual build-up of the firm's own resources, developing new products, acquiring more plant and machinery, hiring extra labour and so on. Organic growth is often a slow but steady process.

(b) **Growth through mergers and takeovers,** which is the combination of two or more firms into one.

3.2 The nature of a merger or takeover can be categorised according to which firms are coming together: are they in exactly the same line of business? Are they in very similar businesses? Are they in related businesses, but operating in different stages of the production and selling process? Are they in unrelated lines of business?

KEY TERMS

Horizontal integration. When two firms in the same business merge, there is horizontal integration. Horizontal integration tends to create monopolies, so that if, for example, All-England Chocolate plc with a 15% share of the UK chocolate market were to merge with British Choc plc which has a 20% share of the UK market, the enlarged company might expect to hold a 35% share of the market.

Vertical integration. Two firms operating at different stages in the production and selling process might merge. When they do, vertical integration occurs. For example a company which operates exclusively in oil refining might take over an oil shipping company, and perhaps an oil extraction company too. This would be backward vertical integration, back through stages in production towards the raw material growing/ extracting stage. The same company might take over a company with a distribution fleet of petrol tanker lorries, and perhaps a chain of petrol stations too. This would be forward vertical integration, forward through stages in production and selling towards the end consumer sales stage.

Conglomerate diversification. A company might take over or merge with another company in a different business altogether. This form of merger is diversification, and a group of diversified companies is referred to as a conglomerate organisation.

The advantages and disadvantages of these different types of business expansion are summarised in the table on the next page.

<table>
<tr><th colspan="2">Horizontal expansion or integration</th></tr>
<tr><td>Advantages

• Economies of scale from larger production quantities, ie lower costs.
◦ Technical economies (use of larger machines or more specialised machines)
◦ Managerial economies (greater specialisation of middle managers)
◦ Commercial economies (bulk buying and selling)
◦ Financial economies (ability to borrow money more cheaply)
◦ Risk-bearing economies (some greater spread of products made within the same general market should help the firm to spread its risks)

• Possibility of achieving monopoly or oligopoly status, and so having greater influence in the market and chance to earn superprofits and raise prices.</td><td>Disadvantages

• Top management might be unable to handle the running of a large firm efficiently, ie there might be management diseconomies of scale.

• The creation of a monopoly will be unacceptable to government.</td></tr>
<tr><th colspan="2">Vertical integration</th></tr>
<tr><td>Advantages

• Gives the firm greater control over its sources of supply (backward vertical integration) or over its end markets (forward vertical integration).

• Financial economies of scale and possibly some commercial economies. Otherwise few economies of scale unless production now becomes better co-ordinated through its various stages.</td><td>Disadvantages

• Possible management diseconomies of scale, owing to lack of familiarity with businesses acquired.</td></tr>
<tr><th colspan="2">Diversification</th></tr>
<tr><td>Advantages

• Risks are spread by operating in several industries. If one industry declines, others may thrive.</td><td>Disadvantages

• No economies of scale apart from financial economies.

• Possible management diseconomies of scale, owing to lack of familiarity with businesses acquired.</td></tr>
</table>

Advantages of small firms

3.3 If there are economies of scale, it is reasonable to ask why small firms continue to prosper. In some industries and professions, small firms predominate (eg building, the legal profession) and in some, small and large firms co-exist. The number of small firms in the UK has grown in recent years. The reasons for the survival of the small firm may be divided into three categories.

(a) **Diseconomies of scale in large firms**, meaning that small firms face lower costs, and the other disadvantages of large firms

(b) **Economic advantages of small firms**

(c) **Financial and managerial challenges of expansion**. Entrepreneurs may be unwilling to use outside capital as this erodes their autonomy, while their business may not generate enough funds to pay for expansion. Also, they may be temperamentally unsuited to management by delegation, preferring to make all decisions themselves; this will place a limit on their firms' expansion.

3.4 **Small firms have certain advantages over large firms which may outweigh economies of scale**.

(a) Since they are small, they are more likely to operate in competitive markets, in which prices will tend to be lower and the most efficient firms will survive at the expense of the inefficient.

(b) They are more likely to be risk takers, investing 'venture capital' in projects which might yield high rewards. Innovation and entrepreneurial activity are important ingredients for economic recovery or growth.

(c) Management-employee relations are more likely to be co-operative, with direct personal contacts between managers at the top and all their employees.

(d) Small firms tend to specialise, and so contribute efficiently towards the division of labour in an economy.

(e) The structure of a small firm may allow for greater flexibility (eg an employee or manager can switch from one task to another much more readily).

(f) Small firms often sell to a local market; large firms need wider markets, and may incur relatively higher costs of transport.

(g) Managerial economies can be obtained by hiring expert consultants, possibly at a cheaper cost than permanent management specialists.

(h) Some small firms act as suppliers or sub-contractors to larger firms. Market demand may be insufficient to justify large scale production.

4 INDUSTRY LOCATION DECISIONS

4.1 We now turn to the question of how decisions are made about where new businesses ought to be located. For the multinational company, the question may be one of where in the world a production facility should be located.

4.2 A firm's location decision will be influenced by the factors listed below.

(a) The cost, nature and quality of resources at the possible location

(b) The costs of transportation of raw materials to the place of production and finished goods to the market

(c) The location of markets

(d) 'Agglomeration' economies of scale (bigger industrial units should be able to produce more cheaply)

(e) Management preferences

(f) Government policies

4.3 The resources we are concerned with are the factors of production: land labour and capital (the firm provides the enterprise).

(a) The **characteristics** of land only sometimes affect a location decision; however, the cheaper cost of land might attract a firm into a particular region.

(b) Capital is a very mobile resource and should not influence the location decision. However, the level of **business risk** in one region may be very high, so that firms are unwilling to invest capital there.

(c) Labour costs may influence the location decision, provided that sufficient labour skills exist in a number of alternative regions. However, low **wage rates** in one region might be offset by poor **productivity**, so that labour costs can be cheaper in a region of comparatively high wages.

4.4 The comparatively low costs of **transporting raw materials** makes the cost of materials in different regions a less important factor in location decisions for many industries. By comparison, it is often much more costly to transport **finished goods** from the place of production to the market (because they are more bulky and may require more careful transportation) and the **nearness of selling markets** will then be more significant than the nearness of raw materials.

4.5 **Management preferences** may be a significant factor in location decisions, with some areas being favoured because of their climate, amenities or desirable residential accommodation. This factor may help to explain the concentration of 'sunrise' industries along the M4 corridor between Bristol and London. Managers might also prefer not to locate too far from an existing location.

4.6 There may be **localisation economies of scale** when several firms decide to locate their business in the same area.

(a) Localised specialist component suppliers can produce components for different firms in the same industry.

(b) Specialist consultancy firms or legal firms, with expertise in a particular industry, may be created in an area where the industry is centrally located.

(c) Local training schemes (eg at technical colleges) might specialise in work associated with the industry, so that skilled labour is available in that particular region.

4.7 These **localisation** (or agglomeration) economies of scale are **external economies of scale,** as distinct from internal economies. However, a distinction is sometimes made between **localisation** economies (which are benefits of size accruing to all firms in the **same** industry in a particular region) and **external** economies, which are benefits of size accruing to all firms in **any** industry in a particular region. Relevant examples of such external economies would be a highly developed infrastructure of fast roads, railways, ports, airline facilities, warehousing facilities, financial services (for example, banks) and a pool of skilled general management.

Government policies and location of industry

4.8 **Government policies**, including **regional policy**, exert an influence on firms' location decisions. Planning permission may be refused for target sites on environmental grounds. On the other hand, governments may wish to encourage industries to locate in particular areas, using tax incentives or subsidies as a means of influence.

4.9 Whether the location policy is to attract more economic activity into the country as a whole or into one region of the country rather than another, a key feature of such a policy is the use of government measures to persuade firms to locate their business in a different place from where they would otherwise have gone. The implication is that, if the firms pursue rational objectives, the government is **diverting resources from more efficient to less efficient use.**

4.10 The need for a regional policy arises when a particular region of the country goes into economic decline, usually because of a slump in the region's main industry (eg in agriculture, textiles, shipbuilding, steel production or mining). The decline of a major industry results in an **industrial imbalance** between regions, with the affected region falling into a depressed state in comparison with other regions, and with high regional unemployment.

4.11 One might suppose that regional disparities in unemployment should be self-correcting, because wages ought to be lower in the depressed regions, and lower wages ought to attract more firms into the region. At the same time, workers ought to move out of regions with unemployment, and go where jobs are available.

4.12 However, this 'self-correcting' process does not necessarily happen, or at least, does not happen very quickly.

(a) Wage structures are fairly rigid, and wages are slow to fall in areas with high unemployment.

(b) Labour is fairly immobile, and the movement of workers to the work is a slow process.

4.13 A government has two policy options.

(a) To encourage workers to move to where there is work, encouraging greater mobility of labour.

(b) To encourage work to go to the workers, encouraging firms to invest in areas of high unemployment.

4.14 A government can encourage firms to set up operations in a particular region.

(a) Financial incentives, such as **subsidies** and **tax incentives**, have been mentioned already, and will be discussed in more detail below.

(b) The government might also use regulatory deterrents, such as making it much more difficult for a firm to obtain planning permissions for new developments in more prosperous regions.

(c) The government can provide indirect incentives in the form of a well-developed infrastructure of roads and so on (for example, the motorway network in North West England).

4.15 There are some difficulties for a policy of encouraging firms to invest in depressed regions.

(a) Firms will need to be convinced that the cost advantages (for example, subsidies) outweigh any disadvantages of higher unit costs (for example, because of higher transportation costs for finished goods).

(b) Firms do not make major decisions to build new plants or offices regularly. Opportunities to influence the location decision of big firms, which would create a large number of new jobs in a region, are 'one-off' events. (However, there might be a cumulative effect on employment from the location decisions of large numbers of small and expanding firms.) Location decisions may be deferred in conditions of economic recession.

(c) Manufacturing firms are becoming more heavily technology-based, and even large production plants might create only a small number of new jobs.

(d) Subsidies and tax incentives make no distinction between inefficient and efficient firms. Inefficient firms are unlikely to bring long-lasting benefits to a region by setting up operations there, because they are unlikely to remain in operation for long.

(e) The administration of subsidies (for example, grants) can be a costly and time-consuming exercise, and perhaps not worth the advantages the scheme provides.

Subsidies to attract industrial investment

4.16 A subsidy may be given in the form of a cash grant or cash aid from the government to help to finance business activity in the private sector of the economy.

4.17 **Purposes of subsidies**

(a) To **preserve jobs or create new jobs**, either nationally or in targeted local areas. This would help the government to keep down unemployment levels, and at the same time have the fiscal advantages of saving payments of unemployment benefits and of having more people in a job and so paying income tax and National Insurance contributions.

(b) To **protect strategic domestic industries**. For example, if the UK wanted to protect its domestic defence equipment industry, it might subsidise UK manufacturers by contributing towards research and development costs.

(c) To **protect domestic industries against competition from foreign producers who are also subsidised by their own government**. For example, if one government were to subsidise its steel producers, another government might respond by subsidising its own steel producers, to counteract what it sees as unfair competition.

(d) To **encourage the development of new and advanced technologies.** Examples are micro-electronics and biotechnology.

(e) To promote an increase in national income and economic welfare.

Disadvantages of subsidies

4.18 **A serious criticism of subsidies is that they might be used to support inefficient industries**. They are usually given to firms in a situation where there would be losses or negligible profits from the business activity, and the subsidy turns a loss or negligible profit into a profit large enough to encourage the firm to develop its business.

(a) Subsidies allow firms to sell their output at a price that is lower than it would otherwise be. A subsidy reduces the average cost per unit of output, and so a profit can be earned at a lower (subsidised) price.

(b) Consumers will demand more at the subsidised price than they would at the higher price which would have to be charged if no subsidy were given.

4.19 **Resources are therefore used to produce goods for which there would not be demand in a free market**. This mis-allocation of resources needs to be justified by the government in terms of the social benefits of lower unemployment, protection of domestic industries, or encouragement of emerging industries.

4.20 The administration of subsidies and subsidy payments is also likely to involve a lot of bureaucracy, and the wasted costs of this officialdom are a further drawback to a scheme of subsidies.

Tax incentives

4.21 Subsidies are cash payments by a government, but the government can also give firms a financial incentive to make new investments by offering **tax incentives**.

4.22 UK firms investing in plant and equipment are able to claim 40% of its cost against tax in the first year and 100% for investment in IT equipment. 100% first year allowances are also available for investment in plant and machinery in designated **enterprise zones**. These are located in depressed areas.

Chapter roundup

- We have described the various types of organisation found in the mixed economy, and we have looked at how the economy can be divided into primary, secondary and tertiary sectors.
- You do not need to have detailed knowledge of the economics of particular **industries**, but understanding the characteristics of different **sectors** of the economy is important. Many of the developmental changes which happen to economies such as that of the UK over a relatively long period of time can be analysed in terms of changes in output and trade involving the sectors of the economy.
- Although it is convenient for economists to assume that profit maximisation is the central objective of firms, we should not overlook the fact that in reality the motives of managers may operate to serve alternative goals.
- It is important that you appreciate the general motives for growth and the means by which business growth is achieved.
- For your exam, you should be aware of the reasons for and methods of government intervention in firms' location decisions, although detailed knowledge of the development of regional policy in the UK or elsewhere is not required.

Quick quiz

1 Distinguish the primary, secondary and tertiary sectors of the economy.

2 What are the general problems associated with changes in economic structure?

3 Why might a profit maximisation model be inadequate in identifying the goals of firms?

4 For a firm, what are the advantages of:

(a) horizontal integration
(b) vertical integration
(c) diversification

5 What are likely to be the main factors influencing a firm's location decision?

Answers to quick quiz

1 The primary sector of the economy is concerned with the production of raw materials such as crops and minerals. The secondary sector processes these raw materials to produce goods. The tertiary sector provides services including goods distribution.

2 Changes in economic structure lead to the contraction of some industries and the expansion of others. Contraction leads to unemployment, consequent reductions in spending power and hence local recession; and possibly regional depopulation as people leave to seek work. Expansion puts strain on local infrastructure such as housing and the transport system and makes substantial demands on available finance.

3 The separation of ownership from control in large organisations means that managerial rather than entrepreneurial goals might be pursued.

4 Horizontal integration offers economies of scale of all types and the possibility of achieving some element of monopoly power over the market. Vertical integration may achieve financial and commercial economies of scale, but its greatest advantages are control over end markets and security of sources of supply. Diversification spreads risk over several industries, so that a decline in one may be compensated for by expansion in another.

5 Local resource costs
Transportation costs
The location of markets
Government policy and inducements
Management preferences
Localisation (agglomeration) economies of scale

Now try the questions below from the Question Bank

Number	Level	Marks	Time
Q19	Introductory	8	10 mins
Q20	Introductory - Interactive	–	–
Q21	Introductory - MCQ	–	–

Chapter 8

PERFECT COMPETITION AND MONOPOLY

	Topic list	Syllabus reference	Ability required
1	Equilibrium under perfect competition	(ii)	Evaluation
2	Equilibrium for a monopoly	(ii)	Evaluation
3	More about monopoly	(ii)	Evaluation

Introduction

Businesses operate in two sets of markets, one for inputs, such as labour, and one for output. The objectives of the businesses may vary, as may the structure and nature of the markets in which they operate. To understand the immediate environment within which a business operates, you need to be aware of the implications of these variations. We look at these implications in this part of the Study Text.

The purpose of this chapter is to consider output decisions by firms which operate with the different forms of market structure characterised as **perfect competition** and **monopoly**.

In Chapter 10, we will go on to look at two other forms of 'imperfect' market structure: **oligopoly** and **monopolistic competition**.

A full understanding of each of these four models of market structure is needed for your exam.

Learning outcome covered in this chapter

- Analyse the process of competition in different market structures

Syllabus content covered in this chapter

- Forms of market structure: competition and economic welfare; competition policy; regulation and deregulation; the public sector and privatisation

1 EQUILIBRIUM UNDER PERFECT COMPETITION

KEY TERM

Perfect competition: a theoretical market structure in which no supplier has an advantage over another.

1.1 **Perfect competition acts as a useful theoretical benchmark.**

(a) We can use it to **judge or predict what firms might do** in markets where competition shows some or most of the characteristics of being perfect

(b) We can also **contrast the behaviour of firms in less perfect markets.** We shall be looking in this chapter and the next at imperfect types of market structure - namely, monopoly, monopolistic competition and oligopoly.

1.2 **Characteristics of perfect competition**

- There is a large number of buyers and sellers in the market.
- Firms are 'price takers', unable to influence the market price individually.
- Producers and consumers act rationally and have the same information.
- The product is homogeneous: one unit of the product is the same as any other unit.
- There is free entry of firms into and free exit of firms out of the market.
- There are no transport costs or information gathering costs.

Exam focus point

You should be ready to quote the above assumptions of the 'perfect competition' model in an exam answer.

Question 1

Think about the market for a particular product - say motor cars. To what extent is this market 'perfect', as defined by the six criteria above?

Answer

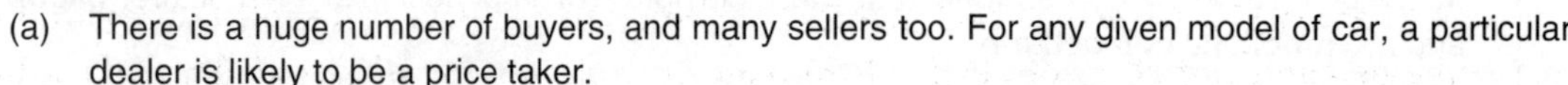

(a) There is a huge number of buyers, and many sellers too. For any given model of car, a particular dealer is likely to be a price taker.

(b) Communication is generally good. Product features are well known and list prices are freely available. And discount levels too are widely commented on, in the press and by word of mouth.

(c) Consumers don't always act rationally. A car which appeals to a buyer's self-image, or snobbishness, may command a higher price than another model apparently similar in all material respects.

(d) The product is very far from homogeneous.

(e) Entry to the market is not easy, whether we are talking about manufacturers of motor cars (very high start-up costs), or dealers.

(f) Transport costs are *not* absent. On the contrary, significant geographical price differentiation is possible because of the high transport costs involved.

Equilibrium in the short run

1.3 How are price and output determined in the case of the profit-maximising firm operating under conditions of perfect competition in the short run?

1.4 The short run is a period in which the number of firms in the market is **temporarily fixed.** In these circumstances it is possible for firms to make supernormal profits or losses as the following diagrams show.

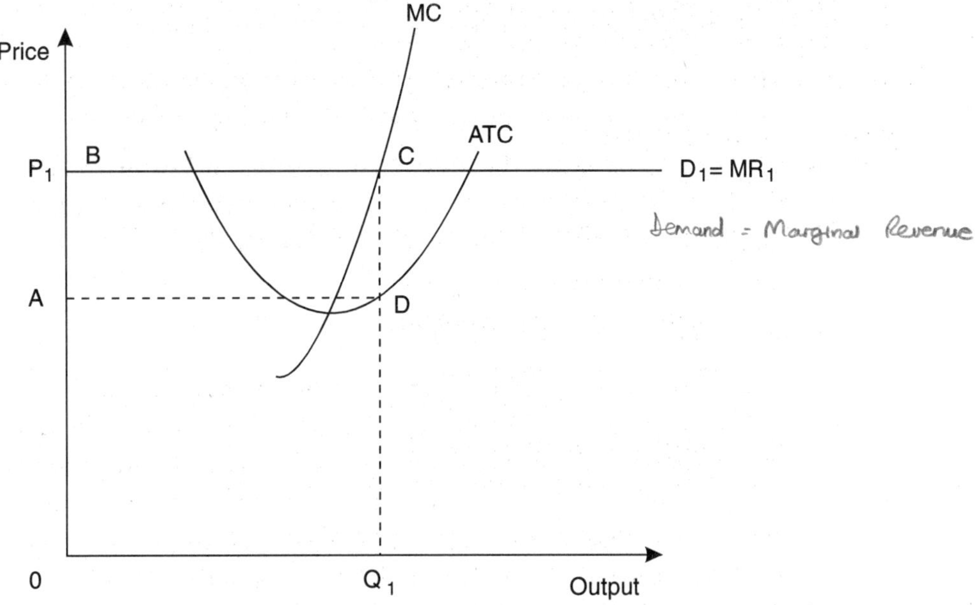

Figure 1 Supernormal profits in the short run

1.5 Figure 1 shows the cost and demand curves of a firm in the short run making supernormal profits. The demand curve is the horizontal line D_1 at price P_1. The curve is a horizontal line indicating that **the firm has to accept the price that the market as a whole fixes** for it. If the firm were to charge a higher price it would lose all its sales and there is no point charging a lower price as it can sell all its output at the given price. The demand curve is thus also the marginal revenue curve; every new unit sold at price P_1 increases total revenue by an amount P_1.

1.6 Figure 1 also shows the average total cost curve (ATC) and the marginal cost curve (MC), with the MC cutting the ATC at the lowest point of the ATC. Given these cost curves and the demand curve D_1, the firm will produce the output Q_1, where the MC curves cuts the MR horizontal curve at the point C. This is the **profit maximising level of output** (see Chapter 5 Section 3).

1.7 At the output Q_1 the firm is making **supernormal profits** indicated by the rectangle ABCD. This will attract new firms into the industry and the price will be bid down, possibly to price P_2 as shown in Figure 2. Here the firm makes a loss shown by the rectangle WXYZ. Once again the firm produces where MC = MR giving an output of Q_2. A firm could choose to do this for a short period so long as revenues covered its **variable** costs, since any excess of revenue **over** variable cost will help to pay the fixed costs. In the long term, however, revenues must cover both fixed and variable costs in full.

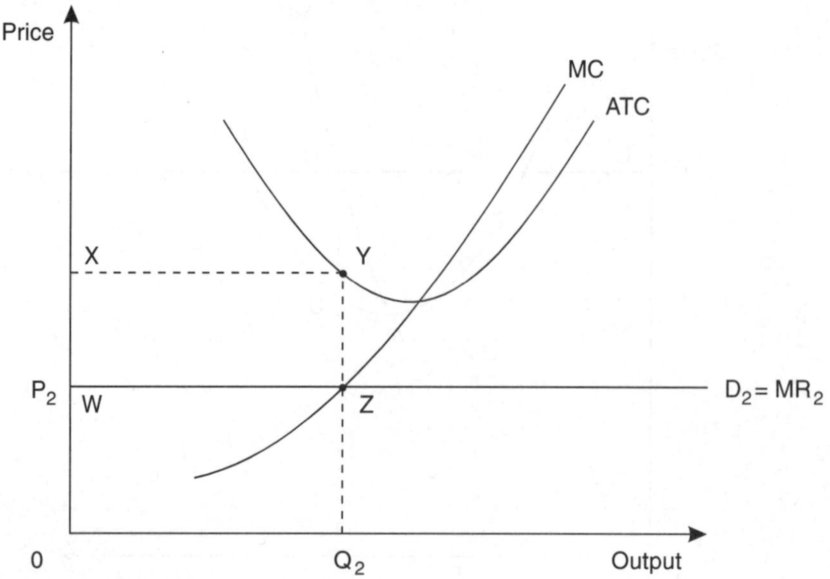

Figure 2 Losses in the short run

1.8 In the long run, whenever profits are being made new firms will enter the industry and the price will fall. Similarly, when losses are made firms will leave the industry and the price will rise.

Question 2

In conditions of perfect competition, the demand curve for a firm's product is:

(a) identical to the firm's marginal revenue curve. True or false?
(b) perfectly inelastic. True or false?

Answer

(a) True. The firm can sell whatever output it produces at the market price.
(b) False. (a) above implies that the demand curve is perfectly elastic.

Equilibrium in the long run

1.9 In a perfectly competitive market in the **long run**, the firm **cannot influence** the market price and its average revenue curve is horizontal. The firm's average cost curve is U shaped. The firm is in equilibrium and earns normal profits only (and so no supernormal profits) when the AC curve is at a tangent to the AR curve as shown in Figure 3(b). In other words, long-term equilibrium will exist when supernormal profits and losses are eliminated. There is no incentive for firms to enter or leave the industry and the price will remain at P with the firm making normal profits only.

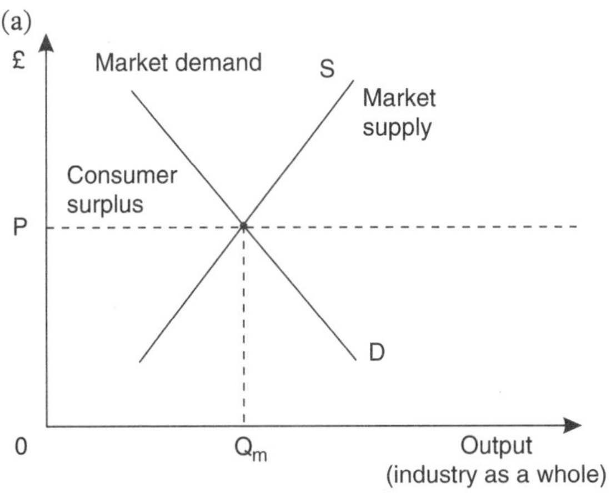

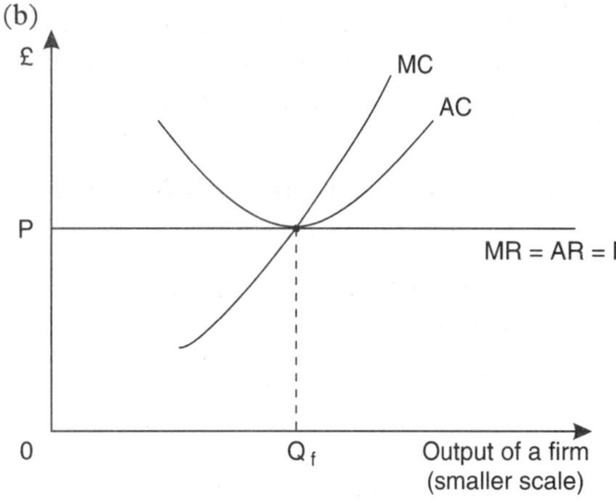

(a) Market as a whole *(b) Individual firm in perfectly competitive market*

Figure 3

1.10 Note the following points about Figure 3.

(a) The market price P is the price which all individual firms in the market must take.

(b) If the firm must accept a given MR (as it must in conditions of perfect competition) and it sets MR = MC, then **the MC curve is in effect the individual firm's supply curve** (Figure 3(b)). The **market supply curve** in Figure 3(a) is derived by aggregating the individual supply curves of every firm in the industry.

(c) Consumer surplus is represented by the area to the left of the demand curve above P.

1.11 Long-run equilibrium will, then, occur in the industry when there are no more firms entering or leaving the industry because no new firm thinks it could earn higher profits by entering and no existing firm thinks it could do better by leaving. In the **long run**, then, all firms in the industry will have MR = MC = AC = AR = price, as in Figure 3(b).

Exam focus point

This explanation of long run equilibrium under perfect competition and the accompanying diagrams are fundamental knowledge for your exam

Question 3

A perfectly competitive firm will be in equilibrium where price is equal to marginal cost. True or false?

Answer

True. Price is at average revenue (AR) which is equal to MC.

Question 4

A small perfectly competitive firm manufactures 200 wooden garden benches each month which it sells for £40 each. The table below shows the firm's costs

Total variable cost	£7,200
Marginal cost	£40
Total fixed cost	£1,800

What should the firm do in the short term?

A Increase output
B Cease production
C Lower its price
D Maintain output at its present level

Answer

D The firm is producing and selling at a level of output where marginal cost is equal to marginal revenue. It is therefore already maximising its profit or minimising its loss. In fact, its monthly total revenue is £40 × 200 units = £8,000. This covers the variable costs and makes a contribution of £800 towards its fixed costs. Ceasing production would cause this contribution to be lost. There would be no point to reducing price since under perfect competition it can sell as much as it can produce at the prevailing market price. If it increased production it would find that its marginal cost rose.

2 EQUILIBRIUM FOR A MONOPOLY 5/02

The monopoly market

KEY TERM

In a **monopoly,** there is only one firm, the sole producer of a good which has no closely competing substitutes

2.1 A firm's monopolistic position may result from some natural factor which makes it too costly for another firm to enter the industry. For example, in the domestic water supply industry it will normally be too costly for a second firm to lay a second water supply system to compete for part of the business of an existing sole supplier: the sole supplier enjoys a **natural monopoly**. In other cases, a monopoly may be formed by mergers of a number of firms in an industry. However formed, **monopoly can only exist if potential competitors are kept out of the market by barriers to entry** (see below). For a monopoly, the total market supply is identical with the single firm's supply and the average revenue curve in monopoly is the same as the total market demand curve.

2.2 If price must be reduced to increase unit sales, average revenue is falling and marginal revenue will always be lower than average revenue; if the monopolist increases output by one unit the price per unit received will fall, so the **extra revenue** generated by the sale of the extra unit of the good is **less** than the **price** of that unit. The monopolist therefore faces a downward sloping AR curve with an MR curve below the AR curve (Figure 4).

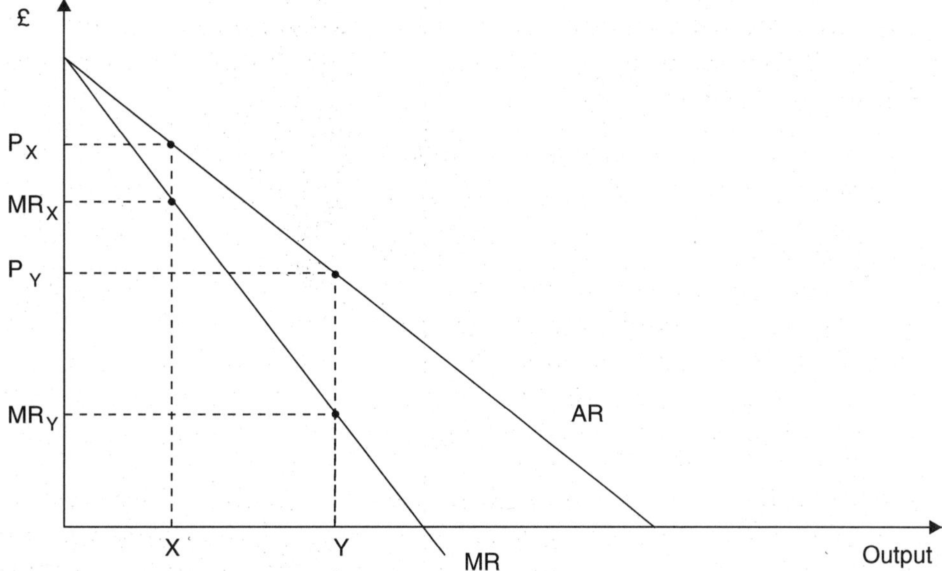

Figure 4 A monopolist's average revenue (AR) and marginal revenue (MR) curves

2.3 Marginal revenue can be negative. This occurs when demand is price inelastic and although lowering the price increases sales demand, the volume increase is small and so total revenue falls.

Question 5

Study the diagram above. At what price and output level would the firm maximise its sales revenue?

Answer

At the point where MR = 0. Further sales will lead to negative MR, and hence a reduction in total revenue.

2.4 It is obviously important that you should understand what the MR and AR (demand) curves are showing us in Figure 4.

(a) At output quantity X, the marginal revenue earned from the last unit produced and sold is MR_X, but the price at which all the X units would be sold is P_X. This is found by looking at the price level on the AR curve associated with output X.

(b) Similarly, at output quantity Y, the marginal revenue from the last unit produced and sold is MR_Y, but the price at which all Y units would be sold on the market is, from the AR curve for Y output, P_Y.

Profit-maximising equilibrium of a monopoly 5/02

2.5 The condition for profit maximisation is, as we have seen, that marginal revenue should equal marginal cost. This is true for any firm. As long as marginal revenue exceeds marginal cost, an increase in output will add more to revenues than to costs, and therefore increase profits.

2.6 Figure 5 shows a monopoly equilibrium where the AC curve touches the AR curve at a tangent, at exactly the same output level where MC = MR. Since AC = AR and AC includes normal profits, the monopolist will be earning normal profits but no supernormal profits.

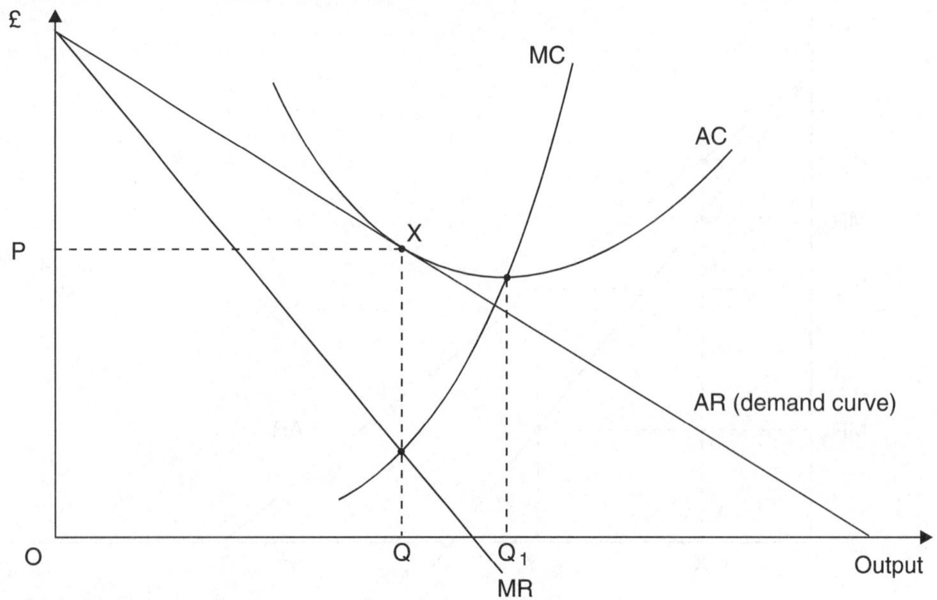

Figure 5 Equilibrium of a monopoly firm earning normal profits

2.7 In this situation, the monopoly will make a loss by producing at output higher than Q, and so it will have to produce at an output level which is well below the capacity at which its average costs are minimised (output Q_1).

2.8 Monopolies are usually able to earn 'monopoly' or supernormal profits in the **long run** as well as the short run, and the situation illustrated in Figure 5 will be **rare** for a monopoly, although (as we shall see later) it is a long-run equilibrium situation for firms in the type of market structure known as monopolistic competition.

2.9 In perfect competition, a firm should not be able to earn supernormal profits in the long run because they would be 'competed away' by new entrants to the industry. A monopoly firm can however earn **supernormal profits** in the long run as well as in the short run, because there are **barriers to entry** which prevent rivals entering the market.

2.10 Figure 6 shows the position of the monopolist earning supernormal profits in the short run. SMC is the short-run marginal cost curve and SAC represents short-run average costs.

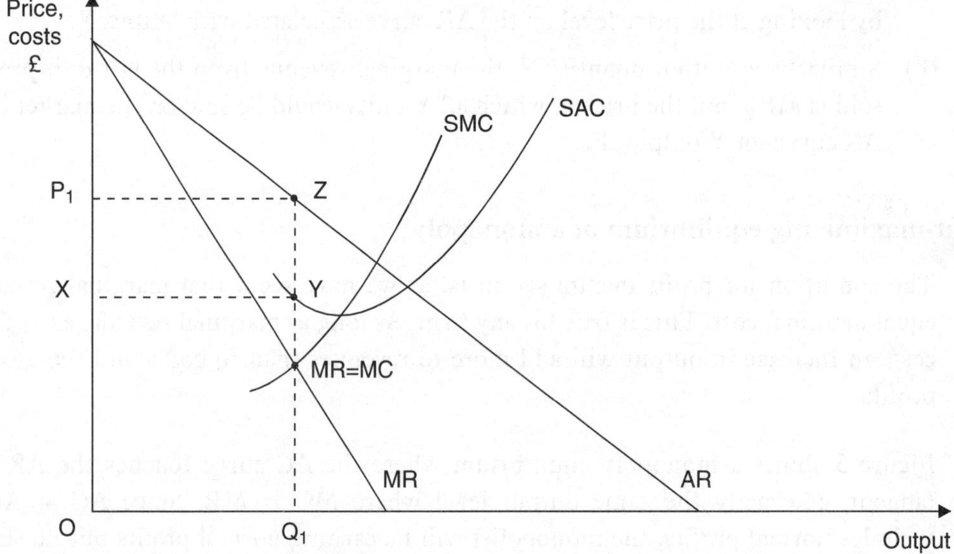

Figure 6 Monopolist's short-run equilibrium

2.11 In Figure 6, the monopolist's profit is maximised at output Q_1, where marginal cost (MC) equals marginal revenue (MR), and the price charged is the average revenue P_1. The monopolist is earning supernormal profits represented by the rectangular area P_1 ZYX.

2.12 **The monopolist will charge a higher price than a perfectly competitive firm, and produce less output. The output of the monopolist will be at a level where AC is not at a minimum.**

2.13 If we superimpose the perfect completion demand curve on Figure 6 we can see a further potential effect of monopoly on economic welfare.

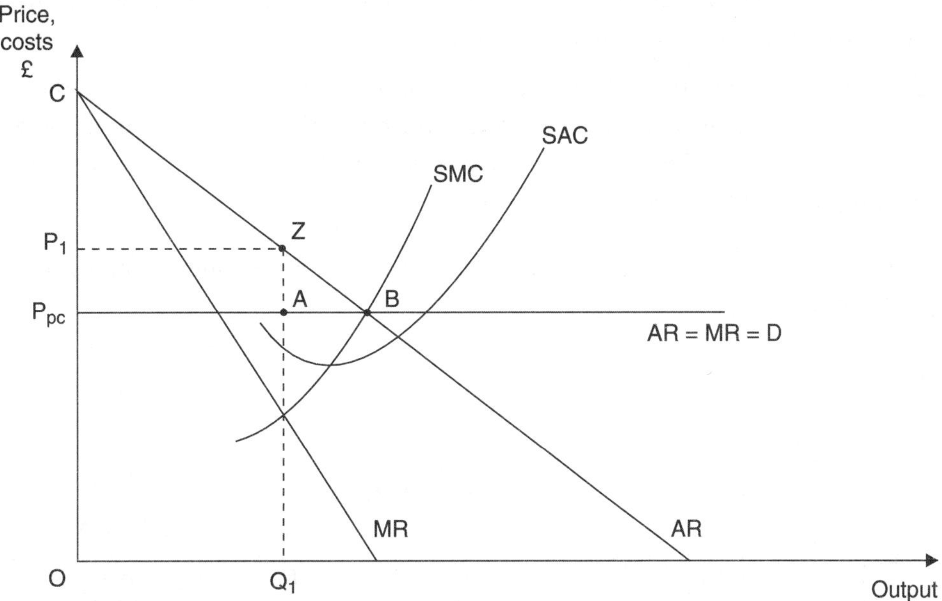

Figure 7 Consumer surplus and dead weight loss

2.14 Under perfect competition, the area CBPpc would constitute consumer surplus. Under monopoly, with price P_1 being charged, this is reduced to CZP_1. Part of the consumer surplus has been transformed into super normal profit.

2.15 The small triangular area ZBA is called the **dead weight loss** due to monopoly, since it is a benefit totally lost.

3 MORE ABOUT MONOPOLY

Price discrimination

3.1 **Price discrimination** occurs when a firm sells the same product at different prices in different markets.

Question 6

You are likely to have encountered examples of price discrimination in practice. Can you recall any?

Answer

You might have thought of:

- Telephone calls (different prices for peak and off-peak calls)
- Rail travel (there are many different tickets you can buy for an identical journey)
- Package holidays (more expensive during school holidays)

3.2 **Three basic conditions are necessary for price discrimination to be effective and profitable**

(a) The seller must be able to **control the supply of the product**. Clearly, this will apply under monopoly conditions. The monopoly seller has control over the quantity of the product offered to a particular buyer.

(b) The seller must be able to **prevent the resale of the good** by one buyer to another. The markets must, therefore, be clearly separated so that those paying lower prices cannot resell to those paying higher prices. The ability to prevent resale tends to be associated with the character of the product, or the ability to classify buyers into readily identifiable groups. Services are less easily resold than goods while transportation costs, tariff barriers or import quotas may separate classes of buyers geographically and thus make price discrimination possible.

(c) There must be significant differences in the willingness to pay among the different classes of buyers. In effect this means that the **elasticity of demand must be different in at least two of the separate markets** so that total profits may be increased by charging different prices.

3.3 We can see how the monopolist seller practising price discrimination can maximise revenue using a diagram.

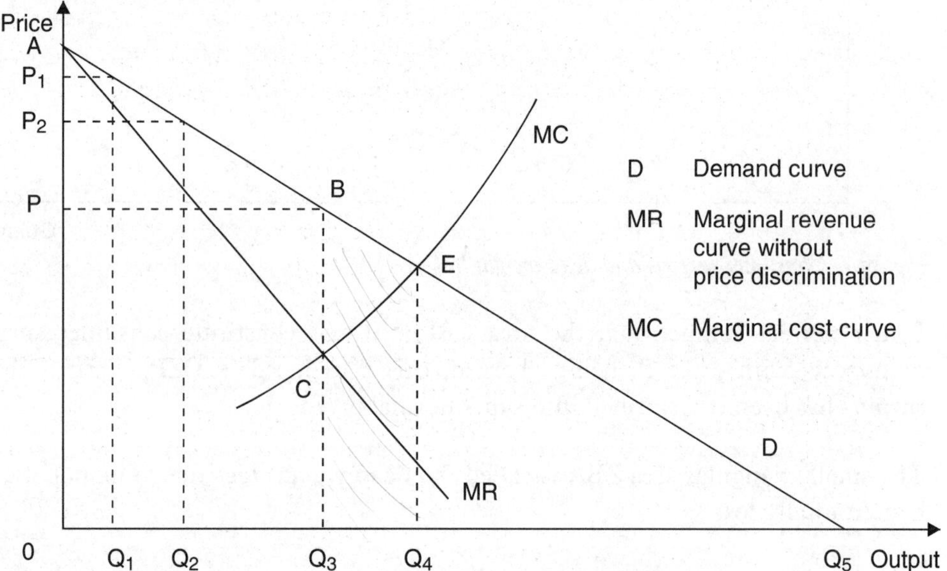

Figure 9 Price discrimination

3.4 Figure 9 demonstrates firstly the equilibrium position of a monopolist who does not discriminate. He produces at the point C where marginal cost equals marginal revenue, producing output Q_3 and selling at price P. His total revenue is given by the rectangle $OPBQ_3$.

3.5 Figure 9 also illustrates how the monopolist can improve on this position, both from the point of increased revenue and increased profits. **The discriminating monopolist does not charge the same price for all units sold.** If we assume that the monopolist can discriminate **perfectly,** then he can sell each unit for a different price as indicated on the demand curve. Thus he can sell the first unit Q_1 at the price P_1, and the second unit Q_2 at the price P_2. This follows for all units sold so that the demand curve now becomes the marginal revenue curve; each extra unit sold is sold for the price indicated on the demand curve, each previous unit being sold for the higher price relevant to that unit.

3.6 The perfectly discriminating monopolist will still maximise profits by producing at the level of output where MC = MR, but the marginal revenue curve is now the curve D, the demand curve. He thus produces at the point E where marginal cost equals the new marginal revenue, producing Q_4 units.

3.7 Recall that the total revenue for the non-discriminating monopolist by producing at the level of output was equivalent to area $OPBQ_3$. The **additional** revenue of the discriminating monopolist is represented by the areas APB plus Q_3BEQ_4. The discriminating monopolist has thus maximised his revenue (consistent of course with maximising his profit). If the monopolist did not wish to maximise profit but wished simply to maximise revenue he would expand production to the point Q_5 when his total revenue would be the area OAQ_5.

3.8 **Take care not to confuse maximising revenue with maximising profit**. Increasing output beyond Q_4 in the example will not increase profit as marginal costs exceed marginal revenue for each additional unit sold.

Examples of price discrimination

3.9 Various examples show that these conditions can be met and that it is possible for a monopolist to engage in price discrimination. Markets may be separated by a **time barrier**, for example where the cost of telephone calls varies according to the time of day at which they are made. Rail operating companies charge cheaper rates for off peak travel. Holiday companies charging a higher price for a given holiday at certain times of the year is another example. These are examples of services which cannot be transferred from the cheaper to the more expensive market.

3.10 Price discrimination also occurs where it is possible to separate buyers into clearly defined **groups**. Industrial users of gas and electricity are able to purchase these fuels more cheaply than are domestic users. Similarly milk is sold more cheaply to industrial users, for example for making into cheese or ice cream, than to private households.

Question 7

Explain why it is possible for a railway or airline to charge different fares for passengers using the same service.

Answer

(a) **Consumers' ignorance**. Not all consumers may be aware of the availability of low-rate tickets such as lower prices for booking in advance, special offers and so on. This means that two customers on the same journey and in similar seats might pay different prices because one of the customers is unaware that a cheaper price could have been obtained.

(b) **The nature of the good**

(i) Prices can be varied according to the time of day or day of the week. Many customers will be forced to travel at peak times and pay top prices and some will switch to travelling at a cheaper time when the railway or airline has spare capacity to be filled up. Demand for journeys at peak times will be relatively inelastic, since demand will be from commuters who must travel in these periods in order to reach their workplace on time.

(ii) A cheaper rate might be offered to children. Since a child cannot transfer his ticket to an adult there is no danger that adults can buy cheaper tickets by using children to obtain tickets on their behalf.

(c) **Geographical separation of market segments**: a railway can sell cheap travel to customers travelling from say, Manchester to London, but still charge full rates to customers travelling from London to Manchester.

Are monopolies beneficial or harmful?

3.11 We have now seen two things.

(a) A monopolist is likely to produce less output but charge a higher price for it than a comparable firm operating in conditions of perfect competition, unless the monopolist can achieve economies of scale that a smaller firm could not. This leads to the monopolist earning extra profits and also a social cost or **deadweight burden** of monopoly.

(b) Monopolists can practise price discrimination.

These two points might suggest that monopolies are a bad thing. But there are economic arguments both for and against monopolies.

3.12 **Arguments in favour of monopolies** **5/01**

(a) **A firm might need a monopoly share of the market if it is to achieve maximum economies of scale**. Economies of scale mean lower unit costs, and lower marginal costs of production. The consumer is likely to benefit from these cost efficiencies through lower prices from the monopoly supplier. Economies of scale shift the firm's cost curves to the right, which means that it will maximise profits at a higher output level, and quite possibly at a **lower selling price** per unit too.

(b) So-called **natural monopolies** exist because of a very high ratio of fixed costs to variable costs. Such a cost structure makes it very likely that significant economies of scale will exist.

(c) **Monopolies can afford to spend more on research and development**, and are able to exploit innovation and technological progress much better than small firms.

(d) **Monopolies may find it easier than small firms to raise new capital** on the capital markets, and so they can finance new technology and new products. This may help a country's economy to grow.

(e) Monopolies will make large profits in the short term, but in many cases their profits will eventually encourage rival firms to break into their market, by developing rival products which might have a better design, better quality or lower price. It can therefore be argued that **temporary monopolies can stimulate competition**, and are in the longer term interests of consumers.

(f) There is also an argument that firms which show entrepreneurial flair and innovation deserve rewarding for the risks they have taken and the new products they have made. They should therefore be rewarded by legal protection of the monopoly through the award of **patent rights**. Monopolies can spend more on research and development and will therefore tend to be innovative.

3.13 **Arguments against monopolies**

(a) The profit-maximising output of a monopolist is likely to be at a price and output level which give it **supernormal profits**. This is a benefit for the monopoly producer at the expense of the consumer.

(b) The profit-maximising output of a monopoly is at a point where **total market output is lower and prices are higher** than they would be if there were a competitive market instead of a monopoly.

(c) **Monopolies do not use resources in the most efficient way possible**. Efficient use of resources can be defined as combining factors of production so as to minimise average unit costs. The profit-maximising output of a monopoly is not where average costs

(AC) are minimised (at the lowest point of the firm's AC curve), and so monopolies are not efficient producers.

(d) Monopolists can carry out restrictive practices, such as price discrimination, to increase their supernormal profits.

(e) The higher prices and supernormal profits encourage firms in competitive markets to want to become monopolies, and they can do this by trying to create **product differentiation**, by introducing differences between their own products and the products of rival competitors. These differences might be real product design or quality differences, or imaginary differences created by a brand name and a brand image. This can be beneficial for producers, but at the expense of consumers.

(f) Because they are not threatened by competition and can earn supernormal profits, **monopolies might become slack about cost control**, so that they fail to achieve the lowest unit costs they ought to be capable of. They may also adopt a complacent attitude to innovation, instead of investing in it.

(g) Monopolies might stifle competition, by taking over smaller competitors who try to enter the market or by exploiting barriers to entry against other firms trying to enter the market.

(h) If a monopoly controls a vital resource, it might make decisions which are damaging to the public interest. This is why the government often chooses to put vital industries under state control (for example, health care, the fire service and the nuclear power industry at the time of writing).

(i) There might be diseconomies of scale in a large monopoly firm.

Barriers to entry — 5/01, 11/01, 5/02

KEY TERM

Barriers to entry: factors which make it difficult for suppliers to enter a market.

3.14 **Barriers to entry** can be classified into several groups.

(a) **Product differentiation barriers**. An existing monopolist or oligopolist would be able to exploit his position as supplier of an established product that the consumer/ customer can be persuaded to believe is better. A new entrant to the market would have to design a better product, or convince customers of the product's qualities, and this might involve spending substantial sums of money on research and development, advertising and sales promotion.

(b) **Absolute cost barriers**. These exist where an existing monopolist or oligopolist has access to cheaper raw material sources or to know-how that the new entrant would not have. This gives the existing monopolist an advantage because his input costs would be cheaper in absolute terms than those of a new entrant.

(c) **Economy of scale barriers**. These exist where the long run average cost curve for firms in the market is downward sloping, and where the minimum level of production needed to achieve the greatest economies of scale is at a high level. New entrants to the market would have to be able to achieve a substantial market share before they could gain full advantage of potential scale economies, and so the existing monopolist would be able to produce its output more cheaply.

(d) The amount of **fixed costs** that a firm would have to sustain, regardless of its market share, could be a significant entry barrier.

(e) **Legal barriers**. These are barriers where a monopoly is fully or partially protected by law. For example, there are some legal monopolies (nationalised industries perhaps) and a company's products might be protected by patent (for example computer hardware or software).

Allocative inefficiency and X-inefficiency

3.15 One of the arguments against monopolies is that they are inefficient compared with firms in conditions of perfect competition because, unlike perfectly competitive firms, they do not produce at an output level that minimises average costs. Instead, they restrict production and raise price to the level that **maximises profit**. As a result, less is produced and consumed than would be the case under perfect competition. The resources that would have been used are diverted elsewhere, to produce things that households actually want less than the monopolist's product. This implies **that monopolies are inefficient in allocating resources**. This is called **allocative inefficiency**.

3.16 A second and different criticism of monopolies is that they are wasteful of costs, and spend more than they need to. The lack of competition, perhaps, makes monopolies **complacent,** and **resources are not used with maximum efficiency**. This type of over-spending inefficiency is called **X- inefficiency**.

3.17 The difference between allocative inefficiency and X-inefficiency is illustrated in Figure 10.

(a) **Figure 10(a).** If a monopolist maximises profit at output level Q_2, there is allocative inefficiency because the firm would produce more at lower cost at output Q_1. (This diagram also illustrates **technical** (or productive) inefficiency, which exists when a firm does not achieve the lowest possible cost per unit of output.)

(b) **Figure 10(b).** If a monopolist has an average cost curve AC_1, when it ought to use resources more efficiently and have an average cost curve AC_2, there is X-inefficiency.

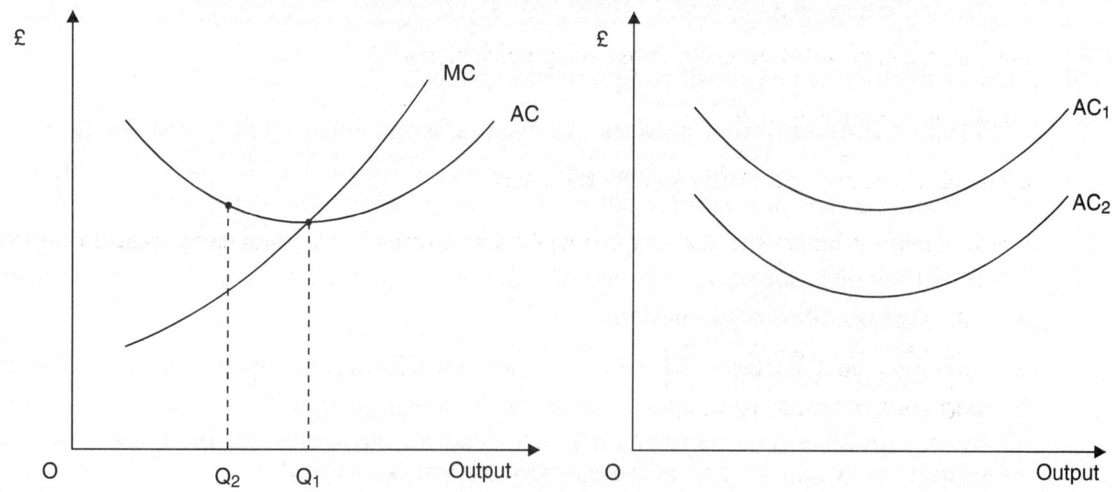

(a) Allocative inefficiency *(b) X-inefficiency*

Figure 10

3.18 All monopolies might be accused of some X-inefficiency, but there has been a view that **state owned monopolies** have a tendency to be more X-inefficient than monopolies which

are private companies. This may be because they have different objectives from those of private sector organisations.

Chapter roundup

- In this chapter, we have examined conditions of perfect competition. In perfectly competitive markets, firms are price takers, and so their decisions are concerned with what output level will maximise profits. In imperfect competition, firms can influence the market price, and so their decisions are about what price to set as well as what volumes of output to produce. Pure monopoly is an extreme form of imperfect competition.
- Firms will generally try to earn supernormal profits if they can. Competition, though, tends to erode supernormal profits, and firms may have to be satisfied, when equilibrium is reached, with just normal profits. The ability to sustain supernormal profits depends on the nature of competition.
- We have noted that monopoly may be beneficial (because of economies of scale) or harmful. Government policies have been directed at the harmful aspects of monopoly. Rather than keeping nationalised monopolies in public ownership, the UK government has privatised them, setting up consumer watchdog bodies to regulate the newly privatised industries.
- It may be that monopolies encourage complacency about costs (X-inefficiency) and may produce allocative inefficiency. Goals other than profit maximisation pursued in large companies could also result in inefficiencies.
- In the next chapter, as we go on to consider monopolistic competition and oligopoly, you should bear in mind that many of the arguments for and against monopolies also apply to firms which operate in these other conditions of imperfect competition.

Quick quiz

1 In what way does monopoly differ from perfect competition?

In a monopoly:

A Products are differentiated
B Supernormal profit is possible
C There are barriers to entry
D There are economies of scale

2 How can a firm in perfect competition make supernormal profits?

3 What is price discrimination?

4 Distinguish allocative inefficiency from X-inefficiency.

5 Which of the following defines the long-run equilibrium position of a firm operating under conditions of perfect competition?

A MC = MR, AC < AR, MR < AR
B MC = MR, AC = AR, MR < AR
C MC > MR, AC = AR, MR = AR
D MC = MR, AC = AR, MR = AR

6 Selling the same good at different prices to different customers is termed:

A Monopolistic exploitation
B Protectionism
C Price discrimination
D Non-price competition

7 In the diagram the firm is currently producing at output level E. The firm will seek to:

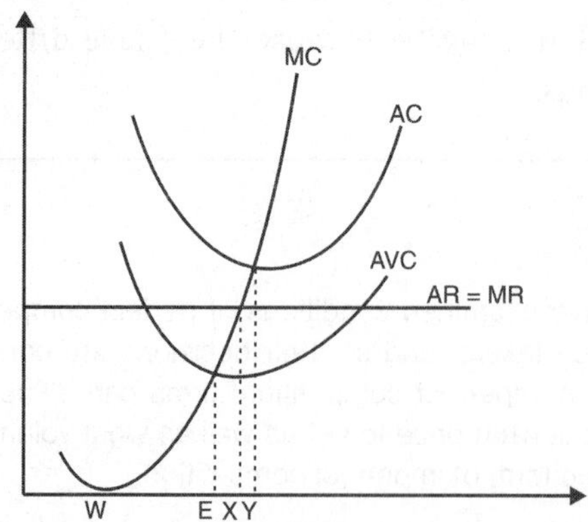

A Leave the industry because AC > MR at all outputs and so losses are inevitable
B Increase output to point Y in order to maximise profits
C Reduce output to point W in order to maximise profits
D Increase output to point X in order to maximise profits

8 The diagram shows the cost curves and revenue curves for Hans Tordam Ltd, a firm of tulip growers. Which of the following statements is true? 1. Price P and output Q are the profit-maximising price and output levels for the firm. 2. Price P and output Q are price and output levels at which the firm makes normal profits. 3. Price P and output Q are the revenue-maximising price and output levels.

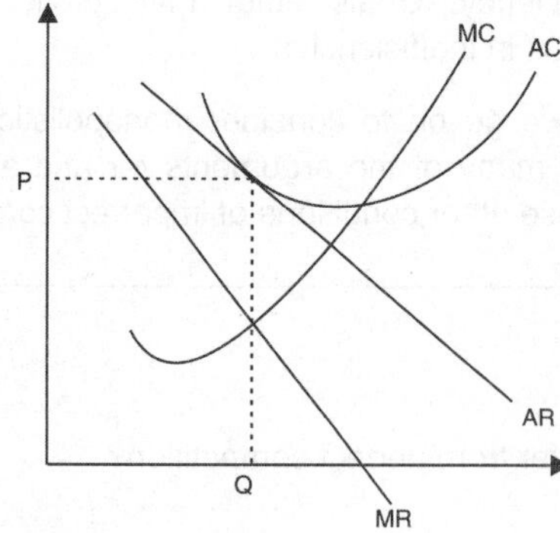

A Statement 1 only is correct
B Statements 1 and 2 are correct
C Statements 2 and 3 are correct
D Statements 1, 2 and 3 are correct

9 The diagram shows the revenue and cost curves for a profit-maximising monopoly firm, Lord and Masters Ltd. Which of the following statements are correct? 1. If the firm has zero marginal costs and 100% fixed costs, its profit-maximising output would be OZ; 2. At profit-maximising output OY, supernormal profits for Lord and Masters Ltd are STWX; 3. If the firm's fixed costs increased, so that the AC curve rose to a level where it is at a tangent to the AR curve at point W, it would cease to make supernormal profit.

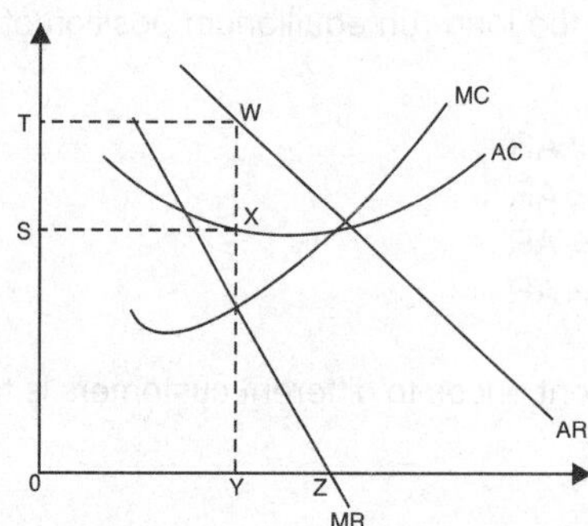

A Statements 1 and 2 are correct
B Statements 2 and 3 are correct
C Statements 1 and 3 are correct
D Statements 1, 2 and 3 are all correct

10 These diagrams show long term equilibrium under perfect competition for both the firm and the industry.

Label these diagrams.

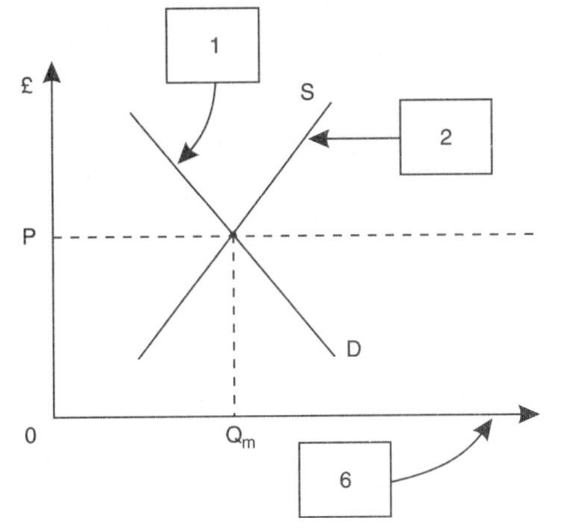

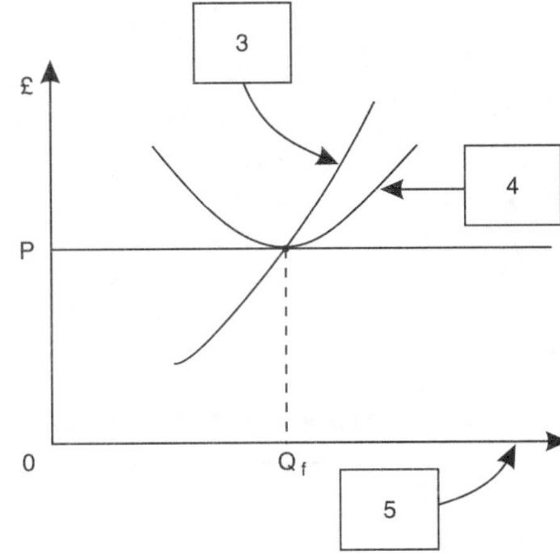

A Firm's average cost
B Output of the firm
C Market supply
D Firm's marginal cost
E Market demand
F Total industry output

Answers to quick quiz

1 C All firms produce homogenous goods under perfect competition. Under a monopoly there is only one producer so the concept of product differentiation is not applicable. Both market forms permit supernormal profit (however, only the monopoly can make supernormal profit indefinitely). Economies of scale may be possible under any market form, though they are, perhaps, less likely under perfect competition.

2 In the short run, the number of firms in the market is fixed. If the prevailing market price is above the lowest point on a firm's average total cost curve, it will make supernormal profits. This will continue until new entrants are attracted into the market and drive the market price down by increasing supply.

3 Price discrimination exists when the same product is sold at different prices in different markets or market segments.

4 A monopolist will produce at a lower level of output and therefore higher cost than a perfectly competitive firm. There is thus inefficient allocation of resources in a monopoly. X-inefficiency arises because monopolists need not control their costs in order to survive. They tend to be inefficient in their use of resources.

5 D For long run equilibrium, MC = MR = AC = AR.

6 C

7 D The firm will produce where MR = MC.

8 B 1. Profit is maximised at price P and output Q, because this is where MC = MR; 2. At this price/output level, average cost equals average revenue. Normal profit is included in cost, and so the firm is making normal profits only, but no supernormal profits; 3.Total revenue is not being maximised because this price/output level is not where MR = 0.

9 D Statement 1 is correct, because if MC = 0, profits would be maximised where MC = MR, which would be at output OZ, where MR = 0. Statement 2 is correct. Supernormal profits per unit are the difference between AR and AC (price and average cost). This is (W - X) or (T - S). Total supernormal profits for output OY are therefore illustrated by area STWX. Statement 3 is probably more difficult to understand. If fixed costs increase, but variable costs remain the same, the MC curve will be unchanged, and so the profit-maximising price will still be OT and the profit-maximising output OY. But if higher fixed costs have raised average costs (AC) to point W, at this price and output level AR = AC, and so there will be no supernormal profits.

10 1 E

2 C

3 D The profit maximising level of output is where marginal costs equals marginal revenue.

4 A Long-term equilibrium is at an output where average cost equals marginal cost and marginal revenue.

5 B

6 F

Now try the questions below from the Question Bank

Number	Level	Marks	Time
Q22	Introductory	8	20 mins
Q23	Introductory - MCQ	–	–
Q24	Introductory - Interactive	–	–

Chapter 9

MONOPOLISTIC COMPETITION AND OLIGOPOLY

Topic list		Syllabus reference	Ability required
1	**Monopolistic competition and non-price competition**	(ii)	Evaluation
2	**Oligopoly**	(ii)	Evaluation
3	**Contestable markets**	(ii)	Evaluation

Introduction

Economic theorists have noted that actual market structures often do not correspond with either of the extreme cases of perfect competition and monopoly, which we examined in Chapter 8.

This led to the analysis of other forms of imperfect market structure, including monopolistic competition and oligopoly, which we now consider.

Learning outcome covered in this chapter

- Analyse the process of competition in different market structures

Syllabus content covered in this chapter

- Forms of market structure: competition and economic welfare; competition policy; regulation and deregulation; the public sector and privatisation

1 MONOPOLISTIC COMPETITION AND NON-PRICE COMPETITION 5/01

Monopolistic competition

KEY TERMS

Monopolistic competition is a market structure in which firms' products are comparable rather than homogeneous. **Product differentiation** gives the products some market power by acting as a barrier to entry.

1.1 A firm which operates in conditions of **monopolistic competition** has a downward sloping demand curve like a monopoly (the quantity of output demanded responds to the price at which the firm is prepared to sell). The downward sloping demand curve is possible because of product differentiation created by the firm. Also, unlike a monopoly firm, it is unable to utilise barriers to entry against other firms. (Indeed, the firm already competes with rivals, which can take retaliatory competitive action if the firm makes big profits.)

1.2 Firms in monopolistic competition (as well as oligopoly, which we discuss later in this chapter) will **try to avoid competition on price** in order to preserve their position as price maker. They will often resort to **non-price competition** instead, perhaps through advertising and sales promotion, or through **product differentiation**. With product differentiation, suppliers try to create differences between their products and other similar products. These differences might be real (for example, design differences) or largely imaginary and created mainly by advertising and brand image (for example, 'designer label' clothing and washing powders).

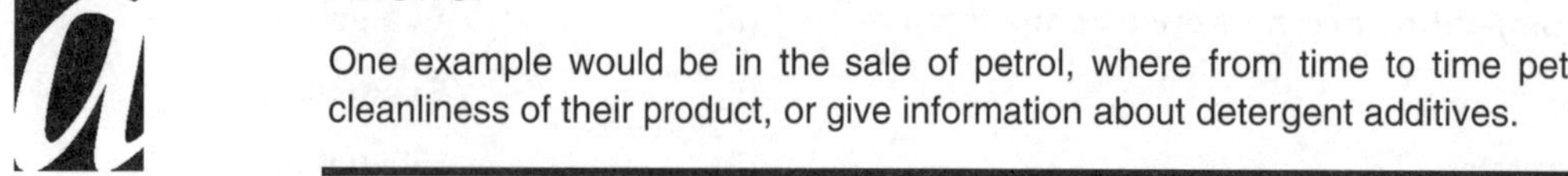

Question 1

See if you can think of other examples of product differentiation.

Answer

One example would be in the sale of petrol, where from time to time petrol suppliers advertise the cleanliness of their product, or give information about detergent additives.

Profit-maximising equilibrium of a firm in monopolistic competition

1.3 A firm which operates in conditions of monopolistic competition will have a **short-run** equilibrium, in which it can make **supernormal profits** and a **long-run** equilibrium in which it cannot. In the **long run**, the monopolistic competitor **cannot** earn supernormal profits since there are no **entry barriers**. Its short-run supernormal profits will be **competed away** by new entrants. As a result of competition, the demand curve will move to the left and the firm will eventually be able to achieve normal profits only.

1.4 The **short-run equilibrium** for a firm in monopolistic competition is illustrated in Figure 1 below. This is the same as the equilibrium of a monopoly firm earning supernormal profits. The firm makes supernormal profits of (P – A) × Q units, shown by the area of the rectangle PQBA.

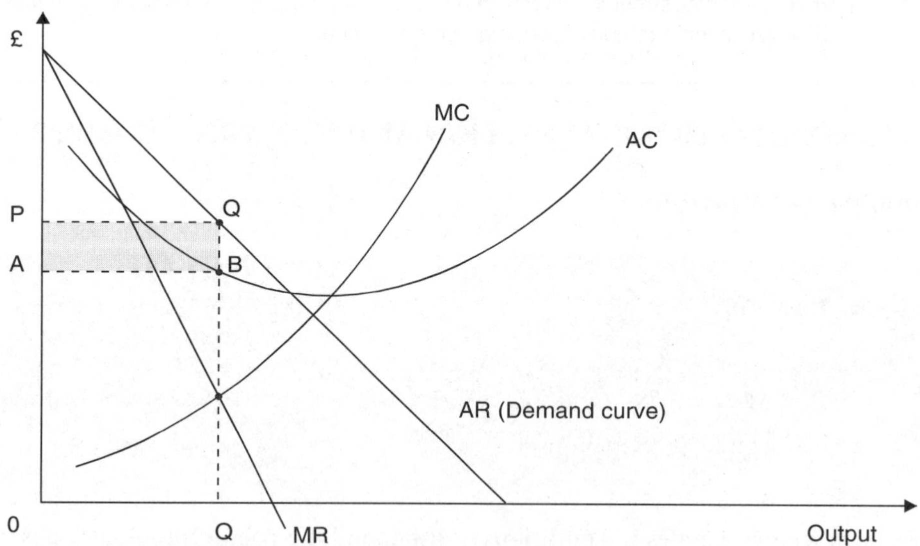

Figure 1 The short-run equilibrium of a firm in monopolistic competition

1.5 The **long-run equilibrium** for a firm in monopolistic competition is illustrated by Figure 2. This is the same as the equilibrium of a monopoly firm which earns no supernormal profits, and so normal profits only.

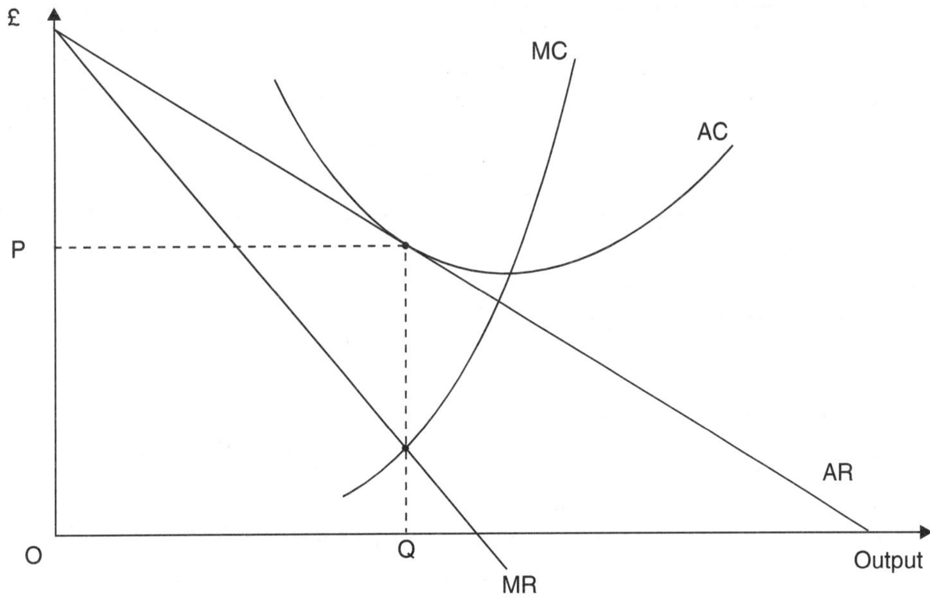

Figure 2 The long-run equilibrium of a firm in monopolistic competition

Price is higher and output lower than in perfect competition for the same reasons described earlier when comparing monopoly with perfect competition.

Implications of monopolistic competition

1.6 Because profit-maximising output is lower compared to perfect competition and is at a point where average costs are not minimised, monopolistic competition, like monopoly, is arguably more **wasteful of resources** than perfect competition.

1.7 Since firms in monopolistic competition cannot expand their output to the level of minimum average cost output without making a loss, the **excess capacity theorem** predicts that industries marked by monopolistic competition will always tend to have excess capacity. (Check this in Figure 2, where profit is maximised at output Q, and output Q is lower than the output level where AC would be minimised.)

1.8 It can be argued that it is wasteful to produce a wide variety of differentiated versions of the same product. If a single version of the same product were made, firms might be able to achieve economies of scale with large-volume production (and so shift their cost curves to the right).

1.9 Some methods that are used to create product differentiation are a waste of resources. Advertising costs are arguably an example of this, although some would argue that promotional activity actually adds utility to a product.

1.10 There is reason to argue that monopolistic competition is **not** so wasteful of resources.

(a) Some product differentiation is 'real', where there are technical differences between similar goods from rival firms. Consumers therefore have more to choose from when there is product differentiation. Their requirements are likely to be satisfied better than if there were just a single, basic, low-price good, without any choice.

(b) If product differentiation is entirely imaginary, created by brand image and advertising when the goods of rival firms are exactly the same, rational buyers should opt for the least-cost good anyway.

Question 2

Now draw a diagram yourself showing the long-run profit-maximising equilibrium of a firm in monopolistic competition.

Compare your diagram with Figure 2 in this chapter.

2 OLIGOPOLY 5/01, 5/02

The nature of oligopoly

KEY TERM

Oligopoly: a market structure where a few large suppliers dominate.

2.1 **Oligopoly** differs from **monopoly** in that there is more than one firm in the market and from **monopolistic competition** because in oligopoly the number of rival firms is small. An oligopoly consisting of only two firms is a **duopoly**.

2.2 Oligopolists may produce a homogeneous product (oil, for example) or there may be **product differentiation** (cigarettes and cars, for example).

2.3 The essence of oligopoly is that **firms' production decisions are interdependent**. One firm cannot set price and output without considering how its rivals' response will affect its own profits. How an oligopolist will actually set his output and price depends on what assumption firms make about their competitors' behaviour.

Exam focus point

The examiner regards this **interdependence of decision making** as fundamentally important to any discussion of oligopoly.

Price cartels by oligopolist producers

2.4 A **price cartel** or **price ring** is created when a group of oligopoly firms combine to **agree** on a price at which they will sell their product to the market. The market might be willing to demand more of the product at a lower price, while the cartel agreement attempts to impose a higher price (for higher unit profits) by restricting supply to the market to a level which is consistent with the volume of demand at the price they wish to charge.

2.5 Each oligopoly firm could increase its profits if all the big firms in the market charge the same price as a monopolist would, and split the output between them. This is known as **collusion,** which can either be tacit or openly admitted.

2.6 Cartels are illegal but difficult to prevent. There might still be price leadership. This occurs when all firms realise that one of them is initiating a price change that will be of benefit to them all, and so follow the leader and change their own price in the same way.

2.7 Figure 3 shows that in a competitive market, with a market supply curve S_1 and demand curve D, the price would be P_1 and output Q_1. A cartel of producers might agree to fix the market price at P_2, higher than P_1. But to do so, the cartel must also agree to cut market supply from Q_1 to Q_2, and so fix the market supply curve at S_2.

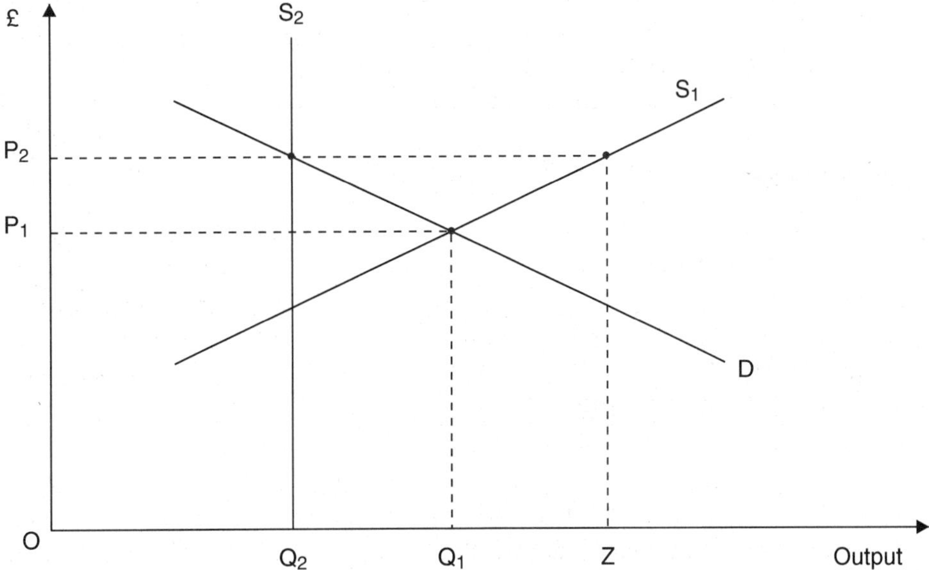

Figure 3 Price cartel

2.8 Establishing a cartel depends on two things.

- The firms in the cartel must be able to control supply to the market.
- The firms must agree on a price and on the output each should produce.

In Figure 3, if the market price is fixed at P_2, firms would want to supply output Z in a free market. This cannot be allowed to happen; otherwise market price P_2 could not be sustained.

2.9 The main **weakness** with cartels is that each firm is still seeking the best results for itself, and so there is an incentive for an individual firm to break the cartel agreement by secretly increasing its output and selling it at the fixed cartel price. However, if all firms increased their output in this way, the cartel would collapse because the high price could not be sustained without a restricted output, and excess supply on the market would force down the price.

2.10 This has been the common experience of the oil-producing countries of the Organisation of Petroleum Exporting Countries. Attempts to agree on a restricted output quota for each country in order to push up oil prices have often broken down because some member countries exceeded their quota, or sold below the cartel's agreed price.

2.11 The **success** of a price cartel will depend on several factors.

(a) Whether it consists of most or all of the **producers** of the product.

(b) Whether or not there are **close substitutes** for the product. For example, a price cartel by taxi drivers might lead to a shift in demand for transport services to buses, cars and trains.

(c) The ease with which supply can be **regulated**. In the case of primary commodities, such as wheat, rice, tea and coffee, total supply is dependent on weather conditions and even political events in the producing country.

(d) The **price elasticity** of demand for the product. An attempt to raise prices by cutting output might result in such a large a fall in demand and such a small rise in price that the total income of producers also falls (price elasticity is greater than 1).

(e) Whether producers can agree on their **individual shares** of the total restricted supply to the market. This is often the greatest difficulty of all.

The kinked oligopoly demand curve **11/01**

2.12 Price cartels do not always exist in an oligopoly market. So how does an oligopoly firm which is **competing** with rival oligopoly firms decide on its price and output level? A feature of oligopoly markets, remember, is that each firm's pricing and output decisions are influenced by what its rivals might do.

2.13 When demand conditions are stable, the major problem confronting an oligopolist in fixing his price and output is judging the response of his competitor(s) to the prices he has set. An oligopolist is faced with a downward sloping demand curve, but the nature of the demand curve is dependent on the reactions of his rivals. Any change in price will invite a competitive response. This situation is described by the **kinked oligopoly demand curve** in Figure 4, in which the oligopolist is currently charging price P, for output OQ, which is at the kink on the demand curve DD.

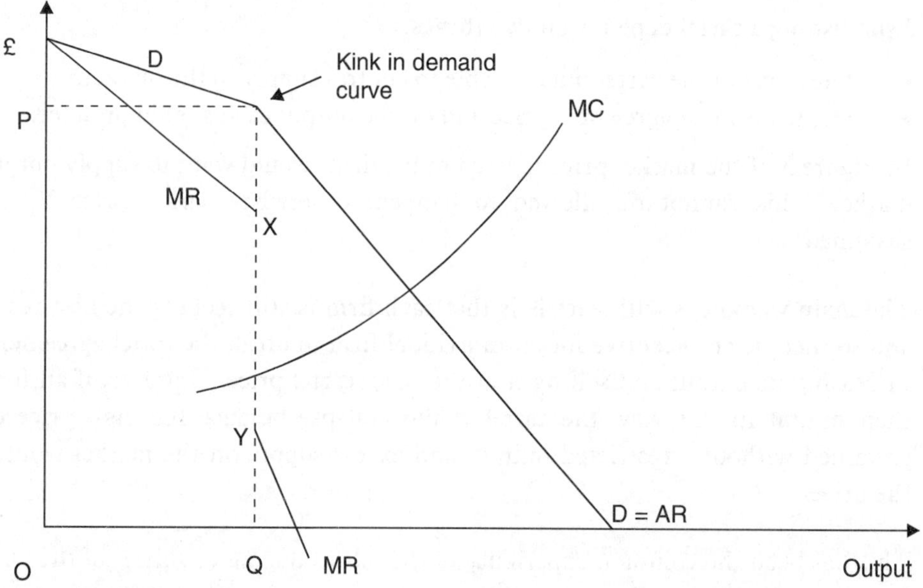

Figure 4 Kinked oligopoly demand curve

2.14 The kinked demand curve is used to explain how an oligopolist might have to **accept** price stability in the market.

(a) If the oligopolist were to **raise** his prices above P, his competitors would keep their price **lower** and so many consumers would buy from them instead. An example is the difficulty which individual petrol companies have in raising the price of petrol at garages. If competitors do not raise their prices too, the firm usually soon has to restore its prices to their previous level. The demand curve would therefore be quite **elastic** at these higher prices.

(b) If, on the other hand, the oligopolist were to **reduce** his prices below P, competitors would probably **do the same**. Total market demand might rise, but the increase in demand for the oligopolist's products would probably be quite low. Demand is thus likely to be **inelastic** at prices below P hence the kink in the demand curve.

2.15 The marginal revenue (MR) curve is **discontinuous** at the output level where there is the kink in the demand curve. The kink in the demand curve explains the nature of the marginal revenue curve MR. At price P, output OQ, the MR curve falls vertically because at higher prices the MR curve corresponds to the more elastic demand curve, and at prices below P the MR curve corresponds to the less elastic demand.

2.16 A firm maximises its profit at the point where MR = MC. The more inelastic the demand curve is below price P, the longer the discontinuous portion (XY) of the MR curve will be. There is thus a wide range of possible positions for the MC curve that produce the same profit maximising level of output.

2.17 The oligopolist's cost structure can change, with worsening or improved efficiencies, but as long as the MC curve cuts the MR curve through its vertical portion XY, the oligopolist's price and output decision should not alter. Hence, there will be price and output stability, with cost changes for the oligopoly firm, which change its MC curve, not affecting output and price.

2.18 Only if marginal costs rise far enough for the MC curve to pass through the MR curve above point X in Figure 4 is there a case for raising price, and only if MC falls far enough to pass through the MR curve below point Y is there a case for lowering price.

2.19 In general, oligopoly prices will rise only if all the firms follow the lead of a rival in raising its price, so that the AR curve shifts outwards. The kink rises to the new common price level, which is again stable. The converse holds for price falls, perhaps occurring because of technological advance.

Price leadership and price wars in oligopoly markets

2.20 In oligopoly markets there is a tendency for one firm to set the general industry price, with the other firms following suit. This is called **price leadership**. It is one source of stability in a market where there may be cartels which tend to be undercut, and price wars.

2.21 When demand conditions change, the situation becomes somewhat different and price stability might no longer exist.

(a) If total market demand falls, oligopolists might try to increase their share of the market by cutting prices.

(b) Similarly, if one oligopolist begins to lose his share of the market, he might try to restore it by cutting prices. The consequence would be a price war. In the UK in recent years there have been price wars by supermarkets and oil companies in selling petrol, for example. The effect of price wars is usually beneficial to consumers, but they are of limited duration because it is not in the interests of oligopolists to sustain them for long.

2.22 Economists sometimes model the strategies of oligopolists and market participants in other types of market structure using **game theory**, which involves examining participants' strategies according to what they stand to gain or lose from each strategy.

Question 3

(a) Draw a diagram to show the effect of a cartel on price and output to the market.
(b) Draw a diagram to show a kinked oligopoly demand curve.

Compare your diagrams with Figures 3 and 4 respectively in this chapter.

3 CONTESTABLE MARKETS

3.1 The theory of contestable markets postulates that although there might be just a **few firms** in the market, the market might operate more efficiently than an oligopoly (or monopolistic competition). In equilibrium, a firm in a **contestable market** in which there are close substitutes will earn normal profits only and no supernormal profits and produce at an output level where AC is minimised. Thus the firm will be at equilibrium MR = MC = AC = AR, just as in perfect competition. Here is an exercise to help you to refresh your memory.

Question 4

Draw a diagram to show the long-run equilibrium position for a firm in a perfectly competitive market. Include on your diagram marginal cost (MC), average cost (AC), marginal revenue (MR) and average revenue (AR).

Compare your diagram with Figure 3(b) in Chapter 8.

3.2 Firms in contestable markets are forced into this situation because there are neither entry or exit barriers.

If they were to be inefficient and produce at a level where AC is *not* minimised, or if they were to raise prices to earn supernormal profits, other firms would quickly enter the market knowing they could just as easily leave if supernormal profits were to be eroded by the extra competition.

3.3 Thus, the theory of contestable markets shows that **it is not necessary to have many firms supplying to a market for conditions similar to perfect competition to apply**. It is enough for the few firms in the market to know that many more firms **could** enter the market for the few firms to act in a **similar way** to firms in the **perfect competition** model.

Exam focus point

For essay questions on market structures, being able to draw relevant diagrams is vital. In your revision, check that you understand how the diagram is built up, and why curves slope in a particular direction.

Chapter roundup

- We have explained that, when price competition is restricted, firms usually go in for other forms of competition, such as sales promotion and product differentiation.
- In some industries, there are many firms, but competition is reduced because each firm seeks to achieve some product differentiation. Each firm can build up a customer loyalty or market niche, and act in many ways like a monopolist, making prices and facing a downward-sloping demand curve.
- In advanced economies, many industries and markets display characteristics of monopolistic competition and/or oligopoly. When industries consist of a small number of firms, then one thing that managers will have to consider is the reaction of rivals to their own pricing and output decisions and to the non-price competitive activities which they pursue. (This is referred to as **competitor analysis**.)
- Oligopolies might collude and make a formal or informal cartel agreement on the price for the industry and output levels for each firm. We have seen that the kinked oligopoly demand curve may explain why there is price stability (and non-price competition) in many oligopoly markets.
- You should by now be able to discuss the four models of market structure we have examined - perfect competition, monopoly, monopolistic competition and oligopoly - in terms of the number of firms, the nature of the product and the ease of entry and exit in the industry. For the exam, you should be able to use appropriate diagrams of cost and revenue to illustrate your arguments and to demonstrate the concepts of equilibrium and efficiency in each market structure.

Quick quiz

1 What is meant by non-price competition?

2 What forms does product differentiation take?

3 What are the implications of the kinked oligopoly demand curve for price and output by an oligopoly firm?

4 What is meant by the term 'contestable market'?

5 Which of the following statements best describes long run equilibrium in a market where there is monopolistic competition?

A Marginal revenue equals average cost
B There is excess capacity in the industry since firms reduce average costs by expanding output
C Firms will earn supernormal profits because price exceeds marginal cost
D Price equals marginal cost, but does not equal average cost

6 Which one of the following statements about price discrimination is incorrect?

A Dumping is a form of price discrimination.

B For price discrimination to be possible, the seller must be able to control the supply of the product.

C Price discrimination is only profitable where the elasticity of demand is different in at least two of the markets.

D An example of price discrimination is the sale of first class and second class tickets on an aeroplane journey.

7 The oligopolist is *least* likely to compete through:

A advertising
B improving product quality
C cutting price
D providing incidental services as an 'add-on' to the basic good

8 This question consists of two statements. Which, if either, is correct? First statement: In conditions of *monopolistic competition,* firms will eventually reach an equilibrium output which is less than the output level at which average total cost is at a minimum. Second statement: In *perfect competition,* at the

output level where marginal revenue equals marginal cost, a firm's average variable costs are minimised.

A Both statements are correct
B The first statement is correct but the second statement is false
C The first statement is false but the second statement is correct
D Both statements are false

9 Which of the following factors would weaken the long-term survival of a cartel?

A Greater price elasticity of demand for the product in the long run
B A high concentration of production in the hands of a few firms
C Substantial costs associated with entry into the industry
D Broadly similar cost structures between industry members

10 Is either of the following statements correct?

1 Firms operating under conditions of monopolistic competition will often engage in advertising

2 The profits of a firm operating under conditions of monopolistic competition can be increased by a shift of its average revenue curve or a fall in the elasticity of demand for the firm's product

A Both statements are correct
B The first statement is correct but the second statement is false
C The first statement is false but the second statement is correct
D Both statements are false

Answers to quick quiz

1 Non-price competition occurs when firms attempt to increase their sales by product differentiation or various forms of promotion.

2 Product differentiation can be achieved by actual differences in design or level of service. It can also be achieved by advertising and promotion, when there may be no actual material differences at all.

3 The kinked demand is a descriptive device which illustrates the tendency to stability of prices in oligopoly markets. Oligopolists avoid price competition since a price cut will be matched by competitors and produce little lasting benefit.

4 A contestable market is one in which just a few firms operate but there are no barriers to entry or exit. Firms therefore tend to operate as under perfect competition since they know that any abnormal profits will attract new entrants very rapidly.

5 B For long run equilibrium in monopolistic competition, MR = MC and AR = AC, but it is *wrong* to say that MR = AC or that AR = MC Since AR = AC, the firm does *not* earn any supernormal profits. There is excess capacity because at the profit-maximising output, average cost is not at a minimum. AC is minimised at a higher output. Since firms could produce more output at a lower AC, we would say that there is excess capacity in the industry.

6 D First and second class tickets are not an example of price discrimination, because even though they are tickets for the same aeroplane journey, they are different products - e.g. in terms of service and travel comfort - rather than the same product being sold at two or more different prices. All the other statements are true.

7 C Oligopoly is usually characterised by price stability, as illustrated by the so-called kinked oligopoly demand curve. Oligopolists are unlikely to cut prices, and are more likely to resort to *non-price competition* such as advertising and sales promotion, innovation and technical differences and incidental services.

8 B In monopolistic competition, a firm's equilibrium is where MR = MC, and this is at an output level below minimum AC. Statement 2 is false because although average *total* cost is minimised, average *variable* costs are not at a minimum and diminishing returns already apply.

9 A Few suppliers; barriers to entry and similar cost structures are prerequisites for an effective collusive oligopoly. Greater elasticity of demand for a product in the long run would affect the cartel's ability to charge a higher price whilst maintaining the same volume of sales. This would lead to firms leaving the cartel and cutting prices in order to sell more of their own production.

10 A The second statement in fact *explains* why the first statement is correct. Firms in monopolistic competition will often use advertising to try to shift their demand curve to the right, or to make demand for their product more price-inelastic (enabling them to earn bigger profits by raising prices).

Now try the questions below from the Question Bank

Number	Level	Marks	Time
Q25	Exam	8	10 mins
Q26	Exam - MCQ	2	–
Q27	Introductory - Interactive	–	–

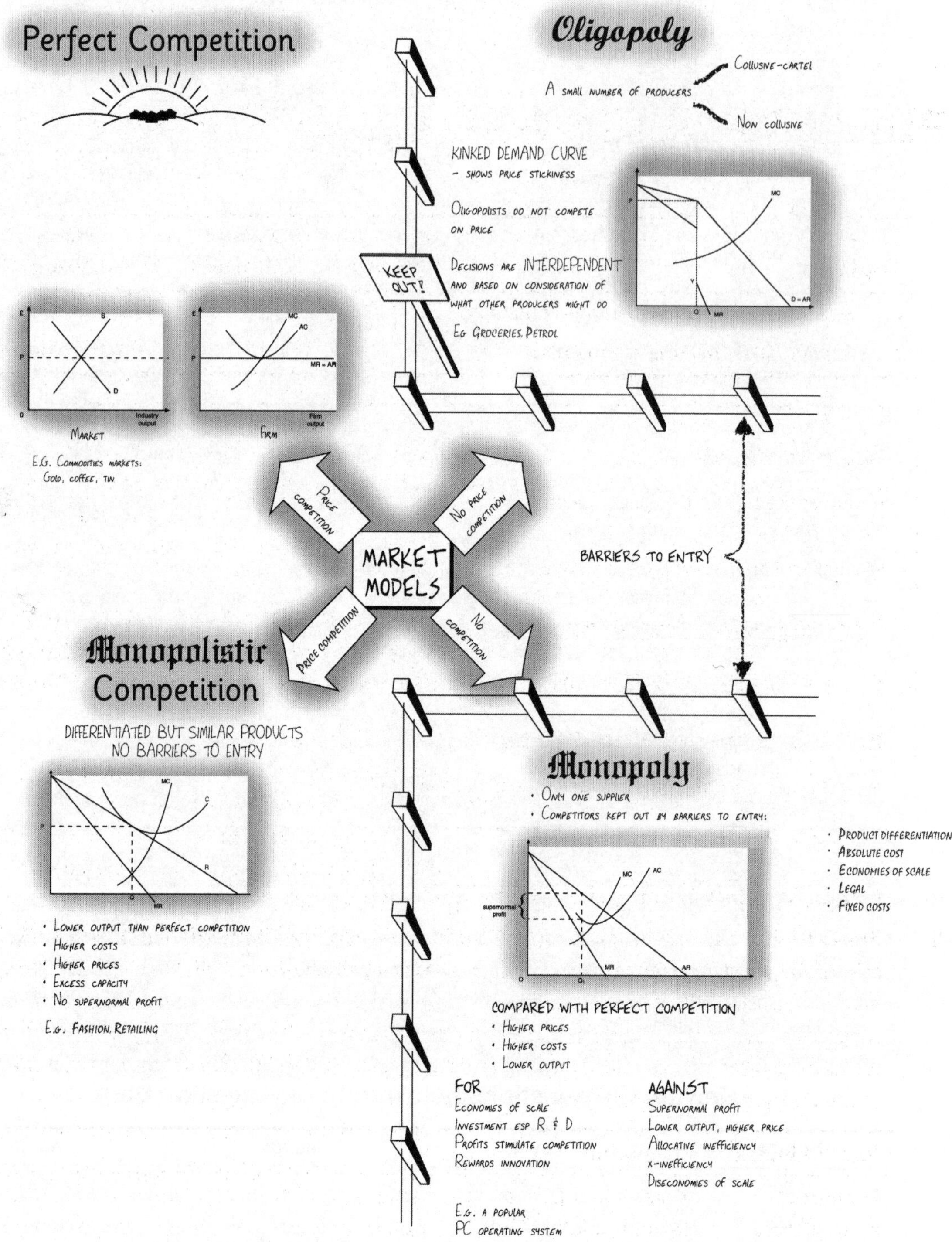

Perfect Competition
Market
Firm
E.G. Commodities markets: Gold, coffee, tin
Oligopoly
A small number of producers
Collusive-cartel
Non collusive
KINKED DEMAND CURVE
– shows price stickiness
Oligopolists do not compete on price
Decisions are INTERDEPENDENT and based on consideration of what other producers might do
E.g. Groceries, Petrol
KEEP OUT!
MARKET MODELS
Price competition
No price competition
Price competition
No competition
BARRIERS TO ENTRY
Monopolistic Competition
DIFFERENTIATED BUT SIMILAR PRODUCTS
NO BARRIERS TO ENTRY
• Lower output than perfect competition
• Higher costs
• Higher prices
• Excess capacity
• No supernormal profit
E.g. Fashion, Retailing
Monopoly
• Only one supplier
• Competitors kept out by barriers to entry:
• Product differentiation
• Absolute cost
• Economies of scale
• Legal
• Fixed costs
supernormal profit
COMPARED WITH PERFECT COMPETITION
• Higher prices
• Higher costs
• Lower output
FOR
Economies of scale
Investment esp R & D
Profits stimulate competition
Rewards innovation
AGAINST
Supernormal profit
Lower output, higher price
Allocative inefficiency
X-inefficiency
Diseconomies of scale
E.g. A popular PC operating system

Chapter 10

PUBLIC POLICY AND COMPETITION

Topic list	Syllabus reference	Ability required
1 Government regulation and privatisation	(ii)	Comprehension
2 Public policy towards monopolies	(ii)	Comprehension

Introduction

An important role of the government is the regulation of private markets where these fail to bring about an efficient use of resources.

We now examine this role of government in relation to monopolies and other aspects of competition.

Learning outcome covered in this chapter

- Explain how governments might respond to the effects of business and the environment

Syllabus content covered in this chapter

- Business and the environment; externalities and public policy

1 GOVERNMENT REGULATION AND PRIVATISATION

1.1 **Market failure is said to occur when the market mechanism fails to result in economic efficiency, and therefore the outcome is sub-optimal.** In response to the existence of market failure, and as an alternative to taxation and public provision of production, the state often resorts to **regulation of economic activity** in a variety of ways. Of the various forms of market failure, the following are the cases where regulation of markets can often be the most appropriate policy response.

Market failure	Regulation
Imperfect competition	Where monopoly power is leading to inefficiency, the state will intervene through controls on, say, prices or profits in order to try to reduce the effects of the monopoly.
Externalities	A possible means of dealing with the problem of external costs and benefits is via some form of regulation. Regulations might include, for example, controls on emissions of pollutants, restrictions on car use in urban areas, the banning of smoking in public buildings, compulsory car insurance and compulsory education.

Market failure	Regulation
Imperfect information	Regulation is often the best form of government action whenever informational inadequacies are undermining the efficient operation of private markets. This is particularly so when consumer choice is being distorted. Examples here would include legally enforced product quality/safety standards, consumer protection legislation, the provision of job centres and other means of improving information flows in the labour market and so on.
Equity	The government may also resort to regulation for social reasons. For example, legislation to prevent racial and/or sexual discrimination in the labour market; regulation to ensure equal access to goods such as health care, education and housing; minimum wage regulations and equal pay legislation.

Types of regulation

1.2 Regulation can be defined as any form of state interference with the operation of the free market. This could involve regulating demand, supply, price, profit, quantity, quality, entry, exit, information, technology, or any other aspect of production and consumption in the market.

Self-regulation

1.3 Bear in mind that in many markets the participants (especially the firms) may decide to maintain a system of voluntary self-regulation, possibly in order to try to avert the imposition of government controls. Areas where self-regulation often exists are the professions (eg the Law Society, the Chartered Institute of Management Accountants, the British Medical Association and other professional bodies), and financial markets (eg the Council of the Stock Exchange, the Take-over Panel and the Securities and Investments Board).

Costs of regulation

1.4 Potential costs of regulation

(a) **Enforcement costs.** Direct costs of enforcement include the setting up and running of the regulatory agencies. Indirect costs are those incurred by those regulated in conforming to the restrictions. These requirements will add to the firms' costs of production and ultimately to their prices.

(b) **Regulatory capture** refers to the process by which the regulator becomes dominated and controlled by the regulated firms, such that it acts increasingly in the latter's interests, rather than those of consumers. This is a phenomenon which has been observed in the USA.

(c) **Unintended consequences of regulation.** Firms will not react passively to regulatory constraints on their behaviour; they will instead try to limit their effectiveness. In general, theory and observation suggest that firms will substitute away from the regulated activity towards those which are less constrained or completely unregulated.

Deregulation

1.5 Deregulation can be defined as the removal or weakening of any form of statutory (or voluntary) regulation of free market activity. Deregulation allows free market forces more scope to determine the outcome.

When should there be deregulation?

1.6 There was a shift in policy in the 1980s in the UK and in the USA towards greater deregulation of markets, in the belief that this would improve efficiency. Indeed, many politicians and commentators believed that it was over-regulation of British industry that was largely responsible for Britain's comparatively uncompetitive and inefficient performance.

1.7 A rational assessment of deregulation should weigh the potential **social** benefits against the **social** costs. If there will be a net gain to society, we can say that the deregulation should proceed. It would be simplistic to contend that **all** regulation is detrimental to the economy. As we have seen, where there is a clear case of market failure, then state regulation may be required.

Advantages and disadvantages of deregulation

1.8 Deregulation measures, whose main aim is to introduce more competition into an industry by removing statutory or other entry barriers, are also known as **liberalisation**. The benefits of liberalising an industry include the following.

(a) **Improved incentives for internal/cost efficiency**. Greater competition compels managers to try harder to keep down costs.

(b) **Improved allocative efficiency**. Competition keeps down prices closer to marginal cost, and firms therefore produce closer to the socially optimal output level.

1.9 In some industries, liberalisation could have certain disadvantages.

(a) **Loss of economies of scale**. If increased competition means that each firm produces less output on a smaller scale, unit costs will be higher.

(b) **Lower quality or quantity of service**. The need to reduce costs may lead firms to reduce quality or eliminate unprofitable but socially valuable services.

(c) **Need to protect competition**. It may be necessary to **implement** a regulatory regime to protect competition where inherent forces have a tendency to eliminate it, for example if there is a dominant firm already in the industry, such as BT in telecommunications. In this type of situation, effective regulation for competition will be required, ie regulatory measures aimed at maintaining competitive pressures, whether existing or potential.

The extent of deregulation and liberalisation in the UK

1.10 In the UK deregulation and liberalisation have taken place in the areas of financial markets, broadcasting, transport and the professions.

(a) **The 1986 'Big Bang' in the Stock Exchange** abolished the old system of separate jobbers and brokers, and fixed brokerage commissions. Barriers to the entry of new firms were also lifted. One result of this was the merging of many broking and jobbing firms in the City into larger groupings, owned in most cases by 'outside' financial institutions.

(b) The Cable and Broadcasting Act (1984) laid the groundwork for both **cable and direct satellite broadcasting** to develop, in competition with the existing over-the-air BBC and ITV transmissions.

(c) Liberalisation of **road passenger transport** - both buses (stage services) and coaches (express services) - was brought about by the Transport Acts of 1980 and 1985. There is now effective free entry into both markets (except in London).

(d) The monopoly position enjoyed by some **professions** has been removed; for example, in opticians' supply of spectacles and solicitors' monopoly over house conveyancing. In addition, the controls on advertising by professionals have been loosened.

1.11 A further instance of liberalisation was the introduction of **compulsory competitive tendering** into public sector organisations. Both local authorities (eg refuse collection, office cleaning and management of leisure facilities) and health authorities (eg hospital cleaning, laundry and catering) have had to contract out the supply of these services, where private sector firms have offered to provide the services at a lower price than their own internal producers.

Privatisation and denationalisation 5/02

KEY TERM

Privatisation: the sale by government of state owned enterprises.

1.12 **Privatisation** takes three broad forms.

(a) The **deregulation of industries**, to allow private firms to compete against state owned businesses where they were not allowed to compete before (for example, deregulation of bus and coach services; deregulation of postal services).

(b) **Contracting out** work to private firms, where the work was previously done by government employees - for example, refuse collection or hospital laundry work.

(c) **Transferring the ownership of assets** from the state to private shareholders, for example the denationalisation of British Gas, BT and many other enterprises.

1.13 The UK government, like many other governments of developed countries, has carried out a policy of denationalisation in recent years. British Gas, BT, the regional water authorities and much of the electricity industry have been among the enterprises which have been privatised. Many of the utility industries which have been privatised are still subject to regulations, for example limiting price increases to the rate of retail price inflation (RPI) minus a specified percentage.

1.14 **Privatisation can improve efficiency** (see below).

1.15 There are **other possible advantages of privatisation**.

(a) Denationalisation provides an immediate source of money for the government.

(b) Privatisation reduces bureaucratic and political meddling in the industries concerned.

(c) There is a view that wider share ownership should be encouraged. Denationalisation is one method of creating wider share ownership, as the sale of BT, British Gas and some other nationalised industries have shown in the UK.

1.16 There are **arguments against privatisation** too.

(a) State owned industries are more likely to respond to the **public interest**, ahead of the profit motive. For example, state owned industries are more likely to cross-subsidise unprofitable operations from profitable ones; for example the Post Office will continue to deliver letters to the isles of Scotland even though the service might be very unprofitable.

(b) Encouraging private competition to state-run industries might be inadvisable where **significant economies of scale** can be achieved by monopoly operations.

(c) Government can provide capital more cheaply than the market to industries whose earning potential is low, but which are deemed to be of strategic importance, such as aircraft manufacture. Opponents of this idea suggest that the very idea of a strategic industry is spurious.

(d) State-owned industries can be run in a way that protects employment, as was the case in the UK coal industry, for instance. The problem with this is that the taxpayer is effectively subsidising technical inefficiency.

(e) Surpluses from state-run industries can be used for public welfare rather than private wealth. The problem here is that points (a) and (d) above tend to preclude the creation of surpluses.

Privatisation, efficiency and competition

1.17 The inefficiency associated with state monopolies was discussed in Chapter 8 and could be said to be of three types.

(a) **Technical inefficiency**. A firm is technically efficient when it uses the **least-cost combination of productive resources** for a given level of output. Failure to do this leads to its not operating at the lowest possible cost per unit of output. This is also known as **productive** inefficiency.

(b) **Allocative inefficiency**. Secondly, there is allocative inefficiency where price is higher than marginal cost such that the good or service is under-produced and under-consumed.

(c) **X-inefficiency**. The monopolist's privileged position relieves it of the need to exert constant effort to keep costs down. The resulting rise in costs is called x-inefficiency.

1.18 The contention that privatisation will lead to efficiency improvements is based on a number of assumptions. The most important assumption is that privatisation will place the industry in a market subject to **competitive pressures** approaching the perfectly competitive ideal. In practice, however, there are few examples of perfectly competitive markets and the likelihood is of restricted competition between a small number of large firms, with a degree of inefficiency persisting. If there are no legal restrictions, it is also possible that state monopolies will merely become private monopolies with even less regard than before for the consumer.

1.19 Another assumption of the analysis is that there are no economies of scale. Where there are significant economies of scale there *may* be a **natural monopoly**, with room in the market for one firm only, and monopoly may be productively more efficient than a market with competing firms.

1.20 It is believed that **management and working practices** will be changed under private sector control. Management will become largely free of interference from the government, working practices should become more efficient and trade union power may be reduced.

1.21 It is claimed that with the central objective of profit maximisation, privatised firms will be **responsive to the wants of consumers** as revealed by market research and signalled by the operation of the price mechanism. The profit objective induces firms to innovate and to seek out new markets, a process which promotes the efficient allocation of resources.

1.22 Where privatisation increases competition, the **greater competition** is likely to make firms produce output more cheaply and to sell it at a lower price. Nationalised organisations have often acted as monopolists, with the consequences of higher prices and lower output characteristic of non-competitive markets.

1.23 In the UK, there has been only a limited increase in competition following some privatisations. Indeed, some organisations have been sold as monopolies to increase their attractiveness to shareholders. The example of BT can be used to illustrate the attempt to encourage competition along with privatisation. Firstly, BT's pricing is regulated by a 'Retail Prices Index minus *x* percent' formula. Secondly, a relatively small competitor, Mercury, a subsidiary of Cable and Wireless, was licensed to compete for part of BT's activities. However, these were relatively minor restrictions on a company with great market power (although since the mid-1990s, new operators have been entering as competitors in the market). The alternative strategy adopted in the USA for the telecommunications giant AT&T was to break down its operations into smaller units which could compete with one another.

1.24 Privatisation alone is often not sufficient to improve the performance of a monopoly and other steps may need to be taken to increase competition. On the other hand, improvements to the competitive environment might equally be achieved without privatisation.

1.25 Some arguments are put forward in favour of privatisation itself. It is argued that it is necessary to take activities out of the public sector in order to take advantage of an improved and more flexible **management culture**: many believe public sector organisations to be inherently inefficient. Against this argument, an alternative policy is to improve the management culture within public sector organisations.

1.26 Privatisation, it is argued, allows **wider share ownership** as well as a temporary boost to the government's finances. It is however arguable that the UK privatisations have **failed to produce deeper share ownership** as still only a low proportion of shareholders own shares in more than one company.

Question 1

What economic arguments could be used to justify the public provision of education?

Answer

Education is widely considered to be a merit good, that is, a good judged to be desirable for people to consume or to receive, regardless of their income. There are various moral and political grounds on which education could be judged as desirable. However, here we are concerned with economic arguments. Arguments for the public provision of education may focus on the desirability of education, or alternatively on its provision by the public sector rather than by the private sector. Below, we look first at economic arguments in favour of education in general before considering arguments specifically in favour of its public provision as compared with private provision.

Economic benefits of education

Basic literacy and numeracy are requirements for a wide range of productive tasks, while at higher levels of skill vocational education helps individuals acquire the competence necessary for specific job roles. The existence of widespread illiteracy and innumeracy in the population necessarily diminishes the prospect of economic growth. Third world countries, in particular, are aware of the difficulties of poor education: it may be impossible to train enough people to cope with new technology, because of their inability to read or manipulate simple numbers.

How should education be provided?

It might be argued that since education equips labour with appropriate skills, then it should be provided by employers. However, although many employers do provide 'on-the-job' training and education to employees, it is not practicable for them to make full educational provision for individuals. This is because most education needs to take place before adulthood when people enter employment and in the case of employees the benefit to employers of providing education is limited by the problem that individuals may leave the employer soon after the education is provided, a problem which often inhibits the provision of any training by employers.

Where employers provide education to employees, there is an externality effect since the education provided may benefit the wider economy. Such benefits will be evident when the employees move to other employment and use their skills more widely. (It is also arguable that more education raises productivity (output per worker) not just for the individual involved but for other workers with whom this individual co-operates.)

Given such externality effects, and given the wider moral or political arguments in favour of education, society should encourage the provision of education if individuals are likely to demand too little of it. They may demand too little because they do not take full account of the social benefits (externality effects) of their receiving education or because they do not take full account of the private benefits to themselves. One way to achieve this is the public provision of free schooling to ensure a minimum level of education and socialisation.

Types of public provision

It is important however to note that a government can ensure the provision of minimum levels of education in different ways. In particular, it is not necessary for the education to be provided by government-run organisations. As with many other activities within government's responsibility, such as refuse collection and road building, it could be 'contracted out' to private sector organisations. 'Vouchers' could be issued for all individuals of school age, which parents could use at the recognised school of their choice, whether in the private or public sector. The school would then redeem the voucher with the government, which would pay the individual's fees. As at present, some regulation would be necessary to ensure that all children are schooled - in other words, to ensure that parents 'spend' their vouchers. Alternatively, government could fund individual places at private sector schools.

2 PUBLIC POLICY TOWARDS MONOPOLIES

Public policy towards private enterprise monopolies

2.1 Since monopolies have both economic disadvantages and economic advantages, there are reasons why a government might wish either to restrict or encourage the development of private enterprise monopolies within its country. Monopolies might be harmful or beneficial to the public interest.

(a) A beneficial monopoly is one that succeeds in achieving economies of scale in an industry where the minimum efficiency scale is at a level of production that would mean having to achieve a large share of the total market supply.

(b) A monopoly would be detrimental to the public interest if cost efficiencies are not achieved. *Oliver Williamson* suggested that monopolies might be inefficient if 'market power provides the firm with the opportunity to pursue a variety of other-than-profit objectives'. For example, managers might instead try to maximise sales, or try to maximise their own prestige.

Government control over monopolies, mergers and restrictive practices

2.2 There are several different ways in which a government can attempt to control monopolies.

(a) It can stop them from developing, or it can break them up once they have been created. Preventing monopolies from being created is the reason why a government might have a public policy on mergers.

(b) It can take them over. Nationalised industries are often government-run monopolies, and central and/or local government also have virtual monopolies in the supply of other services, such as health, the police, education and social services. Government-run monopolies are **potentially advantageous.**

(i) They need not have a profit-maximising objective so that the government can decide whether or not to supply a good or service to a household on grounds other than cost or profit.

(ii) The government can regulate the quality of the good or service provided more easily than if the industry were operated by private firms.

(iii) Key industries can be protected (for example health, education).

(c) It can allow monopolies or oligopolies (firms with few competitors) to operate, but try to control their activities in order to protect the consumer. For example, it can try to prohibit the worst forms of restrictive practice, such as price cartels. Or it may set up regulatory 'consumer watchdog' bodies to protect consumers' interests where conditions of natural monopoly apply, as in the recently privatised utility industries of the UK.

2.3 **Basic ideas behind consumer protection policies**

(a) Control over markets can arise by firms eliminating the opposition, either by merging with or taking over rivals or stopping other firms from entering the market. When a single firm controls a big enough share of the market it can begin to behave as a monopolist even though its market share is below 100%.

(b) Several firms could behave as monopolists by agreeing with each other not to compete. This could be done in a variety of ways - for example by exchanging information, by setting common prices or by splitting up the market into geographical areas and operating only within allocated boundaries.

2.4 In a perfect monopoly, there is only one firm that is the sole producer of a good that has no closely competing substitutes, so that the firm controls the supply of the good to the market. The definition of a monopoly in practice is wider than this, because governments seeking to control the growth of monopoly firms will probably choose to regard any firm that acquires a certain share of the market as a potential monopolist.

The Competition Commission in the UK

Exam focus point

Although the Competition Commission is specific to the UK, questions may be set on it in relation to public control of monopolies and mergers.

2.5 The Director General of Fair Trading may ask the Competition Commission (CC) to investigate if any firm or group of firms controls 25% or more of the market, or the Secretary of State may do the same if any proposed takeover or merger would create a firm that controlled 25% or more of the market. The CC may also investigate proposed mergers where the assets involved exceed £70 million in value. The Commission will then investigate the proposed merger or takeover and recommend whether or not it should be allowed to proceed.

2.6 The **public interest** includes the promotion of competition and the extension of consumer sovereignty, efficiency and enterprise.

2.7 The **interpretation** of the public interest leads to conflicts in many cases. For example, actions which enhance competition and consumer sovereignty may conflict with the objective of allowing firms to be large enough to take advantage of competitive conditions in the international economy.

(a) The CC may agree to a merger, but set conditions which are designed to protect consumers, or it may require that some assets be sold by the merged enterprise in order to prevent a dominant market position being established in a particular area of its operations.

(b) The CC will consider whether any **excessive profits** have been made. In the Roche Products case for example, a return on capital of 70% was deemed to be evidence of **excessive pricing.** In another case, Pedigree Petfoods, 44% was held to be **not excessive.**

(c) The CC will also see whether there is on the face of it a **high degree of interdependence** between a small number of firms. This evidence could be in the form of parallel pricing, predatory pricing or price discriminating policies, sometime prevalent in oligopolies in which there are say only four or five firms.

(d) A firm carrying out 'anti-competitive' practices will not be favoured. An example of this could be 'socially unproductive advertising', where firms in a dominant position have huge advertising spends with the objective of building a barrier over which firms unable to spend a lot on advertising cannot climb. If the merger involves any anti-competitive **distribution policies** such as single supplier agreements, it could be opposed.

(e) The CC will wish to avoid splitting up large companies, thus depriving them of economies of sale. The CC may also throw out applications if they could aggravate unemployment in an area in which unemployment is already significantly high.

(f) The CC will be mindful to protect the needs of merging firms to secure adequate returns for enterprise, risk taking, innovation, improved efficiency research and development, and the need to compete with multinational firms on a global scale. Supernormal profits will not in themselves be a reason to refer merger proposals.

The conflicts between objectives present one problem for the CC, while another problem is that governments may be motivated by other political and economic considerations in deciding whether to adopt CC recommendations.

Chapter roundup

- In the *Economics for Business* exam, you may be expected to use your understanding of market structures in discussing matters of government policy on competition. You will not be expected to have knowledge of particular cases of government intervention, but you should have a general awareness of the issues involved and of the role of the Competition Commission.
- You should understand the various arguments in favour of public (or 'nationalised') ownership of production concerning public goods, merit goods and natural monopoly. You should also be aware of the efficiency arguments against public ownership.
- In the exam, you may be required to explain both the benefits and the limitations of privatisation as a government policy.

Quick quiz

1. In what circumstances might government regulation of markets have an economic justification?
2. What different forms can privatisation take?
3. Why might a government wish to control monopolies?
4. How might a government be able to control monopolies?
5. What cases may the Competition Commission investigate?
6. Which one of the following statements is incorrect?

   A If the effect of privatisation is to increase competition, the effect might be to reduce or eliminate allocative inefficiency

   B Privatisation means selling off nationalised industries by the government to the private sector

   C The effect of denationalisation could be to make firms more cost-conscious, because they will be under the scrutiny of stock market investors

   D The government might appoint consumer watchdogs to regulate privatised industries

Answers to quick quiz

1. The undesirable effects of various forms of market failure can be reduced by government action. Monopoly power can be attacked by regulation of price or profit or even the break-up of the monopoly firm. Externalities can be reduced by bans on some forms of behaviour, such as dangerous pollution, and by levying taxes on others such as the consumption of alcohol. Where imperfect information distorts consumer choice, legally enforceable product standards and disclosure requirements can improve the operation of the market. Finally, governments may intervene for social and political reasons, banning racial discrimination and enforcing a minimum wage, for example.
2. Privatisation can take three forms.
   - Deregulation allows private firms to compete against state owned organisations.
   - Work done by government employees may be contracted out.
   - State owned businesses may be sold to private shareholders.
3. There are arguments both for and against monopolies. Monopolies are detrimental to the public interest when they are inefficient in their allocation of resources and their operations generally. They may also be objected too on the grounds that they obtain higher prices, and hence profits, than would be possible under competition; and they restrict choice.
4. Governments can regulate monopolies, particularly their prices and the quality of their goods and services; prevent them from developing; break them up; or take them into public ownership.

5 The Director General of Fair Trading may ask the Competition Commission (CC) to investigate if any firm or group of firms controls 25% or more of the market, or the Secretary of State may do the same if any proposed takeover or merger would create a firm that controlled 25% or more of the market. The CC may also investigate proposed mergers where the assets involved exceed £70 million in value. The Commission will then investigate the proposed merger or takeover and recommend whether or not it should be allowed to proceed.

6 B Privatisation *could* mean selling off nationalised industries, but it can also refer to deregulation of industries to allow private firms to compete with state-run business (eg private bus companies) and contracting out work previously done by government employees to private firms (eg refuse collection).

Now try the questions below from the Question Bank

Number	Level	Marks	Time
Q28	Exam	16	20 mins
Q29	Exam - MCQ	2	–
Q30	Exam - MCQ	2	–

Part C

The macroeconomic framework

Chapter 11

THE NATURE OF MONEY AND CREDIT

Topic list		Syllabus reference	Ability required
1	Money and credit	(iii)	Comprehension
2	The flow of funds and financial intermediation	(iii)	Comprehension
3	Rates of interest	(iii)	Comprehension

Introduction

All economic activities, whether in the private or public sector, take place within a monetary economy. Thus government and businesses have financial aspects to their operations. Money acts not merely as a measuring rod, thus making accounting possible, but also acts as a means of exchange. Access to finance and the terms on which it is available, most importantly the rate of interest, are crucial elements of the economic environment.

In this first chapter of Part C, we shall be considering:

(a) the function of money - ie what does money do?

(b) how we define money

(c) how money is lent and borrowed, to move it from people who have more money than they can use to people who want to use it.

Learning outcomes covered in this chapter

- Identify the main elements of the monetary and financial system
- Explain the importance of the monetary environment to the business sector

Syllabus content covered in this chapter

- The monetary environment: inflation and the money supply; the banking and financial system; interest rates and monetary policy

1 MONEY AND CREDIT

The functions of money

Question 1

Surely 'money' is a concept very easily understood? Yet we will see in this chapter that it is not necessarily as simple as you might think. Before beginning on the chapter, try to analyse what constitutes money (for example, is a bank deposit account 'money'?) and what are the functions of money. Revise your answers in the light of what you learn while reading this chapter.

1.1 In modern economies, money is used as a means of paying for goods and services, and paying for labour, capital and other resources. Money is important because it provides an easy method for exchanging goods and services (ie buying and selling). It is also important because the total amount of money in a national economy may have a significant influence on economic activity and inflation.

1.2 Attempts to define money have traditionally started with identifying what money does. What are the **functions** of money? We can identify four different functions of money.

- A means of exchange
- A unit of account
- A standard of deferred payment
- A store of value

Money as a means of exchange

1.3 This is arguably the most important function of money in an economy, because without money, the only way of exchanging goods and services would be by means of **barter**, ie by a **direct exchange** of goods or services. In other words, if a shoemaker wanted to buy a horse, he would have two alternative courses open to him.

(a) To find a horse-owner prepared to exchange a horse for a sufficient quantity of shoes of equal value to the horse

(b) To find other people willing to exchange different goods such as clothes or food for shoes, and then trade these goods in exchange for a horse from the horse-owner

1.4 A monetary economy is the only alternative to a barter economy, and it is a means of encouraging economic development and growth.

(a) People are prepared to organise and work for an employer, and in return receive money wages.

(b) A business will exchange its goods or services for money in return.

(c) People will pay out money in order to obtain goods or services.

Money as a unit of account

1.5 This function of money is associated with the use of money as a means of exchange. Money should be able to measure exactly what something is worth. It should provide an agreed standard measure by which the **value** of different goods and services can be compared.

1.6 For example, suppose that only four products are traded in a market. These are pigs, sheep, hens and corn. The relative value of these products must be agreed before exchange can take place in the market. It might be decided that:

- 1 pig has the same value as 0.75 sheep, 3 hens or 1.5 bags of corn
- 1 sheep is the same value as 1.33 pigs, 4 hens or 2 bags of corn
- 1 hen is worth 0.33 pigs, 0.25 sheep or 0.5 bags of corn
- 1 bag of corn has the same value as 0.67 pigs, 0.5 sheep or 2 hens

(In a market with more than four products, the relative values of each product compared with others could be worked out in the same way, although there would be many more value or price ratios to calculate.)

1.7 The function of money in the economy would be to establish a **common unit of value** measurement or account by which the relative exchange values or prices of goods can be established.

Question 2

In the above example of a four-product market, simplify the value relationship by expressing the worth of a pig, a sheep, a hen and a bag of corn in terms of a common unit of money.

Answer

You might have calculated as follows.

A pig	=	3 units
A sheep	=	4 units
A hen	=	1 unit
A bag of corn	=	2 units

Other results (such as 6, 8, 2 and 4 respectively) would work just as well.

Money as a standard for deferred payments

1.8 When a person buys a good or service, he might not want to pay for it straightaway, perhaps because he has not yet got the money. Instead, he might ask for **credit**. Selling goods on credit is not an essential feature of an economy, but it certainly helps to stimulate trade. The function of money in this respect is to establish, by agreement between buyer and seller, how much **value** will be given in return at some future date for **goods** provided **now**. Similarly, when a buyer and seller agree now to make a contract for the supply of certain goods in the future, the function of money is to establish the value of the contract, that is, how much the buyer will eventually pay the seller for the goods.

1.9 **In order to provide an acceptable standard for deferred payments, it is important that money should maintain its value over a period of time**. Suppose, for example, that a customer buys goods for an agreed sum of money, but on three months' credit. Now if the value of money falls in the three-month credit period, the sum of money which the seller eventually receives will be worth less than it was at the time of sale. The seller will have lost value by allowing the credit.

1.10 When the value of money falls (or rises) over time, sellers (or buyers) will be reluctant to arrange credit, or to agree the price for future contracts. Money would then be failing to fulfil its function as a standard for deferred payments.

1.11 One major reason why money might lose value is because of price inflation.

(a) When inflation is high sellers will be reluctant to allow credit to buyers. For example, if a buyer asks for three months credit, and inflation is running at 20% per annum, the 'real' value of the debt that the buyer owes will fall by about 5% over the three month credit period.

(b) Sellers will be reluctant to agree to a fixed price for long-term contracts. For example, a house-builder might refuse to quote a price for building a house over a twelve month period, and instead insist on asking a price which is 'index-linked' and rises in step with the general rate of inflation.

Money as a store of value

1.12 Money acts as a store of value, or wealth. So too do many other assets (eg land, buildings, art treasures, motorcars, machinery) some of which maintain or increase their money value over time, and some of which depreciate in value. This means of course that money is not the only asset which acts as a store of wealth, and we need to extend our definition of this function of money.

1.13 Money is more properly described as acting as a **liquid** store of value. This definition has two parts to it.

(a) Money is a store of value or wealth. A person can hold money for an extended period, for the purpose of exchanging it for services or goods or other assets.

(b) Money is a liquid asset.

Liquidity

1.14 The fact that money is a liquid store of value means that the wealth can be converted immediately (or at least very quickly) into a means of exchange for obtaining goods or services. Liquidity is therefore 'the ability to transform wealth holding into any form without delay or loss of face value'. Liquidity is sometimes defined as 'readily convertible into cash', and the most liquid asset of all is cash itself.

1.15 There are two parts to this definition of liquidity: a liquid asset is one which can be converted into cash (or into a means of exchange for goods or services) without significant delay and without significant penalty or loss of face value.

Delay

1.16 Liquidity is the ability to transform an asset into a means of exchange with minimum delay.

1.17 A liquid store of wealth can therefore be drawn on by its owner to obtain goods and services whenever he wants, and without having to wait to convert the store of wealth into a means of exchange. A painting is a store of wealth, but if its owner wishes to use this wealth to buy something else, he must first sell the painting and then use the proceeds from the sale to make his purchase. Since selling a painting takes time, a painting is not a liquid asset (and nor is a house).

Loss of face value, or significant penalty

1.18 A non-cash asset is liquid if it can be converted into cash within a short period of time without significant penalty. Significant penalty means has two aspects.

(a) Loss of capital value, or face value

(b) Loss or forfeit of a substantial amount of interest (for example, say, loss of 14 days' interest or more)

Question 3

Shares in a quoted company can be bought and sold very rapidly. Could they therefore serve as a form of money?

Answer

No. Although shares can indeed be sold rapidly, the cost of doing so may be a loss on sale.

Liquidity and interest

1.19 An alternative to holding money as banknotes, or money in a non-interest-bearing current bank account, is to hold on to an **interest bearing financial asset** such as the ones below.

- An interest bearing current account
- A bond or debenture

1.20 These provide the holder with two things.

(a) An interest yield on the value of the asset

(b) The certainty of a money repayment to the holder of the asset at the end of a certain period of time or after a certain period of notice has been given by the asset holder

The holder of a financial asset sacrifices some liquidity in exchange for an interest yield on his store of wealth.

Commodity money and non-commodity money

1.21 **Commodity money is money that is made from a valuable commodity, such as gold or silver.** In the past, gold, silver and bronze have been used as money, because they could perform the functions of money and had the attributes of money.

1.22 Commodity money, however, has now given way to **non-commodity money or token money** - that is, money whose exchange value is greater than its inherent 'physical' or commodity value.

(a) Banknotes are one form of non-commodity money.

(b) Bank accounts and cheques are ways of holding and transferring money respectively in non-commodity form.

1.23 Non-commodity money is more easily divisible into small units than commodity money, and it is more portable and more easily transferred. In today's world of highly developed economic activity, commodity money would not be able to perform the functions of money as efficiently as non-commodity money.

Changes in the value of money

1.24 **Inflation** erodes the real value of money. Real value is best defined as the **purchasing power** of money. The erosion of the value of money due to inflation provides one good reason why someone with wealth to store should hold assets which are not money.

1.25 Banknotes, or money held in a non-interest-bearing current bank account, retain their face value. A five pound note, for example, is always worth five pounds. It does not drop in value to, say, £4.50 because of inflation. What happens with inflation is that **the amount of goods five pounds will buy gets progressively less** as time (and inflation) goes on.

1.26 Suppose that a person has £100 in banknotes on 1 January. He does not spend them during the year, so that he still has £100 at the end of the year. During the course of the year, say, the average price of food has gone up 10%, the cost of mortgages and rents has gone up 8%, the cost of energy (gas, electricity, coal) has gone up by 7%, clothing by 3%, household electrical goods by 2% and household electronic goods have gone down by 6%. How much has the value of his banknotes declined in real terms during the year, and how much money would the person need to have at 31 December to have the same spending power or purchasing power that he had on 1 January?

1.27 As you no doubt realise, these questions cannot be answered simply, because different products and services have different price changes. Money is not a **stable** unit of account over time, because the equivalent of £100 of goods on 1 January would, on 31 December, be £110 for food, £108 for mortgages, £107 for energy, £103 for clothing, £102 for electrical goods and £94 for electronic goods.

The effect of inflation on the functions of money

1.28 **Inflation prevents money from performing its functions effectively.**

(a) **Money should be a store of wealth.** In a period of inflation, although money retains its nominal value, it loses some of its purchasing power or real value. If people are worried about money's loss of value, they will prefer to store their wealth in different assets (eg paintings, property, or interest-bearing investments) which they do not expect to lose value.

(b) **Money should be a standard for deferred payment.**

(i) In a period of inflation someone who incurs a debt will profit at the expense of the lender or creditor, because when the debt has to be repaid, its real value will have declined.

(ii) For the same reason, someone who lends money or allows credit will lose out, and might therefore be reluctant to extend credit except at a high rate of interest.

(iii) Long-term contracts (eg to construct and equip an industrial building) might only be agreed if they contain a **price variation clause**, whereby the customer must pay the builder for the cost of any price inflation during the course of construction.

(c) **Money should be a stable unit of account**, but as we have seen, the **relative value** of different goods and services varies over time, because individual products or services do not rise in price by the same percentage amount.

(d) **Money should be an acceptable means of exchange.** When inflation is not excessive, money will probably perform this function adequately. However, when inflation is very high (and there is 'hyperinflation') people might prefer not to use money at all. Instead, they might revert back to a barter economy, or use money alternatives such as gold (because it has an intrinsic value) or a foreign currency such as yen or deutschmarks (whose exchange value will rise against the currency of the hyperinflation economy, and so maintain its real value).

The stock of money

1.29 The money supply is the total amount of money in the economy. It is also referred to as the money stock. A **monetary aggregate** is a measure of the money stock or money supply.

KEY TERM

A **monetary aggregate** is a measure of the money stock or money supply.

1.30 The main purpose of measuring a monetary aggregate is to discover by how much (and how rapidly) the money supply is rising in the economy. There are two further purposes.

(a) To predict from this rise what future changes in economic activity might be

(b) To discover whether past changes in the money supply help to explain changes in economic activity which have already occurred

There is also the view that by controlling the rate of increase in the money supply, inflation can be brought under control and economic conditions made more suitable for achieving economic growth and fuller employment.

Narrow money and broad money

1.31 It is not always easy to decide whether a particular financial asset, for example a bank deposit, is money or not, and it is now considered appropriate to distinguish between narrow money and broad money.

1.32 Financial assets must have a high degree of liquidity to be regarded as narrow money. A definition of narrow money is '**money balances which are readily available to finance current spending, that is to say for transactions purposes**' *(Economic Progress Report).*

1.33 **Broad money,** in contrast, includes financial assets which are **relatively** liquid, **but not as liquid as narrow money items.** A financial asset which would be regarded as narrow money would also fall within the definition of broad money; but broad money, as its name implies, extends the range of assets which are regarded as money.

Broad money is 'money held for transactions purposes and money held as a form of saving. It provides an indicator of the private sector's holdings of relatively liquid assets - assets which could be converted with relative ease and without capital loss into spending on goods and services' *(Economic Progress Report).*

1.34 Narrow money can be defined in different ways, depending on how narrowly 'liquidity' is defined; similarly, broad money can be defined in a variety of ways. Even the broadest definition of money will exclude some financial assets. **There will never be a clear dividing line between what is narrow money, what is broad money, and what is not money at all.**

Question 4

Which of the following best defines narrow money?

A Money balances that are readily available to finance current spending
B Money that is made from a valuable commodity such as gold or silver
C Notes and coins in circulation
D Interest bearing financial assets

Answer

A B is a definition of commodity money, which is irrelevant to modern monetary theory. C is attractive but incorrect since it is an **incomplete** definition of UK M_0, which also includes banks operational deposits at the Bank of England and banks' and building societies' till money. D is part of broad money.

A comparison of the different aggregates

1.35 Definitions of different monetary aggregates currently in use in the UK are shown in the diagram on the next page.

(a) M0 is the 'narrowest' definition of money, the great majority of which is made up of **notes and coin** in circulation outside the Bank of England.

(b) M4 is a 'broad' definition of money, including deposits held for **savings** as well as **spending** purposes. The Bank of England also now publishes statistics for various 'liquid assets outside M4' for the benefit of those who are interested in a still broader definition of the money stock.

1.36 Note also that M4 itself contains some comparatively illiquid elements. For example, M4 contains deposits of any maturity with banks and building societies and certain paper and other capital market instruments of not more than five years' original maturity, although in practice the bulk of M4 is of under three months' residual maturity.

Exam focus point

In the exam, you will not be expected to reproduce the details of different monetary aggregates. You should be able to show an understanding of the difference between narrow and broad money. You might be expected to discuss monetary aggregates figures given in a data response question.

CURRENT UK MONETARY AGGREGATES

Notes and coins in circulation with the M4 private sector

plus Banks' and building societies' till money

plus Banks' operational balances with the Bank of England

equals M0

plus M4 private sector's retail sterling deposits with UK banks and building societies

equals M2

plus M4 private sector's sterling deposits (including sterling certificates of deposit) at UK banks and building societies

equals M4 — *plus* Data is published on a range of liquid assets outside M4

plus Foreign currency deposits of UK residents with UK banks and building societies

plus Sterling and foreign currency deposits of UK public corporations with UK banks and building societies

equals M3H

Note: The 'M4 private sector' means the non-bank non-building society private sector, comprising UK domestic residents and UK based businesses.

Monetary aggregates figures

1.37 To give you some idea of the relative sizes of each of these definitions of money, figures for the money stock in the UK in June 2001 are shown below. It is clear that physical notes and coin form a very small part of the larger aggregates.

			£ billion
M0	=	Notes and coin in circulation outside the Bank of England	32.8
	+	banks' operational deposits with the Bank of England	0.1
			32.9
M4	=	M4 private sector holdings of:	
		notes and coin	27.6
	+	banks' retail deposits	485.3
	+	building societies' shares and deposits	124.6
	+	other interest bearing deposits (including Certificates of Deposit)	281.3
			918.8

2 THE FLOW OF FUNDS AND FINANCIAL INTERMEDIATION 11/01

The flow of funds

2.1 The flow of funds describes the movement of funds or money between one group of people or institutions in the economic system and other groups.

If we begin by ignoring imports and exports and foreign investments, we can start to build up a picture of the flow of funds by identifying three sectors in the economy.

(a) The **personal sector** - mainly individuals or households

(b) The **business sector** (or industrial and commercial sector) - ie companies and other businesses

(c) The **government sector** - ie central government, local government and public corporations

2.2 Within each of these three sectors, there is a continual movement of funds.

(a) Individuals will give money or lend money to other individuals.

(b) Companies will buy goods and services from other companies, and may occasionally lend money direct to other companies.

(c) Central government will provide funds for local government authorities and loss-making nationalised industries.

2.3 As well as movements of funds within each sector, there is also a flow of funds between different sectors of the economy.

2.4 These flows of funds can be shown in a diagram.

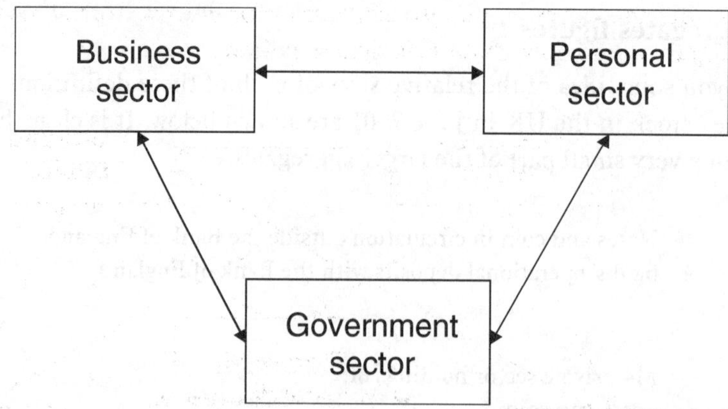

Flow of funds ignoring financial intermediation

2.5 But reality is not quite so simple, and our analysis of the flow of funds in the UK has to take account of two other main factors.

(a) The **overseas sector** comprises businesses, individuals and governments in other countries. The UK economy is influenced by trade with the foreign sector and flows of capital both from and to it.

(b) **Financial intermediaries**

2.6 An intermediary is a go-between, and a financial intermediary is an institution which **links lenders with borrowers,** by obtaining deposits from lenders and then re-lending them to borrowers. They can, for example, provide a link between savers and investors.

KEY TERM

The role of **financial intermediaries** such as banks and building societies in an economy is to provide means by which funds can be transferred from **surplus units** in the economy to **deficit units**. Financial intermediaries develop the facilities and **financial instruments** which make lending and borrowing possible.

2.7 **Intermediation**

If no financial intermediation takes place, lending and borrowing will be direct.

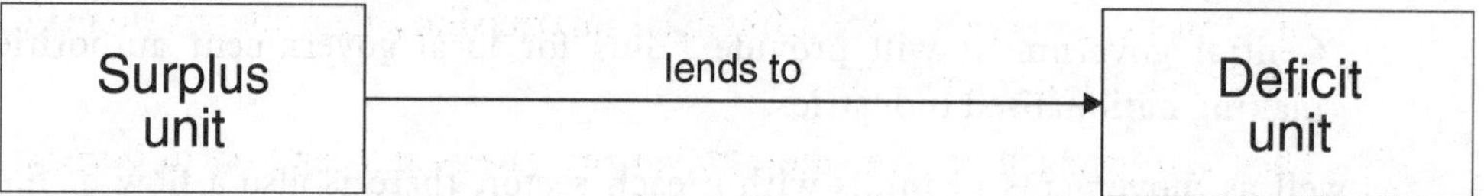

If financial intermediation does take place, the intermediary provides a service to both the surplus unit and the deficit unit.

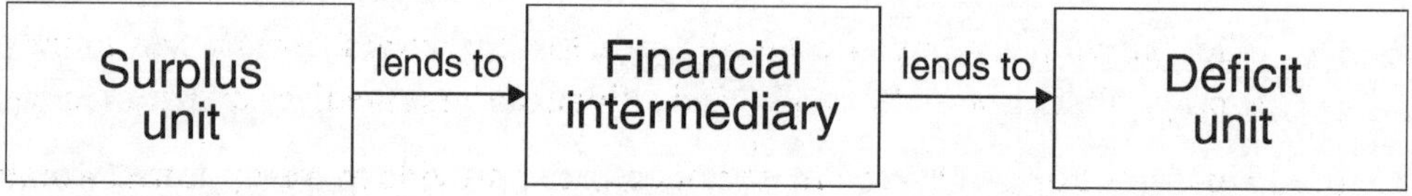

For example, a person might deposit savings with a bank, and the bank might use it collective deposits of savings to provide a loan to a company.

2.8 Financial intermediaries might also lend abroad or borrow from abroad, and a fuller version of the diagram of the flow of funds is thus as follows.

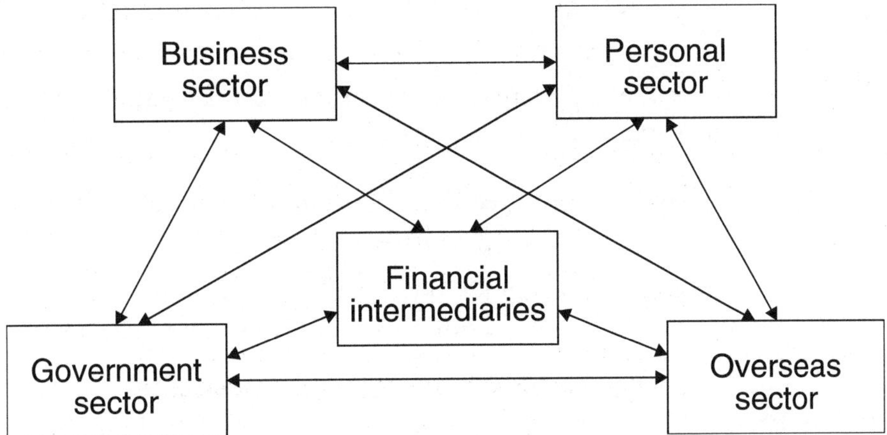

Flow of funds in an open economy, showing the role of financial intermediation

Financial intermediaries

2.9 **UK financial intermediaries**

(a) Banks

(b) Building societies

(c) Insurance companies, pension funds, unit trust companies and investment trust companies.

2.10 In spite of competition from building societies, insurance companies and other financial institutions, banks arguably remain the major financial intermediaries in the UK.

(a) The clearing banks are the biggest operators in the retail banking market, although competition from the building societies has been growing in the UK.

(b) There is greater competition between different banks (overseas banks and the clearing banks especially) for business in the wholesale lending market.

2.11 **Benefits of financial intermediation**

(a) Financial intermediaries provide obvious and convenient ways in which a lender can **save money**. Instead of having to find a suitable borrower for his money, the lender can deposit his money with a financial intermediary that offers a financial instrument to suit his requirements.

(b) They can package up the amounts lent by savers and lend on to borrowers in bigger amounts (a process called **aggregation**).

(c) Provided that the financial intermediary is itself financially sound, **the lender's capital is secure**. Bad debts would be borne by the financial intermediary in its re-lending operations.

(d) They provide a **ready source of funds for borrowers**. Even when money is in short supply, a borrower will usually find a financial intermediary prepared to lend some.

(e) Financial intermediaries, most importantly, provide **maturity transformation**; ie they bridge the gap between the wish of most lenders for liquidity and the desire of most borrowers for loans over longer periods. They do this by providing investors with financial instruments which are liquid enough for the investors' needs and by providing funds to borrowers in a different longer term form.

Credit

2.12 Credit for the purpose of this chapter and the next concerns **lending and borrowing money**, rather than with buying goods on **trade** credit.

2.13 The functions of credit can be seen from the point of view either of the borrower or the lender.

(a) For the borrower, the reason for borrowing money is to be able to purchase goods or services now that he might not otherwise be able to afford. The borrower wants to buy now and pay later.

(b) For the lender, the reason for lending money is that there is nothing that he now particularly wants to spend his money on, and by lending it, he can earn some interest.

2.14 The borrower can be described as a **deficit unit** with not enough money to buy all the goods and services he wants. The lender can be described as a **surplus unit** with more money at the moment than he needs to spend. **Credit involves the transfer of money from a surplus unit to a deficit unit, in return for a promise to pay interest.**

Sources of credit for business

2.15 Credit for businesses comes from a variety of sources, including the following.

Short-term	*Medium-term (say 1 - 5 years)*	*Long-term (over 5 years or so)*
Bank overdraft	Bank loans	Debentures
Trade credit	Hire purchase credit	Mortgage loans
Other creditors	Finance leases	Eurobond loans
Bills of exchange payable	Foreign currency loans (eurocurrency loans)	Other loan stock
		Bank loans

(a) **Trade credit** is credit from suppliers in the normal course of trade. Creditors may allow 30 days, 60 days or even longer for payment of invoices.

(b) **Other creditors** are creditors for items such as taxation payments due to the Inland Revenue or Customs and Excise, or rent and rates payable.

(c) **Hire purchase and instalment credit.** A firm might purchase fixed assets under a hire purchase arrangement, whereby the supplier is paid over several months or years in instalments.

(d) **Lease finance.** A firm might arrange to lease a fixed asset, instead of buying it. With a finance lease, the asset is bought by a leasing company (a lessor) who then leases the asset to the firm (the lessee) for most or all of the asset's useful life. The lease payments eventually cover the cost of the asset plus interest for the lessor.

(e) **Foreign currency loans.** Firms can obtain medium-term or short-term loans in foreign currency from a bank in their own country. This is known as a eurocurrency loan.

(f) **Debentures and other loan stock.** Debentures are long-term loans, the terms of which are set out in a debenture trust deed. Debentures issued by large companies are traded on the stock market.

(g) **Eurobonds.** Very large firms can raise loans on a worldwide market in the form of an issue of eurobonds, which are issued in foreign markets and sold internationally.

2.16 Credit helps to finance assets, and a firm will try to obtain credit to help with financing its business.

(a) Short-term credit is seen as a way of helping to finance current assets, but to make sure that it retains sufficient liquidity to pay its debts on time, a firm should keep its **current ratio** (ratio of current assets to current liabilities) at a sufficiently high level. All businesses have some short-term credit.

(b) Medium-term credit and long-term credit ought to be used to finance **fixed assets**.

(c) Much medium-term and long-term credit (and some bank overdrafts) is secured; that is, the bank or other lenders will receive some security for the loan.

2.17 Long-term debts and preference share capital together are known as **prior charge capital**, because debt interest charges and preference share dividends are prior charges on a company's profits, before any profits left over are attributable to shareholders. The ratio of a company's prior charge capital to its total capital is its **gearing** level, and a company should not allow its gearing level to become too high. This would be a sign that it is getting too heavily into debt.

The structure of a firm's credit

2.18 Credit may be short-term, medium-term or long-term. The length of credit ought to match the life of the assets they finance, and should not exceed the asset's life.

(a) The amount of short-term credit taken by a firm should be limited by considerations of liquidity. The firm must have the cash to pay creditors on time, and so short-term credit should not become excessive in relation to current assets, which are short-term sources of cash.

(b) The amount of long-term credit is effectively measured by the gearing ratio, which should remain at an acceptable level.

Banks and credit

2.19 Banks are major providers of credit. Banks create money when they give credit (see chapter 12), and so bank lending has two aspects which are important for the economy.

- The growth of credit and hence expenditure in the economy
- Increases in the money supply

2.20 Banks lend money that has been deposited with them by customers. A bank is really only a go-between or intermediary between the initial lender and the ultimate borrower. To understand the role of financial intermediaries such as banks, it will help to look at the concept of the flow of funds within an economy.

3 RATES OF INTEREST

3.1 Credit is a scarce commodity, priced through **interest rates**. Although there are many different interest rates in an economy, including building society mortgage rates, banks' base rates and yields on gilt-edged securities, they tend to move up or down together.

(a) If some interest rates go up, for example the banks' base rates, it is quite likely that other interest rates will move up too, if they have not gone up already.

(b) Similarly, if some interest rates go down, other interest rates will move down too.

It is the general level of interest rates, but short-term interest rates in particular, that the government might try to influence.

The term structure of interest rates

3.2 The structure of interest rates refers to the many different interest rates that there are. These various interest rates can be grouped into three broad classes, according to the length of time until the associated debts reach maturity.

- Short-term interest rates
- Medium-term interest rates
- Long-term interest rates

3.3 **Longer term financial assets should in general offer a higher yield than short-term lending.**

(a) The investor must be compensated for tying up his money in the asset for a longer period of time. If the government were to make two issues of 9% Treasury Stock on the same date, one with a term of five years and one with a term of 20 years (and if there were no expectations of changes in interest rates in the future) then the **liquidity preference** of investors would make them prefer the five year stock.

(b) The only way to overcome the liquidity preference of investors is to compensate them for the loss of liquidity; in other words, to offer a higher rate of interest on longer dated stock.

(c) There is a greater **risk** in lending longer term than shorter term for two reasons.

(i) **Inflation**. The longer the term of the asset, the greater is the possibility that the rate of inflation will increase, so that the fixed rate of interest paid on the asset will be overtaken by interest yields on new lending now that inflation is higher.

(ii) **Uncertain economic prospects**. The future state of the economy cannot be predicted with certainty. If an organisation wishes to borrow money now for, say, 15 years, there is no certainty about what might happen to that organisation during that time. It might thrive and prosper or it might run into economic difficulties for one reason or another.

Investors will require a higher return to compensate them for the increased risk.

(d) Note, however, that 2 other factors also affect the cost of borrowing.

(i) The risk associated with the perceived ability of the borrower to fulfil the terms of the loan.

(ii) Whether to not the loan is secured by a mortgage on an asset.

This is covered in more detail later in this chapter.

Yield curve

3.4 A yield curve shows the relationship between interest rates on similar assets with different terms to maturity. A normal yield curve will be upward-sloping, as shown in Figure 1, because of the higher interest rates which are likely to apply to longer terms of lending for the reasons explained in the previous paragraph.

Exam focus point

In the exam, you would not be expected to do more than to state what a yield curve is and what it shows: more detailed knowledge is not expected.

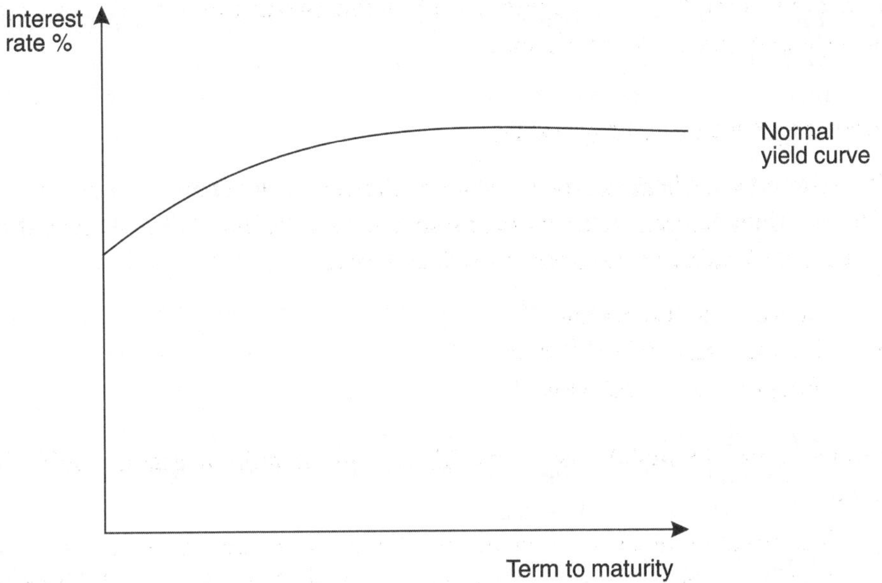

Figure 1 Yield curve

Nominal and real rates of interest 5/01

3.5 **Nominal rates of interest are rates expressed in money terms**. For example, if interest paid per annum on a loan of £1,000 is £150, the rate of interest would be 15%. The nominal rate of interest might also be referred to as the **money rate of interest**, or the **actual money yield** on an investment.

3.6 Real rates of interest are the rates of return that investors get from their investment, adjusted for the rate of inflation. The real rate of interest is therefore a measure of the increase in the real wealth, expressed in terms of buying power, of the investor or lender. Real rates of interest are lower than nominal rates when there is price inflation. For example, if the nominal rate of interest is 12% per annum and the annual rate of inflation is 8% per annum, the real rate of interest is the interest earned after allowing for the return needed just to keep pace with inflation.

3.7 The relationship between the inflation rate, the real rate of interest and the money rate of interest is:

1+ real rate of interest x 1+ inflation rate = 1+ money rate of interest.

We may rearrange this to find the real rate of interest in the example above.

$$\frac{1 + \text{money rate}}{1 + \text{inflation rate}} = 1 + \text{real rate}$$

$$\frac{1.12}{1.08} = 1.037$$

The real rate of interest is thus 3.7%.

The real rate of interest is commonly measured approximately, however, as the difference between the nominal rate of interest and the rate of inflation. In our example, this would be 12% – 8% = 4%.

Variations in the general level of interest rates over time

3.8 Interest rates on any one type of financial asset will vary over time. In other words, the general level of interest rates might go up or down. The general level of interest rates is affected by several factors.

(a) **The need for a real return.** It is generally accepted that investors will want to earn a 'real' rate of return on their investment, that is, a return which exceeds the rate of inflation. The suitable real rate of return will depend on factors such as investment risk.

(b) **Uncertainty about future rates of inflation.** When investors are uncertain about what future nominal and real interest rates will be, they are likely to require higher interest yields to persuade them to take the risk of investing, especially in the longer term.

(c) **Changes in the level of government borrowing.** When the demand for credit increases, interest rates will go up. A high level of borrowing by the government, is likely to result in upward pressure on interest rates.

(d) **Higher demand for borrowing from individuals.** If individuals want to borrow more, for example because they feel confident about their level of future earnings, then interest rates will tend to rise.

(e) **Monetary policy.** Governments control the level of investment rates in order to control inflation (see Chapter 13).

(f) **Interest rates abroad.** An appropriate real rate of interest in one country will be influenced by external factors, such as interest rates in other countries and expectations about the exchange rate.

Interest rate on loans

3.9 The influences affecting interest rates in general will play a background part in determining the rate of interest for a particular loan. The main emphasis will be on specific factors concerning the nature of the borrowing and the status of the borrower.

3.10 The fundamental consideration in any lending decision is **risk**. The more **speculative** any borrowing proposal is believed to be, the higher will be the rate of interest. The lender is concerned not only with recovering the capital sum on the due maturity date, but also with earning a return on the money lent over the period of the loan. The time period of lending influences risk: the longer the time period, the greater is uncertainty about the ability of the borrower to repay the loan or as to the erosion in the value of money by inflation.

3.11 Borrowers and lenders will both take into account real interest rates. Consideration as to **future inflation levels** will therefore help determine the nominal rate of interest.

3.12 The status of the borrower will influence perceived risk. Those with a higher credit rating and moderate financial gearing will be granted more favourable borrowing terms and therefore relatively lower interest rates than those with a poor financial record. Whether a borrower can offer security for a loan and the quality of that security will be important: the better the collateral, the lower the rate of interest.

3.13 From both parties' points of view, but particularly that of the lender, the type of any asset purchased by the loan is important: is the security non-marketable on the one hand, or is it either marketable or redeemable on the other? In the latter case, there is possible escape from the financial commitment and risk, and means of adjustment to changed conditions. The more marketable/redeemable a security, the lower the interest rate.

3.14 The amount of any proposed loan will also be of some importance. Larger individual amounts will be less costly for a borrower to administer and this may be reflected in a marginally higher rate of interest on offer.

3.15 A lender will also be concerned in some instances with the purpose of any loan and the competence of the borrower in use of the funds. The reputation of a financial institution may be jeopardised by ill-considered lending which subsequently is adversely publicised. The greater the risk in this regard is considered to be, the higher will be the rate of interest.

Chapter roundup

- Money oils the wheels of an economy and helps it to function more smoothly. Its main function is as a means of exchange.
- A second important function of money is to provide a liquid store of value - ie a means of saving and preserving wealth. Inflation can undermine this function, because money loses 'real' exchange value when there is price inflation, and it cannot buy as many goods as before.
- Money can be defined in different 'narrow' or 'broad' ways, depending on what financial assets are considered to be money.
- Within an economy, some people, firms and organisations will have money which is surplus to their needs, and others will have less money than they need for their spending requirements. Credit involves lending money, and the transfer (usually in return for interest payments) of money from surplus units to deficit units. Financial intermediaries, such as banks and building societies, make the provision of credit much easier, by taking deposits from savers and re-lending to borrowers.
- In practice, there is a variety of interest rates. To make a profit, institutions that borrow money to re-lend, or that accept deposits which they re-lend (eg banks) must pay lower interest on deposits than they charge to customers who borrow.

Quick quiz

1 What are the main functions of money?

2 What is a liquid asset?

3 Distinguish narrow money and broad money.

4 How does inflation affect the way money performs its functions?

5 List the main sources of credit available to businesses.

6 What is meant by 'maturity transformation'?

7 What are the main factors influencing the general level of interest rates? (3.8)

8 Which combination of demand and supply curves would be appropriate for a firm attempting to increase its profits by increasing its market share?

A Inelastic demand, inelastic supply
B Elastic demand, elastic supply
C Elastic demand, elastic supply
D Elastic demand, inelastic supply

9 The functions of commercial financial intermediaries include all the following except:

A Maturity transformation
B Reduction of transactions costs
C Aggregation
D Gilt issuing

10 What are the functions of money?

Match the descriptions with the functions.

(i) Means of exchange
(ii) Unit of account
(iii) Standard of deferred payment
(iv) Store of value

A Establishes the value of a contract for future settlement
B An alternative to barter
C A liquid asset which can be held for the purpose of exchange
D a measure of value in goods and services

Answers to quick quiz

1. Means of exchange
   Unit of account
   Standard of deferred payment
   Store of value

2. A liquid asset is one which can be transformed into another form without delay or loss of value.

3. Narrow money is highly liquid and may be used immediately for transactions. Broad money assets include narrow money but not all are as liquid as narrow money. It includes assets held as savings but which can be converted into liquid money easily and without capital loss.

4. Inflation erodes the purchasing power of money over time. As a result, money cannot be a satisfactory store of wealth or standard for deferred payment since it loses its value as time passes. Similarly, it cannot be a stable unit of account since individual goods do not rise in price by the same percentage amount. Its acceptability as a means of exchange is undermined by higher rates of inflation since under hyperinflation no one knows what it is worth at any given moment. As a result people turn to barter, foreign currency or commodity money such as cigarettes.

5. Short term credit may be had in the form of overdraft, trade credit and the issue of bills of exchange. Medium term credit often takes the form of term loans from banks, hire purchase and finance leases. Longer term credit may be obtained by issuing debentures and mortgages.

6. Financial intermediaries accept sight deposits but make term loans. They thus convert the immediate maturity of their own short term borrowings into loan assets which will mature at some more distant future time.

7. Interest rates generally are determined by the rate at which the central bank borrows. Banks will generally charge rather more than this. The structure of interest rates is then determined by two things.

   - Longer term loans are riskier than short term loans because of the greater uncertainty about inflation and the likelihood of recovery associated with the more distant future. They therefore attract higher interest rates.
   - Loans which are secured on property are less risky than unsecured loans. They are therefore cheaper.

8. B To increase market share requires greater quantities both demanded and supplied. To sell more, a firm needs to lower price. For this to be profitable, demand must be elastic. To produce more, supply must also be elastic.

9. D This is a function of the Bank of England.

10. 1 B Without money, trade would depend on matching providers and users of goods and services in complex chains.
    2 D A consistent measure of value makes exchange easier to arrange.
    3 A To fulfil this function, money must maintain its value over time.
    4 C Other stores of value vary in their liquidity and the ultimate value they will realise in money terms.

Now try the questions below from the Question Bank

Number	Level	Marks	Time
Q31	Introductory	11	15 mins
Q32	Exam - MCQ	2	–
Q33	Exam - MCQ	2	–

Chapter 12

FINANCIAL INSTITUTIONS AND SOURCES OF FINANCE

Topic list		Syllabus reference	Ability required
1	Credit creation and the banking system	(iii)	Comprehension
2	Capital markets and money markets	(iii)	Comprehension
3	Sources of capital for companies	(iii)	Comprehension

Introduction

In this chapter, we look at aspects of the institutional framework of finance.

This chapter gives a number of examples which refer to the UK banking system. This is for convenience only; the same principles apply to the banking systems of other countries.

Learning outcomes covered in this chapter

- Identify the main elements of the monetary and financial system
- Explain the importance of the monetary environment to the business sector

Syllabus content covered in this chapter

- The monetary environment: inflation and the money supply; the banking and financial system; interest rates and monetary policy

1 CREDIT CREATION AND THE BANKING SYSTEM

The banks and the banking system

1.1 There are different types of banks which operate within a banking system, and you will probably have come across a number of terms which describe them.

(a) **Clearing banks** operate the clearing system for settling payments (eg payments by cheque by bank customers).

(b) The term **retail banks** is used to describe the traditional High Street banks. The term **wholesale banks** refers to banks which specialise in lending in large quantities to major customers. The clearing banks are involved in both retail and wholesale banking but are commonly regarded as the main retail banks.

(c) **Merchant banks** offer services, often of a specialised nature, to corporate customers.

(d) **Commercial banks** make commercial banking transactions with customers. They are distinct from the country's central bank.

Question 1

In the balance sheet of a retail bank, which one of the following items do you think would constitute the largest asset?

(a) Customers' overdrafts and bank loans
(b) Customers' deposits
(c) Land and buildings

Answer

The answer is (a). Item (b) is not an asset of the bank - it is a liability (a sum of money owed by the bank to its customers). It might be tempting to choose item (c), if you think about the large number of High Street sites owned by the retail banks, but in fact the value of this asset is dwarfed by the financial assets of the banks.

The functions of the commercial banks

1.2 **Main functions of the commercial banks.**

(a) **Providing a payments mechanism**. The clearing system is the major payments mechanism in the UK, and it enables individuals and firms to make payments by cheque. The banks are also a source from which individuals and firms can obtain notes and coin.

(b) **Providing a place for individuals, firms and government to store their wealth.** Banks compete with other financial institutions to attract the funds of individuals and firms.

(c) **Lending money** in the form of loans or overdrafts.

(d) **Acting as financial intermediaries** by accepting deposits and lending, and in doing so transforming the risk characteristics and maturity characteristics of the lending.

(e) **Providing customers with a means of obtaining foreign currency, or selling foreign currency**, whenever they require it. Banks play a central role in the foreign exchange markets.

1.3 The banks also provide a wide range of other **commercial services** to customers.

(a) Advising and assisting companies, for example advising firms in a takeover bid and assisting companies to issue shares on the stock market.

(b) Providing assistance to exporters and importers, for example helping exporters to obtain payment from buyers abroad, and helping importers to pay for goods they buy from foreign suppliers

(c) Leasing

(d) Debt factoring services

(e) Executorship and trustee services

(f) Acting as insurance brokers for insurance companies by selling some insurance policies

(g) Selling insurance policies of their own, notably life assurance policies

(h) Selling pensions

(i) Share registration and share dealing services

(j) Unit trust business

(k) Giving investment advice

1.4 Because banks are a major source of lending to firms and individuals, they play a crucial role in the monetary aspects of a country's economy. The government's monetary policy will therefore be concerned with what the banks are doing, and with trying to influence or to control the banks' lending activities, interest rates and the creation of credit. The government will use the central bank to help it to influence the activities of the commercial banks.

Credit creation

KEY TERM

The **bank multiplier** or **credit multiplier** is the name given to banks' ability to create credit, and hence money, by maintaining their cash reserves at less than 100% of the value of their deposits.

1.5 When someone deposits money in a bank, the banks are able as a result to 'create' credit of a much greater magnitude than the amount of money originally deposited.

1.6 Suppose, for example, that in a country with a single bank, customer deposits total £100,000. The bank, we will assume, re-lends all these deposits to other customers. The customers will use the money they have borrowed to buy goods and services and they will pay various firms and individuals for these purchases. If the firms and individuals receiving payment then put the money into their own accounts with the bank, the **bank's deposits will have doubled**.

1.7 It is this fact **that most additions to bank lending end up as money in someone's bank account,** adding to total customer deposits with the banks, that give banks this special **ability to create credit**. This is an ability that is also shared in the UK by building societies, since building society deposits are included in definitions of the money supply (M2 and M4).

1.8 Illustrating the process with some figures may be helpful. We shall assume for simplicity that there is only one bank in the banking system, and that all money lent by the bank is re-deposited by various customers.

1.9 A customer depositing £1,000 in cash with the bank **creates an asset**, in the sense that the bank, in return for the deposit, gives the customer a promise to pay on demand, or subject to notice, the £1,000 deposited. The promise is, of course, an account opened under the name of the client. To the bank, the deposit is a **liability**. However, the deposit provides funds for the bank to acquire **assets**. We shall begin by assuming that the bank holds these assets entirely in the form of cash.

1.10 If the bank keeps the full £1,000 and does nothing with it, then it would simply operate as a 'cloakroom' in which the client's money is deposited. However, if the bank believes that the client is unlikely to claim the full £1,000 for some time, there will be some incentive to use the money rather than to keep it idle. One possibility would be to lend it; the bank would be taking a risk that it will not have the cash when its customer wants to have it back, but at the same time it would expect to make a profit by charging interest on the sum of money so lent.

1.11 On one hand the deposit of the £1,000 creates the opportunity for the bank to make a profit in the form of the interest that it can charge on the money it lends (the incentive being all the stronger if the bank is paying interest on the deposits it accepts), but on the other hand there is a risk that when the money is out on loan the client may claim it back. The bank will then be unable to meet its obligation to repay the cash to the client unless it can recall the loan instantly, which is unlikely.

1.12 As long as the bank feels that the likelihood is small that its depositors will demand a substantial proportion of their deposits in cash, then it faces an acceptable risk in lending some of the money. In other words, the bank strikes a balance between the desire to play safe by holding the cash and the desire to make profits by lending.

1.13 In the example in the table below, it is assumed that the bank has decided on the basis of past experience and observation to keep 50 pence in cash for every £1 deposited, and then lend out the other 50 pence. In other words, the bank in this example is operating a **50% cash ratio**. At step (1) below, the bank has £1,000 in cash. This is enough to support total liabilities of £2,000 and maintain a 50% cash ratio. If the bank now lends £1,000, and if all of that £1,000 is then spent by the borrowers but ends up back with the bank as deposits of other customers, the new situation for the bank will be as in (2) below.

Bank's liabilities (= customer deposits)	*Bank's assets (= cash or loans to customers)*
(1) £1,000 deposits	£1,000 cash
(2) £2,000 deposits	£1,000 cash £1,000 loans

The bank has doubled the money supply.

The credit multiplier

1.14 If at any stage the bank decided that the 50% cash ratio was too conservative and reduced it to 25%, then for £1,000 cash deposited with the bank, deposits could be expanded fourfold. It is important to understand that banks in the process of lending are also potentially creating money because clients either borrowing or receiving the proceeds of borrowers' expenditure can use their deposits to make money transactions. In a modern economy most money transactions are by cheque or other bank transfer such as direct debits or standing order, thus transferring bank deposits from person to person or from firm to firm. Consumers and producers thus use the liabilities of a private institution as money.

1.15 The fact that banks do not need to keep a 100% cash reserve ratio automatically implies that they have the capacity to create money out of nothing. The size of this credit expansion depends primarily on the size of their cash reserve ratio.

1.16 We can summarise the quantitative side of credit creation in banks as follows:

$$\text{Deposits} = \frac{\text{Cash}}{\text{Cash ratio}} \quad \text{or} \quad D = \frac{c}{r}$$

The smaller the cash ratio or **credit multiplier**, the bigger the size of the deposits that a given amount of cash will be able to support and hence the larger the money supply.

1.17 This theoretical description of the credit multiplier applies only to some extent in practice. If a bank decides to keep a cash reserve ratio of 10%, and it receives additional deposits of

£1,000, the total increase in bank deposits will not be £1,000 ÷ 10% = £10,000, but considerably less than this.

Question 2

Suppose that all the commercial banks in an economy operated on a cash reserve ratio of 20%. How much cash would have to flow into the banks for the money supply to increase by £80 million?

Answer

Call the extra cash £C. Then:

$$\frac{C}{20\%} = 80 + C$$

$$C = 20\% \times (80 + C)$$

$$0.8C = 16$$

$$C = £20 \text{ million}$$

If an extra £20 million is deposited, the total money supply will rise to £20 million ÷ 20% = £100 million. This includes the initial £20 million, so the increase is £80 million.

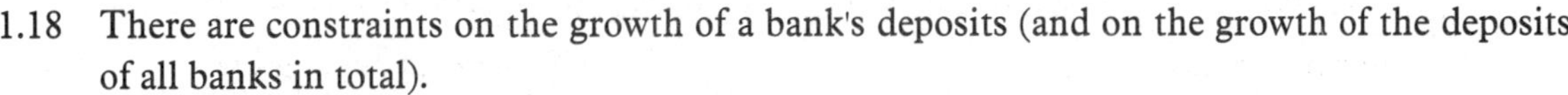

1.18 There are constraints on the growth of a bank's deposits (and on the growth of the deposits of all banks in total).

- Cash leaks out of the banking system into less formal accumulations.
- Customers might not want to borrow at the interest rates the bank would charge.
- Banks should not lend to high-risk customers without good security.

1.19 A **cash ratio** or similar **fractional reserve system** might be imposed on banks by the government. Until 1971, a mandatory cash ratio of 8% was applied to the London clearing banks. Between 1971 and 1981 banks were required to maintain 12½% reserve asset ratio requirement. Although not intended as a direct monetary control (on credit growth), in effect it applied a credit multiplier limit of 8 - ie every initial £1 increase in bank deposits would result in up to £8 more in deposits. Since 1981, the Bank of England has supervised the liquidity and capital structure of banks, but an 'official' minimum reserve asset ratio requirement has not been applied.

Liquidity, profitability and security: aims of the banks

1.20 A commercial bank has three different and potentially conflicting aims which it must try to keep in balance. These are as follows.

(a) **Profitability.** A bank must make a profit for its shareholders. The biggest profits come from lending at higher interest rates. These are obtained with long-term lending and lending to higher risk customers.

(b) **Liquidity**. A bank must have some liquid assets. It needs notes and coin (till money) to meet demands from depositors for cash withdrawals. It also needs to be able to settle debts with other banks. For example, if on a particular day, customers of the Midland Bank make payments by cheque to customers of Lloyds totalling £200 millions, and customers of Lloyds Bank make payments by cheque to customers of the Midland totalling £170 millions, the Midland will be expected to pay Lloyds £30 million to settle the net value of transactions. This is done by transferring funds between the bank accounts of the Midland and Lloyds, which they keep with the Bank of England (as 'operational deposits'). A bank might also need to have some 'near liquid' assets which it can turn into liquid assets quickly, should it find itself with a need for more liquidity. Near-liquid assets earn relatively little interest. A bank will try to keep the quantity of such assets it holds to a safe minimum.

(c) **Security**. People deposit their money with banks because they are regarded as stable and secure institutions. A bank might lend to some high-risk customers, and suffer some bad debts, but on the whole, a bank will be expected to lend wisely and securely, with a strong likelihood that the loans will be repaid in full and with interest. If it did not, people might put their money somewhere else instead, not with the bank. This is why banks usually give careful consideration to the reliability of the borrower. Often, in doubtful cases, they will ask for security for a loan or overdraft. Security means that in the event of a default on loan repayments by the borrower, the bank can realise the security by selling the secured asset or assets and using the sale proceeds to pay off the debt.

Assets and liabilities of commercial banks

1.21 The distribution of assets for all UK commercial banks aggregated together is summarised in the table below.

UK commercial banks' assets, May 1993

	%
Cash	0.5
Balance with Bank of England	0.2
Market loans	24.0
Bills of exchange	1.8
Investments	6.7
Advances	62.0
Miscellaneous	4.8
	100.0

1.22 The triple aspects of bank lending - profitability, liquidity, and security - are evident in a commercial bank's **asset structure**.

(a) About 0.5% to 2% or so of a retail bank's assets might be till money (notes and coin) and deposits with the Bank of England. Most of these assets are held to meet the need for immediate liquidity, and earn no interest.

(b) Some assets are 'near-liquid' which means that they can quickly be converted into liquid deposits.

(i) The most important near-liquid assets are loans to the money markets and other money market securities.

(ii) Other near-liquid assets are bills, mainly eligible bank bills. Bills are short- term debt instruments. Eligible bills are bills of exchange that the Bank of England would be prepared to buy when the banking system is short of money. Most eligible bills are issued by top-class banks who are granted eligible status by the Bank of England.

(iii) Banks also hold some gilt-edged securities, mainly British government stocks. These can be sold on the stock market should a bank wish to obtain immediate liquid funds, but often, banks will buy gilts on the stock market with a fairly short term to maturity, and then hold them until they mature and the government redeems the debt.

Near-liquid assets - market loans, bills of exchange and **gilt-edged security investments** - might represent around 25% to 30% of a retail bank's assets.

(c) The biggest returns are earned by banks on their longer term **illiquid assets** - ie their overdrafts and bank loans to customers. Advances to customers are the biggest proportion of a retail bank's assets (over 70%) and the rate of interest on the loans varies according to the perceived risk of the customer as well as current interest rates.

(d) Banks' assets include the normal type of fixed assets found in any large organisation - eg property and equipment. However, the value of these operational assets is small in relation to the size of loans, even for the big clearing banks.

1.23 **Sterling sight and time deposits** of the retail banks account for most of their **liabilities**. Most sterling deposits are provided by the UK private sector (individuals and firms). **Other currency deposits** are the other main type of liability, consisting of deposits held by customers of UK banks in US dollars, deutschmarks and so on. In the UK there are no exchange control regulations currently in operation, and so private individuals as well as commercial firms and financial institutions are allowed to maintain foreign currency accounts. The bulk of other currency deposits, however, are held by overseas customers of UK banks.

Building societies

1.24 The building societies of the UK are **mutual** organisations whose main assets are mortgages of their members, and whose main liabilities are to the investor members who hold savings accounts with the society. The building societies are supervised by a special Building Societies Commission, while UK banks are supervised by the Bank of England.

1.25 Building societies are allowed to provide certain limited banking services, such as personal lending to customers for purposes other than house buying. Some building societies now offer cheque book accounts, cash cards and many other facilities that compete directly with the banks. The distinction between building societies and banks has become increasingly blurred, as the societies have taken to providing a range of services formerly the province mainly of banks, and banks have themselves made inroads into the housing mortgage market.

1.26 The growing similarity between banks and building societies is recognised by the inclusion of building society deposits in the broader monetary aggregate M4. The building society sector has shrunk in size as a number of the major societies have either converted to public limited companies and therefore become banks or have been taken over by banks or other financial institutions.

The central bank

Exam focus point

The examiner has stated that, where possible, references to institutions will be to generic types (eg central banks) rather than to particular national institutions. You might be able to make use of your knowledge of institutions in any country in answering questions.

1.27 A central bank is a bank which acts on behalf of the government. The central bank for the UK is the Bank of England. The Bank of England ('the Bank') is a nationalised corporation run by a Court of Directors, consisting of the Governor, Deputy Governor, and some Executive Directors and part-time Directors.

1.28 Functions of the Bank of England.

(a) It acts as **banker to the central government** and holds the 'public deposits'. Public deposits include the National Loans Fund, the Consolidated Fund and the account of the Paymaster General, which in turn includes the Exchange Equalisation Account.

(b) It is the **central note-issuing authority** in the UK - it is responsible for issuing bank notes in England.

(c) It is the **manager of the National Debt** - ie it deals with long-term and short-term borrowing by the central government and the repayment of central government debt.

(d) It is the manager of the Exchange Equalisation Account (ie the UK's **foreign currency reserves**).

(e) It acts as advisor to the government on **monetary policy**.

(f) It acts as agent for the government in carrying out its monetary policies. Since May 1997, it has had operational responsibility for **setting interest rates** at the level it considers appropriate in order to meet the government's inflation target.

(g) It acts as a **banker to the commercial banks**. The commercial banks keep a bank account with the Bank of England.

(h) It acts as a **lender to the banking system**. When the banking system is short of money, the Bank of England will provide the money the banks need - at a suitable rate of interest.

Supervision of the banking system has been transferred to the Financial Services Authority

The Bank as lender of last resort to the commercial banking system

1.29 In the UK, the short-term money market provides a link between the banking system and the government (Bank of England) whereby the Bank of England lends money to the banking system, when banks which need cash cannot get it from anywhere else.

(a) The Bank will supply cash to the banking system on days when the banks have a cash shortage. It does this by buying eligible bills and other short-term financial investments from approved financial institutions in exchange for cash.

(b) The Bank will remove excess cash from the banking system on days when the banks have a cash surplus. It does this by selling bills to institutions, so that the short-term money markets obtain interest-bearing bills in place of the cash that they do not want.

1.30 The process whereby this is done currently is known as **open market operations** by the Bank. This simply describes the buying and selling of eligible bills and other short-term assets between the Bank and the short-term money market.

Open market operations and short-term interest rates

KEY TERM

Open market operations: the Bank of England's dealings in the capital market. The bank uses open market operations to control interest rates.

1.31 Open market operations provide the Bank of England with a method of control over short-term interest rates. They are thus an important feature of the government's monetary policy, which the Bank implements on its behalf.

1.32 When bills are bought and sold, they are traded at a discount to their face value, and there is an implied interest rate in the rate of discount obtained. Discounts on bills traded in open market operations have an immediate influence on other money market interest rates, such as the London Inter-Bank Offered Rate (LIBOR), and these in turn influence the 'benchmark' base rates of the major banks.

1.33 Because the eligible bills and other assets which the Bank of England acquires in its money market operations are short-term assets, a proportion mature each day. The market is then obliged to redeem these claims and must seek further refinancing from the bank. This continual turnover of assets gives the Bank of England the opportunity to determine the level of interest rates day by day.

The independence of the Bank of England

1.34 The Bank is an adviser to the government, but not an agent of the government. How much independence of action does the Bank have?

1.35 Proponents of **independence for central banks** argue that independence can prevent the worst government monetary excesses, which in some cases result in **hyperinflation**. High levels of existing public expenditure commitments combined with electoral pressures (along with other factors) build in strong underlying inflationary pressures. An independent central bank is seen as an essential counterweight to the potentially reckless decisions of politicians. As well as avoiding the worst excesses, a strong central bank is regarded as vital for the shorter term stability of domestic prices and of the currency, and so is important to overseas trade. Any government wishing to reduce an already high rate of inflation will, however, have to listen carefully to the advice of its central bank if it is to have any real success.

1.36 Those arguing against independence point out that the central bank is an unelected body and therefore does not have the open responsibility of politicians. Danger in this respect is minimised by the formal publication of decisions and recommendations of the central bank.

1.37 Further, it is claimed that central bank views on monetary policy could be in conflict with other economic objectives of the government. For example, excessively strict pursuit of monetary policy in order to pursue an inflation target might result in prolonged recession and heavy under-utilisation of resources.

1997 changes

1.38 In May 1997, the new Labour government of the UK announced important changes to the role of the UK central bank, the Bank of England. As already mentioned, the Chancellor of the Exchequer handed over to the Bank the power to set interest rates. Rates are set by a new Monetary Policy Committee including the Governor of the Bank, his two deputies and four outsiders, but no politicians. The Committee sets interest rates with the aim of meeting the inflation target set by government.

1.39 The 1997 changes do not make the Bank of England fully independent, as the UK government can still override the Bank in an emergency. The role of the Bank of England also falls short of that of many other central banks in that responsibility for setting inflation or monetary targets rests with government.

1.40 The most independent central bank of all looks likely to be the European Central Bank which is designed to be totally free of political interference. It came into existence at the end of 1998, ready for the European single currency.

2 CAPITAL MARKETS AND MONEY MARKETS 5/01

2.1 These are types of market for dealing in capital.

(a) **Capital markets** are financial markets for **raising** and **investing** largely long-term capital.

(b) **Money markets** are financial markets for lending and borrowing largely short-term capital.

2.2 What do we mean by **long-term** and **short-term** capital?

(a) By **short-term capital**, we mean capital that is lent or borrowed for a period which might range from as short as overnight up to about one year, and sometimes longer.

(b) By **long-term capital**, we mean capital invested or lent and borrowed for a period of about five years or more, but sometimes shorter.

(c) There is a **grey area** between long-term and short-term capital, which is lending and borrowing for a period from about 1-2 years up to about 5 years, which is not surprisingly referred to as **medium-term** capital.

Question 3

Try to think of some of the markets that firms can use to obtain finance. A number of them will be listed in the next few paragraphs.

2.3 **Firms** may obtain long-term or medium-term capital as share capital or as loan capital. Debentures, loan stock, bonds and commercial paper are all types of loan capital.

The Stock Exchange

2.4 The **London Stock Exchange** is an organised capital market based in London which plays an important role in the functioning of the UK economy. It is the main capital market in the UK.

(a) It makes it easier for large firms and the government to raise long-term capital, by providing a market place for borrowers and investors to come together.

(b) The Stock Exchange publicises the prices of quoted (or 'listed') securities, which are then reported in daily national newspapers such as the Financial Times. Investors can therefore keep an eye on the value of their stocks and shares, and make buying and selling decisions accordingly.

(c) The Stock Exchange tries to enforce certain rules of conduct for its listed firms and for operators in the market, so that investors have the assurance that companies whose shares are traded on the Exchange and traders who operate there are reputable. Confidence in the Stock Exchange will make investors more willing to put their money into stocks and shares.

2.5 The **Alternative Investment Market** (AIM), which opened in 1995, is a market where smaller companies which cannot meet the more stringent requirements needed to obtain a full listing on the Stock Exchange can raise new capital by issuing shares. Like the Stock Exchange main market, the AIM is also a market in which investors can trade in shares already issued. It is regulated by the Stock Exchange.

2.6 The price of shares on a stock market fluctuate up and down.

(a) The price of shares in a particular company might remain unchanged for quite a long time; alternatively, a company's share price might fluctuate continually throughout each day.

(b) The **general level** of share prices, as measured by share price indices such as the All-Share Index and the FT-SE 100 Index, may go up or down each minute of the day.

2.7 The indices of share prices on the Stock Exchange act as indicators of the state of **investor confidence** in the country's economy. For example, if investors believe that interest rates are too low to curb inflation, they may sell shares and move their funds to other countries, causing a decline in share prices.

Question 4

From your reading of business pages (which should be a central feature in anyone's study of economics) what factors have you noticed as having an influence on share prices?

Answer

Share prices respond to:

(a) factors related to the circumstances of individual companies - eg news of a company's annual profits, or a proposed takeover bid.

(b) factors related to the circumstances of a particular industry - eg new government legislation or regulations for an industry, such as new laws on pollution controls or customer protection measures.

(c) factors related to the circumstances of the national economy - eg changes in interest rates, the latest official figures for the balance of trade, or price inflation.

Exam focus point

You should be aware of the types of factors set out in the Exercise above, but detailed knowledge of theories of share price behaviour is not expected.

Over-the-counter markets

2.8 Shares and other financial instruments are also bought and sold outside the supervised and regulated official exchanges in the over-the-counter (OTC) markets. OTC market prices are negotiated rather than set by auction, as is the case in most stock exchanges. In the USA, OTC market prices are reported via the National Association of Securities Dealers Automatic Quotation System (NASDAQ). Most OTC trading deals with shares that are not quoted on any public stock exchange.

Day trading

2.9 Trading by individuals over the internet has grown enormously in the USA. No doubt this trend will spread to other countries in due course. Several UK stockbrokers have set up e-broking operations.

Banks

2.10 Banks can be approached directly by firms and individuals for medium-term and long-term loans as well as short-term loans or overdrafts. The major clearing banks, many merchant banks and foreign banks operating in the UK are increasingly willing to lend medium-term capital, especially to well established companies.

The gilt-edged market

2.11 The gilt-edged market is a further major capital market in the UK. The government borrows over the medium and longer term by issuing government stocks (called 'gilt-edged stock'). Trade in second hand gilts will continue until the debt eventually matures and the government redeems the stock. Gilts may be issued either by selling them direct to dealers, or by selling them to the Bank of England first, and then releasing them gradually ('on tap') to the market at a suitable time.

2.12 The primary gilts market is the market for the sale of new gilt issues. There is an active market in second-hand gilts with existing holders selling their holdings of gilts to other investors in the gilts market.

Providers of capital

2.13 The providers of capital include private individuals, such as those who buy stocks and shares on the Stock Exchange, and those who deposit money with banks, building societies and National Savings. (National Savings is a government institution set up to borrow on behalf of the government, mainly from the non-bank private sector of the economy. The National Savings Bank operates through Post Offices throughout the UK, so that individuals can deposit and withdraw savings with relative ease.)

2.14 There are also important groups of **institutional investors** which specialise in providing capital and act as financial intermediaries between suppliers and demanders of funds. Many financial services organisations now have diversified operations covering a range of the following activities.

(a) **Pension funds**. Pension funds invest the pension contributions of individuals who subscribe to a pension fund, and of organisations with a company pension fund.

(b) **Insurance**. Insurance companies invest premiums paid on insurance policies by policy holders. If you think about it, insurance companies, like pension funds, must do something with the premiums they receive, and in practice, they invest the money to earn a return.

(c) **Investment trusts**. The business of investment trust companies is investing in the stocks and shares of other companies and the government. In other words, they trade in investments.

(d) **Unit trusts**. Unit trusts are similar to investment trusts, in the sense that they invest in stocks and shares of other companies. A unit trust comprises a 'portfolio' - ie a holding of stocks or shares in a range of companies or gilts, perhaps with all the shares or stocks having a special characteristic, such as all shares in property companies or all shares in mining companies. The trust will then create a large number of small units of low nominal value, with each unit representing a stake in the total portfolio. These units are then sold to individual investors and investors will benefit from the income and capital gain on their units - ie their proportion of the portfolio.

(e) **Venture capital.** Venture capital providers are organisations that specialise in raising funds for new business ventures, such as 'management buy-outs' (ie purchases of firms by their management staff). These organisations are therefore providing capital for fairly risky ventures. A venture capital organisation that has operated for many years in the UK is Investors in Industry plc, usually known as '3i'. In recent years, many more venture capital organisations have been set up, for example by large financial institutions such as pension funds.

2.15 The role of financial intermediaries in capital markets is illustrated in the diagram below.

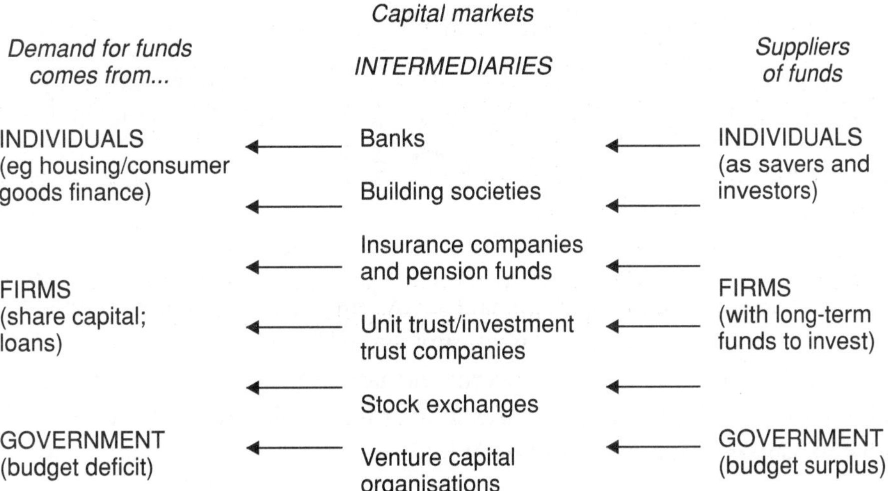

Changes in the capital markets

2.16 Recent years have seen very big changes in the capital markets of the world.

(a) **Globalisation of capital markets**

The capital markets of each country have become internationally integrated. Securities issued in one country can now be traded in capital markets around the world. For example, shares in many UK companies are traded in the USA. The shares are bought by US banks, which then issue ADRs (American depository receipts) which are a form in which foreign shares can be traded in US markets without a local listing.

(b) **Securitisation of debt**

Securitisation of debt means creating tradable securities which are backed by less liquid assets such as mortgages and other long term loans.

(c) **Risk management (and risk assessment)**

Various techniques have been developed for companies to manage their financial risk such as swaps and options. These 'derivative' financial instruments may allow transactions to take place off-balance sheet and the existence of such transactions may make it more difficult for banks and other would-be lenders to assess the financial risk of a company that is asking to borrow money.

(d) **Increased competition**

There is much fiercer competition than there used to be between financial institutions for business. For example, building societies have emerged as competitors to the banks, and foreign banks have competed successfully in the UK with the big clearing banks. Banks have changed too, with some shift towards more fee-based activities (such as selling advice and selling insurance products for commission) and away from the traditional transaction-based activities (holding deposits, making loans).

Securitisation of debt

2.17 The securitisation of debt involves disintermediation. **Financial disintermediation** is a process whereby ultimate borrowers and lenders by-pass the normal methods of financial intermediation (such as depositing money with and borrowing money from banks) and find other ways of lending or borrowing funds; or lend and borrow directly with each other, avoiding financial intermediation altogether.

2.18 Securitisation of debt provides firms with a method of borrowing directly from non-banks. Although banks might act as managers of the debt issue, finding lenders who will buy the securitised debt, banks are not doing the lending themselves.

The money markets

2.19 The UK money markets are operated by the banks and other financial institutions. Although the money markets largely involve wholesale borrowing and lending by banks, some large companies and the government are also involved in money market operations. **The money markets are essentially shorter term debt markets,** with loans being made for a specified period at a specified rate of interest.

2.20 The money markets operate both as a **primary market**, in which new financial claims are issued and as a **secondary market,** where previously issued financial claims are traded.

2.21 Amounts dealt in are relatively large, generally being above £50,000 and often in millions of pounds. Loans are transacted on extremely 'fine' terms - ie with small margins between lending and borrowing rates - reflecting the **economies of scale** involved. The emphasis is on liquidity: the efficiency of the money markets can make the financial claims dealt in virtually the equivalent of cash.

2.22 There are several markets.

(a) **The primary market** is the market where, as already described, the Bank of England carries out 'open market operations' in short-term financial instruments in order to ensure the liquidity of the banking system and to exert influence over interest rates.

(b) **The interbank market** is the market in which banks lend short-term funds to one another. The principal interest rate in this market is the London Inter-Bank Offer Rate or LIBOR, which is used by individual banks to establish their own base interest rates and interest rates for wholesale lending to large borrowers.

(c) **The Certificate of Deposit market** is a market for trading in Certificates of Deposit, a form of deposit which can be sold by the investor before maturity.

(d) **The local authority market** is a market in which local authorities borrow short-term funds from banks and other investors, by issuing and selling short-term 'debt instruments'.

(e) **The finance house market** covers the short-term loans raised from the money markets by finance houses (eg hire purchase finance companies).

(f) **The inter-company market** refers to direct short-term lending between companies, without any financial intermediary. This market is very small, and restricted to the treasury departments of large companies, and has largely been superseded by the sterling commercial paper market.

(g) **The sterling commercial paper market** is a market in which companies issue debt securities carrying interest, known as commercial paper (CP) with a maturity of up to one year, or medium term notes (MTNs) with a period of between one and five years.

2.23 A distinction is sometimes made between the primary market and all the other money markets which are referred to collectively as the parallel markets or 'unofficial' markets. Bear in mind also the existence of eurocurrency markets, which were explained earlier in this chapter.

3 SOURCES OF CAPITAL FOR COMPANIES

3.1 A company must have capital to carry out its operations. Many companies start in a small way, often as family businesses, then grow to become public companies, which can invite the public to subscribe for shares. New capital is thus made available which enables the firm to expand its activities and achieve the advantages of large-scale production.

3.2 **Principal sources of capital for a company**

(a) **Issued share capital**. Share capital might be in the form of ordinary shares (equity) or preference shares. Bear in mind that only the ordinary shareholders are owners of the company, and preference shares are comparatively rare.

(b) **Retained profits and other reserves**. Retained profits are profits that have been kept within the company, rather than paid out to shareholders as dividends.

(c) **Borrowing**. Companies borrow from banks and from private or institutional investors. Investors might purchase debt securities issued by the company. The company promises to repay the debt at a date in the future, and until then, pays the investors interest on the debt. Debt capital includes debentures and, for larger companies, eurobonds and commercial paper.

(d) **Venture capital**. Venture capitalists are prepared to finance risky ventures such as start ups. Because they accept a high degree of risk (with many of their ventures producing little or no return) they require a very high return from the ones that do succeed. They also require a clear exit route that allows them to realise their capital, such as a public flotation issue of shares.

3.3 If a company wants to raise new capital from sources other than retained profits, it should establish whether it needs long-term (usually meaning three years or longer) or short-term capital. Short-term capital can be obtained either by taking longer credit from suppliers, or by asking the company's bank for a short-term loan or bigger overdraft facility. Ideally, a company should use long-term finance to finance commitments with a long payback period, such as fixed assets or research and development.

3.4 **Raising more long-term capital would require the issue of more share capital or more debt**. The ability to raise capital by issuing new shares will depend on the status of the company. A company listed on the Stock Exchange or AIM could go to the market to raise funds. A private company would have to try to raise new share capital privately, without being able to use the institutions of an organised market place; the task for private companies is therefore much more difficult.

3.5 A large public limited company is usually in a better position to raise capital than smaller companies, private companies and non-incorporated businesses.

(a) The high standing of such companies makes investors and other creditors more willing to offer finance.

(b) There is a well established machinery for raising capital through the Stock Exchange. A share issue will be organised for a firm by a merchant bank (known as an issuing house) or similar organisation.

(c) The limited liability of company shareholders usually makes large companies more willing to borrow, in contrast to small company owner-directors, sole traders and partners, who accept greater personal financial risks when they borrow large amounts of capital.

3.6 **The main source of external lending to companies, both long and short-term, is the banks.** New debenture (loan) stock is not often issued by companies to raise new funds because this stock must compete with government loan stock (gilts) to attract investors, and because they are higher risk, company debentures must generally offer a higher rate of interest than the interest rate on gilts, which has been very high itself in recent years.

3.7 **Advantages of funds generated from retained earnings**

- Absence of brokerage costs
- Simplicity and flexibility
- All gains from investment will accrue to existing shareholders

Disadvantages

(a) Shareholders' expectation of dividends may present a problem, particularly for a public company quoted on the Stock Exchange.

(b) Insufficient earnings may be available.

3.8 Despite the existence of various capital markets and money markets, it is not necessarily easy for firms to raise new capital, except by retaining profits. Small firms in particular find it difficult to attract investors without surrendering a measure of **control**, with the banks remaining as the major source of funds for such companies. The capital markets are dominated by institutional investors who have tended to channel their funds into safe investments such as 'blue chip' stocks and shares which are traded on the Stock Exchange main market or on the AIM, as well as government securities. The venture capital providers take a more adventurous approach, although it should be noted that some of the venture capital organisations have been set up by the large institutional investors.

3.9 Banks in the UK have also traditionally been thought of as conservative in their approach to finance, avoiding risky investments. However, the high number of company receiverships experienced in the economic recession of 1990 to 1992 suggests that bankers' traditional reputation for excessive caution may have been undeserved during the late 1980s.

Chapter roundup

- The commercial banks provide a payments mechanism as well as financial intermediation.
- Banks (and building societies) create credit when they lend or grant overdrafts, and their activities thus contribute significantly to the increase in the money supply. In practice, the size of the credit multiplier is restricted by 'leakages' and by central bank controls over the liquidity and capital structure of banks.
- Government monetary policy may be concerned with bank lending activities.

  Bank deposits are included in most definitions of the money supply, which the government may wish to control.

  The government might wish to control interest rates, including interest rates on bank lending.
- Commercial banks will operate in a way and at a level of activity which seeks to keep a suitable balance between liquidity, profitability and security.
- The central bank has various functions. These include acting as a banker to the central government and to the commercial banks.
- The Bank of England acts as administrator or agent for carrying out the government's monetary policies. These policies in the UK include attempts to influence the level of short-term interest rates. The process by which the Bank can control or influence short-term interest rates is known as open market operations.
- We have discussed the role of the capital markets and the money markets and have outlined the main sources of capital available to an enterprise.
- A key development in the financial markets in recent years has been disintermediation. Building societies and banks are being by-passed by borrowers and lenders. Corporate finance in particular is now being raised more and more by marketable securities. This explains the emergence of the term 'securitisation' as a term for what is happening in the capital markets.

Quick quiz

1 Define the credit multiplier.

2 What three aims must a commercial bank keep in balance?

3 List the likely functions of a central bank.

4 If the banking system has liquid reserves of £225bn and seeks to maintain a reserve ratio of 13%, what will broad money supply be?

A £17bn
B £1,731bn
C £2,925bn
D £292,599bn

5 A 'money market' is best defined as:

A A market where organisations raise any form of finance.
B A market where organisations raise long-term finance.
C A market where organisations raise short-term finance.
D A market where Treasury Bills are traded.

6 Advantages of obtaining a stock market listing include all the following except:

A Better access to capital markets
B Ability to make share for share deals
C Ability to liquidate holdings
D Greater public scrutiny

7 The ability of the banks to create credit is constrained by all the following except:

A Leakages of cash out of the banking system
B A reduced reserve ratio
C Low demand for loans
D Prudent lending operations

8 A money market financial intermediary is best defined as:

A An institution which matches surplus funds holders to deficit funds units.

B An institution which operates on the Stock Exchange, matching buyers and sellers of stocks and shares.

C An institution which allows firms to obtain equipment from suppliers by providing leasing or hire purchase finance.

D An institution which acts as a buffer between the Bank of England and the rest of the UK banking system.

Answers to quick quiz

1 The credit multiplier (or bank multiplier) is the name given to banks' ability to create credit, and hence money, by maintaining their cash reserves at less than 100% of the value of their deposits.

2 Liquidity, profitability and security.

3 Setting interest rates
Banker to the government
Central issuer of banknotes
Manager of the national debt
Manager of the nation's foreign currency reserves
Banker to the clearing banks
Supervision of the banking system

4 B £225bn * credit multiplier = total deposits (broad money) therefore £225bn *(1/0.13) = £1,731bn

5 C

6 D Greater public scrutiny may attract takeover bidders and will require the firm to pay more attention to public relations.

7 B A falling reserve ratio will increase the credit multiplier.

8 A An institution on the Stock Exchange is a capital market player. C is a financial intermediary but is not the best definition. D is a financial intermediary but is not the best definition.

Now try the questions below from the Question Bank

Number	Level	Marks	Time
Q34	Introductory	8	10 mins
Q35	Exam - MCQ	2	–
Q36	Exam - MCQ	2	–

Chapter 13

NATIONAL INCOME AND ITS MEASUREMENT

	Topic list	Syllabus reference	Ability required
1	The concept of national income	(iii)	Comprehension
2	The circular flow of income in the economy	(iii)	Comprehension
3	Definition and measurement of national income	(iii)	Comprehension

Introduction

Businesses operate in the economy as a whole and changes in the macroeconomic environment can have major implications for them.

We look in this chapter at how we can measure the total amount of economic activity in a country. This provides a foundation from which to develop the following chapters on the macroeconomic environment.

Learning outcomes covered in this chapter

- Identify the appropriate macroeconomic concepts to explain the measurement and determination of national income
- Explain macroeconomic phenomena by demonstrating a simple circular flow of income model
- Identify the main indicators of macroeconomic performance and demonstrate their significance

Syllabus content covered in this chapter

- National income: its measurement and determination; the circular flow of income and a simple aggregate demand and supply model; unemployment and the price level

Exam focus point

For the exam, you need to develop an understanding of how the economy as a whole functions and the way in which government policy operates. A basic understanding of the concept of the economy as a system and an appreciation of the way the economy performs in terms of employment, output and prices are essential. You should also be aware of the debates within economics about the nature of the macroeconomy, particularly where this affects the conduct of government economic policy.

1 THE CONCEPT OF NATIONAL INCOME

1.1 There are three key measures of national economic output.

- National income
- Gross national product (GNP)
- Gross domestic product (GDP)

Question 1

These are terms which are often encountered in news reports, and yet are often only vaguely understood. Jot down what you think is the meaning of each, and review what you have written once you come to the end of the chapter.

1.2 These are related but different measures of the amount of economic wealth that a country creates or earns over a period of time, usually one year. Why is **national income** so important?

(a) National income is an important measure because it is an aggregate of personal incomes. The bigger the national income in a country, the more income its individual inhabitants will be earning on average. More income means more spending on the output of firms, and more spending (ignoring inflation) means more output of goods and services and hence a rise in the standard of living.

(b) Growth in national income is an economic policy objective of most, if not all, governments, as discussed in Chapter 1.

1.3 **National income** can be viewed from a number of aspects.

(a) The people or organisations that **spend money** to buy the goods and services such as consumers (or **households**), the government and foreign buyers (the **overseas sector**)

(b) The factors of production, which **earn** factor incomes

(c) The firms (or government departments and corporations) which **produce** the goods or services in the national economy

1.4 The three approaches give rise to three ways of analysing the creation of economic wealth.

- The expenditure approach
- The income approach
- The value added approach (until recently, called the output approach)

Question 2

Before proceeding, recall from an earlier chapter what the factors of production are, and what reward is earned by each.

2 THE CIRCULAR FLOW OF INCOME IN THE ECONOMY 5/01

2.1 Firms must pay households for the factors of production, and households must pay firms for goods. The income of firms is the sales revenue from the sales of goods and services. This creates a **circular flow** of income and expenditure, as illustrated in Figure 1. This is a basic **closed economy**, without foreign trade.

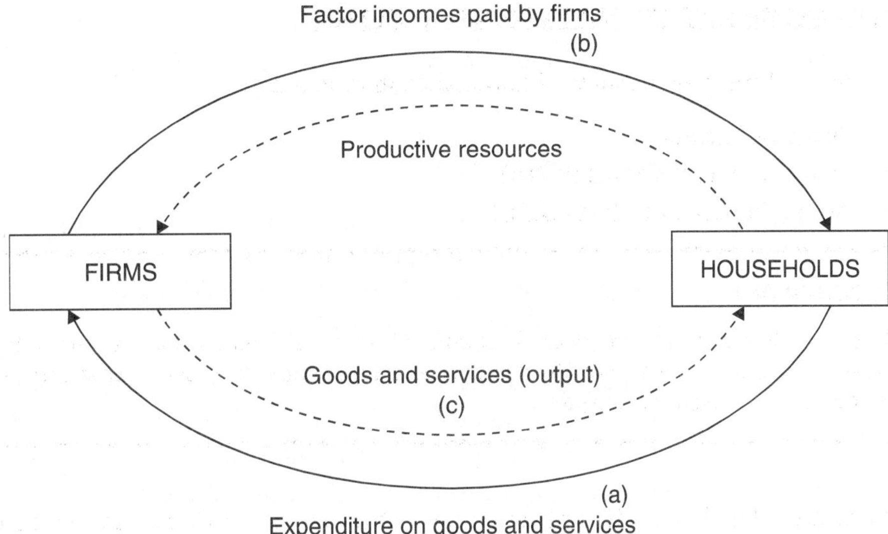

Figure 1 Circular flow of income

2.2 Households earn **income** because they have provided the factors of production which enable firms to output goods and services. The income earned is used as **expenditure** on these goods and services that are made. The total sales value of goods produced (output) should equal the total expenditure on goods, assuming that all goods that are produced are also sold. The amount of expenditure should also equal the total income of households, because it is households that consume the goods and they must have income to afford to pay for them.

Withdrawals and injections into the circular flow of income 5/02

2.3 Our simplified diagram of the circular flow of income needs to be amended to allow for two things.

- **Withdrawals** from the circular flow of income
- **Injections** into the circular flow of income

> **KEY TERMS**
>
> - **Withdrawals**: movements of funds out of the cycle of income and expenditure between firms and households.
> - **Injections**: movements of funds in the other direction

2.4 **Withdrawals** from the circular flow

(a) **Savings (S).** Households do not spend all of their income. They save some, and these savings out of income are withdrawals from the circular flow of income.

(b) **Taxation (T).** Households must pay some of their income to the government, as taxation. Taxes cannot be spent by households.

(c) **Imports (M).** When we consider national income, we are interested in the economic wealth that a particular country is earning. Spending on imports is expenditure, but on goods made by firms in other countries. The payments for imports go to firms in other countries, for output created in other countries. Spending on imports therefore withdraws funds out of a country's circular flow of income.

Be aware that **saving** is different from **investment**; saving simply means withdrawing money from circulation. Think of it as cash kept in a money box rather than being put into a bank to earn interest.

2.5 **Injections** into the circular flow of income.

(a) **Investment (I).** Investment in capital goods is a form of spending on output, which is additional to expenditure by households. Just as savings are a withdrawal of funds, investment is an injection of funds into the circular flow of income, adding to the total economic wealth that is being created by the country.

(b) **Government spending (G).** Government spending is also an injection into the circular flow of income. In most mixed economies, total spending by the government on goods and services represents a large proportion of total national expenditure. The funds to spend come from either taxation income or government borrowing.

(c) **Exports (X).** Firms produce goods and services for export. Exports earn income from abroad, and therefore provide an injection into a country's circular flow of income.

2.6 Figure 2 shows the circular flow of income, taking account of withdrawals and injections. This is an **open economy**, since it participates in foreign trade.

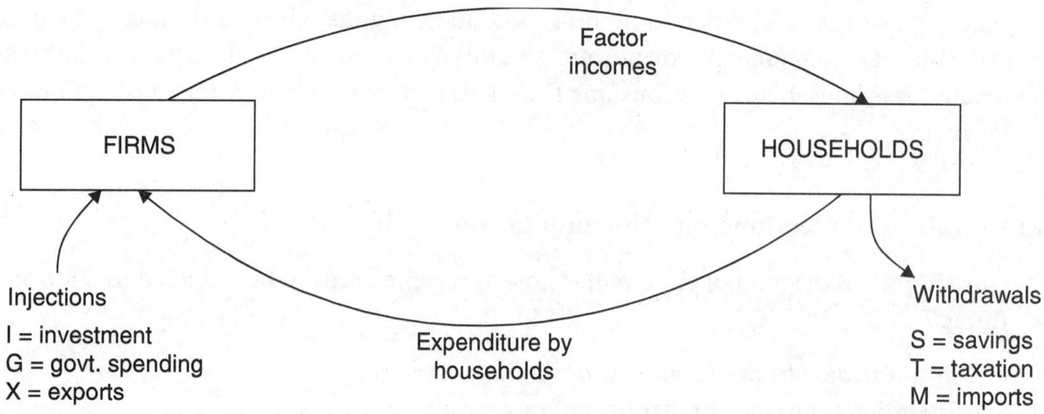

Figure 2 Circular flow of income showing withdrawals and injections

Three approaches to measuring national income

2.7 There are three main approaches.

(a) **The expenditure approach**. The economic wealth created in a period can be measured by the amount of expenditure on the goods and services that are produced by the nation's economy.

(i) The expenditures will be incurred by consumers, the government and foreign buyers of exports. Expenditures on **imports** represent wealth created by other countries, and so the value of expenditure on imports must be deducted from the total expenditure figure.

(ii) Expenditures by firms are **excluded,** to avoid double-counting. Firms buy goods and services which become costs of the goods or services that they produce and sell themselves. If we included expenditure by firms, we would be double-counting the value of the wealth created by the suppliers of raw materials and components and the providers of services to other firms.

(b) **The income approach**. This approach measures the income of individuals from employment and from self-employment, the profits of firms and public corporations and rent on property. (Interest earnings will be included within the profits of companies or the income of individuals.)

(c) **The value added or output approach.** This approach is to measure the value added by all activities which produce goods and services, that is their net output in the period.

2.8 All three approaches will in theory result in the same total amount for economic wealth created in the period, which we call **national income.** In practice, statistical discrepancies arise which cause differences between the figures.

Question 3

We stated above that, in the expenditure approach to measuring national income, expenditures by firms are excluded to avoid double counting. Think carefully about this and ensure that you understand exactly what is meant. Jot down an explanation.

Answer

Firms buy goods and services which become costs of the goods or services that they produce and sell themselves. If we included expenditure by firms, we would be double-counting the value of the wealth created by the suppliers of raw materials and components and the providers of services to other firms.

2.9 It will be useful to look at some simplified examples which illustrate the three approaches to measuring national income.

2.10 EXAMPLE: NATIONAL INCOME

Suppose that a small national economy consists of one firm. During a certain period of time, the firm undertakes certain transactions.

- It imports raw materials from abroad, costing £4,000.
- It hires labour, who are paid wages of £9,000.
- It sells all its output for £20,000 and so makes a profit of £7,000.
- It pays its post-tax profits of £4,000 to shareholders as dividends.

The country's government taxes the labour force £2,000 and the company £3,000.

The firm's sales of £20,000 are to three types of customer.

(a) Domestic consumers spend £11,000. This £11,000 is the post-tax wages earned by the labour force (£7,000) plus the £4,000 in dividends earned by the company's shareholders.

(b) The government spends the £5,000 it has raised in taxes.

(c) Foreign buyers spend £4,000.

Required

Calculate the gross domestic product.

2.11 SOLUTION

As we have seen, there are three ways of calculating national income.

(a) **The expenditure approach**

	£
Consumers' expenditure	11,000
Government expenditure	5,000
	16,000
Add exports	4,000
	20,000
Subtract imports	(4,000)
GDP	16,000

(b) **The income approach**

	£
Income from employment (here pre-tax wages)	9,000
Gross (pre-tax) profit of the firm	7,000
GDP	16,000

The income is measured before deducting tax.

(c) **The value added or output approach**

	£
Output of firm at sales value	20,000
Less cost (sales value) of goods or services purchased from outside firms	(4,000)
GDP	16,000

The cost of goods and services purchased from outside firms - here just the imported materials of £4,000 - has to be subtracted so as either to avoid the double-counting of output, or to remove the value of output produced by firms in other countries.

The government and national income 5/02

2.12 The government has several functions within the national economy, and so plays several different roles in the circular flow of income.

(a) It acts as the **producer** of certain goods and services instead of privately-owned firms, and the production of public administration services, education and health services, the police force, armed forces, fire services and public transport are all aspects of output. The government in this respect acts, like firms, as a producer and must also pay wages to its employees.

(b) It acts as the **purchaser** of final goods and services and adds to total consumption expenditure. National and local government obtain funds from the firms or households of the economy in the form of taxation and then use these funds to buy goods and services from other firms.

(c) It **invests** by purchasing capital goods, for example building roads, schools and hospitals.

(d) It makes **transfer payments** from one section of economy to another, for example by taxing working households and paying pensions, and by paying unemployment benefits and social security benefits.

3 DEFINITION AND MEASUREMENT OF NATIONAL INCOME

Definition of national income 5/01

> **KEY TERM**
>
> **National income**: the sum of all incomes which arise as a result of economic activity, that is from the production of goods and services.

3.1 The incomes which make up national income, which include rent, employment income interest and profit, are known as **factor incomes** because they are earned by the factors of production: land, labour, capital and entrepreneurship.

3.2 National income is also called **net national product**.

(a) The terms **income** and **product** are just two different aspects of the same circular flow of income.

(b) The term **net** means 'after deducting an amount for capital consumption or depreciation of fixed assets'. (We shall return to this point later.)

Gross domestic product (GDP)

3.3 Most UK national income is derived from economic activity **within the UK**. Economic activity within the UK is referred to as total **domestic income** or **domestic product**. It is measured **gross** ie before deducting an amount for capital consumption or depreciation of fixed assets and the term **gross domestic product** therefore refers in the UK to **the total value of income/production from economic activity within the UK**.

Gross national product (GNP)

3.4 'Some national income arises from overseas investments while some of the income generated within the UK is earned by non-residents. The difference between these items is **net property income from abroad**'.

Gross national product (GNP) is therefore the gross domestic product (GDP) plus the net property income from abroad - or after subtracting the net property income from abroad, if it is a negative value.

> **KEY TERMS**
>
> - **Gross domestic product**: the value of the goods and services produced by an economy in a given period.
> - **Gross national product**: GDP **plus** income accruing to domestic residents from investments abroad **less** income accruing to foreign residents from investments in the domestic economy.

The relationship between GDP, GNP and national income

3.5 The relationship between GDP, GNP and national income is therefore this.

	GDP
plus	Net property income from abroad
equals	GNP
minus	Capital consumption
equals	National income (net)

Question 4

Which of the following will cause a rise in national income?

A An increase in capital consumption (depreciation)
B A rise in imports
C A rise in subsidies
D A rise in indirect taxes

Answer

D All the others have effect as reductions in national income.

The expenditure approach to measuring national income

3.6 Probably the most widely used measure of national income is the measurement of total spending or expenditure, and it is worth looking at this in some detail. The table below shows figures for the UK for a recent year.

UK national income 1995: expenditure approach

	£bn
At current market prices	
Consumers' expenditure	447.2
General government consumption	148.6
Gross domestic fixed capital formation	105.4
Value of increase/(decrease) in stocks and work in progress	3.9
Total domestic expenditure	705.1
Exports of goods and services	197.6
Imports of goods and services	(203.1)
Statistical discrepancy	0.5
Gross domestic product (GDP) at current market prices	700.1
Taxes on expenditure (indirect taxes)	(103.6)
Subsidies	7.0
Gross domestic product (GDP) at factor cost	603.5
Net property income from abroad	9.6
Gross national product (GNP) at current factor cost	613.1
Capital consumption (depreciation)	(72.6)
National income at factor cost	540.5

(Source: Annual Abstract of Statistics)

Adjustments to GDP at market prices

3.7 Since the prices of many goods and services are distorted by sales taxes (for example, alcohol and cigarettes) and some are distorted by subsidies (for example, many agricultural products), we often wish to view the situation without these distortions and convert GDP at market prices to **GDP at factor cost**.

KEY TERMS

Expenditure at market prices is the actual amounts paid for the goods by their buyers, but **expenditure at factor cost** is expenditure at market prices minus indirect taxes plus any government subsidies.

3.8 It is necessary to include property income from abroad to give a fuller picture of what is happening in the domestic economy. When this extra item is included we now have a measure called gross national product or GNP.

3.9 **National income** is technically GNP **minus** an allowance for depreciation of the nation's capital. In other words, national income is 'net' national product. Just as firms calculate depreciation in arriving at accounting profits, so too do economists assess a value for depreciation of the nation's capital (referred to as **capital consumption**) to arrive at net national income.

3.10 Although technically national income has a particular definition, generally you will find all these measures (GDP, GNP and NI) loosely referred to as 'national income'.

The income approach to measuring national income

3.11 The second method of calculating national income is the income method. Since money spent by an individual or firm must become income to another we should not be surprised to find that except for a residual error the results of the two methods are the same.

UK national income 1995: income approach

	£bn
At current factor cost	
Income from employment (wages and salaries plus employers' national Insurance contributions)	377.9
Income from self-employment	67.7
Gross trading profits of companies	91.0
Gross trading surplus of public corporations	4.6
Gross trading surplus of government enterprises	0.6
Rent	62.8
Imputed charge for consumption of non-trading capital	3.0
Total domestic income	608.5
Less stock appreciation	(4.9)
GDP – income based	603.6
Residual error	(0.1)
GDP – expenditure based (see earlier Table)	603.5

(Source: Annual Abstract of Statistics)

3.12 The table showing the income based approach shows several separate items of income.

(a) **Income from employment** (ie wages and salaries before deducting tax and including employers' national insurance contributions)

(b) **Pre-tax profits of companies**

(c) **Pre-tax profits of public corporations** (including nationalised industries)

(d) The **pre-tax 'surplus'** of other government enterprises

Interest earned by individuals and companies on any investments they hold is included in the first two figures.

3.13 You might notice that these income figures do not include two elements.

(a) Income from government pensions or social security payments are **transfer payments.**

(b) Any value for work done by individuals for no monetary reward, such as housework done by housewives or do-it-yourself home improvements are activities for which no money value can be given, and so are not economic activities.

3.14 **Transfer payments** are payments such as state pensions and benefits that are made by government, where the recipient does not make any contribution to output in return. They are payments which involve the transfer of wealth, rather than a reward for creating new economic wealth. Transfer payments do not lead directly to any increase in marketable output of goods and are therefore excluded from the income figures.

Question 5

Which of the following is or are transfer payments?

(a) Salaries paid to Members of Parliament
(b) Invalidity benefit

Answer

(a) are *not* transfer payments. MPs are like any other employees - they just happen to be employed by the Government.

(b) *is* a transfer payment. It falls within the category of social security payments.

The value added method of measuring national income

3.15 The third method of calculating national income is the value added or output method. Since the goods and services we spend our money on must have been produced by some industry or another it is not surprising to find the amount we have all spent is the same as the total value of the output goods and services produced. This total value of output can be calculated by adding up the 'values added' at the various stages of the production and distribution process.

3.16 The value added approach to calculating national income is illustrated in the table below, and provides an overview of GDP by industry.

UK national income 1995: value added approach

	£bn
At current factor cost	
Agriculture, forestry and fishing	11.8
Mining and quarrying, oil and gas exploration	14.5
Manufacturing	131.6
Electricity, gas and water supply	15.7
Construction	31.8
Wholesale and retail trade, hotels, catering, repairs	84.7
Transport, storage and communication	50.8
Financial intermediation, real estate, renting and business activities	158.2
Public administration, national defence, compulsory social security	39.5
Education, health and social work	72.9
Other services	23.2
Gross domestic product (GDP) - output based	634.7
Adjustment for financial services	(30.8)
GDP – income based	603.9
Residual error (as with income approach)	(0.4)
GDP – expenditure based	603.5

(Source: Annual Abstract of Statistics)

Difficulties in calculating national income

3.17 Estimates have to be made when accurate figures are unobtainable, and there are omissions in obtaining some figures, and deliberate errors in other. For example, tax evasion might occur on a large scale. Because of errors, the three approaches will produce slightly different figures, and one of them must be taken as correct. In practice, the **expenditure based figures are considered most reliable**, and the income based and output based GDP figures are adjusted to the expenditure based GDP figure, by inserting a **balancing item** known as a residual error.

Question 6

The following data relates to the economy of a country over a one year period.

	£million
Consumers' expenditure	18,400
General government final consumption	4,540
Gross domestic fixed capital formation	4,920
Value of physical decrease in stocks	20
Exports of goods and services	6,450
Imports of goods and services	6,240
Taxes on expenditure	2,760
Subsidies	300
Net property income from abroad	210
Capital consumption	1,750

Required

Calculate the following from the above data.

(a) Gross domestic product (GDP) at factor cost
(b) Gross national product (GNP) at factor cost
(c) National income at factor cost

Answer

The calculation below also shows GDP and GNP at market prices, although these are not required in the exercise.

		£million
Consumers' expenditure		18,400
General government final consumption		4,540
Gross domestic fixed capital formation		4,920
Value of physical decrease in stocks		(20)
Total domestic expenditure		27,840
Exports		6,450
Imports		(6,240)
GDP at market prices		28,050
Net property income from abroad		210
GNP at market prices		28,260
GDP at market prices (see above)		28,050
Factor cost adjustment		
Taxes on expenditure		(2,760)
Subsidies		300
GDP at factor cost	(a)	25,590
Net property income from abroad		210
GNP at factor cost	(b)	25,800
Capital consumption		(1,750)
National income at factor cost	(c)	24,050

3.18 General difficulties arise in the calculation of national income because arbitrary definitions must be made, for example as follows.

(a) **Production** includes goods and services paid for but excludes **work done by people for themselves.**

(b) **Goods which have a serviceable life of several years** are included in national income at their full value in the year they are bought (with the exception of owner-occupied houses).

(c) Data from which the national income figure is estimated contain errors. The value of the unmeasured **black economy** could be very high.

(d) Although transfer payments do not affect national income, net income from abroad does increase the total size of a nation's income and must be calculated.

(e) **Services provided to the public** by the government, such as policing, many health services, and education, are valued at cost whereas output of private firms include profit in their valuation.

National income and inflation

3.19 Inflation is a particular problem in using national income as a measure of national wealth. Price inflation increases the **money value** of national income. We should be careful not to interpret this as meaning that there is more economic activity going on in our economy. All that has happened is that the prices of the things we are measuring have increased. To see if there has been any real change in the level of activity we must deduct any influence due to inflation. Although this is not a simple operation, the standard method for turning money GDP or GNP into real measures is to use what is called the **GDP deflator** in order to take inflation out of the figures.

The purposes of calculating national income 5/02

3.20 Calculating the national income serves several purposes.

(a) It measures the **standard of living** in a country (national income per head).

(b) It allows comparisons between the **wealth** of different countries.

(c) It makes it possible to measure the **improvement** (or deterioration) in national wealth and the standard of living.

(d) It assists central government in its **economic planning.**

3.21 National income or GNP per head of the population gives an indication of the **trend over time** in a country's standard of living, because GNP is measured consistently from year to year, whatever the weaknesses of thc mcasurcment system that is used. **GNP per head of population is however less reliable as a guide to comparing the standard of living in different countries.**

(a) GNP excludes work done by a person for himself. It also excludes barter trade. In some countries, do-it-yourself production and barter trade are more common than in others, and so the total GNP of the various countries would not be properly comparable.

(b) In measuring GNP, government services which are not paid for are valued at cost. If one country has a large state-owned sector which provides services free (eg health and education) whereas another country has only a small state-owned sector, output which is valued at cost in one country would be valued at market price in the other, and so there would be different valuations given to the same physical product.

(c) Spending on items which produce a benefit over several years is included in GNP in one year only, which is the year the expenditure takes place. If a country is still enjoying benefits from past investments, this will not be reflected in its current GNP.

(d) Every country will have difficulty in obtaining accurate data about output and GNP. Thus a country with a strong 'black economy' will be much wealthier than its official GNP per head of population might suggest. Given differences in the strength of the black economy from country to country, their figures for GNP will not be properly comparable.

(e) The needs of people in one country will differ widely from the needs of people in another country. This will be due to differences in social attitudes, customs and habits, religious beliefs, climate, density of population and so on. A country with a hot climate might spend large sums on air conditioning and similar anti-heat products, whereas a country with a cold climate will want central heating and insulation products instead. When people in different countries want entirely different things, it is not really possible to presume that their comparative standards of living can be measured on a single money scale.

(f) Countries will produce items that may be seen as being of little or no relevance to their immediate standards of living. Spending on defence equipment and space programmes are examples. These add to GNP per head of the population without people in the population getting direct benefit out of them. The GNP per capita of a country with high defence spending and one with little such spending would therefore not be properly comparable.

3.22 These drawbacks to using GNP per head of population for international comparisons mean that simpler and more direct comparisons are sometimes used instead. One way of doing this is to select a number of products which are widely in demand. Examples might be television sets and motor cars. Measurements can then be obtained of the average number of cars or TV sets per household or per head of the population and how long it takes an average worker to earn enough in wages to buy a car or a TV set.

Question 7

Which of the following is not a valid reason for treating with caution inter-country standard of living comparisons based on GNP per head?

A Government services provided without charge at the point of delivery are valued at cost

B GNP includes barter trade, which is particularly difficult to value

C Continuing benefit from past public sector investment is not reflected in GNP per head

D There may be important differences from country to country in the scale of the unofficial or illegal economy

Answer

B Barter trade is not included in GNP

Chapter roundup

- We started this chapter by observing that there is a circular flow of income in an economy, which means that expenditure, output and income will all have the same total value.
- There are withdrawals from the circular flow of income (savings, taxation, import expenditure) and injections into the circular flow (investment, government spending, export income).
- We saw that national income can be measured by an expenditure method, income method or value added (output) method. Allowing for statistical errors in collecting the data, all three methods should give the same total for GDP, GNP and national income.
- A useful formula to learn is that for the expenditure method: $Y = C + I + G + (X - M)$.
- National income figures can be used to measure growth in the economy, although 'real' growth can only be measured by 'taking out inflation' and using figures on a common price basis.
- Economic wealth is perhaps best measured by GDP, GNP or national income per head of the population. However, national income is a measure of *annual* income, not the nation's total stock of wealth.
- For reasons mentioned in this chapter, national income has serious limitations as a measure of economic wealth and welfare. It remains an important indicator nonetheless, and in planning its economic policy, a government will probably seek to improve the standard of living of its population by setting as targets:
  - growth in national income
  - growth in national income per head of the population

Quick quiz

1 What are the withdrawals from and injections into the circular flow of income?

2 Outline the three approaches used in calculating national income.

3 Explain the relationship between national income, GDP and GNP.

4 What are the difficulties in calculating national income?

5 What adjustments must be made to GDP at market prices to arrive at GNP at factor cost?

A Add indirect taxes, deduct subsidies, add net property income from abroad
B Add indirect taxes, deduct subsidies, add capital consumption (depreciation)
C Deduct indirect taxes, add subsidies, deduct capital consumption (depreciation)
D Deduct indirect taxes, add subsidies, add net property income from abroad

Answers to quick quiz

1 Withdrawals are savings (S), taxation (T) and imports (M).
Injections are investment (I), government spending (G) and exports (X).

2 The expenditure approach is based on measuring total expenditure on goods and services produced in the economy.

The income approach totals individual incomes from employment and self employment, the profits of firms and rent on property.

The value added approach is based on measuring the total output of goods and services in the economy.

3 GDP is the total value of income or production within a national economy. GNP is GDP plus property income from abroad, less property income paid to foreign investors. National income, or net national product is GNP less capital consumption (depreciation of fixed assets).

4 Calculation of national income requires the collection of large quantities of statistical data. This can only be done on a sample basis and so is subject to sampling errors and omissions. The data may also be deliberately distorted by illicit factors such as tax evasion and smuggling.

5 D

Now try the questions below from the Question Bank

Number	Level	Marks	Time
Q37	Introductory	8	10 mins
Q38	Introductory - MCQ	–	–
Q39	Introductory - Interactive	–	–

Chapter 14

THE DETERMINATION OF NATIONAL INCOME

	Topic list	Syllabus reference	Ability required
1	The Keynesian approach	(iii)	Comprehension
2	Consumption, savings and investment	(iii)	Comprehension
3	The multiplier and the accelerator	(iii)	Comprehension
4	The business cycle	(iii)	Comprehension
5	Government policies and objectives	(iii)	Comprehension
6	The supply side	(iii)	Comprehension

Introduction

In macroeconomics we are looking, not at individual spending decisions, investment decisions, pricing decisions, employment decisions, and output decisions but at spending, investment, price levels, employment and output in the economy as a whole and at total income (national income).

In this chapter, we study the basic elements of the Keynesian model for national income determination and equilibrium.

Broadly speaking, macroeconomists divide into the two camps of the **Keynesians** and the **monetarists**. These two camps have had differing ideas about how national income can be made to grow, how full employment can be achieved and how booms and slumps of trade cycles can be smoothed out. They differ in their views about the causes of inflation, the extent to which inflation creates unemployment and prevents economic growth, and the effectiveness of government measures to stimulate the economy.

This chapter also provides a short introduction to the place of government policy in the wider economy.

Learning objectives covered in this chapter

- Explain the economic role of government through fiscal and monetary policy and demonstrate the impact of such policies on the business sector
- Explain the nature of the trade cycle, its causes and consequences
- Explain the debates concerning the nature of the macroeconomy and appropriate government policy

Syllabus content covered in this chapter

- Macroeconomic stability: economic fluctuations and their causes; macroeconomic forecasting and stabilisation policy

1 THE KEYNESIAN APPROACH

The origin of Keynesianism

1.1 Keynesian economics originated with *John Maynard Keynes*, an English economist whose book *The General Theory of Employment, Interest And Money* (1936), revolutionised macroeconomic analysis. Keynes put forward his ideas following a period in which there was an economic boom (after the First World War), followed by the Wall Street Crash in 1929, and the depression in the 1930s when unemployment levels soared.

1.2 Pre-Keynesian economists had tried to explain unemployment as a temporary phenomenon. They believed that if there is a surplus of labour available (unemployment) then the forces of demand and supply, through the wages (price) mechanism, would restore equilibrium by bringing down wage levels, thus stimulating demand for labour. Any unemployment would only last as long as the labour market was adjusting to new equilibrium conditions. The pre-Keynesian theory was challenged during the 1930s. If pre-Keynesian theory was right, wages should have fallen and full employment should have been restored. However, this did not happen, and the depression continued for a long time.

1.3 It is instructive to note that it was during this economic situation that Keynes put forward his new theory. Its fundamental advance on earlier theory was to explain how **equilibrium could exist in the macroeconomy, but there could still be persistent unemployment and slow growth**.

1.4 The term **full employment national income** is used to describe the total national income that a country must earn in order to achieve full employment. By **full employment** we mean that the country's economic resources are fully employed. However, as far as labour is concerned, full employment does not mean that everyone has a job all the time. There will always be some **normal** or **transitional** unemployment as people lose their job or give up one job for another, and so **full** employment might mean, say, that 3-5% of the total working population is unemployed at any time.

1.5 Keynes also tried to explain the causes of **trade cycles** which are the continuous cycles of alternating economic boom and slump. Why does an economy not grow at a steady rate, or remain stable, instead of suffering the harmful effects of trade cycles?

Aggregate demand and aggregate supply

1.6 Keynes' basic idea was that demand and supply analysis could be applied to macroeconomic activity as well as microeconomic activity.

KEY TERMS

Aggregate demand (AD) means the total demand in the economy for goods and services.

Aggregate supply (AS) means the total supply of goods and services in the economy.

1.7 AS depends on physical production conditions - the availability and cost of factors of production and technical know-how. Keynes was concerned with short-run measures to affect the economy, and he also wrote in a period of high unemployment when there was obviously no constraint on the availability of factors of production. His analysis therefore concentrated on the **demand side**. Supply side economics (discussed later in this chapter) describes the views of economists who do not subscribe to the Keynesian approach to

dealing with current problems of national income and employment, and prefer instead to concentrate on the **supply side** - in other words, production factors.

1.8 The **aggregate supply curve** will be upward sloping, for the reasons applying to the microeconomic supply curves mentioned in earlier chapters. A higher price means that it is worthwhile for firms to hire more labour and produce more because of the higher revenue-earning capability. So at the macroeconomic level, an increasing price level implies that many firms will be receiving higher prices for their products and will increase their output.

1.9 In the economy as a whole, supply will at some point reach a labour constraint, when the entire labour force is employed. When there is full employment, and firms cannot find extra labour to hire, they cannot produce more even when prices rise, unless there is some technical progress in production methods. The aggregate supply curve will therefore rise vertically when the full employment level of output is reached (AS in Figure 1).

1.10 AD is total planned or desired consumption demand in the economy for consumer goods and services and also for capital goods, no matter whether the buyers are households, firms or government. AD is a concept of fundamental importance in Keynesian economic analysis. Keynes believed that national economy could be managed by taking measures to influence AD up or down.

1.11 The AD curve will be downward sloping because at higher prices, total quantities demanded will be less.

1.12 Keynes argued that a national economy will reach equilibrium where the aggregate demand curve and aggregate supply curve intersect.

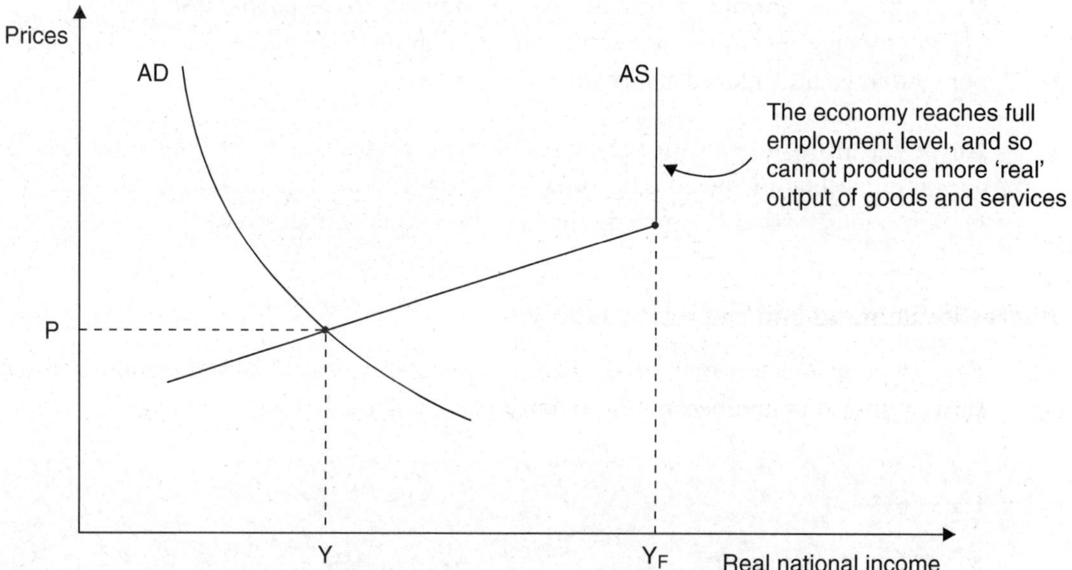

Figure 1 Equilibrium national income, using aggregate supply and aggregate demand analysis

1.13 The actual level of national income will be at the intersection of the AD curve and AS curves - ie at Y (Figure 1). The difference between the equilibrium national income Y and the full employment national income Y_F shows how much national income could be increased with the resources at the economy's disposal. Price levels will be at P. Y therefore represents the level of **satisfied** demand in the economy. Note that the aggregate demand function assumes constant prices.

1.14 Two points follow on immediately from this initial analysis.

- Equilibrium national income Y might be at a level of national income below full employment national income Y_F. This is the situation in Figure 1.
- On the other hand, the AD curve might cut the AS curve above the point at which it becomes vertical, in which case the economy will be fully employed, but price levels will be higher than they need to be. There will be inflationary pressures in the economy, as shown in Figure 2, if aggregate demand is AD_1.

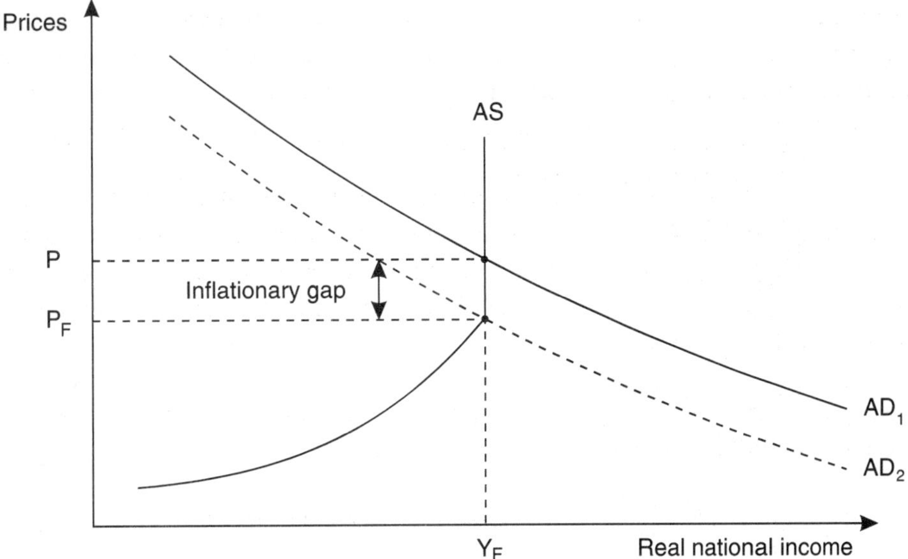

Figure 2 Equilibrium national income at full employment, but with inflationary pressures (an inflationary gap)

Exam focus point

This diagram and the accompanying ideas are vital for your examination.

Shifts in the AD curve

1.15 As with demand and supply analysis in microeconomics, we can predict in macroeconomics that equilibrium national income can be increased by either of two things.

- Shifting the AD curve to the right
- Shifting the AS curve to the right

As suggested already, Keynesian economists concentrate on shifts in AD.

Deflationary and inflationary gaps 5/01

1.16 In a situation where resources are already fully employed, there may be an **inflationary gap** since increases in aggregate demand will cause price changes and not variations in real output. An inflationary gap can be described as the extent to which the aggregate demand function would have to shift downward to produce the full employment level of national income without inflation.

1.17 You should also note that a shift in the AD curve or the AS curve will not only change the national income, it will also change price levels (P). In Figure 2, an inflationary gap can be removed by shifting the aggregate demand curve to the left, from AD_1 to AD_2.

1.18 If you are not sure about this point, a simple numerical example might help to explain it better. Suppose that in Ruritania there is full employment and all other economic resources are fully employed. The country produces 1,000 units of output with these resources. Total expenditure (that is, aggregate demand) in the economy is 100,000 Ruritanian dollars, or 100 dollars per unit. The country does not have any external trade, and so it cannot obtain extra goods by importing them. Because of pay rises and easier credit terms for consumers, total expenditure now rises to 120,000 Ruritanian dollars. The economy is fully employed, and cannot produce more than 1,000 units. If expenditure rises by 20%, to buy the same number of units, it follows that prices must rise by 20% too. In other words, when an economy is at full employment, any increase in aggregate demand will result in price inflation.

1.19 The Keynesian argument is that if a country's economy is going to move from one equilibrium to a different equilibrium, there needs to be a shift in the aggregate demand curve. To achieve equilibrium at the full employment level of national income, it may therefore be necessary to shift the AD curve to the right (upward) or the left (downwards).

1.20 In a situation **where there is unemployment of resources** there is said to be a **deflationary gap** (Figure 3). Prices are fairly constant and real output changes as aggregate demand varies. A deflationary gap can be described as the extent to which the aggregate demand function will have to shift upward to produce the full employment level of national income.

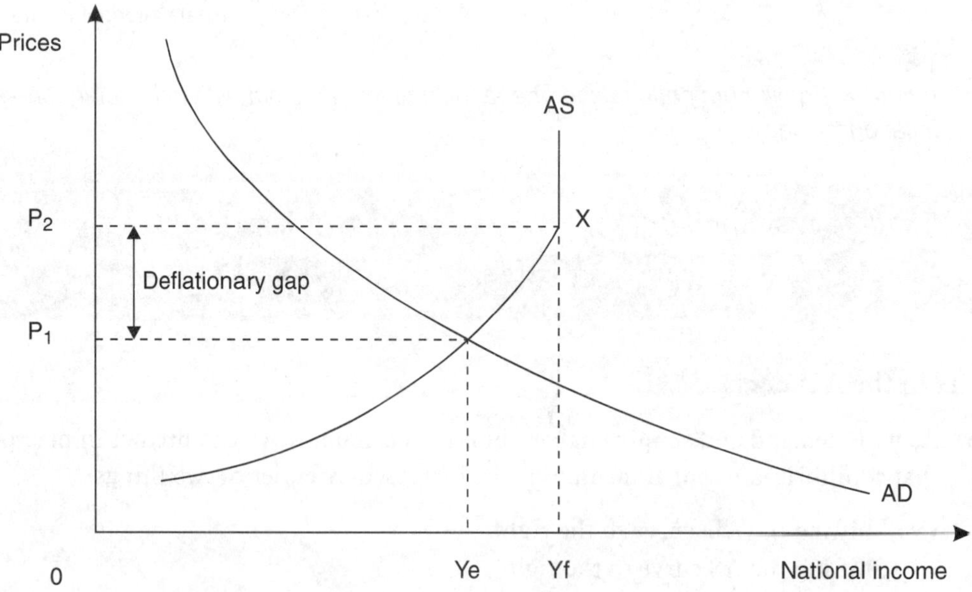

Figure 3 Deflationary gap

The ideal equilibrium national income

1.21 If one aim of a country's economic policy is full employment, then the ideal equilibrium level of national income will be where AD and AS are in balance at the full employment level of national income, without any inflationary gap - in other words, where aggregate demand at current price levels is exactly sufficient to encourage firms to produce at an output capacity where the country's resources are fully employed. This is shown in Figure 4, where equilibrium output will be Y (full employment level) with price level P.

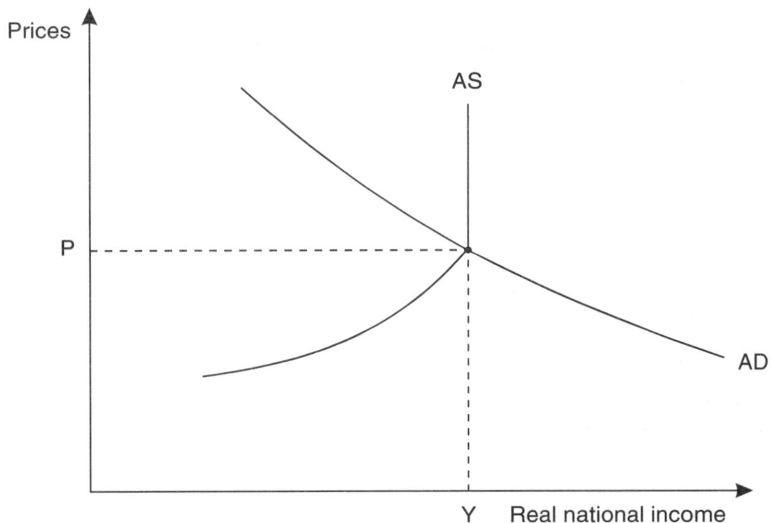

Figure 4 Equilibrium national income

(A country will also seek economic growth, but to achieve a real increase in living standards, both AD and AS curves will now have to shift to the right.)

Demand management

1.22 For Keynesian analysis to have practical value for the management of a national economy, it is necessary to establish how aggregate demand can be shifted.

1.23 To understand shifts in AD, we need to turn our attention to expenditure in the economy. A formula for the GNP (= total national expenditure) which was described in the previous chapter is:

$E = C + I + G + (X - M)$

where		
	E is the total national expenditure	(GNP)
	C is the total domestic consumption	(money spent on consumer goods)
	I is the total industrial investment	(money spent by private sector firms and the public sector on capital items) *
	G is the total government spending	(government 'current' or 'consumption' spending)
	X is the total exports	(including income from property abroad)
	M is the total imports	(including money paid as income to residents in other countries for property they hold in the country)

* Alternatively, government investment spending on capital items can be included in G leaving I to represent investment by firms only.

KEY TERM

Demand management policies involve the manipulation of E (eg achieving economic growth) by influencing C, I, G or net exports.

1.24 If we ignore capital consumption, we can equate E (GNP) with national income. This is what we shall do in our analysis of the Keynesian model.

Withdrawals and injections into the circular flow of income 5/01

1.25 In the previous chapter on national income, the different approaches to calculating national income - the expenditure, income and value added approaches - were explained in terms of the circular flow of income round the economy.

1.26 For a national economy, there are certain withdrawals from and injections into this circular flow of income. Withdrawals divert funds out of the circular flow and injections add funds into it.

(a) **Withdrawals** from the circular flow of income (W) consist of imports (M), taxation (T) and savings (S).

(b) **Injections** into the circular flow of income (J) consist of exports (X), government spending (G), and investment spending by firms (I).

1.27 Keynes argued that for an equilibrium to be reached in the national income, not only must AD = AS, but also total **planned** withdrawals from the circular flow of funds **must be equal to total planned injections**. Thus, for equilibrium:

W = J, and so M + T + S = X + G + I

1.28 In the long term W will always equal J.

(a) The difference between the value of imports M and the value of exports X is the **balance of payments deficit** (or **surplus**). Even in the short term, this difference must be balanced by borrowing (or lending abroad), as we shall see in a later chapter.

(b) The difference between government spending and taxation can only be made up by government borrowing. Loans are eventually repaid.

(c) In the long run, savings will also equal investments, even though the people who save and the firms who invest are not the same. We shall look more closely at savings and investment later.

1.29 However, although W and J will be equal retrospectively and in the long run, it does not follow that **planned** J and **planned** W will equal each other **in the short run**, since injections and withdrawals are made by different people.

1.30 This frustration of plans in the short run causes national income to change over time. The imbalance between J and W creates factors which can make the level of national income change. Keynes argued that the imbalance between planned withdrawals and planned injections explained **trade cycles** - the fluctuations in national income which give rise to booms and slumps - which prevent an economy from settling down at an equilibrium level.

Summary so far

1.31 Keynes argued that an equilibrium national income will be reached where aggregate demand equals aggregate supply. There are two possible equilibria.

(a) One is at a level of employment which is below the full employment level of national income. The difference between actual national income and full employment national income is called a **deflationary gap**. To create full employment, the total national income (expenditure) must be increased by the amount of the deflationary gap.

(b) The other is at a level of demand which exceeds the productive capabilities of the economy at full employment, and there is insufficient output capacity in the economy to meet demand at current prices. There is then an **inflationary gap**.

1.32 The equilibrium national income will change if there are shifts in the AD curve.

1.33 When there is some unemployment in the economy, the aggregate demand curve will be further to the **left** than it could be. In other words, unemployment indicates a lower than necessary aggregate demand, and so a low AD. Although there might be some inflation when there is unemployment, very high levels of inflation are associated with full employment and over-strong aggregate demand.

1.34 You should notice that the aggregate supply curve begins to slope upwards before full employment income is reached. This is because the employment of less efficient labour, competition by firms for labour, possibly lower plant efficiency as factories approach capacity output and so on, will raise prices as well as output. In other words, there can be some inflation when there is some unemployment.

2 CONSUMPTION, SAVINGS AND INVESTMENT 5/01

Consumption and savings (C and S)

2.1 Let us now go into a bit more detail on Keynesian analysis, and concentrate particularly on consumption, savings and investment. To simplify our analysis, we shall ignore government spending, taxation, imports and exports for the time being. By ignoring imports and exports, we are concentrating on a **closed economy** which is not in any way dependent on foreign trade.

2.2 If we ignore G, T, X, and M, we can look at a circular flow of income in which households divide all their income between two uses: consumption and saving.

2.3 Provided that national income is in equilibrium, we will have:

$$Y \equiv C + S$$

where Y = national income, C = consumption and S = saving.

This should seem logical to you. Income can only be either spent or saved. Since we have a closed economy, consumption must be of goods produced by the economy itself.

Savings

2.4 There are two ways of saving. One is to hold the income as money (banknotes and coin, or in a current bank account). The other way is put money into some form of interest-bearing investment. In the long run, there is no reason for people to hold banknotes or keep money in a current bank account, unless they intend to spend it fairly soon. If this is so, income that is not spent will be saved and income that is saved will, eventually, be invested. (The people who put their money into interest-bearing savings are not making any investment themselves in capital goods, but the institutions with whom they save will use the deposits to lend to investors and so indirectly there will be a real increase in investment when people save money in this way.)

Question 1

What do you think are the main factors which influence the amount that people will save?

Answer

The amount that people save will depend on:

(a) how much income they are getting, and how much of this they want to spend on consumption

(b) how much income they want to save for precautionary reasons, for the future

(c) interest rates. If the interest rate goes up we would expect people to consume less of their income, and to be willing to save and invest more.

2.5 We can therefore conclude that in **conditions of equilibrium** for national income:

$$Y \equiv C + S$$

and, $$Y \equiv C + I$$

and so, $$I \equiv S$$

In the short run, however, savings and investment might not be equal and so there might not be equilibrium.

The propensities to consume and save 5/01

2.6 Even when a household has zero income, it will still spend. This spending will be financed by earlier **savings** (and, in the real world, by **welfare receipts**). There is thus a constant, basic level of consumption. This called **autonomous** consumption. When the household receives an income, some will be spent and some will be saved. The **proportion** which is spent is called the **marginal propensity to consume** (MPC) while the **proportion** which is saved is equal to the **marginal propensity to save** (MPS).

2.7 In our analysis (ignoring G, T, X and M) saving and consumption are the only two uses for income, MPC + MPS = 1.

2.8 Therefore, we may say that a household's expenditure in a given period is made up of 2 elements.

(a) A fixed amount (£a) which is the autonomous consumption.
(b) A further **constant** percentage of its income (b% of Y) representing the MPC.

Similarly, a national economy as a whole will spend a fixed amount £a, plus a constant percentage (b%) of national income Y.

We can then state a **consumption function** as $C = a + bY$.

2.9 Given a consumption function $C = a + bY$:

(a) The marginal propensity to consume is b, where b is the proportion of each extra £1 earned that is spent on consumption.

(b) The average propensity to consume will be the ratio of consumption to income:

$$\frac{C}{Y} = \frac{A+bY}{Y}$$

2.10 For example, suppose an individual household has fixed spending of £100 per month, plus extra spending equal to 80% of its monthly income.

(a) When its monthly income is £800, its consumption will be:

£100 + 80% of £800 = £740

(b) When its monthly income is £1,000 its consumption will be:

£100 + 80% of £1,000 = £900

2.11 The household's marginal propensity to consume is 80%.

Question 2

Using the above figures, calculate the household's average propensity to consume:

(a) when its income is £800
(b) when its income is £1,000

Answer

(a) $\text{APC} = \frac{740}{800} = 92.5\%$

(b) $\text{APC} = \frac{900}{1,000} = 90\%$

2.12 **Changes** in the marginal propensity to consume and the marginal propensity to save will involve a change of preference by households between current consumption and saving for future benefits. A cause of such a change might be a change in interest rates, which makes the investment of savings more or less attractive than before.

What factors influence the amount of consumption?

2.13 There will always be a minimum fixed amount of total consumption. Total consumption by households, however, is affected by five influences.

(a) **Changes in disposable income, and the marginal propensity to consume**. Changes in disposable income are affected by matters such as pay rises and changes in tax rates. An increase in household wealth may reduce levels of saving thus increasing consumption.

(b) **Changes in the distribution of national income**. Some sections of the population will have a higher marginal propensity to consume than others and so a redistribution of wealth might affect consumption. (A redistribution of wealth might be accomplished by taxing the rich and giving to the poor in the form of more government allowances).

(c) **The development of major new products**. When such developments happen, they can create a significant increase in spending by consumers who want to buy the goods or services.

(d) **Interest rates**. Changes in interest rates will influence the amount of income that households decide to **save**, and also the amount that they might elect to borrow for spending.

(e) **Price expectations**. Expectations of price increases may increase current consumption while expectations of price reductions may have the opposite effect.

2.14 One of the determinants of the MPC is **taste and attitude**. If a household believes that saving is a virtue it will save as much as possible and spend as little as possible; and in the economy as a whole, a general belief in the value of thrift may mean that the MPC is low. Nowadays the prestige attached to the possession of consumer goods may have overcome the admiration for thrift, making the MPC higher than it once was.

2.15 A further determinant of MPC is the **attractiveness of savings**. If interest rates are high, households will wish to save more of their income to benefit from the higher rates of interest. The more they save, the less they consume. Conversely some goods are so expensive that they tend to be bought on credit; if interest rates are high there is less incentive to borrow and thus a lower tendency to purchase high-cost goods.

2.16 Given C = a + bY, the value of b may also be affected by the value of a. If the cost of essential commodities rises in relation to all other commodities, the value of a will rise. This means that a greater proportion of household consumption becomes fixed and there is less available for variable consumption bY. Thus a rise in a causes a fall in b.

We can show the consumption function in a graph, which shows the relationship between consumption, savings and (disposable) income (Figure 6).

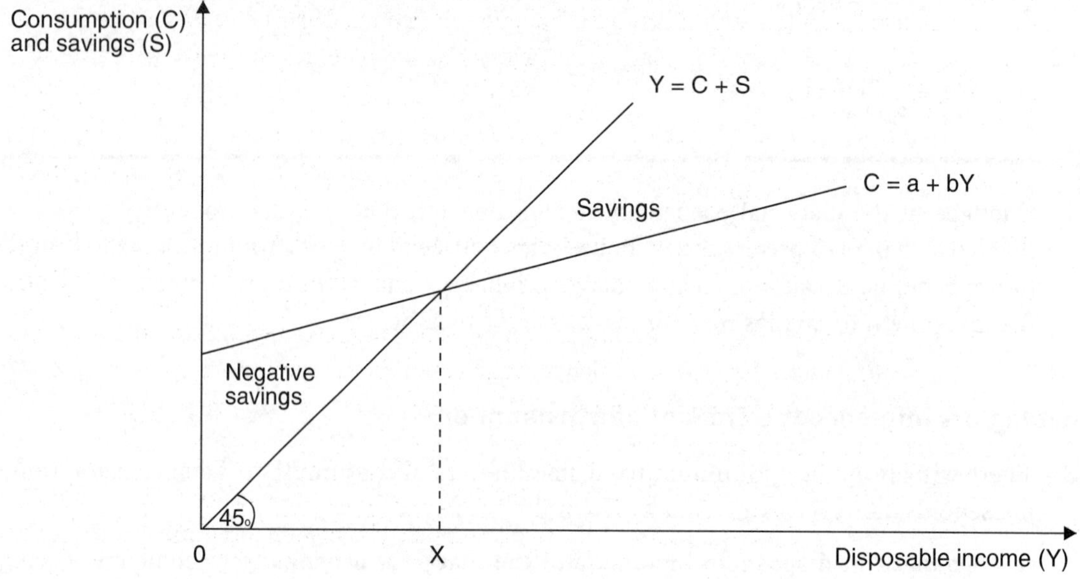

Figure 6 Income, consumption and savings (closed economy)

2.17 As we have seen, in a closed economy with no government sector, income must equal the sum of consumption and savings. Consumption will always be a minimum amount, and at lower levels of national income (below X in Figure 6) consumption will exceed national income. This means that households will be using up savings to buy goods.

Investment (I)

2.18 The total volume of desired investment in the economy depends on factors similar to those influencing 'micro-level' investment decisions by firms.

- The rate of interest on capital
- The marginal efficiency of capital invested
- Expectations about the future and business confidence
- The strength of consumer demand for goods

2.19 The demand for funds to invest by firms and the willingness of investors to lend their savings for investment (the supply of funds) should adjust to one another through the price mechanism of the interest rate.

(a) **Higher interest rates** should make firms less willing to invest, because the marginal efficiency of capital will have to be higher to justify the higher interest cost. However, firms cannot always cut their investment plans quickly and at short notice.

Higher interest rates should have two other effects.

(i) They will tempt individuals to consume less of their income and save more, with a view to investing it.

(ii) They will also tempt individuals to invest more of their savings - that is, to hold less cash and more interest-bearing investments.

(b) **Lower interest rates** should have the opposite effect.

2.20 An investment involves the acquisition of more buildings, machinery, plant and equipment or stocks of goods and so on. The importance of the interest rate for investment should therefore be apparent in the marginal efficiency of capital. Firms should go on adding to their capital provided that the marginal efficiency of capital exceeds the interest rate, which is its marginal cost.

New technology and investment

2.21 When new technology emerges which changes methods of production (such as robotics) or provides opportunities to produce new types of good, there will be a boost to investment.

(a) New technology which reduces the unit costs of production will increase profitability. The supply curve for the goods that are affected by the new production methods will shift to the right. Firms will invest in the new technology in order to achieve lower costs and remain competitive.

(b) New technology which leads to new types of good will give a stimulus to consumption demand. Firms will invest to make the product and meet the consumer demand.

Investment and economic recovery

2.22 **Investment represents one of the major injections in the circular flow of income.** Variations in the level of investment can, through the multiplier, affect the level of national income and the level of aggregate demand in the economy. A major conclusion from Keynesian analysis is that in order to achieve economic recovery from a recession, there should be major investment, which will create further growth through the workings of the **multiplier** (see below).

2.23 Investment can be in either the public or the private sector of the economy, although the money to finance the investment might need to come from different sources.

(a) Private sector investment will come from retained profits, new issues of shares, or borrowing. However, in an economic recession profits might be low, and investors might lack confidence in a recovery, so that new share issues are impossible on a large scale.

(b) Public sector investment might be financed by higher taxation, or by an increased deficit between government income and expenditure, that is, a higher **public sector net cash requirement** (PSNCR).

(c) Public sector spending should have socially valuable spin-off effects, such as improved roads, sewers and public buildings.

(d) However, a high PSBR, meaning large government borrowings, might force up interest rates in the capital markets and **crowd out** private sector investment, by making it too expensive for firms to borrow and invest profitably. (Keynesian economists deny that such crowding out takes place, however.)

2.24 There are two additional reasons why investment is very important.

(a) The act of investment represents consumption forgone now in order to increase the capacity to produce, and therefore to consume, in the future. It is through investment (or lack of it) that the future shape and pattern of economic activity is pre-determined.

(b) The growth rate of the economy is determined not only by the technological progress or the increases in the size and quality of the labour force but also by the rate at which the capital stock is increased or replaced. Investment represents an addition to the existing capital stock. If that addition is greater than the amount by which the capital stock depreciates, then the capital stock of the economy is growing and so is the capacity of the economy to produce more goods and services. Hence investment is an important determinant of the long-term growth rate of an economy.

Government influence on investment

2.25 The government can influence the level of private investment in several ways.

(a) **It can attempt to control interest rates.** By keeping interest rates low, for example, the government might encourage a higher volume of investments, whereas by allowing interest rates to rise, the government would probably cause the volume of investment to fall. Governments can influence interest rates. In the UK, this is done mainly through operations in the money markets.

(b) **It can provide direct encouragement to investing firms**, by offering investment grants, perhaps directed at particular regions, or by providing tax incentives. A grant involves a cash payment by the government towards the cost of the investment. Tax incentives may also take the form of capital allowances. The size of grants or tax allowances can be varied, according to government policy. It is questionable, however, whether the widespread use of grants and generous capital allowances have a significant effect on the volume of investment.

(c) **The government can seek to stimulate business confidence**, for example by developing and announcing an economic policy for continued growth, and then achieving policy targets. The success of the government in stabilising the economy, controlling inflation and preventing industrial unrest provides a very important influence on business confidence.

(d) **The government can try to encourage technological developments**, perhaps by financing research schemes of its own, and perhaps by entering into a research partnership with private firms. In the long run, investment in education might be significant for the strength of innovative research and development by the country's industries.

(e) **Government policy might be directed towards influencing the volume of consumption**. A policy to control the growth in the money supply, for example, would involve trying to reduce the growth in credit. Credit control in turn would affect consumer spending, especially in consumer durable goods and changes in consumption affect investment levels.

(f) The government can spend money itself, and higher government spending might stimulate investment by the private sector.

3 THE MULTIPLIER AND THE ACCELERATOR

The multiplier

3.1 The **multiplier** is the **process of circulation of income** in the national economy, whereby an injection of a certain size leads to a much larger increase in national income. The firms or households receiving the injection use at least part of the money to increase their own consumption. This provides money for other firms and households to repeat the process and so on.

3.2 The level of national income might increase or decrease for a number of reasons; for example, there might be a pay rise for workers or an increase in the country's exports. Keynes showed that if there is an **initial** change in expenditure due to an increase in exports, or government spending or investment or consumer spending, a new equilibrium national income level will be reached.

3.3 **The eventual total increase in national income will be greater in size than the initial increase in expenditure**. This is because of the continuing circulation of the funds concerned.

KEY TERM

The ratio of the **total** increase in national income to an initial increase is called the **multiplier**.

3.4 $$\text{Multiplier} = \frac{\text{Total increase in national income}}{\text{Initial increase in national income}}$$

3.5 The multiplier can be defined as a measure of the effect on total national income of a unit change in a component of aggregate demand: I, G or X.

Multiplier values can therefore be measured specifically for each of these separately.

$$\text{Investment multiplier} = \frac{\text{Eventual change in national income}}{\text{Initial change in investment spending}}$$

$$\text{Government spending multiplier} = \frac{\text{Eventual change in national income}}{\text{Initial change in government spending}}$$

$$\text{Export multiplier} = \frac{\text{Eventual change in national income}}{\text{Initial change in exports}}$$

Numerical illustration of the multiplier

3.6 A numerical illustration of the multiplier might help to explain it more clearly. In this example, we shall again ignore taxes, government spending, exports and imports, and assume a simple closed economy in which all income is either spent on consumption (C) or saved (S). Let us suppose that in this closed economy, marginal propensity to consume (MPC) is 90% or 0.9. Then, out of any addition to household income, 90% is consumed and 10% saved.

(a) If income goes up by £200, £180 would be spent on consumption, and £20 saved.

(b) The £180 spent on consumption increases the income of other people, who spend 90% (£162) and save £18.

(c) The £162 spent on consumption in turn becomes additional income to others, so that a snowball effect on consumption (and income and output) occurs, as follows.

			Increase in expenditure £	*Increase in savings* £
Stage	1	Income rises	200.00	-
	2	90% is consumed	180.00	20.00
	3	A further 90% is consumed	162.00	18.00
	4	"	145.80	16.20
	5	"	131.22	14.58
		etc	...	.....
		Total increase in income	2,000.00	200.00

3.7 In this example, an initial increase in income of £200 results in a final increase in national income of £2,000. The multiplier is 10.

3.8 **The multiplier is the reciprocal of the marginal propensity to save.** Since MPC = 0.9, MPS = 0.1.

$$\text{Multiplier} = \frac{1}{\text{MPS}} \text{ or } \frac{1}{1 - \text{MPC}}$$

$$\text{Increase in national income} = \frac{\text{Initial increase in expenditure}}{\text{MPS}} = \frac{£200}{0.1} = £2{,}000$$

Note that at the new equilibrium, savings of £200 equal the initial increase in expenditure of £200 but national income has risen £2,000.

3.9 If the marginal propensity to consume were 80%, the marginal propensity to save would be 20% and the multiplier would only be 5. Because people save more of their extra income, the total increase in national income through extra consumption will be less.

3.10 The multiplier in a national economy works in the same way. **An initial increase in expenditure will have a snowball effect**, leading to further and further expenditures in the economy. Since total expenditure in the economy is one way of measuring national income, it follows that an initial increase in expenditure will cause an even larger increase in national income. The increase in national income will be a multiplier of the initial increase in spending, with the size of the multiple depending on factors which include the marginal propensity to save.

3.11 If you find this hard to visualise, think of an increase in government spending on the construction of roads. The government would spend money paying firms of road contractors, who in turn will purchase raw materials from suppliers, and sub-contract other work. All these firms employ workers who will receive wages that they can spend on goods and services of other firms. The new roads in turn might stimulate new economic activity, for example amongst road hauliers, housebuilders and estate agents.

3.12 Depending on the size of the multiplier, an increase in investment would therefore have repercussions throughout the economy, increasing the size of the national income by a multiple of the size of the original increase in investment.

3.13 If, for example, the national income were £10,000 million and the average and the marginal propensity to consume were both 75%, in equilibrium, ignoring G, T, X and M:

Y = £10,000 million
C = £7,500 million
I = S = £2,500 million

Since MPC = 75%, MPS = 25%, and the multiplier is 4.

3.14 An increase in investment of £1,000 million would upset the equilibrium, which would not be restored until the multiplier had taken effect, and national income increased by 4 × £1,000 million = £4,000 million, with:

Y = £14,000 million
C = £10,500 million (75%)
I = S = £3,500 million (25%)

3.15 A downward multiplier or **demultiplier** effect also exists. A reduction in investment will have repercussions throughout the economy, so that a small disinvestment (reduction in expenditure/output) will result in a multiplied reduction in national income

3.16 You should also be aware of factors which might influence the MPC and MPS in any economy, for example the age distribution of the population, the income distribution of the population, expectations of the future and other socio-economic factors.

The importance of the multiplier

3.17 **The importance of the multiplier is that an increase in one of the components of aggregate demand will increase national income by more than the initial increase itself.** Therefore if the government takes any action to increase expenditure (for example by raising government current expenditure, or lowering interest rates to raise investment) it will set off a general expansionary process, and the eventual rise in national income will exceed the initial increase in aggregate demand.

3.18 This can have important implications for a government when it is planning for growth in national income. By an initial increase in expenditure, a government can 'engineer' an even greater increase in national income, (provided that the country's industries can increase their output capacity), depending on the size of the multiplier.

The multiplier in an open economy 11/01

3.19 So far we have been considering a simplified economy in which income is either saved or spent on domestic production. The real world is more complex and we must now consider the effect of taxation and imports. Like savings, these are **withdrawals from the circular flow** and they therefore affect the multiplier. Thus, in an open economy, the value of the multiplier depends on three things.

(a) The **marginal propensity to save** (MPS)

(b) **The marginal propensity to import**, because imports reduce national income, and if households spend much of their extra income on imports, the snowball increase in total national income will be restricted because imports are a withdrawal out of the circular flow of income. One of the reasons for a low multiplier in the UK is the high marginal propensity to import.

(c) **Tax rates**, because taxes reduce the ability of people to consume and so are likely to affect the marginal propensity to consume and the marginal propensity to save.

3.20 Whereas the multiplier in a closed economy is the reciprocal of the marginal propensity to save, the multiplier in an open economy, taking into account government spending and taxation, and imports and exports, will be less. This is because government taxation and spending on imports reduces the multiplier effect on a country's economy.

3.21 For an open economy:

$$\text{Multiplier} = \frac{1}{s+m+t}$$

where
s is the marginal propensity to save
m is the marginal propensity to import
t is the marginal propensity to tax - ie the amount of any increase in income that will be paid in taxes.

3.22 The multiplier as defined in this way may still be represented as below.

$$\text{Multiplier} = \frac{1}{1-\text{MPC}}$$

since any increase in income is totally accounted for by savings, tax imports and consumption.

3.23 For example, if in a country the marginal propensity to save is 10%, the marginal propensity to import is 45% and the marginal propensity to tax is 25%, the size of the multiplier would be:

$$\frac{1}{0.1+0.45+0.25} = \frac{1}{0.80} = 1.25$$

Changes in equilibrium national income and the multiplier: a graphical representation

3.24 It is possible to show the multiplier effect in the form of a diagram.

Exam focus point

The multiplier is a vital part of macroeconomic theory. You must be able to draw this diagram and explain it.

3.25 In Figure 7, the horizontal axis represents national income (Y). The vertical axis represents planned or desired expenditure. The national economy is in equilibrium when actual output (which is the same as national income) is equal to desired expenditure. This occurs at any point along the 45° line Y=E.

3.26 On to this basic picture we have superimposed two other lines.

(a) The lower is the consumption function we described in Section 2. This consists of autonomous expenditure (a), which occurs even when income is zero, plus the proportion of income which is spent in accordance with the marginal propensity to consume (bY).

(b) Desired expenditure within the economy is not limited to consumption; we must also consider the **injections**, government spending (G), investment (I), and net exports (X-M). If we assume these are constant, total actual expenditure for any level of national income is shown by the upper line E=C+G+I+(X-M).

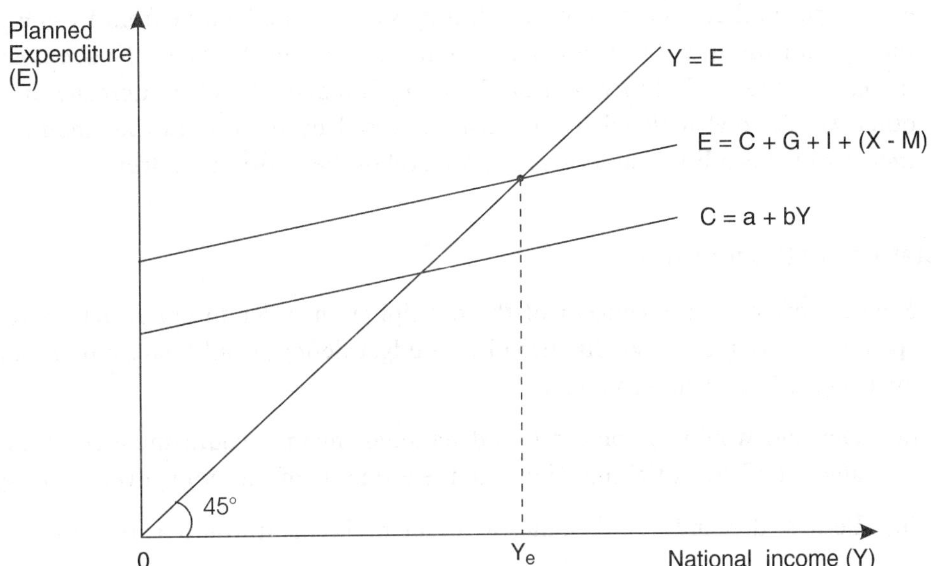

Figure 7 Equilibrium national income

3.27 Equilibrium national income in Figure 7 is at Y_e, where Y = E = C + G + I + (X – M).

3.28 What will happen if the economy has unemployed resources at national income Y_e, and total expenditure is increased - ie C, G, I or (X – M) increases. By how much will national income increase? This is shown in Figure 8.

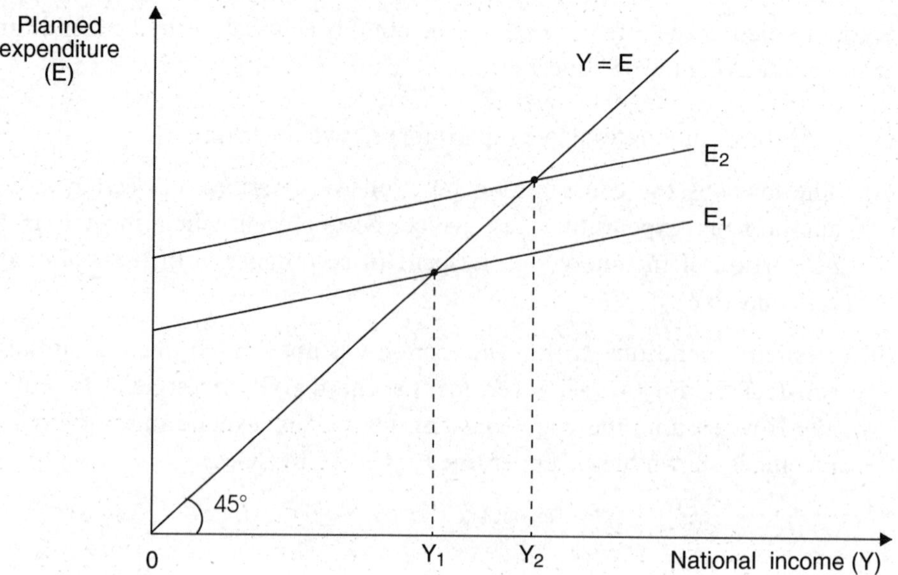

Figure 8 Multiplier effect

3.29 If injections were made to increase (for example, an increase in government spending or extra exports) then there would be a shift upwards in the E curve from E_1 to E_2. In Figure 8, the equilibrium level of income has now increased from Y_1 to Y_2. Notice however that the increase in the level of income from Y_1 to Y_2 is **bigger than the increase in injections**. In other words, total national income has increased by more than the amount of the initial increase in expenditure, and this is a portrayal of the multiplier effect.

Limitations of the multiplier

3.30 Keynes developed the concept of the multiplier in order to argue that extra government spending on public works, financed by a budget deficit, would have a pump-priming effect on a demand-deficient economy.

(a) Demand would be increased and national income would increase by more than the amount of the initial injection into the economy of the extra government spending.

(b) Because demand would be increased, unemployment would be reduced.

3.31 However, there are several important factors that limit the significance of the multiplier.

(a) It is relevant to a demand-deficient economy with high unemployment of resources. **If there is full employment, any increase in demand will be inflationary.**

(b) The **leakages** from the circular flow of income might make the value of the multiplier very low. This is relevant to the UK, where there is a high marginal propensity to import.

(c) There may be a **long period of adjustment** before the benefits of the multiplier are felt. If a government wants immediate action to improve the economy, relying on demand management and the multiplier could be too slow.

(d) The consumption function in advanced economies is probably more volatile than Keynes believed. If consumption is unpredictable, measures to influence national income through the multiplier will be impossible to predict too.

The accelerator principle

KEY TERM

Accelerator principle: the theory that investment changes disproportionately in response to change in output.

3.32 The accelerator principle states that if there is a **small change** in the output of **consumer** goods, there will be a **much greater change** in the output of **capital** equipment required to make those consumer goods. This change in production of capital equipment (investment spending) speeds up the rate of economic growth, or slump.

3.33 A numerical example might help to illustrate this principle. Suppose that a firm makes biscuits and has 100 ovens in operation. The life of each oven is 5 years.

(a) If the demand for biscuits is constant, on average, 20 ovens must be replaced each year.

(b) If the demand for biscuits now rises by, say, 10% the firm will need 110 ovens in operation. During the first year of the increase, the demand for ovens will be 30 units. This is made up of replacement of 20 ovens and an extra requirement of 10 ovens to bring the total to 110.

A 10% rise in demand for consumer goods results in a 50% rise in demand for capital goods, in the short term. The accelerator is at work! The accelerator principle indicates how, when the demand for consumer goods rises, there will be an even greater proportional increase in the demand for capital goods. This speeds up growth in national income.

(a) If demand for biscuits now remains constant at the new level, annual replacement of capital equipment will average 22. There is consequently the danger that there will be over-capacity in the oven-making industry because the short-term peak demand of 30 ovens per annum is not maintained.

(b) This means that unless the rate of increase in consumer demand is maintained, over-capacity in capital goods industries is likely to occur.

3.34 The accelerator also works in reverse. **A decline in demand for consumer goods will result in a much sharper decline in demand for the capital goods which make them.**

3.35 **The accelerator implies that investment and hence national income remain high only as long as consumption is rising.**

3.36 So as income approaches the peak level dictated by available capacity, new investment will fall towards zero, reducing aggregate demand and hence national income. (The sharp fall in investment caused by the fall in consumption, due to the accelerator effect, will be compounded by the 'demultiplier', so that the accelerator and the demultiplier will combine to reduce national income more severely than the initial fall in consumption. The recovery in investment when demand stops falling will stimulate the economy again and cause income and thus demand to rise again.)

3.37 Note carefully that the accelerator comes into effect as a consequence of **changes in the rate of consumer demand**.

3.38 The extent of the change in investment depends on two things.

(a) The size of the change in consumer demand

(b) The **capital-output ratio**. This is the ratio of capital investment to the volume of output, in other words how much capital investment is needed to produce a quantity of output. For example, if the capital output ratio is 1:3, it would need capital investment of £1 to produce an extra £3 of output pa, and so if demand went up by say, £3 billion, it would need an extra £1 billion of investment to produce the extra output to meet the demand.

3.39 Economists at one time believed that the accelerator helped to explain the upswings and downturns of the trade cycle and therefore that the trade cycle was inevitable.

The paradox of thrift

3.40 The **paradox of thrift** is an illustration of the workings of a 'demultiplier' in a situation where savings and investment are temporarily out of balance. The demultiplier operates because households increase savings but there is **not a corresponding increase in investment**.

3.41 The paradox of thrift draws attention to the point that the amount of income saved by people is not necessarily invested, because people might choose to hold their savings as money (ie non-interest bearing wealth) rather than to invest the savings, at least in the short term.

3.42 Since extra saving does not necessarily result in additional investment (either because people do not want to invest or because entrepreneurs are not prepared to invest), three conclusions follow.

(a) The fall in consumption resulting from a rise in saving adversely affects entrepreneurs' expectations, and therefore they decide to reduce investment.

(b) A reduction in investment, through the multiplier, causes greater reductions in national income.

(c) Since national income falls, households have smaller income and therefore save less.

Thus greater saving without greater investment ends with smaller incomes and smaller savings. This is the paradox of thrift.

4 THE BUSINESS CYCLE 11/01, 5/02

4.1 Business cycles or trade cycles are the continual sequence of rapid growth in national income, followed by a slow-down in growth and then a fall in national income. After this recession comes growth again, and when this has reached a peak, the cycle turns into recession once more.

4.2 Four main phases of the business cycle can be distinguished.

- Recession
- Depression
- Recovery
- Boom

4.3 Recession tends to occur quickly, while recovery is typically a slower process. Figure 9 can be used to help explain how this is so. You may find it of interest to relate the processes which we are describing in this section to your knowledge of the recession in the UK economy from 1990 to 1992.

4.4 At point A in Figure 9, the economy is entering a recession. In the recession phase, consumer demand falls and many investment projects already undertaken begin to look unprofitable. Orders will be cut, stock levels will be reduced and business failures will occur as firms find themselves unable to sell their goods. Production and employment will fall. The general price level will begin to fall. Business and consumer confidence are diminished and investment remains low, while the economic outlook appears to be poor. Eventually, in the absence of any stimulus to aggregate demand, a period of full **depression** sets in and the economy will reach point B.

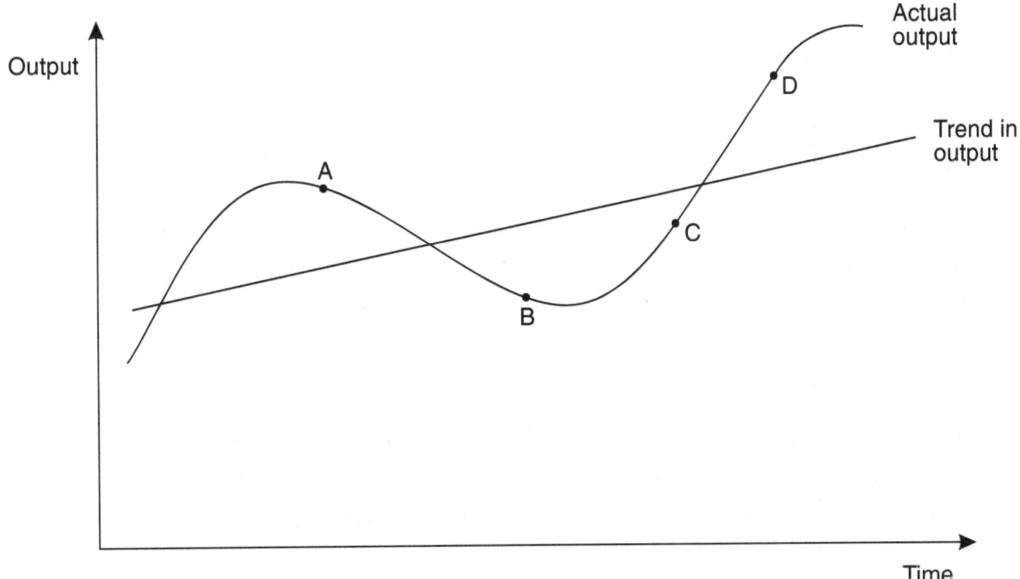

Figure 9 The business cycle

4.5 **Recession** can begin relatively quickly because of the speed with which the effects of declining demand will be felt by businesses suffering a loss in sales revenue. The knock-on effects of destocking and cutting back on investment exacerbate the situation and add momentum to the recession. Recovery can be slow to begin because of the effect of recession on levels of confidence.

4.6 At point C the economy has reached the **recovery** phase of the cycle. Once begun, the phase of recovery is likely to quicken as confidence returns. Output, employment and income will all begin to rise. Rising production, sales and profit levels will lead to optimistic business expectations, and new investment will be more readily undertaken. The rising level of demand can be met through increased production by bringing existing capacity into use and by hiring unemployed labour. The average price level will remain constant or begin to rise slowly.

4.7 In the recovery phase, decisions to purchase new materials and machinery may lead to benefits in efficiency from new technology. This can enhance the relative rate of economic growth in the recovery phase once it is under way.

4.8 As recovery proceeds, the output level climbs above its trend path, reaching point D, in the **boom** phase of the cycle. During the boom, capacity and labour will become fully utilised. This may cause bottlenecks in some industries which are unable to meet increases in demand, for example because they have no spare capacity or they lack certain categories of skilled labour, or they face shortages of key material inputs. Further rises in demand will, therefore, tend to be met by increases in prices rather than by increases in production. In general, business will be profitable, with few firms facing losses. Expectations of the future may be very optimistic and the level of investment expenditure high.

4.9 **It can be argued that wide fluctuations in levels of economic activity are damaging to the overall economic well-being of society**. The inflation and speculation which accompanies boom periods may be inequitable in their impact on different sections of the population, while the bottom of the trade cycle may bring high unemployment. Governments generally seek to stabilise the economic system, trying to avoid the distortions of a widely fluctuating trade cycle.

Multiplier-accelerator theory

4.10 Keynes suggested that a combination of the multiplier and the accelerator explained the upswings and downswings of the trade cycle.

4.11 Suppose that there is an actual or even an **expected** increase in consumption, so that a small initial increase in national income occurs or is expected to occur. If firms are to be able to meet the extra demand from consumers, they will have to invest in more capital equipment, and therefore there will be an increase in investment, which in turn increases spending and national income.

4.12 The **multiplier comes into effect** and the small initial increases in consumption and investment result in an even bigger total increase in national income. As national income grows, **investment grows faster than the growth in consumption because of the accelerator**.

4.13 If consumption demand stabilises, the rate of investment falls to the new maintenance level. The reduction in new investment causes a fall in national income and so consumption demand begins to fall too.

4.14 Since the multiplier effect increases (or decreases) national income as a result of increases (or decreases) in injections to the circular flow, the accelerator effect also comes into operation, and investment demand rises (or falls) as a result of actual and expected changes in consumption.

4.15 The connecting link between the change in consumption, the level of investment and national income is the view that entrepreneurs take about whether the increase in demand will be maintained in the future, and so whether it is worth investing more capital. If an increase in demand is only expected to be temporary, firms might decide not to invest, so that the extra consumption spending will be met by higher imports. (The value of imports per £1 spent, as mentioned earlier, has a bearing on the size of the multiplier.)

4.16 Combined together, the multiplier and accelerator build up the momentum of initial small changes in demand, so that the multiplier-accelerator process explains the cumulative tendencies of upswings and downswings in the economy, ie trade cycles.

4.17 The implications of Keynes' analysis, and in particular of multiplier-accelerator theory, are that large increases or decreases in national income occur because of small initial changes in consumption or investment. Even expected changes in demand should result in new investment and the multiplier and accelerator would then come into operation.

4.18 Although business upswings and downswings can be large and rapid, there will eventually be a limit to the upswing or the downswing. A ceiling or a floor in the level of national income will be reached. Why should this be so?

(a) **Ceilings**. Ceilings are reached when the full employment level of national income is reached. Unless firms can invest in new labour-saving equipment, or increase labour productivity, the total volume of output will eventually be restricted to the limited availability of labour. If labour is fully employed, it cannot produce more unless it becomes more productive, or unless machines can be introduced to do work that labour did before.

(b) **Floors**. A floor will also be reached. At its worst level business confidence would be so low that firms do not invest much at all. If investment is nil, savings will fall to zero too, and national income will equal consumption only. There must always be some consumption, and national income could never fall below this minimum fixed consumption level.

4.19 **Turning points** in upturns and downturns can be explained by accelerator theory. The **multiplier-accelerator effect**, combined with floors and ceilings, could explain how there might be never-ending business cycles of upturns and downturns in a national economy.

How long was the last UK recession?

4.20 Officially, the definition of an economic recession is a **decline in economic output for two consecutive quarters** or more. On the basis of this definition, the UK last experienced a recession from the first quarter of 1990 (the second consecutive quarter of falling output or gross domestic product (GDP)) until the last quarter of 1992 - a total of seven quarters.

4.21 When the recession was over according to the official definition, the continuation of significant unemployment, company failures and weak consumer confidence suggested that it still had further to run. This is to some extent the result of lags in the economy: it takes time for improvements in GDP to feed through to jobs and investment. Unemployment could still be rising when a recession has officially ended.

5 GOVERNMENT POLICIES AND OBJECTIVES

Economic policy objectives

5.1 All modern governments are expected to manage their national economies to some extent. Electorates generally suppose that government action can support or hinder the growth of prosperity and look to them for serviceable macroeconomic policies. There are four main objective of economic policy, though debate continues about their relative priority.

(a) **To achieve economic growth**, and growth in national income per head of the population. Growth implies an increase in national income in real terms. Increases caused by price inflation are not real increases at all.

(b) **To control price inflation** (to achieve stable prices). This has become a central objective of UK economic policy in recent years.

(c) **To achieve full employment**. Full employment does not mean that everyone who wants a job has one all the time, but it does mean that unemployment levels are low, and involuntary unemployment is short-term.

(d) **To achieve a balance between exports and imports** (on the country's balance of payments accounts) over a period of years. The wealth of a country relative to others, a country's creditworthiness as a borrower, and the goodwill between countries in international relations might all depend on the achievement of an external balance over time.

KEY TERMS

Monetary policy: government policy on the money supply, the monetary system, interest rates, exchange rates and the availability of credit.

Fiscal policy: government policy on taxation, public borrowing and public spending.

Policy instruments

5.2 To try to achieve its intermediate and overall objectives, a government will use a number of different policy tools or policy instruments.

(a) **Monetary policy**. Monetarist economists believe that control over the growth of the money supply is necessary to reduce inflation and that inflation is harmful to the economy because it creates economic uncertainty which deters growth. We discuss monetary policy in Chapter 16.

(b) **Fiscal policy**. Keynesian economists believe that when an economy has spare production capacity and unemployment, investment and output can be stimulated (through government spending or tax cuts) so as to reduce unemployment without creating more inflation. We discuss fiscal policy and taxation in Chapter 17.

(c) **Prices and incomes policy**. Some economists have argued that inflation can be tackled directly through government controls over prices and incomes.

(d) **Industrial and regional policy**. Some governments have policies to encourage industrial investment, for example through grants and tax incentives and to develop particular regions, for example by targeting grants on specific areas.

(e) **Exchange rate policy**. Some economists argue that economic objectives can be achieved through management of the exchange rate by the government. The strength or weakness of sterling's value, for example, will influence the volume of UK imports and exports, the balance of payments and interest rates.

(f) **External trade policy**. A government might have a policy for promoting economic growth by stimulating exports. Another argument is that there should be import controls to provide some form of protection for domestic manufacturing industries by making the cost of imports higher and the volume of imports lower. Protection should encourage domestic output to rise, thus stimulating the domestic economy.

5.3 These policy tools are not mutually exclusive: for example, a government might adopt a policy mix of monetary policy, fiscal policy and exchange rate policy in an attempt to achieve its economic objectives.

5.4 In practice, economic policy-making is complicated by a range of problems.

- **Inadequate information**
- **Time lags** between use of policy and effects being noticeable
- **Political pressures** for short-term solutions
- Unpredictable **side-effects** of policies
- The **influence of other countries**
- **Conflict between policy instruments**

5.5 **Conflicts between policy instruments**

(a) A fiscal deficit intended to stimulate AD by increasing G necessitates government borrowing. This may force up interest rates and discourage investment (the **crowding out** effect) thus reducing AD.

(b) Tighter **monetary policy** to limit inflation will force up interest rates. This in turn will increase the Retail Prices Index (as mortgage costs are part of the RPI) and could discourage investment. Lower investment means lower efficiency and higher costs.

(c) Prices and incomes policy introduced to reduce inflation may lead to industrial disruption in turn causing a fall in output and possible difficulties on the balance of international trade.

The changing emphasis of economic policy

5.6 The emphasis on different policy objectives has changed in line with political, social and economic events. The objective of **full employment** was central to UK policy thinking following the Second World War, as it was in other developed countries also. Later, other macroeconomic objectives came to the fore, and explicit policy commitments have been made by governments at different times to the objectives of **low inflation, balance of payments equilibrium** and the maximisation of **economic growth**.

5.7 Changing policy emphases reflect changing views about how the economy works, and value judgements about which objectives are most desirable.

6 THE SUPPLY SIDE 11/01

6.1 The Keynesian policy of demand management relies upon the proposition that the level of aggregate demand determines the level of national income and prices, since demand creates supply. The **supply side approach** advocated by monetarists, on the other hand, focuses policy upon the **conditions of aggregate supply**, taking the view that the availability, quality and cost of resources are the long term determinants of national income and prices. Supply side economists argue that by putting resources to work, an economy will automatically generate the additional incomes necessary to purchase the higher outputs.

KEY TERM

Supply side economics can be defined as an approach to economic policymaking which advocates measures to improve the supply of goods and services (eg through deregulation) rather than measures to affect aggregate demand.

6.2 Supply side economics is characterised by the following propositions.

(a) The predominant long-term influences upon output, prices, and employment are the conditions of aggregate supply.

(b) Left to itself, the **free market** will automatically generate the highest level of national income and employment available to the economy.

(c) **Inflexibility in the labour market** through the existence of trade unions and other restrictive practices retain wages at uncompetitively high levels. This creates unemployment and restricts aggregate supply.

(d) The rates of **direct taxation** have a major influence upon aggregate supply through their effects upon the **incentive** to work.

(e) There is only a **limited role for government** in the economic system. Demand management can only influence output and employment 'artificially' in the short run, whilst in the long run creating inflation and hampering growth. Similarly state owned industries are likely to be uncompetitive and accordingly restrict aggregate supply.

6.3 The **central role of aggregate supply** is demonstrated in Figures 4(a) and (b).

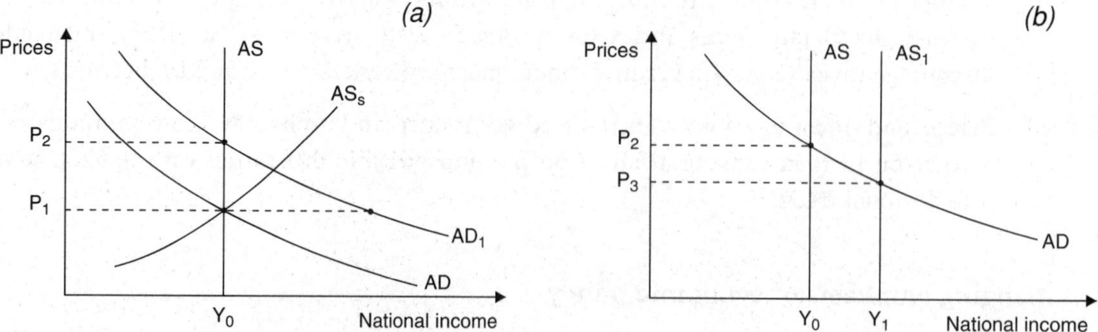

Figure 3 The importance of aggregate supply

6.4 Figure 3(a) shows the effect of a rise in aggregate demand, perhaps as the result of expansionary demand management policies, as a shift in the aggregate demand schedule from AD to AD_1, but in the long run national income remains at Y_0. As_s is the short run supply schedule. In the long run, aggregate supply is inelastic, represented by AS. The effect of the rise in aggregate demand is due to increased prices from P_1 to P_2. Supply side theorists accept that in the short run, national income may rise along the short-run aggregate supply curve AS_s but contend that ultimately national income will fall to its long-run level of Y_0 because supply cannot be maintained above its long run level. Consequently aggregate demand is powerless to increase long-run output or employment.

6.5 Figure 3(b) illustrates a rise in aggregate supply from AS to AS_1. The income generated from the higher employment causes aggregate demand to extend and consequently national income rises from Y_0 to Y_1. This demonstrates the supply side view that **only changes in the conditions of aggregate supply can lead to a sustained increase in output and employment**. The vertical aggregate supply curve suggests that changes in aggregate demand do not affect output but rather only influence prices.

6.6 The economy will self-regulate through the action of the price mechanism in each market. Flexible prices in goods and factor markets will ensure that at the microeconomic level each market tends towards a market-clearing equilibrium. At the macroeconomic level the maximum attainable level of national income is at the level of full employment. The exponent of supply side economics argues that **flexible wages** will ensure the economy reaches this point.

6.7 The importance of flexible wages is shown in Figure 4. When the wage rate is at W_0 the demand for labour is Q_d whilst the total supply of labour stands at Q_s. This creates involuntary unemployment of $(Q_s - Q_d)$ at the prevailing wage rate. By accepting lower wages workers can 'price themselves back into jobs' and consequently unemployment falls. If wages were perfectly flexible downwards then the market would restore full employment at wage rate W_1. This would leave unemployment at its natural rate.

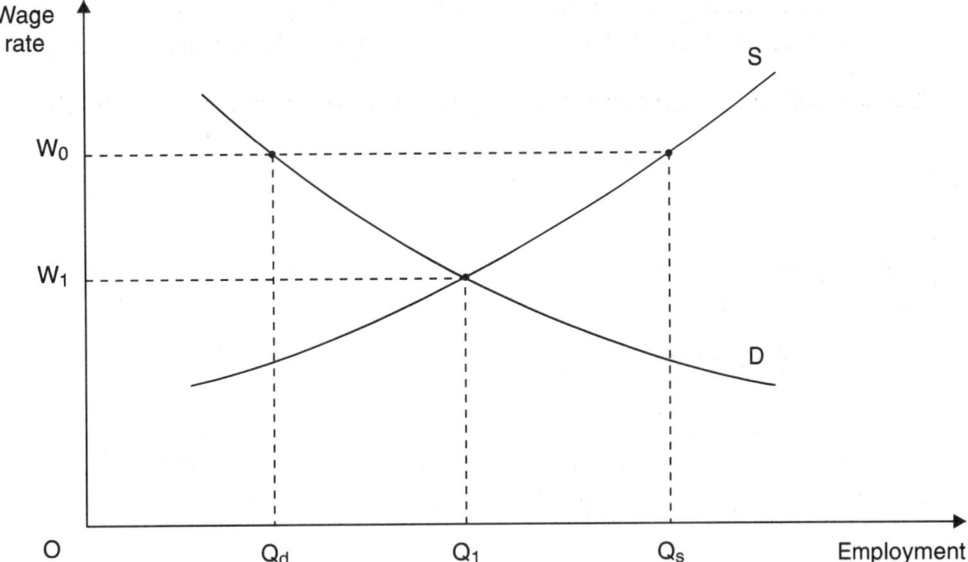

Figure 4 The labour market

6.8 **Stagflation.** In the 1970s there was a problem with **stagflation:** a combination of unacceptably high unemployment and unacceptably high inflation. One of the causes was diagnosed as the major rises in the price of crude oil that took place. The cost of energy rose and this had the effect of rendering some production unprofitable. The supply curve shifted to the left as a result. The continuing stagnation is illustrated in Figure 5.

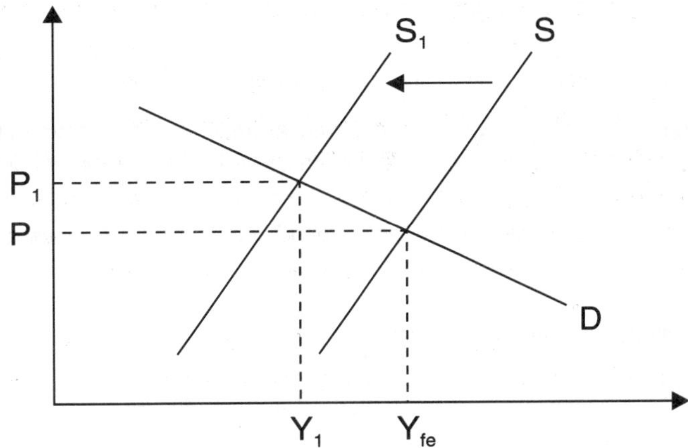

Figure 5 Stagflation

Unemployment falls and prices rise. Any long term major increase in costs (a **price shock**) is likely to have this effect.

Supply side economic policies

6.9 Supply side economists advise **against government intervention** in the economy at both the microeconomic and macroeconomic levels. **Microeconomic intervention** by government is disliked by supply side economists for a number of reasons.

(a) **Price regulation** distorts the signalling function essential for markets to reach optimal equilibrium.

(b) **Wage regulation** distorts the labour market's ability to ensure full employment.

(c) **Public ownership** blunts the incentive effects of the profit motive and leads to inefficiency.

(d) **Government grants and subsidies** encourage inefficient and 'lame duck' industries.

(e) **Public provision of services** may not encourage efficiency and can limit the discipline of consumer choice.

(f) **Employment legislation** such as employment protection limits market flexibility through discouraging recruitment and encouraging over-manning.

6.10 **Macroeconomic intervention** by government is regarded by supply side economists as harmful for several reasons.

(a) **Demand management** will be inflationary in the long run.

(b) High taxes will act as a **disincentive.**

(c) The possibility of **politically motivated policy changes** will create damaging uncertainty in the economy. This will discourage long-term investment.

6.11 Although most would accept the need for **expansion of the money stock** by government to accommodate increases in aggregate demand, some supply-siders have denied even this role to the government.

Chapter roundup

- We have looked at the Keynesian model, as a way of explaining how national income is determined, and how national income equilibrium is reached.
- To achieve full employment national income, it might be possible for a government to take measures to boost aggregate demand in the economy, although some price inflation will probably result. (Remember, Y = C + I + G + (X – M).) When there is inflation in the economy, measures could be taken to suppress aggregate demand.
- Changes in national income begin with a small change in expenditure, leading to an even larger eventual change in national income, due to the multiplier effect.
- The value of the multiplier is $\frac{1}{s}$ in a closed economy with no government sector.
- The value of the multiplier is $\frac{1}{s+m+t}$ in an open economy.
- A multiplier value can be measured specifically for investment, government spending and exports separately.
- Changes in national income can also be explained partially by the accelerator principle, which is that changes in investment spending are proportionally greater than changes in consumption spending, and therefore investment spending is more susceptible to bigger upturns and downturns.
- Trade cycles are explained in Keynesian economics as the combined effect of the multiplier and the accelerator.
- Macroeconomic policy aims cannot necessarily all be sustained together for a long period of time; attempts to achieve one objective will often have adverse effects on others, sooner or later.
- To some extent, there is a conflict between steady balanced growth in the economy and full employment. Although a growing economy should be able to provide more jobs, there is some concern that since an economy must be modernised to grow and modern technology is labour-saving, it might be possible to achieve growth without creating many more jobs, and so keeping unemployment at a high level.

- Monetarist economists argue that a Keynesian government policy to boost demand in the economy is likely to be inflationary and inflation will create more unemployment. They generally prefer to concentrate on the 'supply side' of the economy advocating policies which will affect supply and the costs of production rather than policies for influencing demand.

Quick quiz

1 For an equilibrium national income level to be reached, withdrawals from and injections into the circular flow of income must be equal. Why are they not always in balance?

2 What are the marginal propensity to consume and the marginal propensity to save?

3 How might a government try to influence the volume of investment by firms?

4 What are typically the main phases in a trade cycle?

5 What is the main implication of multiplier-accelerator theory?

6 Injections into the economy are:

A Consumption and Investment
B Investment and Government Expenditure
C Investment, Government Expenditure and Export Demand
D Consumption, Investment, Government Expenditure and Export Demand

7 If a consumption function has the formula C = 750 + 0.4Y where is Y the change in national income, and injections are 500, then equilibrium national income will be at:

A 833
B 1250
C 2083
D 3125

8 If the MPC is greater for the poor than the rich then a redistribution of national income in favour of the rich will:

A Raise savings out of a given income
B Increase the multiplier
C Decrease the MPS
D Stimulate import demand

9 A deflationary gap occurs when:

A Aggregate demand is insufficient to buy up all the goods and services the company is capable of producing.
B Aggregate demand is more than sufficient to buy up all the goods and services produced by an economy.
C A government attempts to spend its way out of recession.
D A government is cutting its level of expenditure.

10 The accelerator principle states:

A How a rise in investment causes national income to rise by more than the rise in investment.
B That a small rise in production of capital goods will cause a substantial rise in demand for consumer goods.
C That investment is a function of the level of national income.
D That investment is a function of the rate of change of national income.

Answers to quick quiz

1 The withdrawals and injections are not made by the same people.

2 When a household receives an increase in income, some will be spent and some will be saved. The proportion which is spent is the marginal propensity to consume, while the proportion which is saved is the marginal propensity to consume.

3 Lower interest rates, investment grants and tax incentives may encourage investment. Governments can also stimulate demand by tax cuts or lower interest rates and improve business confidence by business friendly and growth enhancing policies like deregulation and controlling inflation. Policies to encourage technological development may also lead to increased investment.

4 Recession, depression, recovery and boom.

5 The interaction of the multiplier and the accelerator may explain the variations in the trade cycle.

6 C

7 C Equilibrium occurs when E = Y. E = C + J = 750 + 0.4Y + 500. Therefore 0.6Y = 1,250, therefore Y= 2,083.

8 A The rich will save more, not spend.

9 A

10 D

Now try the questions below from the Question Bank

Number	Level	Marks	Time
Q40	Introductory	8	10 mins
Q41	Introductory - Interactive	–	–
Q42	Exam - MCQ	2	–

Chapter 15

MONEY AND INFLATION

Topic list		Syllabus reference	Ability required
1	The quantity theory of money	(iii)	Comprehension
2	The Keynesian theory of money	(iii)	Comprehension
3	The monetarist viewpoint	(iii)	Comprehension
4	Inflation and its consequences	(iii)	Comprehension

Introduction

In this chapter and the next we return to money and its place in the economy. We looked at the nature of money and the creation of credit in Chapters 11 and 12. We must now consider the role of government policy relating to money as it affects the management of the economy. This is called monetary policy.

Initially, this chapter deals with the theoretical framework and describes the different approaches economists have taken to explaining why money is needed and how it should be managed. The important names here are *Fisher, Keynes* and *Friedman.*

An important aspect of monetary policy is the control of inflation. Section 3 of this chapter therefore deals with the nature of inflation and its impact on the macroeconomy.

Learning outcome covered in this chapter

- Identify the main elements of the monetary and financial system

Syllabus content covered in this chapter

- The monetary environment: inflation and the money supply; the banking and financial system; interest rates and monetary policy

1 THE QUANTITY THEORY OF MONEY

The classical quantity theory of money

1.1 The **classical quantity theory of money**, goes back many years. It is associated with *Irving Fisher's* book *The Purchasing Power of Money*, which was published in 1911. The classical quantity theory is based on the view that money is used only as a **medium of exchange** and people require it only in order to settle transactions in good and services.

1.2 However, Keynesian economists argue that there are other reasons for wanting to hold money, as we shall see later.

1.3 If the number of transactions in the economy is fixed, and independent of the amount of the money supply, then the total money value of transactions will be PT, where

P is the price level of goods and services bought and sold
T is the number or quantity of transactions.

1.4 The amount of money needed to pay for these transactions will depend on the **velocity of circulation**. Money changes hands. A person receiving money can use it to make his own purchases. For example, if A pays B £2 for transaction X, B can use the £2 to pay C for transaction Y and C can use the same £2 to pay D for transaction Z. If the three transactions X, Y, and Z all occur within a given period of time then the money value of the transactions is:

£2 price level × 3 transactions = £6.

1.5 The total amount of money is the same £2 in circulation for all three transactions but this money has exchanged hands three times. The velocity of circulation is 3 and MV = 6, where M is the money supply and V is the velocity of circulation.

1.6 The quantity theory of money is summarised by this identity:

$$\mathbf{MV \equiv PT}$$

This is known as the **Fisher equation.**

1.7 MV **must** be equivalent to PT because they are two different ways of measuring the same transactions. In practice, the velocity of circulation V is calculated as the balancing figure in the equation below.

$$V = \frac{PT}{M}$$

Question 1

Which of the following definitions correctly describes the velocity of circulation?

(a) The money stock in a given time period divided by the level of prices
(b) The number of times in a given period that a unit of money is used to purchase final output
(c) The total value of transactions in a given time period divided by the average price level

Answer

According to the quantity theory, $V = \frac{PT}{M}$. This is described by (b), which is therefore the correct answer.

Answer (a) implies that $V = \frac{M}{P}$, and answer (c) implies that $V = \frac{PT}{P}$, both of which are incorrect.

KEY TERM

Quantity theory of money: the theory which holds that changes in the level of prices are caused predominantly by changes in the supply of money. This derives from the Fisher equation, MV = PT, assuming that the velocity of circulation V and the number of transactions T are stable.

1.8 Three further **assumptions** are made.

(a) **V has a roughly constant value.** The velocity of circulation of money remains the same at all times, or at least only changes very slowly over time.

(b) **T is either given or it is independent of the amount of money, M**. The reason why T should be a given total was that the supporters of the quantity theory argued that full employment of resources is the norm and if all resources are fully utilised, the volume of transactions T must be a constant value.

(c) **The amount of M is determined by other factors and is independent of V, T or (most significantly) P.** The money supply could be controlled by government authorities, including the central bank.

1.9 Given these assumptions, the quantity theory of money becomes a theory of **price levels** because, since MV = PT, then

$$P = \frac{MV}{T}$$

1.10 If V and T are roughly constant values, P will vary directly with increases or decreases in the amount of M: changes in the money supply M cause prices P to change. In other words, inflation is **directly related to** the money supply, and a 10% increase in the money supply, say, would result in 10% inflation.

1.11 There is a logic behind the algebra of the classical quantity theory and it relates to the basic assumption that money is used only for transactions relating to goods and services. If this is true, it follows that an excess of money will lead to increased attempts to spend it. Similarly, a shortage of money will have the effect of reducing demand. If the economy is utilising its productive resources to the full (that is, if there is full employment) it will not be possible to increase output. Any increase in demand will therefore cause prices to rise by the action of market forces. Similarly, any reduction in demand will cause prices to fall.

1.12 This theory is very satisfactory in explaining past experience of price rises and falls over long periods, as during the nineteenth century. In the first half of the nineteenth century there was large scale economic expansion, but the money supply was based on the gold standard and expanded only slowly: prices generally fell. In the second half of the century there were extensive increases in the supply of gold as a result of mining in Australia and America. The growth of economic activity, and hence output, did not match the growth in the gold supply and prices rose.

The money supply and inflation

1.13 **Important conclusions** from the quantity theory of money equation.

(a) If the velocity of circulation of money, V, is more or less constant, then any **growth in the money supply**, M, over and above the potential in the economy to increase T, will cause **inflation.**

(b) If **output in the economy, T, is** growing and if the velocity of circulation, V, is constant, then a **matching growth in the money supply,** M, is needed to avoid deflation.

(c) Government's monetary policy should be to allow some growth in the money supply **if the economy is growing,** but not to let the growth in the money supply get out of hand.

1.14 The extent to which these conclusions are valid depends largely on whether the velocity of circulation of money is roughly constant or not. For example, if the money supply increases by 10%, and real growth in the economy (the increase in the volume of transactions) is 3%, we could predict that inflation will be about 7% - but only if the velocity of circulation is constant.

1.15 The quantity theory of money relates the money supply directly to the general level of prices. It has no close connection to the classical theory of interest rates. This was simply a supply and demand equilibrium price model for liquid funds. The rate of interest is effectively the price of borrowing and the reward of lending. This model was discussed in the chapter on markets for factors of production.

2 THE KEYNESIAN THEORY OF MONEY

The demand for money

KEY TERM

Liquidity preference is the preference of people to hold on to their savings as money (in liquid form) rather than investing it.

2.1 Keynes identified three reasons why people hold wealth as money rather than as interest-bearing securities.

KEY TERMS

The **transactions motive.** Households need money to pay for their day-to-day purchases. The level of transactions demand for money depends on household incomes.

The **precautionary motive.** People choose to keep money on hand or in the bank as a precaution for when it might suddenly be needed.

The **speculative motive.** Some people choose to keep ready money to take advantage of a profitable opportunity to invest in bonds which may arise (or they may sell bonds for money when they fear a fall in the market prices of bonds).

2.2 There is an important contrast here with the classical quantity theory of money. The **quantity theory** assumes that the demand for money is governed by **transactions** only. By proposing two further reasons, Keynes strikes out into new territory.

2.3 The precautionary motive is really just an extension of the transactions motive. However, the **speculative motive** for holding money needs explaining a bit further.

(a) If individuals hold money for speculative purposes, this means that they are not using the money to invest in bonds. They are holding on to their savings for speculative reasons. Hence, savings and investment might not be in equilibrium, with consequences for changes in national income.

(b) The reason for holding money instead of investing in bonds is that **interest rates are expected to go up**. If interest rates go up, bond prices will fall. For example, if the current *market price* of bonds which pay 5% interest on face value is £100, and interest rates doubled to 10%, the market value of the bonds would fall, perhaps to £50. This is because the interest paid on a bond is fixed at a percentage of *face value*. The ratio between the income paid and the *market value* adjusts to the current prevailing interest rate by means of changes in the market value. So if interest rates are expected to go up, any bonds held now will be expected to lose value, and bond holders would make a capital loss. Thus, it makes sense to hold on to money, for investing in bonds later, *after* interest rates have gone up. Keynes called such money holdings **idle balances.**

(c) What causes individuals to have expectations about interest rate changes in the future? Keynes argued that each individual has some expectation of a **normal rate of interest.** This concept of a normal interest rate reflects past levels and movements in the interest rate, and expectations of the future rate level, obtained from available market information.

Question 2

Following this Keynesian analysis, how would you expect an individual to act if:

(a) he thinks that the current level of interest is below the 'normal' rate?
(b) he thinks that the current level of interest is above the 'normal' rate?

Answer

(a) If someone believes that the normal rate of interest is above the current level, he will expect the interest rate to rise and will therefore expect bond prices to fall. To avoid a capital loss the individual will sell bonds and hold money.

(b) Conversely, if an individual believes that the normal rate of interest is below the current market interest rate, he will expect the market interest rate to fall and bond prices to rise. Hence he will buy bonds, and run down speculative money holdings, in order to make a capital gain.

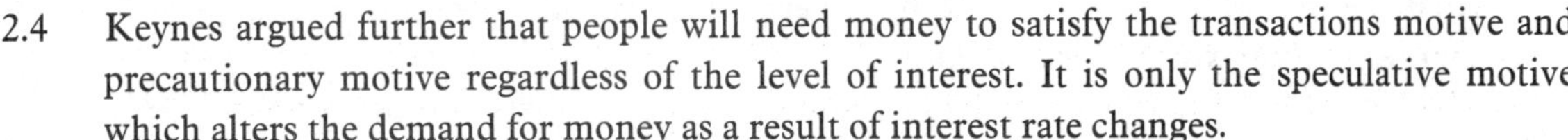

2.4 Keynes argued further that people will need money to satisfy the transactions motive and precautionary motive regardless of the level of interest. It is only the speculative motive which alters the demand for money as a result of interest rate changes.

(a) If interest rates are high, people will expect them to fall and will expect the price of bonds to rise. They will therefore purchase bonds in anticipation of a capital gain and will therefore have **low liquidity preference.**

(b) If interest rates are low but are expected to rise, this implies that bond prices are likely to fall. People will therefore hold liquid funds in order to be able to invest in bonds later on. Their **liquidity preference will be high.**

2.5 The conclusion is that the demand for money will be high (liquidity preference will be high) when interest rates are low. This is because the speculative demand for money will be high. Similarly, the demand for money will be low when interest rates are high, because the speculative demand for money will be low.

2.6 There is thus a **minimum fixed demand** for money (transactions and precautionary motives) and **some demand** for money that varies with interest rates (speculative motive). This can be shown as a liquidity preference curve (Figure 1). A minimum quantity of money is needed, regardless of interest rate, to satisfy the minimum demand arising from the transactions and precautionary motives for holding money.

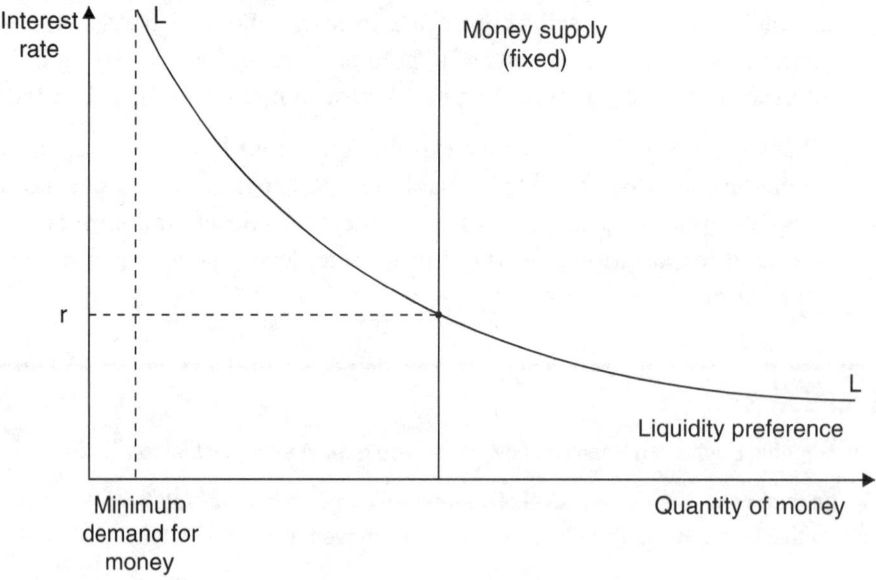

Figure 1 Interest rates, money demand and the money supply

Interest rates

2.7 Keynes' view on the determination of interest rates is, like the classical view, a market model. He argued that the level of interest rates is determined by the interaction of demand for and supply of money. While the liquidity preference curve may be thought of as a normal demand curve, with the rate of interest being the price of money, Keynes suggested that the money supply was fixed by government and therefore inelastic: a vertical supply curve, in other words, as shown in Figure 1.

2.8 The **quantity theory** assumes that an increase in the money supply will automatically lead to an increase in AD. Since the economy is assumed to be operating at full employment and therefore not able to produce more goods and services, this increase in AD will cause a rise in the level of prices generally. **Keynes took a different view**. He said that an increase in the money supply would lead to a fall in interest rates.

2.9 **It is a very important aspect of this theory, and a contrast with the quantity theory, that an increase in the money supply would not lead directly to an increase in AD.**

2.10 If there is an increase in the money supply, from MS_1 to MS_2 in Figure 2, not surprisingly, it will become cheaper and interest rates will fall from r_1 to r_2. There will be some increase in the level of investment spending, since it now becomes more profitable for firms to invest in new capital because of the fall in the cost of borrowing. The increase in investment, being an injection into the circular flow of income, causes some increase in the level of national income through the multiplier process. According to the Keynesians, therefore, **a change in the money supply only indirectly affects the demand for goods and services**, and hence the level of income, via a change in the rate of interest. This is called an **indirect transmission mechanism**.

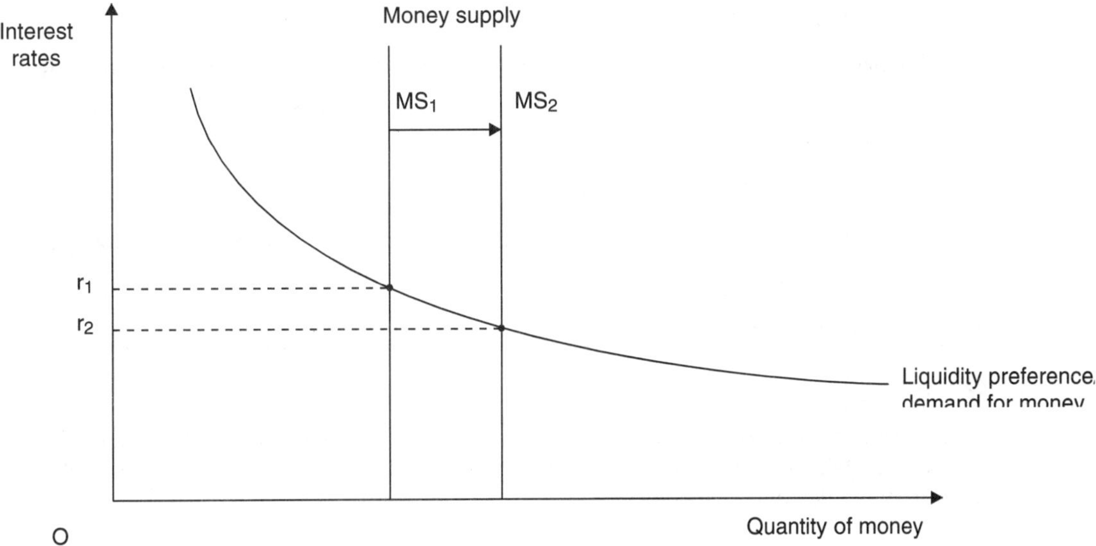

Figure 2 Consequence of an increase in the money supply

2.11 The impact on the economy of the increase in the money supply therefore depends on the effect that the fall in interest rates produces. According to the Keynesian view, both investment demand and consumer spending are **relatively insensitive** to interest rate changes, that is, they are relatively interest-inelastic. The **volume of investment** depends heavily, Keynes argued, on **technological changes** and **business confidence and expectations** too. It follows that the increase in the money supply will have only a limited effect on aggregate demand and consequently relatively little effect on output and employment or on price levels. This view implies that the velocity of circulation, V, is **not fixed**, since a varying amount of money is held as investment in bonds.

2.12 Keynesians therefore argue that monetary policy to control the money supply would, have an effect on interest rates and changes in interest rates might in the longer term affect investment. In other respects, however, monetary policy would not really affect the economy and national income, because increases in the money supply would be neutralised by reductions in the velocity of circulation, leaving PT unaffected.

What makes the money supply grow?

2.13 We have looked at the demand for and supply of money without yet asking what it is that makes the money supply grow in the first place. If we define money broadly, to include bank deposits, **four main factors contribute to money supply growth.**

(a) Government short term borrowing has a direct effect on the money supply since the banks can use the Treasury bills they receive as part of their liquid reserves. Government borrowing thus releases cash into circulation that would otherwise be tied up in bank reserves.
(b) Who the government borrows from, banks or non-banks, since only banks have the ability to create money by lending
(c) Bank lending generally
(d) Flows of money between the country and foreign traders/investors

Approaches to controlling the growth of the broad money supply

2.14 A government might take any of four broad approaches to controlling the growth of the money supply.

(a) To reduce or control government borrowing

(b) To finance as much government borrowing as possible by borrowing from the UK non-bank private sector, for example by encouraging National Savings in preference to issuing gilts

(c) To control the increase in bank lending

(d) To control external and foreign currency items, for example by keeping the balance of payments under control

---

Question 3

In an earlier chapter we identified four functions of money: a means of exchange, a unit of account, a standard of deferred payment and a store of value. Which one of these is central to the Keynesian analysis of the demand for money?

Answer

It is the function of money as a liquid store of value or wealth which is central to the concept of liquidity preference.

---

3 THE MONETARIST VIEWPOINT 5/01

3.1 **Friedman** argued that there is a much more direct link between the money supply and national income. Whereas Keynes argued that an increase in the money supply would merely result in lower interest rates, with no immediate effect on national income, monetarists argue that an increase in the money supply will lead directly and quickly to changes in national income and PT, with the velocity of circulation V remaining fairly constant.

3.2 In his analysis of the demand for money, Friedman argued that money is just one of five broad ways of holding wealth.

- **Money**
- **Bonds**
- **Equities**
- **Physical goods**
- **Human wealth**

(Human wealth here is a special concept and may be ignored for the purpose of our analysis.)

3.3 Each method of holding wealth brings some form of return or yield to the holder.

(a) The main yield from money is the **convenience** of having it when it is needed. This cannot be measured in money terms.

(b) The return on **bonds** is the interest plus any capital gain (or loss).

(c) **Equities** should provide dividends and capital growth which keep ahead of the rate of inflation.

(d) **Physical assets in this analysis,** do not waste away through use, because assets which are consumed cannot be a store of wealth. There might be an increase in their capital value but the yield also includes the non-monetary return, such as the use of furniture, the enjoyment from paintings and so on.

3.4 Friedman argued that the demand for money is related to the demand for holding wealth in its other forms. While Keynes believed that if people did not want to hold money, they would invest it to earn interest, monetarists believe that they might also use it instead to buy equities or physical assets.

3.5 Friedman argued that money gives a convenience yield but it is not an asset which is held for its own sake. It is a 'temporary abode of purchasing power' waiting to be spent on other types of financial or physical asset. The **demand for money** is therefore a function of the yield on money and the yield on other forms of holding wealth. **Yield** as defined here includes non-monetary yield such as convenience and enjoyment.

3.6 Monetarists would argue, further, that the demand for money is fairly interest-inelastic. The demand for money is related to a transactions motive, but not to any speculative motive. An expected rise in interest rates might persuade individuals to sell bonds and buy other assets, but not to hold speculative money.

The loanable funds theory of interest rates

3.7 According to Keynesians, the level of interest rates is determined by the interaction of the speculative demand for money and the money supply.

3.8 Monetarists hold the traditional view that the reasons for demanding money are for transactions only, not speculation about future investment. Monetarists argue instead that interest rates are determined by the demand and supply of **loanable funds**. An increase in the money supply, without any increase in demand for money (investment), will increase the amount of loanable funds available (savings). Interest rates will fall, and investment will rise.

The transmission mechanism and imbalances between money supply and demand

3.9 Monetarists say that the connection between the demand for money, the money supply and national income can be explained by **a direct transmission mechanism**.

3.10 Starting from a position of equilibrium holding of assets of all kinds, **an increase in the money supply** would leave individuals holding an excess of money balances. In order to restore the level of money holdings to its desired level, individuals will substitute **assets of all kinds** for money: the demand for goods and services will increase, not just demand for financial assets.

(a) The increase in the quantity of money means a fall in the rate of interest. This will not lead to an increase in the demand for money, according to the monetarists, because they believe that the **demand for money is interest-inelastic**.

(b) The increase in direct spending on goods and services will, however, lead to a **rise in the level of money national income**.

By assuming that money is a substitute for all assets, the monetarists conclude that variations in the money supply have a great influence on the level of national income. In terms of the classical quantity theory of money, if M goes up, and MV = PT, there will be an increase in PT, but this could mean an increase in either real output (T) or in prices and inflation (P).

3.11 Suppose that the demand for money goes up, but the authorities stop the money supply from increasing, so that there is an **excess demand** for money. The transmission

mechanism will work the other way. Households will sell bonds and equities and reduce consumption on other goods in order to acquire more money. Interest rates will go up. There will be a decline in total spending in the economy until money supply and demand are again in equilibrium. Since MV = PT, a decline in PT will have one of two effects.

(a) If the economy is operating below its full employment national income level, there will be a decline in T leading to even less output and so more unemployment.

(b) If the economy has an inflationary gap, there will be a decline in P, and inflation will be brought under control.

The new quantity theory of money

3.12 Friedman re-stated the quantity theory of money, as follow.

$MV \equiv PQ$

where M is the **money supply**
V is the **velocity of circulation** of money
P is the **average price level**
Q is the physical quantity of **national output per period** (ie the real volume of economic output)

Thus, PQ is the **money value of national output** (ie national income Y at current prices). Remember that in Fisher's version of this equation P was the **general level** of prices rather than a numerical average and T was the number of transactions. PT was therefore the money value of transactions and **proportional** to national income, **not equal** to it.

3.13 Monetarists argue that V and Q are independent of M. Therefore, an increase in money supply M will tend to raise prices P, via the direct transmission mechanism.

(a) Individuals will have more money than they want.

(b) They will spend this excess money, buying not just 'bonds' (as Keynes believed) but also equities and physical goods.

(c) The greater demand for physical goods will boost expenditure in the economy (and so the money value of national income).

(d) However, a rapid increase in the money supply will increase spending at a faster rate than the economy will be able to produce more physical output.

(e) A rapid increase in the money supply will therefore inevitably be inflationary.

3.14 In conclusion, for monetarists, changes in the money supply cause changes in the money value of national income. Remember that Keynes believed there was only a weak link between changes in the money supply and changes in aggregate demand.

Question 4

According to monetarist economics, which of the following consequences will result from an increase in the money supply?

1 Households will have excess money.
2 Households will use this money to buy more bonds, equities and physical goods.
3 Interest rates will rise.
4 The demand for money will respond to the change in interest rates.
5 Expenditure in the economy will increase.

Answer

Consequences 1, 2 and 5 (but not 3 and 4) will result. According to monetarists, an increase in the money supply creates excess supply over demand. Households use the excess money to buy bonds (and so interest rates *fall*), equities and physical goods (and so expenditure in the economy rises). The demand for money is interest-rate inelastic, according to monetarists (but not according to Keynesians) and so this does not increase in response to any interest rate fall.

The monetarist view of money supply and inflation in the economy

3.15 Monetarists argue that since money is a direct substitute for all other assets, an increase in the money supply, given a fairly stable velocity of circulation, will have a direct effect on demand for other assets because there will be more money to spend on those assets. If the total output of the economy is fixed, then an increase in the money supply will lead directly to higher prices.

3.16 Monetarists therefore reach the same basic conclusion as the old quantity theory of money. A rise in the money supply will lead to a rise in prices and probably also to a rise in money incomes. (It is also assumed by monetarists that the velocity of circulation remains fairly constant, again taking a view similar to the old quantity theory.) In the short run, monetarists argue that an increase in the money supply might cause some increase in real output and so an increase in employment. In the long run, however, all increases in the money supply will be reflected in higher prices unless there is longer term growth in the economy.

Weaknesses in monetarist theory

3.17 There are certain **complications with the monetarist views**, for example the following.

(a) The velocity of circulation is known to fluctuate up and down by small amounts.

(b) Increases in prices will not affect all goods equally. Some goods will rise in price more than others and so the relative price of goods will change. For example, the price of houses might exceed the average rate of inflation but the price of electronic goods might rise more slowly.

(c) A higher rate of inflation in one country than another might affect the country's balance of payments and currency value, thereby introducing complications for the economy from international trade movements.

(d) Prices in the economy might take some time to adjust to an increase in the money supply.

3.18 **Comparison of theories**

	Classical Quantity Theory	*Keynesian Theory*	*New Quantity Theory*
Name	Fisher	Keynes	Friedman
Keyword/symbol	MV≡PT	'liquidity preference'	MV≡PQ
Use for money	Transactions	Transaction motive Precautionary motive Speculative motive	Cash Bonds Equities Physical goods Human wealth
Assumptions	T, V constant M independently determined	Only speculative demand varies Money supply usually fixed	Demand for money is interest-inelastic
Effect if rise in money supply when economy at full employment	AD up, price rises	Price of bonds up, interest rate falls, small rise in AD and prices	Spending on assets of all kinds up, AD up, prices up
Transmission mechanism	Direct	Indirect, via interest rate	Direct
Determination of interest rate	Supply and demand for money	Since money supply fixed, depends on speculative demand for bonds	Supply and demand of loanable funds

4 INFLATION AND ITS CONSEQUENCES 11/01

KEY TERM

Inflation is the name given to an increase in price levels generally. It is also manifest in the decline in the purchasing power of money.

4.1 Historically, there have been very few periods when inflation has not been present. We discuss below why high rates of inflation are considered to be harmful. However, it is important to remember that **deflation** (falling prices) is normally associated with low rates of growth and even recession. It would seem that a healthy economy may require some inflation. This is recognised in the current UK inflation target of 2½%, and the European Central Bank's target of 2%. Certainly, if an economy is to grow, the money supply must expand, and the presence of a low level of inflation will ensure that growth is not hampered by a shortage of liquid funds.

Why is inflation a problem? 5/01

4.2 An economic policy objective which now has a central place in the policy approaches of the governments of many developed countries is that of stable prices. Why is a *high* rate of price inflation harmful and undesirable?

Redistribution of income and wealth

4.3 Inflation leads to a redistribution of income and wealth in ways which may be undesirable. Redistribution of wealth might take place from creditors to debtors. This is because debts lose 'real' value with inflation. For example, if you owed £1,000, and prices then doubled, you would still owe £1,000, but the **real value** of your debt would have been halved. In general, in times of inflation those with economic power tend to gain at the expense of the weak, particularly those on fixed incomes.

Balance of payments effects

4.4 If a country has a higher rate of inflation than its major trading partners, its exports will become relatively expensive and imports relatively cheap. As a result, the balance of trade will suffer, affecting employment in exporting industries and in industries producing import-substitutes. Eventually, the exchange rate will be affected (see Chapter 19).

Uncertainty of the value of money and prices

4.5 If the rate of inflation is imperfectly anticipated, no one has certain knowledge of the true rate of inflation. As a result, no one has certain knowledge of the value of money or of the real meaning of prices. If the rate of inflation becomes excessive, and there is 'hyperinflation', this problem becomes so exaggerated that money becomes worthless, so that people are unwilling to use it and are forced to resort to barter. In less extreme circumstances, the results are less dramatic, but the same problem exists. As prices convey less information, the process of resource allocation is less efficient and rational decision-making is almost impossible.

Resource costs of changing prices

4.6 A fourth reason to aim for stable prices is the resource cost of frequently changing prices. In times of high inflation substantial labour time is spent on planning and implementing price changes. Customers may also have to spend more time making price comparisons if they seek to buy from the lowest cost source.

Economic growth and investment

4.7 It is sometimes claimed that inflation is harmful to a country's economic growth and level of investment. A study by *Robert Barro* (*Bank of England Quarterly Bulletin*, May 1995) examined whether the evidence available supports this view. Barro found from data covering over 100 countries from 1960 to 1990 that, on average, an increase in inflation of ten percentage points per year reduced the growth rate of real GDP per capita by 0.2 to 0.3 percentage points per year, and lowered the ratio of investment to GDP by 0.4 to 0.6 percentage points. Although the adverse influence of inflation on economic growth and investment appears small, some causal effect would appear to exist, which could affect a country's standard of living fairly significantly over the long term.

Consumer price indices 5/02

4.8 We have already referred to the way in which inflation erodes the real value of money. In order to measure changes in the real value of money as a single figure, we need to group all goods and services into a single price index.

4.9 A consumer price index is based on a chosen 'basket' of items which consumers purchase. A weighting is decided for each item according to the average spending on the item by consumers.

4.10 Consumer price indices may be used for several purposes, for example as an indicator of inflationary pressures in the economy, as a benchmark for wage negotiations and to determine annual increases in government benefits payments. Countries commonly have more than one consumer price index because one composite index may be considered too wide a grouping for different purposes.

The Retail Prices Index

4.11 The most important measure of the general rate of inflation in the UK is the **Retail Prices Index (RPI)**. The RPI measures the percentage changes month by month in the average level of prices of the commodities and services, including housing costs, purchased by the great majority of households in the UK. The items of expenditure within the RPI are intended to be a representative list of items, current prices for which are collected at regular intervals.

The underlying rate of inflation

4.12 The term **underlying rate of inflation** is usually used to refer to the RPI adjusted to exclude mortgage costs and sometimes other elements as well (such as the local council tax). The effects of interest rate changes on mortgage costs help to make the RPI fluctuate more widely than the underlying rate of inflation.

4.13 The UK government's target rate for inflation is defined in terms of **RPIX**, which is the underlying rate of inflation measured as the increase in the RPI excluding mortgage interest payments. Another measure, called **RPIY**, goes further and excludes the effects of VAT changes as well.

4.14 **Causes of inflation**

- Demand pull factors
- Cost push factors
- Import cost factors
- Expectations
- Excessive growth in the money supply

4.15 **Demand pull inflation** occurs when the economy is buoyant and there is a high aggregate demand, in excess of the economy's ability to supply.

(a) Because aggregate demand exceeds supply, prices rise.

(b) Since supply needs to be raised to meet the higher demand, there will be an increase in demand for factors of production, and so factor rewards (wages, interest rates, and so on) will also rise.

(c) Since aggregate demand exceeds the output capability of the economy, it should follow that Demand pull inflation can only exist when unemployment is low. A feature of inflation in the UK in the 1970s and early 1980s, however, was high inflation coupled with high unemployment.

> **KEY TERM**
>
> **Demand pull inflation:** inflation resulting from a persistent excess of aggregate demand over aggregate supply. Supply reaches a limit on capacity at the full employment level.

4.16 Traditionally Keynesian economists saw inflation as being caused by Demand pull factors. However, they now accept that Cost push factors are involved as well.

4.17 **Cost push inflation** occurs where the costs of factors of production rise regardless of whether or not they are in short supply. This appears to be particularly the case with wages.

> **KEY TERM**
>
> **Cost push inflation**: inflation resulting from an increase in the costs of production of goods and services, eg through escalating prices of imported raw materials or from wage increases.

4.18 **Import Cost push inflation** occurs when the cost of essential imports rise regardless of whether or not they are in short supply. This has occurred in the past with the oil price rises of the 1970s. Additionally, a fall in the value of a country's currency will have import Cost push effects since a weakening currency increases the price of imports.

4.19 A further problem is that once the rate of inflation has begun to increase, a serious danger of **expectational inflation** will occur. This means, regardless of whether the factors that have caused inflation are still persistent or not, there will arise a generally held view of what inflation is likely to be, and so to protect future income, wages and prices will be raised now by the expected amount of future inflation. This can lead to the vicious circle known as the **wage-price spiral**, in which inflation becomes a relatively permanent feature because of people's expectations that it will occur.

4.20 Monetarists have argued that inflation is caused by **increases in the supply of money**. There is a considerable debate as to whether increases in the money supply are a **cause** of inflation or whether increases in the money supply are a **symptom** of inflation. Monetarists have argued that since inflation is caused by an increase in the money supply, inflation can be brought under control by reducing the rate of growth of the money supply.

Question 5

(a) A government can help to counter Demand pull inflation by reducing interest rates. True or false?

(b) A government can help to counter Demand pull inflation by increasing value added tax. True or false?

(c) A government can help to counter Cost push inflation by increasing income tax rates. True or false?

(d) A government can help to counter Cost push inflation by linking wage increases to productivity improvements. True or false?

Answer

(a) *False.* On the contrary, this would increase consumer borrowing and hence stimulate Demand pull inflation.

(b) *True.* This might increase total spending on goods and services *inclusive* of the tax, but spending *net* of tax will probably fall.

(c) *False.* Increasing direct taxation will reduce consumers' disposable income, and is therefore a measure aimed at countering Demand pull inflation, not Cost push inflation.

(d) *True.* This will reduce the unit costs of production.

4.21 However, if the government controls the money supply without telling anyone what its planned targets of growth are, then people's **expectations** of inflation will run ahead of the growth in the money supply. Wage demands will remain at levels in keeping with these expectations and so the rate of increase in P will exceed the rate of increase in M. If the government succeeds in its aim of limiting the growth of the money supply, but wages rise at a faster rate, then higher wages will mean less real income (Y) and less real output (T). In other words, the economy will slump even further.

4.22 It is for this reason that the government must announce its targets for growth in the money supply.

(a) Most monetarists argue that the government must give a clear announcement of its targets for monetary growth so as to influence people's expectations of inflation.

(b) Some economists might argue that an **incomes policy** should be imposed by the government to prevent wage rises in excess of government targets.

4.23 Monetarists pointed to the high inflation of the mid-1970s as evidence in support of their views since very rapid monetary growth preceded the price inflation. However, later research suggested that soaring oil and commodity prices were the culprits. Falling commodity prices helped subsequently to reduce inflation.

How does controlling inflation help the economy to grow?

4.24 Monetarists argue that monetary control will put the brake on inflation, but how does this help the economy? We have already noted *Robert Barro's* finding that inflation seems to hinder economic growth. We might argue like this.

(a) High inflation increases **economic uncertainty**. Bringing inflation under control will restore business confidence and help international trade by stabilising the exchange rate.

(b) A resurgence of business confidence through lower interest rates (due to less uncertainty and lower inflation) will **stimulate investment** and real output.

(c) A **controlled growth in the money supply** will provide higher incomes for individuals to purchase the higher output.

The control of inflation

4.25 The best way of controlling inflation will depend on the causes of it. In practice, it may be difficult to know which cause is most significant. The table below sets out various policies designed to control inflation.

Anti-inflation policies

Cause of inflation	*Policy to control inflation*
Demand pull (high consumer demand)	Take steps to reduce demand in the economy ◦ Higher taxation, to cut consumer spending ◦ Lower government expenditure (and lower government borrowing to finance its expenditure) ◦ Higher interest rates
Cost push factors (higher wage costs and other costs working through to higher prices)	Take steps to reduce production costs and price rises ◦ De-regulate labour markets ◦ Encourage greater productivity in industry ◦ Apply controls over wage and price rises (prices and incomes policy)
Import Cost push factors	Take steps to reduce the quantities or the price of imports. Such a policy might involve trying to achieve either an appreciation or depreciation of the domestic currency
Excessively fast growth in the money supply	Take steps to try to reduce the rate of money supply growth ◦ Reduced government borrowing and borrow from the non-bank private sector ◦ Try to control or reduce bank lending ◦ Try to achieve a balance of trade surplus ◦ Maintain interest rates at a level that might deter money supply growth
Expectations of inflation	Pursue clear policies which indicate the government's determination to reduce the rate of inflation

High interest rates and inflation

4.26 A government may adopt a policy of raising **interest rates** as a means of trying to reduce the rate of inflation, when inflation is being caused by a boom in consumer demand (with demand rising faster than the ability of industry to increase its output to meet the demand). In the UK however, as already mentioned, the Government has transferred the power to set interest rates to the Bank of England from 1997.

(a) When interest rates go up, there will be an initial increase in the rate of inflation. (As we have seen, mortgage interest payments are included in the retail prices index in the UK.)

(b) If interest rates are high enough, there should eventually be a reduction in the rate of growth in consumer spending.

(i) People who borrow must pay more in interest out of their income. This will leave them less income, after paying the interest, to spend on other things. (The government would not want wages to rise, though, because if people build up their income again with high wage settlements, the consumer spending boom could continue.)

(ii) High interest rates might deter people from borrowing, and so there would be less spending with borrowed funds.

(iii) High interest rates should encourage more saving, with individuals therefore spending less of their income on consumption.

(iv) High interest rates will tend to depress the values of non-monetary assets, such as houses, and the reduction in people's perceived wealth may make people feel 'poorer' and consequently reduce the amounts they spend on consumer goods.

Prices and incomes policy

4.27 **Control of prices and incomes** by government regulation (or voluntary agreement) is a further approach to keeping inflation down. In Britain, this was last tried in the 'social contract' of the Labour government of James Callaghan in the late 1970s. A prices and incomes policy is likely to be treated as a temporary policy. Such policies have been used in the past as a last resort when other policies to govern the economy have failed.

4.28 **Problems with wage controls**

- Non-comparable wages between work groups and erosion of pay differentials
- The problem of rewarding productivity improvements
- Evasion of the controls
- Trade union resistance

4.29 A policy for controlling prices also has particular problems to overcome.

- Administrative difficulty of imposing control
- Rising prices of imports which should be passed on
- Special cases needing price rises to avoid insolvency

4.30 There is also the enormous practical problem of establishing a policing agency or agencies to monitor, control and approve increases in prices and incomes. If this agency has to vet every individual price rise and wages settlement, it would need a very large staff, and might easily become a slow-working bureaucracy, denounced by firms and employees for its delayed decisions. If price controls are too rigid, the government might face the problem that a black market economy might develop in certain goods, with prices on the black market rising to levels that are far in excess of the government's limits.

Chapter roundup

- We have seen that the quantity theory of money is based on the identity $MV \equiv PT$. On the assumption that V is constant and T can only increase slowly, large increases in the money supply M will be inflationary.
- According to monetarists, an increase in the money supply will have clear consequences.
  - Individuals will have more money than they want.
  - They will spend this excess money, buying not just 'bonds' (as Keynes believed) but also equities and physical goods.
  - The greater demand for physical goods will boost expenditure in the economy (and so the money value of national income).
  - However, a rapid increase in the money supply will increase spending at a faster rate than the economy will be able to produce more physical output.
  - A rapid increase in the money supply will therefore inevitably be inflationary.

- Keynes argued that money is held for transactions and precautionary motives (for spending) and for speculative reasons. Transaction spending is independent of the money supply. Changes in the money supply will have implications for speculative holdings of money, and interest rates, but will have little or no consequence for spending on goods and services.
- Keynesians argue that interest rates are determined by the interaction of the supply of money and the demand for money rather than bonds (liquidity preference). Monetarists argue that interest rates are determined by the supply and demand for loanable funds.
- Keynes argued that increases in the money supply will affect interest rates and the demand for money, but changes in interest rates only have a limited and relatively insignificant effect on consumer spending and investment spending. This is a view which is now not generally favoured.
- High rates of **inflation** are harmful to an economy.
  - Inflation redistributes income and wealth improperly.
  - Inflation can harm the balance of payments and effect the exchange rate.
  - Uncertainty about the value of money makes business planning more difficult.
  - Constantly changing prices impose extra costs.
  - High inflation appears to cut economic growth.
- Inflation is measured by means of **price indices** such as RPI, RPIX and RPIY.
- **Demand pull inflation** arises from an excess of aggregate demand over the productive capacity of the economy.
- **Cost push inflation** arises from increases in the costs of production.
- Economists do not all agree about the relationship between inflation and **growth in the money supply**. If a government wishes to reduce inflation by controlling the growth of the money supply, it should announce its intentions in order to reduce **expectations of inflation**.

Quick quiz

1 Write the equation for the classical quantity theory of money.

2 According to Keynes, what are the three motives for wanting to hold money?

3 What will be the consequence for bond prices of an increase in interest rates?

4 What are the two main types of inflation?

5 What effect does a high interest rate have on the exchange rate?

6 For the Quantity Theory of Money identity $MV \equiv PT$ to explain short-run price behaviour, it is necessary that:

A P varies inversely with M
B Interest rates remain unchanged
C Changes in V in the short run are predictable
D T remains unchanged

7 According to Keynes, which one of the following is very sensitive to changes in interest rates?

A The money supply
B The speculative demand for money
C The precautionary demand for money
D Transactions demand for money

8 Other things remaining the same, according to Keynes, an increase in the money supply will tend to reduce:

A Interest rates
B Liquidity preference
C The volume of bank overdrafts
D Prices and incomes

9 According to monetarist economists, which of the following consequences will result from an increase in the money supply? 1. Households will have excess money. 2. Households will use this money to buy more bonds, equities and physical goods. 3. Interest rates will rise. 4. The demand for money will respond to the change in interest rates. 5. Expenditure in the economy will increase.

A 1, 2, 5 only will happen
B 3, 5 only will happen
C 1, 2, 4, 5 only will happen
D 3, 4 and 5 will all happen

Answers to quick quiz

1 MV ≡ PT

2 The transactions, precautionary and speculative motives.

3 Bond prices will fall until the fixed income they provide equates to the rate of interest.

4 Demand pull and Cost push

5 It attracts foreign investment, thus increasing the demand for the currency. The exchange rate rises as a result.

6 D T has to be unchanged for MV ≡ PT to be a predictor of price behaviour. Any increase in M, given no change in V in the short run, would result in a matching percentage increase in prices P.

7 B According to Keynes the money supply would be fixed by the authorities. The demand for money depends on three motives (transactions, precautionary and speculative) but it is the speculative demand for money that is sensitive to changes in interest rates, and this explains the liquidity preference schedule.

8 A Lower interest rates should be a consequence of an increase in the money supply, with a movement along the liquidity preference curve rather than a shift in the liquidity preference curve.

9 A The question describes the transmission mechanism, which is the link between an excess of money supply over demand (or money demand over supply) and changes in expenditure in the economy. According to monetarists, an increase in the money supply creates excess supply over demand. Households use the excess money to buy bonds (and so interest rates *fall*), equities and physical goods (and so expenditure in the economy rises). The demand for money is interest-rate inelastic, according to monetarists (but not according to Keynesians) and so this does not increase in response to any interest rate fall..

Now try the questions below from the Question Bank

Number	Level	Marks	Time
Q43	Introductory	8	10 mins
Q44	Exam - MCQ	2	–
Q45	Exam - MCQ	2	–

Chapter 16

MONETARY POLICY, UNEMPLOYMENT AND INFLATION

Topic list		Syllabus reference	Ability required
1	Unemployment	(iii)	Comprehension
2	Unemployment and inflation	(iii)	Comprehension
3	Monetary policy	(iii)	Comprehension

Introduction

In the previous chapter we began our examination of monetary policy by looking at money and inflation. In this chapter, we discuss government monetary policy and, in particular, dealing with inflation. Government policy on inflation is complicated by a clear link between inflation and unemployment; at one time it was believed that it was not possible to reduce them both simultaneously. We therefore start this chapter with a discussion of unemployment and continue with a description of the link with inflation in Section 2. The way is then clear for us to consider monetary policy in Section 3. We round off this chapter with a section on supply side policies, which have been associated with monetarist economists.

Learning outcomes covered in this chapter

- Explain the importance of the monetary environment to the business sector
- Explain the economic role of government through fiscal and monetary policy and demonstrate the impact of such policies on the business sector
- Explain the debates concerning the nature of the macroeconomy and appropriate government policy

Syllabus content covered in this chapter

- National income: its measurement and determination; the circular flow of income and a simple aggregate demand and supply model; unemployment and the price level
- The monetary environment: inflation and the money supply; the banking and financial system; interest rates and monetary policy

1 UNEMPLOYMENT

1.1 The **rate of unemployment** can be calculated as:

$$\frac{\text{Number of unemployed}}{\text{Total workforce}} \times 100\%$$

The number of unemployed at any time is measured by government statistics. If the flow of workers through unemployment is constant then the size of the unemployed labour force will also be constant.

1.2 **Flows into unemployment**

(a) Members of the working labour force **becoming** unemployed

- Redundancies
- Lay-offs
- Voluntary quitting from a job

(b) People **out** of the labour force **joining** the unemployed

- School leavers without a job
- Others (for example, carers) rejoining the workforce but having no job yet

1.3 **Flows out of unemployment**

- Unemployed people finding jobs
- Laid-off workers being re-employed
- Unemployed people stopping the search for work

In the UK, the monthly unemployment statistics published by the Office for National Statistics (ONS) count only the jobless who receive benefits. The ONS announced in 1997 that it wishes to introduce a new 'headline' measure of unemployment, based on a household survey, to include up to an estimated 300,000 additional people who are seeking work but not claiming benefits. This would bring the UK published measures closer into line with standard international definitions of unemployment.

Consequences of unemployment

1.4 Unemployment results in the following problems.

(a) **Loss of output**. If labour is unemployed, the economy is not producing as much output as it could. Thus, total national income is less than it could be.

(b) **Loss of human capital**. If there is unemployment, the unemployed labour will gradually lose its skills, because skills can only be maintained by working.

(c) **Increasing inequalities in the distribution of income**. Unemployed people earn less than employed people, and so when unemployment is increasing, the poor get poorer.

(d) **Social costs**. Unemployment brings social problems of personal suffering and distress, and possibly also increases in crime such as theft and vandalism.

(e) **Increased burden of welfare payments**. This can have a major impact on government fiscal policy.

Categories of unemployment

5/01

1.5 Unemployment may be classified into categories.

Category	Comment
Frictional	It is inevitable that some unemployment is caused not so much because there are not enough jobs to go round, but because of the *friction* in the labour market (difficulty in matching quickly workers with jobs), caused perhaps by a lack of knowledge about job opportunities. In general, it takes time to match prospective employees with employers, and individuals will be unemployed during the search period for a new job. Frictional unemployment is temporary, lasting for the period of transition from one job to the next.
Seasonal	This occurs in certain industries, for example building, tourism and farming, where the demand for labour fluctuates in seasonal patterns throughout the year.
Structural	This occurs where **long-term changes in the conditions of an industry occur**. The feature of structural unemployment is high regional unemployment in the location of the industry affected.
Technological	This is a form of structural unemployment, which occurs when new technologies are introduced. (a) Old skills are no longer required. (b) There is likely to be a labour saving aspect, with machines doing the job that people used to do. With automation, employment levels in an industry can fall sharply, even when the industry's total output is increasing.
Cyclical or demand-deficient	It has been the experience of the past that domestic and foreign trade go through cycles of boom, decline, recession, recovery, then boom again, and so on. (a) During recovery and boom years, the demand for output and jobs is high, and unemployment is low. (b) During decline and recession years, the demand for output and jobs falls; and unemployment rises to a high level. Cyclical unemployment can be long-term, and a government might try to reduce it by doing what it can to minimise a recession or to encourage faster economic growth.

1.6 Seasonal employment and frictional unemployment will be short-term. Structural unemployment, technological unemployment, and cyclical unemployment are all longer term, and more serious.

Government employment policies

1.7 Job creation and reducing unemployment should often mean the same thing, but it is possible to create more jobs without reducing unemployment.

(a) This can happen when there is a greater number of people entering the jobs market than there are new jobs being created. For example, if 500,000 new jobs are created during the course of one year, but 750,000 extra school leavers are looking for jobs, there will be an increase in unemployment of 250,000.

(b) It is also possible to reduce the official unemployment figures without creating jobs. For example, individuals who enrol for a government financed training scheme are taken off the unemployment register, even though they do not have full-time jobs.

1.8 A government can try several options to create jobs or reduce unemployment.

(a) **Spending more money directly on jobs** (for example hiring more civil servants)

(b) **Encouraging growth** in the private sector of the economy. When aggregate demand is growing, firms will probably want to increase output to meet demand, and so will hire more labour.

(c) **Encouraging training in job skills**. There might be a high level of unemployment amongst unskilled workers, and at the same time a shortage of skilled workers. A government can help to finance training schemes, in order to provide a 'pool' of workers who have the skills that firms need and will pay for.

(d) **Offering grant assistance to employers** in key regional areas

(e) **Encouraging labour mobility** by offering individuals financial assistance with relocation expenses, and improving the flow of information on vacancies

1.9 **Other policies may be directed at reducing real wages to market clearing levels**

(a) Abolishing **closed shop** agreements, which restrict certain jobs to trade union members

(b) Abolishing **minimum wage regulations,** where such regulations exist

Question 1

Match the terms (a), (b) and (c) below with definitions A, B and C.

(a) Structural unemployment
(b) Cyclical unemployment
(c) Frictional unemployment

A Unemployment arising from a difficulty in matching unemployed workers with available jobs
B Unemployment occurring in the downswing of an economy in between two booms
C Unemployment arising from a long-term decline in a particular industry

Answer

The pairings are (a) C, (b) B and (c) A.

2 UNEMPLOYMENT AND INFLATION

2.1 The problems of unemployment and inflation were very severe for many countries in recent years. It has been found that boosting demand to increase the level of employment can cause a higher rate of inflation. However, growth in *unemployment* can also be associated with a rising rate of inflation.

The meaning of full employment

2.2 The term full employment does not mean a situation in which everyone has a job. There will always be at least a certain **natural rate of unemployment,** which is the minimum level of unemployment that an economy can expect to achieve.

2.3 An aim of government policy might be to reduce unemployment to this minimum natural rate, and so get as close as possible to the goal of full employment. On the basis that unemployment cannot be kept below its natural rate without causing inflation, the natural rate of unemployment is sometimes called the **non-accelerating inflation rate of unemployment (NAIRU)**. But in order to understand the idea of a natural rate of unemployment more fully, we need to examine in more detail the idea that there is a **trade-off between unemployment and inflation**.

Inflationary gaps and deflationary gaps

2.4 As we saw earlier when looking at the Keynesian model, equilibrium national income can be shown using an aggregate demand curve (AD), where AD is the total demand for all goods in the economy, at different price levels and an aggregate supply curve (AS), where AS is the total supply of all goods in the economy, at different price levels.

2.5 According to Keynes, **demand management** by the government could be based on government **spending and taxation policies** (fiscal policy). These could be used for two purposes.

(a) **To eliminate a deflationary gap** and create full employment. A small initial increase in government spending will start off a **multiplier-accelerator** effect, and so the actual government spending required to eliminate a deflationary gap should be less than the size of the gap itself.

(b) **To eliminate an inflationary gap** and take inflation out of the economy. This can be done by reducing government spending, or by increasing total taxation and not spending the taxes raised.

2.6 Keynesians accept that reductions in unemployment can only be achieved if prices are allowed to rise: reducing unemployment goes hand in hand with allowing some inflation.

The Phillips curve

2.7 In 1958 *A W Phillips* found a statistical relationship between unemployment and the rate of money wage inflation which implied that, in general, **the rate of inflation falls unemployment rose and vice versa**. A curve, known as a **Phillips curve**, can be drawn linking inflation and unemployment (Figure 1).

KEY TERM

Phillips curve: a graphical illustration of the historic inverse relationship between the rate of wage inflation and the rate of unemployment.

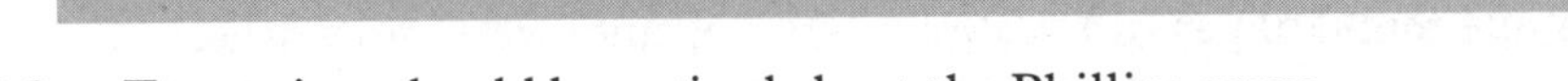

2.8 Two points should be noticed about the Phillips curve.

(a) The curve crosses the horizontal axis at a positive value for the unemployment rate. This means that zero inflation will be associated with some unemployment; it is not possible to achieve zero inflation and zero unemployment at the same time.

(b) The shape of the curve means that the lower the level of unemployment, the higher the **rate of increase** in inflation.

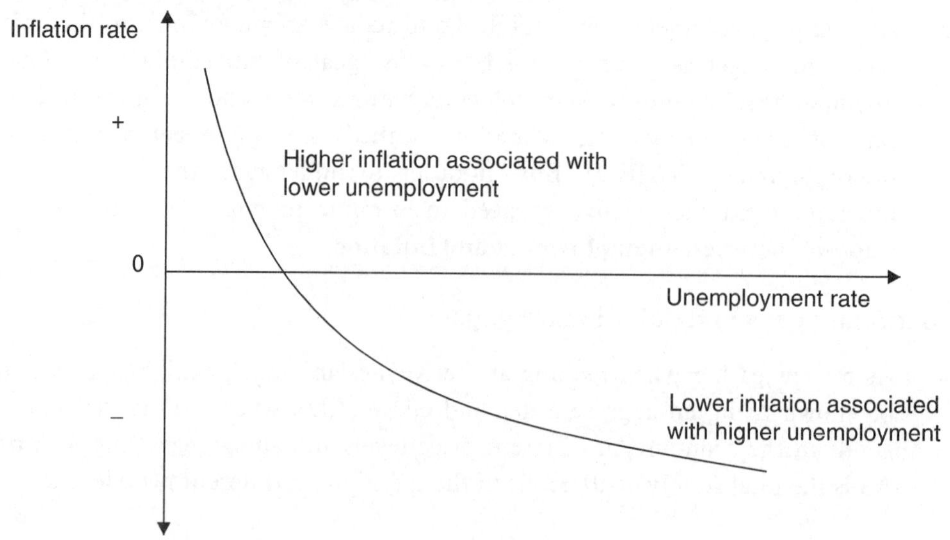

Figure 1 Phillips curve

2.9 The existence of a relationship between inflation and unemployment of the type indicated by the Phillips curve suggests that the government should be able to use demand management policies to take the economy to acceptable levels of inflation and unemployment.

2.10 This re-emphasises the argument of Keynesian economists that in order to achieve full employment, some inflation is unavoidable. If achieving full employment is an economic policy objective, a government must therefore be prepared to accept a certain level of inflation as a necessary evil.

2.11 However, the Phillips curve relationship between inflation and unemployment broke down at the end of the 1960s when Britain began to experience **rising inflation at the same time as rising unemployment.**

Inflationary expectations: monetarists' refinements to the Phillips curve

2.12 An explanation of rising inflation rates combined with rising unemployment was put forward, based on **inflationary expectations.** This **natural rate hypothesis** is supported by monetarist economists.

2.13 **Inflationary expectations** reflect the rates of inflation that are **expected** in the future. The inflationary expectations of the work force will be reflected in the level of wage rises that is demanded in the annual round of pay negotiations between employers and workers.

(a) If the work force expects inflation next year to be 3%, they will demand a 3% wage increase in order to maintain the real value of their wages.

(b) If we now accept that any increase in wages will result in price inflation then a 3% pay rise to cover expected inflation will result in an actual rate of inflation of 3%.

(c) The work force might also try to achieve some increase in the real value of wages. If inflation next year is expected to be 3%, the work force might demand a pay rise of say, 4%. According to monetarist economists, a pay rise of 4% would simply mean inflation of 4%. If workers wish to achieve a 1% increase in real wages each year, then during each successive period the rate of inflation will begin to accelerate from 5% to 6% to 7% and so on, and the real increases in wages will not happen.

(d) To compound the problem of inflation still further, it is argued that if mistakes are made over expectations, then money wages will be adjusted upwards next period in order to rectify the mistake made last period.

(i) For example, in one year the work force might expect inflation to be 3%, and so demand a 3% increase in wages. If this is achieved, but the actual rate of inflation during the year is 5%, the work force will try to put things right. They will demand a 2% pay increase, just to cover the 'lost ground' last year, as well as an increase to cover expected inflation next year.

(ii) It follows that if expected inflation next year is 5%, the pay demand will be 7% (plus any demand for an increase in the value of wages). If a 7% pay rise is granted, inflation will go up to 7% pa.

(e) Any 'external' factor (such as increases in the prices of imported goods, or higher indirect taxes) which may lead wage earners to expect higher prices in the near future will of course result in even higher wage claims.

2.14 The example used here is simplified because expectations change and adapt. However, many economists believe that events in the UK from about 1967 well into the 1970s followed a sequence of events not unlike that described above.

Question 2

Which of the following conclusions is supported by the Phillips curve?

(a) Higher inflation causes unemployment
(b) Higher unemployment causes inflation
(c) Full employment and low inflation cannot be achieved together

Answer

The answer is (c). The Phillips curve expresses an assumed relationship between unemployment and inflation. It does not purport to offer a causal explanation of the link.

The natural rate hypothesis

2.15 The **natural rate hypothesis** incorporates these views on inflationary expectations, to produce a refinement of the Phillips curve.

2.16 Suppose that the economy is characterised by the Phillips curve PC_1 in Figure 2. Initially, say, that is at an unemployment rate of 5% and zero price and wage inflation.

(a) Suppose now that the government expands aggregate demand so as to reduce unemployment to, say, 3% of the labour force. There is a movement along the Phillips curve, and the new unemployment level turns out to be associated with 4% inflation.

(b) As employers realise that they are paying higher wages as well as higher prices, they cut their costs by laying workers off and the unemployment rate rises to 5% again.

(c) But in the meantime the period of positive inflation has generated inflationary expectations and 5% unemployment is now associated with 4% inflation, because the Phillips curve has shifted from PC_1 to PC_2.

2.17 In effect, the **short-run** Phillips curve has shifted outwards from PC_1 to PC_2 in Figure 2.

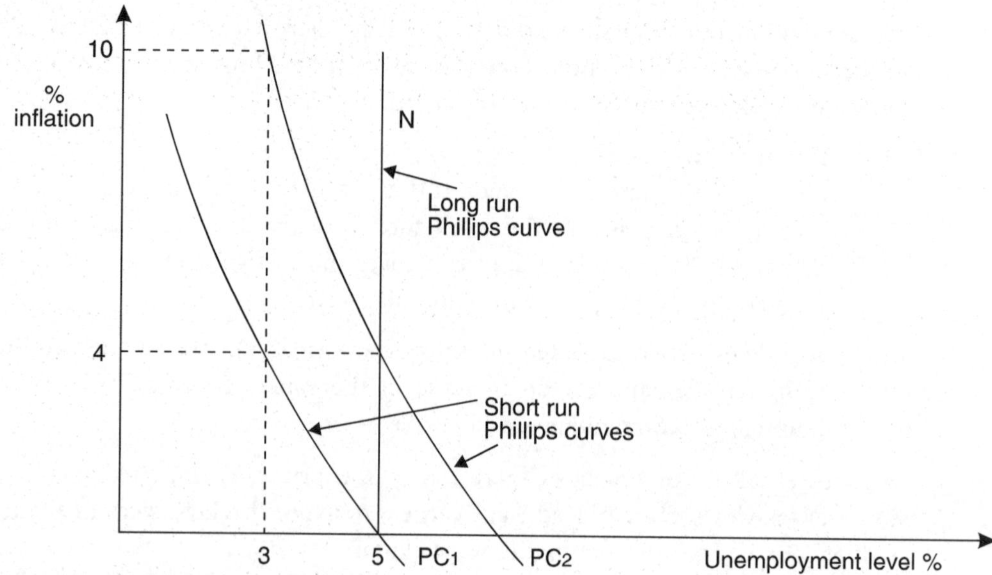

Figure 2 Natural rate hypothesis

2.18 Moderate monetarist economists state that the **long-run Phillips curve is vertical at the natural rate of unemployment.** In our example, monetarists would claim that the long-run Phillips curve is line N in Figure 2 so that there is a natural unemployment rate of 5% (but note that this figure of 5% is simply being used as an example here). This rate of unemployment is sometimes called the non-accelerating inflation rate of unemployment and referred to as the NAIRU.

2.19 In the long run, unemployment will revert towards its natural level. The rate of inflation, however, will be determined by the short-run Phillips curve, which will shift upwards as inflationary expectations increase. The distinction between short and long-run Phillips curves can help explain the observation that in the UK unemployment and inflation have often both risen at the same time.

KEY TERMS

The **natural rate hypothesis** says that the expansion of AD to reduce unemployment below its natural rate will only produce inflation. The natural rate is also called the **non-accelerating inflation rate of unemployment (NAIRU)**

Question 3

To check whether you understand this point, suppose that the short-run Phillips curve is now PC_2 in Figure 2, with unemployment at 5% and annual inflation at 4%. What would happen if the government now took measures to reduce unemployment to 3%?

Answer

Inflation would rise to about 10%, which is the rate of inflation on PC_2 associated with 3% unemployment. However, according to the natural rate hypothesis, in the longer run, unemployment would move back to 5%. A new short-run Phillips curve would be established, according to which an unemployment rate of 5% would be associated with 10% inflation.

2.20 Monetarist economists argue that the only way to reduce the rate of inflation is to get inflationary expectations out of the system. In doing so, excessive demands for wage rises should be resisted by employers. However a firm approach to reducing the rate of inflation could mean having to accept high levels of unemployment for a while.

2.21 The **new classical school** of monetarist believes that the aggregate supply and Phillips curves are **vertical in the short run**. Therefore, they condemn any policy to expand demand as leading only to increased inflation. They suggest that human behaviour is governed by **rational expectations**; that is, by a rational assessment of all the information currently available. The implication is that the public will recognise inflation-producing policies as soon as they are introduced and adjust their expectations of inflation **immediately**. This will lead to increased wage demands and the expected inflation will ensue.

2.22 The new classical school sees unemployment as unrelated to inflation. They suggest that unemployment should be tackled by supply-side measures designed to reduce the NAIRU, while the sole aim of monetary policy should be to control inflation. Governments should announce clear monetary rules and then stick to them.

3 MONETARY POLICY 5/01

Exam focus point

Questions on monetary policy will typically require you to consider its impact on the business sector.

The role of monetary policy

3.1 Monetary policy can be used as a means towards achieving ultimate economic objectives for inflation, the balance of trade, full employment and real economic growth. To achieve these **ultimate objectives**, the authorities will set **intermediate objectives** for monetary policy.

3.2 In the UK, the ultimate objective of monetary policy in recent years has been principally to reduce the rate of inflation to a sustainable low level. The intermediate objectives of monetary policy have related to the level of interest rates, growth in the money supply, the exchange rate for sterling, the expansion of credit and the growth of national income.

The money supply as a target of monetary policy

3.3 To monetarist economists, the **money supply** is an obvious intermediate target of economic policy. This is because they claim that an increase in the money supply will raise prices and incomes and this in turn will raise the demand for money to spend.

3.4 When such a policy is first introduced, the short-term effect would be unpredictable for three reasons.

(a) The effect on interest rates might be erratic.

(b) There might be a time lag before anything can be done. For example, it takes time to cut government spending and hence to use reduction in government borrowing as an instrument of monetary policy to control the growth in M0 or M4.

(c) There might be a time lag before control of the money supply alters expectations about inflation and wage demands.

3.5 Growth in the money supply, if it is a monetary policy target, should therefore be a **medium-term target**. When the UK government set targets for the growth of the money supply as a main feature of its economic policy strategy from 1980, it was consequently prepared to wait for some years to see any benefits from its policies and therefore set out its policy targets in a **medium-term** financial strategy.

3.6 There are other problems with using growth in the money supply as an intermediate policy target.

(a) There will be difficulty in selecting a suitable monetary aggregate, whose growth rate will either affect or reflect changes in economic conditions. For example, if the aim of controlling the money supply is to control inflation, but if M4 increases by 20% per annum when the rate of inflation is just 5% per annum, targets for M4 growth would be an unsuitable monetary policy objective.

(b) It is debatable whether controlling the growth in the money supply will result in control over the rate of inflation. In the UK, the fall in the velocity of circulation of the broad money supply aggregates through the 1980s has meant that the broad money supply has risen at a much faster rate than inflation.

Interest rates as a target for monetary policy

3.7 The authorities might decide that **interest rates** - the price of money - should be a target of monetary policy. This would be appropriate if it is considered that there is a direct relationship between interest rates and the level of expenditure in the economy, or between interest rates and the rate of inflation.

3.8 **A rise in interest rates will raise the price of borrowing** in the internal economy for both companies and individuals. If companies see the rise as relatively permanent, rates of return on investments will become less attractive and **investment plans may be curtailed**. Corporate profits will fall as a result of higher interest payments. Companies will reduce stock levels as the cost of having money tied up in stocks rises. Individuals should be expected to reduce or postpone consumption in order to reduce borrowings, and should become less willing to borrow for house purchase.

3.9 Although it is generally accepted that there is likely to be a connection between interest rates and investment (by companies) and consumer expenditure, **the connection is not a stable and predictable one**, and interest rate changes are only likely to affect the level of expenditure after a **considerable time lag**.

3.10 **Other effects of raising interest rates**

(a) High interest rates will keep the value of sterling higher than it would otherwise be. This will keep the cost of imports high, and so discourage the purchase of imports. This may be necessary to protect the balance of payments and to prevent 'import-cost-push' inflation. UK manufacturers have complained bitterly about this effect in recent years and BMW cited it as one of the reasons for disposing of Rover.

(b) High interest rates will attract foreign investors into sterling investments, and so provide capital inflows which help to finance the large UK balance of payments deficit.

3.11 An important reason for pursuing an interest rate policy is that the authorities are able to influence interest rates much more effectively and rapidly than they can influence other policy targets, such as the money supply or the volume of credit. As we have already seen, in 1997 the new Labour Government of the UK placed responsibility for interest rate decisions with the Bank of England, which sets rates with the objective of meeting the government's inflation target.

The exchange rate as a target of monetary policy

3.12 **Why the exchange rate is a target**

(a) If the exchange rate falls, exports become cheaper to overseas buyers and so more competitive in export markets. Imports will become more expensive and so less competitive against goods produced by manufacturers at home. A fall in the exchange rate might therefore be good for a domestic economy, by giving a **stimulus to exports** and **reducing demand for imports**.

(b) An increase in the exchange rate will have the opposite effect, with dearer exports and cheaper imports. If the exchange rate rises and imports become cheaper, there should be a reduction in the rate of domestic inflation. A fall in the exchange rate, on the other hand, tends to increase the cost of imports and adds to the rate of domestic inflation.

3.13 When a country's economy is heavily dependent on overseas trade, as the UK economy is, it might be appropriate for government policy to establish a target exchange value for the domestic currency. However, the exchange rate is dependent on both the domestic rate of inflation and the level of interest rates. Targets for the exchange rate cannot be achieved unless the rate of inflation at home is first brought under control.

Growth in money national income as a target of monetary policy

3.14 The authorities might set targets for the level of national income in the economy. For example, the policy might be for the growth in the national income (or GNP or GDP) to be X% per annum for Y years. However, it takes time to collect information about national income whereas targets of monetary policy should be items for which statistical data can be collected regularly and easily.

3.15 For this reason, although a target growth rate in national income itself is, in theory, probably the most suitable target of monetary policy, it is the least practical because the authorities would always be working with out-of-date information.

Targets and indicators

3.16 An economic indicator provides information about economic conditions and might be used as a way of judging the performance of government.

(a) A **leading indicator** is one which gives an advance indication of what will happen to the economy in the future. It can therefore be used to predict future conditions. For example, a fall in the value of sterling by, say, 2% might be used to predict what will happen to the balance of payments and to the rate of inflation.

(b) A **coincident indicator** is one which gives an indication of changes in economic conditions **at the same time** that these changes are occurring. For example, if the narrow money supply rises by 5%, this might 'confirm' that the rate of increase in GDP over the same period of time has been about the same, 5% in 'money' terms.

(c) A **lagging indicator**, you will have guessed, is one which 'lags behind' the economic cycle. Unemployment, to take an example, often continues to rise until after a recession has ended and only starts to fall again after recovery has begun.

3.17 Items which are selected as monetary targets will also be indicators, but not all indicators are selected by the authorities as targets. There are a number of monetary indicators.

(a) The size of the money stock

(b) Interest rates such as the banks' base rate of interest, the Treasury bill rate and the yield on long-dated government securities

(c) The exchange rate against the US dollar, or the trade-weighted exchange rate index

(d) The size of the government's borrowing

(e) Government borrowing as a percentage of Gross Domestic Product

The interrelationship between targets: the money supply and interest rate targets

3.18 The authorities can set intermediate targets for the growth of the money supply, but to achieve their targets of growth it will be necessary to allow interest rates to adjust to a level at which the demand for money matches the size of the money supply. For example, a policy to cut the growth of the money supply might result in higher real interest rates.

3.19 On the other hand, the authorities might set targets for the level of interest rates. If they do so, they must allow whatever demand for money there is to be met at that rate of interest by allowing the money supply to meet the demand. If they did not, interest rates would then rise above or fall below the target level.

3.20 This means that the authorities can set a target for the money supply or a target for interest rates, but **they cannot set independent targets for both at the same time.**

Instruments of monetary policy

3.21 There are a number of **techniques** or **instruments** which are available to the authorities to achieve their targets for monetary policies.

- Changing the level and/or structure of **interest rates** through **open market operations**
- **Reserve requirements**
- **Direct controls**, which might be either quantitative or qualitative
- **Intervention to influence the exchange rate**

Control over the level and structure of interest rates

3.22 When a government uses interest rates as an instrument of policy, it can try to influence either the general level of interest rates or the term structure of interest rates. It could do this by influencing either short-term interest rates or long-term interest rates. In the UK since 1997, the Bank of England has had responsibility for setting short-term interest rates. Long-term rates could possibly be influenced by increasing or reducing the PSBR.

Reserve requirements on banks as a means of controlling the money supply

3.23 As another technique for controlling money supply growth, the government might impose **reserve requirements** on banks. A reserve requirement might be a compulsory minimum cash reserve ratio (ie ratio of cash to total assets) or a minimum liquid asset ratio.

3.24 You will recall that any initial increase in bank deposits or building society deposits will result in a much greater eventual increase in deposits, because of the credit multiplier.

Ignoring leakages, the formula for the credit multiplier is:

$$D = \frac{C}{r}$$

where C is the initial increase in deposits
r is the liquid assets ratio or reserve assets ratio

D is the eventual total increase in deposits

3.25 If the authorities wished to control the rate of increase in bank lending and building society lending, they could impose minimum reserve requirements - ie a minimum value for r. **The bigger the value or r, the lower size of the credit multiplier would be.**

3.26 There are drawbacks to reserve requirements as a monetary policy instrument.

(a) Unless the same requirements apply to all financial institutions in the country, some institutions will simply take business from others. For example, reserve requirements on UK banks but not on building societies would give the building societies a competitive advantage over the banks, without having any effect on the control of total credit/money supply growth.

(b) Similarly, restrictions on domestic financial institutions which do not apply to foreign banks would put the domestic financial institutions at a competitive disadvantage in international markets. This is one reason why international co-operation on the capital adequacy of banks (the Basle agreement) is an important step towards better regulation of financial markets.

Direct controls as a technique of monetary control

3.27 Another way of controlling the growth of the money supply is to impose direct controls on bank lending. Direct controls may be either quantitative or qualitative.

(a) **Quantitative controls** might be imposed on either bank lending (assets), for example a 'lending ceiling' limiting annual lending growth, or bank deposits (liabilities). The purpose of quantitative controls might be seen as a means of keeping bank lending in check without having to resort to higher interest rates.

(b) **Qualitative controls** might be used to alter the type of lending by banks. For example, the government (via the Bank) can ask the banks to limit their lending to the personal sector, and lend more to industry, or to lend less to a particular type of firm (such as, for example, property companies) and more to manufacturing businesses.

Quantitative controls

3.28 Controls might be temporary, in which case, in time, interest rates would still tend to rise if the money supply growth is to be kept under control. However, the advantage of a temporary scheme of direct quantitative controls is that it gives the authorities time to implement longer term policy. Quantitative controls are therefore a way of bridging the time-lag before these other policies take effect.

3.29 Quantitative controls might be more permanent. If they are, they will probably be unsuccessful because there will be financial institutions that manage to escape the control regulations, and so thrive at the expense of controlled institutions.

3.30 Direct controls on banks, for example, might succeed in reducing bank deposits but they will not succeed in controlling the level of demand and expenditure in the economy if lending is re-directed into other non-controlled financial instruments of non-controlled financial institutions. For example, large companies might use their own bank deposits to set up a scheme of lending themselves.

3.31 Direct controls are therefore rarely effective in dealing with the source rather than the symptom of the problem. Direct controls tend to divert financial flows into other, often less efficient, channels, rather than to stop the financial flows altogether, ie 'leakages' are inevitable.

Qualitative controls

3.32 Qualitative controls might be **mandatory** or they might be applied through **moral suasion**. Mandatory directives of a qualitative nature are unlikely in practice, because they are difficult to enforce without the co-operation of banks and other financial institutions. Moral suasion, on the other hand, might be used frequently. This is a process whereby the Central Bank appeals to the banks to do one or more things.

- To restrain lending
- To give priority to certain types of lending such as finance for exports or for investment
- Refuse other types of lending such as loans to private individuals

3.33 Moral suasion might therefore be a temporary form of control. As just one example, in 1989, the governor of the Bank of England 'advised' the banks to be wary of lending in such large amounts to property companies, thereby trying to influence banks' lending decisions without giving them directives or instructions.

Exchange rate control as an instrument of monetary policy

3.34 The exchange rate and changes in the exchange rate, have implications for the balance of payments, inflation and economic growth. The government might therefore seek to achieve a target exchange rate for its currency. More will be said about exchange rates later.

Chapter roundup

- The monetarist concept of a stable equilibrium implies that with zero price inflation, there is a natural optimal level of unemployment, and a rate of economic growth and balance of trade position from which the economy will not deviate. Monetarism focuses on economic stability in the medium to long term, which can only be achieved by abandoning short-term demand management goals.
- There appears to be a connection between the rate of inflation and unemployment. The Phillips curve has been used to show that when there is zero inflation, there will be some unemployment.
- A conclusion from the link between unemployment and inflation is that if the government wants to reduce unemployment, it must accept a faster rate of inflation in the economy, which will damage prospects of economic growth. On the other hand, by trying to reduce inflation in order to stimulate economic growth and more employment in the longer term, there will have to be some unemployment in the short term.
- Efforts to control inflation might be directed at high taxes or high interest rates to reduce consumer demand, exchange rates to control the cost of imported goods, control of the money supply, direct controls over price and wage increases, or supply side reforms freeing up labour markets.

Quick quiz

1 What does a Phillips curve show?

2 What is meant by inflationary expectations?

3 All of the following measures might be used by a government to help to control cost-push inflation EXCEPT:

A A revaluation/appreciation of the currency
B Higher direct taxation
C Measures to control 'wage drift'
D Linking public sector pay increases to productivity improvements

4 Which of the following measures is likely to be deflationary?

A A depreciation of the currency
B Reducing interest rates
C Raising tax allowances by less than the rate of inflation
D Running a budget deficit in a recession

5 Which of the following would be a *fiscal* measure by a government which would have the effect of restricting the growth in the money supply?

A An increase in short term (money market) interest rates.
B An increase in the rate of value added tax.
C An increase in the Public Sector Borrowing Requirement.
D The imposition of a prices and incomes policy.

6 Inflation caused by rising wages during times of high growth and low unemployment is termed:

A Wage cost-push inflation
B Demand-pull inflation
C Import cost-push inflation
D Inflationary expectations

7 When resources in a country's economy are fully employed, which of the following changes would have an inflationary effect? 1. A decline in the liquidity preference of households. 2. Wage increases in most industries. 3. The issue and sale of new gilt-edged securities by the Bank of England.

A Changes 1 and 2 only
B Changes 2 and 3 only
C Changes 1 and 3 only
D Changes 1, 2 and 3

8 What causes inflation?

Match the characteristics with the types.

(i) Demand – pull
(ii) Cost – push
(iii) Expectational
(iv) Money supply growth

A Leads to the vicious circle called the wage – price spiral
B The economy is buoyant and there is pressure on its ability to supply
C Keynesians argue that this is a symptom rather than a cause
D Factor rewards rise whether or not they are in short supply

9 The short-run Phillips curve is likely to

A Have a negative slope
B Have a positive slope
C Be horizontal
D Be vertical

10 Causes of unemployment

Match the characteristics with the names.

(i) Frictional
(ii) Structural
(iii) Technological
(iv) Demand-deficient

A Long term changes in the conditions of an industry
B Trade cycle leads to changes in requirement for output
C Old skills no longer required. Output may increase
D Temporary, during transfer from one job to another

Answers to quick quiz

1 Phillips' original curve plotted the apparent inverse relationship between inflation and unemployment.

2 Inflationary expectations are expectations about what the rate of inflation will be in the future. They arise when it appears that inflation is high and likely to increase. They lead to accelerating pay demands and to some extent are a self-fulfilling prophecy.

3 B An increase in direct taxation will not reduce pressures for higher costs; if anything, it will encourage workers to demand higher wages, which will add to cost-push inflationary pressures.

A revaluation of the currency should make import costs cheaper.

Wage drift is the tendency for annual wages increases to run ahead of the rate of inflation and to 'drift' upwards, and controlling this would reduce inflationary pressures from higher costs.

Linking wage and salary increases to productivity improvements will help to keep unit costs down, and so reduce cost-push inflationary pressures.

4 C Deflationary measures are those that reduce demand in the economy. Raising tax allowances by less than the rate of inflation will have the effect of reducing individuals' disposable income, and so be deflationary.

5 B Higher value added tax rates would reduce spending in the economy (net of VAT) and by possibly increasing government tax revenue, would reduce the PSBR (or add to the PSDR); these effects would keep down the money supply growth *and* be a fiscal measure.

Higher short term interest rates would result in higher bank lending rates and lower bank borrowing, but this is a monetary policy measure, not a fiscal measure.

A higher PSBR will *add* to broad money supply growth.

A prices and incomes policy, by keeping down the rate of inflation, should also restrict the money supply growth, but this is not a fiscal measure either.

6 B Shortages of labour caused by high demand are causing wages to rise. This is demand-pull inflation.

7 A A decline in the demand for money (change 1) is likely to make households spend some of their unwanted money on goods and services, and this will be inflationary. Wage increases without productivity improvements will create cost-push inflation (change 2). The effect of an issue of securities by the Bank of England is to take money away from households/firms, and can have a contractionary effect on the money supply. This is not inflationary.

8 (i) B Aggregate demand exceeds the output capacity of the economy. Keynesians saw this as the main cause of inflation and predicted it could only occur when unemployment was low.

(ii) D Particularly caused by rises in wages but also by rises in the prices of imported materials and components.

(iii) A The expectation of inflation can cause it to persist even when the underlying causes have been removed, since higher wages will be demanded.

(iv) C Monetarists argue that expansion of the money supply beyond the rate of real growth will be inflationary.

9 A The short-run Phillips curve has a negative slope implying that there is a trade-off between the rate of inflation and the level of unemployment.

10 (i) D Time is needed to match workers and employers.
(ii) A Industries decline for a variety of reasons.
(iii) C A form of structural unemployment. New methods use less labour.
(iv) B Sometimes called cyclical unemployment

Now try the questions below from the Question Bank

Number	Level	Marks	Time
Q46	Introductory	8	10 mins
Q47	Introductory - Interactive	–	–
Q48	Exam - MCQ	–	–

Chapter 17

FISCAL POLICY AND TAXATION

Topic list		Syllabus reference	Ability required
1	Fiscal policy	(iii)	Comprehension
2	Principles of taxation	(iii)	Comprehension

Introduction

The word 'fisc' means the state treasury or the public purse, and fiscal policy relates to matters concerning the state or government treasury.

Bear in mind that the coverage in this chapter of the different forms of taxation in the UK is an overview only, to meet the knowledge requirements of the examination. It is not designed to help you fill in your tax return: that would require rather more detail.

Learning outcome covered in this chapter

- Explain the economic role of government through fiscal and monetary policy and demonstrate the impact of such policies on the business sector

Syllabus content covered in this chapter

- The fiscal environment: taxation and public spending; the budget and government borrowing; demand management and supply side policy

1 FISCAL POLICY

Fiscal policy and national income

1.1 A government's fiscal policy concerns its plans for taxation, borrowing and spending. Remember that **government spending is an injection** into the economy, adding to aggregate demand = expenditure = national income, whereas **taxes are a withdrawal**. A government's '**fiscal stance**' may be **neutral, expansionary** or **contractionary,** according too its effect on national income.

(a) **Spending more money** and financing this expenditure by borrowing would indicate an expansionary fiscal stance.

(b) **Collecting more in taxes** without increasing spending would indicate a contractionary fiscal stance.

(c) Collecting more in taxes in order to **increase spending**, thus diverting income from one part of the economy to another would indicate a broadly neutral fiscal stance.

Three elements of public finance 5/02

1.2 There are three broad elements in public finance.

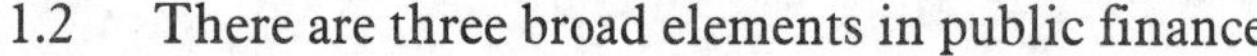

(a) **Expenditure**. The government, at a national and local level, spends money to provide goods and services, such as a health service, public education, a police force, roads, public buildings and so on, and to pay its administrative work force. It may also, perhaps, provide finance to encourage investment by private industry, for example by means of grants.

(b) **Income**. Expenditure must be financed, and the government must have income. Most government income comes from **taxation**, bit some income is obtained from **direct charges** to users of government services such as National Health Service charges.

(c) **Borrowing**. To the extent that a government's expenditure exceeds its income it must borrow to make up the difference. The amount that the government must borrow each year is now known as the **Public Sector Net Cash Requirement(PSNCR)** in the UK. Its former name was **Public Sector Borrowing Requirement (PSBR)** and you may be more familiar with this term.

KEY TERMS

The **public sector net cash requirement (PSNCR)** is the **annual** excess of spending over income for the entire sector- not just the central government.

Fiscal policy and macroeconomic objectives 5/01

1.3 **Fiscal policy** is concerned with **government spending** (an injection into the circular flow of income) and **taxation** (a withdrawal).

(a) If government spending is increased, there will be an increase in the amount of injections, expenditure in the economy will rise and so national income will rise (either in real terms, or in terms of price levels only; ie the increase in national income might be real or inflationary).

(b) If government taxation is increased, there will be an increase in withdrawals from the economy, and expenditure and national income will fall. A government might deliberately raise taxation to take inflationary pressures out of the economy.

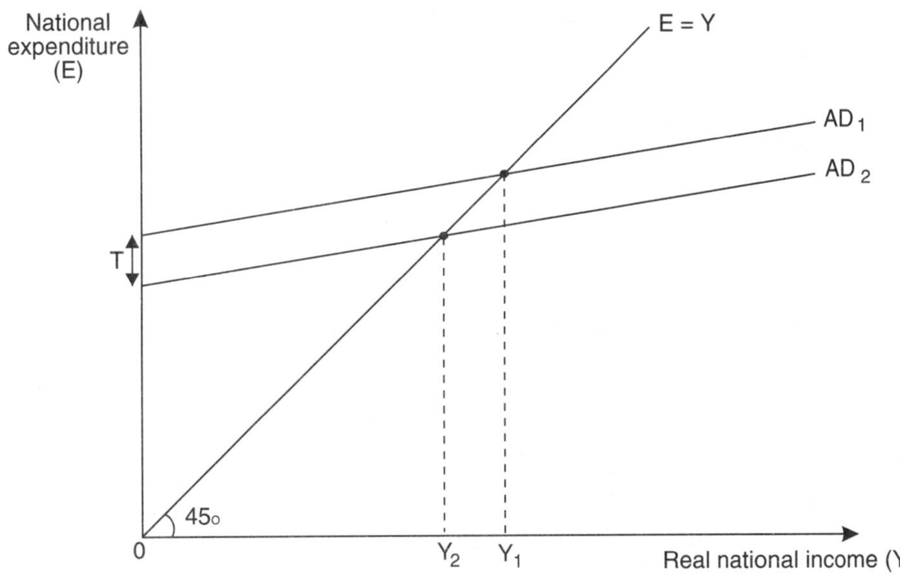

Figure 1 Increase in taxation

1.4 An increase in taxation by £T in Figure 1, without any matching increase in government expenditure, would **reduce** the aggregate expenditure in the economy from AD_1 to AD_2 and so the money value of national income would fall from Y_1 to Y_2. This would result in either a fall in real output or it would dampen inflationary pressures.

1.5 Similarly, a reduction in taxation without any reduction in government spending would **increase** the money value of national income. This would either cause real output to increase, or it would give a boost to price rises and inflation.

1.6 Fiscal policy can be used to reduce unemployment and provide jobs.

(a) More government spending on capital projects would create jobs in the construction industries.

(b) Government-funded training schemes are a means of spending by government to improve training, so as to make people more qualified for jobs in private industry.

(c) A government might tax companies on the basis of the numbers and pay levels of people they employ (as with employers' national insurance contributions). Lower employment taxes would possibly make employers more willing to take on extra numbers of employees.

If government raises taxes and spending by the same amount, so that the budget remains in balance, there will be an **increase in aggregate monetary demand**. This is because tax payers would have saved some of the money they pay in increased tax and the government spends all of it within the economy. This effect is called the **balanced budget multiplier**.

1.7 Government spending, however, might create inflationary pressures, and inflation tends to create more unemployment. Fiscal policy must therefore be used with care, even to create new jobs.

1.8 Since government spending or tax reductions might be inflationary, and higher domestic prices make imports relatively cheaper and exports less competitive in foreign markets, fiscal policy has possible implications for the **balance of payments** (discussed later in this Study Text).

1.9 The impact of changes in fiscal policy is not always certain, and fiscal policy to pursue one aim (eg lower inflation) might for a while create barriers to the pursuit of other aims (eg employment).

Budget surplus and budget deficit 5/02

1.10 If a government decides to use fiscal policy to influence demand in the economy, it can choose either expenditure changes or tax changes as its policy instrument. Suppose, for example, that the government wants to stimulate demand in the economy.

(a) **It can increase demand directly by spending more itself** - eg on the health service or education, and by employing more people itself.

(i) This extra spending could be financed by higher taxes, but this would reduce spending by the private sector of the economy because the private sector's after-tax income would be lower.

(ii) The extra government spending could also be financed by extra government borrowing. Just as individuals can borrow money for spending, so too can a government.

(b) **It can increase demand indirectly by reducing taxation** and so allowing firms and individuals more after-tax income to spend (or save).

(i) Cuts in taxation can be matched by cuts in government spending, in which case total demand in the economy will not be stimulated significantly, if at all.

(ii) Alternatively, tax cuts can be financed by more government borrowing.

1.11 Just as aggregate demand in the economy can be boosted by either more government spending or by tax cuts, financed in either case by a higher PSNCR, so too can demand in the economy be reduced by cutting government spending or by raising taxes, and using the savings or higher income to cut government borrowing.

1.12 Expenditure changes and tax changes are not mutually exclusive options, of course. A government has several options.

(a) Increase expenditure and reduce taxes, with these changes financed by a higher PSNCR

(b) Reduce expenditure and increase taxes, with these changes reducing the size of the PSNCR

(c) Increase expenditure and partly or wholly finance this extra spending with higher taxes

(d) Reduce expenditure and use these savings to reduce taxes

1.13 When a government's income exceeds its expenditure, and there is a negative PSNCR or **Public Sector Debt Repayment (PSDR),** we say that the government is running a **budget surplus**. When a government's expenditure exceeds its income, so that it must borrow to make up the difference, there is a PSNCR and we say that the government is running a **budget deficit**.

1.14 **Crowding out**. Deficit budgets have been criticised on the grounds that they 'crowd out' public sector activity; that is, the government spending merely replaces private spending with no net increase in AD. In particular, it is suggested that increased government borrowing inevitably leads to higher interest rates, which, in turn, lead to a reduction in private borrowing for both consumption and investment. The Keynesian response to this criticism is to day that crowding out will not occur when there are **idle resources** within the economy, such as a large number of unemployed.

Fiscal policy and the Budget

1.15 A feature of fiscal policy is that a government must **plan** what it wants to spend, and so how much it needs to raise in income or by borrowing. It needs to make a plan in order to establish how much taxation there should be, what form the taxes should take and so which sectors of the economy (firms or households, high income earners or low income earners) the money should come from. This formal planning of fiscal policy is usually done once a year and is set out in **the Budget**.

Monetary policy and fiscal policy

1.16 **Monetary policy can be made to act as a subsidiary support to fiscal policy and demand management**. Since budgets are once-a-year events, a government must use non-fiscal measures in between budgets to make adjustments to its control of the economy.

(a) A policy of **low interest rates** or the absence of any form of credit control might stimulate bank lending, which in turn would increase expenditure (demand) in the economy.

(b) **High interest rates might** act as a deterrent to borrowing and so reduce spending in the economy.

(c) Strict **credit controls** (for example restrictions on bank lending) might be introduced to reduce lending and so reduce demand in the economy.

1.17 Alternatively, monetary policy might be given prominence over fiscal policy as the most effective approach by a government to achieving its main economic policy objectives. This might not however be possible: from 1990 to 1992, for example, monetary policy in the UK was heavily constrained by the need to set interest rates at levels which maintained sterling's position in the European exchange rate mechanism (ERM). From 1997, the Government has given the Bank of England the role of setting interest rates, although it is still the government which sets an inflation target. If the UK joined a single European currency, interest rates would largely be determined at the European level.

The success of fiscal policy as a method of demand management

1.18 The success of fiscal policy as a means of influencing the economy sufficiently has been called into question.

(a) At the end of the 1970s, *Lewis and Ormerod* concluded that the multiplier effect of various fiscal policies is quite small (perhaps less than 1.0 after the first year). The implication of this conclusion is that to increase government spending by borrowing more might have a disappointingly small effect on demand and employment in the UK.

(b) Expansion and contraction of the economy are both subject to the effect of **automatic stabilisers**. There are two types.

(i) Tax revenues that *rise* as national income *rises*. Nearly all taxes fall into this category.

(ii) Government expenditures that *fall* as national income *rises*. Welfare payments associated with unemployment and low incomes make up the bulk of this category.

The effect of automatic stabilisers is to reduce the value of the **multiplier**, thus dampening the rate of both expansion and contraction. When the economy is in the process of recovering from a recession the effect of the automatic stabilisers is called **fiscal drag**.

The National Debt

KEY TERMS

The **National Debt** is the amount of debt owed by the **central** government of a country to its various creditors.

1.19 Creditors of the government may be nationals of the country (eg investors in government loan stock) or foreign nationals (perhaps foreign banks or even the International Monetary Fund).

1.20 When the National Debt is high, interest repayments will account for a large proportion of central government expenditure. It is therefore important that when a government borrows money, it should be invested or spent in such a way as to ensure that sufficient income is eventually generated to repay the interest and debt capital. If a government is unable to do this (as in the case of many developing and less developed countries at the moment) it will lose its creditworthiness and find future loans much harder to come by.

1.21 The National Debt exists in the form of debt instruments of two types.

(a) **Marketable debt**

- Short-term debt, which consists of **Treasury bills**. This is a very small amount.
- Long-term debt, which consists of **gilt-edged securities**.

(b) **Non-marketable debt**

- National Savings
- Any non-marketable loans raised by the government

Servicing the National Debt and the burden on society

1.22 To service the National Debt, a government must pay interest on the debt and make capital repayments when they fall due. However, the problem of making capital repayments can be overcome, if required, by taking out new loans when old loans mature (eg to repay a loan of £100 million, a government can borrow a further £100 million).

1.23 If the loan is obtained from the private sector of the country's economy, the National Debt and servicing the debt involve the transfer of funds between different sections of society. When the government borrows, it takes money from one group and spends it on other sections of society. When the government pays interest, it will raise money in taxes from the rest of society and pay this money to its creditors. Once again, this involves a transfer of the funds.

1.24 Servicing the National Debt thus involves two processes.

(a) A redistribution of funds within society, through government borrowing and spending, or through taxation to pay debt interest.

(b) Borrowing to spend now and only repaying the debt with interest later. In other words, society benefits now, and the payment burden falls on society in later years, perhaps in some cases as long as a generation or so later.

1.25 When money is borrowed from abroad, the flow of funds in obtaining the money and in repaying the debt crosses national boundaries, and so there are implications for the balance of payments and the exchange rate of the domestic currency. Repaying a debt to foreign debtors also places a burden on society, because the money raised from taxes to service the debt must be paid abroad.

Public expenditure control

1.26 If the entire public sector had a balanced budget, the PSNCR would be nil. When there is an annual excess of income over expenditure, some of the National Debt can be repaid and so there is a Public Sector Debt Repayment.

1.27 To reduce the size of the PSNCR, a government must either reduce its expenditure or raise its income from taxation. The sale of nationalised industries to the private sector is another source of funds.

1.28 Keynesian economists argue the need for **more government spending in a recession** to boost demand in the economy and create jobs. An argument put forward is that it makes sound financial sense to use current revenues from taxation to meet current expenditures and interest payments on debt, but to use borrowing for capital expenditure needs. Since taxation revenue exceeds current spending, the argument concludes that the government should borrow more for capital spending. The UK government has rejected this argument, and believes that the upward spiral of public expenditure of earlier years made the burden of taxation on companies and individuals intolerable.

2 PRINCIPLES OF TAXATION 5/02

Functions of taxation

2.1 Taxation has several functions.

(a) **To raise revenues for the government** as well as for local authorities and similar public bodies (eg the European Union).

(b) **To discourage certain activities regarded as undesirable.** The imposition of Development Land Tax in the United Kingdom in the mid-70s (since abolished) was partially in response to growth in property speculation.

(c) **To cause certain products to be priced to take into account their social costs**. For example, smoking entails certain social costs, including especially the cost of hospital care for those suffering from smoking-related diseases, and the government sees fit to make the price of tobacco reflect these social costs.

(d) **To redistribute income and wealth.** Higher rates of tax on higher incomes will serve to redistribute income. UK inheritance tax goes some way towards redistributing wealth.

(e) **To protect industries from foreign competition.** If the government levies a duty on all imported goods much of the duty will be passed on to the consumer in the form of higher prices, making imported goods more expensive. This has the effect of transferring a certain amount of demand from imported goods to domestically produced goods.

(f) **To provide a stabilising effect on national income**. Taxation reduces the effect of the multiplier, and so can be used to dampen upswings in a trade cycle - ie higher taxation when the economy shows signs of a boom will slow down the growth of money GNP and so take some inflationary pressures out of the economy.

The size of the multiplier, remember, is $\left(\frac{1}{s + m + t}\right)$ where t is the marginal rate of taxation.

Qualities of a good tax

2.2 *Adam Smith* in his *Wealth of Nations* ascribed **four features to a good tax system.**

(a) **Equity**. Persons should pay according to their ability.

(b) **Certainty**. The tax should be well-defined and easily understood by all concerned.

(c) **Convenience**. The payment of tax should ideally be related to how and when people receive and spend their income (eg PAYE is deducted when wages are paid, and VAT is charged when goods are bought).

(d) **Economy**. The cost of collection should be small relative to the yield (eg by this criterion, the car road tax is an inefficient tax).

2.3 Further features of a good tax can be identified.

- **Flexibility**. It should be adjustable so that rates may be altered up or down.
- **Efficiency**. It should not harm initiative, but evasion should be difficult.
- It should attain its purpose without distorting economic behaviour.

2.4 Note the following distinctions.

(a) A **regressive tax** takes a higher **proportion** of a poor person's salary than of a rich person's. Television licences and road tax are examples of regressive taxes since they are the same for all people. High income earners, even though individual charges can vary from one local authority to another, and in spite of some rebates for the least well-off groups.

(b) A **proportional tax** takes the **same proportion** of income in tax from all levels of income. Schedule E income tax with a basic of tax at 23% is proportional tax, but only within a limited range of income.

(c) A **progressive tax** takes a **higher proportion** of income in tax as income rises. Income tax as a whole is progressive, since the first part of an individual's income is tax-free due to personal allowances and the rate of tax increases in steps from 20p in £1 to 40p in £1 as taxable income rises.

Advantages and disadvantages of progressive taxation

2.5 **Arguments in favour of progressive direct taxes**

(a) **They are levied according to the ability of individuals to pay**. Individuals with a higher income are more able to afford to give up more of their income in tax than low income earners, who need a greater proportion of their earnings for the basic necessities of life. If taxes are to be raised according to the ability of people to pay (which is one of the features of a good tax suggested by Adam Smith) then there must be some progressiveness in them.

(b) **Progressive taxes enable a government to redistribute wealth from the rich to the poor in society**. Such a redistribution of wealth will alter the consumption patterns in society since the poorer members of society will spend their earnings and social security benefits on different types of goods than if the income had remained in the hands of the richer people.

(c) **Indirect taxes tend to be regressive and progressive taxes are needed as a counter-balance** to make the tax system as a whole more fair.

2.6 **Arguments against progressive taxes**

(a) **In an affluent society, there is less need for progressive taxes than in a poorer society.** Fewer people will live in poverty in such a society if taxes are not progressive than in a poorer society.

(b) **Higher taxes on extra corporate profits might deter entrepreneurs** from developing new companies because the potential increase in after-tax profits would not be worth the risks involved in undertaking new investments.

(c) **Individuals and firms that suffer from high taxes might try to avoid or evade paying tax** by transferring their wealth to other countries, or by setting up companies in tax havens where corporate tax rates are low. However, tax avoidance and evasion are practised whether tax rates are high or low. High taxes will simply raise the relative gains which can be made from avoidance or evasion.

(d) When progressive taxes are harsh, and either tax high income earners at very high marginal rates or tax the wealthy at high rates on their wealth, **they could act as a deterrent to initiative.** Skilled workers might leave the country and look for employment in countries where they can earn more money.

The 'poverty trap'

2.7 If one considers the effects of state benefits on income as a form of 'negative taxation', then the highest marginal rates of taxation/loss of benefit in recent years in the UK have fallen on low income earners receiving state benefits. For example, where the benefit rules state than an individual loses £1 of benefit for each £1 of extra part-time earnings, then the individual is suffering a marginal rate of taxation/loss of benefit of 100% and there is no financial incentive for him to work at all. This is sometimes called a poverty trap.

A proportional tax

2.8 It is often argued that tax burdens should be proportional to income in order to be fair, although a proportional tax has the following disadvantages.

(a) A large administrative system is needed to calculate personal tax liabilities on a proportional basis. The costs of collecting income tax relative to tax revenues earned can be high, particularly in the case of lower income taxpayers.

(b) Such a tax does not contribute towards a redistribution of wealth among the population.

A regressive tax

2.9 In the case of a regressive tax, a greater proportionate tax burden falls on those least able to afford it. The main disadvantage of a regressive tax is that it is not fair or equitable. The main advantage of a regressive tax is that it is often relatively easy to administer and collect. This is the case with motor vehicle tax, for example. However, a regressive tax might also be expensive to collect.

Question 1

Below are details of three taxation systems, one of which is regressive, one proportional and one progressive. Which is which?

	Income before tax	*Income after tax*
	£	£
System 1	10,000	8,000
	20,000	15,000
System 2	10,000	7,000
	20,000	14,000
System 3	10,000	9,000
	20,000	19,000

Answer

	Tax paid on low income	*Tax paid on high income*	*Nature of tax*
System 1	20%	25%	Progressive
System 2	30%	30%	Proportional
System 3	10%	5%	Regressive

Direct and indirect taxes

2.10 A **direct tax** is paid direct by a person to the Revenue authority. Examples of direct taxes in the UK are income tax, corporation tax, capital gains tax and inheritance tax. A direct tax can be levied on income and profits, or on wealth. Direct taxes tend to be progressive or proportional taxes. They are also usually unavoidable, which means that they must be paid by everyone.

2.11 An **indirect tax** is collected by the Revenue authority from an intermediary (a supplier) who then attempts to pass on the tax to consumers in the price of goods they sell. Indirect taxes are of two types.

> **KEY TERMS**
>
> A **specific tax** is charged as a *fixed sum* per unit sold.
>
> An **ad valorem tax** is charged as a *fixed percentage* of the price of the good.

Direct taxation on income: advantages and disadvantages

2.12 The main advantages of direct taxes on income are that they can be made fair and equitable by being designed as progressive or proportional to the degree desired. Because of their generally progressive nature they also tend to stabilise the economy, automatically taking more money out of the system during a boom and less during depression. Moreover, because they are more difficult to pass on, they are less inflationary than indirect taxes. Finally, taxpayers know what their tax liability is.

2.13 When income tax is levied at a high rate, it could **discourage** the geographical and the occupational mobility of labour.

(a) There might be higher gross income levels in one region of the country where jobs are in plentiful supply than in an area of high unemployment. High income tax rates, however, might make the after-tax increase in income an insufficient incentive to

move. High marginal rates of taxation might also cause a migration of highly skilled and therefore highly paid workers to countries with a more favourable tax regime.

(b) High marginal tax rates, by narrowing the differentials in the after-tax pay of skilled and unskilled labour, may reduce the incentive to train and thereby cause a shortage of skilled labour.

2.14 High marginal rates of tax could **encourage tax avoidance** (finding legal loopholes in the tax rules so as to avoid paying tax). In Britain, high tax rates led to a growth of making income payments-in-kind by way of fringe benefits, for example, free medical and life insurance, preferential loans and favourable pension rights. The tax authorities responded to this by bringing an increasing number of fringe benefits into the tax net - for example, the private use of a company car.

2.15 In some cases individuals and companies may resort to **tax evasion**, which is the illegal non-payment of tax. Employed people have limited scope for tax evasion, because of the **pay as you earn** (PAYE) tax system in the UK. Undoubtedly, the self-employed have a greater ability to evade tax by failing to declare earnings. If evasion becomes widespread the cost of enforcing the tax laws may become very expensive.

2.16 A direct tax on **profits is likely to act as a disincentive to risk-taking and enterprise**. The tax will reduce the net return from a new investment and any disincentive effects will be greater when the tax is progressive. In addition, a tax on profits will reduce the ability to invest. A considerable part of the finance for new investment comes from retained profits so any tax on corporate profits will reduce the ability of firms to save and therefore limit the sources of funds for investment.

2.17 High taxation acts as a disincentive to work because if marginal tax rates (ie the proportion of additional income taken as tax) are high, individuals are likely to behave in one of two ways.

(a) They may forgo opportunities to increase income through additional effort on the basis that the increase in net income does not adequately reward the effort or risk.

(b) They may resort to working in the parallel 'black' economy to avoid paying the tax.

2.18 The **Laffer curve** (named after Professor Arthur Laffer) illustrates the effect of tax rates upon government revenue and national income.

2.19 In the hypothetical economy depicted in Figure 3 a tax rate of 0% results in the government receiving no tax revenue irrespective of the level of national income. If the rate is 100% then nobody will work because they keep none of their earnings and so once again total tax revenue is zero. At 25% tax rates the government will achieve a total tax take of £30bn; the same as the revenue they enjoy at rates of 75%. By deduction the level of national income when taxes are 25% must be £120bn compared with only £40bn if taxes are 75%. High taxation appears to operate as a disincentive and reduce national income.

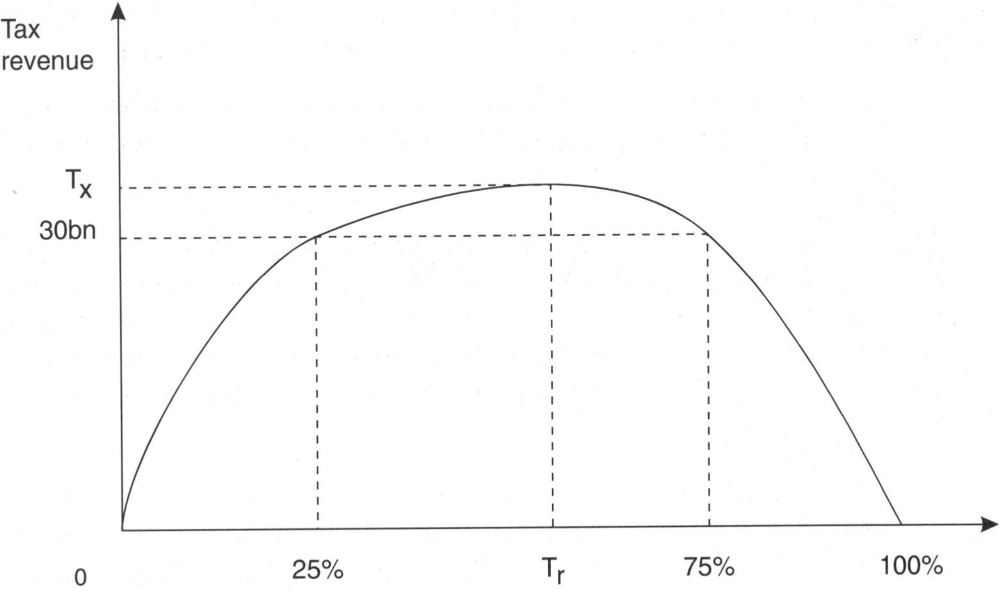

Figure 3 Laffer curve for a hypothetical economy

2.20 Three consequences flow from this Laffer curve analysis.

(a) High rates of taxation act as a disincentive to work and accordingly reduce output and employment.

(b) Governments cannot always expect to increase tax revenue by increasing tax rates. There appears to be a crucial tax rate beyond which the fall in national income resulting from the erosion of incentives and effort outweighs the increased tax rate. In Figure 3 the maximum tax revenue is T_x, at average tax rate T_r. If tax rates are above T_r, the government can increase tax revenues by cutting tax rates.

(c) There will always be two tax rates available which can yield the same total tax revenue: one associated with a high level of national income and another associated with a lower level. In consequence, governments committed to high government expenditure need not necessarily be associated with high rates of tax.

KEY TERMS

Laffer curve: a curve depicting the relationship between tax revenue and the average tax rate, designed to illustrate the thesis that there is an optimal tax rate at which tax revenues are maximised.

Indirect taxation: advantages and disadvantages

2.21 **Indirect** taxes are hidden in the sense that the taxpayer is frequently unaware of the amount of tax he is paying, so that it is almost painlessly extracted (eg the high rate of tax on beer and spirits). This has considerable advantages from the government's point of view.

2.22 **Indirect taxation can be used to encourage or discourage the production or consumption of particular goods and services** and hence affect the allocation of resources. For example, the production of goods that produce environmental pollution may be taxed as a means of raising the price in order to reduce demand and output. Similarly, the consumption of cigarettes can be discouraged by high indirect taxation.

Question 2

The burden of an indirect tax must either be borne by the producer or passed on by the producer to consumers. If a producer feels able to pass on the whole of the burden, what can you deduce about the elasticity of demand for his product?

Answer

Demand for the product must presumably be inelastic, at least in the opinion of the producer. Otherwise he would fear to pass on the tax burden by increasing his prices as this would lead to a fall in demand.

2.23 Indirect taxation is a relatively **flexible instrument of economic policy**. The rates of indirect taxes may be changed to take effect immediately. For example, if the Chancellor wished to boost aggregate demand in the economy he could reduce rates of indirect taxation and this would have an immediate effect on private consumption. In the case of direct taxes, more notice must be given to the taxpayer.

2.24 Indirect taxes can be **cheap to collect**. Traders and companies are required to act as collectors of value added tax in the UK, thus reducing the administrative burden on government.

2.25 Indirect taxes do have disadvantages however.

(a) **They can be inflationary**. In the UK, a switch from direct tax to indirect tax in the budget of 1979, when VAT rates were increased, resulted in a large increase in the reported rate of inflation. When prices are rising the burden of *ad valorem* indirect taxes will naturally rise also. However, a specific indirect tax will only be inflationary if the rate at which it is applied is changed.

(b) **Indirect taxes also tend to be regressive.** A broadly levied indirect tax like VAT is likely to be quite regressive because the poorer members of the community spend a very much larger fraction of their income than very rich people. A system of indirect taxes on luxury goods would not be regressive, however.

(c) **Indirect taxes are not completely impartial in their application in other ways.** For example, someone who seeks to relax with a cigarette in a pub is going to be much more heavily hit by indirect taxes than someone who likes walking. The differential taxes, moreover, prevent resources from being distributed optimally according to consumer preference. Unlike an income tax, indirect taxes change the relative price of goods. This means that consumers have to arrange their patterns of expenditure accordingly. This substitution may involve loss of satisfaction.

(d) Like taxes on incomes, **indirect taxes may be evaded by some.** The so-called 'black economy', in which cash payments are made and income is not declared for tax purposes, is undoubtedly large and widespread in the UK, particularly in the self-employed sector.

Chapter roundup

- Fiscal policy provides a method of managing aggregate demand in the economy. We can summarise the points raised so far as follows.
- If the government spends more, for example on public works such as hospitals, roads and sewers, without raising more money in taxation (ie by borrowing more) it will increase expenditure in the economy, and so raise demand. Keynes argued that owing to the workings of the multiplier and accelerator, an initial boost of extra government spending on public works would stimulate demand by a multiple of the initial spending increase.
- If the government kept its own spending at the same level, but reduced levels of taxation, it would also stimulate demand in the economy because firms and households would have more of their own money after tax for consumption or saving/investing.
- In the same way, a government can reduce demand in the economy by raising taxes or reducing its expenditure.
- A government must decide how it intends to raise tax revenues, from direct or indirect taxes, and in what proportions tax revenues will be raised from each source.
- Direct taxes have the quality of being progressive or proportional. Income tax is usually progressive, with high rates of tax charged on higher bands of taxable income. Indirect taxes can be regressive, when the taxes are placed on essential commodities or commodities consumed by poorer people in greater quantities.

Quick quiz

1 What is the difference between fiscal policy and monetary policy?

2 What are the components of the UK National Debt?

3 Outline how the government may use fiscal policy to influence aggregate demand.

4 What is:

(a) a regressive tax?
(b) a proportional tax?
(c) a progressive tax?

5 Distinguish between direct taxation and indirect taxation.

6 The government of a certain country decides to introduce a poll tax, which will involve a flat rate levy of £200 on every adult member of the population. This new tax could be described as:

A Regressive
B Proportional
C Progressive
D Ad valorem

7 High rates of personal income tax are thought to have a disincentive effect. This refers to the likelihood that the high rates of tax will:

A Encourage illegal tax evasion by individuals
B Lead to a reduction in the supply of labour
C Lead to a reduction in savings by individuals
D Discourage consumer spending and company investments

8 The total yield from an indirect tax levied on a good is likely to be greatest when:

A Demand is inelastic, supply is elastic
B Demand is inelastic, supply is inelastic
C Demand in elastic, supply is elastic
D Demand is elastic, supply is inelastic

9 Which of the following will *not* be the immediate purpose of a tax measure by the government?

A To discourage an activity regarded as socially undesirable.
B To influence interest rates.
C To protect a domestic industry from foreign competition.
D To price certain products so as to take into account their social cost.

10 Which of the following government aims might be achieved by means of fiscal policy? 1. A redistribution of income between firms and households. 2. A reduction in aggregate monetary demand. 3. A change in the pattern of consumer demand.

A Objectives 1 and 2 only
B Objectives 1 and 3 only
C Objectives 2 and 3 only
D Objectives 1, 2 and 3

Answers to quick quiz

1 A government's fiscal policy is concerned with taxation, borrowing and spending; and their effects upon the economy. Monetary policy is concerned with money, the money supply, interest rates, inflation and the exchange rate.

2 The UK National Debt has two main parts: marketable instruments (Treasury bills and gilt-edged securities) and non marketable debt, which consists chiefly of National Savings.

3 A government can increase demand by spending more itself or by reducing taxation so that firms and households have more after-tax income to spend.

4 A regressive tax takes a higher proportion of a poor person's income than a rich person's. A progressive tax takes a higher proportion of a rich person's income and a lower proportion of a poor person's. A proportional tax take the same proportion of all incomes.

5 Direct taxes are levied on income while indirect taxes are levied on expenditure. Indirect taxes are regressive. Direct taxes can be progressive.

6 A A flat-rate poll tax, with no concession for the lower-paid, would take a higher proportion of the income of lower-income earners than of higher income earners. This is a regressive tax system.

7 B The disincentive effect refers specifically to the disincentive of individuals to work.

8 B The total yield from an indirect tax is likely to be greatest when (a) demand for the good is relatively unaffected by the addition of a tax on to the price and (b) supply is relatively unaffected, even though suppliers will be receiving the price net of the tax.

9 B The main purpose of taxation will be to raise revenue for the government. Other aims might be to redistribute wealth or affect demand in the economy. Changes in rate of tax do not have a direct influence on interest rates, which can be influenced by a government's *monetary* policies.

10 D Objective 1 could be achieved by raising (or lowering) taxes on firms and lowering (or raising) taxes on households. Objective 2 could be achieved by raising taxation in order to reduce consumers' disposable income and so to reduce aggregate expenditure in the economy: these consequences should lead to a fall in the demand for money. Objective 3 can be achieved either by taxing income or by means of selective indirect taxes on certain goods.

Now try the questions below from the Question Bank

Number	Level	Marks	Time
Q49	Introductory	8	10 mins
Q50	Introductory - MCQ	–	–
Q51	Exam - MCQ	–	–

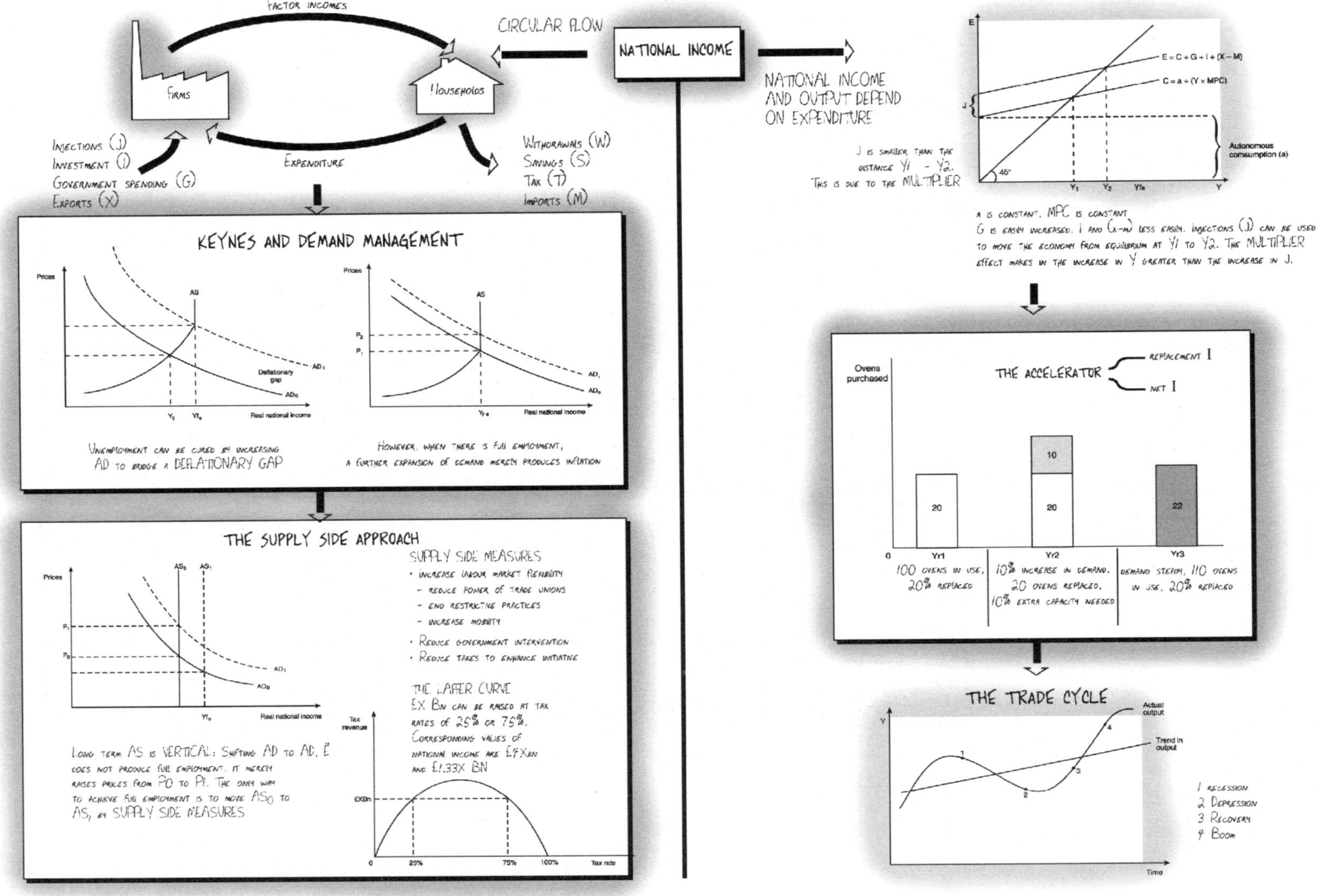

NATIONAL INCOME
CIRCULAR FLOW
Factor incomes
Firms
Households
Expenditure
Injections (J)
Investment (I)
Government spending (G)
Exports (X)
Withdrawals (W)
Savings (S)
Tax (T)
Imports (M)
NATIONAL INCOME AND OUTPUT DEPEND ON EXPENDITURE
E = C + G + I + (X – M)
C = a + (Y × MPC)
Autonomous consumption (a)
J is smaller than the distance Y1 – Y2. This is due to the MULTIPLIER
a is constant. MPC is constant. G is easily increased. I and (X–M) less easily. Injections (J) can be used to move the economy from equilibrium at Y1 to Y2. The MULTIPLIER effect makes the increase in Y greater than the increase in J.
KEYNES AND DEMAND MANAGEMENT
Prices
Deflationary gap
Real national income
Unemployment can be cured by increasing AD to bridge a DEFLATIONARY GAP
However, when there's full employment, a further expansion of demand merely produces inflation
THE SUPPLY SIDE APPROACH
Long term AS is VERTICAL: Shifting AD to AD1 does not produce full employment. It merely raises prices from P0 to P1. The only way to achieve full employment is to move AS0 to AS1 by SUPPLY SIDE MEASURES
SUPPLY SIDE MEASURES
• Increase labour market flexibility
– Reduce power of trade unions
– End restrictive practices
– Increase mobility
• Reduce government intervention
• Reduce taxes to enhance initiative
THE LAFFER CURVE
£X Bn can be raised at tax rates of 25% or 75%. Corresponding values of national income are £4X bn and £1.33X BN
Tax revenue
Tax rate
THE ACCELERATOR
Replacement I
Net I
Ovens purchased
100 ovens in use, 20% replaced
10% increase in demand. 20 ovens replaced, 10% extra capacity needed
Demand steady, 110 ovens in use, 20% replaced
THE TRADE CYCLE
Actual output
Trend in output
Time
1 Recession
2 Depression
3 Recovery
4 Boom

Part D
The open economy

Chapter 18

INTERNATIONAL TRADE

Topic list		Syllabus reference	Ability required
1	**Multinational enterprises and globalisation of markets**	(iv)	Comprehension
2	**International trade and its economic advantages**	(iv)	Comprehension
3	**Free trade agreements**	(iv)	Comprehension

Introduction

One of the most important changes in the economic environment in recent years has been the internationalisation of economic activity. This is reflected in the growth of trade and capital flows between economies and the subsequent increased openness of those economies. The final section of the syllabus introduces those aspects of the international economy most relevant to the chartered management accountant.

In this chapter, we look at the nature and operations of multinational enterprises and the economic advantages of international trade to the nations participating in it.

Learning outcomes covered in this chapter

- Explain patterns of international trade and the sources of international specialisation
- Identify the international movement of factors of production and the role of transnational companies in this process
- Identify and explain the concepts and consequences of globalisation for businesses and national economies
- Identify the main elements of national policy with respect to external economic relations, especially in the context of regional trading blocs

Syllabus content covered in this chapter

- Patterns of international trade and trade policy; regional trading blocs; the globalisation of production
- International factor movements; international capital markets; international investment flows; the movement of labour and technology; the nature and role of transnational companies

1 MULTINATIONAL ENTERPRISES AND GLOBALISATION OF MARKETS 5/01, 11/01

The size and significance of multinational enterprises

1.1 A multinational company is one that has production or service facilities in more than one country. Multinational enterprises range from medium-sized companies having only a few facilities (or subsidiaries or 'affiliates') abroad to giant companies having an annual turnover larger than the gross national product (GNP) of some smaller countries of the world. Indeed the largest - the US multinationals Ford, General Motors and Exxon have each been reported to have a turnover larger than the GNPs of all but 14 countries of the world.

1.2 The size and significance of multinationals is increasing. Many companies in middle-income countries such as Singapore are now becoming multinationals, and the annual growth in output of existing multinationals is in the range 10-15%.

Globalisation of production

1.3 Transitional companies are tending more and more to take a global view of production. This process has been accelerated by improvements in communications, including the expansion and falling cost of air travel; the development of Internet based systems; and improvements in telecommunications generally, such as satellite telephone systems. Production facilities may be located in particular countries for a variety of reasons.

(a) To give access to markets protected by tariffs
(b) To reduce transport costs
(c) To exploit national or regional differences in demand for goods
(d) To take advantage of low labour costs

1.4 Centralisation of manufacturing can bring important **economies of scale**. These must be balanced against transport costs and barriers to trade.

Globalisation of capital markets

1.5 Globalisation describes the process by which the capital markets of each country have become internationally integrated. The process of integration is facilitated by improved telecommunications and the deregulation of markets in many countries (for example, the UK stock market's so-called Big Bang of 1986). Securities issued in one country can now be traded in capital markets around the world. This trend can only increase as stock exchanges are linked electronically as has happened with the London and Frankfurt markets.

1.6 For companies planning international investment activities (also known as foreign direct investment (FDI)), easy access to large amounts of funds denominated in foreign currencies can be very useful. Such funds are available in the eurocurrency markets, whose continued expansion during the 1980s, although slower than during the 1970s, has encouraged FDI. The eurocurrency markets can also help to bypass official constraints on international business activities.

Problems in managing international operations

1.7 Although multinationals can exploit a number of advantages over smaller firms (for example economies of scale, access to capital markets worldwide, and the ability to manufacture and produce in countries where material and labour resources are cheap), they also suffer from a number of **specific managerial problems.**

Problem	Comment
Planning	The environmental variables within which an organisation operates make planning difficult even in local terms. But a multinational faces problems of forecasting environmental variables over many countries. Plans which look promising in the local environment may founder abroad.
Organising	The possible structures of an organisation have been discussed in earlier chapters. Multinationals face the problem that no one structure can meet the needs of the many different environments in which they operate.

Problem	Comment
Staffing	The basic problem here is whether managers should be chosen from the home country or selected locally. Home-grown managers may be familiar with headquarters philosophy, but may find it difficult to get on with local staff from a different background. On the other hand, use of locally-selected managers may lead to a lack of homogeneity in the multinational's trading efforts.
Leading	In some countries a participative style of management is practised. But this may be difficult to transfer to other countries where there is a tradition of autocratic rule.
Controlling	Effective controlling depends on accurate measurement of performance. When many aspects of performance are measured in monetary terms this means that currency differences are a serious obstacle to control. In addition, accounting practices, financial reporting and taxation may all vary from country to country. Inflation rates may be different, and exchange rates will exacerbate the problem. The sheer size and geographical dispersion of multinationals mean that delays elapse between the measurement of performance and the taking of corrective action.

Forms of foreign investment

1.8 FDI provides an alternative to growth restricted to a firm's domestic market. A firm might develop horizontally in different countries, replicating its existing operations on a global basis (**horizontal integration**). **Vertical integration** might have an international dimension through FDI to acquire raw material or component sources overseas (backwards integration) or to establish final production and distribution in other countries (forward integration). Diversification might alternatively provide the impetus to developing international interests.

2 INTERNATIONAL TRADE AND ITS ECONOMIC ADVANTAGES 11/01, 5/02

International trade in goods and services

2.1 Economists distinguish the concepts of **comparative advantage** and **absolute advantage** in international trade. Our explanation of this distinction makes the following assumptions.

- There are only two countries, country X and country Y
- Only two goods are produced, lorries and wheat
- There are no transport costs and no barriers to trade
- Resources within each country are easily transferred from one industry to another

Absolute advantage

2.2 A country is said to have an absolute advantage in the production of a good when it is more efficient than another country in the production of that good, ie when it can produce more of a particular good with a given amount of resources than another country. It is a fairly common situation for one country to be more efficient than another in the production of a particular good.

2.3 Assuming that Y produces wheat more efficiently than country X, while country X has an absolute advantage in producing lorries, a simple arithmetical example can illustrate the potential gains from trade. The table below shows the amounts of lorries and wheat that

each country can produce in year 0, assuming that each country has an equal quantity of resources and devotes half of its resources to lorry production and half to wheat production.

Year 0

	Lorries	*Wheat (tons)*
Country X	20	100
Country Y	10	150
World total	30	250

2.4 The relative cost of lorry production is lower in country X than in country Y, but the situation is reversed in the case of wheat production. Country X has an absolute advantage in lorry production and country Y has an absolute advantage in wheat production. Greater specialisation will, however, increase total output.

Question 1

Suppose that each country devotes its entire production resources to the product for which it enjoys an absolute advantage. What will be the total output of lorries and wheat?

Answer

Total world output will be 40 lorries (produced by country X) and 300 tons of wheat (produced by country Y).

2.5 By specialising, total world output is now (see Exercise 1 solution) greater with ten more lorries and 50 tons more wheat now available for consumption. In order to obtain the benefits of specialisation these countries can exchange some part of their individual outputs. It is not possible to specify the exact rate of exchange but the limits of the exchange rate must be somewhere between the domestic opportunity cost ratios of the two countries. These are: for country X, 5 tons of wheat per lorry; for country Y, 15 tons of wheat per lorry. One country will not benefit from international trade if the 'exchange rate' is not between these ratios.

Comparative advantage

KEY TERM

The law of **comparative advantage** (or comparative costs) states that two countries can gain from trade when each specialises in the industries in which it has lowest opportunity costs.

2.6 The theory of **comparative advantage** is based on the idea of **opportunity cost** and the **production possibility frontier**. Within a country, opportunity cost for any category of product may be established in terms of the next most advantageous use of national resources. If two countries produce different goods most efficiently and can exchange them at an advantageous rate in terms of the comparative opportunity costs of importing and home production, then it will be beneficial for them to specialise and trade. Total production of each good will be higher than if they each produce both goods. This is true even if one country has an absolute advantage in both goods.

2.7 The principle of comparative costs can be shown by an arithmetical example. It is now assumed that in year 10 country X is more efficient in the production of both lorries and

wheat. If each country devotes half its resources to each industry the assumed daily production totals are as shown below.

Year 10

	Lorries	*Wheat (tons)*
Country X	20	200
Country Y	10	150
World total	30	350

2.8 In terms of resources used, the costs of production in both industries are lower in country X. If we consider the opportunity costs, however, the picture is rather different. In country X the cost of one lorry is ten tons of wheat: in devoting resources to the production of one lorry in country X there is a sacrifice in terms of ten tons of wheat forgone. The opportunity cost of one lorry in country Y is fifteen tons of wheat. Country X therefore has a comparative advantage in the production of lorries.

2.9 In country X the opportunity cost of a ton of wheat is now $^1/_{10}$ of a lorry, while in country Y the opportunity cost is $^1/_{15}$ of a lorry. In terms of the output of lorries forgone, wheat is cheaper in country Y than in country X. Country Y has a comparative advantage in wheat. It would now be possible for country Y to buy 10 lorries from country X in exchange for 200 tons of wheat. Country X would transfer some of its resources from the production of wheat to the production of lorries, while country Y would put all of its resources into the production of Wheat. Total production would now look like this.

	Lorries	*Wheat* (tons)
Country X	30	100
Country Y	0	300
World total	30	400

There is an increase in the world output of wheat.

2.10 Alternatively, country X might buy 150 tons of wheat form country Y in exchange for 15 lorries. Country X would transfer even more resources to the production of lorries and the total production figures would change again.

	Lorries	*Wheat* (tons)
Country X	35	50
Country Y	0	300
	35	350

There has now been an increase in the world output of lorries.

2.11 Clearly, the two countries could adjust their trade between these extremes, achieving overall increases in **both** types of good.

2.12 **Other advantages of free international trade**

(a) Some countries have a surplus of **raw materials**, and others have a deficit. A country with a surplus can take advantage of its resources to export them. A country with a deficit of a raw material must either import it, or accept restrictions on its economic prosperity and standard of living.

(b) International trade increases **competition** among suppliers in the world's markets. Greater competition reduces the likelihood of a market for a good in a country being dominated by a monopolist. The greater competition will force firms to be competitive and so will increase the pressures on them to be efficient, and also perhaps to produce goods of a high quality.

(c) International trade creates **larger markets** for a firm's output, and so some firms can benefit from **economies of scale** by engaging in export activities. Economies of scale improve the efficiency of the use of resources, reduce the output costs and also increase the likelihood of output being sold to the consumer at lower prices than if international trade did not exist.

(d) There may be **political advantages** to international trade, because the development of trading links provides a foundation for closer political links. An example of the development of political links based on trade is the European Union.

Exam focus point

Make sure that you can clearly explain comparative advantage. Fundamentally, the comparative advantage model explains trade in terms of the benefits of international specialisation. Note that it is trade that leads to specialisation and not the other way round.

Transport costs

2.13 In the earlier example, we assumed that transport costs in international trade are negligible. High transport costs, however, can negate the advantages of specialisation and international trade.

Free movement of capital

2.14 Free trade is associated with the free movement of goods (and services) between countries. Another important aspect of international trade is the free movement of capital.

(a) If a UK company (or investor) wishes to set up a business in a different country, or to take over a company in another country, how easily can it transfer capital from the UK to the country in question, to pay for the investment?

(b) Similarly, if a Japanese company wishes to invest in the UK, how easily can it transfer funds out of Japan and into the UK to pay for the investment?

2.15 Some countries (including the UK, since the abolition of exchange controls in 1979) have allowed a fairly free flow of capital into and out of the country. Other countries have been more cautious, mainly for one of two reasons:

(a) The free inflow of foreign capital will make it easier for foreign companies to take over domestic companies. There is often a belief that certain key industries should be owned by residents of the country. Even in the UK, for example, there have been restrictions on the total foreign ownership of shares in companies such as British Aerospace and Rolls Royce.

(b) Less developed countries especially, but other more advanced economies too, are reluctant to allow the free flow of capital out of the country. After all, they need capital to come into the country to develop the domestic economy.

2.16 For countries with a large and continuing balance of trade deficit, such as the UK and the USA, it is **essential** that capital should come into the country to finance the deficit. The balance of payments is discussed in detail in the next chapter.

Barriers to free international trade

2.17 In practice many barriers to free trade exist because governments try to protect home industries against foreign competition.

2.18 **Protectionism** can be practised by a government in several ways.

- Tariffs or customs duties
- Import quotas
- Embargoes
- Hidden subsidies for exporters and domestic producers
- Import restrictions

Tariffs or customs duties

2.19 Tariffs or customs duties are taxes on imported goods. The effect of a tariff is to raise the price paid for the imported goods by domestic consumers, while leaving the price paid to foreign producers the same, or even lower. The difference is transferred to the government sector.

Import quotas

2.20 **Import quotas** are restrictions on the **quantity** of a product that is allowed to be imported into the country. The quota has a similar effect on consumer welfare to that of import tariffs, but the overall effects are more complicated.

(a) Both domestic and foreign suppliers enjoy a higher price, while consumers buy less at the higher price.

(b) Domestic producers supply more.

(c) There are fewer imports (in volume).

(d) The government collects no revenue.

2.21 An **embargo** on imports from one particular country is a total ban, ie effectively a zero quota.

Hidden export subsidies and import restrictions

2.22 There has been an enormous range of government subsidies and assistance for exports and deterrents against imports. Some examples are given below.

(a) **For exports** - export credit guarantees (insurance against bad debts for overseas sales), financial help (such as government grants to the aircraft or shipbuilding industry) and state assistance via the Foreign Office;

(b) **For imports** - complex import regulations and documentation, or special safety standards demanded from imported goods and so on.

2.23 When a government gives grants to its domestic producers, for example regional development grants for new investments in certain areas of the country or grants to investments in new industries, the effect of these grants is to make unit production costs lower. These give the domestic producer a cost advantage over foreign producers in export markets as well as domestic markets.

Arguments in favour of protection

2.24 Protectionist measures may be taken against imports of cheap goods that compete with higher-priced domestically produced goods, and so **preserve output and employment** in domestic industries. In the UK, advocates of protection have argued that UK industries are declining because of competition from overseas, and the advantages of more employment at a reasonably high wage for UK labour are greater than the disadvantages that protectionist measures would bring.

(a) Measures might be necessary to **counter dumping of surplus production** by other countries at an uneconomically low price. For example, if the European Union (EU) were to over-produce, it might decide to dump the surpluses on other countries. The losses from overproduction would be subsidised by the EU governments, and the domestic industries of countries receiving dumped goods would be facing unfair competition from abroad. Although dumping has short-term benefits for the countries receiving the cheap goods, the longer term consequences would be a reduction in domestic output and employment, even when domestic industries in the longer term might be more efficient.

(b) Protectionist measures by one country are often implemented in **retaliation** against measures taken by another country that are thought to be unfair. This is why protection tends to spiral once it has begun. Any country that does not take protectionist measures when other countries are doing so is likely to find that it suffers all of the disadvantages and none of the advantages of protection.

(c) There is an argument that protectionism is necessary, at least in the short term, to protect a country's **infant industries** that have not yet developed to the size where they can compete in international markets. Less developed countries in particular might need to protect industries against competition from advanced or developing countries.

(d) Protection might also help a country in the short term to deal with the problems of a **declining industry**. Without protection, the industry might quickly collapse and there would be severe problems of sudden mass unemployment. By imposing some protectionist measures, the decline in the industry might be slowed down, and the task of switching resources to new industries could be undertaken over a longer period of time.

(e) Protection is often seen as a means for a country to **reduce its balance of trade deficit,** by imposing tariffs or quotas on imports. However, because of retaliation by other countries, the success of such measures by one country would depend on the demand by other countries for its exports being inelastic with regard to price and its demand for imports being fairly elastic.

Undesirable effects of protection **11/01, 5/02**

2.25 As well as reducing the benefits brought by trade, protection can have direct disadvantageous effects on a country's businesses.

2.26 **Higher costs**. Protection is likely to raise costs to domestic business for three reasons.

(a) Imports of raw materials, components, fuel and so on will be more expensive.

(b) Domestic producers of inputs will take advantage of the reduction in competition to raise their prices.

(c) Rising prices of both imports and domestic goods will lead to increased wage demands.

2.27 **Reduced demand.** Domestic producers will face reduced demand for two reasons.

(a) Foreign trading partners are likely to retaliate with protective measures of their own, thus reducing export demand.

(b) Home consumers will find their real income declines as costs rise (see above) and thus domestic demand will decline.

3 FREE TRADE AGREEMENTS 5/01

The World Trade Organisation

3.1 The World Trade Organisation (WTO) was formed in 1995 as successor to the General Agreement on Tariffs and Trade (GATT). The GATT was originally signed by 23 countries in 1947. GATT had three aims.

(a) To reduce existing barriers to free trade.

(b) To eliminate discrimination in international trade.

(c) To prevent the growth of protection by getting member countries to consult with others before taking any protectionist measures.

3.2 It has been estimated that the opening up of markets for agricultural and industrial goods following the 1993 GATT accord could add around US$200-300 billion to world income by the year 2002. Ratification of the agreement by member governments followed during 1994. The new World Trade Organisation (WTO), which GATT members have now joined, was set up in 1995 as a result of the agreement. GATT itself officially ceased to exist at the end of 1995.

The European Union

3.3 The European Union (EU) (formerly the European Community) is one of several international economic associations. It was formed in 1957 by the Treaty of Rome and now consists of Austria, Belgium, Denmark, Finland, France, Germany, Greece, Ireland, Italy, Luxembourg, the Netherlands, Portugal, Spain, Sweden and the United Kingdom. Over the coming years, more nations are expected to join, including a number of Eastern European countries which were formerly operated as centralised command economies under Communist regimes.

3.4 The European Union has a **common market** combining different aspects, including **a free trade area** and a **customs union**.

(a) A **free trade area** exists when there is no restriction on the movement of goods and services between countries. This may be extended into a **customs union** when there is a free trade area between all member countries of the union, and in addition, there are common external tariffs applying to imports from non-member countries into any part of the union. In other words, the union promotes free trade among its members but acts as a protectionist bloc against the rest of the world.

(b) A **common market** encompasses the idea of a customs union but has a number of additional features. In addition to free trade among member countries there are also free markets in each of the **factors of production**. A British citizen has the freedom to work in any other country of the European Union, for example. A common market will also aim to achieve stronger links between member countries, for example by

harmonising government economic policies and by establishing a closer political confederation.

The single European market

3.5 The EU set the end of 1992 as the target date for the removal of all existing physical, technical and fiscal barriers among member states, thus creating a large multinational European Single Market. This objective was embodied in the Single European Act of 1985. In practice, these changes have not occurred overnight, and many of them are still in progress.

3.6 Elimination of trade restrictions covers the following areas.

(a) **Physical barriers** (eg customs inspection) on good and services have been removed for most products. Companies have had to adjust to a new VAT regime as a consequence.

(b) **Technical standards** (eg for quality and safety) should be harmonised.

(c) Governments should not discriminate between EU companies in awarding **public works contracts.**

(d) **Telecommunications** should be subject to greater competition.

(e) It should be possible to provide **financial services** in any country.

(f) There should be **free movement of capital** within the community.

(g) **Professional qualifications** awarded in one member state should be recognised in the others.

(h) The EU is taking a co-ordinated stand on matters related to **consumer protection.**

3.7 At the same time, you should not assume that there will be a completely 'level playing field'. There are many areas where harmonisation is a long way from being achieved. Here are some examples.

(a) **Company taxation**. Tax rates, which can affect the viability of investment plans, vary from country to country within the EU.

(b) **Indirect taxation** (eg *VAT*). Whilst there have been moves to harmonisation, there are still differences between rates imposed by member states.

(c) **Differences in prosperity**. There are considerable differences in prosperity between the wealthiest EU economy (Germany), and the poorest (eg Greece). The UK comes somewhere in the middle.

(d) **Differences in workforce skills**. Again, this can have a significant effect on investment decisions. The workforce in Germany is perhaps the most highly trained, but also the most highly paid, and so might be suitable for products of a high added value.

(e) **Infrastructure**. Some countries are better provided with road and rail than others. Where accessibility to a market is an important issue, infrastructure can mean significant variations in distribution costs.

The European Free Trade Association (EFTA)

3.8 The European Free Trade Association (EFTA) was established in 1959, with seven member countries, one of which was the UK. The UK, Denmark and Portugal have since transferred to the EU, while Finland and Iceland joined the other original member states, Sweden,

Norway, Austria and Switzerland. More recently, Finland, Sweden and Austria have also joined the EU. There is free trade between EFTA member countries but there is no harmonisation of tariffs with non-EFTA countries.

The European Economic Area (EEA)

3.9 On 1 January 1993, EFTA forged a link with the EU to create a European Economic Area (EEA) with a population of 380 million, so extending the benefits of the EU single market to the EFTA member countries (excluding Switzerland, which stayed out of the EEA). The membership of the EEA now comprises the EU countries plus Norway and Iceland.

The North American Free Trade Agreement (NAFTA)

3.10 Canada, the USA and Mexico formed the North American Free Trade Agreement (NAFTA) in 1993. This free trade area covering a population of 360 million is similar in size to the European Economic Area.

Chapter roundup

- The growth of multinational enterprises has taken place in an environment of increasing globalisation of markets.
- We have looked at the benefits of international trade from an economic point of view. World output of goods and services will increase if countries specialise in the production of goods/services in which they have a comparative advantage. Just how this total wealth is shared out between countries depends on circumstances.

Quick quiz

1 Define a multinational enterprise.

2 Outline the main problems encountered in managing international business operations.

3 What is meant by the law of comparative advantage?

4 What is meant by:

(a) a free trade area
(b) a customs union
(c) a common market

5 Assume that two small countries, X and Y, produce two commodities P and Q, and that there are no transport costs. One unit of resource in Country X produces 4 units of P or 8 units of Q. One unit of resource in Country Y produces 1 unit of P or 3 units of Q. which of the following statements is true?

A Country X has an absolute advantage over Country Y in producing P and Q, and so will not trade.
B Country X does not have an absolute advantage over Country Y in producing P and Q.
C Country Y has a comparative advantage over Country X in producing Q.
D Country X has a comparative advantage over Country Y in producing both P and Q.

Answers to quick quiz

1 A multinational enterprise is one which has a physical presence or property interests in more than one country.

2
- Planning is complicated by the wide variation in conditions between countries.
- It is difficult to structure an organisation to meet the demands of operations in different countries.
- Multinationals have to achieve a balance between local and ex-patriate staff
- Successful management styles vary from country to country.
- Control by reference to monetary measures is complicated by varying inflation rates, exchange rates, taxation rates and financial reporting practices.

3 The law of comparative advantage or comparative costs states that two countries can gain from trade when each specialises in the industries in which it has the lowest opportunity costs.

4 A free trade area exists when there is no restriction on trade between countries. This is extended into a customs union when common external tariffs are levied on imports from non-member countries. A common market adds free movement of the factors of production, including labour and may harmonise economic policy.

5 C Country X has an *absolute* advantage over Country Y in making P and Q, because 1 unit of resource in Country X will make more of either P or Q than one unit of resource in Country Y. However, international trade should still take place because of *comparative* advantage in producing P and Q. The opportunity costs of producing a unit of P is 2 units of Q in Country X and 3 units of Q in Country Y. Similarly, the opportunity cost of producing a unit of Q is $\frac{1}{2}$ a unit of P in Country X and $\frac{1}{3}$ of a unit of P in Country Y. Country X has a comparative advantage in producing P and Country Y has a comparative advantage in the production of Q. International trade should be beneficial for both countries, with country X exporting P and Country Y exporting Q.

Now try the questions below from the Question Bank

Number	Level	Marks	Time
Q52	Introductory	8	10 mins
Q53	Exam – MCQ	2	–
Q54	Introductory - MCQ	–	–

Chapter 19

THE BALANCE OF PAYMENTS AND EXCHANGE RATES

Topic list		Syllabus reference	Ability required
1	The balance of payments	(iii)	Comprehension
2	The terms of trade	(iii)	Comprehension
3	Exchange rates and exchange rate systems	(iii)	Comprehension

Introduction

In this final chapter, we examine two things.

- The balance of payments and the economic policies affecting it
- Policies on exchange rates, and the effects of these policies

Learning outcomes covered in this chapter

- Explain the concept of the balance of payments and its determinants
- Distinguish between different exchange rate regimes and their implications for the business sector

Syllabus content covered in this chapter

- The balance of payments; structure and determinants of the balance of payments; foreign exchange rate regimes; European monetary union

1 THE BALANCE OF PAYMENTS 5/01, 11/01, 5/02

The nature of the balance of payments

1.1 The balance of payments is a statistical 'accounting' record of a country's international trade transactions (the purchase and sale of goods and services) and capital transactions (the acquisition and disposal of assets and liabilities) with other countries during a period of time.

Exam focus point

Confusion of the balance of payments with the government budget is common in exams. Make sure that the distinction is clear in *your* mind.

1.2 Under the current method of presentation of the UK balance of payments statistics, **current account** transactions are sub-divided into four parts.

- Trade in goods
- Trade in services
- Income
- Transfers

Before 1996, the term **visibles** was used in official statistics for trade in goods and the term **invisibles** was used for the rest. These terms have now been dropped in order to give more emphasis to the balances for trade in goods and services, although you may still find them mentioned.

1.3 Income is divided into two parts.

- Income from employment of UK residents by overseas firms
- Income from capital investment overseas

Transfers are also divided into two parts.

(a) Public sector payments to and receipts from overseas bodies such as the EU. Typically these are interest payments.

(b) Non-government sector payments to and receipts from bodies such as the EU.

1.4 The **capital account** balance is made up of public sector flows of **capital** into and out of the country, such as government loans to other countries.

1.5 The balance on the **financial account** is made up of flows of capital to and from the non-government sector, such as direct investment in overseas facilities; portfolio investment (in shares, bonds and so on); and speculative flows of currency. Movements on government foreign currency reserves are also included under this heading.

The sum of the balance of payments accounts is zero

Net errors and omissions

1.6 A balancing item appears in the balance of payments accounts because of errors and omissions in collecting statistics for the accounts (for example, sampling errors for items such as foreign investment and tourist expenditure and omissions from the data gathered about exports or imports).

1.7 The sum of the balance of payments accounts must always be zero (ignoring statistical errors in collecting the figures). This is for the same reason that a balance sheet must always balance: for every debit there must be a credit.

The UK balance of payments accounts

1.8 A recent UK balance of payment account is summarised below.

UK balance of payments accounts

	£ billions
Current account	
Trade in goods	-26,767
Trade in services	11,538
Income	8,332
Transfers	-4,084
Current balance	-10,981
Capital account	776
Financial account	5,853
Net errors and omissions	4,352
	0

1.9 Given that the balance of payments in principle sums to zero, you may wonder what is meant by a surplus or deficit on the balance of payments. When journalists or economists speak of the balance of payments they are usually referring to the deficit or surplus on the **current account**, or possibly to the surplus or deficit on trade in goods only (this is also known as the **balance of trade**).

Question 1

'If the balance of payments always balances why do we hear about deficits and surpluses?'

Answer

The sum of the three balance of payments accounts must always be zero because every transaction in international trade has a double aspect. Just as accounting transactions are recorded by matching debit and credit entries, so too are international trade and financing transactions recorded by means of matching plus and minus transactions.

If a UK exporter sells goods to a foreign buyer:

(a) the value of the export is a plus in the current account of the balance of payments.

(b) the payment for the export results in a reduction in the deposits held by foreigners in UK banks. (A minus in the assets and liabilities section.)

When we use the phrases 'deficit' or 'surplus on the balance of payments' what we actually mean is a deficit or surplus on the current account. If there is a surplus (+) on the current account we would expect this to be matched by a similar negative amount on the assets and liabilities section. This will take the form of:

(a) additional claims on non-residents (for example, overseas loans).
(b) decreased liabilities to non-residents (paying off our loans abroad).

This will involve not only banks and other firms but it may also involve the government too, since it is responsible for the 'reserves'.

If there is a deficit (-) on the current account the result will be a similar positive amount on the assets and liabilities section. This will consist of inward investment and/or increased overseas indebtedness, representing how the deficit has been 'financed'. This means that banks and other firms will owe more money abroad and the government may also be borrowing from abroad.

Exam focus point

Do not, as some students do, equate a trade surplus or deficit with a 'profit' or 'loss' for the country. 'A country is not like a company and the trade balance has nothing to do with profits and losses', comments the Examiner.

Foreign currency and international trade

1.10 Whenever there is international trade, there is a need for foreign currency for at least one of the parties to the transaction.

(a) If a UK exporter sells goods to a US buyer, and charges the buyer £20,000, the US buyer must somehow obtain the sterling in order to pay the UK supplier. The US buyer will do this by using some of his US dollars to buy the £20,000 sterling, probably from a bank in the USA;

(b) If a UK importer buys goods from Germany, he might be invoiced in deutschmarks, say DM100,000. He must obtain this foreign currency to pay his debt, and he will do so by purchasing the deutschmarks from a UK bank in exchange for sterling;

(c) If a UK investor wishes to invest in US capital bonds, he would have to pay for them in US dollars, and so he would have to sell sterling to obtain the dollars.

1.11 Thus **capital outflows**, such as investing overseas, not just payments for imports, cause a demand to sell the domestic currency and buy foreign currencies. On the other hand, exports and capital inflows to a country cause a demand to buy the domestic currency in exchange for foreign currencies.

1.12 Exporters might want to sell foreign currency earnings to a bank in exchange for domestic currency, and importers may want to buy foreign currency from a bank in order to pay a foreign supplier.

Exchange rates and the UK balance of payments

1.13 As in any other market, the market for foreign exchange is a market in which buyers and suppliers come into contact, and 'prices' (exchange rates) are set by supply and demand. Exchange rates change continually. Significant movements in the exchange rate for a country's currency can have important implications for the country's balance of payments.

Equilibrium in the balance of payments

1.14 A balance of payments is in equilibrium if, over a period of years, the exchange rate remains stable and autonomous credits and debits are equal in value (the annual trade in goods and services is in overall balance). However, equilibrium will not exist if these things require the government to introduce measures which create unemployment or higher prices, sacrifice economic growth or impose trade barriers (eg import tariffs and import quotas).

Surplus or deficit in the balance of payments

1.15 A problem arises for a country's balance of payments when the country has a deficit on current account year after year, although there can be problems too for a country which enjoys a continual current account **surplus**.

1.16 The problems of a **deficit** on the current account are probably the more obvious. When a country is continually in deficit, it is importing more goods and services that it is exporting. This leads to two possible consequences.

(a) It may borrow more and more from abroad, to build up external liabilities which match the deficit on current account, for example encouraging foreign investors to lend more by purchasing the government's gilt-edged securities.

(b) It may sell more and more of its assets. This has been happening recently in the USA, for example, where a large deficit on the US current account has resulted in large purchases of shares in US companies by foreign firms.

1.17 Even so, the demand to buy the country's currency in the foreign exchange markets will be weaker than the supply of the country's currency for sale. As a consequence, there will be pressure on the exchange rate to depreciate in value.

1.18 If a country has a **surplus** on current account year after year, it might invest the surplus abroad or add it to official reserves. The balance of payments position would be strong. There is the problem, however, that if one country which is a major trading nation (such as Japan) has a continuous surplus on its balance of payments current account, other countries must be in continual deficit. These other countries can run down their official reserves, perhaps to nothing, and borrow as much as they can to meet the payments overseas, but eventually, they will run out of money entirely and be unable even to pay their debts. Political pressure might therefore build up within the importing countries to impose tariffs or import quotas.

How can a government rectify a current account deficit?

1.19 The government of a country with a balance of payments deficit will usually be expected to take measures to reduce or eliminate the deficit. A deficit on current account may be rectified by one or more of the following measures.

(a) A depreciation of the currency (called **devaluation** when deliberately instigated by the government, for example by changing the value of the currency within a controlled exchange rate system).

(b) Direct measures to restrict imports, such as tariffs or import quotas or exchange control regulations.

(c) Domestic deflation to reduce aggregate demand in the domestic economy.

The first two are **expenditure switching** policies, which transfer resources and expenditure away from imports and towards domestic products while the last is an **expenditure reducing** policy.

Depreciation/devaluation of the currency 5/01

1.20 A rising (ie appreciating) exchange rate may reflect relatively low inflation and strong trade and general economic performance, as in the case of Japan in recent years. Conversely, poor economic performance and high inflation will result in **currency depreciation**. As a result of a fall in the value of the currency, exports would be relatively cheaper to foreign buyers, and so the demand for exports would rise.

1.21 The extent of the increase in export revenue would depend on several factors.

(a) The price elasticity of demand for the goods in export markets.

(b) The extent to which industry is able to respond to the export opportunities by either producing more goods, or switching from domestic to export markets.

(c) Perhaps also the price elasticity of supply. With greater demand for their goods, producers should be able to achieve some increase in prices (according to the law of supply and demand), and the willingness of suppliers to produce more would then depend on the price elasticity of supply.

(Appreciation of a currency will have converse effects to those of a depreciation.)

1.22 The cost of imports would rise as a result of **currency depreciation** because more domestic currency would be needed to obtain the foreign currency to pay for imported goods. The volume of imports would fall, although whether or not the total value of imports fell too would depend on the elasticity of demand for imports.

(a) If demand for imports is inelastic, the volume of demand would fall by less than their cost goes up, so that the total value of imports would rise.

(b) If demand for imports is elastic, the total value of imports would fall since the fall in volume would outweigh the increase in unit costs.

1.23 If a country imports raw materials and exports manufactured goods which are made with those materials, the cost of imported raw materials will rise, and so producers will have to put up their prices to cover their higher costs. There will be a net fall in export prices, as explained above, but perhaps not by much.

Effects of a fall in exchange rate on the balance of payments 11/01

1.24 The effects of a fall in the exchange rate (for example, due to a government policy of devaluation) are likely to vary in the short term and the long term. The immediate effects will depend on the elasticity of demand for imports. Demand is likely to be fairly inelastic in the short term and so total expenditure on imports will rise. Exports will be cheaper in overseas markets (in foreign currency) but in the short term exporters might be unable to increase their output to meet the higher demand.

1.25 Until domestic industry adjusts to the change and increases its output of exported goods and home produced substitutes for imported goods, there will be a deterioration in the current account of the balance of payments.

1.26 After a time lag, production of exports and import substitutes can be expected to rise, so that the volume of exports will rise, thereby increasing the sterling value of exports (regardless of sterling's lower exchange rate) and the volume of imports will fall further. This will improve the current account balance.

1.27 The improvement in the balance of payments will have some limit, and the current balance should eventually level off. The effect of the falling exchange rate on the current balance through time has been portrayed in the form of the so-called *J* **curve** (Figure 1).

KEY TERMS

J curve effect: the effect on the balance of payments of a falling exchange rate. Inelasticity of both supply and demand means that the current account will deteriorate at first but then improve.

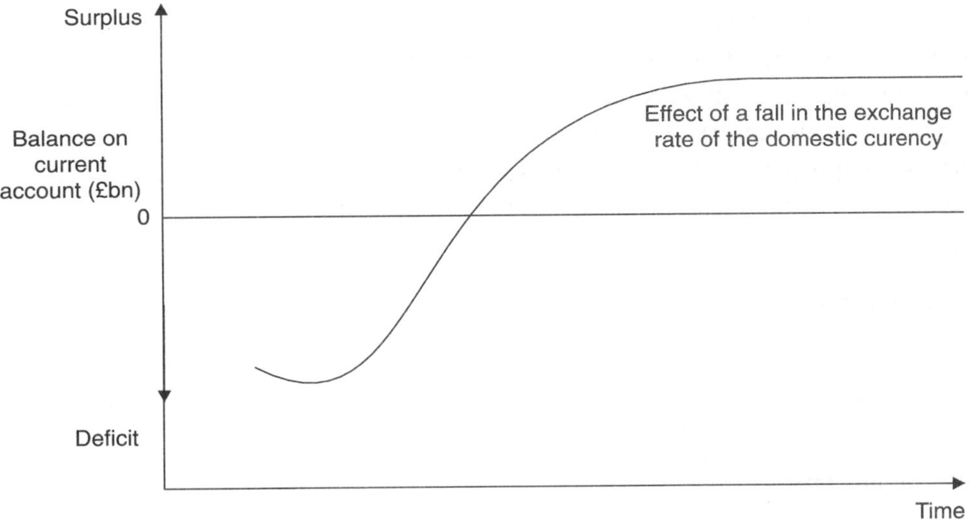

Figure 1 J curve

Effects of currency appreciation 5/01, 5/02

1.28 A **strongly rising (ie appreciating) exchange rate** may reflect relatively low inflation and strong trade and general economic performance, as in the case of Japan in the 1970s and 80s. (Conversely, poor economic performance and high inflation will result in currency depreciation.) To consider the implications for an economy such as Japan's of a rise in the value of the currency in more detail, we may look first at the effects on exports and then on imports required to buy 100 yen rises.

1.29 As the yen rises in value, so other currencies weaken relatively. Over the years, the number of dollars, pounds, marks and so on required to buy 100 yen rises. **The result is to increase the effective price of Japanese goods abroad, so that with price elasticity of demand the volume of exports would be depressed**. The diminished volume of exports would have domestic consequences.

- Stocks would gradually build up, leading to a curtailment of production.
- In turn, this could result in higher unit costs as fixed costs are less effectively spread.
- Short-time working and possibly labour redundancies might follow.
- Some investment decisions might be deferred or even cancelled altogether.

These reductions in the level of economic activity would have negative multiplier effects.

1.30 **A strong currency means that imports become cheaper**. Therefore costs of imported raw materials and foodstuffs fall. Input costs for industry therefore fall and any rises in retail prices are restrained. Inflationary pressures in the system are thus lessened. This may be used to advantage on exports to offset partially the effect of the rising currency: firms may be able to hold down their ex-factory price and so enable the net price overseas to rise very little. Any advantage on the import side of a stronger currency would depend on the relative importance of imports: a country having to import much of its raw materials and fuel could find this a useful advantage.

1.31 With a strong currency, there will also be an increased attraction in buying foreign consumer goods. Invisible imports may begin to rise: more Japanese residents might venture abroad on holiday, so increasing the supply of yen in currency markets and raising the demand for other currencies. This would exert some downward pressure on the yen. Any recessionary effects on industry would, of course, tend to lessen these import pressures.

1.32 The overall effect would depend on the balance between export and import effects - some unfavourable, some favourable. Any significant decline in the net inflow of capital as economic expansion slows could have a de-stabilising effect. The overall effect would also depend upon the ability of the economy to adjust to the changed conditions, for example through improved efficiency, so enabling ex-factory prices to be reduced. It would also depend upon economic conditions in the rest of the world.

Protectionist measures

1.33 Another way of attempting to rectify a balance of payments deficit is to take direct protectionist measures like those we have already described to reduce the volume of imports. These measures might include these below.

(a) **Import tariffs**

(b) **Import quotas**

(c) A **total ban or embargo** on imports from a certain country

(d) Placing **administrative burdens** on importers (for example increasing the documentation required or safety standards that imported goods must comply with)

(e) **Exchange control regulations** which make it difficult for importers to obtain foreign currency to buy goods from abroad

(f) Providing **export subsidies** to encourage exports, and other measures of financial support to exporters

1.34 Import restrictions and export subsidies give rise to counter-measures by other countries. They are therefore potentially dangerous measures for a country whose economy relies heavily on external trade. Exchange control regulations might be essential, however, for a country with a balance of payments deficit, low official reserves and one which has great difficulty in borrowing capital from abroad.

Domestic deflation

1.35 Deflation can be used to adjust a balance of trade deficit. When the total volume of expenditure and demand for goods in a country's economy is too high, the government can take steps to reduce it, by reducing its own expenditure, raising interest rates to deter borrowing, and cutting private consumption by raising taxes. This fall in demand should lead to a fall in prices or at least to a reduction in the rate of domestic inflation. Unfortunately, it might also lead, in the short term at least, to a reduction in industrial output and a loss of jobs in the country's economy. Certainly, the country must accept a lowering of its standard of living if severe deflationary measures are taken. The effect of deflation is not only to dampen domestic inflation rates, but to force domestic manufacturers, who will be faced with lower domestic demand for their goods, to switch more effort into selling to export markets.

1.36 **Deflationary measures include cutting government spending, increasing taxation and raising interest rates**. They have three purposes.

(a) To reduce the demand for goods and services at home, and so to reduce imports.

(b) To encourage industry to switch to export markets, because of the fall in domestic demand.

(c) To tackle domestic inflation, which might be undermining the beneficial effect for exports of a depreciating domestic currency by raising the prices of exported goods in terms of the domestic currency.

1.37 Sometimes, a government's domestic economic policies are not deflationary, despite a balance of payments deficit, and on the contrary, the government's economic policies might encourage increasing demand, which will both boost demand for imports, and cause more inflation and a falling exchange rate. Economic policies which boost demand in the economy in spite of a balance of payments deficit will worsen, rather than improve, the deficit.

The balance of payments and the domestic economy

1.38 You should try to view any country's balance of payments position in the context of its domestic economy.

(a) When a country's exports exceed its imports, or *vice versa*, there may be a lack of equilibrium between withdrawals from the circular flow of income in the domestic economy (remember that these withdrawals include imports) and injections into the circular flow of income (which include exports). Equilibrium in the balance of payments (external equilibrium) will also help a country to achieve equilibrium in its circular flow of income (internal equilibrium).

(b) If a country's international trade is only small in size compared with its domestic economy, problems with any balance of payments deficit will be much less than for a country which relies heavily on international trade.

Interest rates and the balance of payments

1.39 Comparative interest rates between one country and another, and changes in interest rates, affect the balance of payments in two ways.

(a) Directly, by stimulating or discouraging foreign investment, and so inflows and outflows of capital.

(b) Indirectly, through the exchange rate. Foreign investment creates a demand for the currency and keeps the exchange rate at a high level.

1.40 Is a high interest rate policy a good solution to the problem of a deficit on the balance of payments current account?

(a) If a country relies on inflows of capital to finance a continuing balance of trade deficit, the country's balance of payments will never get into equilibrium. High interest rates will keep the exchange rate high for the country's currency, and this will make it more difficult to export (high export prices to foreign buyers) and encourage imports (cheaper prices). The country might therefore be unable to rectify its balance of trade deficit.

(b) If there is a continuing balance of trade deficit, there will always be a threat that the country's currency will eventually depreciate in value. This will deter investors. The UK is in this position at the time of writing.

1.41 Investors will only put money into capital investments abroad if they have satisfactory expectations about what the exchange rate for the foreign currency will be. Interest rates alone are not the only factor on which to base an investment decision. After all, what is the value to an investor of high interest rates from investments in a foreign currency when the exchange value of the currency is falling?

External debt

1.42 A country's external debt is the total amount that the country owes to foreign creditors. It can include several elements.

(a) Loans from specialist international lending organisations, in particular the International Monetary Fund (IMF) and the World Bank.

(b) Loans from foreign governments.

(c) Loans from private foreign investors, in particular foreign banks.

Question 2

See if you can think through what the effect of a balance of payments current account deficit will be on a country's external debt.

Answer

A country's external debt increases whenever it has a balance of payments deficit on current account.

(a) A deficit on current account must be balanced (that is, equalled) by a matching surplus in transactions in external assets and liabilities, in other words, by:

(i) borrowing from abroad
(ii) selling assets that are owned abroad

(b) If a country's balance of trade deficit is very high, it must borrow heavily from abroad. Borrowing could be:

(i) borrowing by the government

(ii) borrowing by the private sector

(iii) increasing investments in the country's private sector by foreign firms, eg takeovers of domestic companies by foreign companies

(c) There would be fears of a depreciation in the exchange rate of the country's currency, as a consequence of the balance of trade deficit. How can a country succeed in attracting foreign investors if they fear that the value of their investment might fall because of a currency depreciation?

Interest rates will probably have to remain high to compensate foreign investors for this risk.

(d) If the country's external debt becomes very high, the cost of servicing the debt by meeting interest payment schedules could become a severe burden on the country's economy.

2 THE TERMS OF TRADE 5/02

2.1 The **balance of trade** for any country depends on two things.

- The volume of goods exported and imported
- The relative prices of exports and imports

KEY TERMS

Terms of trade: the quantities of domestic goods that a country must give up to obtain a unit of imported goods.

2.2 In effect, the terms of trade are an export: import price ratio, which measures the relative prices of a country's exports and imports. The terms of trade for a country continually change as export prices and import prices change.

2.3 The terms of trade determine the volume of exports necessary to pay for a given volume of imports or, meaning the same thing, the volume of imports that can be purchased with the proceeds of a given volume of exports.

2.4 Other things being equal, if the price of exports falls relative to that of imports (a fall in the terms of trade) the trade balance will deteriorate, or *vice versa*.

2.5 Note that trade balance depends not just on the physical volume of exports and imports, but on the prices at which they are traded.

Question 3

A country's electronics industry, which is its major export industry, switches from the production of mass low cost, low profit margin microchips to the production of more high powered, high cost, high profit margin custom-built microchips. Which one of the following effects would you expect to occur?

A An improvement in the balance of trade
B A deterioration in the balance of trade
C An improvement in the terms of trade
D A worsening in the terms of trade

Answer

The answer is C. This is one example of how a country's terms of trade might improve. By switching from low priced to high priced products in a major export industry, unit export prices will go up and the terms of trade will improve. The change in the *balance* of trade depends on changes in the *volume* of exports and imports *as well as changes in export and import prices.*

Measuring the terms of trade

2.6 The terms of trade are measured as:

$$\frac{\text{Unit value of exports}}{\text{Unit value of imports}}$$

2.7 In practice economists are usually concerned not with a measurable value for the terms of trade but with a measure of *changes* in the terms of trade, (eg from one year to the next).

Using indices for the average prices of imports and exports, the movement in the terms of trade between 1998 and 1997 would be computed as:

$$\frac{\text{Price of exports in 1998/price of exports 1997}}{\text{Price of imports 1998/price of imports 1997}}$$

Changes in the terms of trade

2.8 Change in a country's terms of trade occur for two reasons.

(a) A change in the composition of exports or imports; in the UK, two main things have improved the UK's terms: lower oil imports and manufacturers trading up to higher-price products for export.

(b) Lower or higher prices of imports/exports - such as the oil price collapse in 1985, which worsened the terms of trade for the UK.

2.9 A government has limited powers to influence its country's terms of trade, since it cannot directly influence the composition nor the prices of imports and exports - although it *can* affect the terms of trade through a revaluation or devaluation of the currency which would alter relative import/export prices.

(a) If a country's terms of trade **worsen,** the unit value of its imports will rise by a bigger percentage than the unit value of its exports. The terms of trade will worsen when the exchange rate of the currency depreciates in value against other currencies.

(b) If a country's terms of trade **improve,** the unit value of its exports will rise by a bigger percentage than the unit value of its imports. The terms of trade will improve when the exchange rate of the country's currency appreciates in value against other currencies.

2.10 It would seem logical to assume that an improving terms of trade is good for a country and a worsening terms of trade is bad for it. But **this is not necessarily the case**.

2.11 The effect of a change in the terms of trade should be considered in the context of the country's balance of payments. If the terms of trade worsen for a country, the country will be unable to afford the same volume of imports, or else its balance of payment position will deteriorate. In contrast, a country with improving terms of trade will be able to afford more imports or will improve its balance of payments.

2.12 Changes in the terms of trade affect a country's balance of payments via the price elasticity of demand for the goods traded. If a country's terms of trade improve, so that the price of its exported goods rises relative to the price of its imported goods, there will be a relative fall in the volume of goods exported and a rise in the volume of imports. The size of this fall in exports and increase in imports will depend on the price elasticities of demand for exported goods in foreign markets and imported goods in the country's domestic markets.

Question 4

From your knowledge of the theory of elasticity of demand, analyse what will happen to the current balance of trade when the terms of trade improve, on the assumptions:

(a) that demand for exported goods and demand for imported goods are both *inelastic*
(b) that both demands are *elastic*

Answer

(a) If the demand for exported goods is inelastic the total value of exports will rise if their price goes up.

(b) If the demand for imported goods is inelastic the total value of imports will fall if their price falls.

Provided that price elasticity of demand for both exports and imports is inelastic, an improvement in the terms of trade will result in an improvement in the current balance of trade.

On the other hand if the price elasticity of demand for both exports and imports is elastic, an improvement in the terms of trade will lead to a worsening current balance of trade, because:

(a) a rise in export prices would reduce total export revenue
(b) a fall in import prices would increase total payments for imports

An improvement in the terms of trade might therefore result in a better or a worse balance of payments position. The same applies to worsening terms of trade.

3 EXCHANGE RATES AND EXCHANGE RATE SYSTEMS

Definition of the rate of exchange

3.1 An exchange rate is the rate at which one country's currency can be traded in exchange for another country's currency. Dealers in foreign exchange - ie banks - make their profit by buying currency at one exchange rate, and selling it at a different rate. This means that there is a selling rate and a buying rate for a currency.

The foreign exchange market

3.2 International trade involves foreign currency, for either the buyer, the seller, or both (eg a Saudi Arabian firm might sell goods to a UK buyer and invoice for the goods in US dollars). As a consequence, it is quite likely that exporters might want to sell foreign currency earnings to a bank in exchange for domestic currency, and that importers might want to buy foreign currency from a bank in order to pay a foreign supplier.

3.3 This buying and selling of foreign currency between firms and banks is one element in the foreign exchange market.

3.4 Although demand to buy and sell foreign currencies arises from the demand of individuals (for example tourists going abroad) and firms (for example importers, exporters, firms investing overseas and governments), the main bulk buying and selling of foreign currencies is done mainly by banks in the foreign exchange markets of the world, such as London.

3.5 The foreign exchange markets are worldwide; the main dealers are banks. The largest currency dealing centre is London, with a huge **daily turnover of US $464 billion** according to a 1995 survey (60% up on three years earlier). Around 350 banks deal regularly in the London market.

(a) Banks buy currency from customers and sell currency to customers - typically, exporting and importing firms.

(b) Banks may buy currency from the government or sell currency to the government - this is how a government builds up or uses its official reserves.

(c) Banks also buy and sell currency between themselves.

Dealing on the foreign exchange markets

3.6 Since most foreign exchange rates are not fixed but are allowed to vary, rates are continually changing, and each bank will offer new rates for new customer enquiries according to how its dealers judge the market situation. Dealers are kept continually informed of rates at which deals are currently being made, by means of computerised information services.

3.7 Deals are settled immediately by telephone (and confirmed in writing later). This method of buying and selling means that exchange rates do change continually, responding rapidly to changes in demand and supply.

3.8 Exchange rates will often change by just small amounts up or down. Sometimes, when the supply (selling) of a currency is stronger than demand, the exchange rate for that currency will fall sharply. Similarly, strong demand might push up the exchange rate of a currency substantially.

Spot rates and forward rates

3.9 Broadly speaking, there are two ways in which foreign currency is bought and sold.

- **Spot**: for immediate delivery
- **Forward**: for delivery at a date in the future

3.10 Thus, a UK firm might receive US$150,000 from a US customer, and sell it spot to a bank, to receive sterling immediately (in practice normally two working days after the contract is made). If the exchange rate is $1.5000 to £1, the UK firm would receive £100,000.

3.11 If a firm knows that it is going to receive some foreign currency in the near future, which it will want to sell in exchange for domestic currency, it can make a forward exchange contract with a bank, at an exchange rate that is specified in the contract. Thus, if a firm knows that it is going to receive US$100,000 in 3 months' time, it can make a forward exchange contract now to sell the US dollars in 3 months' time at a specified exchange rate. If the spot rate is $1.5000 to £1, the forward rate may be higher or lower than $1.5000 (depending on comparative interest rates in the USA and the UK).

Factors influencing the exchange rate for a currency 5/01, 5/02

3.12 The exchange rate between two currencies is determined primarily by supply and demand in the foreign exchange markets. Demand comes from individuals, firms and governments who want to buy a currency and supply comes from those who want to sell it.

3.13 Supply and demand in turn are subject to a number of influences.

- The rate of inflation, compared with the rate of inflation in other countries
- Interest rates, compared with interest rates in other countries
- The balance of payments
- Speculation
- Government policy on intervention to influence the exchange rate

3.14 Other factors influence the exchange rate through their relationship with the items identified above.

(a) Total income and expenditure (demand) in the domestic economy determines the demand for goods. This includes imported goods and demand for goods produced in the country which would otherwise be exported if demand for them did not exist in the home markets.

(b) Output capacity and the level of employment in the domestic economy might influence the balance of payments, because if the domestic economy has full employment already, it will be unable to increase its volume of production for exports.

(c) The growth in the money supply influences interest rates and domestic inflation.

Inflation and the exchange rate

3.15 **If the rate of inflation is higher in one country than in another country, the value of its currency will tend to weaken against the other country's currency.**

3.16 **Purchasing power parity theory** attempts to explain changes in the exchange rate exclusively by the rate of inflation in different countries. The theory predicts that the exchange value of a foreign currency depends on the relative purchasing power of each currency in its own country. As a simple example, suppose that there is only one commodity, which costs £110 in the UK and 165 Euros in France. The exchange rate would be £1 = 1.5 Euros. If, as a result of inflation, the cost of the commodity in the UK rises to £120, the exchange rate would adjust to:

$$1.5 \times \frac{110}{120} \times £1 = 1.375 \text{ Euros}$$

3.17 If the exchange rate remained at £1 = 1.5 Euros, it would be cheaper to import more of the commodity from France for £110 and the UK would have a balance of trade deficit. This would only be corrected by an alteration in the exchange rate, with the pound weakening against the franc.

3.18 Purchasing power parity theory states that an exchange rate varies according to relative price changes, so that:

$$\text{'Old' exchange rate} \times \frac{\text{Price level in country A}}{\text{Price level in country B}} = \text{'New' exchange rate}$$

3.19 The theory was soon found to be inadequate to explain movements in exchange rates **in the short term**, mainly because it ignores payments between countries (ie demand and supply transactions) and the influence of supply and demand for currency on exchange rates.

Interest rates and the exchange rate

3.20 It would seem logical to assume that if one country raises its interest rates, it will become more profitable to invest in that country, and so an increase in (mainly short-term) investment from overseas will push up the exchange rate because of the extra demand for the currency from overseas investors.

3.21 This is true, but there is a limit to the amount of investment capital that will flow into a country because of higher interest rates. A major reason this is that investors may expect a **risk premium** for investing in a high interest rate currency if they fear that the currency will depreciate in value.

The balance of payments and the exchange rate

3.22 Purchasing power parity theory is more likely to have some validity in the long run, and it is certainly true that the currency of a country which has a much higher rate of inflation than other countries will weaken on the foreign exchange market. In other words, the rate of inflation relative to other countries is certainly a factor which influences the exchange rate.

3.23 Although this influence is obvious, it is not predominant. This is apparent from the fact that if exchange rates did respond to demand and supply for current account items, then the balance of payments on the current account of all countries would tend towards equilibrium. This is not so, and **in practice other factors influence exchange rates more strongly**.

3.24 **Demand for currency to invest in overseas capital investments and supply of currency from firms disinvesting in an overseas currency have more influence on the exchange rate, in the short term at least, than the demand and supply of goods and services.**

3.25 If a country has a persistent deficit in its balance of payments current account, international confidence in that country's currency will eventually be eroded, and in the long term, its exchange rate will fall as capital inflows are no longer sufficient to counterbalance the country's trade deficit.

Speculation and exchange rate fluctuations

3.26 Speculators in foreign exchange are investors who buy or sell assets in a foreign currency, in the expectation of a rise or fall in the exchange rate, from which they seek to make a profit. Speculation could be destabilising if it creates such a high volume of demand to buy or sell a particular currency that the exchange rate fluctuates to levels where it is overvalued or undervalued in terms of what hard economic facts suggest it should be. If a currency does become undervalued by heavy speculative selling, investors can make a further profit by purchasing it at the undervalued price and selling it later when its price rises.

3.27 Speculation, when it is destabilising, could damage a country's economy because the uncertainty about exchange rates disrupts trade in goods and services.

Government intervention in foreign exchange markets

3.28 The government can intervene in the foreign exchange markets in two ways.

(a) It can sell its own currency in exchange for foreign currencies, when it wants to keep down the exchange rate of its domestic currency. The foreign currencies it buys can be added to the official reserves.

(b) It can buy its own currency and pay for it with the foreign currencies in its official reserves. It will do this when it wants to keep up the exchange rate when market forces are pushing it down.

3.29 The government can also intervene indirectly, by changing domestic interest rates, and so either attracting or discouraging investors in financial investments which are denominated in the domestic currency.

3.30 By managing the exchange rate for its currency, a government does not stop all fluctuations in the exchange rate, but it tries to keep the fluctuations within certain limits. Limits might be unofficial or official.

(a) **Unofficial limits**: a government might intervene in the foreign exchange markets and sell foreign currency from its official reserves to buy the domestic currency, and so support its exchange rate, even though there is no officially declared exchange rate that it is trying to support.

(b) **Official limits**: for example countries in the European ERM, used to allow their domestic currency to fluctuate against each other's currency only within specified limits. Devaluation or revaluation beyond those limits was only permitted following a 'realignment' of ERM currencies.

Question 5

The diagram shows supply and demand curves for the UK pound in US dollars.

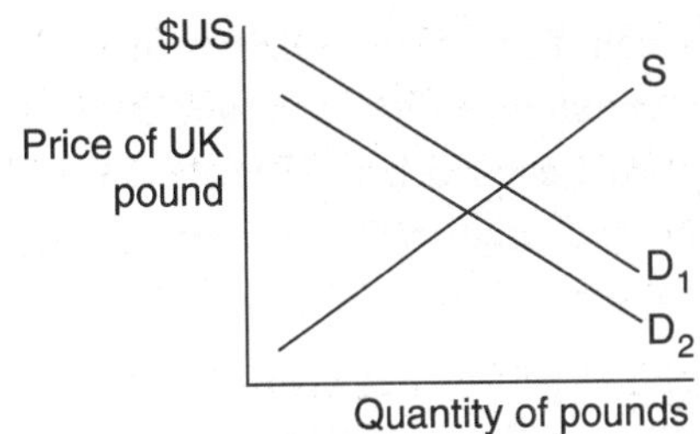

Which of the following could cause a shift in the demand curve from D_1 to D_2?

A An increase in demand for UK exports in the US
B A fall in US interest rates
C A fall in UK interest rates
D An increase in the number of US tourists visiting the UK

Answer

C A and D would both increase demand for pounds in order to pay for the increased trade in goods and services. The immediate effect of B would be an increase in the quantity of dollars supplied at any price; if this had any effect on demand for pounds it would be more likely to increase it than reduce it.

Consequences of an exchange rate policy

3.31 **Reasons for a policy of controlling the exchange rate**

(a) To rectify a balance of trade deficit, by trying to bring about a fall in the exchange rate.

(b) To prevent a balance of trade surplus from getting too large, by trying to bring about a limited rise in the exchange rate.

(c) To emulate economic conditions in other countries. The UK's membership of the ERM (from October 1990 until suspended in 1992) had as one of its aims that of emulating the conditions of lower inflation which exist in other ERM member countries.

(d) To stabilise the exchange rate of its currency. Exporters and importers will then face less risk of exchange rate movements wiping out their profits. A stable currency increases confidence in the currency and promotes international trade.

Exchange rate policies of governments 11/01

3.32 The different exchange rate policies which are open to governments fall into four categories.

- Fixed exchange rates
- Free floating exchange rates
- Margins around a moveable peg
- Managed floating

Fixed exchange rates

3.33 A policy of rigidly fixed exchange rates means that the government of every country in the international monetary system must use its **official reserves** to create an exact match between supply and demand for its currency in the foreign exchange markets, in order to keep the exchange rate unchanged. Using the official reserves will therefore cancel out a surplus or deficit on the current account and non-official capital transactions in their balance of payments. A balance of payments surplus would call for an addition to the official reserves, and a deficit calls for drawings on official reserves.

3.34 The official reserves could in theory consist of any foreign currency (or gold) within the fixed exchange rate agreement. The exchange rates of the various currencies in the system might all be fixed against each other. However, for simplicity and convenience, it is more appropriate to fix the exchange rate for every currency against a standard. The standard might be one of the following.

- **Gold**
- **A major currency**
- **A basket of major trading currencies**

3.35 A fixed exchange rate system removes exchange rate uncertainty and so encourages international trade. It also imposes economic disciplines on countries in deficit (or surplus). However, this restricts independence of domestic economic policies. A government might be forced to keep interest rates high or to reduce demand in the domestic economy (for example by raising taxes and so cutting the demand for imports) in order to maintain a currency's exchange rate and avoid a devaluation.

3.36 If levels of inflation differ widely in countries subscribing to a fixed exchange rate regime, the regime may not survive for long. The high inflation countries will be forced to devalue in order to keep their exports competitive and to reduce imports.

3.37 There is inevitably some loss of flexibility in economic policy making once a country joins a fixed exchange rate regime. The UK is a case in point: Norman Lamont, the Chancellor of the Exchequer, acknowledged in his 1992 Budget speech that within the semi-fixed ERM system monetary policy was primarily directed at the maintenance of sterling's parity within the system.

Free floating exchange rates

3.38 Free floating at flexible exchange rates are at the opposite end of the spectrum to rigidly fixed rates. **Exchange rates are left to the free play of market forces** and there is no official financing at all. There is no need for the government to hold any official reserves, because it will not want to use them.

3.39 Floating exchange rates are the only option available to governments when other systems break down and fail. Friedman has remarked that 'floating exchange rates have often been adopted by countries experiencing financial crises when all other devices have failed. That is a major reason why they have such a bad reputation.' In practice, governments prefer generally to operate **managed floating** of their currency and a policy of allowing a currency to float entirely freely is rare.

A moveable peg system

3.40 A moveable or adjustable peg system is a system of fixed exchange rates, but with a provision for the devaluation or revaluation of a currency.

Margins around a moveable peg

3.41 A moveable peg system provides some flexibility. Exchange rates, although fixed, are not rigidly fixed, because adjustments are permitted. Even so, it is still fairly inflexible, because governments only have the choice between a revaluation/devaluation or holding the exchange rate steady. A more flexible system would allow some minor variations in exchange rates. The European ERM involved margins around a moveable peg, as did the earlier Bretton Woods international agreement on exchange rates, which lasted from 1944 to 1971.

Consequences of membership of an exchange rate system

3.42 Exchange rate stability within an exchange rate regime may help dampen inflation by preventing a government from allowing the currency to drift downwards in value to compensate for price inflation. At the same time, it means that interest rate policy must be consistent with keeping the currency stable. If interest rates are too high, foreign investors will buy sterling, leading to capital inflows, much of which may be of short term 'hot money', and there will be upward pressure on the currency. If interest rates are too low, there will conversely be downward pressure on the currency.

3.43 Other possible consequences of stabilisation within an exchange rate system are that there may be effects on people's expectations and on the perceived risk of exchange rate movements between member currencies. As well as allowing firms to plan and forecast with greater certainty, exchange rate stability ought to make a currency less risky to hold.

European Economic and Monetary Union

3.44 There are three main aspects to the proposed European monetary union.

(a) **A common currency.**

(b) **A European central bank**. The European central bank has several roles.

- Issuing the common currency
- Conducting monetary policy on behalf of the central government authorities
- Acting as lender of last resort to all European banks
- Managing the exchange rate for the common currency

(c) A **centralised monetary policy** would apply across all the countries within the union. This would involve the surrender of control over aspects of economic policy and therefore surrender of some political sovereignty by the government of each member state to the central government body of the union.

The EMU timetable

3.45 EMU is a topical issue. 1 May 1998 saw the meeting of those European Union countries wishing to join the monetary union at the outset. Italy, France, Ireland, Germany, Belgium, Luxembourg, the Netherlands, Finland, Spain, Portugal and Austria all signed up for the first phase of EMU starting on 1 January 1999. The UK decided to opt out but retains the right to join at a later stage. The European Central Bank (ECB) running a single monetary policy was established in 1998 and *Wim Duisenberg* of the Netherlands was appointed as its president. (Some argue that the credibility of the ECB has been undermined by the political horse-trading prior to his appointment.) Irrevocably locked exchange rates were fixed between the old currencies of participating countries.

3.46 *Gordon Brown*, Chancellor of the Exchequer, explained in the House of Commons that in reaching this decision, the Government Treasury department 'made a detailed assessment of five economic tests' believed to define whether a clear and unambiguous case could be made to support Britain joining a single currency.

- Whether there can be sustainable convergence between Britain and the economies of a single currency

- Whether there is sufficient flexibility to cope with economic change
- The effect on investment
- The impact on the financial services industry
- Whether it is good for employment

3.47 He concluded that applying these economic tests revealed that 'it is not in the interest of the UK to join in the first wave of EMU starting on 1 January 1999 and - barring some fundamental and unforeseen change in economic circumstances - making a decision, this parliament, to join is not realistic'. However, he went on to urge Government and business to prepare intensively during this parliament, so that Britain will be in a position to join early in the next parliament, should that be desired.

For and against EMU *11/01*

3.48 The arguments for and against EMU can be summarised as follows, with particular reference to the UK's position.

For	Against
Economic policy stability. • EMU members will be required to keep to strict economic criteria. • Politicians in member countries will be less able to pursue short-term economic policies, for example just before an election, to gain political advantage.	**Confusion in the transition to EMU.** • Introduction of a new currency and coinage would cause confusion to businesses and consumers • Firms might use it as an opportunity to push through price rises.
Facilitation of trade. • Will eliminate risk of currency fluctuations affecting trade and investment between EMU member countries. • Will eliminate need to hedge against such risks. • Will be savings in foreign exchange transaction costs for companies, as well as tourists. • Will enhance ease of trade with non EU countries. • Transparency of prices	**Loss of national control over economic policy.** • Under EMU, monetary policy would largely be in the hands of the new European Central Bank, which has little experience and has demonstrated greater interest in holding down inflation than in economic growth. • Individual countries' fiscal policies would also need to stay in line with European policy criteria. • The European economic policy framework puts great emphasis on price stability. • Restrictive monetary policies have resulted in disproportionate unemployment and output effects.
Lower interest rates. • Will remove risk of inflation and depreciating currencies, reducing interest rates. • Will stabilise interest rates at a low level.	**Consequences for the financial services industry** • Forecasts that the City of London would enter an immediate decline if the UK did not join have proved untrue.

For	Against
Seigneurage	
• Seigneurage is the benefit accruing from the right to issue currency. If the euro becomes a global reserve currency, non-EU nations will buy it to hold rather than for the purposes of trade. This will support the exchange rate and allow interest rates to be lower.	

3.49 EMU is now widely recognised as principally a political initiative rather than an economic one. It is a major step towards the creation of an over-arching European state.

Chapter roundup

- The balance of payments accounts consist of a current account with visibles and invisibles sections and transactions in capital (external assets and liabilities including official financing). The sum of the balances on these accounts must be zero, although in practice there is a balancing figure for measurement errors.
- A surplus or deficit on the balance of payments usually means a surplus or deficit on the current account. It is possible for countries to try to finance a deficit on the current account from a surplus on capital account, temporarily at least. However, to do so, the country must be able to attract finance (including investment capital) from abroad, and so the country needs to remain 'creditworthy', with investors having confidence in the stability of the exchange rate for the country's currency.
- A country can rectify a balance of payments deficit in three ways.
  - Allowing its currency to depreciate or devalue in foreign exchange value
  - Imposing protectionist measures or exchange control regulations
  - Deflationary economic measures in the domestic economy
- The balance of trade depends not only on the volumes of goods traded, but on the relative *prices* of exports and imports (ie on the terms of trade).
- The traditional view that exchange rates will depend on the country's balance of trade (more exactly, on its current account surplus or deficit) still has some validity in the longer term. However, capital transactions can influence the exchange rate significantly, especially in the short term. Factors other than the underlying balance of payments position influencing the exchange rate are the comparative rates of inflation in different countries, comparative interest rates in different countries, the speculation and government policy on managing or fixing exchange rates.
- Exchange rates are determined by supply and demand, even under fixed exchange rate systems, and governments can intervene to influence the exchange rate by, for example, adjusting interest rates. Government policies on exchange rates might be fixed exchange rates or free floating exchange rates as two extreme policies. In practice, 'in-between' schemes have been of two types.
  - Fixed rates, but with provision for devaluations or revaluations of currencies from time to time ('adjustable pegs') and also some fluctuations ('margins') around the fixed exchange value permitted – for example, the ERM
  - Managed floating – for example the US dollar, the yen and sterling since leaving the ERM
- Introduction of the single European currency will have significant implications for how monetary policy is carried out within the single currency area.

Quick quiz

1 What does the J curve describe?

2 How do deflationary measures help to eliminate a balance of payments deficit?

3 What is meant by the terms of trade?

4 What does the theory of purchasing power parity say?

5 How may the government intervene in the foreign exchange markets?

6 What is the balance of trade?

A The balance of payments on current account
B Net visible trade
C Net visible and invisible trade
D The theory of gains from trade

7 Which of the following statements concerning international trade are true? (1) The J curve effect will work in reverse if there is a depreciation when the current account is in deficit. (2) Protectionism could reduce exports. (3) Devaluation of the domestic currency will reverse a current account deficit.

A (1) and (3) only
B (1), (2) and (3)
C (1) and (2) only
D (2) and (3) only

8 The table of figures shows the domestic prices of two products, P and Q, in the UK and the USA. Assuming that producers in each country will not export either product unless they obtain a price that is at least as high as they can get in their domestic market, then full specialisation of production will occur in accordance with the law of comparative advantage at which of the following exchange rates?

	P	Q
Price in UK (£)	1.0	2.5
Price in USA ($)	2.0	6.0

A $1.60 = £1
B $1.90 = £1
C £2.20 = £1
D $2.50 = £1

9 From a given base year, a country's export prices rise by 8% and import prices rise by 20%. During this period, the terms of trade will have:

A Risen from 100 to 111.1
B Risen from 100 to 112
C Fallen from 100 to 90
D Fallen from 100 to 88

10 A devaluation will only benefit the UK balance of payments if:

A The sum of the price elasticities of demand for imports and exports is less than 1
B The sum of the price elasticities of demand for imports and exports is greater than 1
C The sum of the price elasticities of demand for imports and exports is less than 0
D The sum of the price elasticities of demand for imports and exports is greater than 0

Answers to quick quiz

1 The J curve shows the effect on the balance of payments of a falling exchange rate. A falling exchange rate will eventually reduce demand for imports and increase demand for exports. However, in the short term, both domestic and export demand are likely to be inelastic and the ability of domestic industry to meet any increase in export demand will be limited. The volume of goods and services traded is therefore unlikely to change in the short term, but imports will cost more in foreign currency and exports will sell for less. It is therefore likely that there will be a deterioration in the balance of payments in the short term.

2 Domestic deflation cuts demand, including demand for imports. Industry is therefore encouraged to switch to export markets.

3 The terms of trade are the ratio of export prices to import prices. This ratio determines the volume of exports necessary to pay for a given volume of imports.

4 Purchasing power parity theory suggests that exchange rates are determined by relative inflation rates. The currency of the country with high inflation will tend to weaken against those of countries with lower inflation rates, since more of its currency will be required to buy any given good.

5 Governments may intervene directly by buying and selling currency. They may also influence exchange rates by adjusting their interest rates and by direct currency controls such as limiting the amount of foreign currency which individuals are allowed to buy.

6 B Learn this definition.

7 D The J curve would work in reverse if there were a surplus and the currency appreciated.

8 C According to the law of comparative advantage, the UK should specialise in producing Q and the USA should specialise in producing P. UK firms will want to earn at least £2.50 for each unit of Q they make, but US buyers won't pay more than $6 per unit, and so the exchange rate must be no more than (6 / 2.5) $2.40 = £1. US firms will want to earn at least $2 for each unit of P they make, but UK buyers won't pay more than £1, and so the exchange rate has to be at least $2 = £1. A range of exchange rates at which specialisation and international trade will take place is therefore $2 to $2.40 to £1. In the UK opportunity cost of making P = 2.5 units of Q and opportunity cost of making Q =0.4 units of P. In the USA opportunity cost of making P = 3 units of Q and opportunity cost of making Q = 0.33 units of P.

9 C 108/120*100=90.

10 B In order to benefit, internal demand must react to a rise in the price of imports and external demand must react to a fall in the price of UK exported goods.

Now try the questions below from the Question Bank

Number	Level	Marks	Time
Q55	Exam	8	10 mins
Q56	Exam - MCQ	2	–
Q57	Introductory - MCQ	–	–

Question bank

1 ALLOCATION OF RESOURCES *10 mins*

Explain the meaning and importance of the term 'the allocation of resources'. **8 Marks**

2 In economics, the central economic problem means:

A Consumers do not have as much money as they would wish
B There will always be a certain level of unemployment
C Resources are not always allocated in an optimum way
D Output is restricted by the limited availability of resources

3 Which of the following would cause the production possibility frontier for an economy to shift outwards?

(i) A reduction in the level of unemployment
(ii) A rise in the rate of investment
(iii) A fall in the price of one factor of production
(iv) A rise in output per worker

A (i) and (ii) only
B (i), (ii) and (iii) only
C (i), (iii) and (iv) only
D (ii) and (iv) only

4 SECOND HAND CARS

Examine the likely effects on the price and quantity sold of second hand cars in the event of:

(a) a large increase in petrol prices **4 Marks**
(b) a legal requirement that all cars fitted with expensive emission controls **4 Marks**
(c) a big increase in the price of new cars **4 Marks**
(d) a massive investment in public transport **4 Marks**

Total Marks = 16

5 In the diagram below, point 5 represents equilibrium. If the government starts to pay a cash subsidy to producers of the commodity, what will the new equilibrium be?

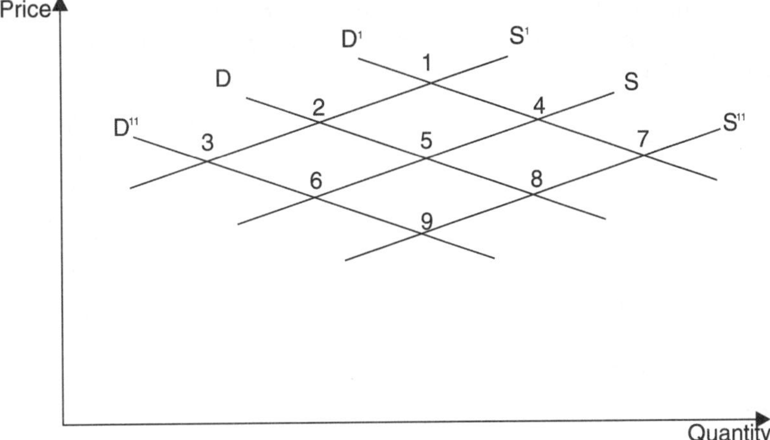

A Point 2
B Point 4
C Point 6
D Point 8

6 Surpluses will be enjoyed by some suppliers and some consumers even when the market clears under perfect competition.

Match the correct labels to the boxes on this diagram.

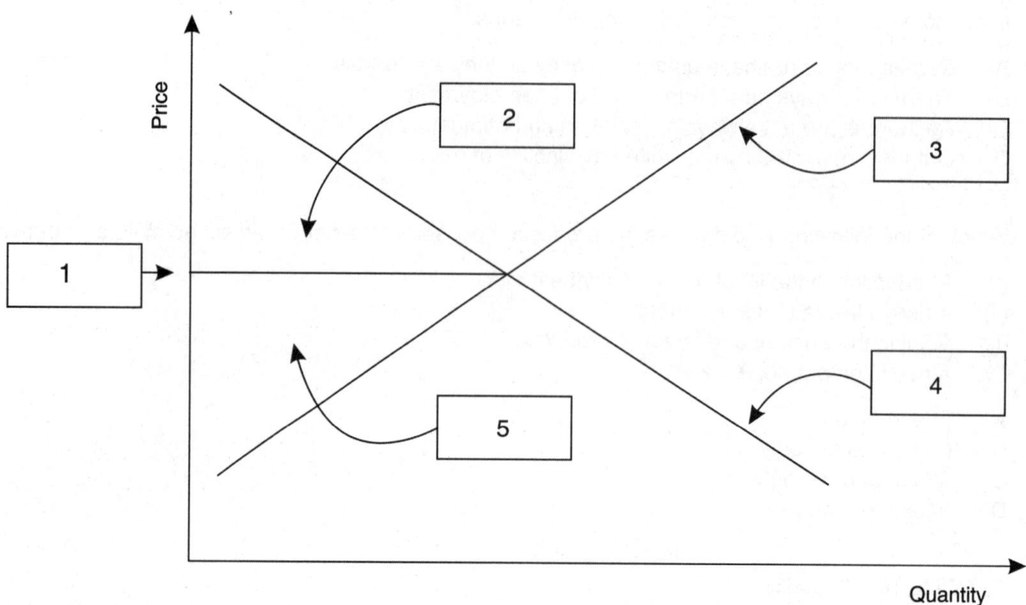

Labels:

A Equilibrium price
B Consumer surplus
C Market supply
D market demand
E Producer surplus

7 **DATA RESPONSE QUESTION: DEMAND AND SUPPLY** *20 mins*

Data

The government plans to introduce a subsidy of 10 pence per pint on milk. Set out below are a demand schedule and a supply schedule for milk in a fictional town before the subsidy is introduced, when the market price is 35 pence.

Price per pint	Quantity demanded per day Pints	Quantity supplied per day Pints
60p	22,000	40,000
50p	23,000	35,000
40p	25,000	30,000
30p	30,000	25,000
20p	35,000	20,000
10p	37,000	15,000

Required

(a) What is a change in the quantity supplied and how is it caused? **4 Marks**

(b) Explain the effects of the subsidy on the market price and the quantity of milk sold per day. **6 Marks**

(c) Of what relevance is the price elasticity of demand to business people and governments? **6 Marks**

Total Marks = 16

8 The price elasticity of demand (PED) of good A is negative, its income elasticity of demand (IED) is positive and its cross elasticity of demand (XED) with respect to good X is negative. What is the nature of good A?

A A good bought for purposes of ostentation, complementary to X
B An inferior good, substitute for X
C A normal good, complementary to X
D A Giffen good, substitute for X

9 There are 3 special cases of elasticity of supply.

Put the correct labels in the boxes on this diagram.

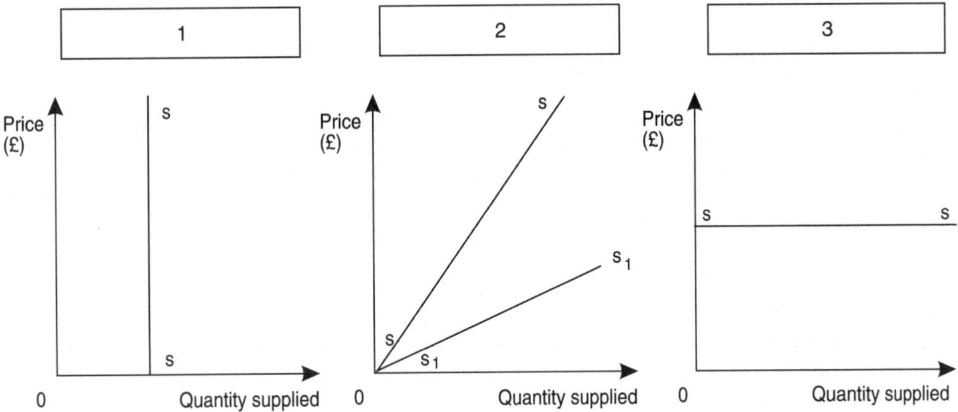

A Unit elastic supply
B Perfectly elastic supply
C Perfectly inelastic supply

10 SOCIAL COSTS *10 mins*

How might governments attempt to correct the distortions in resource allocation caused by social costs? **8 Marks**

11 A selective indirect tax will have predictable effects.

In this diagram, an indirect tax has been imposed and supply has shifted from S_0 to S_1.

Put the correct labels in the boxes on the diagram.

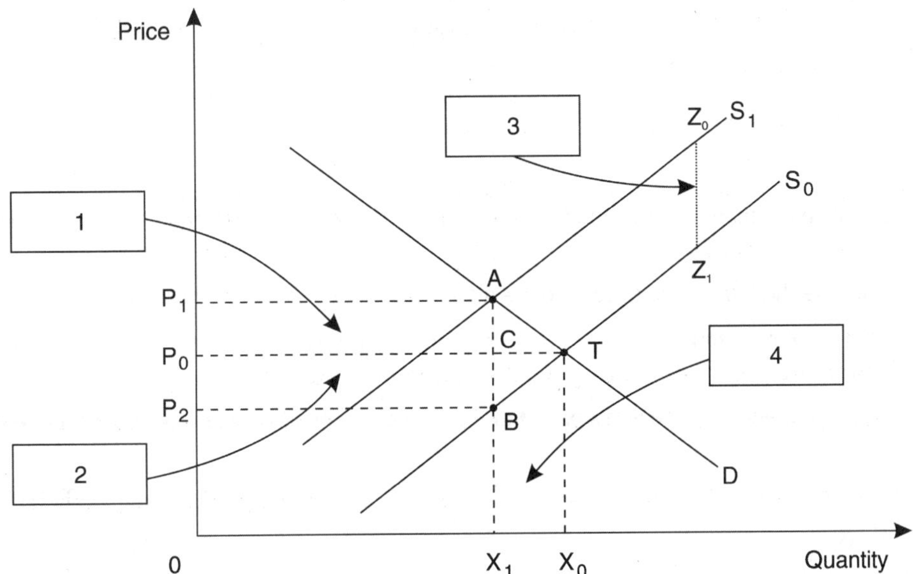

A Fall in output
B Tax paid by supplier
C Tax paid by customer
D Supernormal profit
E Tax imposed per unit

12 The table below shows a market demand schedule and a market supply schedule for beans.

Price per tonne	*Quantity demanded per month*	*Quantity supplied per month*
£	('000 tonnes)	('000 tonnes)
280	4,000	9,200
260	5,000	8,800
240	6,400	8,200
220	7,400	7, 400
200	8,200	6,600
180	9,000	5,800
160	9,800	4,800

What would be the consequences of the introduction by the government of a maximum price for beans of £200 per tonne? Assume that supply quantities can be readily adjusted to any new market conditions.

1 There would be a need for rationing of beans
2 There would be a 'bean mountain'
3 There would be a shortage of 1,600,000 tonnes per month
4 There would be a surplus of 1,600,000 tonnes per month
5 The price for beans would be unchanged

A Consequences 1 and 3
B Consequences 2 and 4
C Consequence 5 only
D Consequence 4 only

13 **DATA RESPONSE QUESTION: REVENUE AND COSTS** *20 mins*

The following data refer to the revenue and costs of a firm.

Output	*Total revenue*	*Total costs*
	£	£
0	-	110
1	50	140
2	100	162
3	150	175
4	200	180
5	250	185
6	300	194
7	350	229
8	400	269
9	450	325
10	500	425

Required

(a) Calculate the marginal revenue for the firm and state which sort of market it is operating in. **3 Marks**

(b) Calculate the firm's fixed costs and the marginal cost at each level of output. **3 Marks**

(c) What level of output will the firm aim to produce and what amount of profit will it make at this level? **4 Marks**

(d) Explain the effect on the firm's output and profits of the entry of new producers into the industry. **6 Marks**

Total Marks = 16

14 The table below shows a firm's total cost (TC), average cost (AC) and marginal cost (MC) for certain levels of output. Which is which?

Units of output	*1*	*2*	*3*
	£	£	£
1	1.10	1.10	1.10
2	0.80	0.50	1.60
3	0.58	0.15	1.75
4	0.50	0.25	2.00
5	0.50	0.50	2.50
6	0.52	0.62	3.12

A 1 = AC, 2 = TC, 3 = MC
B 1 = AC, 2 = MC, 3 = TC
C 1 = MC, 2 = AC, 3 = TC
D 1 = TC, 2 = AC, 3 = MC

15 Put the correct labels in the boxes on this diagram of short run costs.

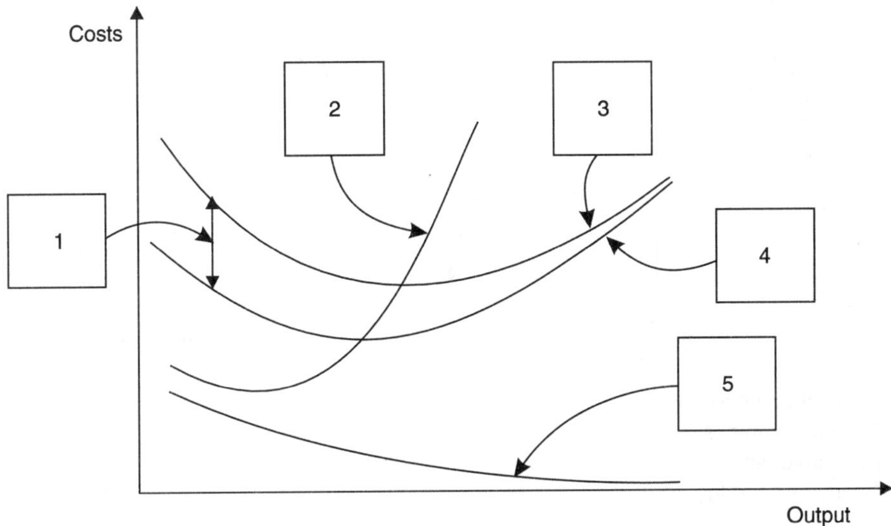

A Marginal cost
B Average fixed cost at this output
C Average total cost
D Average fixed cost curve
E Average variable cost

16 TYPES OF PROFIT *10 mins*

Explain what economists mean by the term 'profit', and distinguish between normal and supernormal profits. **8 Marks**

17 The output table below shows to the labour productivity of Helen Highwater Ltd, a firm manufacturing bars of scented soap.

Number of workers	*Total product per day (bars of soap)*
4	22
5	32
6	49
7	67
8	85
9	99
10	107
11	114
12	120

Each bar of soap sells for £2 after deducting costs of materials. The firm can have any number of workers at a wage of £16 per day. How many workers should it have in order to maximise profits?

A 6
B 8
C 10
D 12

18 Transfer earnings are the reward a factor would receive in its next best employment i.e. its opportunity cost.

Economic rent is the difference between transfer earnings and actual reward.

Put the correct labels in the boxes in this diagram.

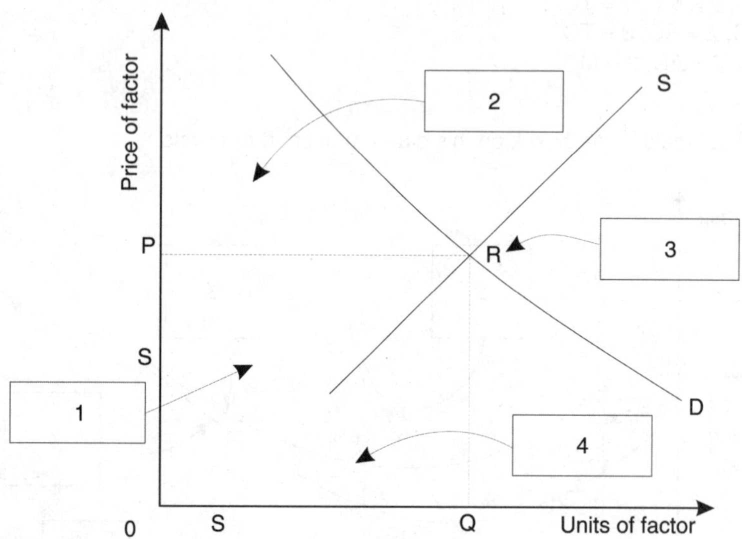

A Equilibrium price
B Transfer earnings
C Economic rent
D Consumer surplus

19 **HIGHER REAL COSTS** *10 mins*

Does government intervention in the location of industry cause an efficiency loss in the form of higher real costs of production? **8 Marks**

20 Write alongside each of the following industries the sector of the economy to which it belongs – primary, secondary, tertiary.

(a) Processing of fish to produce cod-liver oil.
(b) Sale of chipped wood bark from sawmills as ornamental garden mulch.
(c) Insurance of fishing vessels.
(d) A water supply company.
(e) Provision of capital for the purchase of mature woodland.

21 With what famous economist is the sales maximisation model associated?

(a) Keynes
(b) Cyert
(c) Baumol
(d) Adam Smith

22 **MONOPOLY** *10 mins*

Explain why consumers may not always suffer if a competitive industry becomes monopolised.

8 Marks

23 Which diagram shows marginal cost and marginal revenue under perfect competition?

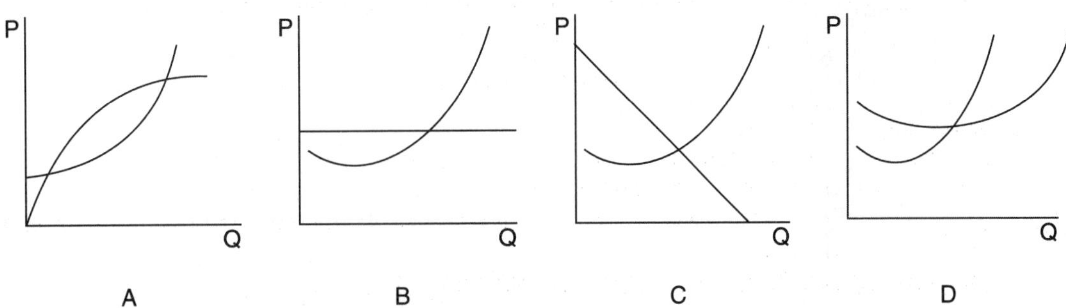

24 This diagram shows equilibrium under monopoly.

Label the diagram.

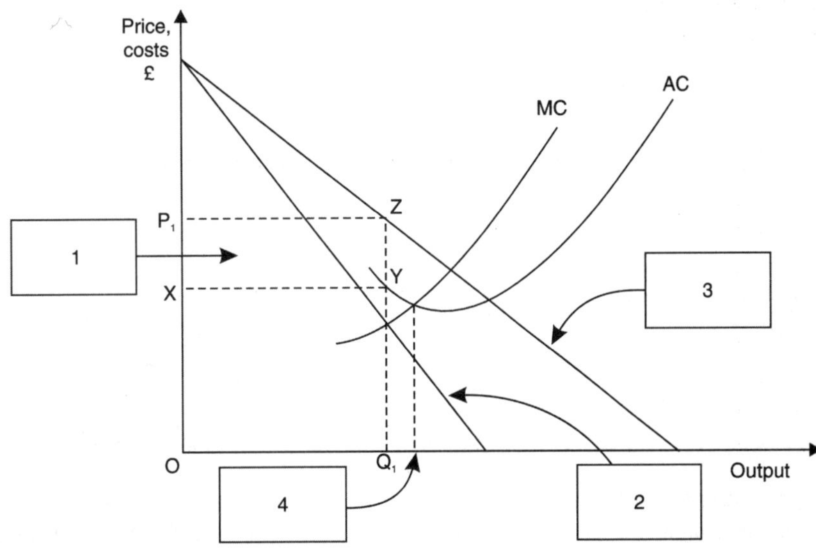

A Supernormal profit
B Marginal Revenue
C Transfer earnings
D Profit maximising output
E Average revenue
F Most efficient level of output

25 DISTINCTIONS *10 mins*

(a) Distinguish between monopolistic competition and oligopoly.
(b) Give an example of an industry which approximates to each of these market structures. **8 Marks**

26 In what way does monopolistic competition differ from monopoly?

Under monopolistic competition:

A There is no possibility of supernormal profit
B There are no barriers to entry
C The excess capacity theorem does not apply
D The average revenue curve slopes downwards

27 Oligopoly markets usually show little price competition.

Label the diagram.

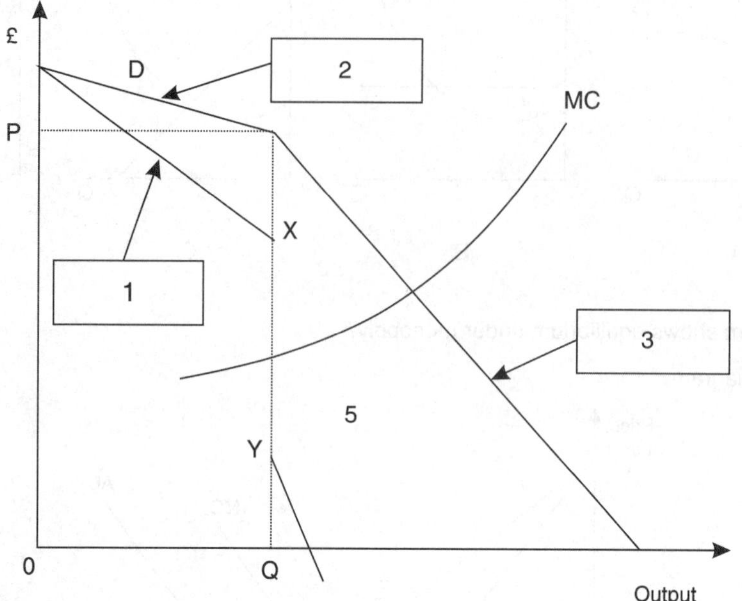

A Average cost
B Very inelastic demand
C Marginal revenue
D Very elastic demand

28 DATA RESPONSE QUESTION: PRIVATISATION *20 mins*

Read the following extract and answer the following questions.

'In Eastern Europe new governments are urgently looking for ways of increasing the role of the private sector of their economies. In the Third World, privatisation appeals to governments as a way of raising finance without increasing their debt burden.

'The policy stems from the traditional conservative antipathy to the state and the new emphasis on markets. 'Privatisation exposes the industries to market forces. If a state monopoly is broken then consumers may choose the more satisfactory service, which will generate profits and expand, thus resources are allocated in response to consumer demand. The pressure to meet market requirements should improve internal efficiency. '

(Adapted from A Griffiths and S Wall, *Applied Economics*)

(a) Explain what is meant by 'privatisation'. **4 Marks**
(b) Explain the argument used by the authors in support of privatisation. **4 Marks**
(c) What, in practice, might limit the benefits to be derived from privatisation? **8 Marks**

Total Marks = 16

29 Which of the following is not generally regarded as tending to justify government regulation of markets?

A Imperfect competition
B Externalities
C Regulatory capture
D Imperfect information

30 Which one of the following statements is incorrect?

A If the effect of privatisation is to increase competition, the effect might be to reduce or eliminate allocative inefficiency

B Privatisation means selling off nationalised industries by the government to the private sector

C The effect of denationalisation could be to make firms more cost-conscious, because they will be under the scrutiny of stock market investors

D The government might appoint consumer watchdogs to regulate privatised industries

31 INTEREST RATES *15 mins*

(a) Explain briefly the various factors that can influence the levels of interest rates. **6 Marks**

(b) The *Financial Times* publishes daily money market interest rates on deposits ranging from periods of one day (overnight) to one year.

Explain briefly why and how long-term interest rates may differ from short-term interest rates. **5 Marks**

Total Marks = 11

32 The slope of a normal yield curve is:

A Upwards because of government monetary policy
B Upwards because of uncertainty about the future
C Downwards because of price inflation
D Downwards because of reducing demand

33 The relationship between the inflation rate (i), the money rate of interest (m) and the real rate of interest (r) is:

A $(1 + m) \times (1 + i) = (1 + r)$

B $\frac{(1 + m)}{(1 + i)} = (1 + r)$

C $(1 + m) \times (1 + r) = (1 + i)$

D $\frac{(1 + r)}{(1 + i)} = (1 + m)$

34 BANK DEPOSITS *10 mins*

'Bank deposits ... are largely created by the commercial banks themselves.' (Hanson)

Explain this statement. **8 Marks**

35 The narrow money supply in Psychomania is currently 4,800 million Psychomanian florins. All the Psychomanian banks operate a 15% cash ratio. By how much would the cash ratio have to change if the money supply was to be reduced to 4,000 million florins.

A Decrease to 12.5%
B Increase to 18%
C Increase to 20%
D Decrease to 12%

36 Which of the following is the most liquid asset of a commercial bank?

A Money at call
B Government Bonds
C Cash
D Operational balances with the Bank of England

37 GNP *10 mins*

Can Gross National Product (GNP) per head fairly be used to compare international standards of living? **8 Marks**

38 Here are some entries from the national accounts of Psychomania. All entries are in millions of Psychomanian groats.

Income from employment before tax	9,000
Output of firms at sales value	20,000
Government expenditure	2,000
Firms' pre-tax profit	7,000
Firms' investment	3,000
Consumers' expenditure	11,000
Exports	4,000

What is the value of imports?

A It is impossible to say
B 8,000
C 4,000
D 9,000

39 There is a circular flow of value around the macroeconomy

Label the diagram.

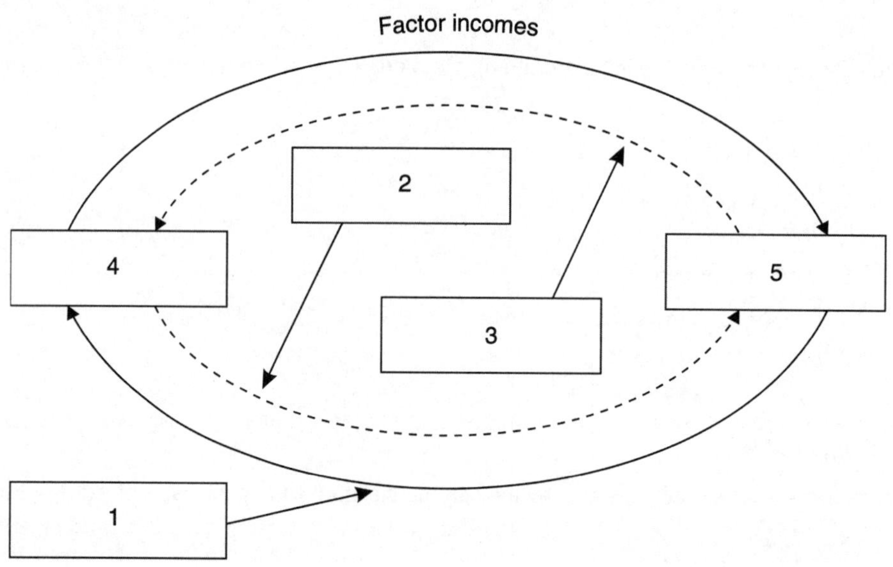

A Households
B Expenditure on goods and services
C Factors of production
D Firms
E Goods and services produced and sold

40 CONSUMPTION *10 mins*

Why are governments concerned by changes in the overall level of consumption? **8 Marks**

41 Keynes applied the idea of supply and demand to the macroeconomy.

Label the diagram.

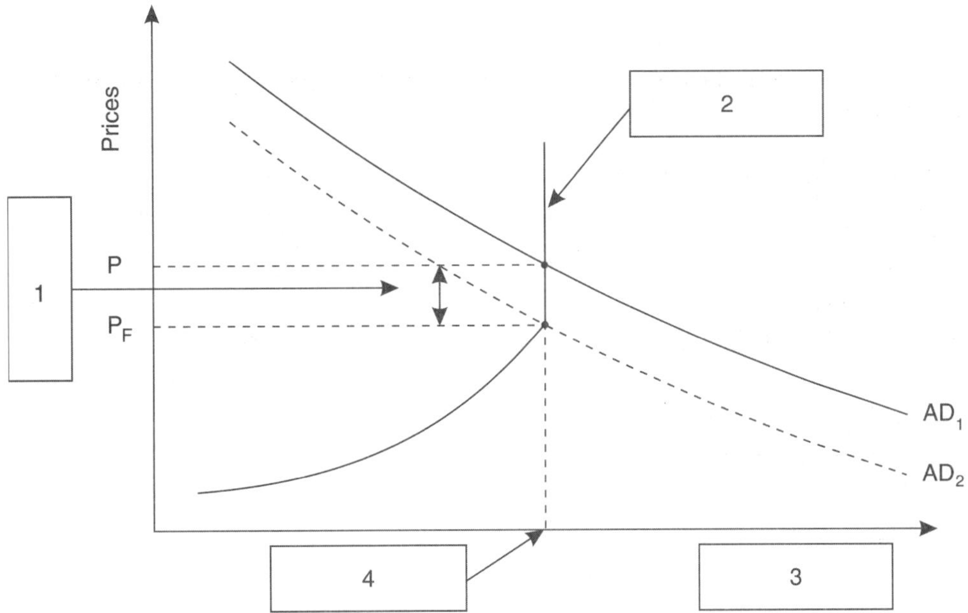

A Full employment level of output
B Real national income
C Inflationary gap
D Aggregate supply

42 Withdrawals from the circular flow of income in an economy are:

A Savings, investments and exports
B Investment, taxation and imports
C Investment, government spending and exports minus imports
D Savings, taxation and imports

43 MONEY SUPPLY *10 mins*

Why do monetarist economists think that the size of the money supply should be controlled? **8 Marks**

44 Fixed interest securities that pay £1.50 every six months are trading at a price of £40 each, though their face value is £50 each. What is the current rate of annual interest available on investments of this type?

A 6%
B 3¾%
C 7½%
D 3%

45 The relationship between money supply and prices can be expressed in the quantity theory of money identity as follows.

A M/V = P/T
B MV = PT
C MP = VT
D MT = VP

46 UNEMPLOYMENT *10 mins*

Distinguish between structural unemployment and demand deficient (cyclical) unemployment. **8 Marks**

47 The Phillips curve was at first seen as describing a method for the government to control the economy.

Label the diagram.

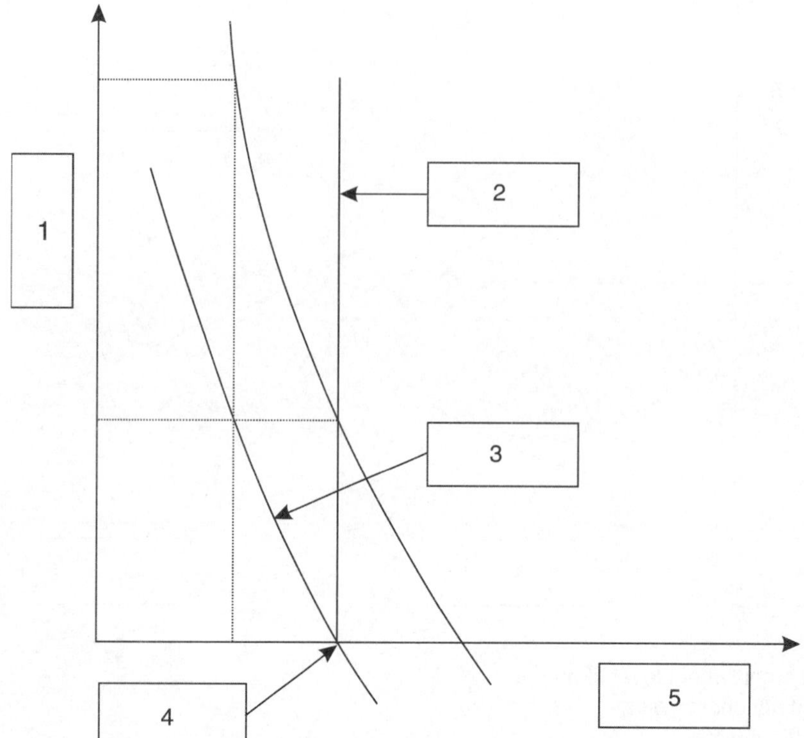

A Short run Phillips curve
B Unemployment
C Inflation
D Long run Phillips curve
E NAIRU

48 Which of the following diagrams shows an inflationary gap?

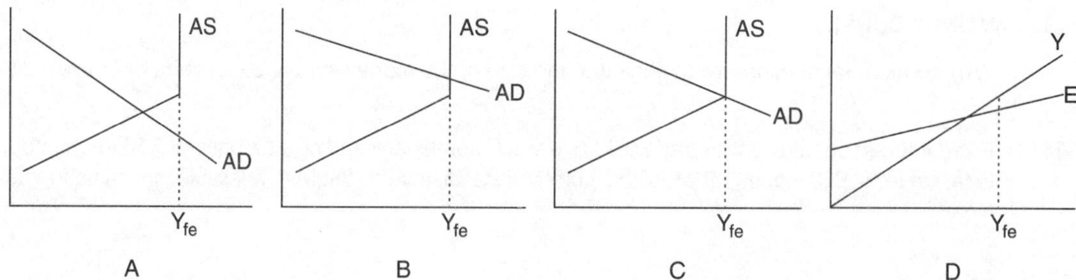

49 *10 mins*

Why might a government's budget vary from time to time, sometimes being in balance, sometimes in surplus and sometimes in deficit? **10 Marks**

50 During a period of inflation, which of the following taxes would rise as a proportion of taxpayers' income assuming no change in the rates or allowances?

(i) Capital gains tax
(ii) A progressive income tax
(iii) Valued added tax

A (i) and (ii)
B (ii) only
C (i) only
D (ii) and (iii)

51 A government wishes to continue to combine an expansionary fiscal stance with anti-inflationary monetary policy. What combination of policy instruments should it choose?

A Taxation up, borrowing down, interest rates up
B Spending down, taxation down, interest rates down
C Interest rates stable, taxation greater than spending
D Spending greater than taxation, interest rates up

52 BENEFITS OF TRADE *10 mins*

What are the principal economic benefits that a country obtains from international trade? **8 Marks**

53 According to the law of comparative advantage, the consequences of protectionism in international trade are that protectionist measures will prevent

A Each country of the world from maximising its economic wealth
B Each country of the world from maximising the value of its exports
C The countries of the world from maximising their total output with their economic resources
D Each country of the world from achieving equilibrium in its balance of payments

54

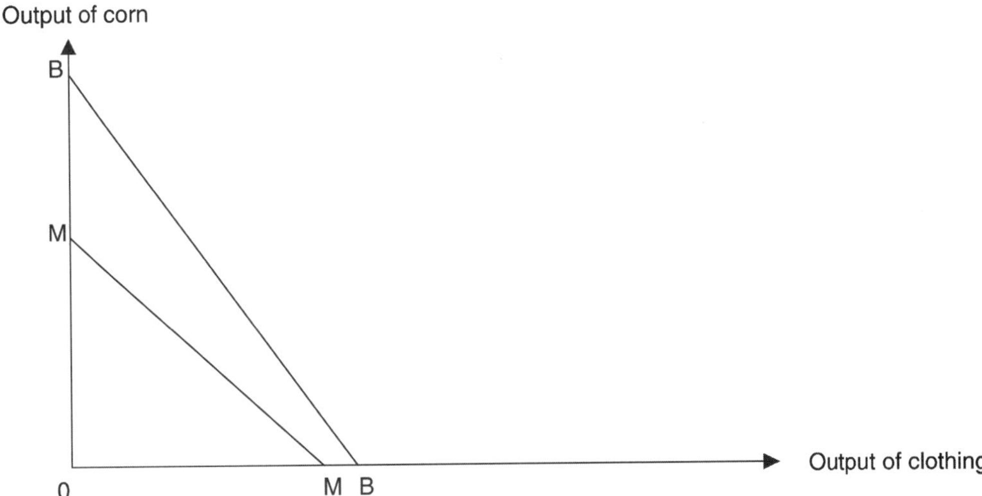

MM and BB represent production possibility boundaries of two countries, Mula and Burra respectively. Each country produces just two goods, corn and clothing. From the diagram, it can be seen that

A Mula has a comparative advantage in the production of clothing

B Burra has an absolute advantage in the production of both corn and clothing

C in the absence of international trade, Burra has a higher national income per head of the population than Mula

D Burra has a comparative advantage in the production of clothing

55 BALANCE OF PAYMENTS DEFICIT *10 mins*

Suppose that the balance of payments is massively in deficit. How could the Chancellor of the Exchequer remove the deficit? **8 Marks**

56 The most likely effect of a cut in the basic rate of UK income tax is:

A A rise in the value of the pound
B A fall in the value of the pound
C A fall in the PSBR
D A fall in the amount of VAT receipts

57 Suppose that the US dollar - £ sterling exchange rate is initially $1.50 =£1. During the subsequent period of time, inflation in the USA is 2% and in the UK it is 12%. If the only movement in the exchange rate during this period could be explained by purchasing power parity theory, the exchange rate at the end of the time period would be

A $1.3500 = £1
B $1.3660 = £1
C $1.6470 = £1
D $1.6500 = £1

Answer bank

1 **ALLOCATION OF RESOURCES**

The resources available to a society can be classified into four types of factor of production:

(i) land
(ii) labour
(iii) capital
(iv) enterprise

In all societies, resources are scarce and the wants of consumers exceed the capacity of society to meets those wants. The scarcity of resources means that choices need to be made. These choices encompass:

(i) production decisions (How much to produce? What combination of factors of production should be used for production?)

(ii) decisions about for whom the output is produced.

The choice to produce some goods or services from the factors of production available implies the choice not to produce other goods or services using the same economic resources. The implied sacrifice of the next best alternative forgone is called the *opportunity cost* of producing those goods or services.

The process of allocating resources is important because if the economic welfare gained from the scarce resources available is to be maximised, the right decisions need to be made about the basic choices of resource allocation.

2 D

3 D

4 **SECOND HAND CARS**

(a) Petrol and cars are **complementary** products; hence, any change in the market for petrol would be expected to affect the market for second-hand cars. The demand for petrol, however, is likely to be **price inelastic** so that a major change in its price will be necessary to affect the demand for any complementary product. Figure 1 assumes that there is a large increase in the price of fuel

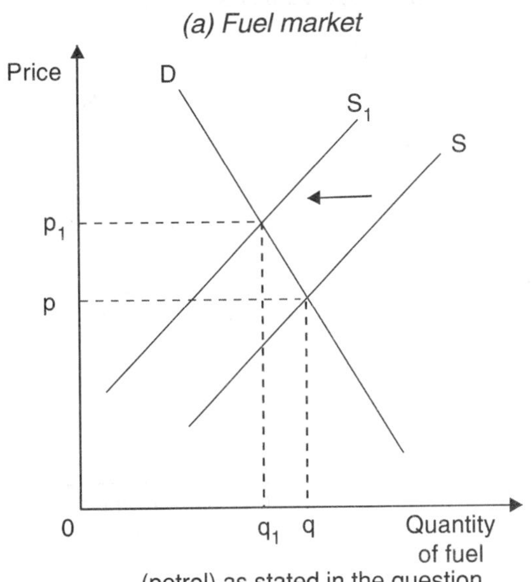

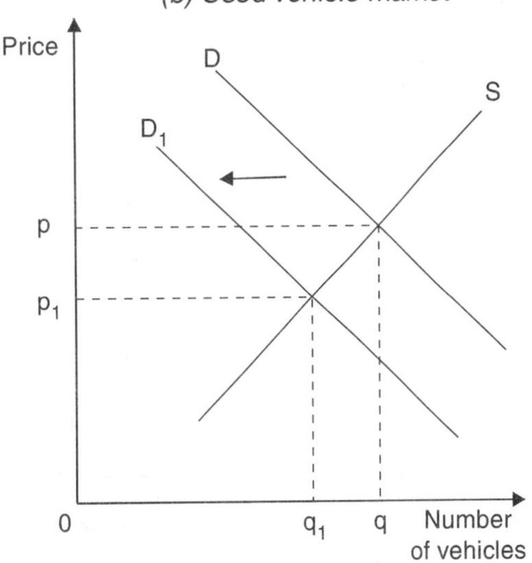

(petrol) as stated in the question.

Figure 1

In this instance, the rise in the price of fuel results from a change in the conditions of supply. This is the basis of the new supply curve S_1 to the left of the existing one (Figure 1(a)). A rise in the price of fuel is a rise in the cost of owning and running a car. There will thus be a fall in the demand for second-hand cars and a fall in the price and quantity sold (Figure 1(b)).

(b) The requirement to have expensive emission controls fitted would raise the supply price of second-hand vehicles and result in a fall in the numbers sold. Consequently the **supply curve** would move **upwards**, representing an increase in price at each level of output.

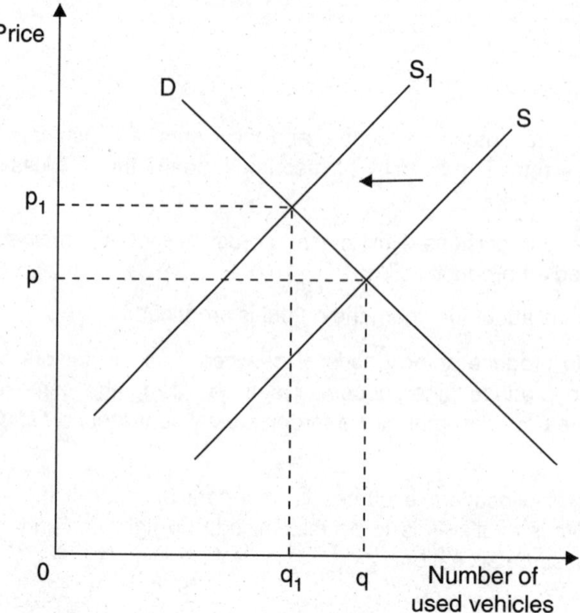

Figure 2

Expensive emission controls could well involve an outlay which is large in relation to the market value of many second-hand cars. Such controls fitted in the factory to new vehicles could make only a relatively small difference in their price. This could result in an increased preference for new cars as against second-hand cars. The supply curve shifts to the left (from S to S_1 in Figure 2) and the quantity of vehicles traded falls (from q to q_1). Any fall in the demand for second-hand vehicles would then depress the price, offsetting in part the increase resulting from the new requirements.

(c) This involves new vehicles and used vehicles as **substitute** products, touched upon in the answer to part (b) of the question.

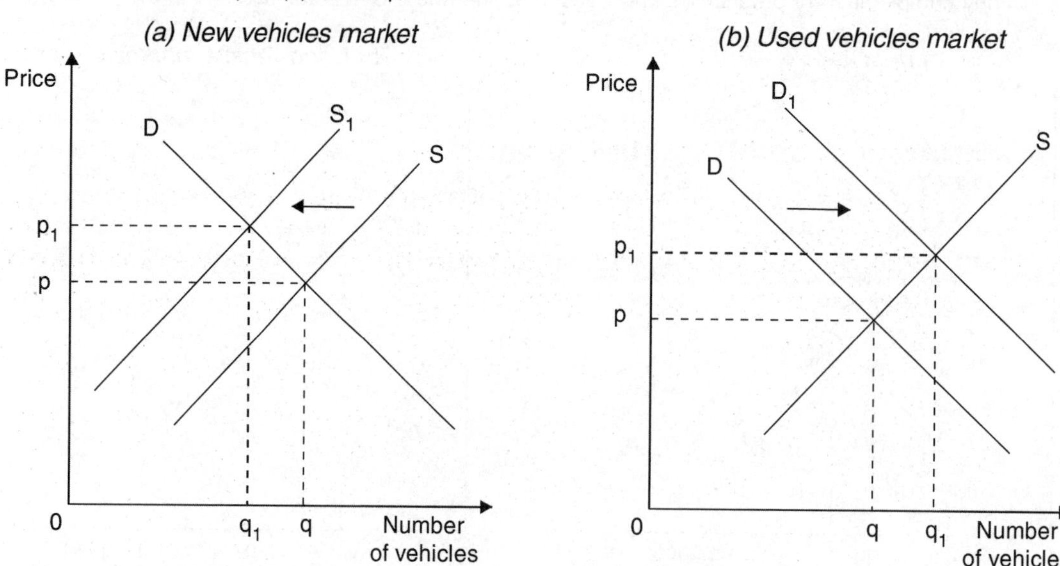

Figure 3

It is assumed here that the increase in the price of new cars is the result of a major increase in supply costs. The rise in price causes a switch of demand into second-hand vehicles, so pushing up their price and leading to an increase in the number sold (Figure 3(b)).

The increased price of new vehicles could alternatively result from an increase in the demand for them.

(d) This involves another 'product' which is in competition with second-hand cars. If there is a reduction in the price of public transport services, the following could be the result (Figure 4).

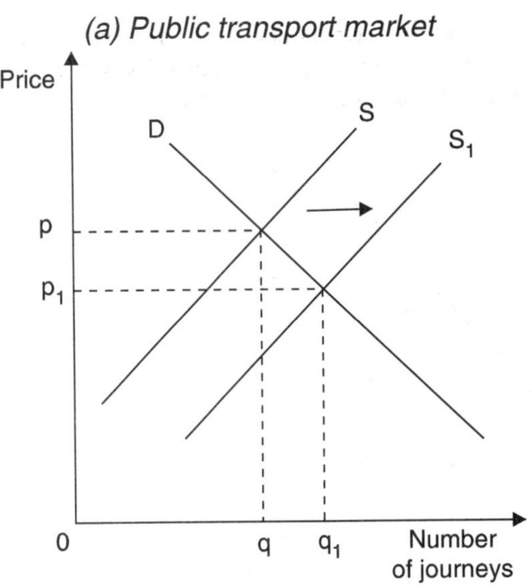

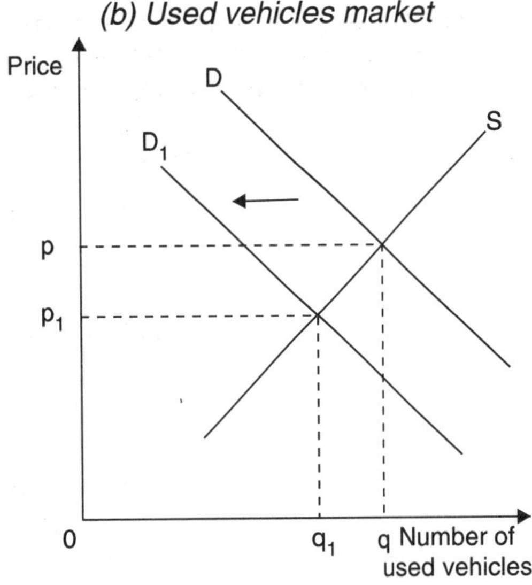

Figure 4

Here the fall in public transport prices leads to an expansion in demand for public transport (Figure 4(a)) while the demand for second-hand cars falls (with a new demand line D_1 in Figure 4(b)) together with a fall in price. However, the relationship between public transport and the market for second-hand cars is likely to be a highly complex and indeterminate one. Thus, people might make greater use of public transport while the ownership of cars (including second-hand cars) could continue to increase.

5 D The effect of a cash subsidy is to shift the supply curve to the right. Producers are willing to supply bigger quantities at the same market price, because they will get a cash subsidy from the government in addition to the market price. The new supply curve goes through points 7, 8 and 9, and so the new equilibrium, given no change in demand, is at point 8.

6

1 A The market clears at the equilibrium price – there is neither surplus nor shortage.
2 B Some consumers would have paid a higher price.
3 C The higher the price, the more attractive it is to suppliers.
4 D The demand curve usually slopes downwards.
5 E Some suppliers would have sold at lower price.

7 **DATA RESPONSE QUESTION: DEMAND AND SUPPLY**

(a) A 'change in the quantity supplied' is illustrated in Figure 2 and is sometimes referred to as a movement along the supply curve. It is caused solely by a change in the price of the good supplied, a higher price causing more to be supplied and a lower price causing less. In all of these cases the supply curve itself does not move.

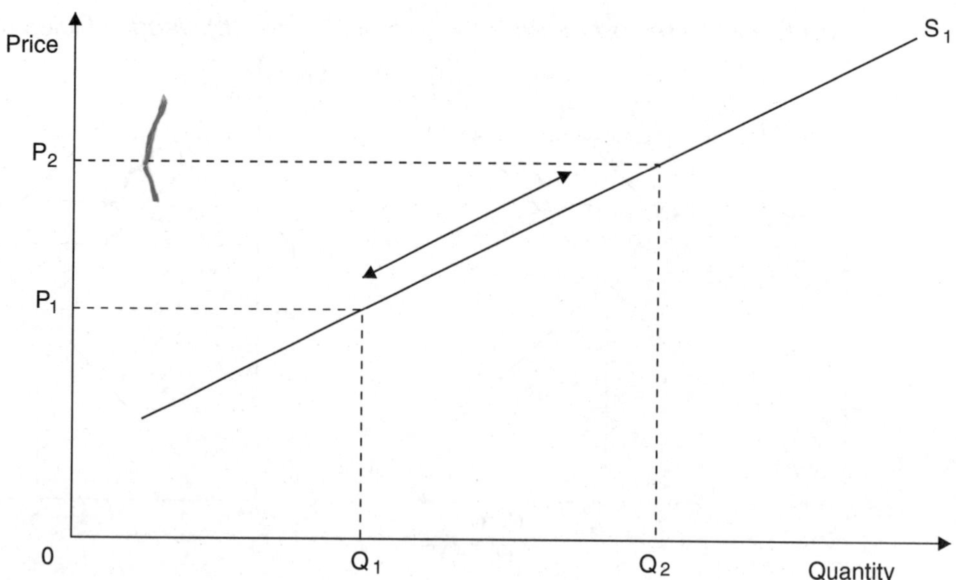

Figure 2

(b) If the market price of the milk is 10p the supplier will receive 10p from the consumer plus another 10p from the government, making 20p in all. If the market price is 20p the supplier actually receives 30p (20p from the consumer plus 10p from the government). As shown in the table below, the result will be that suppliers will increase supply by the amount of the subsidy, shifting the supply schedule downwards. What the farmers used to supply at a market price of 30p, they will now supply at a market price of 20p and so on, since the government will top this up to 30p with the 10p subsidy.

Price	*Quantity supplied without subsidy*	*Quantity supplied after 10p subsidy*
60p	40,000	-
50p	35,000	40,000
40p	30,000	35,000
30p	25,000	30,000
20p	20,000	25,000
10p	15,000	20,000

This can be shown diagrammatically as a shift of the supply curve downwards by the amount of the subsidy.

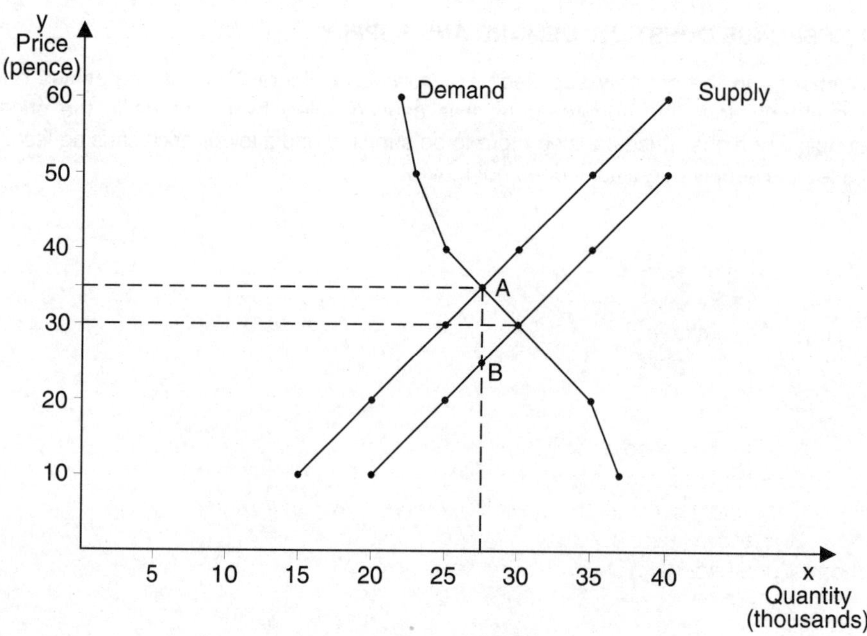

Figure 3

The vertical distance (A – B) is the amount of the subsidy.

Before the subsidy is applied, it can be estimated that 27,500 pints per day will be supplied and sold.

Following the application of the subsidy, demand equates with supply at a price of 30p. At this new equilibrium price, a quantity of 30,000 pints per day is supplied and sold.

The effect of the subsidy on the market quantity and price depends upon the elasticity of demand and the elasticity of supply, changes in which alter the slope of the demand and supply curves. For example, if demand were more inelastic over the range of price at which the demand curve crosses the supply schedules, there would be a larger reduction in the market price and a smaller increase in the size of the market.

(c) The price elasticity of demand indicates the effects that changes in price have on sales. If demand is relatively elastic, it may be unwise for a business to raise prices, since demand may fall significantly enough to reduce total revenue and possibly to reduce profits. If, on the other hand, demand is relatively inelastic, increasing prices may allow total revenue to be increased.

One area of government policy in which demand elasticity is important is that of indirect taxation. The degree to which increasing taxes or duties on goods is successful in increasing total revenues will depend upon the elasticity of demand. Above a particular level of price, there may be elasticity, and revenues may fall if the taxes are increased. However, indirect taxation may be applied for objectives other than the raising of revenue. A government may, for instance, apply high taxes to cigarettes and tobacco with the objective of cutting consumption of those products on health grounds.

8 C Ostentation goods and Giffen goods have positive PED. Inferior goods have negative IED. Substitutes have positive XED.

9 1 C Quantity available to purchase remains the same no matter what price is offered.
2 A Any straight line passing through the origin shows unit elasticity.
3 B Any desired quantity is available at the prevailing price, none at a lower price.

10 **SOCIAL COSTS**

A government might attempt to correct the distortions in resource allocation caused by social costs by bringing social costs and private costs into line.

Using pollution as an example, the output of polluting industries is generally greater than is optimal because the polluters often take little or no account of the costs imposed on others by their actions. One approach for government is to levy a tax on polluters equal to the cost of removing the effects of the externality they generate. This will encourage firms to cut emissions and provide an incentive for them to research ways of permanently reducing pollution.

A second approach is to impose regulations. Waste may only be disposed of with prior consent and if none is given, or if it is exceeded, the polluter is fined. There may also be standards of, for example, air and water quality, with appropriate penalties for not conforming to the standards. Problems with this approach are the administrative burden it creates and the costs involved in monitoring and enforcement.

The government may also consider the use of subsidies to 'persuade' polluters to cut back on their output and hence pollution, or to assist with expenditure on new machinery, for example air filters, which reduce or eliminate pollution. The problem with subsidies is that they provide no incentive to reduce pollution any further.

11 1 C Customer now pays P_1 instead of P_0
2 B Supplier receives P_2 net of tax instead of P_0
3 E The supply curve shifts vertically by the amount of the tax
4 A Demand is lower at the higher price
Supernormal profit does not appear in the diagram

12 A Before the maximum price regulations were introduced, the equilibrium price was £220, with 7,400,000 tonnes demanded and supplied each month. With a maximum price of £200, demand will be 8,200,000 tonnes per month and supply only 6,600,000 tonnes per month. With demand exceeding supply, there will be a bean shortage and a need for rationing - since prices cannot be raised to eliminate the excess demand.

13 DATA RESPONSE QUESTION: REVENUE AND COSTS

It is assumed below that total revenue and total cost are stated in pounds (£).

Output	*Total revenue (TR)* £	*(a) Marginal revenue* $TR_n - TR_{(n-1)}$ £	*Total costs (TC)* £	*(b) Marginal costs* $TC_n - TC_{(n-1)}$ £	*Total profit TR - TC* £
0	-	-	110	-	(110)
1	50	50	140	30	(90)
2	100	50	162	22	(62)
3	150	50	175	13	(25)
4	200	50	180	5	20
5	250	50	185	5	65
6	300	50	194	9	106
7	350	50	229	35	122(max)
8	400	50	269	50	131(max)
9	450	50	325	56	125
10	500	50	425	100	75

(a) Marginal revenue is the additional revenue which results from the sale of the last unit of output.

The figures in the table above show that marginal revenue is a constant £50 at all levels of output given. This means that average revenue (price) must also be a constant £50. The firm's demand curve is perfectly elastic, indicating that the firm is operating in a perfectly competitive market.

(b) The fixed costs of the firm are those costs which do not vary with output. The level of fixed costs are therefore the total costs of £110 at the output level of zero.

Marginal cost is the change in total cost arising from the production of the last unit of output. The marginal cost for each level of output is shown in the table.

(c) As stated in (a) above, the firm is operating in a perfectly competitive market. The firm will seek to maximise profits by producing at a level of output at which marginal cost equals marginal revenue. It can be seen from the table that this occurs at output level 8. Total profit (total revenues minus total costs) at this levels of output is £131.

(d) When a firm is earning normal profits only, it is just covering all of its costs (measured in terms of alternatives forgone). New producers will only wish to enter the industry if it is possible to earn supernormal profits.

The entry of new firms will increase quantities supplied at different levels of price, thus shifting the industry supply curve to the right. Given a downward-sloping industry demand curve, the market price will fall. This is shown in the diagram: as supply shifts from curve S^1 to curve S^2, the average revenue curve for individual firms falls from AR^1 to AR^2. The firm's average revenue curve is the same as its marginal revenue (MR) curve.

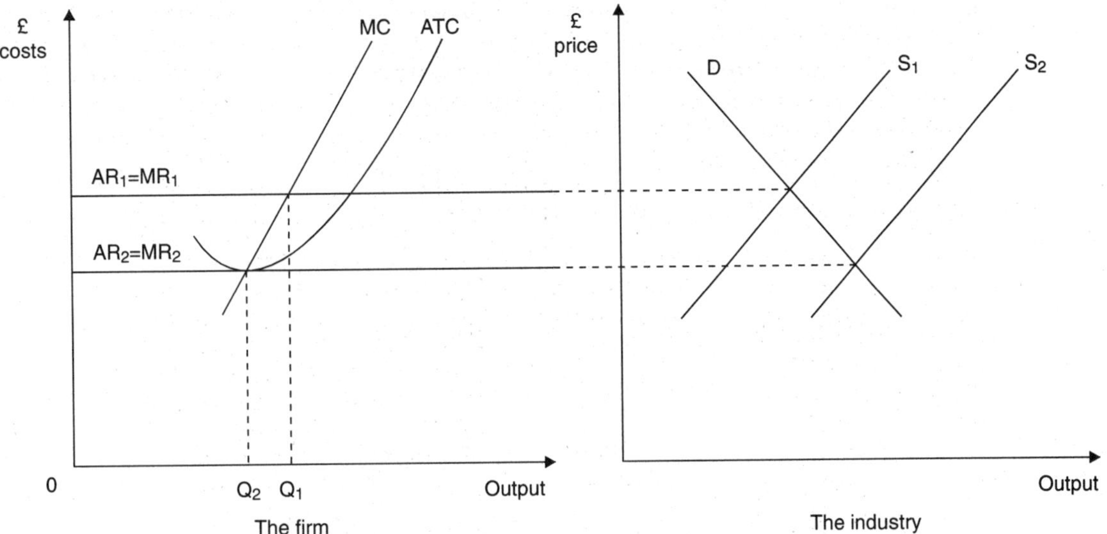

The profit-maximising position for the firm is where MC = MR. As marginal revenue falls from MR_1 to MR_2, the individual firm's profit-maximising level of output falls from Q_1 to Q_2. As more firms enter the industry, each firm's output will continue to fall until average revenue equals average total costs (ATC) for each firm. This occurs when average revenue falls to AR_2 and the individual firm's output is Q_2. All firms will now be earning normal profits only and it will no longer be worthwhile for new firms to enter the industry.

14 B 3 must be TC as it is the largest of any level of output greater than one unit. 2 is MC since it shows the increase in TC for each extra unit of production. Therefore 1 must be AC. Also 1 is equal to 3 divided by the units of output. It is also possible to discern that 2 begins to increase at a lower level of output than 1, and is equal to 1 at its lowest point. This is the relationship between MC and AC.

15

1	B	Fixed costs plus variable costs equals total costs.
2	A	Marginal cost crosses the average cost lines at their lowest points.
3	C	Average total cost equals average fixed cost plus average variable cost.
4	E	Average costs fall while marginal costs are lower and rise when they are higher.
5	D	Fixed costs are spread over more units as output increases.

16 TYPES OF PROFIT

> *Tutorial note.* In economics, profit is the reward to the entrepreneur for bearing risk and because of this it is included as a cost of production. This is the essence of part (a) and should be used to illustrate the difference between normal profits, the minimum acceptable for the entrepreneur to stay in the industry, and supernormal profits. Do not, as some candidates did when the question was set in the exam, go into too much detail for this part, which is only worth 8 marks. Part (b) requires a discussion of the role of profits in the operation of the price mechanism, as a guide to resource allocation.

Profit is the difference between total revenue and total costs. It is the reward to enterprise (a factor of production), in return for its risk-bearing role in the production process.

In economics, the concept of opportunity cost is used, measuring the cost of production in terms of the alternatives foregone. Hence, the profits of a business must take into account the cost of the entrepreneur valued in terms of his employment in his best alternative occupation.

Of the four factors of production, enterprise is the only one which cannot be certain of gaining a reward, for example if the business makes a loss. The entrepreneur bears the burden of this uncertainty, profit being the reward for doing so.

Normal profit is defined as the minimum reward acceptable to the entrepreneur in the long run: any entrepreneur not earning at least normal profit will transfer to an alternative occupation. Hence, normal profit is regarded as a cost of production: unless the business will generate sufficient revenue to cover the cost of the entrepreneur, as well as paying for the services of the other factors, production will not go ahead. Normal profit is therefore the transfer earnings of the entrepreneur (the minimum necessary to keep him in his present occupation). Anything the business generates in excess of normal profit is known as *supernormal* or excess profit and represents economic rent to the entrepreneur. Supernormal profits are generally competed away in the long run unless the firm maintains a monopoly position through effective barriers to entry.

17 C

Employees	*Sales value of total product*	*Marginal revenue product*	*Marginal cost*
	£	£	£
4	44	-	-
5	64	+20	+16
6	98	+34	+16
7	134	+36	+16
8	170	+36	+16
9	198	+28	+16
10	214	+16	+16 *
11	228	+14	+16
12	240	+12	+16

*Profits are increased up to the point where the MRP of labour exceeds the MC of labour, and are maximised where MRP = MC, which is at an employment level of 10.

18
1 C
2 D
3 A
4 B

19 **HIGHER REAL COSTS**

In the long run a perfectly competitive market will lead to the optimal allocation of resources and the optimal location of economic activity. If resources are scarce, their price will rise, and if they are in excess supply their price will fall. Higher prices in one region than another will result in a movement of resources (labour) from the low price to the high price regions, until an equilibrium is achieved whereby all resources are located optimally. The optimal location of resources in a perfectly competitive market implies that output is produced at the minimum cost in the optimal place. Location is relevant to this situation, because of transport costs from the location of production to the location of markets.

Factor prices will not necessarily reflect regional scarcities. National wage agreements might exist, so that wage levels are the same in regions with unemployment as they are in regions with job vacancies. Also labour immobility might prevent the migration of individuals from a low wage region with unemployment to a high wage region with jobs to offer.

Regional policy might involve the payment of government grants to industries that invest in a depressed region, but such grants, if applied to all investments, would fail to distinguish between efficient and inefficient investments. High-cost producers might remain competitive because of government subsidies. When government assistance is selective, and bureaucrats or politicians are empowered to decide which investments should be given public money, and the consequences might be uneconomic investment decisions.

20
(a) Secondary. This is manufacture, using a primary sector output.
(b) Tertiary. This is distribution of a secondary sector by-product.
(c) Tertiary. Insurance of primary sector capital equipment.
(d) Secondary. By definition.
(e) Tertiary. Finance for a primary sector asset.

21 (c) Baumol. This is a name worth having up your sleeve. You will come across him again in other subjects.

22 MONOPOLY

The larger size of monopoly firms compared with smaller firms in competition with one another means that monopolists may be able to take advantage of economies of scale. For example, there are considerable economies in operating a single domestic gas supply network compared with a number of networks competing in the same areas. Monopolist firms may be able to spread fixed costs over larger amounts of output. They may also gain from economies in bulk buying of inputs and in marketing and distribution costs.

Monopoly firms may be in a stronger position to finance research and development activities, enabling them to make technological advances which will lower unit costs of production and also to develop new products to meet consumers' needs.

The presence of economies of scale could reduce monopolists' production costs below that of firms in a competitive market. Equilibrium will then be at a point further down the monopolist's downward sloping demand curve than it would be without the scale economies, and the resultant profit maximising position will be at a lower price and higher output level than in the competitive market.

If a competitive industry were to become monopolised, consumers' interests might also be served by some form of regulation of the industry. Some monopolistic companies in the UK are subject to price regulation, such as BT, the telecommunications operator. Such regulation may enable scale economies to be achieved while preventing consumers from suffering from the full effects of monopolistic pricing policies.

23 B A shows total cost and total revenue and C shows marginal cost and marginal revenue, both where perfect competition does not exist. D shows marginal cost and average cost for a typical firm.

24
1 A Profits are maximised at output Q_1; revenues exceed opportunity costs.
2 B Marginal and average revenue must both fall if sales are to increase.
3 E
4 F Efficiency is highest when average costs are lowest, which is where MC cuts AC.

There is no label for profit maximising output.
Transfer earnings does not appear on the diagram.

25 DISTINCTIONS

Monopolistic competition occurs where there is a large number of firms whose outputs are close but not perfect substitutes, either because of product differentiation or geographical fragmentation of the market. The fact that the products are not homogeneous means that any one firm may raise its price relative to the prices of its competitors without losing all its sales, so that its demand curve is downward sloping rather than a horizontal straight line (as in perfect competition). The combination of a large number of firms, as in perfect competition with downward sloping demand curves as in monopoly, is responsible for the term 'monopolistic competition'.

In monopolistic competition the firm maximises profits where marginal cost equals marginal revenue. Supernormal profits are earned in the short run, but these are competed away in the long run due to new firms being attracted into the industry. An example of monopolistic competition might be the retail trade, where there are a large number of firms. There is freedom of entry in the long term and products are differentiated by advertising, opening hours, service and so on.

Oligopoly is a type of market in which there is a small number of firms account for a large proportion of output, employment and so on. The essential feature of this market form is the high degree of interdependence among the decisions of the firms. The result of this is that each seller must predict the reactions of his competitors before he can determine the consequences of any decision he might take. This obviously creates considerable uncertainty in the industry, and partly because of this and partly because their profits will be higher, it is generally argued that oligopolists will adopt a policy of collusion. The most usual form will be an agreement to avoid price competition although the firms may well compete through product differentiation, particularly in consumer good industries.

Oligopoly is a very common market structure, an example in the UK being the washing powder industry. There are only a few firms producing products which are basically similar but differentiated by advertising.

26 B However, firms attempt to differentiate their products. Supernormal profits can be made, but they are likely to be competed away in the longer term. The excess capacity theorem applies. The AR curve slopes downwards in all market models except perfect competition.

27 1 C
2 D Customers will desert an oligopolist who increases prices
3 B A price cut will be matched by the other oligopolists, with little eventual change in market share.

Average cost is not shown on this diagram

28 **DATA RESPONSE QUESTION: PRIVATISATION**

(a) Privatisation in its broadest sense takes three forms.

(i) The deregulation of industries, to allow private firms to compete against state-owned businesses where they were not allowed to compete before (eg the deregulation of bus and coach services and of postal services).

(ii) Contracting out work to private firms, where the work was previously done by government employees - eg refuse collection, hospital laundry work.

(iii) Transfer of the ownership of assets from the state to private shareholders. There has been a policy in the UK in recent years of 'de-nationalising' and 'privatising' certain industries, eg telecommunications, gas, water and electricity.

(b) Privatisation should encourage efficiency. Nationalised industries often use their resources inefficiently and wastefully. The effect of denationalisation might be to make the industries more cost-conscious, because they will be directly answerable to shareholders, and under scrutiny from stock market investors. Inefficiencies might therefore be reduced or eliminated.

If the effect of privatisation is to increase competition, the greater competition is likely to make firms produce output more cheaply and sell it at a lower price. Nationalised organisations have often acted as monopolists, with the consequences of higher prices and lower output characteristic of non-competitive markets.

With the central objective of profit maximisation, privatised firms should prove to be responsive to the wants of consumers as signalled by market research and the operation of the price mechanism. The profit objective induces firms to innovate and to seek out new markets, a process which promotes the efficient allocation of resources.

(c) In practice, there has been little evidence of increased competition following some privatisations. Indeed, some organisations have been sold as monopolies to increase their attractiveness to shareholders. It might be claimed that there was little alternative in the case of industries which are clearly natural monopolies and that, in any case, as private firms they must compete for funds on the capital market with other private sector organisations. Nevertheless, it is argued that monopolies do not have to be efficient to be profitable, and it is profitability that is the main determinant of a firm's ability to raise those funds.

State-owned industries are more likely to respond to the public interest, ahead of the profit motive. For example, state-owned industries are more likely to cross-subsidise unprofitable operations from profitable ones; eg the Post Office will deliver letters to the isles of Scotland even though the service might be very unprofitable.

The gain to the government's finances is a temporary one only. The selling off of major industries reduces the government's influence over the economy, although some would argue that this is a benefit of privatisation.

29 C The others are types of market failure. Regulatory capture occurs when the regulator becomes unduly influenced by the regulated firms.

30 B Privatisation *could* mean selling off nationalised industries, but it can also refer to deregulation of industries to allow private firms to compete with state-run business (eg private bus companies) and contracting out work previously done by government employees to private firms (eg refuse collection).

Statement C is correct, and refers to the influence of stock market competition on newly-privatised monopolies. Statement D is correct: an example in the UK is the regulatory body Oftel for BT (formerly British Telecom).

31 INTEREST RATES

(a) The following factors may influence the levels of interest rates.

(i) Supply and demand for money are important influences. If people decide they would rather spend money than save it, perhaps because of high inflation, the shortage of funds may drive up interest rates.

(ii) Changing expectations of future trends in interest rates will affect the relationship between short-term and long-term interest rates, as new expectations that the general level of interest rates will rise or fall will cause long-term interest rates to rise or fall respectively.

(iii) Investors' desire for liquidity may increase in times of political or economic uncertainty. Long-term interest rates will then have to rise to attract investors to make long-term commitments.

(iv) Government policy, signalled in the UK through public statements and through the Bank of England, may influence interest rates. The government may attempt to control the exchange rate through interest rates, raising interest rates when the pound weakens so as to increase the demand for sterling.

Such government action is applied to short-term interest rates. After a while, long-term interest rates may be affected, since if they are not increased following a rise in short-term rates investors will only invest short-term.

(b) Investors seek not only high returns but also liquidity (the ability to convert their investments into cash quickly) and a low risk of being forced to accept a low interest rate (or take a capital loss on marketable fixed interest securities) should interest rates rise. For these reasons, investors may be expected to favour short-term over long-term investments, and short-term interest rates should therefore be lower.

If there are expectations that interest rates will fall, investors will prefer to lock in at higher long-term rates, while borrowers will not wish to be committed to higher long-term rates and will prefer to 'borrow short'. There will be an excess supply of funds at long maturities and a shortage of funds at short maturities. Long-term interest rates will fall relative to short-term rates.

If interest rates are now expected to rise, investors will not wish to lock in to lower interest rates and will therefore 'sell short'. Borrowers will wish to borrow at lower long-term rates to avoid exposure to the higher rates expected in the future. These demand and supply factors will result in a shortage of long-term funds, which will push up long-term money market rates, and to an excess supply of short-term funds, which will lead to a reduction in short-term rates.

32 B The interest charged on a long term loan is likely, *ceteris paribus*, to be higher than that charged on a short term loan because of the greater risk involved in committing money for the longer term.

33 B

34 BANK DEPOSITS

On any particular day only a relatively small portion of the funds held by banks will be withdrawn. There may be a very substantial outflow of funds, but there is also likely to be a very substantial inflow. Hence, the net change in a bank's holdings of cash on any particular day is likely to be relatively small. The banks are therefore able to lend a substantial part of the funds deposited with them. As lending is the most profitable of a bank's activities, it is to be expected that all banks in the system do this. The effect will be a multiple expansion of credit following an initial deposit of cash.

This process may be illustrated in the following example. It is assumed that banks wish to maintain a cash ratio of 10%, ie they maintain a ratio of 10% cash to total deposits. This means that banks will

lend 90% of all cash deposited with them. If therefore a bank receives a cash deposit of £10,000 it will lend £9,000 in the form of advances.

The bank has not made the loan in cash, but simply credited the sum of £9,000 to the borrowers. Bank deposits have increased by £9,000 but so have the bank's assets in the form of a claim against the borrowers. Having been granted loans, borrowers will seek to spend them, with cash being withdrawn from the bank to meet these expenditures. The £9,000 used by borrowers to make purchases will flow back into the banking system as someone else's deposits. A further 90% of these deposits (ie £8,100) will be re-lent. Again, this will flow back into the banking system with 90% of these deposits (ie £7,290) being re-lent.

It is apparent that this process will continue, and as a result of the initial cash deposit, there will be an expansion of bank lending in the form of a diminishing series:

$$£10,000 + £9,000 + £8,100 + £7,290 + \ldots$$

Clearly, the initial deposit of £10,000 leads to an eventual increase in bank deposits many times greater than the initial cash deposit. The increase in bank deposits comes about because of the lending activities of the banks in their search for profits.

35 B The existing relationship is $4,800 \times 0.15 = 720$
The desired relationship is $4,000 \times 0.18 = 720$

36 C Cash is the most liquid asset of all.

37 GNP

Gross domestic product (GDP) is the value of all the goods and services produced in the domestic economy over a given period of time, typically one year. This includes the value of goods produced for exports as well as goods produced within the country for its own domestic markets. It is the gross value of the domestic product because it does not make any allowance for the cost of depreciation of the capital which has been used to produce the output.

The gross national product (GNP) is GDP plus the amount of net income earned by the country's inhabitants from property or investments abroad (or minus the amount of net payments to individuals and firms in other countries for the property or investments they own in the country).

People's standard of living in economic terms is viewed in terms of how much they consume. GNP is commonly divided by the number of inhabitants in the country to arrive at a value for GNP or GDP per head of the population. Changes in GNP per capita can then be used to measure the increase or decrease in a country's standard of living over time.

GNP per head of population is less reliable as a guide to comparing the standard of living in different countries, however.

(a) In defining GNP, 'product' includes goods and services which are paid for, but excludes work done by a person for himself. It also excludes barter trade. In some countries, do-it-yourself production and barter trade are more common than in others, and so the total GNP of the various countries would not be properly comparable.

(b) In measuring GNP, government services which are not paid for are valued at cost. If one country has a large state-owned sector which provides services free (eg health and education) whereas another country has only a small state-owned sector, output which is valued at cost in one country would be valued at market price in the other and so there would be different valuations given to the same physical product.

(c) Spending on items which produce a benefit over several years is included in GNP in one year only, which is the year the expenditure takes place. If a country is still enjoying benefits from past investments, this will not be reflected in its current GNP.

(d) Every country will have difficulty in obtaining accurate data about output and GNP. Statistical errors and omissions will be large, and in particular, any output of a country's black economy will not be reflected in the official records. Thus a country with a strong black economy will be much wealthier than its official GNP per head of population might suggest.

(e) GNP per head does not take into account the distribution of income. Two countries with the same average GNP per head might have very different income distributions, with one having a relatively even distribution among its people while the other has a small very wealthy class and a large section of the population is living in poverty. We would want to say that the population of the former country enjoys a higher standard of living.

(f) The needs of people in one country will differ widely from the needs of people in another. This will be due to differences in social attitudes, customs and habits, religious beliefs, climate, density of population and so on. Different countries will also produce different outputs. When people in different countries want entirely different things, it is not really possible to presume that their comparative standards of living can be measured on a single money scale.

(g) Countries will spend on some items that may be of little direct relevance to their immediate standard of living. Spending on armaments is an example. The GNP per capita of a country with high defence spending and one with little such spending would therefore not be properly comparable. Some countries may devote resources to various 'prestige' projects from which their people gain little.

38 C

National income	=	income from employment + firms' profit (income approach) = 16,000.
Also, national income	=	Total expenditure + exports – imports (expenditure approach)
⇒ 16,000	=	3,000 + 2,000 + 11,000 + 4,000 – imports
⇒ imports	=	5,000 + 11,000 + 4,000 – 16,000
	=	4,000

39

1 B Expenditure is financed by factor incomes
2 E Goods and services are produced by firms and consumed by households
3 C Productive resources are land, labour, capital and enterprise
4 D Firms produce for consumption by households
5 A Households supply factors of production to firms

40 CONSUMPTION

The economy may be visualised as a single huge market with a downward sloping aggregate demand curve and an upward sloping aggregate supply curve. National income is determined by the interaction of aggregate demand and aggregate supply. The intersection of the two curves determines the overall level of prices and the overall level of output. Consumption is a major component of aggregate demand. It is therefore an important influence upon the level of national income.

If the economy reaches an equilibrium at a level of national income which leaves some productive resources unused, the practical result of this is continuing unemployment. On the other hand, if aggregate demand exceeds the productive capacity of the economy, an increase in inflation is likely to occur. Governments therefore try to influence the level of consumption as a means of influencing aggregate demand. They aim to achieve a level of aggregate demand which minimises unemployment while not causing shortages of labour which are likely to lead to inflation.

41

1 C With the economy at full employment, there is no spare capacity so an increase in aggregate demand produces inflation.

2 D Aggregate supply cannot increase once full employment is reached.

3 B National income and national output are the same thing.

4 A Full employment places an upper limit on output.

42 D

43 MONEY SUPPLY

Monetarists argue that since money is a direct substitute for all other assets, an increase in the money supply, given a fairly stable velocity of circulation, will have a direct effect on demand for other assets

because there will be more money to spend on those assets. If the total output of the economy is fixed, then an increase in the money supply will lead directly to higher prices.

Monetarists therefore reach the same basic conclusion as the old quantity theory of money. A rise in the money supply will lead to a rise in prices and probably also to a rise in money incomes. (It is also assumed by monetarists that the velocity of circulation remains fairly constant, again taking a view similar to the old quantity theory.)

In the short run, monetarists argue that an increase in the money supply might cause some increase in real output and so an increase in employment. In the long run, however, all increases in the money supply will be reflected in higher prices unless there is longer term growth in the economy.

44 C A £40 investment produces an annual return of £3. This is equivalent to 7½%.

45 B The quantity theory of money identity states that MV = PT.

46 UNEMPLOYMENT

Structural unemployment arises from the decline in existing industries and the development of new industries which takes place in all modern economies in response to change, for example in the structure of demand. The demand for certain products may be declining alongside the growth of new or alternative products and this, together with an inability to compete with foreign competition, is one of the main causes of the decline of particular industries and consequent unemployment in that industry. Structural unemployment is often localised because those industries which have declined, such as steel, shipbuilding and coalmining, have tended to be localised. A special case of structural unemployment is known as technological unemployment which results from the success of new industries using advanced technology and a higher degree of automation, enabling the same amount of output to be achieved with considerably less labour.

Cyclical unemployment or *'demand deficient' unemployment* results from a downswing in the trade cycle. The trade or business cycle refers to the regular recurring changes in the pattern of aggregate demand and in its recession phase, when demand falls, there is a general reduction in the demand for labour and hence unemployment. The Keynesian argument was based on the belief that the economy could settle into a less than full-employment equilibrium because of a continuing lack of aggregate demand, emphasising the role of the government in pursuing demand management policies. The pre-Keynesian or classical economists, however, believed that large scale unemployment was caused by an excessively high level of real wages and could be dealt with by allowing real wages to fall. This view has been revived to some extent by monetarist and new classical economists who criticise demand management as having only temporary results, leading ultimately to higher inflation.

47
1 C
2 D Once NAIRU is reached, increases in aggregate demand only produce inflation.
3 A
4 E
5 B

48 B A and D show a deflationary gap. C shows an economy at ideal equilibrium.

49 A budget deficit occurs where expenditure exceeds income and a budget surplus occurs where expenditure is less than income.

In a **mixed economy** like that of the United Kingdom, the level of economic activity fluctuates depending upon where we are in the trade cycle. During the **upturn** in the trade cycle production is rising, firms and individuals earn more profits and wages so the government should collect more revenue. Unemployment should also fall during this period, and so government expenditure should fall. At this stage of the cycle, the budget may be in surplus.

During the **downturn** of a trade cycle, the reverse applies. Profits and incomes fall and government revenue falls, but unemployment rises and government expenditure on unemployment benefit rises. There is then more likely to be a budget deficit.

Keynes suggested that budget deficits should be used to help an economy out of recession. According to Keynes, unemployment was caused by a lack of aggregate demand in the economy. So if the government increased its expenditure, this would raise aggregate demand.

Using Keynesian policies, a government may plan a budget deficit to boost aggregate monetary demand. Increased government expenditure might be on infrastructure such as roads, schools or the health service. Alternatively, taxes could be cut to increase consumers' disposable incomes. The objective would be to close the 'deflationary gap' that is seen to be preventing the economy reaching a level of full employment. Thus, variations in the budget balance can be the result of deliberate government budgetary policy.

50 B Inflation brings more taxpayers into the higher tax bracket. Value added tax and capital gains tax would continue as the same proportions of income, assuming no significant changes in patterns of investment and spending.

51 D B would reduce the size of the state sector, which would be contractionary; the reduction in interest rates might lead to sufficient private sector demand for the economy to expand overall, or it may not. The effect of such a policy combination on inflation is impossible to say.

A would control inflation by making a public sector debt repayment possible, as well as via interest rate control. However, this is not an expansionary fiscal stance.

C is a contractionary fiscal stance and a neutral policy on inflation.

52 BENEFITS OF TRADE

International trade arises for various reasons. The most obvious economic benefit is that different countries have different factor endowments and hence are able to specialise in the production of particular goods. The standard of living may be improved if countries specialise, as specialisation enables a greater variety and a larger number of goods to be consumed. However, the vast majority of goods which countries buy from abroad they could produce for themselves domestically. The main reason they are imported is that they can be produced with greater relative efficiency by foreign firms than by domestic firms. The law of comparative advantage shows that countries gain when they specialise in the production of those goods in which they have the greater relative efficiency. These goods can then be traded for other goods that are required.

A country is said to have an absolute advantage in the production of a commodity when it is more efficient that other countries at producing that commodity. Absolute advantage occurs therefore when one country can produce more of a commodity than other countries using the same amount of resources. If two countries each have an absolute advantage in the production of different goods, total world output can be increased and both countries can gain when each country specialises in the production of the good in which it has an absolute advantage.

53 C A conclusion from the law of comparative advantage is that if free trade is allowed, countries will specialise in the production of goods and services in which they have a comparative advantage over other countries. As a result, the world's economic resources will be put to their most productive uses, and total output will be maximised. It does not follow that each country of the world will maximise its own national income or economic wealth (statement A), because the distribution of wealth between the individual countries in the world could be uneven, with some countries earning much more than others from their output and their exports.

54 A A production possibility boundary shows the possible combinations of two goods that a country can produce with its resources. The slope of the line for each country indicates the opportunity cost of producing corn in terms of lost production of clothing, and the opportunity cost of producing clothing in terms of lost production of corn. In Burra, the opportunity cost of producing corn is a lot less than it is in Mula. (If it were the *same* in both countries, the slopes of the production possibility boundaries would be parallel to each other.) This means that Burra has a comparative advantage in the production of corn. By the same analysis, we can conclude that Mula has a comparative advantage in the production of clothing.

Statement B cannot be proved or disproved. *Absolute* advantage cannot be ascertained from the diagram. Burra might be a country with *many more resources* than Mula, and absolute advantage refers to the production capabilities of each country *per unit of resource*.

Statement C cannot be proved or disproved either, because although Burra can produce more output in total than Mula, its national income per head of population depends on *population size*, for which we do not have any information.

55 BALANCE OF PAYMENTS DEFICIT

If the balance of payments is in deficit, then our imports exceed our exports. This excess of imports must be paid for either by movements on the capital account of the balance of payments, ie sales of our overseas assets or purchases of UK assets by foreigners, or by transfers out of our reserves (or a combination of the two).

In order to remove the deficit, the Chancellor must reduce imports and/or increase exports. The policies which he can use fall into three main categories:

(a) Currency devaluation
(b) Import restrictions
(c) Domestic deflation

The principal impact of devaluation is to make our goods and services cheaper for foreigners to buy, thereby increasing their demand for our goods, and to make imports more expensive in the UK, thus reducing demand for them. A devaluation will only benefit the balance of payments if the impact on the total value of our exports is opposite to or greater than the impact on the total value of our imports.

Looked at in sterling terms, the total value of our exports will rise as they become cheaper in foreign currency terms and demand for them therefore increases. The extent of this increase depends upon the elasticity of demand for our exports. The total value of imports may rise or fall in sterling terms depending on the relationship between the rise in prices and the fall in demand, known as the elasticity of demand for imports.

In the short term, demand is usually inelastic and so a devaluation often results in a short term deterioration in the balance of payments before any improvement is seen. This is known as the 'J-curve' effect.

The Chancellor could impose physical or price restrictions on imports, within the constraints imposed by international treaties and agreements.

Physical restrictions can take the form of quotas for certain items or even a total ban on imports of specific items or items from specific countries. Other physical measures include exchange controls which limit the amount of money which can be spent overseas.

Price restrictions usually take the form of tariffs which increase the price of imports and thereby reduce demand for them. As with devaluation, the benefit of tariffs depends on the elasticity of demand for imports. This is why price restrictions are more often used in conjunction with physical restrictions than in isolation.

It should be noted that both devaluation and import restrictions (the latter in particular) can lead to retaliation from other countries whose actions might well negate the effects of these measures.

Finally, the Chancellor could deflate demand within the UK, a measure which should reduce the demand for imports and encourage UK businesses to try harder to export to cover reduced demand in the home market.

56 B Consumption of all goods will increase, including imports. This will increase the supply of sterling on the foreign-exchange markets and the price of sterling will therefore fall.

57 B Purchasing power parity theory predicts that changes in exchange rates between two currencies are attributable to the different rates of price inflation in each country.

$$\text{New exchange rate} = \text{old exchange rate} \times \frac{1 + \text{inflation rate in currency's country}}{1 + \text{inflation rate in other country}}$$

The inflation rate is a proportion, and so 10% = 0.10 etc.

Therefore we have a new US dollar/pound sterling exchange rate of

$$\$1.50 \times \left(\frac{1.02}{1.12}\right) = \$1.3660.$$

The dollar has strengthened in value against sterling because the rate of inflation has been lower in the USA than in the UK.

Index

Note: Key Terms and their page references are given in **bold**

Absolute advantage, 315
Accelerator principle, 245
Accounting profits, 74
Ad volerem tax, 303
Agglomeration economies of scale, 125
Aggregate demand, 227
Aggregate supply, 227
Aggregation (in financial intermediation), 185
Allocative efficiency, 163
Allocative inefficiency, 144, 165
Alternative Investment Market, 203
Arc elasticity of demand, 40
Automatic stabilisers, 298
Average cost, **71**, 72
Average revenue, 79

Backwards integration, 315
Balance of payments equilibrium, 251
Balance of payments, 269,325
Balance of trade, 327
Balancing item, 326
Bank accounts, 179
Bank multiplier, 195
Bank of England, 199
Banknotes, 179
Banks, 187, 193
Barriers to entry, 138,143
Barriers to entry, 143
Benchmark, 201
Big Bang, 163
Black marketeers, 34
Bretton Woods agreement, 342
Budget deficit, 296
Budget surplus, 296
Budget, 297
Building societies, 199
Business confidence, 263
Business cycles, 246
Business expansion, 123

Capital markets, 202
Capital, 91, 92
Capital-output ratio, 246
Cartels, 152
Cash reserve ratio, 288
Central bank, 199
Certificates of Deposit, 206
Ceteris paribus, 4, 24
Circular flow of income, 212
Clearing system, 194
Coincident indicator, 287
Collective bargaining, 99
Collusion, 152
Command economy, 56
Commercial banks, 194
Commercial paper, 207
Commodity money, 179
Comparative advantage, 315, **316**
Competition Commission, 168
Competitor analysis, 157
Complements, 24
Compulsory competitive tendering, 164
Conflicts between policy instruments, 250
Conglomerate diversification, 123
Constant returns to scale, 82
Constituents of the firm, 122
Consumer price indices, 269
Consumer surplus, 32
Consumer watchdog bodies, 168
Consumption function, 234
Consumption, 233
Contestable markets, 156
Cost accounting, 74
Cost of production, 70
Cost-push inflation, 271
Credit controls, 298
Credit creation, 195
Credit multiplier, 195
Credit multiplier, 196
Cross elasticity of demand, 49
Crowding out,238, 297
Current account, 327
Current ratio, 187
Customs duties, 319
Customs union, 321

Dead weight loss, 139
Deadweight burden, 142
Debentures, 207
Deficit on current account, 328
Deficit units, 184
Deflation, 329
Deflationary gap, 230, 281
De-industrialisation, 119

Demand curve, 22
Demand for factors of production, 91
Demand for labour, 95
Demand management, 231, **281**
Demand schedule, 21
Demand, 21, 39
Demand-pull inflation, 270, **271**
Demerit good, 61
'Demultiplier', 241, 246
Derivative financial instruments, 205
Derived demand, 20, **91**
Dimensional economies of scale, 84
Diminishing returns, 77
Direct tax, 104, 303
Discrimination, 99
Diseconomies of scale, 82, 83, 85
Disintermediation, 206
Distribution of income, 25
Diversification, 315
Division of labour, 9
Domestic deflation, 332
Dumping, 35, 320
Duopoly, 152

Economic growth, 249
Economic indicator, 287
Economic policy objectives, 249
Economic profits, 74
Economic rent, 111
Economic reorganisation, 14
Economic system, 8
Economic value, 9
Economic wealth, 10, 212
Economic welfare, 11
Economics, 5
Economies of scale, 82
Elasticities, 65
Elasticity of demand for imports, 329
Elasticity of demand for labour, 102
Elasticity, 39, 40
Eligible bills, 198
Embargo on imports, 319
Entrepreneurship, 5, 82, 91, 108
Equilibrium in the balance of payments, 328
Equilibrium price, 31, **32**
Equity, 207
Eurobonds, 186, 205, 207
European Economic and Monetary Union, 343
European Economic Area, 323
European Free Trade Area (EFTA), 322
European Free Trade Association, 322
European Union, 300, 318, 321
Excess capacity theorem, 151
Exchange controls, 318
Exchange rate mechanism, 342
Exchange rate policies, 250, 341
Exchange rate stability, 342
Exchange rate, 336, 338
Exchange value, 9
Exchange, 9
Expectational inflation, 271
Expenditure approach to measuring national income, 218
Expenditure at factor cost, 219
Expenditure at market prices, 219
Expenditure reducing, 329
Expenditure switching, 329
Explicit costs, 74
Export credit guarantees, 319
Export multiplier, 239
Export subsidies, 319
Exports, 214
External balance, 249
External debt, 333
External economies of scale, 85
External trade policy, 250
Externalities, **57**, 59
Externality, 59

Factor incomes, 217
Factor markets, 90
Factor mobility, 98
Factor pricing, 110
Factors of production, 4, 70
Financial instruments, 184
Financial intermediaries, 204, 184
Firm, 121
Firms, 20
Fiscal drag, 298
Fiscal policy, 250
Fixed costs, 71, 76
Fixed exchange rates, 341
Floating exchange rates, 342
Flow of funds, 183
Footsie (FT-SE 100) Index, 203
Foreign currency, 327
Foreign exchange markets, 119, 336
Forward integration, 315
Fractional reserve system, 197
Free riders, 59
Free trade area, 321
Full employment national income, 227
Full employment, 249, 280

Game theory, 155
'GDP deflator', 222
Gearing, 187
Geographical immobility of labour, 99
Giffen goods, 47
Gilt-edged market, 204
Globalisation of capital markets, 205
Globalisation, 120, 314
Gold, 341
Government intervention in foreign exchange markets, 340
Government spending multiplier, 239
Government spending, 214
Great Depression, 227
Gross domestic product (GDP), 217
Gross national product, 217

Horizontal integration, 123
Horizontal integration, 123
Horizontal integration, 315
Households, 20
Hyperinflation, 180, 269

Imperfections in a market, 57
Implicit costs, 74
Import cost-push inflation, 271
Import quotas, 319, 329
Import restrictions, 319
Imports, 213
Incentives, 105
Income approach, 214
Income effect, 47
Income elasticity of demand, 48
Incomes policy, 272
Indirect taxes, 46, 61, **62**, 303
Industrial imbalance, 127
Inelastic demand, 42
Infant industries, 320
Inferior good, 25, 49
Inflation, 222, 249, 259, 267, **268**, 280
Inflationary expectations, 282
Inflationary gaps, 229, 281
Injections into the circular flow of income, 213
Injections, 213
Institutional, 204
Interaction of demand and supply, 19
Interest rates and the balance of payments, 333
Interest rates, 92, 187, 273, 288
Interest, 91, 92
Internal economies of scale, 85
International Monetary Fund (IMF), 333
International trade, 315
Investment multiplier, 239
Investment trust, 204
Investment, 214, 236

J curve effect, 330
J curve, 330
Japan, 329

Keynesians, 226

Labour immobility, 98
Labour productivity, 103, 105
Labour, 90
Laffer curve, 304, 305
Lagging indicator, 287
Land, 5, 90, 105
Law of diminishing returns, 77
Leading indicator, 287
Lease finance, 186
Lender of last resort, 200
Less developed countries, 12, 320
Liberalisation, 163
Limited liability, 117
Liquidity preference, 188, 260
Liquidity preference, 260
Liquidity, 178, 197
Loanable funds theory of interest rates, 265
Location decision, 125
London Inter-Bank Offered Rate, 201
Long run, 51, **71**
Long-run costs, 81

Management buy-outs, 205
Management discretion model, 122
Managerial economies, 85
Managerial model of the firm, 122
Managerial objectives, 122
Marginal cost, 71, 72
Marginal efficiency of capital, 92
Marginal productivity theory, 95
Marginal revenue product (MRP) of labour, 95
Marginal revenue, 79
Marginal utility, 20
Market clearing price, 31, 32
Market demand curve, 23
Market demand, 25
Market economy, 8

Market failure, 57, 161
Market period, 51
Market supply curve, 29
Market, 19, **20**
Maturity transformation, 185
Maximum prices, 33
Mergers, 123
Merit goods, 60, 61
Minimum efficient scale, 86
Minimum price legislation, 34
Minimum prices, 34
Mixed economy, 8
Monetarists, 226, 267, 271
Monetary aggregate, 180
Monetary policy, 250, 251, 285, 297
Money markets, 202, 206
Money stock, 180
Money supply, 267
Money, 176
Monopolistic competition, 149
Monopoly, 57, **136**
Monopsonists, 57
Moral suasion, 290
Moveable peg system, 342
Multinational enterprises, 313
Multiplier, 239
Multiplier-accelerator theory, 248

NAIRU, 281
National Debt, 298
National income, 212, 217
Nationalised industries, 168
Natural monopoly, 136
Natural rate hypothesism, 282
Natural rate hypothesis, 284
Natural rate of unemployment, 280, 284
Natural resources, 13
Net national product, 217
New quantity theory, 266
Nominal rates of interest, 189
Non-accelerating inflation rate of unemployment, 284
Non-accelerating rate of unemployment, 284
Non-commodity money, 179
Non-price competition, 150
Normal goods, 25, 49
Normal profit, 71, 110
North American Free Trade Agreement (NAFTA), 323

Objectives of firms, 121
Occupational immobility, 99
Oligopolies, 48
Oligopoly, 152
OPEC, 153
Open market operations, 200, 201, 206
Opportunity cost, 7, 75, **111**, 316
Optimum, 57
Options, 205
Organisational coalition, 123
Ostentation, 47
Output approach, 215
Over the counter (OTC) markets, 203

Pacific Basin, 120
Paradox of thrift, 246
Parallel markets, 207
Pension funds, 204
Perfect competition, 57, 131, 132
Phillips curve, 281
Point elasticity of demand, 40
Pollution policies, 62
Pollution, 58, 61
Poverty trap, 302
Precautionary motive, 260
Price and output determination, 19
Price discrimination, 139
Price elasticity of supply, 39, 49
Price leadership, 155
Price legislation, 61
Price mechanism, 31, 58
Price regulation, 33
Price signals, 31
Price theory, 20
Prices and incomes policy, 250, 251, 274
Primary sector, 118
Prior charge capital, 187
Private benefit, 58
Private cost, 58
Private sector, 117
Privitisation, 164
Producer surplus, 33
Product differentiation, 149, 150, 152
Production possibility curve, 5
Production quotas, 35
Productive inefficiency, 165
Productivity, 126
Professional associations, 99
Profit maximisation, 79, 121, 122
Profit, 74, **79**, 91, 108
Profitability, 197
Progressive tax, 301
Proportional tax, 301

Protectionism, 319
Protectionist measures, 331
Public finance, 294
Public goods, 60
Public sector borrowing requirement (PSBR), 295, 305
Public Sector Borrowing Requirement, 295
Public sector organisations, 117
Purchasing power parity theory, 338
Purchasing power, 179

Qualitative controls, 289
Quantity theory of money, 257, **258**

Rationality, 20
Rationing, 34
Raw materials costs, 29
Real rates of interest, 189
Recession, 246
Redistribution of wealth, 61, 269
Regional policy, 126
Regressive tax, 301
Regulation of markets, 161
Rent, 90, 105
Research and development, 85
Reserve requirements, 288
Retail Prices Index(RPIX), 270
Retained earnings, 208
Retraining schemes, 99
Risk management, 205
Risk, 109, 190
RPIY, 270

Sales maximisation model, 122
'Satisficing', 122
Savings, 213, 233
Savings, 93
Scarce resource, 5
Scarcity, 4
Secondary sector, 118
Secular period, 51
Security, 197
Selective indirect tax, 62
Self-regulation, 162
Set-aside, 35
Share price indices, 203
Share prices, 203
Short run, 51, **71**
Short-run average cost (SAC) curve, 76
Short-run costs, 71
Small firms, 124
Social benefit, 58
Social contract, 274
Social cost, 58
Specialisation, 316
Specialisation, 9
Specific tax, 303
Speculation, 338
Speculative motive, 260
Stagflation, 253
Stakeholders, 121
Statutory minimum wage, 101
Stock Exchange, 163, 202
Store of value, 178
Structural unemployment, 279
Subsidies, 61, 127
Substitute goods, 24
Substitutes, 24
Substitution effect, 47
Sunk costs, 74
Supernormal profit, 71, 110, 138
Supply curve for labour, 96
Supply curve, 28
Supply of capital, 93
Supply schedule, 28
Supply side economics, 227, 251, 253
Supply, 27
Surplus on current account, 328
Surplus units, 184
Swaps, 205

Takeovers, 123
Tariffs, 319, 329
Tax incentives, 125
Taxation, 213
Technical inefficiency, 165
Technological changes, 263
Technological developments, 29
Technological progress, 13, 142
Term structure of interest rates, 188
Terms of trade, 14
Terms of trade, 334
Tertiary sector, 119
Time horizon, 48
Time lags, 250
Token money, 179
Total cost, 71, **72**
Total revenue, 79
Trade credit, 186
Trade cycles, 12, 232, 246
Trade unions, 99, 274
Transactions motive, 260
Transfer earnings, 111

Transfer payments, 112, 216
Transformation curve, 5
Transmission mechanism, 265

Uncertainty, 109
Underlying rate of inflation, 270
Unemployment, 278
Unit trusts, 204
Utility, 10, 20

Value added method of measuring national income, 220
Variable costs, 71, 76
Velocity of circulation, 258
Venture capital, 205
Vertical integration, 123, 315

Wage-price spiral, 271
Wages, 90, 95
Wall Street Crash, 227
Wealth, 10
Withdrawals from the circular flow of income, 213
Withdrawals, 213
World Bank, 333
World Trade Organisation (WTO), 321

X-Inefficiency, 144

Yield curve, 188

REVIEW FORM & FREE PRIZE DRAW

All original review forms from the entire BPP range, completed with genuine comments, will be entered into one of two draws on 31 January 2003 and 31 July 2003. The names on the first four forms picked out on each occasion will be sent a cheque for £50.

Name: ______________________ **Address:** ______________________

____

How have you used this Text?
(Tick one box only)

- ☐ Self study (book only)
- ☐ On a course: college (please state)__________
- ☐ With 'correspondence' package
- ☐ Other __________

Why did you decide to purchase this Text?
(Tick one box only)

- ☐ Have used BPP Texts in the past
- ☐ Recommendation by friend/colleague
- ☐ Recommendation by a lecturer at college
- ☐ Saw advertising
- ☐ Other __________

During the past six months do you recall seeing/receiving any of the following?
(Tick as many boxes as are relevant)

- ☐ Our advertisement in CIMA *Insider*
- ☐ Our advertisement in *Financial Management*
- ☐ Our advertisement in *Pass*
- ☐ Our brochure with a letter through the post
- ☐ Our website www.bpp.com

Which (if any) aspects of our advertising do you find useful?
(Tick as many boxes as are relevant)

- ☐ Prices and publication dates of new editions
- ☐ Information on product content
- ☐ Facility to order books off-the-page
- ☐ None of the above

Which BPP products have you used?

Text	☐	**MCQ cards**	☐	**i-Learn**	☐
Kit	☐	**Tape**	☐	**i-Pass**	☐
Passcard	☐	**Video**	☐	**Virtual Campus**	☐

How did you/will you take the exam for this paper? (Tick one box only)

Written exam	☐
Computer-based assessment	☐

Your ratings, comments and suggestions would be appreciated on the following areas.

	Very useful	*Useful*	*Not useful*
Introductory section (Key study steps, personal study)	☐	☐	☐
Chapter introductions	☐	☐	☐
Key terms	☐	☐	☐
Quality of explanations	☐	☐	☐
Case examples and other examples	☐	☐	☐
Questions and answers in each chapter	☐	☐	☐
Chapter roundups	☐	☐	☐
Quick quizzes	☐	☐	☐
Exam focus points	☐	☐	☐
Question bank	☐	☐	☐
Answer bank	☐	☐	☐
Index	☐	☐	☐
Icons	☐	☐	☐
Mind maps	☐	☐	☐

Overall opinion of this Study Text *Excellent* ☐ *Good* ☐ *Adequate* ☐ *Poor* ☐

Do you intend to continue using BPP products? Yes ☐ No ☐

On the reverse of this page are noted particular areas of the text about which we would welcome your feedback. Please note any further comments and suggestions/errors on the reverse of this page as well. The BPP author of this edition can be e-mailed at: nickweller@bpp.com

Please return this form to: Nick Weller, CIMA Range Manager, BPP Publishing Ltd, FREEPOST, London, W12 8BR

TELL US WHAT YOU THINK

Because the following specific areas of the text contain new material your comments on their usefulness are particularly welcome.

Economic Systems	(Chapter 1)
Dead weight loss	(Chapter 8)
Privatisation	(Chapter 10)
New classical economics and stagflation	(Chapter 14)
Undesirable effects of protection	(Chapter 18)

Please note any further comments and suggestions/errors below.

FREE PRIZE DRAW RULES

1 Closing date for 31 January 2003 draw is 31 December 2002. Closing date for 31 July 2003 draw is 30 June 2003.

2 Restricted to entries with UK and Eire addresses only. BPP employees, their families and business associates are excluded.

3 No purchase necessary. Entry forms are available upon request from BPP Publishing. No more than one entry per title, per person. Draw restricted to persons aged 16 and over.

4 Winners will be notified by post and receive their cheques not later than 6 weeks after the relevant draw date.

5 The decision of the promoter in all matters is final and binding. No correspondence will be entered into.

See overleaf for information on other
BPP products and how to order

CIMA Order

To BPP Publishing Ltd, Aldine Place, London W12 8AW
Tel: 020 8740 2211. Fax: 020 8740 1184
www.bpp.com Email publishing@bpp.com
Order online www.bpp.com

Mr/Mrs/Ms (Full name)

Daytime delivery address

Postcode

Daytime Tel | Email | Date of exam (month/year)

	7/02 Texts	1/02 Kits	1/02 Passcards	9/00 Tapes	7/00 Videos	Virtual Campus	7/02 i-Pass	7/02 i-Learn	7/02 MCQ cards
FOUNDATION									
1 Financial Accounting Fundamentals	£20.95 ☐	£10.95 ☐	£6.95 ☐	£12.95 ☐	£25.95 ☐	£50 ☐	£24.95 ☐		£5.95 ☐
2 Management Accounting Fundamentals	£20.95 ☐	£10.95 ☐	£6.95 ☐	£12.95 ☐	£25.95 ☐	£50 ☐	£24.95 ☐		£5.95 ☐
3A Economics for Business	£20.95 ☐	£10.95 ☐	£6.95 ☐	£12.95 ☐	£25.95 ☐	£50 ☐	£24.95 ☐		£5.95 ☐
3B Business Law	£20.95 ☐	£10.95 ☐	£6.95 ☐	£12.95 ☐	£25.95 ☐	£50 ☐	£24.95 ☐		£5.95 ☐
3C Business Mathematics	£20.95 ☐	£10.95 ☐	£6.95 ☐	£12.95 ☐	£25.95 ☐	£50 ☐	£24.95 ☐		£5.95 ☐
INTERMEDIATE									
4 Finance	£20.95 ☐	£10.95 ☐	£6.95 ☐	£12.95 ☐	£25.95 ☐	£80 ☐	£24.95 ☐	£34.95 ☐	£5.95 ☐
5 Business Tax (FA 2002)	£20.95 ☐ (10/02)	£10.95 ☐	£6.95 ☐	£12.95 ☐	£25.95 ☐	£80 ☐	£24.95 ☐	£34.95 ☐	£5.95 ☐
6 Financial Accounting	£20.95 ☐	£10.95 ☐	£6.95 ☐	£12.95 ☐	£25.95 ☐	£80 ☐	£24.95 ☐	£34.95 ☐	£5.95 ☐
6i Financial Accounting International	£20.95 ☐	£10.95 ☐							
7 Financial Reporting	£20.95 ☐	£10.95 ☐	£6.95 ☐	£12.95 ☐	£25.95 ☐	£80 ☐	£24.95 ☐	£34.95 ☐	£5.95 ☐
7i Financial Reporting International	£20.95 ☐	£10.95 ☐							
8 Management Accounting - Performance Management *	£20.95 ☐ 11/02 ☐ 5/03 ☐	£10.95 ☐	£6.95 ☐	£12.95 ☐	£25.95 ☐	£80 ☐	£24.95 ☐	£34.95 ☐	£5.95 ☐
9 Management Accounting - Decision Making *	£20.95 ☐ 11/02 ☐ 5/03 ☐	£10.95 ☐	£6.95 ☐	£12.95 ☐	£25.95 ☐	£80 ☐	£24.95 ☐	£34.95 ☐	£5.95 ☐
10 Systems and Project Management	£20.95 ☐	£10.95 ☐	£6.95 ☐	£12.95 ☐	£25.95 ☐	£80 ☐	£24.95 ☐	£34.95 ☐	£5.95 ☐
11 Organisational Management	£20.95 ☐	£10.95 ☐	£6.95 ☐	£12.95 ☐	£25.95 ☐	£80 ☐	£24.95 ☐	£34.95 ☐	£5.95 ☐
FINAL									
12 Management Accounting - Business Strategy	£20.95 ☐	£10.95 ☐	£6.95 ☐	£12.95 ☐	£25.95 ☐				
13 Management Accounting - Financial Strategy	£20.95 ☐	£10.95 ☐	£6.95 ☐	£12.95 ☐	£25.95 ☐				
14 Management Accounting - Information Strategy	£20.95 ☐	£10.95 ☐	£6.95 ☐	£12.95 ☐	£25.95 ☐				
15 Case Study				£12.95 ☐	£25.95 ☐				
(1) Workbook	£20.95 ☐								
(2) Toolkit		£19.95 ☐ (For 11/02: available 9/02. For 5/03: available 3/03)							
Learning to Learn (7/02)	£9.95 ☐								

* BPP is producing separate editions for the November 2002 and May 2003 exams. Please tick the exam you will be sitting.

Total ☐

POSTAGE & PACKING

Study Texts

	First	Each extra	
UK	£3.00	£2.00	£
Europe***	£5.00	£4.00	£
Rest of world	£20.00	£10.00	£

Kits/Passcards/Success Tapes

	First	Each extra	
UK	£2.00	£1.00	£
Europe*	£2.50	£1.00	£
Rest of world	£15.00	£8.00	£

MCQ cards	£1.00	£1.00	£

CDs each

		£
UK	£2.00	£
Europe*	£2.00	£
Rest of world	£10.00	

Breakthrough Videos

	First	Each extra	
			£
UK	£2.00	£2.00	£
Europe*	£2.00	£2.00	£
Rest of world	£20.00	£10.00	

Grand Total (Cheques to *BPP Publishing*) I enclose a cheque for (incl. Postage) £

Or charge to Access/Visa/Switch

Card Number

Expiry date Start Date

Issue Number (Switch Only)

Signature

We aim to deliver to all UK addresses inside 5 working days. A signature will be required. Orders to all EU addresses should be delivered within 6 working days. All other orders to overseas addresses should be delivered within 8 working days. *Europe includes the Republic of Ireland and the Channel Islands.